Revised Second Edition

PRISONERS' SELF-HELP LITIGATION MANUAL

Written by
DANIEL E. MANVILLE

Edited by
JOHN BOSTON

Introduction by
ALVIN J. BRONSTEIN

Contributing authors
JAMES LAWRENCE
JACK GUTTENBERG
GEORGE N. BREZNA

OCEANA PUBLICATIONS, INC./NEW YORK • LONDON • ROME

Library of Congress Cataloging in Publication Data

Manville, Daniel E.
   Prisoners' self-help litigation manual.

   Rev. ed. of: Prisoners' self-help litigation manual /
James L. Potts, Alvin J. Bronstein. c1976.
   Includes index.
   1. Prisoners—Legal status, laws, etc.—United
States.   2. Actions and defenses—United States.
I. Boston, John, 1948-   II. Potts, James L.
Prisoners' self-help litigation manual.   III. Title.
KF9731.M36   1983   344.73'0356   83-15406
ISBN 0-379-20830-X   347.304356

Manufactured in the United States of America

To
Buck and Lula Mae,
my parents,
and
David Emmet
and
to those incarcerated individuals
who have refused to do time,
requiring time to do them.
I deliver into your hands
a weapon
that knows no boundaries
— except —
that which you impose upon it.

A Personal Statement

One of the reasons you are confined under such atrocious conditions is the failure of all of you (Hispanics, blacks, native Americans, whites, etc.) to set aside your petty jealousies and dislikes and your claims to machismo in order to form a united concrete legal organization which will have a say concerning the conditions under which you are incarcerated. Every person I knew while incarcerated hated those confining them. But, almost every prisoner of any ethnic group or gang hated each other even more. This prevented prisoners from organizing into a single united political force.

Until you can set aside the societal conditioning that keeps you from working together toward common ends, you can expect to remain confined under brutal and dehumanizing conditions.

You look to your pleasures while your brothers rot in these concrete and steel tombs—where you hide your mistakes.

D.E.M.
Washington, DC
July 1983

Summary of Contents

Table of Contents

Acknowledgments

Special acknowledgment is given to all the people who have travelled the rocky and winding road with me since my release from prison in 1976 as I have endeavored to become a prisoners' rights attorney. It has not been an easy road to travel. Many times I felt that what society was requiring of me to achieve my dream was not worth the price; I longed for the complacent life of prison. Friends would not allow my prison mentality to become my reality. Because of them, to a large extent, this *Manual* is produced. I wish to acknowledge a few of them: Carol Fallis, Lenny Esquina, Jr., Stuart Lev, Ronald Steinberg, Bill Goodman, Jim Lawrence, Bob Hodge and family, Ken Birch and family, Linda Ojala, the yearly backpacking gang, and the National Lawyers Guild (especially the Lansing Chapter).

Special acknowledgment is given to Ed Koren of the National Prison Project with whom I have had the pleasure of working closely over the past few years. He not only has helped me refine my legal analysis but has always treated me as a colleague and associate. Ed has been instrumental in keeping John and me on track in the production of the *Manual*. He also has been our spiritual guide when we have had differences of opinion.

Acknowledgment must also be given to John Boston. John has not only been the editor of the *Manual,* but is primarily responsible for this opus magnum. He has continually encouraged (one could say, pushed) me to make this a complete *Manual*. We threw in not only the kitchen sink but every other item that a prisoner will need to litigate and enforce a favorable decision.

The Legal Aid Society of New York and the National Prison Project are thanked for use of their libraries and other facilities.

The following are some of the people who have contributed their time and energy to make this *Manual* what it is: Elizabeth Figueroa, David A. Lewis, Martha Allerton, John O'Leary, Mary Glover, Tom Clark, Jim Gaylord, Kim Berger, Stuart Dowty, and Steve Ney. Thanks beyond what words can express are given to Bill Straub, the Production Manager, and to Scott Custin, Layout Person.

Introduction

By Alvin J. Bronstein*

For almost a century, the prevailing view in our society was that prisoners suffered a total deprivation of liberty and that their rights were non-existent. The courts concurred in the notion that incarceration in prison was exclusively for punishment and adopted a "hands-off" policy which prevented prisoners from securing any rights except those allowed by their jailers. Few persons, including lawyers, attempted to challenge this policy. The abdication of judicial responsibility reinforced the status quo of prison life and, because no other political or social institutions responded to the complaints of prisoners, the penal system became isolated from public scrutiny.

The practical effect of the "hands-off" policy was to place all decisions concerning internal affairs of the prison within the discretion of prison officials, no matter how inhumane or arbitrary the results. The courts continually deferred to the so-called expertise of the prison administration in refusing to hear complaints by prisoners concerning violations even of their most fundamental rights.

As a natural outgrowth of the post World War II civil rights movement, and aided by the public awareness that resulted from the explosion at Attica in 1971, judicial attitudes began to change drastically from the de facto rightlessness that had been almost universally accepted for prisoners. Although the principle prevailed that a prisoner's rights were diminished to some extent by virtue of incarceration, it was recognized that "there is no iron curtain drawn between the Constitution and the prisons of this country." Thus, for a period of almost ten years, the courts began to carefully examine what went on behind the curtain and to set forth limits on the government's curtailment of the rights of prisoners. In addition to a series of decisions protecting the civil liberties of prisoners in narrow single issue cases, such as disciplinary due process and the right to uncensored communication with the outside world, by the early part of this decade there were thirty states in which the entire state prison system or one or more major prisons in the state were operating under a federal court order because of a finding that the

---

* Executive Director, National Prison Project ACLUF, Editor of the 1976 *Prisoners' Self-Help Litigation Manual.*

totality of conditions in that system or prison constituted cruel and unusual punishment.

Many of the significant legal victories for prisoners in the past fifteen years originated with lawsuits prepared and filed by prisoners themselves. The landmark Alabama prison case in which, for the first time, a court found that the totality of conditions in an entire state prison system actually made people worse and therefore constituted cruel and unusual punishment, was originally submitted to the court as a hand-written petition by an elderly prisoner.

However, beginning in the last half of the 1970's, the Burger-Rehnquist court has moved us back in history. In what is best characterized by Justice Rehnquist's callous comment that "nobody promised them a rose garden," a majority of the Supreme Court has seen as its principle role the halting of the expansion of prisoners' rights law. In a series of cases beginning in 1976, we began to see a return to the "hands-off" doctrine with language about a wide spectrum of discretionary actions that traditionally have been the business of prison administrators rather than federal courts and that the day-to-day functioning of state prisons involves issues and discretionary decisions that are not the business of federal judges. In the first case in which the Supreme Court considered the limitations that the Eighth Amendment imposes upon the conditions in which a state may confine prisoners, the court discussed the deference that should be given to prison administrators and then said that "to the extent that such conditions are restrictive and even harsh, they are part of the penalty that criminals pay for their offenses against society."

In spite of the prevailing conservative attitude of the courts, if we are to be a democratic society that pays more than lip service to the principle that we are to be governed by the rule of law rather than the rule of men, all persons and especially prisoners must have access to the courts and the means with which to have their grievances adequately aired. Because there are so few lawyers willing and able to represent prisoners in matters where they challenge the conditions and practices that govern their confinement, this new edition of the *Self-Help Litigation Manual* represents a substantial effort towards providing that means.

Experienced observers and commentators have acknowledged the remarkable and important role of the courts. Professor James Jacobs wrote that "Prison litigation may be the peaceful equivalent of a riot in bringing prisoners' grievances to public attention and in mobilizing political support for change." Federal Bureau of Prisons Director Norman Carlson said that "the federal judiciary as a whole is the most effective force for constructive change in prisons." According to Allen Breed, Director of the National Institute for Corrections, "the role of the courts over the past fifteen years in acting as a catalyst for much needed change in our nation's prisons cannot be overemphasized."

Because we need more prison change and fewer prison riots, this *Manual* is both timely and important.

I
Using This Manual and Using the Courts

A. Introduction

This manual belongs to those who are incarcerated and must suffer the daily indignities of the American prison system. It is our hope that through your use of this manual you may gain for yourself and others a few more of the rights guaranteed you by the law.

Protecting your and others' rights cannot be done in a haphazard manner. You should therefore be very familiar with all the relevant chapters of this manual before you actually start a legal action. Chapters I, II, III, IV, and XI should be read by any prisoner who plans to bring a lawsuit of any type. If you wish to challenge your criminal conviction, Chapter IX will also be relevant; if your problem relates to parole or probation, you should also read Chapters VI, VII, and VIII; detainers are dealt with in Chapter X; and if you wish to challenge prison rules, conditions, or practices, you should read Chapters V, VI, and VII. You will increase your chances of success in the courts if you follow the procedures outlined throughout the manual.

The importance of doing this basic self-education is demonstrated by the poor results obtained by most prisoners in court. In fiscal year 1979, the federal courts dismissed 9,943 of the 10,301 civil rights cases filed by prisoners *pro se* upon the initial reading of the complaint.[1] Many of these prisoners did not have valid legal claims. However, many others lost their cases because they did not know what to do; they sued the wrong people, filed in the wrong court, waited too long, or failed to put the right information in their papers.

Despite the overwhelming lack of success, prisoners continue to go to court in record numbers. This is partly because prisons have not

---

[1] The Federal Judicial Center, "Recommended Procedures for Handling Prisoner Civil Rights Cases in the Federal Courts," at 9-10 (1980).

1

established adequate grievance or compensation systems to handle complaints from prisoners. Also, it is because prisons are often run in a lawless manner. At least twenty-eight states have a prison or their entire prison system under comprehensive court order for failure to provide those incarcerated with the minimum civilized conditions of confinement.[2] Until prisoners are confined under conditions that are civilized and given a way to resolve their grievances fairly, the courts will continue to receive large numbers of pleadings from those incarcerated.

B.   How To Use This Manual

This manual presents the basic information you will need to bring lawsuits concerning prison conditions and practices, parole matters, detainers, and post-conviction proceedings such as petitions for a writ of habeas corpus challenging your criminal conviction. We do not deal with how to defend yourself in a criminal trial or how to conduct a criminal appeal because space does not permit and because you have the right to appointed counsel in these proceedings.[3]

We do not provide any magical answers on how to become a successful jailhouse lawyer. This is only achieved through hard work on your part. The manual seeks to provide you with the basic information concerning the different rights of prisoners, the possible remedies you can obtain from a court, the forms to use, etc.

This book is divided into eleven chapters on different subjects. There are a number of other features designed to help you find what you need to know:

Sections and subsections. We have divided each chapter into smaller parts with separate headings, all of which are listed in the Table of Contents. Sometimes, scanning the Table of Contents is the fastest way to locate the subject you want.

Index. At the end of the book, there is an alphabetical list of topics and the places in the book where they are discussed. Looking in the Index will help you find topics that do not have a special subsection (such as

---

[2]*See* Rhodes v. Chapman, 452 U.S. 337, 101 S.Ct. 2392, 2402 n.1 (1981) (Brennan, J., concurring).

[3]*See* Gideon v. Wainwright, 372 U.S. 335, 83 S.Ct. 792 (1963) (indigent criminal defendants entitled to assistance from appointed counsel); Scott v. Illinois, 440 U.S. 376, 99 S.Ct. 1158 (1979) (defendant cannot be sentenced to imprisonment, whether felony or misdemeanor, unless state has afforded indigent the right to assistance of appointed counsel in his/her defense); Douglas v. California, 372 U.S. 353, 83 S.Ct. 814 (1963) (required appointment of counsel for an indigent defendant's first appeal as of right); *but see* Ross v. Moffitt, 417 U.S. 600, 94 S.Ct. 2439 (1974) (state not required to provide indigent defendant with appointed counsel for discretionary appeal).

"John Doe defendants"), or that are mentioned in several places (such as "assaults").

Footnotes. At the bottom of each page are footnotes which contain case citations, statutory references, and other information backing up or explaining the statements on the page. These footnotes are a fast way of finding case law dealing with a particular subject.

Table of cases. After the index at the end of the book, there is an alphabetical list of all cases and where in the book they are discussed.

Forms. In the Appendix at the end of the book, there are actual examples of various kinds of legal papers that you may wish to use as models.

Chapter II describes how to do legal research in a prison law library. There is a lot more to know about legal research than we have had space to tell you. It is suggested that you, or the prison law librarian, order one or more of the other books mentioned in Chapter II to supplement the limited knowledge provided here on legal research.

Chapter III discusses the drafting of legal documents such as complaints, motions, orders, briefs, etc. This is a chapter that you should review very closely since most prisoners' lawsuits are dismissed by judges because they cannot understand what problems are being complained about by the *pro se* prisoner.

Chapter IV is a summary of the working of the federal and state court systems.

Chapter V is an overview of the law of the rights of prisoners with respect to prison conditions and practices, which includes a fairly detailed discussion of federal procedural and substantive rights, equal protection, and pretrial detainees' rights.

Chapter VI discusses the type of civil actions state and federal prisoners may bring and the remedies they may obtain. The chapter details what you must allege to state a cause of action, the jurisdictional requirements, and the remedies (damages, injunctive relief, or declaratory judgment) you may be entitled to from the courts or administrative agencies. The requirements, if any, for exhaustion of remedies and the possible advantages of exhausting these remedies are discussed. Also discussed are the types of defenses prison officials can raise and possible methods of defeating these defenses.

Chapter VII tells you how to litigate your action in federal court. This chapter discusses the requirements of a complaint; how to file it and then get the summons and complaint served; how to file for indigency and appointed counsel; methods of preparing your factual case; how to handle your own trial if you cannot obtain appointed counsel (*e.g.,* the type of evidence admissible; how to do *voir dire,* examine witnesses, and introduce documents, etc.); for prisoners who have won, the methods of enforcement or modification of the judgment are discussed. Your appeal rights and how to appeal are also explained.

Chapter VIII concerns your parole and parole revocation rights. The U.S. Supreme Court has recently held that prisoners have no per se constitutional right to parole. If a right to parole does exist, it must be created by state statute. Cases that have found a right to parole and those that have not are discussed and the distinctions between them are explained. Parole revocation in the early 1970s was held by the Supreme Court to be a "conditional liberty" entitled to due process protection. The minimal due process protection you are entitled to in a revocation hearing is also discussed.

Chapter IX discusses post-conviction procedures and some of the grounds for relief. A post-conviction challenge is an attack on your criminal conviction alleging that some aspect of the conviction is illegal and that you should be released. This is the only chapter that deals directly with your criminal conviction.

Chapter X provides a detailed look at detainers and how to remove them when one has been filed against you. Different factual situations are provided with a discussion of the possible courses of action you could take and the pros and cons of each one. A discussion is also provided concerning the right to a speedy trial as it relates to detainers.

Chapter XI seeks to provide methods you can use to protect yourself against prison officials' retaliation for litigation against them. Since you are in a very vulnerable position, under the almost absolute control of prison officials, we suggest that you form an organization inside and, if you can, outside prison to keep an eye on the activist jailhouse lawyers.

There are also numerous appendices following the text of the manual. Each of these appendices provides information to supplement one or more of the chapters. Become very familiar with the appendices and what they contain.

If you wish to be effective as a jailhouse lawyer, you must organize. It is impossible for one person to keep up with the law in the area of prisoners' rights, to handle complaints of prisoners, and to file administrative grievances, pleadings, briefs, etc. If you are able to work with two or more other jailhouse lawyers, you can produce a larger volume of work of a higher caliber. It is even better if you can join, or form, a prison chapter of an organization such as the National Lawyers Guild, the National Conference of Black Lawyers, or the Jaycees.

C. Before You Go To Court

This manual contains a large amount of information for prisoners who wish to represent themselves. We hope it is organized and explained in a way that makes it easy to use. However, there are certain basic ideas which every *pro se* litigant should understand before undertaking any kind of legal action. Because they are so important, we think they are worth repeating in this introductory chapter.

1. *Understand who you are dealing with.* When you go to court, you will be dealing with judges. Even if you ultimately have a jury trial, there will be months—sometimes even years—of pretrial proceedings supervised by the judge. Judges are mostly white, middle-class, middle-aged (and older) males who have been successful lawyers or politicians. In short, they are members of the establishment. Even judges who are women, members of minority groups, or young are likely to have more in common with other judges than with prisoners. Very few of them will ever have been in a prison or jail except on a tour conducted by the warden.

This does not mean that judges cannot or will not be fair. It does mean that their experiences and perspectives are very different from yours and you must understand where they are coming from in order to get through to them. They are likely to assume that authority figures, including prison officials, are honest people acting in good faith unless you prove otherwise. Thus, for example, they will not assume that prison guards falsify disciplinary reports to cover up their own misbehavior. If this is an element of your case, you must be prepared to *prove* to their satisfaction that it happened.

Judges frequently have certain assumptions, biases, or prejudices about prisoners as well. They may assume that prisoners—people they think of as criminals—are likely to be irresponsible or dishonest people. (After all, in most jurisdictions you will be dealing with judges that preside in criminal proceedings.) You must conduct yourself in a restrained and dignified way or you will play directly into this stereotype. Do not use the courts as a place to blow off steam; do not make accusations you cannot prove; do your best to follow the rules of the court. Otherwise, you will not only guarantee losing your own case, but you will leave an impression that will hurt the next prisoner to bring a case in that court.

2. *Do not try to sound like a lawyer.* Prisoners often try to use the most formal and technical language they know when they write legal papers because they think this is how lawyers do it and they can impress the court in that way. In fact, the tide is running the other way. The world in general is sick of lawyers and their jargon, and most good lawyers are doing their best to sound like ordinary sensible people. (Some states have even passed "plain English statutes" requiring that legal documents be written so ordinary people can understand them.) A judge reading your legal papers wants to know two things: What does this person want me to do? Why does s/he think I should do it? The easier it is for the judge to find that out, the better off you are.[4] But most importantly, the judge is going to be far more concerned with the facts of your case than with legal

---

[4]See Ch. III for a discussion of legal writing. See also Appendix B, Form 1, for a sample complaint.

citations.[5]The judge already knows something about the law, and can find out what s/he does not know by sending a clerk to the library. However, the judge knows nothing about the facts except what the parties say. Explain the facts, keep it simple, keep it short, and do not try to decorate it with fancy phrases.

3. *Follow through.* Do not bring a case unless you intend to pursue it. If you bring a case and for some reason you cannot or do not wish to do the work to bring it to completion, do not just forget about it; withdraw it by filing a motion for a dismissal.[6] There are several reasons for this. First, if you bring a case and never follow it up, you will contribute to the stereotype many judges have of prisoners, which we referred to above. Second, the defendants' lawyer will make a motion to dismiss or a motion for summary judgment, and if you do not respond, the court will make a decision based only on the defendants' submission. The result will be another bad precedent cluttering up the law books and hurting later prisoner litigants.

4. *Use the grievance system and administrative remedies in your prison or jail.*[7] Sometimes these procedures actually work. Even if you know they do not, it is a good idea to use them anyway, because it will make you look more like a reasonable and orderly person when you do go to court. It will tell the court that you gave the authorities an opportunity to correct the error initially. In addition, sometimes prison officials will give you a statement of their policy or of the reasons for their actions that will be very useful later on in court.

5. *Sue in the right court.* Untold numbers of prisoners have their lawsuits dismissed because they go to federal court when they should go to state court, or because they go to the wrong state court. The federal courts may generally be used by prisoners only if the defendants are federal or state officials or employees, the case raises issues of federal law, or the plaintiff and the defendants live in different states.[8] Many grievances that state prisoners take to court—for example, accidents in the workplace or violation of prison classification regulations—do not raise any federal law issue;[9] these cases should be brought in state court.[10] Some states require that claims against individuals be brought in

[5]See Ch. II, Sec. A, for a discussion of "marshalling the facts."

[6]*See* Rule 41, Federal Rules of Civil Procedure, for a discussion of voluntary dismissal of a lawsuit.

[7]See Ch. VI, Sec. D, for a discussion of exhaustion of remedies.

[8]For a discussion of the requirements of suing federal or state officials, state prisoners should read Ch. VI, Sec. B, and federal prisoners should read Ch. VI, Sec. C.

[9]See Ch. V for a discussion of your substantive and procedural rights.

[10]See Ch. IV, Secs. B and D for a discussion of state courts.

one court and that claims against the state itself, or against state agencies, be brought in a different court. Find out before you sue what court the case belongs in.

6. *Sue the right defendants.* We have not counted, but we suspect that the single most frequent cause of dismissal of prisoners' lawsuits is naming the wrong people or agencies as defendants.[11] In federal court, you generally cannot sue a state;[12] you can sue a city or county only under limited circumstances;[13] and you can usually sue supervisory officials only for acts that they were personally involved in, not acts that their subordinates committed without their knowledge.[14] You can sue the United States itself only in certain circumstances;[15] in other circumstances, you are restricted to suing individual federal employees or officials.[16] Sometimes you will have a choice of suing one defendant in one court and a different defendant in another court; for example, if an officer in a state prison assaults you with no justification, you may be able to sue the officer in federal court or the state in a state court. Find out before you get started who the proper defendants are for the kind of case you want to bring.

7. *Remember the statute of limitations.* Statutes of limitations are statutes restricting how long you can wait before suing about an event.[17] These statutes may provide for a long or short time period, and different kinds of suits are subject to different limitation periods even within the same state.

There is always a statute of limitations when you are suing for damages, and sometimes there are statutes of limitations restricting when you can ask for an injunction or other court order. When you think your rights have been violated, find out how long you have to do something about it. If you miss this deadline, your lawsuit will be permanently barred.

In addition to having statutes of limitations, many counties and municipalities require you to give them notice within a certain time period if you intend to sue them. If you do not give notice that you intend to sue, your case may be dismissed even if you bring it before the deadline set by the statute of limitations.

[11]See Ch. VI, Secs. B, C, and E, for a discussion of naming the right defendants.

[12]See Ch. VI, Sec. E1a, for a discussion of the Eleventh Amendment immunity.

[13]See Ch, VI, E2b, for a discussion of local government liability.

[14]See Ch. VI, Sec. E2a, for a discussion of establishing personal involvement.

[15]See Ch. VI, Secs. C2, 4, 5 and E1a, for discussions of suing the United States.

[16]See Ch. VI, Secs. C1, 3 and E1d, for discussions of suing federal officials.

[17]See Ch. VI, Sec. E4, for a discussion of statute of limitations.

D. Getting a Lawyer

You are probably familiar with the old saying that the person who represents himself or herself has a fool for a client. That advice is obviously out of place in this book, if only because many prisoners do not have any option but representing themselves. However, nobody would dispute that having a competent lawyer is better than representing yourself. Whether having a not so good lawyer is better depends on what kind of case you are bringing and what kinds of skills you have. There are certain kinds of cases—for example, medical damage suits—which require technical knowledge that no *pro se* litigant is likely to have.[18] Also, there are certain things that a *pro se* litigant cannot do or cannot do as well as even a mediocre lawyer—for example, getting on the telephone to the other side's lawyers (and having them take the call), or persuading prison officials to turn over security-related documents that they do not want to have circulating in the prison.[19]

Getting a lawyer for a prison case or a post-conviction proceeding[20] is frequently difficult, since few lawyers know much about prisons or prison law and since most of them do know that the percentage of successful post-conviction proceedings is low. Also, private lawyers are out to make a living and they know that most prisoners do not have a lot of money to pay fees or to front the out-of-pocket costs even of meritorious cases.

There are a number of ways in which you can try to obtain a lawyer. You can ask the court to appoint a lawyer for you.[21] In civil cases and post-conviction proceedings, it is generally left to the court's discretion whether to appoint a lawyer for you.[22] Courts will be influenced in their decisions by a variety of factors: how complicated your case is; whether it seems to have any merit; whether you seem to be able to handle it yourself; and—probably the most important factor—how difficult it is to persuade a lawyer to represent you.[23] Courts generally do not have any power to force private lawyers to take cases. However, the bar in some jurisdictions is more willing to get involved in representing prisoners and

---

[18]See Ch. V, Sec. C3, for a discussion of medical damage cases.

[19]See Ch. VII, Sec. E2e, for a discussion of production of documents.

[20]In a criminal prosecution where you may be sentenced to jail or prison, and in a direct appeal from a conviction, you have the right to an appointed lawyer if you cannot afford to hire a lawyer. See *supra* note 3, for a list of cases.

[21]See Ch. VII, Sec. A3b, for a discussion of appointment of counsel.

[22]*Id.*

[23]*Id.*

indigents than in others. In New York City, for example, the federal courts have organized "*pro bono* panels," which have arranged for many prisoners to be represented by prestigious Wall Street law firms; courts in other areas may have no regular means at all for finding counsel, and the judge has only his or her personal knowledge of local lawyers to rely on.

A second avenue for finding counsel is civil rights, civil liberties, and legal services and legal aid offices.[24] Sometimes these organizations represent prisoners; even if you know they cannot, it is worth contacting them because they may be able to refer you to someone else. Bar associations (state, county, and city) often have referral services, although many are not very helpful to prisoners. Of course, you can also write directly to lawyers you may know of or know personally.

Contacting an attorney involves some of the same practical considerations as writing legal papers. Lawyers are busy people, and they too want to find out as quickly as possible what you want from them and why you think they should represent you. Private lawyers usually want to know what is in it for them. They also want to avoid involvement with situations that are complicated or non-productive or with people who are difficult and unreasonable.

When you write to an attorney seeking representation, therefore, you should do your best to sound reasonable. Do not engage in name-calling or rhetoric. Tell the lawyer exactly what has happened that you think provides the basis for a lawsuit. You should do this as briefly as possible and still make yourself understood. (For example, "I was placed in punitive segregation after a hearing. I was found guilty of inciting a riot. The hearing board did not let me tell my side of the story. To my knowledge, none of the witnesses I asked for were called. They gave me a statement of reasons which says only 'We find you guilty based on all the evidence.'") Unless you know that the lawyer is knowledgeable about prison law, you should briefly mention what you believe is the legal basis of a suit—cases, statutes, regulations, etc.[25] If you have any kind of documentary evidence (for example, a disciplinary hearing disposition with a meaningless statement of reasons),[26] it may help to send a copy with your letter. You should also tell the lawyer about any evidence you have to back up your story. However, it is not wise to send voluminous papers, at least initially. If there are particular witnesses that you can identify, or if the prison keeps documents that would help prove your

---

[24]See Ch. XI, Secs. C and D, for a listing of national and state organizations you may wish to write.

[25]See Ch. V for a discussion of your substantive and procedural rights.

[26]See Ch. V, Sec. B2b, for a discussion of disciplinary procedures.

case, explain. You should explain in what way you were injured (physical injury, restrictive conditions in segregation, etc.),[27] so the lawyer will be able to make a quick assessment about the likelihood of a money judgment. Finally, if you are contacting a lawyer who may not be familiar with the kind of case you want to bring, you should mention any applicable attorneys' fee statutes, such as the Civil Rights Attorneys' Fees Award Act, 42 U.S.C. §1988, which provides that the court may award a fee to the plaintiff's lawyer if the plaintiff wins a civil rights suit against state officials.[28] One thing you should *never* do is write to a lawyer and say "I need to see you. It's very important. Come visit me." Lawyers' time is their most valuable possession, and they are rarely willing to commit several hours of it without having some idea in advance of what they will be spending it on.

[27]See Ch. VI, Sec. F, for a discussion of damages.

[28]Other relevant attorneys' fee provisions include the Equal Access to Justice Act, 5 U.S.C. §504, 28 U.S.C. §2412, and the Federal Tort Claims Act, 28 U.S.C. §2678, which deal with suits against federal employees and the federal government. States may also have provisions for attorneys' fees in state court actions. A federal district court has the discretion to appoint counsel to represent prisoners concerning revocation of parole or when seeking relief under 28 U.S.C. §§2241, 2254, 2255 (*see* 18 U.S.C. §3006A(g)), and to compensate the appointed counsel (*see* 18 U.S.C. §3006A(d) and (e)).

II
Legal Research

This chapter focuses on how to do legal research in a prison law library, and how to effectively use this research for preparing a complaint, petition, or motion and the accompanying supporting memorandum of law. Legal research consists of long hours of searching for cases through digests, treatises, and annotations; long hours of reading cases; many frustrations and disappointments; and few victories. But when you do obtain victory, the victory is *sweet*.

In order to research effectively, you must know how to read the law found in federal and state constitutions, statutes, cases, and administrative regulations. To do efficient research, you must develop an understanding of the various legal research tools and techniques. Discussion of every aspect of these tools and techniques is precluded in this manual. But the information in this chapter sets forth the basic skills you need to develop if you wish to become proficient in legal research in a prison law library, which normally is inadequately supplied with research material.[1] The following listed books are a few of the many excellent books available at a reasonable cost that treat legal research, problem-solving, and writing in depth. All of these books are published by West Publishing Company: Statsky and Wernet, *Case Analysis and Fundamentals of Legal Writing* (1977); Statsky, *Introduction to Paralegalism: Perspectives, Problems, and Skills* (1974), with *Supplement* (1977); Statsky, *Legislative Analysis: How to Use Statutes and*

---

[1]Although the Supreme Court, in Bounds v. Smith, 430 U.S. 817, 828, 97 S.Ct. 1491 (1977), held "that the fundamental constitutional right of access to the courts requires prison authorities to assist inmates in the preparation and filing of meaningful legal papers by providing prisoners with adequate law libraries or adequate assistance from persons trained in the law," most prison law libraries are grossly inadequate for complete legal research. *See* Ramos v. Lamm, 485 F. Supp. 122, 151 (D. Colo. 1980) ("law libraries at Old Max fall below any known acceptable standard"), *aff'd,* 639 F.2d 559, 582-85 (10th Cir. 1980) (en banc), *cert. denied,* 101 S.Ct. 1759 (1981). The recommended minimum requirements for a prison law library are listed in Appendix E.

Regulations (1975); Cohen, *How to Find the Law: With Special Chapters on Legal Writing* (7th ed. 1976); and Cohen, *Legal Research in a Nutshell* (3d ed. 1978).

A. Marshalling the Facts

Legal research is based on facts; without them, the law is meaningless. The most common mistake of *pro se* litigants is to fail to state the *facts* clearly and adequately for the court. Remember, the court already knows something about the law; but it knows *nothing* about the facts except what you tell it.

Before you can draft a legal pleading to file in the court, you must have a clear understanding of the problem. You must meticulously write down all the facts that relate to your problem in a narrative (story) form. This narrative is called a *statement of facts,* and it contains information describing a thing, an occurrence, or an event, telling *what* happened, to *whom* it happened, *when* and *where* it happened, *how* it happened, and *why* it happened. This is called "marshalling the facts" because you are putting *all* the *facts* relating to your problem together on paper in the order they occurred. This statement of facts will assist you in organizing your research and you can also use it later when you write your complaint, motion, or brief. The following is an example of "marshalling the facts":

1. At 8:00 p.m. on February 19, 1981, Lt. Smith called you to the control center. Upon your arrival he informed you that you would be placed in the maximum security unit.

2. When you asked why you were being placed in maximum security, Lt. Smith said it was for administrative reasons.

3. You were not given a written notice or a hearing before placement in maximum security.

4. The maximum security cell in which you were placed had no sheets for the bed and the cell was filthy. During your confinement you were not given soap, toothpaste, cigarettes, or any other commissary material.

5. You were allowed to order only one law book a week from the law library, and you had to return it within one hour of receiving it.

6. You appeared before a classification committee after 30 days in maximum security. Their response to your question as to why you were in lock-up was that it was for administrative reasons. You were also told you would be returned to general population after you had spent another 15 days in maximum security.

Next, list any prison rule or regulation concerning your legal problem:[2]

---

[2] See Ch. V, Sec. B1b, for a discussion of how prison rules and regulations may create a constitutional right.

1. The prison rules state you will be placed in maximum security for administrative reasons only if it is found that you are a threat to other prisoners or staff, an escape risk, or for your own protection.

2. The prison rules also state that one confined in maximum security for administrative reasons shall retain all the rights and privileges of prisoners in general population, except those necessary to curtail for security reasons.

Your statement of facts must not contain "conclusory statements,"[3] such as "the warden is trying to stop all litigation against him." The courts will only deal with *facts.*[4] If there is no concrete evidence that the warden is trying to stop all the litigation against him, you should not make the claim, because every statement contained in your complaint or petition will have to be proved by you at trial.

Once you have "marshalled the facts," you will then form "legal questions" based on these facts to guide you in your research. These "legal questions" are just short statements asking what your rights are. For example:

1. Do I have a right to an explanation or to give my point of view when I am placed in maximum security?

2. Can prison officials put me in maximum security for any reason, or are the reasons limited?

3. Do I have a right to soap, toothpaste, cigarettes, etc., while confined in maximum security?

4. What type of access to law library materials am I allowed while confined in maximum security?

Once you have written out your "legal questions," you will do the legal research to determine what the answers are.

Once you have done some research, you will be able to restate the questions in a more precise fashion, using the terms and ideas you have learned through your research. For example, using the statement of facts just given, you would ask:

1. Did prison rules create a liberty interest such that a prisoner would

---

[3]*See* Negrich v. Hohn, 379 F.2d 213 (3d Cir. 1967) (a complaint which contains only vague and conclusory allegations can be dismissed); Marnin v. Pinto, 463 F.2d 583, 584 (3d Cir. 1972) (general conclusory allegations that the food is bad and the living conditions miserable are not enough). See also Ch. VII, Secs. A3a and B.

[4]*See* Estelle v. Gamble, 429 U.S. 97, 97 S.Ct. 285 (1976) (indicated that failure to plead the necessary facts may properly result in a dismissal). Ostrer v. Aronwald, 567 F.2d 551, 553 (2d Cir. 1977) (a complaint containing ". . . unsupported allegations, which fail to specify in detail the factual basis necessary to enable defendants intelligently to prepare their defense, . . ." can be dismissed). See also Ch. VII, Sec. B, Motion To Dismiss or Judgment on the Pleadings.

not be placed in maximum security for administrative reasons unless it was found that s/he was either "a threat to other prisoners or staff, an escape risk, or dangerous to him/herself?"

2. If a state-created liberty interest is established so that a prisoner will not be placed in maximum security for administrative reasons unless certain conditions are found to exist, what procedural due process is s/he entitled to before placement in maximum security?

3. Is a prisoner denied adequate access to law library materials when prison officials allow him/her to order only one law book a week from the law library?

(The above three questions are not exhaustive of the possible questions that could be ascertained from the statement of facts, but are only examples.)

When framing the legal questions, you must keep in mind what you will need to prove in establishing (1) that your facts are true, (2) that your rights were violated, and (3) the damages you suffered. You should only include in the legal questions those facts you have support for, or are quite sure you can obtain during discovery.[5]

Your case is *built* from the *facts*. The facts will direct your legal research, preparation of your complaint, type of discovery, legal memoranda, oral argument, and trial strategy. *Stick to the facts.*[6]

B.   Finding and Reading a Case

There is no magic to legal research; it is usually a long and arduous task. You first must learn how to find a case and, once found, how to use the research aids included in reporters to analyze the case you read. These aids will also assist you in finding additional cases "on point," and analyzing and evaluating them quickly.

1.   "Reports" and "Reporters"

Once a court has decided a lawsuit or legal action that was brought before it, this decision or opinion may be published in a court "report" or "reporter." The difference between a court "report" and "reporter" is simply that the "report" is the official publication of the court, while a "reporter" is the unofficial publication of the original court case by a private publishing company. West Publishing Company publishes the unofficial reporters, which contain all of the decisions of the federal and state courts that will be published in the official reports. Your prison law library should have West's reporters containing federal cases and should

---

[5]See Ch. VII, Sec. E, for a general discussion concerning discovery.

[6]See also Ch. VII, Sec. G, Summary Judgment.

have the national reporter for the region in which your state is located (*e.g.,* the *North Western Reporter* for Michigan[7]). When citing cases in your legal pleadings, the unofficial reporters of West are as valid as the official reports, even though it is preferable to provide the official citation.

United States Supreme Court cases are published in three different sets of books in the Court's exact words. The official publication of Supreme Court decisions is the *United States Reports,* which when cited is abbreviated as "U.S." West publishes Supreme Court decisions in the *Supreme Court Reporter,* abbreviated "S.Ct." This reporter contains a cross-reference from the official *U.S. Reports* citations to the volumes and pages of the *S.Ct.* reporter. The Lawyers' Cooperative Publishing Company publishes the *United States Supreme Court Reports - Lawyers' Edition,* abbreviated "L.Ed." and "L.Ed.2d." This reporter contains a summary of briefs of counsel and annotations on significant legal issues in reported cases, as well as the Supreme Court opinions themselves.

The following is a list of reports and reporters containing decisions of the federal and state courts. Even though most states have their own reports, the reporters listed below are probably what will be available to you:

FEDERAL REPORTS AND REPORTERS OF THE NATIONAL REPORTER SYSTEM

Full Name of Publication	Official Abbreviation	Type of Cases Reported
United States Reports	U.S.	U.S. Supreme Court
Supreme Court Reporter	S.Ct.	U.S. Supreme Court
U.S. Supreme Court Reports—Lawyers' Edition	L.Ed./ L.Ed.2d	U.S. Supreme Court
Federal Reporter, Second Series	F.2d	Federal Appeals Courts
Federal Supplement	F. Supp.	Federal District Courts

REGIONAL REPORTERS OF THE NATIONAL REPORTER SYSTEM

Full Name of Publication	Official Abbreviation	Type of Cases Reported
Atlantic Reporter	A.2d	Reports cases from Pa., Md., N.J., Ct., Vt., R.I., N.H., Me., Del., and D.C.
North Eastern Reporter	N.E.2d	Reports cases from Ill., Ind., Mass., N.Y., and Ohio

---

[7]The prison law library may also contain the official state reporter.

Full Name of Publication	Official Abbreviation	Type of Cases Reported
North Western Reporter	N.W.2d	Reports cases from Iowa, Mich., Minn., Neb., N.D., S.D., and Wis.
Pacific Reporter	P.2d	Reports cases from Alaska, Ariz., Cal., Colo., Hawaii, Idaho, Kan., Mont., Nev., N.M., Okla., Ore., Utah, Wash., and Wyo.
South Eastern Reporter	S.E.2d	Reports cases from Ga., N.C., S.C., Va., and W.Va.
Southern Reporter	So.2d	Reports cases from Ala., Fla., La., and Miss.
South Western Reporter	S.W.2d	Reports cases from Ark., Ky., Mo., Tenn., and Tex.

The "2d" behind the citation of a reporter means it is the *second series* of that reporter. Some reporters may have a third series ("3d"). The second and third series in the reporter system do not indicate that these series are revised editions of the former reporter, but rather that the present series contain the most recently decided cases. Court decisions are overruled only by subsequent decisions.

All West reporters have the following research aids:

1. Parallel cites to the official report can be found on the first page where the case is reported in the hardback reporter.

2. Topical Key Numbers of rules of law are provided with each case, allowing you access to West digests.

3. The "Cumulative Statutes Construed" table lists all the cases in that volume citing a particular federal or state statute.

4. The "Key Number Digest" at the beginning of the book lists cases contained in that volume by subject matter.

5. The "Words and Phrases" table lists all the cases in that volume that define words and phrases.

6. The "Table of Cases" lists all the cases reported in that volume.

7. Some of the reporters will have tables listing the cases that explain the criminal and civil court rules.

2. Citations

Each case has its own individual "citation," consisting of the volume and page number of the reporter where the decision first appears. The citation will tell you in abbreviated form where to find the case. For example, "*Ramos v. Lamm,* 485 F. Supp. 122 (D. Colo. 1979), *aff'd in part, rev'd in part and remanded,* 639 F.2d 559 (10th Cir. 1980), *cert. denied,* 101 S.Ct. 1759 (1981)," tells you that the plaintiff (the person su-, ing) is "Ramos" and the defendant (the person being sued) is "Lamm." Whether the person suing is a "plaintiff" in a civil suit, a "petitioner" in a habeas or mandamus action, or an "appellant" on appeal after an adverse decision against him/her, s/he is always the first name in the title of the action. The second name is always the party being sued, regardless whether s/he is the "defendant" in a civil action the "respondent" in a habeas or mandamus action. A party may be a non-person or an entity, such as the Department of Corrections, the Commissioner of the Parole Board, the warden, a corporation, agency, etc.

The number "485" in the citation is the volume in which the case will be found. The "F. Supp." tells you that the case was decided by a federal district court and is reported in the "Federal Supplement." The "122" indicates the page in volume 485 of the Federal Supplement where the case begins. The "(D. Colo. 1979)" informs you that the case was decided in 1979 by the United States District Court for the State of Colorado.[8] You next see *"aff'd in part, rev'd in part and remanded,* 639 F.2d 559 (10th Cir. 1980)," which tells you the lower court decision was affirmed in part and reversed in part and the case was remanded to the trial court for further consideration by the Tenth Circuit Court of Appeals in 1980 and is reported in volume 639 of the Federal Reporter (F.2d) starting on page 559. You next see *"cert. denied,* 101 S.Ct. 1759 (1981)," which tells you the United States Supreme Court denied in 1981 the request for issuance of a writ of certiorari and is reported at volume 101 of the Supreme Court Reporter (S.Ct.) on page 1759. The proper citation format can be obtained from the Harvard Law Review Association, *A Uniform System of Citation* (13th ed. 1981).

Most of the case books in your prison law library will be the unofficial reporters. Once you have found cases in the unofficial reporters to cite in your memorandum of law, you will also want to cite in your memorandum the citation to the official report. The court may only have the official reporter, and you want to make it easy for an overworked judge to find a case that is helpful to you. For example, you have found the case *Lawrence v. Department of Corrections,* 276 N.W.2d 554 (Mich. Ct. App. 1979), which you are citing in your brief, and you want to obtain the parallel cite to the official report.[9] There are four ways to

---

[8]Most states are divided into two or more districts in which federal courts are located (*e.g.,* Michigan is divided into Eastern and Western Districts). When citing a case from a state which has two or more district courts, you would list which district the court is located in (*e.g.,* "(W.D. Mich. 1983)," tells you the case was decided by the U.S. District Court of the Western District for the State of Michigan).

[9]The citation you would want to put in your brief is Lawrence v. Dept. of Corrections, 88 Mich. App. 167, 276 N.W.2d 554 (1979), *lv. denied,* 407 Mich. 909 (1979).

obtain the parallel citation, once you have a citation from either a
"report" or a "reporter."[10] The major technique of finding a parallel
citation to cases is to use "Shepard's";[11] another method would be to
look immediately above the name of the case on the first page in the
report or reporter where it appears; a third would be to look in the "Table of Cases" volume of the *Modern Federal Practice Digest* or the digest
from the region from which your case is reported;[12] and finally, if your
law library has it, you could use the National Reporter Bluebook to find
the unofficial citation when you have the official citation.

3. Research Aids From a Case

If you open volume 485 of the Federal Supplement to page 122, you
will find the names of the parties, *Ramos v. Lamm,* at the top of the
column where the case begins. Under this is an unofficial summary of the
case, called a "synopsis," written by a member of the publishing
company. The synopsis is not part of the decision and you should not
quote it, but it will help you quickly tell whether the case covers an area
of interest to you.

After the synopsis are short paragraphs called "headnotes," with
numbers, a word or short phrase, and a key followed by a number. Each
headnote paragraph corresponds to a section in the body of the actual
court decision. For example, ¶6, or the sixth headnote, will correspond
to the section in the actual opinion that begins with a [6], found on page
152. After reading the synopsis and determining that the case covers an
area of interest, you would read the headnotes and determine which
of them (usually not all of them) sound relevant to your research. In the
decision, the court will give generally the same rule of law that was
summarized in the headnote.[13] Usually, the section of the opinion

---

[10]Cases reported in the Federal Reporters and Federal Supplements do not
have parallel citations, and some states have abolished the official reports and
rely exclusively on West reporters. When citing cases from these states, such as
Florida, you must list the name of the court deciding the case (*e.g.,* Panzavecchia
v. Crockett, 379 So.2d 1047 (Fla. App. 1980)).

[11]If you have difficulty locating a parallel cite in *Shepard's,* you may be
looking in the wrong book, since *Shepard's* will generally only give the parallel
cite the first time the case is reported in their book. Try an earlier volume. Also,
the parallel cite may not exist yet (an official cite for a report may not be published for up to a year after the decision is rendered), and a parallel cite to an official
report may never exist, see *supra* note 10. The parallel cite will be in parenthesis.

[12]If you have the name of the case and not the citation, you can look in the
"Table of Cases" volume of the appropriate *Digest* to find the citation.

[13]The text of a headnote is not part of the decision, and should not be quoted
in your briefs. Burbank v. Ernst, 232 U.S. 162, 34 S.Ct. 299 (1914) ("We look to

containing the headnote number will provide the court's rationale for using a particular rule of law summarized in the headnote and will give other citations supporting its reasoning. However, you can not rely on a case until you have read the whole thing, concentrating on the sections of the decision containing the relevant headnotes. If you do not read the entire decision, you may miss something that is very helpful.

The phrase and key number "Prisons (Key)13(8)" immediately after the headnote [6] are important for finding other cases which have used the same rule of law. The digest topic and key number "Prisons (Key)13(8)" can be found in all West Digests, *e.g.,* the *Modern Federal Practice Digest.*[14] You can look in the *Modern Federal Practice Digest* or the *General Digest* and find other cases that have been reported which have used that same rule of law, even those that have come to different conclusions under the same rule. You may not find all the cases on a subject under the same key number, the indexing is not always consistent; and you may have to use several key numbers.

The number in brackets (*e.g.,* "[6]") is used in "Shepardizing" the case. "Shepardizing" a case allows you to determine the history and treatment of that particular case, thus finding all subsequent cases that have cited that case and that particular proposition of law. "Shepardizing" is discussed later in this chapter.

At the end of a headnote there may be a citation to a section of federal or state constitutions (such as U.S.C.A. Const., Amends. 5, 14), or to a statute (such as 42 U.S.C. §1983). The headnote has interpreted or construed the citation listed at the end of it.

Court decisions will list the names of the attorneys representing the parties involved. You may want to contact them to obtain some of the legal documents filed in that case. Some attorneys will provide you free copies, while others will charge you for photocopying and postage. The federal courts are another place where you can obtain a copy of a particular legal document; however, they will charge at least 50 cents per page.

4.   Briefing the Case

When you find a case that appears relevant, you should *brief* it. This means writing a short analysis and evaluation of the case. Briefing helps you understand what the case means and helps you separate the *holding* (the court's actual ruling on the facts before it) from *dictum* (statements by the judge about what the law might be on some other set of facts).

---

the opinion for the original and authentic statement of the grounds of [the] decision.").

[14]Most regional reporters have their own digest. If your prison law library does not have the regional digest, you should request the prison to obtain it.

Briefing is the most useful way for you to take notes on your research. You should read a case fully at least once before briefing it. In briefing the case, you will be looking for those *questions* of law the court had to resolve to render a decision, and the *statements* the court had to express to render a decision. The following method[15] of briefing a case is suggested.

a.   Facts

State in a short paragraph the precise facts in the case you are briefing. For example, from *Wolff v. McDonnell*[16] (these facts relate to only one issue in the *Wolff* case),

> Nebraska statute provided that a prisoner could lose statutory good time if found guilty of a major disciplinary violation. The procedures required by state law entitled the prisoner to appear before an Adjustment Committee where the report is read to him/her and s/he could ask questions of the writer of the ticket. The Committee could conduct additional investigations if it desired. A finding of guilty would usually result in loss of good time.

b.   Judicial History

This short paragraph will state the history of the case, which the court writing the opinion will usually summarize. For example,

> The district court, based on prior decisions of the Circuit, had rejected the prisoners' procedural due process claim.[17] The Court of Appeals reversed, holding that the procedural requirements outlined recently by the Supreme Court should be followed in prison disciplinary hearings.[18]

c.   Issue

Usually, there is more than one issue in a decision, and each issue should be stated in a separate short paragraph. For example, "Whether state prisoners are entitled to procedural protection of the Due Process Clause of the Fourteenth Amendment when charged with disciplinary actions that could result in loss of statutory good time?"

---

[15]Adopted from Statsky, *Legal Research, Writing, and Analysis: Some Starting Points,* pp. 413-14 (1974).

[16]418 U.S. 539, 94 S.Ct. 2963 (1974).

[17]McDonnell v. Wolff, 342 F. Supp. 616 (D. Neb. 1972).

[18]McDonnell v. Wolff, 483 F.2d 1059 (8th Cir. 1973).

d. Result/Holding

The holding of the court tells you what the court said about that issue. For example, "Prisoners, when faced with major misconduct that could result in loss of statutory good time, are entitled to the minimum requirements of procedural due process." There may be more than one result/holding, and each of these should be listed in a separate paragraph.

e. Reasoning/Rationale

You want to state exactly what *reasons* the court used in the decision to reach each of its holdings. The rationale consists of the *rule of law and the facts* found by the court in the present case to support its rule of law. For example,

> A state need not create the right to receive statutory good time which results in a shortened prison sentence. But, once it has created a right to good time and its deprivation is a sanction authorized for major misconduct, the prisoner has state-created a "liberty" interest that is entitled to minimum procedural protection to ensure that the state-created right is not arbitrarily abrogated.

f. Procedural Consequences

If the case you briefed is an appellate case, you must state what happened to that case. For example, "Affirmed in part, reversed in part"; "The judgment of the district court is reversed, and the case is remanded to the district court with instructions to dismiss the complaint"; etc. When an appellate court "reverses" a lower court judgment, or "reverses in part," it is saying that the judgment as a whole, or at least part of it, was wrong. The appellate court may reverse the judgment of the lower court and dismiss the case, or send it back to the lower court for further consideration of the issue(s) in light of the appellate court's decision.

g. Subsequent Judicial History

You will usually need to "Shepardize" the citation to determine whether the case was appealed to a higher appellate court or whether, after a remand to the lower court, another judgment has been rendered. The subsequent judicial history is important because an appellate court, or the lower court after a case has been remanded, may reverse its earlier judgment or may decide that the court's earlier rationale was wrong and the case should have been decided as it was on other grounds.

Briefing cases is time-consùming and requires meticulous attention to details. The order or format you use when briefing a case is not important. It is important that you carefully pick out the facts, issues, holdings, and rationale. If you master the discipline of briefing, the quality of your legal work will improve tremendously.

Since litigation usually takes a long time and you will probably refer again to the cases you have cited in your first memorandum, you should thoroughly brief each case the first time so you will not have to reread the entire case later. You must try to find cases where the *facts* are very similar to the facts in your case. Cases which involve different factual situations are not very helpful unless you are prepared to give a reason why the rule of law in another situation should also apply in your situation. (*E.g.,* in *Wolff v. McDonnell,* 418 U.S. 539, 94 S.Ct. 2963 (1974), the Supreme Court held that procedural due process was required in prison disciplinary hearings; later, in *Vitek v. Jones,* 445 U.S. 480, 100 S.Ct. 1254 (1980), it explained why the holding of *Wolff* should also apply to transfers to a prison mental hospital.)

Cases that are similar in facts to your case but have been decided adversely to you must also be briefed thoroughly. You must tell the court why the cases that have been decided adversely to your factual situation should not be relied upon by the court in rendering its decision. If you do not distinguish the cases which are adverse to you, the state will certainly find these cases and stress to the court that it should follow the decisions reached in these cases.

C. Methods of Research

Once you have learned how to marshal the facts in your own case and how to find, read, and brief cases, you will then be ready to learn the different methods of legal research. Since it is usually difficult for prisoners to do exhaustive research of a particular area of the law due to the inadequate resources in a prison law library, the following methods, we hope, will compensate for these inadequacies, and will allow you to obtain enough legal materials to submit a memorandum of law to the court. You must remember that since no two cases are identical, there seldom will be a "right" answer. You must look for cases with factual situations that are very similar to yours.

1. Researching by Words

The "word approach" is generally used in researching a legal problem when you know of no statutes or cases to start your research—you have no idea where to begin. Even though someone around the prison law library often will know about a case that is similar to yours, this approach to research must be learned for that one time someone in the law library will not be able to help you to get started.

Examine the statement of facts contained in Section A, "Marshalling the Facts," at the beginning of this chapter, and separate the words or phrases into a few general categories. Pick out the important words in your statement of facts, such as "maximum security," "administrative reasons," "prison rules," "classification committee," "rights and privileges," "hearing," etc. If you go to the *Modern Federal Practice Digest* (federal cases) or the *General Digest* (both federal and state cases) and look in the separate volumes for the above words, you will not find any of these words or phrases listed. This does not mean that cases dealing with these words or phrases are not contained in the digests; rather, your search is too specific. You must think of general words or phrases that relate to your legal problems (*e.g.,* "constitutional law" and "civil rights"). If you check the digests for these general topics and read some of the headnotes listed under different sections of "constitutional law" and "civil rights," you will not find many cases dealing with prisoners or convicts and their rights. All of the words or phrases have one thing in common in this factual situation: they apply to a prisoner or convict. You must then look in the digest for these words or variations of them, and you will find Prisons and Convicts. You now have a starting point when using the "word" approach.

If the prison law library digest contains the "Descriptive Word Index," you could have looked in these volumes. These volumes list general words alphabetically and where they can be found under Digest Topics and Key Numbers in the regular volumes of the digest. For example, you look up the general word classification and find a subheading of "prisoners" which refers you to the Digest Topic Prison and Key Number 13(5,6).

You should find time to examine the "digest topic" arrangement that West Publishing Company uses in all its digests. It will be listed in the front pages of every volume of the West digests. West has divided its digest topics into seven main divisions of law, with each one of these main divisions subdivided into numerous other general word topics.

If you looked up the word "Prisons" in the *Modern Federal Practice Digest,* you would find the following outline:

1. Establishment and maintenance.
2. Use by United States of state prison or county jail.
3. Use by city of county jail.
4. Regulation and supervision.
   (1) In general.
   (2) Judicial supervision in general.
   (3) ----State prisons.
   (4) Persons held pending trial or on detainer.

(5) Particular rights, privileges, and restrictions.

(6) Communications, visitors, privacy, and censorship in general.

(7) Personal grooming and effects; contraband and searches.

(8) Access to reading matter.

(9) Access to mails for correspondence.

(10) Access to courts.

(11) ----Access to counsel; paralegal counsel, and inmate assistance.

(12) ----Communication with courts, officers, or counsel.

(13) ----Law books and law libraries, legal materials, and opportunity for legal work.

(14) Religious practices and materials.

5. Officers.

6. ----In general.

7. ----Appointment, qualification, and tenure.

8. ----Compensation for services.

9. ----Powers and duties.

10. ----Liabilities in general.

11. ----Liabilities on bonds.

12. Management in general.

13. Custody and control of prisoners.

(1) In general.

(2) Discipline, security, and confinement.

(3) Judicial supervision in general.

(4) Particular violations, punishments, and deprivations; use of force.

(5) Segregation and solitary confinement; classification.

(6) Disciplinary, classification, and grievance proceedings; composition of tribunal.

(7) Requisites of proceedings in general.

(8) ----Notice and hearing; summary proceedings.

(9) ----Counsel and witnesses.

(10) ----Review and judicial supervision.

13.5. Transfer of custody.

(1) In general.

(2) Interstate and state--federal transfers.

(3) Proceedings and judicial supervision.

14. Discharge of prisoners in general.

15. Reduction of term of imprisonment and discharge for good conduct.

(1) In general.

(2) Constitutional and statutory provisions.

(3) Sentences to which applicable; persons entitled.

(4) Computation of credit.

(5) Forfeiture before release.

(6) Conditional release and revocation.

(7) Procedure and review.

16. Escape of prisoners.

17. Maintenance and care of prisoners.

17.5. Bringing articles to or communicating with prisoners.

18. Compensation for keeping and maintenance of prisoners, jail fees, and incidental expenses.

(1) In general.

(2) Board.

(3) Jail fees and discharge of prisoners.

(4) Officers entitled.

(5) Forfeiture of compensation.

(6) Liability of county, city, or town.

(7) Liability of state.

(8) Allowance and payment.

(9) Actions for maintenance.

There are a number of other key numbers in the Digest System that deal with prisons which you should examine. They are contained in such topic headings as Civil Rights, Constitutional Law, Criminal Law (section on Cruel and Unusual Punishment), and Convicts. Unfortunately, some cases may not be listed under any of these headings,[19] so you should be sure to "Shepardize" the important cases in your topic so you can pick up additional cases that are poorly indexed in the key number system.

Glancing down the outline, you would see some topical sections that would assist you in your research (*e.g.,* 4(4) and (13); 13(5), (6), and (7); etc.). If you turned to subsections (4) and (13) of §4 and then (5), (6), and (7) of §13, you would find headnotes of the type contained in reporters. You should read the headnotes of the cases listed under the sections and the subsections of the topic of interest. The cases and their headnotes are listed in the *Modern Federal Practice Digest,* starting first with the highest federal court, the U.S. Supreme Court, and then the federal courts of appeal, followed by the federal district courts listed alphabetically by state. The *General Digests* will list cases decided by the federal courts first and then list alphabetically the state courts' decisions.

Once you have read the headnotes contained in the topic sections and have written down the citations of all cases that look like they are relevant to your factual situation, you should look in the "pocket part"[20]

---

[19]*See, e.g.,* Ariz v. LeFevre, 642 F.2d 1109 (2d Cir. 1981) (Muslim rights case indexed only under Federal Civil Procedure); Marcera v. Chinlund, 91 F.R.D. 579 (W.D.N.Y. 1981) (contact visiting case indexed only under Federal Civil Procedure and Injunction).

[20]A "pocket part" is a paper pamphlet tucked in the pocket in the back of the bound volume. It will list the year it is to be used, *e.g.,* "For use in 1981." If the

of that volume for more cases. In addition to the pocket parts, there may be bound paperback "supplement" volumes to check.

After checking the bound volume, the pocket part, and the paperback supplements, you may realize that there is a period of three to six months for which reported cases can not be found in the digest. For example, the most recent supplement is dated September 1982, and it is now December 1982. To find the most recently reported cases, you will need to go to the paperback "advance sheets," which are issued weekly, for the different reporters in your law library. If the most recent reported case in the supplement is volume 535 F. Supp., you will need to look at each reporter printed after volume 535 of the Federal Supplement. Once you have found these volumes of the reporters you should look at the "Key Number Digest" in the front of each bound volume and the advance sheets under the topic(s) of interest to you, in order to find the most recent cases reported.

Now that you have written down the citations of all the cases that are factually similar to yours, you are ready to begin briefing cases. You should follow the format provided in Section 4 of this chapter, *supra*. Only the cases which are similar to yours factually and which you think you can use in your brief, or cases that the opposing party will use and that you will need to distinguish, should be briefed. The cases that you have briefed should be "Shepardized" to obtain other cases directly on point and to determine whether these cases have been affirmed, reversed, granted certiorari, etc.

There are numerous other research tools you can use that are structured similarly to the *Modern Federal Practice Digest*. If you can master the techniques explained above relating to the *Modern Federal Practice Digest,* you can transfer those skills to the below-listed digests:

(a) West's *Decennial Digest* contains the case law decided for a ten-year period. The most recent edition is called the *Eighth Decennial Digest* and covers the period of 1966 to 1976. The previous *Decennial Digests* each cover a different ten-year period. The cases are listed by the identical topical matter used in the *Modern Federal Practice Digest,* except that in this *Digest* both state and federal cases are reported under each topic.

(b) West's *General Digest* has its volumes printed yearly since the last *Decennial Digest*. Each yearly volume of the *General Digest* (1977, 1978, 1979, 1980, and 1981) will list by the topical matter the federal and state cases decided in that particular year. Since the *Eighth Decennial Digest* covered the ten-year period 1966 to 1976, the *General Digest* will have bound volumes for 1977, 1978, 1979, 1980, and 1981; it will have a

---

pocket part is missing or is not current, you should inform the librarian or guard in charge of the library.

paperback supplement for the year 1982, which will be bound at the end of the year. *General Digests* will be reprinted so that all cases decided between 1976 and 1986 will be listed under their proper topical matter for that particular ten-year period.

(c) *American Jurisprudence* and *Corpus Juris Secundum* are the two major legal encyclopedias which cover almost every area of the law.[21] If there is an area of law with which you are unfamiliar, you should read the treatises on that particular subject contained in one of these encyclopedias to obtain a general overview of that particular area. The treatises will provide case cites and are updated yearly by pocket parts.

(d) *Index to Legal Periodicals:* This publication lists law reviews by a word index. Law review articles can be very helpful when researching an area of law with which you are not familiar, or when trying to apply a standard or test that an earlier court decision had established.

(e) *Words and Phrases:* If you need a case that defines a word or phrase, such as "substantial evidence," "armed with a weapon," or "abuse of discretion," you should look at *Words and Phrases*. These volumes are updated with supplements.

(f) *American Law Reports:* The A.L.R. series contains selected cases decided by federal and state courts, with each case followed by an extensive commentary and annotations. These annotations are updated, superseded, etc., when another series of A.L.R. is published. A.L.R. is presently being published as a new series, the fourth.

(g) *American Law Reports, Federal:* The same as the A.L.R. series, first through the fourth, but contains only federal cases with annotations based on federal law.

2. Researching a Statute

The area of law you are interested in obtaining information about may concern "what must be alleged in a civil rights complaint filed in federal court, if it is to have jurisdiction";[22] "what must be alleged in a complaint to state a cause of action for conspiracy to violate civil rights"; etc. These questions are best answered by referring to statutes concerning each particular question. When determining whether there is a statute that covers your area of interest, you should always use the "Annotated" edition of federal statutes (the *United States Code Annotated*) or state statutes (*Michigan Compiled Law Annotated* or *Michigan Statutes Annotated*). The annotated edition provides "Notes of Decisions"[23] which list cases that interpreted the particular statute.

---

[21]These encyclopedias treat matters of law on a subject or topical basis.

[22]See Ch. VI, Secs. B1 and C1, for a discussion of jurisdiction.

[23]"Notes of Decisions" will provide you with an index by subject matter relevant to how courts have interpreted that particular statute.

If you do not have citations to statutes concerning your area of interest, you will need to look in the index volumes at the end of the statutes.[24] To gain access to this index you should use the "word approach" you just learned. If you want to find the answer to "what must be alleged in a civil rights complaint filed in federal court for it to have jurisdiction," you would want to look under the general topics of "federal court," "district court," "jurisdiction," "civil rights," "complaint," etc. Under each of these general topics would be listed numerous headings and subheadings you would need to scan to find whether you can obtain a citation to a statute. Once you have looked under the previously identified general topics and have listed citations of statutes that might contain the information you seek, you will go to each statute and read the body of those statutes.

One of the statutes you should have listed was 28 U.S.C. §1334. If you will look in the volume of the *United States Code Annotated* which contains volume 28 and includes §§1081 to 1690, you will find §1334. The body of the statute is listed first. You would read this to determine whether it applies to your situation.

After the body of the statute is the reference to the official edition of the statute. These references are explained more fully in the "Historical and Revision Notes" which tells you where to find the legislative history and when, if ever, the statute was amended or revised.[25] Next comes the "Cross References," which refer you to other statutes that cover topics similar to this one.

The next two listings are very helpful to a prisoner litigator. The "Library References" listing will give topical subject matters with their Key Numbers that refer you in turn to the *Digests* of the West Publishing Company, and also will give a reference to one of the legal encyclopedias (such as C.J.S., *Corpus Juris Secundum*) by subject matter and section of that subject. The West's *Federal Forms* will refer you to sections in the form books for samples of complaints, allegations of jurisdiction, or whatever else you are researching.

The "Notes of Decisions" contain a series of paragraph summaries explaining court decisions that have interpreted and applied statutes. At the beginning of each "Notes of Decisions" will be an index to assist you

---

[24]A list of the general subject categories for the entire set of volumes will also be found in the first few pages of the first volume. Some statutes contain this general subject category in the first few pages of every volume for that particular state.

[25]Most prison law libraries will not have the *U.S. Code Congressional and Administrative News* (U.S.C.C.A.N.), which would list the origins of the statute, what committee of the legislative branch worked on it, comments of congressional members during debate of the statute, etc. If available, it can be useful to show the intent of the statute.

in finding cases. Once you have found the phrases in the index that you feel are related to your area of interest, turn to these numbered sections of the annotation and skim them for cases of interest. Remember to check the pocket part for the latest cases and to see if the statute has been amended or revised since the main text was printed. Also check for any bound paperback supplements dated later than the pocket part.

You can also "Shepardize" the statute and its subsections to determine if there have been any legislative changes and to find court decisions interpreting these changes. "Shepardizing" is discussed in subsection 4, *infra*.

3. Researching a Case

This is the easiest way to research, since all you need is one case that deals with your particular point of interest. As mentioned earlier, usually there is someone around the law library who can give you a cite to a case covering your area of interest.

Once you have your one case, you will need to examine the headnotes of that case to find which section of the decision deals with the exact point of law you need. Using the bracketed number appearing before the headnotes, you should turn to that part of the decision where this bracketed number appears. Usually, these bracketed sections will contain citations to other cases which you then can read to get additional citations.

The case that has law concerning your area of interest will provide you with the topic digest name and Key Number by the headnote of your interest. Using the topic digest name and Key Number, you can look in the digests under that name and number and find other cases on the same subject. (See Researching By Words, *supra*.)

Another method or researching is to Shepardize the case you find on point. The drawback to Shepardizing only your case is that this method only provides the cases decided after your initial case of interest, whereas using the digests will give you prior cases related to your issue.

Regardless what method of research is used, you must Shepardize every case you will cite in your memorandum of law, to determine whether a higher court has affirmed, reversed, modified, etc., each of those cases. (*E.g., Ramos v. Lamm,* 485 F. Supp. 122 (D. Colo. 1979), *aff'd in part, reversed in part and remanded,* 639 F.2d 554 (10th Cir. 1980), *cert. denied,* 101 S.Ct. 1759 (1981).)

4. Shepardizing

Shepardizing is an important aspect of legal research which you will have to use when citing cases, statutes, court rules, and law reviews. If you Shepardize a case, you can find the parallel cite and other cases that are part of the same litigation, if any others exist: cases that have mentioned your case; law review publications; and annotations in A.L.R., A.L.R.2d, A.L.R.3d, A.L.R.4th, or A.L.R. Fed. Shepardizing a statute will allow you to find the original legislation number, any legislative changes (appeal, amendment, revision, etc.), cases interpreting the statute, and any other publication citing it. The Shepardizing of court rules and law reviews will provide additional research materials.

There are numerous groups of *Shepard's Citations,* each dealing with a particular court system or area of law.[26] Each set of *Shepard's Citations* will consist of at least one permanent bound volume and temporary supplements.[27] To determine whether you have all the correct *Shepard's* volumes, you need to look at the box on the front cover of the most recent supplemental pamphlet.[28] It will tell you "WHAT YOUR LIBRARY SHOULD CONTAIN."[29]

Once you have found the right set of *Shepard's* and have made sure that all the volumes are there, you should examine the first few pages of one of these volumes. Find the "Table of Abbreviations," located in the front, and familiarize yourself with it. These abbreviations are used throughout *Shepard's Citations* and provide an analysis of the case you are Shepardizing, because they tell you what the other cases citing your decision have held. If you see an "e" before a citation, you know the case is "explained"; an "o" tells you the case has been "overruled"; and an "f" tells you the court that cited the case you are "Shepardizing" "followed" that holding.

If you are Shepardizing a case, you should start with the most recent *Shepard's* and work your way backward. Always make certain that if your case was reported in "N.W.2d," you are in that section of *Shepard's* listings, and not in the section listing the "N.W." cases. Once you have the right section of the most recent *Shepard's,* look for the citation of the case you want to Shepardize—volume and page

---

[26]There are *Shepard's Citations* for all the federal and state courts and their respective statutes and for other areas like the federal regulations.

[27]The bound volumes will be red. Supplemental pamphlets will be red, gold, and white in color.

[28]The most recent pamphlet should be dated no more than two months earlier than the current month and year.

[29]Since most prison law libraries are grossly inadequate and usually do not contain reporters dating back further than 30 or 40 years, they may not stock the early dated bound *Shepard's* volumes. These early volumes are needed to allow you to at least "Shepardize" the cases not in your law library, and to read what other courts have said about them. Have your law librarian order the missing *Shepard's* volumes.

number. Since you are probably not interested in all the headnotes of the case you are Shepardizing, you will look down the list of cases to see which cites have a small elevated number identical to the headnotes you are Shepardizing. This small elevated number will be located following the abbreviation of the reporter and will tell you that the case cited the same proposition of law as you found earlier. Using the headnote Shepardizing method, you will not have to read all the cases listed, and can concentrate on cases right on point.

Since your case relied on earlier cases in arriving at a decision, you should Shepardize those cases. Remember, the case you Shepardize will only provide you with citations of cases decided after that case was decided. If you wish to go back in the law, you must use the case cited in your case and Shepardize them.

Shepardizing a statute, such as 28 U.S.C. §1334(4), is a little different than using case *Shepard's*, in that you must look under the title of the statute first ("Title 28"), then the section ("1334"), then any subsection ("4").

This is a very limited discussion of Shepardizing, and we highly recommend that you read the front page of a bound *Shepard's* volume several times until you have mastered this method of legal researching. Your law library should also contain the pamphlet entitled *How to Use Shepard's Citations.* This publication is free to subscribers and if your law library does not have it, the librarian should be informed to write Shepard's, Inc., P.O. Box 1235, Colorado Springs, CO. 80901, for a free copy.

Any cases or statutes cited in your memorandum of law must be Shepardized to determine if a higher court has affirmed, reversed, modified, etc. It is your responsibility to the court that you are filing your pleadings with to provide it with the latest legal citations supporting your legal contentions. Failure to fully Shepardize your citations can be very harmful, especially if one of the main cases you are relying on has been reversed by a higher court. You should always cover yourself and Shepardize completely.

III
Legal Writing

By James Lawrence*

Legal writing is the art of writing a legal document. The way you write will depend on what kind of document you are writing. Persons using this manual will typically be writing one of the following types of documents:

a) *Complaint or Petition.* This is a document which begins a lawsuit.

b) *Motion or Reply to Motion.* A motion is a request that the judge make a particular order.

c) *Order or Judgment.* You may prepare a written order or judgment hoping that the judge will sign it. Once it is signed, the parties are required to do what it says.

d) *Affidavit.* This is a document in which you or another person swears to certain facts. In many courts it must be notarized, but in others, including federal courts, the signer may simply indicate that s/he is signing under penalty of perjury.[1]

e) *Brief.* A brief is a detailed statement of facts and law which explains to the court why it should rule your way on any particular point. A brief may be filed in support of a motion, before or after trial, or on appeal.

A. Complaint or Petition

A complaint or petition needs a *heading* or *caption* at the top of the first page. The heading or caption states the name of the court, the name or names of all plaintiffs or petitioners, and the name or names of all defendants or respondents.[2] It also should contain the docket number of

---

* Attorney, J.D., University of Michigan, 1979.

[1] *See* 28 U.S.C. §1746.

[2] If you are bringing a civil action, you are called a plaintiff, and the other party is called the defendant. If you are bringing a habeas corpus action or a mandamus action, you are the petitioner, and the opposing party is the respondent. See Appendices B, Form 1a, and C, Form 7a.

the case and the name of the judge, when these are known. When they are not known, a space should be left to fill in the information later.

The document then needs a *title*. "Complaint" is usually good enough.[3] If it is a petition, you should say petition for what (*e.g.,* "Petition for Habeas Corpus" or "Petition for Mandamus").

After the title, but before the numbered paragraphs, you should include a very short introductory paragraph, such as "This is a §1983 action filed by Joseph Smith, a state prisoner, alleging violation of his constitutional rights and seeking injunctive relief. . . ." (List what relief you seek.)

You should then begin with the *paragraphs*. Each paragraph is a *short* statement of a fact or claim. Each paragraph must be numbered. Each paragraph should be *short* (no more than one to four sentences long). *Short* paragraphs are easier for judges and their clerks to read. Further, writing *short* paragraphs will help you to focus on what is important and exclude what is unimportant.

It is important not to mix different facts in the same paragraph. For example, suppose in paragraph 4 of your complaint you state: "The hearing officer did not advise me of the charges against me, and did not give me a copy of the hearing report." In the answer to the complaint, the other side might simply deny that paragraph is true. If they do, you will not know whether they are denying that "the hearing officer did not advise you of the charges against you," or "the hearing officer . . . did not give you a copy of the hearing report," or if the hearing officer did not do either. To avoid this problem, you would divide the above statement into two separate paragraphs.

You also should not mix facts and legal claims in the same paragraph. For example, if you say in paragraph 5: "Officer Johnson cut my hair over my objections, which denied my right to due process and freedom of expression," the other side, in their answer to the complaint, may deny this paragraph. You do not know whether they are denying that "Officer Johnson cut [your] hair," or "Officer Johnson denied your right to due process and freedom of expression," or if Officer Johnson did not do either.

Putting each fact or claim in a separate paragraph requires the other side to answer in more detail, which is to your benefit. If the other side admits the fact situation or legal claim contained in any part of the paragraph, you will have less to prove at trial. Remember, whatever is admitted by the other side in their answer need not be proved at trial by

---

[3] The complaint is the first pleading that you will file in a civil action. If you wish to proceed without payment of filing fees or costs, you will need to file a motion to proceed in forma pauperis, affidavit in support, an order for the judge to sign, and an affidavit of proof of service. See Appendix B, Forms 1, 2, and 7. See also Ch. VII, Sec. A, Starting Your Lawsuit.

you. If the other side disregards any of your facts or claims by not denying or admitting them, they will be considered to have admitted those paragraph(s).

The paragraphs in your pleadings should be divided into two parts: the *allegations common to all claims* and the *claims.*[4] The allegations common to all claims should contain all of the following information.

a) *Jurisdiction.* You must demonstrate, by citation to statutes, court rules, or the facts, that the court has jurisdiction over the case. For example, you may demonstrate jurisdiction by showing that a United States District Court has jurisdiction over your case by citing the relevant Federal statutes.[5]

b) *The parties.* You must identify who the parties are, both by name and by office. You should spell out relationships between the parties. If someone is an agent or employee of a person or agency, you should allege that fact.[6] If a party is an agency of the U.S. government or a particular state government, you should allege that fact.[7] If you are a prisoner, you should allege where you are imprisoned and who has custody of you.

c) *Exhaustion of remedies.* If you are suing a government agency in state or federal court, it is advised that you exhaust your administrative remedies before going to court. This means that you fully presented your claim and appealed the claim within the administrative agency. Exhaustion of these remedies is not required before filing civil rights actions in federal court under 42 U.S.C. §1983.[8] If you are a state prisoner seeking federal habeas corpus, you should show that the issues were duly presented to and rejected by the state courts, including all state

----

[4]The claims will be listed after your facts and consist of the different causes of action. See Appendix B, Form 1a.

[5]If you are a state prisoner bringing a civil rights action, jurisdiction is based on 28 U.S.C. §1343 and venue is based on 28 U.S.C. §1391. If you are a federal prisoner bringing an action against the federal officials for violating your federal civil rights, jurisdiction is based on 28 U.S.C. §§1331 and 1361 and venue is based on 28 U.S.C. §1391. Neither federal nor state prisoners are required any longer to allege a jurisdictional amount in excess of $10,000. See Ch. VI, Secs. B and C, for a full discussion of jurisdiction.

[6]See Ch. VI, Sec. D2, for a discussion of personal involvement of prison officials.

[7]See Ch. VI, Sec. D1, Immunities.

[8]See Ch. VI, Sec. D, for a general discussion concerning the pros and cons of exhausting remedies.

appellate courts. If you have not exhausted your remedies in these cases, go back and do it before filing your petition.[9]

d) *The facts.*[10] You should make an effort to allege only those facts which can be proven. You should include those facts that are relevant, and leave out facts that are irrelevant.

When you have completed the allegations common to all claims, you can begin on the claims themselves. Each claim will have one or more paragraphs. Each claim should have a number of its own (First Cause of Action, Second Cause of Action, etc.), which ordinarily will not be the same as the numbers of the paragraphs within the claim.[11]

Within the claim, you should make reference back to earlier paragraphs where you state the facts you are relying on.[12] Then you should write a paragraph which states why those facts entitle you to judgment. Ordinarily, this will include a citation to a statute, constitutional provision, court rule, or case, but does not have to. (*E.g.,* "The actions of the Defendant stated in paragraphs 3-24 denied Plaintiff due process of law. U.S. Const., Amend. V.")

If you are making a claim of negligence, for example, your cause of action must contain (at a minimum) 4 allegations, each of which should have a separate paragraph:

1) Defendant owed Plaintiff a duty of reasonable care (explain the nature of the duty). Example: The Defendant owed Plaintiff a duty of reasonable care to protect him/her from assaults of other prisoners.

2) Defendant breached that duty by (explain the nature of the breach). Example: The Defendant breached that duty by failing to assign a prison guard to the gym during the time when it is in use by prisoners.

3) The breach of duty resulted in damages (list the damages).

4) The breach of duty proximately caused those damages.

In any negligence or tort case, where you are seeking compensation for damages, you must include the words "proximate cause" or some variation (such as "proximately caused") in the claim.

If you have a case based on one constitutional provision, two statutes, and a principle of common law, you should have claims or four causes of action in your complaint. Common law refers to law stated in court cases

---

[9]See Ch. IX, Sec. B2, for a discussion of exhaustion of state procedures in a habeas corpus action.

[10]The facts are the most important part of your complaint or petition. Courts assume they know the laws and will usually only look at your facts to determine whether your complaint has alleged a violation of the law.

[11]See Appendix B, Form 1a, and C, Form 7.

[12]See Appendix B, Form 1a, the section listing the causes of action.

not based on a statute or constitution, such as the law of negligence or bailment.

Ordinarily, you do not need cases or lengthy legal analysis in a civil complaint.[13] However, your petition for habeas corpus should have attached to it a brief containing cases and legal analysis.[14]

After you have listed all the claims, you should use an unnumbered paragraph to say: "WHEREFORE, Plaintiff moves that this Honorable Court grant the following relief: . . ." You should then use *lettered* paragraphs to list each item of relief you want. You may separate the items either with "ands" or "ors." When you use "ors," this is called *requesting relief in the alternative.* After listing what you want, add a final relief paragraph requesting the court to grant "such other relief as it may appear Plaintiff is entitled to."

You should then sign the document, date it, and include your mailing address.[15]

Some complaints need to be *verified,* and others do not. To make sure you do not make a mistake, you should verify all complaints and petitions. To verify a complaint or petition, you sign an affidavit stating that the facts stated in the complaint are true to your knowledge, and that the facts stated on information and belief are true to the best of your knowledge and belief.[16] It should be notarized or signed under penalty of perjury.[17]

B.   Motion or Reply to Motion

A motion is a request to a court to take an action in a case over which the court already has jurisdiction.[18] The court action that you are

---

[13]In federal court the rules state that a complaint should "be simple, concise, and direct." Rule 8(e)(1), FRCP.

[14]See Appendix C, Form 6b.

[15]See Ch. VII, Sec. A2, Requirements for Filing and Service.

[16]See Appendix B, Form 1.

[17]28 U.S.C. §1746 provides that in all federal court proceedings, written declarations made under penalty of perjury are permissible in lieu of notarized affidavits. *See* Carter v. Clark, 616 F.2d 228 (5th Cir. 1980). Use this form:

"I declare (or certify, verify, or state) under penalty of perjury that the foregoing is true and correct."

Executed on (date). (Signature)

[18]Very rarely will you file a motion before you have filed your complaint or petition with the court or before the plaintiff has served the defendant with the complaint or petition.

requesting will result in an order being issued. The subject matter of motions is virtually unlimited—extension of time to file a brief in opposition to defendant's motion for summary judgment, sanctions against the defendant for failure to comply with your request for discovery, etc.[19] You should not hesitate to draft motions which state in plain language any request which is legally and factually supportable and which is within the power of the court to grant.[20]

Like a complaint, a motion or reply to a motion needs the case caption at the top of the first page. It also needs a title, such as "Motion for Summary Judgment."[21] After the title and before the numbered paragraphs, you should include a short paragraph, such as "Plaintiff Joseph Smith, pursuant to Fed. R. Civ. Proc. 56(a), moves for summary judgment and says: . . . ."

You should then use numbered paragraphs to state your legal position, and lettered paragraphs to state the relief requested.

If there is a court rule which covers the motion, you must carefully read the rule.[22] You should cite it in the motion, and make sure you have met all of the requirements of the rule. For example, if the rule requires that there be no genuine issue of material fact, you should allege in a separate paragraph that there is no genuine issue of material fact.[23] You will then use another paragraph to explain why there is no genuine issue of material fact.

If the other side files a motion,[24] you will file a reply, sometimes called a response or an answer. The reply uses the same general form as a motion. In your reply, you must respond to the legal position contained in the motion.

If the issue involved in the motion is simple, you may include all your legal authority in the motion, and not use a brief in support. If the issue is complex, you should include your authority and legal analysis in a separate brief in support. If you file a brief in support, you should *incorporate* the brief into the motion. You do this by making a paragraph of your motion say something like: "Plaintiff incorporates by reference the Brief in Support of this Motion."

A motion will often be accompanied by affidavits of fact, when the motion depends on facts. Affidavits are generally required in motions for summary judgment and motions in opposition to summary judg-

---

[19] See Appendices B and C for examples of motions.

[20] See Ch. VII, Secs. A3, B, C, E2g, and G-H, for different motions.

[21] See Appendix B, Form 11.

[22] See Ch. VII, Secs. B-D, E2g, G, H, and O, concerning different motions.

[23] *Id.* at Sec. G, Summary Judgment.

[24] See Ch. VII, Sec. B, Motion To Dismiss or Judgment on the Pleadings.

ment.[25] If the motion itself contains facts, and it usually does, you should *verify* the motion with an affidavit of verification.[26]

C.   Order or Judgment

If you write an order or judgment, you are in fact writing a *proposed* order or judgment. It becomes an order or judgment only if signed by the judge. In some rare instances, a court clerk can sign an order or judgment. Anytime you submit a motion to the court, you may also submit a proposed order granting you the relief you requested.[27]

An order may be written or oral, but for your purposes will usually be written. A written order will *require* a party to do something, or will *permit* a party to do something (for example, an order permitting the Plaintiff an extension of time to file a brief).

A judgment is a particular kind of order: one that ends the case.[28]

Often, judges will insist on writing their own orders. Certain types of orders may have to be prepared by the judge because a form is used, and you do not have the form. When you have the opportunity to write the order, you should do so, because you can make sure it says what you want.

An order or judgment requires the case caption at the top of the first page and a title. Below that is a short, indented, single-spaced paragraph stating where the court is and what date the order was signed. Below that is a statement as to which judge is present.[29]

The body of the order should begin with a paragraph stating who moved for what, and the comment that the court has been briefed by the parties. It should then contain one or more paragraphs starting with the words "IT IS ORDERED . . ." or "IT IS FURTHER ORDERED . . ." where you list the specific things to be ordered. At the end, leave a space for the judge's signature and a place for the clerk of the court to countersign the order.[30]

D.   Affidavit

An affidavit should also begin with the case caption and title. Beneath

---

[25]See Ch. VII, Sec. G, Summary Judgment.

[26]*See supra* note 17.

[27]See Appendix B, Forms 13c and 14c.

[28]See Ch. VII, Sec. O2, for a discussion of enforcing or obtaining relief from the judgment.

[29]*See supra* note 27.

[30]*Id.*

that is a short affidavit heading which shows where the affidavit was sworn to, such as:

STATE OF MICHIGAN)
) SS. AFFIDAVIT OF JOSEPH SMITH
COUNTY OF WAYNE   )

You then begin an unnumbered paragraph, such as "Joseph Smith, being first duly sworn, does say and depose the following: . . . ." You will then use numbered paragraphs listing the facts to which you wish to swear. If the affidavit is short, you do not need to use numbered paragraphs.

The person swearing to the facts is called the *affiant* or *deponent*. At the bottom of the affidavit, allow a place for the signature of the affiant. Below the affiant's signature provide a statement that the affidavit was sworn to before the notary on such and such a date, and leave a space for the notary's signature.[31]

Some people conclude affidavits with the phrase "Further deponent says not." This is not necessary, but it is not harmful either.

You should swear only to those facts which are within your personal knowledge. If you believe something is true, but did not observe it, you may state that it is true *on information and belief*. Note carefully that swearing to untrue facts in an affidavit might subject you to criminal liability (conviction and sentence) for perjury, false swearing, contempt of court, or fraud.

The most common forms of affidavits you will use are:

a) *Proof of Service*.[32] The affiant swears that a document was mailed or served on a particular date.

b) *Affidavit of Indigency*.[33] The affiant swears that he is too poor to afford court costs and fees, or is so poor that he cannot afford an attorney, etc. It should include the facts about your financial situation.

c) *Affidavit of Verification*. The affiant swears that the facts stated in another document are true to his knowledge, and that facts stated on information and belief are true to the best of his knowledge and belief.

d) *Affidavit Supporting (or Opposing) Summary Judgment*.[34] A party moving for summary judgment, and a party opposing summary judgment, are often required by court rules to file affidavits in support of their position.

---

[31]When prison officials do not provide a notary, you may make a declaration under penalty of perjury. *See supra* note 17.

[32]See Appendix B, Form 17.

[33]*Id.*, Form 2b. See Ch. VII, Sec. A3, for a full discussion of indigency.

[34]See Ch. VII, Sec. G, for a full discussion of summary judgment.

If other people support your version of the facts, and they have personal knowledge of the facts, they may sign affidavits too. If the facts may be contested (as with a motion for summary judgment), you should submit as many affidavits as you can get. Matters not likely to be contested, such as Proof of Service, can be handled with a single affidavit.

E. Brief (Or Memorandum of Law)

In everyday language, the word "brief" means short. A legal brief can be one page long or a hundred pages long, or even longer. However, some courts have a rule limiting the size of briefs, unless you move for and receive permission to file a longer brief. If your brief will be longer than 50 pages, you should check to see whether there is such a length limitation. The information is commonly available from the court clerk.

A brief consists of the following items.[35]

a) *Cover page.* This lists the title of the contents and includes the case caption.

b) *Table of Contents.* This lists the contents in more detailed form and lists the page numbers where the items can be found. While individual issues are not listed on the cover page, they are listed in the table of contents.

c) *Index of Authorities.* This is a table listing all the authorities (cases, statutes, etc.) you use in the brief, the citation, and the page or pages of the brief where it is used.

d) *Statement of Questions Presented.* This lists the issues in question form. You should provide your answer to each question.

e) *Statement of Facts.*

f) *Argument.* The argument consists of the briefed issues.

g) *Relief Requested.*

h) *Signature.*

i) *Appendix.*

Different courts will have different requirements for the statement of facts. In federal courts, you write a *Statement of the Case, or Statement of Proceedings* which explains the procedural history of the case, and a *Statement of Facts* which contains the facts of the case which are relevant to your legal argument, often, a local court system will have local rules regarding briefs in addition to the general court rules. For example, each federal district court and circuit court has local rules in addition to the general rules of the Federal Rules of Civil Procedure. These rules should always be consulted to determine actual filing requirements.

If you are in an appellate court, you may be required to file a Concise

---

[35]See Appendices B, Form 11c, and C, Form 7b.

Statement of Facts and Proceedings which has been approved by the lower court judge. In some cases, you and the attorney for the other side may be able to stipulate to a statement of facts.

An *appendix* is always required in some appellate courts, and may not be required in others. Check the appropriate local court rules, or ask the court clerk. There are some things which should always be included in an appendix, such as affidavits, important documents (an administrative hearing report, for example), or the decision you are appealing.

The *argument* addresses one or more legal issues which are of consequence to the court action. Each legal issue should have its own portion of the brief. The issues should be numbered. Each issue should have a title, which should be a complete sentence. For example, one issue might be entitled "The District Court erred by refusing to hold an evidentiary hearing," and another issue might be entitled "Summary Judgment was improper because there was a disputed question of material fact."

Each issue in the argument should include relevant authority to support your position. This authority can be cases, statutes, constitutional provisions, court rules, administrative rules, city ordinances, etc. You may also use secondary authority, such as quotations from CJS (Corpus Juris Secundum), Am Jur 2d (American Jurisprudence Second), law review articles, etc.[36]

If a proposition or legal issue is well founded or obvious, you can use a single case to support it. If a proposition is likely to be challenged, you should use all the authorities you can muster.

Your argument should be logical and as short as possible. If your argument is too long, or is sloppy, uses poor English, or is otherwise difficult to read, it may not be thoroughly read by the judge. It may help to have others read over your issues when you have finished them. If your friends cannot understand what you are saying, chances are the judge will not understand either.

Remember, however, that while you are very familiar with the facts of the case, others are not, including the judge. You must make sure in each issue that the reader knows the facts behind your claim. You should *not* write a long scholarly discussion of the law which fails to mention what the facts are. Instead, you should generally organize your issues as follows:

a) facts
b) logic
c) conclusions reached by applying logic to facts
d) authority which supports either your logic, your conclusions, or both.

---

[36]See Ch. II, Legal Research.

Of course, you need not separately label each of these four parts. Often, they may be intertwined so that a label would be impossible.

As you draw your conclusions on the issue, there are several different types of arguments you can make. One or more of these types of arguments may be included in a single issue:

a) *Direct authority.* You show how a case, statute, or other authority directly applies to your case. (*E.g.:* Although the motion to dismiss the indictment was not made before trial as required by Fed. R. Crim. Proc. 12(b), it was nonetheless timely under Rule 12(f). Where the defendant does not learn of the grand jury impropriety until after trial starts, Rule 12(f) excuses him from the requirements of Rule 12(b)(2). *United States v. Cathey,* 591 F.2d 268, 271 (5th Cir. 1979).)

b) *Analogous authority.* A case, statute, or other authority applies to a situation similar to yours, and you argue by analogy that the same rule should apply to your case. (*E.g.:* A person who takes property with the good faith belief that it was abandoned is not guilty of the crime of larceny. *Morissette v. United States,* 342 U.S. 246, 72 S.Ct. 240, 96 L.Ed. 288 (1952). By the same token, a prisoner who left the prison grounds with the good faith belief he was authorized to do so is not legally guilty of the crime of escape.)

c) *Distinguishing authority.* If authority seems to go counter to your position, you can distinguish the authority by showing that it was intended to apply to another type of situation, and not yours. This is the opposite of using analogous authority. (*E.g.:* In many cases, the failure to object in state court precludes consideration of the issue in federal habeas corpus, under *Wainwright v. Sykes,* 433 U.S. 72, 97 S.Ct. 2497, 53 L.Ed.2d 594 (1977). However, the failure to object in state court is no obstacle to federal habeas corpus in this case because the state courts overlooked any alleged failure to object and in fact reached and ruled on the merits of the issues. *Wainwright v. Sykes* applies only if the state court fails to reach the issue because of a failure to object. *See* 433 U.S. at 87; *see also Ulster County Court v. Allen,* 442 U.S. 140, 99 S.Ct. 2213, 60 L.Ed.2d 777 (1979).)

d) *Legislative intent.* If you are relying on a statute, constitutional provision, or court rule, you can argue that the framers of the rule intended to include (or not include) cases of your type within the rule. The argument should show that both the language of the rule and the purposes of the rule support your position. (*E.g.:* Administrative Procedure Act rulemaking provisions apply to the Department of Corrections. *Lundberg v. Corrections Commission,* 57 Mich. App. 204 (1977). Considering the precision with which the APA was drafted, it seems odd that the legislature would have intended to make the Department of Corrections subject to the rulemaking and declaratory judgment provisions, and not the contested case provisions, but would forget to mention it. The plain language of the statute directly contradicts the Department's contention as to the legislative intent. Furthermore, the purpose of the APA is to increase fairness in administrative hearings. That legislative purpose will not be advanced by exempting the Department of Corrections from the contested case provisions of the APA. Every government agency has pressures to resolve cases quickly at the expense of fairness, and the APA is designed as a check on that process. There is nothing in the language of the APA to suggest that the legislature trusted the commitment to fairness of the Department of Corrections any more than they trusted the commitment to fairness of any other agency.)

e) *Unfairness or injustice.* Whether or not you have authority supporting your position, you can argue that failure to rule your way will result in unfairness or injustice in this case. (*E.g.:* It simply would not be fair to allow the defendant to introduce the photograph showing the floor to be clean where the defendant's employee admitted that he mopped the floor after the accident and before the taking of the photograph.)

f) *Public policy.* You can argue that the law should be a certain way as a matter of public policy. You may show that there is a general need, not limited to your case, to adopt a rule such as the one you propose. You may point to the bad results for society if your rule is rejected, and the good results if your rule is adopted. (*E.g.:* There is no judge present during the grand jury proceedings, and the prosecutor runs them as he sees fit. The only checks on the powers of the prosecutor before the grand jury are the provisions of Rule 6. If there is no remedy for violation of Rule 6, then the prosecutor will be able to disregard Rule 6 whenever he pleases, without fear of jeopardizing his case. The sound administration of justice and respect for the law will be severely damaged if Rule 6 continues to exist, but there are no meaningful remedies for its violation.)

g) *"Reductio ad absurdum"*. You can show that if the position of the other side is carried to its logical extreme, the results will be absurd, ridiculous, or unfair. You can list a "parade of horribles" which will result from an adverse ruling. (*E.g.:* If we accept the warden's contention that this court has no jurisdiction to overturn the punishment because of severity alone, we will give a blank check to prison officials to inflict any punishment they please for any infraction of rules. Taking the warden's position to its logical extreme, the warden could have sentenced plaintiff to death for having an untidy cell, and this court would be powerless to intervene.)

h) *Windfall.* You can show that if your position is not adopted, the other side will receive a windfall. A windfall is an unearned and undeserved benefit or advantage. (*E.g.:* According to the district judge, he would have dismissed the case if he had learned of the prosecutor's violation before trial started. However, because the prosecutor managed to conceal the violation until after trial started, the judge refused to dismiss. The prosecutor should not be granted a windfall by virtue of his ability to keep the rule violations a secret until after trial starts.)

i) *Turning the tables.* If there is no direct authority supporting your position, you may often be able to note that there is likewise no direct authority supporting your opponent's position. Similarly, you can argue that your opponent's version of the facts is not supported by the record, or that his logic contains logical flaws. (*E.g.:* As the prosecutor correctly noted, there are no cases holding this rule to be retroactive. However, it is equally true that there are no cases holding this rule not to be retroactive.)

j) *Straddling the issue.* If you are not sure how the court will rule on a particular question, you can show that you should win no matter which way the court decides the issue. Similarly, you can rest one argument on one interpretation of the law, and another on the opposite interpretation of the law. If the court rejects one of your positions, it automatically adopts the other one. (*E.g.:* Either the petitioner was intoxicated or he was not. If he was intoxicated, then his statement cannot be considered voluntary, and it must be suppressed. If he was not intoxicated, then there was no excuse for the police failure to bring plaintiff to court for arraignment, and the statement must be suppressed anyway. Therefore, it makes no difference whether the court believes or disbelieves the testimony that petitioner was intoxicated; the statement must still be suppressed.)

As you write your brief, you should use a style that is plain and clear. You should not use a word if you do not know that it means; look it up. You should not use a rare or unusual word if a more common word can be used. Do not try to "write like a lawyer" to impress the judge. Most judges dislike formal and pretentious language, and may often conclude that such language is being used to cover up some shortcoming in your logic. Furthermore, using such language creates a danger that you will use it incorrectly, or make your argument so incomprehensible that your whole case suffers. Using plain English will make your documents easier to read and reduces the chance of making an embarrassing mistake.

As a general rule, your document will not receive full attention if it is difficult to read. Accordingly, your argument should be as short as possible. You should use relatively short sentences which come right to the point. You should use the best spelling and grammar you can. It is best if you type. If you cannot type, printing is preferable to longhand writing. Whether or not you type, you should be neat, use double spacing, and leave blank margins.

In using authorities, it is important not to claim too much for the authority. You should not say that a case is directly on point if it is not. You should not say that a case proves something if it does not. Instead, you might say that it *suggests* or *implies* something, or that it *supports* or *tends to show* something. If your authority is weaker still, you might say that it is *consistent* with your position. If you say that a case holds something, and the case does not, you have greatly damaged your credibility, and your whole case may suffer.

You should reduce to a minimum your use of words such as *clearly, plainly, obviously,* etc. You should not use these words until and unless you demonstrate that the point is clear, plain, or obvious. A proposition either is obvious, or it is not, and it will not become more obvious by use of the word "obviously." Instead of saying "It is clear that plaintiff's due process rights were violated," you should say "plaintiff submits that his due process rights were violated." There is an old saying that the more a brief writer uses the word "clearly," the less likely it is that the matter is clear.

In writing your issues, you should carefully avoid saying anything which suggests that the judge deciding your case is stupid, lazy, or unfair, even if the judge is stupid, lazy, or unfair. You should never use an insulting term when a more neutral term is available. You should not accuse someone else of misconduct, unless you are prepared to back it up with proof. Instead of saying on appeal that the judge "made up" certain facts, you should say that factual conclusions of the judge are not supported by the record.

Many times you will feel that a judge did not give your complaint, petition, or motion fair consideration: "He ruled that way because I am a prisoner." In your motion for reconsideration or in your appellate documents, you should not let your emotion control your writing. A court is authorized to immediately dismiss a legal pleading that threatens violence, contains disrespectful references to the courts, or is abusive of the judicial process.[37] Emotional outbursts in your legal pleadings can only cause you harm. Use the facts and the law to show why the judge was wrong.

You should not make threats or promises in a brief. If you do, the reader will change his focus from the correctness of your legal position to your own bad character. Similarly, you should avoid using a hostile tone in your writing. By the language you use, you should paint a picture of yourself as a reasonable and thoughtful person.

If your brief is to be filed before your opponent's brief, you will face

---

[37]*Cf.* Theriault v. Silber, 574 F.2d 197 (5th Cir. 1978), *cert. denied,* 440 U.S. 917 (1979) (notice of appeal stricken that contained disrespectful and impertinent remarks concerning trial judge); Carter v. Telectron, Inc., 452 F. Supp. 944 (S.D. Tex. 1977) (plaintiff had filed 178 duplicate suits in 15 years). *See also* Van Meter v. Morgan, 518 F.2d 366 (8th Cir.), *cert. denied,* 423 U.S. 896 (1975).

the difficult problem of whether to answer an argument that you predict your opponent may use against you. As a general rule, you should not do this, because you might call your opponent's attention to an issue he might otherwise miss. However, if the issue is certain to be raised sometime, you should address it head-on in your brief at the earliest possible opportunity.

At the conclusion of each issue, you should have a short paragraph which states what conclusion you want the court to reach on that issue, and what relief you want.

It may help your development of legal writing skills to read briefs written by others. However, as in all things, it is practice, practice, practice which sharpens your skills.

IV
Outline of the Legal System

The United States has a *federal* system of government. This means that both the central government and the state governments have some sovereign (ruling) power. This results in a system of state courts and federal courts.

In order to understand the court system, it is necessary to understand the concepts of *jurisdiction* and *venue.* Jurisdiction refers to the power of a court to hear a particular type of case.[1] If the case can be brought in more than one court, those courts are said to have *concurrent jurisdiction.*[2] If the case may be brought only in one court, that court is said to have *exclusive jurisdiction.* Venue refers to the geographical region over which the court exercises power.

In any court case, there are *parties.* The party bringing a case to court is called the *plaintiff* or *petitioner,* depending on the type of case. The party opposing a plaintiff is called a *defendant,* while the party opposing a petitioner is called a *respondent.* A plaintiff files a *complaint,* while a petitioner files a *petition.* When one wishes to bring a civil rights action under 42 U.S.C. §1983, one ordinarily files a complaint. When one seeks habeas corpus relief, one ordinarily files a petition.

In addition to courts, the legal system includes administrative agencies, such as the Bureau of Prisons or the Federal Trade Commission. While administrative agencies are not courts, they often decide matters and issue orders like a court does, though in a less formal way.

This section describes the federal and state court systems and their relationship to each other and to administrative agencies.

A. The Federal Courts

1. United States District Court

With very few exceptions, prosecutions and lawsuits in federal courts

---

[1]See Ch. VI, Secs. B1a and C1a, for a further discussion of jurisdiction.

[2]See Sec. D, *infra,* for a more detailed discussion of concurrent jurisdiction.

begin in a United States district court. Some states, like Colorado, have a single district court which covers the entire state. Other states, like Florida, are divided into districts, each of which has a separate district court.

The United States district court has jurisdiction over prosecutions for violations of federal criminal statutes, as stated in 18 U.S.C. §3231. Jurisdiction of the U.S. district court in other types of cases is defined in Title 28 of the U.S. Code, §§1330-1363. Venue is covered in Title 28, §§1391-1407.

When one wishes to bring an action in federal court, it is advisable to read the jurisdictional statutes to see if the court has jurisdiction. A U.S. district court has jurisdiction over all the following types of cases, among others:

a) Cases "arising under" the Constitution, statutes, or treaties of the United States. This is often referred to as "federal question" jurisdiction. Formerly, the district courts lacked jurisdiction in federal question cases involving less than $10,000, but this has been changed by statute, and now there is no money limitation. 28 U.S.C. §1331.

b) Any civil case involving diversity of citizenship, but only if the amount in controversy is over $10,000. This applies to cases where the plaintiff is a citizen of a different state than all the defendants. 28 U.S.C. §1332.

c) Bankruptcy. 28 U.S.C. §1334.

d) Any case brought under the federal civil rights statutes. 28 U.S.C. §1343.

e) Any mandamus action against federal officials. 28 U.S.C. §1361.

f) Any cases involving admiralty law, or law of the sea. 28 U.S.C. §1333.

g) Habeas corpus actions, to free the petitioner from either state or federal custody. 28 U.S.C. §§2241, 2254, 2255.

h) Certain cases where the United States government is a party. 28 U.S.C. §§1345, 1346.

Cases in United States district court are governed by the Federal Rules of Evidence (FRE). Criminal cases are governed by the Federal Rules of Criminal Procedure (FRCrP), and civil cases are governed by the Federal Rules of Civil Procedure (FRCP). These rules are found in volumes 18 and 28 of U.S. Code (U.S.), U.S. Code Annotated (USCA), or the U.S. Code Service (USCS).

In a civil case involving diversity of citizenship, the federal court will generally apply the law of the state out of which the lawsuit arose. In other cases, federal law usually governs, although state law issues may be important.

In most cases, the U.S. district court issues its rulings solely on the basis of federal law. Federal law may be classified into the following types:

a) Constitution.

b) Statutes enacted by Congress. This includes Federal Rules of Evidence and Federal Rules of Civil and Criminal Procedure, which are enacted by Congress.

c) Treaties.

d) Administrative rules or regulations.

e) Judicial decisions.

The Constitution of the United States is the supreme law of the land, and is always to be followed. It is written in broad general language which allows a great deal of room for interpretation by judges. Most prisoners' lawsuits involve the amendments to the Constitution, most notably the First, Fourth, Fifth, Sixth, Eighth, and Fourteenth Amendments.

Federal legislation is passed by the United States Congress. It is collected in the United States Code (U.S.) and is found in the book series entitled United States Code Annotated (USCA) and United States Code Service (USCS). Federal legislation is to be followed unless it conflicts with the Constitution, in which case it is said to be unconstitutional.

Treaties are equal in power to statutes, but they cannot override the Constitution. Treaties are often difficult to find in any law library, and more so in prison law libraries. Some treaties are found in USCA and USCS, while others may be found only in United States Statutes (Stat.), which lists statutes and treaties in order according to the date they were passed. United States Statutes can be dangerous to use, because it does not include updates which may show that the statute or treaty was amended or repealed. Fortunately, treaties rarely become an issue to prisoners, except when there is a question regarding extradition or deportation.

Administrative rules are issued by administrative agencies. The issuance of such rules is governed generally by the Administrative Procedures Act (APA), 5 U.S.C. §§551 *et seq.* Administrative rules are binding on the agency which enacts them, except when they violate a statute, treaty, or the Constitution. Administrative rules can be obtained from the agency itself, or from the Code of Federal Regulations (CFR).

Judicial decisions are where most of the law is found. Because constitutions and statutes are often vague and do not cover every point which needs to be covered, it is necessary for courts to construe them. Many important rules of law are found only in court decisions.

A U.S. district court is obligated to follow decisions of the U.S. Supreme Court. A U.S. district court is also obligated to follow decisions of the circuit court of appeals for the circuit in which the district court is located.[3] Cases decided by other circuit courts of appeals, and by U.S. district courts, are persuasive authority, but not binding authority.[4] Decisions of state courts are persuasive, but not binding on federal courts, except in diversitys or other cases where the federal court must use state law.

Orders and opinions of the U.S. district court are sometimes published, and sometimes not. Those that are published are usually found in Federal Supplement (F. Supp.). Some are also found in Federal Rules Decisions (F.R.D.).

2. United States Courts of Appeals (Circuit Courts)

Each United States district court is directly under the control of a circuit court of appeals. There are 12 circuit courts which cover the entire nation. Each circuit court covers a region of several states, except the Court of Appeals for the District of Columbia Circuit. Cases from district courts in Florida, Georgia, and Alabama are now heard by the 11th Circuit Court of Appeals, created in 1981.

Jurisdiction of the circuit courts is covered by 28 U.S.C. §§1291-1294. A circuit court hears appeals from *final decisions* of a United States district court within its region and from orders denying or granting injunctions (but not a temporary restraining order). It may grant leave to appeal a non-final order, and this appeal is known as an *interlocutory appeal*. Many decisions made by a district court, such as decisions granting or denying class action status or ruling on discovery questions, cannot be appealed until the whole case is decided.

A circuit court applies the same law as a district court. It is bound by decisions of the U.S. Supreme Court. When all the judges in a circuit together decide a case, they are said to sit *en banc*. An en banc decision of the same circuit is binding upon all judges of that circuit. A typical court of appeals case is heard by a three-judge panel. The decision of one three-judge panel is binding on other three-judge panels from the same circuit.

Proceedings in the circuit courts are governed by the Federal Rules of Appellate Procedure. Published decisions of circuit courts of appeals are found in Federal Reporter (F.) and Federal Reporter, Second Series (F.2d).

---

[3]The federal district courts of Michigan must follow the decisions of the Sixth Circuit Court of Appeals.

[4]The federal district courts of Michigan need not follow decisions by the Ninth Circuit Court of Appeals or decisions of the federal district courts of Ohio or Wisconsin.

3. United States Supreme Court

The United States Supreme Court is the highest court in the land. Once it has ruled, there is no further court to which one can appeal. However, adverse decisions of the U.S. Supreme Court may sometimes be changed by statute or constitutional amendment.

The jurisdiction of the Supreme Court is defined by Article III of the Constitution and by 28 U.S.C. §§1251-1258. In some rare cases, the Supreme Court has original jurisdiction over a case, bypassing the district court and circuit court.[5] However, most cases get to the Supreme Court by way of *appeal* or *certiorari* from lower courts.

When a case is heard by appeal, the Supreme Court is obligated to hear the case, except that it can dismiss the appeal if it finds that the federal question involved is "insubstantial." When review is sought by certiorari, the Supreme Court can decide to hear the case or not hear the case, in its absolute discretion. Four justices must vote to hear a case before certiorari is granted.

Review of decisions from U.S. circuit courts of appeals is governed generally by 28 U.S.C. §1254. A party may appeal from a decision which holds a state statute unconstitutional as violating the federal Constitution. Other review must be by application for a writ of certiorari.

Review of state court decisions is governed generally by 28 U.S.C. §1257. A party must apply to the highest court of the state for review before seeking review from the U.S. Supreme Court. The party may go to the U.S. Supreme Court even if the highest state court refuses to hear the appeal. A party may appeal to the U.S. Supreme Court when a federal treaty or statute is held unconstitutional. A party may also appeal when a state statute is upheld against a challenge that it violates the federal Constitution. Other cases may be reviewed only upon an application for writ of certiorari. The U.S. Supreme Court does not have the power to hear state court cases unless they involve some question of federal law.

Proceedings in the United States Supreme Court are governed by the Rules of the United States Supreme Court, found in USCA and USCS. The U.S. Supreme Court is not bound by the decisions of any other court. The U.S. Supreme Court generally follows its own prior decisions. Adherence to past decisions constitutes the rule of *stare decisis*. However, sometimes the Supreme Court does overrule prior cases and invents a new rule of law.

Decisions of the U.S. Supreme Court are reported in United States Reports (U.S.), Supreme Court Reporter (S.Ct.), and United States Reports, Lawyers Edition (L.Ed. and L.Ed.2d). It should be noted that a Supreme Court refusal to grant certiorari in a particular case does not

---

[5]12 U.S.C. §1251.

constitute a decision on the merits and, therefore, is not binding on anyone, except in the particular case involved.

A book you may wish to obtain that deals with everything one would want to know about the Supreme Court is *Supreme Court Practice,* by Stern & Gressman, which is published by the Bureau of National Affairs, Inc., Washington, D.C.

B.   The State Courts

Each state has its own court system. The names and jurisdictions of various courts differ from state to state, so it is difficult to give rules that apply to all of them.

A typical state court system is that of Michigan. In Michigan, the two lowest courts are district courts and probate courts. District courts handle misdemeanor prosecutions and preliminary examinations in felony cases. Search and arrest warrants are usually handled by district courts. District courts also handle civil cases involving claims under $10,000.

Probate courts handle juvenile prosecutions. They also handle cases of parental abuse or neglect and child custody cases other than those arising out of divorce or paternity actions. Probate courts handle the affairs of children and mental incompetents and often appoint guardians for them. Probate courts handle wills and the distribution of property of those who have died.

Cases from district court and probate court are appealed to the circuit court. Circuit courts also handle felony prosecutions, divorce, paternity actions, injunctions, mandamus, and civil cases involving claims over $10,000.

Cases from circuit courts are appealed to the court of appeals, and from there, to the Supreme Court of Michigan. Some cases may then be reviewed by the U.S. Supreme Court, depending on whether they involve a substantial federal question.

Outside of Michigan, there are diverse types of courts, including Orphans Court, Prothonotary Court, and Superior Court. The jurisdiction of each depends on state law. Persons going to state courts in New York should be aware of some confusing terminology. In New York, many trials are heard in the Supreme Court, while appeals are taken to the Supreme Court, Appellate Division, and then to the New York Court of Appeals, the highest court in the state. In some states, there are "courts" known as police court or justice of the peace court. These courts can hear cases, but their decisions are usually reviewable de novo by other state courts. When a case is reviewed de novo, the reviewing court ignores what happened in the lower court and hears the case all over again.

Most prisoners who go to court to sue someone believe they will get a better break from a federal court than a state court, and so they file their suit in federal court. However, it often is true that the prisoner would be better off going into a state court. Almost any civil action which can be brought in federal court, including civil rights actions, can be brought in state court as well. Federal courts often have clogged dockets, meaning your case might be heard faster in a state court. Further, state statutes may be of help to state prisoners. Some states have Freedom of Information Acts, or Administrative Procedures Acts, or other statutes upon which the prisoner can rely. Prisoners suing any agency of the state should look up the venue statutes and see if the agency can be sued in the county which includes the state capitol. If so, that can be a big bonus, since lawsuits against the prison will fare better in a place other than a local court in the same county as the prison.

Of course, a state court is always the place to go when the federal court does not have jurisdiction over the case—for example, when a prison official is being sued for violating a state statute or for committing a state law tort, such as medical malpractice.

C. Administrative Agencies

Government in the United States and in each state is divided into three branches: legislative, executive, and judicial. Administrative agencies are part of the executive branch, and are theoretically under the control of the governor or the President. However, administrative agencies usually act independently of the governor or the President in their day-to-day operations.

Administrative agencies are created by state or federal statute. The statute defines the jurisdiction of the agency, what its powers are, and what it is supposed to do with those powers. Any administrative agency may be taken to court to force it to comply with the statutes that govern it. State agencies are taken to state courts, and federal agencies are taken to federal courts.

Agencies are generally required to issue, or promulgate, rules governing their own activities and the activities of the people they regulate.[6] Procedures for enacting rules are often found in an Administrative Procedures Act (APA), such as the federal APA at 5 U.S.C. §§551 *et seq.* Administrative regulations can be obtained from the agency itself, or from books which publish the regulations. Federal regulations are found in the Code of Federal Regulations (CFR). States often have an Administrative Code where rules are published.

---

[6]Pickus v. United States Board of Parole, 507 F.2d 1107, 1112 (D.C. Cir. 1974); King v. United States, 492 F.2d 1337, 1343 (7th Cir. 1974).

Agencies are required to follow their own rules, and courts will usually enforce that duty.[7] Occasionally, the failure of the agency to enact a rule means that the agency is powerless to act against the individual. This is so because without any rules, the individual has no fair notice of what is or is not prohibited, which can be a denial of due process.

Any prison, and any Bureau of Prisons or Department of Corrections which runs prisons, is an administrative agency. Local jails are technically administrative agencies, but may be exempted from Administrative Procedures Acts because they are an agency of the county or city, and not the state.

When a party seeks money damages from an administrative agency, he will often have to go to a court of claims.[8] This is a special court established by statute to handle money claims against state or federal agencies. Mandamus and injunction actions go to regular courts, and not to a court of claims.

D. Relationship Between State and Federal Courts

As a general rule, the state and federal court are completely separate, except for the ultimate review by the U.S. Supreme Court of state court decisions involving federal questions.

In a civil rights case, the plaintiff often complains about the actions of a state agency or state officials. The plaintiff does not have to exhaust the state administrative or court remedies before going to federal courts. But you should check your state law to determine whether you must exhaust administrative remedies before filing in state court. See Ch. VI, Sec. D, for a discussion of exhaustion of remedies.

1. Federal Courts Hearing State Issues

Federal courts usually consider themselves bound by state court decisions which declare what state law is. State courts are bound by U.S. Supreme Court decisions which declare what the federal Constitution provides. However, state courts sometimes refuse to follow constitutional rulings of lower federal courts, even if the federal court sits in the same state.

Except in the most unusual situation, a federal court will not issue an injunction against a state court or prosecutor to stop a state criminal

---

[7]See Ruiz v. Estelle, 503 F. Supp. 1265, 1356-57, n.185 (S.D. Tex. 1980), *aff'd in part and mod. in part,* 679 F.2d 1115 (5th Cir. 1982); Sands v. Wainwright, 491 F.2d 417, 428 (5th Cir. 1973), *cert. denied,* 416 U.S. 992 (1974).

[8]*See* M.C.L.A. 600.419, M.S.A. 27A.6419 (claims against the State of Michigan must be brought in the Court of Claims of Michigan).

prosecution.[9] Needless to say, state courts have no power at all to issue injunctions against federal courts or agencies.

Federal courts use various reasons for refusing to issue injunctions against state courts and agencies. Sometimes such refusal is based on "comity," and sometimes it is based on "the abstention doctrine." Sometimes a federal or state court will refuse to hear an issue because it is deemed not to be "ripe" for review, or because the plaintiff lacks "standing" to raise the issue. The rules governing these are found in court decisions. The governing standards are usually complex and vague.

In a federal court, a party may bring an action under federal law. Once there is a federal claim over which the federal court has jurisdiction, the plaintiff may join in the complaint other causes of action under state law, as long as they arise out of the same transaction or are otherwise factually linked. The federal court may consider these claims under the doctrine of *pendent jurisdiction*.[10] Once the federal court has pendent jurisdiction over the state law claims, it may decide the state law claims without deciding your federal claims.

2. State Courts Hearing Federal Issues

Generally, federal constitutional rights can be enforced in state courts. Many state courts will hear actions brought under §1983, although some will not.[11] Also, some state courts permit the litigation of federal con-

---

[9]Younger v. Harris, 401 U.S. 37, 91 S.Ct. 746 (1971). *See* 28 U.S.C.A. §2283, which prohibits a federal injunction against proceedings in state courts except where authorized by some act of Congress, or where the injunction is necessary to aid the jurisdiction or effectuate the judgment of a federal court. *See also* Moore v. Sims, 442 U.S. 415, 99 S.Ct. 2371 (1979) (abstention doctrine applicable to civil actions); Trainor v. Hernandez, 431 U.S. 434, 97 S.Ct. 1911 (1977); Hicks v. Miranda, 422 U.S. 332, 345-50, 95 S.Ct. 2281 (1975) (federal courts must abstain from exercising jurisdiction if state proceedings are inaugurated after a §1983 complaint has been filed in federal court but before proceedings on the merits have begun in federal court).

[10]See Ch. VI, Sec. B3, for a more detailed discussion concerning pendent jurisdiction.

[11]Bors v. Preston, 111 U.S. 252, 4 S.Ct. 407 (1884); United States v. California, 328 F.2d 729, 733 (9th Cir. 1964), *cert. denied,* 379 U.S. 817 (1965); New Times, Inc. v. Arizona Bd. of Regents, 20 Ariz. App. 422, 426, 513 P.2d 960, 964 (1973), *vacated on other grounds,* 110 Ariz. 367, 519 P.2d 169, 176 (1974). In Aldinger v. Howard, 427 U.S. 1, 36 n.17, 96 S.Ct. 2413 (1976), Justice Brennan, in dissent, said: "The Court today appears to decide *sub silentio* a hitherto unresolved question by implying that §1983 claims are not claims exclusively cognizable in federal courts but may also be entertained by state courts. [Citation omitted.] This is a conclusion with which I agree."

stitutional claims without invoking §1983.[12] Check your state's jurisdictional statutes (and form books, if any) to see how to properly present a constitutional claim in a state court complaint.

Whether to bring your federal claim to a state or federal court is sometimes one of the most important and difficult decisions you must make. You may wish to consider a variety of factors, including the following:

1) Which court has the best "track record" in dealing with prisoners' cases? Which judges are more sympathetic?

2) Where are the courts? If the state court is in a rural county dominated by the prison, you may get a fairer shake from a federal court which is more distant from the prison and in a larger city.

3) How backed up are the two court systems? Depending on where you are, one court system may be able to give you a quicker response than the other.

4) How good is your federal claim? If your federal claim is marginal and there is a chance that a federal court will hold that you have alleged only a state law violation, you may want to go directly into state court and not risk wasting time in a court that will dismiss your case. If it is clear that you have a good state claim, the argument for going into state court in the first place is stronger.

5) Do you have a complex state law issue? Even a strong constitutional claim may be mixed up with state law issues. A state court may be more competent to sort these out, and a federal court may be inclined to "abstain" pending a state court clarification of state law issues.

6) How much discovery do you need? The discovery provisions in federal court are more liberal than those in some state courts; be sure to find out about your state's rules before making your decision.

7) Who are you interested in suing? In damage cases, state and federal courts present different options. In a federal court, you can sue individual prison officials, and under limited circumstances you can sue cities and counties; you cannot sue states.[13] Some states provide a broader right to sue states, cities, and counties under the doctrine of *respondeat superior*. Sometimes this remedy must be pursued in a court of claims. Punitive damages may not be available, and you may not have the right to a jury trial in these courts, depending on the relevant state statutes. If your concern is to get back at the people who mistreated you, you may be better advised to go to federal court; if you just want to get

---

[12]For example, in New York, constitutional cases may be litigated as actions for a declaratory judgment or as "Article 78 proceeding." Kovarshy v. Housing Development Administration, 31 N.Y.2d 191, 335 N.Y.S.2d 383, 286 N.E.2d 882 (1972).

[13]See Ch. VI, Sec. E1a, for a discussion of the Eleventh Amendment and *Monell*.

some compensation for your injuries, a state court may be more advantageous, if you can sue the state, city, or county directly.

In making the decision as to which court to go to, you should remember that in a civil action the doctrine of collateral estoppel and res judicata will apply to state court decisions preventing you from relitigating your claims in federal court.[14]

The purpose of this section has been to make you aware that state courts can be used to litigate federal issues. There are a lot of problems when using state courts but, with the present trend in the Supreme Court, your access to the federal courts is being curtailed,[15] and you may be forced to use the state courts.

---

[14]See Ch. VI, Sec. E3, for a further discussion of res judicata and collateral estoppel.

[15]*See Parratt v. Taylor,* 451 U.S. 527, 101 S. Ct. 1908 (1981) (a state prisoner deprived of property by prison officials is not denied due process if the state has a remedy where s/he can receive compensation).

V

Overview of Prisoners' Rights

Lawful imprisonment necessarily makes unavailable many rights and privileges of the ordinary citizen, a "retraction justified by the considerations underlying our penal system." But though his rights may be diminished by the needs and exigencies of the institutional environment, a prisoner is not wholly stripped of constitutional protections when he is imprisoned for crime. There is no iron curtain drawn between the Constitution and the prisons of this country.[1]

A. Introduction

There are many generalities in the cases on prisoners' rights—some favorable to prisoners, some unfavorable, depending on the issues and the judges involved in the particular case. In litigating your rights, however, you should focus on the specific legal right you are asserting and on the cases and principles that deal with that right, rather than on broad generalities.

As a convicted prisoner, you are protected in some measure by several provisions of the United States Constitution, as well as by certain other provisions of state and federal law. The particular legal provision you will rely on will depend on the factual situation you are trying to remedy. The Eighth Amendment to the Constitution, which prohibits "cruel and unusual punishment," governs most claims relating to physical abuse by guards or other prisoners,[2] deprivation of medical care,[3] overcrowding,[4] inadequate exercise and movement, and dilapidated, unsafe, or unsanitary physical conditions.[5] Claims relating to denial of religious free-

---

[1]Wolff v. McDonnell, 418 U.S. 539, 555-56, 94 S.Ct. 2963 (1974) (citations omitted).

[2]See Sec. C2, *infra,* for a discussion of protection from physical abuse.

[3]See Sec. C3, *infra,* for a discussion of medical care.

[4]See Sec. C10a, *infra,* for a discussion of overcrowding.

[5]See Sec. C10, *infra,* for a discussion of physical conditions and restrictions.

61

dom,[6] freedom of speech, access to reading material, correspondence, and visiting will usually be governed by the First Amendment.[7] Improper searches of your cell or your person will be litigated under the Fourth Amendment, as will some claims of improper seizure of property.[8] Other property claims, plus claims that you have been disciplined or segregated without a hearing or otherwise treated arbitrarily and unfairly, will be governed by the Due Process Clause of the Fifth Amendment (for federal prisoners) or the Fourteenth Amendment (for state prisoners).[9] Claims of denial of access to a law library, consultation with lawyers, or interference with litigation may state claims under the Sixth Amendment, the First Amendment, or the Due Process Clause.[10] Racial discrimination in prison is barred by the Equal Protection Clause of the Fourteenth Amendment (for state prisoners) or the Due Process Clause of the Fifth Amendment (for federal prisoners).[11] (When they were adopted, the First, Fourth, Sixth, and Eighth Amendments applied only to the federal government, but the courts have held that they are "incorporated" by the Due Process Clause of the Fourteenth Amendment and now apply to state officials as well.)

If you are a pretrial detainee, the Eighth Amendment does not apply to you, but the Due Process Clauses of the Fifth and Fourteenth Amendment have been held to prohibit conditions that amount to "punishment" for persons who have not been convicted.[12] You are also entitled to the protection of the First, Fourth, Fifth, and Sixth Amendments described in connection with the rights of convicts.

Courts frequently do not agree about what the Constitution actually requires, even when they are interpreting the same constitutional provision. Only a decision of the United States Supreme Court can guarantee nationwide uniformity in the interpretation of constitutional principles.[13] Thus, a federal court has held that prisoners have a constitutional right to visit, while another federal court has held that there is no such right.[14] Therefore, when you are preparing a lawsuit, be sure to find

---

[6]See Sec. C7, *infra,* for a discussion of religion.

[7]See Sec. C1, *infra,* for a discussion of communication, expression, and association.

[8]See Sec. C5, *infra,* for a discussion of searches, seizures, and privacy.

[9]See Sec. B2, *infra,* for a discussion of procedural rights.

[10]See Sec. C4, *infra,* for a discussion of access to the courts.

[11]See Sec. D, *infra,* for a discussion of equal protection.

[12]See Sec. E, *infra,* for a discussion of pretrial detainees' rights.

[13]See Ch. IV, Sec. A, for a discussion of the federal courts.

[14]*Compare* Lynott v. Henderson, 610 F.2d 340, 342-43 (5th Cir. 1980), *with*

out what the law is in your federal circuit and state. If it is not favorable, you have an added burden of convincing the court to rule in your favor by distinguishing your case from earlier cases, or demonstrating that a change in the law is necessary in light of changes in conditions, policies, etc.[15] Probably the easiest way to argue for a change in the law is to use the same rationale, or reasons, that other courts used to decide similar cases in your favor. Use the *facts* and *rationale* of those cases and show the courts how they are very similar, if not identical, to yours.

In addition to constitutional rights, both state and federal prisoners and detainees may be entitled to other rights based on state or federal statutes and regulations and on state constitutions. This point cannot be overemphasized, even though this chapter focuses on rights under the federal Constitution. It is impossible for us to deal with the nonconstitutional law of fifty states and the federal government. You should always research state, federal, and local statutes, case law, and regulations to determine if there is a legal standard you can use that is more favorable than the federal Constitution.[16]

B. Procedural Due Process Rights[17]

The Due Process Clauses of the Fifth and Fourteenth Amendments prohibit federal and state officials from depriving you of "life, liberty,

---

White v. Keller, 438 F. Supp. 110 (D. Md. 1977), *aff'd,* 588 F.2d 913 (4th Cir. 1978).

[15]See Ch. III, Sec. E, for examples of types of arguments you may make.

[16]See Ch. II for a discussion of how to do legal research.

[17]Procedural due process is distinct from "substantive due process" in that the former deals with the procedures that must be used before the government takes some action against you, while the latter deals with the Due Process Clause's restrictions on what the government can do to you regardless of procedures. Examples of substantive due process include the prohibition on conditions that amount to "punishment" for pretrial detainees, Bell v. Wolfish, 441 U.S. 520, 99 S.Ct. 1861 (1979), see also Sec. E, *infra;* the prohibition on the excessive use of force, Johnson v. Glick, 481 F.2d 1028 (2d Cir. 1973), *cert. denied,* 414 U.S. 1033 (1973), see also Sec. C2, *infra;* and the right of access to courts, Procunier v. Martinez, 416 U.S. 396, 419, 94 S.Ct. 1800 (1974); Henderson v. Counts, 544 F. Supp. 149, 152-53 (E.D. Va. 1982), see also Sec. C4, *infra.* Because the protections of the First, Fourth, Sixth, and Eighth Amendments initially applied only to the federal government, and are now applicable to the states only by way of the Fourteenth Amendment's Due Process Clause, *see* Duncan v. Louisiana, 391 U.S. 145, 147-48, 88 S.Ct. 1444 (1968), these rights are sometimes referred to as part of "substantive due process" as well. *See* Duncan v. Poythress, 657 F.2d 691, 704 (5th Cir. 1981), *writ of cert. dismissed as improvidently granted,* Poythress v. Duncan, 103 S.Ct. 368 (1982); see also Sec. C, *infra,* for a discussion of different "substantive" constitutional rights.

or property without due process of law." To prevail on a due process claim, you must therefore show two things:

(a) You were deprived of life, liberty, or property; and
(b) The deprivation was without due process of law.

A great deal of litigation has been devoted to defining these two elements of a due process violation.[18]

1.   Life, Liberty, or Property

Not every restriction that prison officials place on you deprives you of "liberty" or "property" as these words are used by the courts. The courts have backed away from the idea that any "grievous loss" invokes the protections of due process. Now, the courts hold that "liberty interests" or "property interests" protected by due process may arise in two ways: from the Constitution itself,[19] or from state or federal statutes, rules, or understandings.[20]

a.   Constitutionally Based Liberty Interests

In *Vitek v. Jones,*[21] the Supreme Court held that prisoners have a liberty interest in avoiding being classified and treated as mentally ill; therefore, the state had to provide due process protections before committing a prisoner to a mental hospital.[22] Similarly, in *Procunier v. Martinez,*[23] the Supreme Court held that prisoners have a liberty interest based on the First Amendment in uncensored communication by letter; prisoners are therefore entitled to due process protections when prison officials censor their correspondence. The fact that you have a constitutionally based liberty interest does not mean that the state can never take it away; it does mean that the state cannot do so arbitrarily and that it must provide fair procedures that will prevent arbitrariness.

Few cases have found constitutionally based liberty interests. Most prisoners' due process lawsuits allege deprivation of both constitutional

---

[18]*See* Gaballah v. Johnson, 629 F.2d 1191 (7th Cir. 1980).

[19]See Sec. B1a, *infra,* for a discussion of constitutionally based liberty interests.

[20]See Sec. B1b, *infra,* for a discussion of liberty or property interests created by state law.

[21]445 U.S. 480, 491-94, 100 S.Ct. 1254 (1980).

[22]*See also* Cobb v. Aytch, 643 F.2d 946 (3d Cir. 1981) (notice and hearing required before detainees were transferred to state prison where result was infringement of Sixth Amendment rights to effective counsel and speedy trial).

[23]416 U.S. 396, 417-19, 94 S.Ct. 1800 (1974).

and state-created liberty interests. When courts are presented with these two claims, they prefer to base their decision on nonconstitutional grounds as much as possible.[24]

To qualify as a constitutionally based liberty interest, a right generally must be one that is actually enjoyed at the present time, and not a mere hope. Thus, the Supreme Court has held that *revocation* of parole or probation—a conditional liberty that one already possesses—involves a constitutionally based liberty interest governed by the requirements of due process.[25] However, the initial *grant* of parole does not involve a constitutionally based liberty interest automatically governed by the Due Process Clause because it is "a mere anticipation or hope of freedom."[26]

In short, if prison or parole authorities want to take away some liberty that you have, there may be a constitutionally based liberty interest protected by due process. If they refuse to give you a liberty that you want, there is probably not a constitutionally based liberty interest. This does not mean that you have no due process rights; it means that you must find some basis for your liberty interest in the relevant statutes and regulations, rather than in the U.S. Constitution.

b.   Liberty or Property Interests Created by State Law

The question of when state law creates a liberty or property interest (or "entitlement") protected by due process is still being worked out in the federal courts. You should be sure to read the latest cases in the Supreme Court and in your federal circuit when you have a procedural due process problem.

The Supreme Court has held that state-created liberty or property interests may be found in "statutes or other rules. . . ."[27] It has not spelled out what "other rules" may create these interests. Some lower federal courts have held that state constitutions, and state court decisions

---

[24]*See, e.g.,* Kozlowski v. Coughlin, 539 F. Supp. 852, 855 (S.D.N.Y. 1982) (district court found a liberty interest based on state judicial decisions and prison regulations); United States ex rel. Hoover v. Elsea, 501 F. Supp. 82, 86-87 (N.D. Ill. 1980), *rev'd on other grounds,* 669 F.2d 433 (7th Cir. 1982).

[25]Gagnon v. Scarpelli, 411 U.S. 778, 93 S.Ct. 1756 (1973); Morrissey v. Brewer, 408 U.S. 471, 480-82, 92 S.Ct. 2593 (1972).

[26]Greenholtz v. Inmates of the Nebraska Penal and Correctional Complex, 442 U.S. 1, 10, 99 S.Ct. 2100 (1979), *quoting* United States ex rel. Bey v. Connecticut Board of Parole, 443 F.2d 1079, 1086 (2d Cir. 1971); *see also* Connecticut Board of Pardons v. Dumschat, 452 U.S. 458, 463, 101 S.Ct. 2460 (1981) (hope of sentence commutation not protected by due process). See also Ch. VIII for a discussion of parole.

[27]Connecticut Board of Pardons v. Dunschat, 452 U.S. 458, 465, 101 S.Ct. 2460 (1981).

interpreting them, create liberty interests.[28] Most federal courts have held that a state regulation or directive is sufficient to create a liberty or property interest.[29] In *Hewitt v. Helms,* the Supreme Court suggested that prison regulations may be less likely than other statutes and regulations to create liberty interests; however, it found that the statutes and regulations before it did create a liberty interest in staying in population and out of administrative segregation.[30] The Supreme Court has also held that unwritten "policies and practices" or "mutually explicit understandings" may create a liberty or property interest protected by due process.[31] However, the Supreme Court has also rejected such arguments in two cases involving state parole systems.[32] You should therefore base your due process claim on statutes or regulations, rather than informal practices, whenever possible.[33]

Not every state statute or regulation creates a liberty interest. Only if a statute or regulation limits the discretion of state officials by providing that they may or must take some action only under certain prescribed circumstances does the statute or regulation create a liberty interest or "entitlement." If the statute or regulation contains no explicit standards governing the conduct of state officials, there is no state-created liberty interest.[34]

Thus, in *Greenholtz v. Inmates of the Nebraska Penal and Correc-*

---

[28]Kozlowski v. Coughlin, 539 F. Supp. 852, 855-56 (S.D.N.Y. 1982).

[29]*See, e.g.,* Parker v. Cook, 642 F.2d 865, 868-76 (5th Cir. 1981); Bills v. Henderson, 631 F.2d 1287 (6th Cir. 1980); Stringer v. Rowe, 616 F.2d 993 (7th Cir. 1980); Pugliese v. Nelson, 617 F.2d 916, 922 (2d Cir. 1980); Finney v. Mabry, 528 F. Supp. 567, 570 (E.D. Ark. 1981). *Contra,* Gorham v. Hutto, 667 F.2d 1146 (4th Cir. 1981).

[30]__U.S.__, 103 S.Ct. 864 (1983).

[31]Perry v. Sinderman, 408 U.S. 593, 602-03, 92 S.Ct. 2717 (1972). *Accord,* Stringer v. Rowe, 616 F.2d 993, 996 (7th Cir. 1980); Clifton v. Robinson, 500 F. Supp. 30 (E.D. Pa. 1980).

[32]Jago v. Van Curen, 454 U.S. 14, 102 S.Ct. 31 (1981) ("mutually explicit understandings" create only property interests, not liberty interests); Connecticut Board of Pardons v. Dumschat, 452 U.S. 458, 101 S.Ct. 2460 (1981) (consistent practice of granting commutations did not create liberty interest).

[33]*See* Gibson v. Lynch, 652 F.2d 348, 356-58 (3d Cir. 1981); McGhee v. Belisle, 501 F. Supp. 189 (E.D. La. 1981); Garland v. Polley, 594 F.2d 1220 (8th Cir. 1979).

[34]Connecticut Board of Pardons v. Dumschat, 452 U.S. 458, 466-67, 101 S.Ct. 2460 (1981). *See also* Hughes v. Rowe, 449 U.S. 5, 101 S.Ct. 173, 177-78 (1980); 3 PLM 91 (April 1981).

tional Complex,[35] the state parole statute provided that an eligible prisoner would be released *unless* the Board of Parole found:

> (a) There is a substantial risk that [the inmate] will not conform to the conditions of parole;
> (b) His release would depreciate the seriousness of his crime or promote disrespect for law;
> (c) His release would have a substantially adverse effect on institutional discipline; or
> (d) His continued correctional treatment, medical care, or vocational or other training in the facility will substantially enhance his capacity to lead a law-abiding life when released at a later date.

Because this statute created an "expectancy of release" unless one of these four reasons was found to exist, the Supreme Court held that a "protectable entitlement" was created.[36] By contrast, the Massachusetts statutes governing transfers between prisons contained no specific criteria saying when prison officials could order these transfers. Therefore, the Supreme Court held no liberty interest protected by due process was created.[37]

A useful way to think about the due process analysis of statutes and regulations is: if the statute or regulation can be restated in the form "If . . . then" or "Shall . . . unless," it probably creates a liberty interest or entitlement. For example, a regulation which boils down to "*If* the disciplinary committee finds that a prisoner has committed a major infraction, *then* the prisoner may be placed in punitive segregation" creates a liberty interest. So does a statute or regulation which says in effect, "The Classification Committee *shall* grant work release to a prisoner within two years of his or her release date *unless* the prisoner has one or more major infractions within the previous twelve months or *unless* there is other reason to believe that the prisoner presents a significant risk of escape or violation of law or regulations if granted work release." However, a regulation which says, "The Classification Committee may grant work release to any prisoner whom it deems deserving or appropriate" would not create a liberty interest because the phrase "deserving or appropriate" is too vague to provide any limits or

---

[35]442 U.S. 1, 99 S.Ct. 2100 (1979), *quoting from* Neb. Rev. Stat. §83-1, 114(1) (1976).

[36]*Id.* 442 U.S. at 11-12. *See also* Hewitt v. Helms, __U.S.__, 103 S.Ct. 864, 871 (1983) ("the repeated use of explicitly mandatory language in connection with requiring specific substantive predicates demands a conclusion that the State has created a protected liberty interest").

[37]Meachum v. Fano, 427 U.S. 215, 226-27, 96 S.Ct. 2532 (1976).

specific criteria telling prison officials when they must grant or deny work release.

This may seem like a strange rule because it provides constitutional protection where prison officials' discretion is limited but no protection where state law lets the officials do as they please. However, it is the approach the Supreme Court has taken, and it is therefore the governing law you must use when alleging you have been denied due process.

Procedural regulations by themselves do not create a liberty interest; only a substantive restriction on prison officials' discretion will do so. Thus, where state prison regulations permitted out-of-state transfers for any reason, there was no liberty interest, and the fact that the prison's own procedures were not followed did not violate due process.[38] In this situation, the only legal claim is a state law claim, which you may have to pursue in state court.

2.   Due Process of Law

Once a court finds that you have been deprived of a liberty or property interest, the next question is "what process is due," *i.e.,* what procedures must be followed. The answer may vary from case to case; the Supreme Court has used a balancing test which considers how serious the deprivation is, how much good additional procedures will do, and how expensive or difficult they will be.[39] Thus, in prison disciplinary hearings that may result in loss of good time, prisoners are entitled to fewer procedural protections than in revocation of probation or parole because the effect of loss of good time is less immediate, and because of the possible dangers to security that full-fledged adversary proceedings might cause in prison.[40] In *Greenholtz v. Inmates of Nebraska Penal and Correctional Complex,*[41] the Court held that a formal hearing was not required for parole release decisions because it would not make much difference in the risk of an erroneous decision.

a.   The Parratt v. Taylor Rule

In *Parratt v. Taylor,*[42] the Supreme Court held that when prison of-ficials negligently lose a prisoner's property, due process is not violated

---

[38]Olim v. Wakinekona, __U.S.__, 103 S.Ct. 1741 (1983).

[39]Mathews v. Eldridge, 424 U.S. 319, 335, 96 S.Ct. 843 (1976).

[40]*Compare* Wolff v. McDonnell, 418 U.S. 539, 559-63, 94 S.Ct. 2963 (1974), *with* Morrissey v. Brewer, 408 U.S. 471, 92 S.Ct. 2593 (1972).

[41]*Supra* note 35, at 14-15.

[42]451 U.S. 527, 101 S.Ct. 1908 (1981).

as long as state law provides an adequate means of redress. The *Parratt* decision as it applies to property is discussed in more detail in Sec. C6, *infra*. Some courts, however, have applied *Parratt* to deprivations of liberty without due process as well, despite the statement to the contrary in Justice Blackmun's concurring opinion.[43] In *Rutledge v. Arizona Board of Regents*,[44] the Ninth Circuit held that a claim of excessive force (a deprivation of liberty) did not state a due process claim where the state provided a tort remedy. The same court later held that the *Parratt* rule did *not* apply to a case involving a liberty interest (procedural protections before transfer).[45] Other courts have taken a similar position.[46] Still other decisions have held that *Parratt* governs all *procedural* due process claims but not *substantive* due process[47] claims or claims of denial of a substantive constitutional right.[48]

Because the holding of *Parratt* is new and the courts are still working out its meaning, you must be especially careful to find and read the latest cases interpreting it in your jurisdiction and in the Supreme Court.[49] You must also draft your pleadings very carefully. Avoid relying solely on procedural due process claims when you can. If the facts you allege violate some other constitutional guarantee—substantive due process, the First, Fourth, or Eighth Amendment, etc.—make that argument crystal clear in your pleadings and briefs. And finally, if the law in your federal jurisdiction is not clearly in your favor, give serious consideration to taking your case to state court.

Questions of procedural due process arise in various contexts. Some of the most important ones are discussed below.

---

[43]*Id.* 101 S.Ct. at 1918.

[44]660 F.2d 1345, 1352-53 (9th Cir. 1981), *decided on other grounds sub nom.* Kush v. Rush, __U.S.__, 103 S.Ct. 1483 (1983).

[45]Wakinekona v. Olim, 664 F.2d 708, 715 (9th Cir. 1981), *rev'd on other grounds sub nom.* Olim v. Wakinekona, *supra* note 38.

[46]Brewer v. Blackwell, 692 F.2d 387, 394-95 (5th Cir. 1982); Howse v. DeBerry Correctional Institution, 537 F. Supp. 1177 (M.D. Tenn. 1982); Haygood v. Younger, 527 F. Supp. 808, 813-15 (E.D. Calif. 1981).

[47]*See supra* note 17 for a definition of substantive due process.

[48]Wolf-Lillie v. Sonquist, 699 F.2d 864 (7th Cir. 1983); Palmer v. Hudson, 697 F.2d 1220 (4th Cir. 1983); Duncan v. Poythress, 657 F.2d 691, 704 (5th Cir. 1981), *cert. dismissed as improvidently granted,* 103 S.Ct., 368 (1982); Abraham v. County of Washoe, 547 F. Supp. 548 (D. Nev. 1982); Juncker v. Tinney, 549 F. Supp. 574 (D. Md. 1982); Henderson v. Counts, 544 F. Supp. 149 (E.D. Va. 1982); Al-Mustafa Irshad v. Spann, 543 F. Supp. 922 (E.D. Va. 1982); Holmes v. Wampler, 546 F. Supp. 500 (E.D. Va. 1982).

b. Disciplinary Proceedings

In *Wolff v. McDonnell*,[50] the Supreme Court held that due process safeguards must be observed when prison officials deprive prisoners of statutorily authorized "good time"; the Court indicated that the same safeguards apply to "solitary confinement." Most courts have required that *Wolff* safeguards be observed in disciplinary proceedings that could lead to any form of punitive confinement; they have not required that there be a state-created entitlement.[51] The Second Circuit has held that the *Wolff* requirements are also applicable to "keeplock" (restriction to one's cell).[52]

Under *Wolff,* prisoners facing disciplinary charges are entitled to notice of the charges at least 24 hours before a hearing, a written statement of the evidence that a decision is based on and the reasons for the action taken, and the right to call witnesses and present documentary evidence if doing so will not jeopardize institutional safety or correctional goals. However, prisoners are not entitled to confront and cross-examine witnesses against them or to have the assistance of counsel. The Court assumed that prisoners are entitled to an impartial tribunal but held that a committee of prison officials was sufficiently impartial.[53]

The notice that is given of a disciplinary proceeding must describe "specific conduct upon which the charges are based" and also must give some reasonable indication of the date of the hearing.[54] A finding of guilt must contain a summary of the evidence relied upon and the statement of reasons for the finding of guilt must also be reasonably specific. A disposition that said only "We recognize and consider the resident[']s statement[,] however[,] we accept the reporting officer[']s charges" has been held inadequate because it did not indicate which of two reports was relied on or why one witness was more believable than another.[55]

---

[49]A good summary of the lower courts' interpretation of *Parratt* can be found in Begg v. Moffitt, 555 F. Supp. 1344 (N.D. Ill. 1983).

[50]*Supra* note 40, 418 U.S. at 556-59 and n. 19.

[51]*See, e.g.,* Finney v. Arkansas Board of Corrections, 505 F.2d 194, 208 (8th Cir. 1974); Powell v. Ward, 392 F. Supp. 628, 629 (S.D.N.Y. 1975), *aff'd as modified,* 542 F.2d 101 (2d Cir. 1976).

[52]McKinnon v. Patterson, 568 F.2d 930 (2d Cir. 1977).

[53]*Supra* note 40, 418 U.S. at 563-71.

[54]United States ex rel. Speller v. Lane, 509 F. Supp. 796, 798-99 (S.D. Ill. 1981).

[55]Chavis v. Rowe, 643 F.2d 1281, 1287 (7th Cir. 1981). *See also* Dyson v. Kocik, 689 F.2d 466 (3d Cir. 1982); Hayes v. Walker, 555 F.2d 625, 631 (7th Cir. 1977); Devaney v. Hall, 509 F. Supp. 497 (D. Mass. 1981); United States ex rel. Speller v. Lane, 509 F. Supp. 796, 799 (S.D. Ill. 1981).

There has been much litigation concerning a prisoner's right to call witnesses. In *Wolff,* the Court suggested but did not require that disciplinary committees give reasons for refusing to call witnesses.[56] Some lower federal courts, however, have held that the refusal to call witnesses must be based on individualized reasons and not blanket policy and that prison officials must be able to show the reasons if challenged in court.[57] Other courts have held that prisoners must show that the denial of witnesses was arbitrary and capricious.[58] Among the specific reasons that have been upheld for denying witness requests are that the witnesses would be cumulative and would take too much time or that they would only have dealt with a side issue.[59] Some courts have held that witnesses should, in general, appear at the hearing itself or be interviewed in the accused's presence.[60] Others have held it sufficient for them to be interviewed by the committee or its investigator prior to the hearing.[61] Some courts have also held that the refusal to permit access to records that would support the prisoner's defense is unconstitutional.[62]

While due process obviously requires an impartial tribunal, courts will not find a lack of impartiality just because the committee contains security personnel or because the committee chooses to believe a guard's story rather than yours.[63] To show a lack of impartiality, you must generally prove something more specific. For example, where a prisoner

---

[56]*Supra* note 40, 418 U.S. at 556.

[57]McCann v. Coughlin, 698 F.2d 112 (2d Cir. 1983); Bartholomew v. Watson, 665 F.2d 915 (9th Cir. 1982); Hayes v. Thompson, 637 F.2d 483 (7th Cir. 1980); King v. Wells, 94 F.R.D. 675 (E.D. Mich. 1982); Hendrix v. Faulkner, 525 F. Supp. 435 (N.D. Ind. 1981); Jacobson v. Coughlin, 523 F. Supp. 1247 (N.D.N.Y. 1981); United States ex rel. Speller v. Lane, 509 F. Supp. 796 (S.D. Ill. 1981); Powell v. Ward, 487 F. Supp. 917 (S.D.N.Y. 1980), *aff'd as modified,* 643 F.2d 924 (2d Cir. 1981), *cert. denied,* 454 U.S. 832 (1981).

[58]Thomas v. Estelle, 603 F.2d 488 (5th Cir. 1979); Hurney v. Carvey, 602 F.2d 993 (1st Cir. 1979); *see also* Devaney v. Hall, 509 F. Supp. 497 (D. Mass. 1981) (upholding denial of all witness requests in disciplinary unit).

[59]Ward v. Johnson, 690 F.2d 1098 (4th Cir. 1982) (en banc); Langston v. Berman, 667 F.2d 231 (1st Cir. 1981); Ra Chaka v. Nash, 536 F. Supp. 613 (N.D. Ill. 1982).

[60]Powell v. Ward, *supra* note 57, at 928-24; Jacobson v. Coughlin, *supra* note 57, at 1253.

[61]United States ex rel. Speller v. Lane, 509 F. Supp. 796 (S.D. Ill. 1981).

[62]Chavis v. Rowe, 643 F.2d 1281 (7th Cir. 1981); Pace v. Oliver, 634 F.2d 304 (5th Cir. 1981).

[63]Rhodes v. Robinson, 612 F.2d 766, 773 (3d Cir. 1979); Powell v. Ward, 542 F.2d 101, 103 (2d Cir. 1976); United States ex rel. Silverman v. Commonwealth of Pennsylvania, 527 F. Supp. 742 (W.D. Pa. 1981).

was charged with various offenses for possessing a petition asking that a certain prison official be fired, a disciplinary committee with that official on it was not impartial.[64] Generally, a tribunal is not impartial if the hearing officer or a committee member was involved in the incident that the hearing is about, witnessed it, or investigated it.[65]

You have a right to a hearing within a reasonable length of time, but the courts have not been able to agree on exactly what that means. One court imposed a seven-day time limit,[66] but another court in the same state held that this was not constitutionally required.[67] Other courts have held that a 13-day delay was not justified;[68] that delays of a month or six weeks were not unconstitutional;[69] and that a two-month delay was permissible during an institutional lockdown.[70] In arguing that your hearing was delayed too long, you should emphasize particular facts that made the delay unreasonable in your case, *e.g.,* that the alleged disciplinary offense was simple and required little investigation, that the delay caused witnesses to become unavailable, that you were kept in punitive confinement for a long time waiting for the hearing, etc. You *may* also be able to rely on time limits in prison regulations.[71]

A prisoner may be placed in administrative segregation pending completion of an investigation of misconduct charges.[72] Lower federal courts have suggested that this pre-hearing confinement must be limited to a reasonable period; the Supreme Court did not address this issue directly.[73] In any case, repeated short lockups for "investigation" without charges or a hearing are unconstitutional.[74]

---

[64]Edwards v. White, 501 F. Supp. 8 (M.D. Pa. 1979).

[65]Powell v. Ward, *supra* note 57, 487 F. Supp. at 931.

[66]*Id.* at 931.

[67]Majid v. Henderson, 533 F. Supp. 1257 (N.D.N.Y. 1982).

[68]Pitts v. Kee, 511 F. Supp. 497 (D. Del. 1981).

[69]Dowdy v. Johnson, 510 F. Supp. 836 (E.D. Va. 1981); Vice v. Harvey, 458 F. Supp. 1031 (D.S.C. 1978).

[70]United States ex rel. Houston v. Warden, Stateville Correctional Center, 635 F.2d 656 (7th Cir. 1980).

[71]*See* King v. Milton, 525 F. Supp. 1192 (D.N.J. 1981); *see also* Meeker v. Manning, 540 F. Supp. 131 (D. Conn. 1982); *contra,* Caruth v. Pinkney, 683 F.2d 1044 (7th Cir. 1982).

[72]Hewitt v. Helms, *supra* note 30, 103 S.Ct. at 874.

[73]*Compare* Ra Chaka v. Nash, 536 F. Supp. 613 (N.D. Ill. 1982); Franklin v. Israel, 537 F. Supp. 1112 (W.D. Wisc. 1982); Pitts v. Kee, 511 F. Supp. 497 (D. Del. 1981); Tawney v. McCoy, 462 F. Supp. 752 (N.D. Va. 1978), *with* Hewitt v. Helms, *supra* note 30, 103 S.Ct. at 874 and n.9.

[74]Hendrix v. Faulkner, 525 F. Supp. 435, 462 (N.D. Ind. 1981).

Prison officials' use of confidential informants without disclosing their identity or, sometimes, even the details of their testimony has drawn mixed responses from the courts. In *Helms v. Hewitt,*[75] the lower court condemned reliance on hearsay statements by confidential informants without any guarantees of reliability because it "invites disciplinary sanctions on the basis of trumped up charges." However, the Supreme Court did not bother to mention this danger. Other courts have held that such statements may be used without identifying the informant or even producing him/her before the disciplinary committee.[76] Some courts have even held that the prisoner need not even be informed of the dates and details of the alleged offenses if it would give away the identity of informants.[77]

Courts—especially federal courts—generally will not look into the merits of disciplinary decisions; as long as your procedural rights are respected, the courts will not review the actual decision to see if it is right or wrong.[78] If you have been cleared at a hearing, they probably will not hear your claim that the charges were unfounded in the first place.[79]

In a few cases, courts have been willing to look beyond the procedural aspects when the prisoner alleged that disciplinary actions were brought conspiratorially and in bad faith, to cover up officials' misconduct or retaliate for prisoners' legal action.[80] However, courts are likely to be very suspicious of such claims, and you had better be prepared to support your claim with solid evidence as soon as you file your case.

---

[75]655 F.2d 487 (3d Cir. 1981), *rev'd on other grounds sub nom.* Hewitt v. Helms, __U.S.__, 103 S.Ct. 864 (1983).

[76]Kyle v. Hanberry, 677 F.2d 1386 (11th Cir. 1982); Smith v. Rabalais, 659 F.2d 539 (5th Cir. 1981).

[77]Smith v. Rabalais, *id.* at 544; Franklin v. Israel, 537 F. Supp. 1112 (W.D. Wisc. 1982); *see also* Langston v. Berman, 667 F.2d 231 (1st Cir. 1981); Rinehart v. Brewer, 483 F. Supp. 165 (S.D. Iowa 1980). *But see* McCollum v. Miller, 695 F.2d 1044 (7th Cir. 1982) (additional safeguards might be required where information is withheld).

[78]Cummings v. Dunn, 630 F.2d 649 (8th Cir. 1980); Lewis v. Israel, 528 F. Supp. 960 (E.D. Wisc. 1980); Kelly v. Cooper, 502 F. Supp. 1371 (E.D. Va. 1980); Jordan v. Robinson, 464 F. Supp. 223 (W.D. Pa. 1979); Zaczek v. Huber, 437 F. Supp. 402 (W.D. Va. 1977).

[79]McCoy v. McCoy, 528 F. Supp. 712 (N.D. W. Va. 1981); Riggs v. Miller, 480 F. Supp. 799 (E.D. Va. 1981); *but see* Chavis v. Rowe, 643 F.2d 1281 (7th Cir. 1981) (administrative reversal of disciplinary conviction did not moot damage claim).

[80]Milhouse v. Carlson, 652 F.2d 371 (3d Cir. 1981); Furtado v. Bishop, 604 F.2d 80 (1st Cir. 1979), *cert. denied,* 444 U.S. 1035 (1980); King v. Cuyler, 541 F. Supp. 1230 (E.D. Pa. 1982).

You may also be able to gain reversal of your disciplinary conviction by showing that there is *no* evidence to support the charges. Thus, in *Edwards v. White*,[81] the court held that a prisoner found with a petition containing no signatures could not be convicted of "conspiracy to disrupt prison routine" when there was *no* evidence that he conspired with anyone. In *United States ex rel. Smith v. Robinson*,[82] where the inmate was charged with a contraband offense but there was *no* evidence that he had obtained the material improperly, the conviction was struck down. However, if there is *any* evidence to support the charges, the courts will generally not second-guess the findings of the disciplinary committee.[83]

In an emergency, prison authorities may be excused from complying strictly with due process requirements. However, an emergency justifies only a postponement, not the complete suspension, of ordinary procedural protections.[84]

See Ch. VI, Sec. E1, for a discussion of the immunities that prison officials involved in disciplinary proceedings may have.

c.   Administrative Segregation

Prison officials frequently seek to isolate prisoners from the rest of the population, under conditions equivalent to punitive segregation, without proving prisoners guilty of disciplinary infractions. Instead, they claim that it is done pending investigation of misconduct charges, to prevent future acts of misconduct or other violations of security and order, or to protect the person who is being segregated. This confinement is often of indefinite length. Various names are used for this preventive confinement: "administrative segregation," "maximum security," "involuntary protective custody," etc. In this section, we use "administrative segregation."

The Supreme Court has recently addressed the question of due process in connection with administrative segregation and has severely restricted prisoners' rights in this regard. In *Hewitt v. Helms*,[85] the Court held that there was no constitutionally based liberty interest in remaining in

---

[81]501 F. Supp. 8 (M.D. Pa. 1979).

[82]495 F. Supp. 696 (E.D. Pa. 1980).

[83]Inglese v. Warden, U.S. Penitentiary, 687 F.2d 362 (11th Cir. 1982).

[84]*See, e.g.,* United States ex rel. Houston v. Warden, Stateville Correctional Center, 635 F.2d 656 (7th Cir. 1980) (two-month delay in hearing excused); Carlo v. Gunter, 520 F.2d 1293 (1st Cir. 1975) (hearings to be provided at "earliest practicable opportunity" after emergency).

[85]__U.S.__, 103 S.Ct. 864 (1983).

general population and out of administrative segregation, even though it assumed that conditions were about the same in administrative as in disciplinary segregation.[86] The Court stated that "administrative segregation is the sort of confinement that inmates should reasonably anticipate receiving at some point in their incarceration."[87] However, the Court did find that there was a state-created liberty interest based on statutes and regulations which created some procedural protections and restricted administrative segregation to certain specified circumstances.[88] The Court thus implies that if state law and regulations say you can be put in administrative segregation for no reason or at the whim of prison officials, then you have no federal constitutional protections; several lower court decisions have stated this explicitly.[89]

The Court also restricted the scope of due process protections, holding that

> an informal nonadversary evidentiary review [is] sufficient both for the decision that an inmate represents a security threat and the decision to confine an inmate to administrative segregation pending completion of an investigation into misconduct charges against him. An inmate must merely receive some notice of the charges against him and an opportunity to present his views to the prison officials charged with deciding whether to transfer him to administrative segregation. Ordinarily a written statement by the inmate will accomplish this purpose, although prison administrators may find it more useful to permit oral presentations in cases where they believe a written statement would be ineffective. So long as this occurs, and the decisionmaker reviews the charges and then-available evidence against the prisoner, the Due Process Clause is satisfied.[90]

The Court did not hold that a statement of reasons or an impartial tribunal was necessary; since these issues were not addressed, it is not clear whether the Court meant they were not necessary or whether it simply forgot to mention them. The Court did note that the proceeding "must occur within a reasonable time following an inmate's transfer,"[91] and that "administrative segregation may not be used as a pretext for

---

[86]*Id.* at 867 n.1 and 870-71.

[87]*Id.* at 870.

[88]*Id.* at 872-73.

[89]Bills v. Henderson, 631 F.2d 1287, 1293 (6th Cir. 1980); Mitchell v. Hicks, 614 F.2d 1016, 1019 (5th Cir. 1982); Arsberry v. Sielaff, 586 F.2d 37 (7th Cir. 1978); Four Certain Unnamed Inmates of Massachusetts v. Hall, 550 F.2d 1291 (1st Cir. 1977).

[90]Hewitt v. Helms, *supra* note 30, at 874.

[91]*Id.* at n.8.

indefinite confinement of an inmate."[92] With respect to the latter, the Court required "some sort of periodic review of the confinement of such inmates."[93] However, it noted that this review "will not necessarily require that prison officials permit the submission of any additional evidence or statements."[94]

The *Hewitt* opinion seems designed to maximize prison officials' discretion to lock prisoners up more or less at will and to minimize prisoners' ability to require that they have any substantial basis for their actions. The court endorsed the idea that isolation of a prisoner pending an investigation of misconduct charges "serves important institutional interests relating to the insulating of possible witnesses from coercion or harm,"[95] without any suggestion that prison officials should have to show that there is such a danger in a specific case. *Hewitt* also suggests that there is little limit on what prison officials may base their decisions on:

> In assessing the seriousness of a threat to institutional security, prison administrators necessarily draw on more than the specific facts surrounding a particular incident; instead, they must consider the character of the inmates confined in the institution, recent and longstanding relations between prisoners and guards, prisoners [between themselves], and the like. In the volatile atmosphere of a prison, an inmate easily may constitute an unacceptable threat to the safety of other prisoners even if he himself has committed no misconduct; rumor, reputation, and even more imponderable factors may suffice to spark potentially disastrous incidents. The judgment of prison officials in this context, like that of those making parole decisions, turns largely on "purely subjective evaluations and on predictions of future behavior," . . . ; indeed, the administrators must predict not just one inmate's future actions, as in parole, but those of an entire population. Owing to the central role of these types of intuitive judgments, a decision that an inmate or a group of inmates represents a threat to the institution's security would not be appreciably fostered by . . . trial-type procedural safeguards. . . .[96]

This Supreme Court holding that prison officials can rely on rumor, subjective evaluations, and intuitive judgments in locking up prisoners in conditions equivalent to punitive segregation obviously creates an

---

[92]*Id*. at n.9.

[93]*Id*.

[94]*Id*. Previously, some courts had held that this review must be based on specific criteria and standards. *See, e.g.,* Jackson v. Meachum, 699 F.2d 578 (1st Cir. 1983). It is unclear whether these cases are still good law.

[95]Hewitt v. Helms, *supra* note 30, at 872.

[96]*Id*. at 872-73 (footnote omitted).

enormous risk of arbitary and malicious behavior. For responding to such acts by prison officials, we make the following suggestions.

First, consider your state law remedies. After *Hewitt,* the protections provided by state law and regulations may be greater than federal constitutional protections. You may bring a state law challenge either in state court or as a pendent claim in federal court. (See Ch. VI, Sec. B3, for a discussion of pendent jurisdiction.) It may also be possible to persuade a state court to rule based on the *state* constitution that you are entitled to more procedural protections than *Hewitt* provides. In making this argument, you should rely on the kinds of arguments made in the federal cases that were overruled by *Hewitt.*[97]

Second, if you do base your claim on the federal constitution, try to distinguish *Hewitt.* If you can show that your confinement is in actuality based on an act of alleged misconduct, you should be entitled to the disciplinary safeguards of *Wolff v. McDonnell,*[98] rather than the lesser safeguards of *Hewitt.* Prison officials "cannot avoid their due process responsibilities simply by relabeling the punishments imposed on prisoners."[99] Also, if you can show that your confinement is actually in retaliation for constitutionally protected activities, such as filing lawsuits or grievances or otherwise criticizing prison officials, you should be entitled to relief. (See Sec. C4d, *infra,* for a discussion of retaliation.) However, the courts will require substantial proof, not just unsupported allegations, of such motivations.

Third, where you can, emphasize issues that were not addressed in *Hewitt.* If you are not given a statement of reasons, you should take the position that one is necessary even though *Hewitt* did not mention it. Similarly, if the decisionmaker is someone who was involved in the investigation against you or is someone whom you can show is biased against you, you can argue that you were denied an impartial factfinder. If you are a jailhouse lawyer assisting an inmate who is not literate (or

---

[97]*See* Cooper v. Morin, 49 N.Y.2d 69, 399 N.E.2d 1188, 424 N.Y.S.2d 168 (1979), *cert. denied,* 446 U.S. 984 (1980) (New York State constitution provides more protections for pretrial detainees than federal constitution). *See also, e.g.,* Wright v. Enomoto, 462 F. Supp. 397 (N.D. Calif. 1976), *summarily affirmed,* 434 U.S. 1052, 98 S.Ct. 1223 (1978); Helms v. Hewitt, 655 F.2d 487 (3d Cir. 1981), *rev'd,* __U.S.__, 103 S.Ct. 864 (1983); Finney v. Mabry, 528 F. Supp. 567 (E.D. Ark. 1981); Drayton v. Robinson, 519 F. Supp. 545, 551-52 (M.D. Pa. 1981), and cases cited; Bono v. Saxbe, 450 F. Supp. 935 (E.D. Ill. 1978), *aff'd in pertinent part,* 620 F.2d 609 (7th Cir. 1982).

[98]418 U.S. 539, 94 S.Ct. 2963 (1974). See discussion of *Wolff* in Sec. 2b, *supra.*

[99]Taylor v. Clement, 433 F. Supp. 585, 586-87 (S.D.N.Y. 1977); *accord,* Flowers v. Coughlin, 551 F. Supp. 911, 916 (N.D.N.Y. 1982).

not literate in a language the prison officials read), you can argue that a personal appearance for that prisoner was required by due process. If you are kept in administrative segregation based on something other than the reasons you were first placed there, you can argue that you should have a right to submit new evidence and, in some situations, appear personally. For example, if you are first placed in segregation for investigation and you are kept in segregation on the basis that your attitude is still dangerous, it is hard to see how prison officials can make this judgment without talking with you to determine your current attitude.

d. Transfers

There is no constitutionally based liberty interest entitling you to a hearing or any other procedural protections before transfer from one prison to another. To obtain due process protections, you must show that you have a liberty interest created by statute or regulation by the method discussed in Sec. B1b, *supra*.[100] This is so, according to *Meachum* and *Montanye,* even if the transfer is to a higher-security institution or is motivated by a disciplinary purpose. It is also true even if you are being transferred from state to federal custody;[101] from one state to another;[102] from city to state institution;[103] or to a distant location and an alien cultural climate.[104]

To obtain due process rights in transfer situations, you must show that state or federal statutes or regulations created a liberty interest.[105] This is generally difficult, since most states' laws do not explicitly do so[106] and

---

[100]Meachum v. Fano, 427 U.S. 215, 96 S.Ct. 2532 (1976); Montayne v. Haymes, 427 U.S. 236, 96 S.Ct. 2543 (1976).

[101]Sisbarro v. Warden, Massachusetts State Penitentiary, 592 F.2d 1 (1st Cir. 1979); Fletcher v. Warden, 467 F. Supp. 777 (D. Kan. 1979), and cases cited therein.

[102]Cofone v. Manson, 594 F.2d 934 (2d Cir. 1979); Sisbarro v. Warden, Massachusetts State Penitentiary, *id.*

[103]Cobb v. Aytch, 643 F.2d 946, 955-56 (3d Cir. 1981).

[104]Olim v. Wakinekona, *supra* note 38; Ali v. Gibson, 631 F.2d 1126, 1134-35 (3d Cir. 1980).

[105]*See* Neal v. Director, District of Columbia Dept. of Corrections, 684 F.2d 17 (D.C. Cir. 1982).

[106]*But see* United States ex rel. Hoover v. Elsea, 501 F. Supp. 82, 88 (N.D. Ill. 1980), *rev'd on other grounds,* 669 F.2d 433 (7th Cir. 1982).

the federal courts have been very conservative in interpreting state law to place due process restrictions on transfer.[107] A state regulation requiring particular procedures before transfer does not give you a constitutional due process right to those procedures.[108]

A few other exceptions to the *Meachum* "no due process rights before transfers" rule have been recognized. If you are transferred and committed to a prison mental hospital, you are entitled to a commitment hearing.[109] If you are transferred to a statewide disciplinary unit, you may have due process rights.[110] Where transfer of pretrial detainees to state prison interfered with their Sixth Amendment rights to the effective assistance of counsel and to a speedy trial, a constitutionally based liberty interest was found.[111]

Although transfers are generally not governed by procedural due process protections, there may be substantive rights that are violated by a transfer. Transfers in retaliation for bringing litigation or for other constitutionally protected expression are unlawful.[112] Out-of-state transfers that interfere with access to the courts of the transferring state may also be unlawful, although the remedy may not be return to the transferring state.[113] However, transfers to distant locations that interfere with visiting do not violate the Constitution.[114] Some courts have suggested that the frequent practice of automatically segregating prisoners after they are

---

[107]*See, e.g.,* Gorham v. Hutto, 667 F.2d 1146 (4th Cir. 1981); DeMarco v. Hewitt, 481 F. Supp. 693 (E.D. Pa. 1979).

[108]Olim v. Wakinekona, *supra* note 38. Whether or not violation of a state procedural regulation violates due process, it can be raised as a pure state law question in state court. If there is any doubt as to whether you have a federal due process claim, your wisest course of action may be to file in state court. See Ch. IV, Sec. D, for a discussion of use of state courts.

[109]Vitek v. Jones, 445 U.S. 480, 100 S.Ct. 1254 (1980).

[110]Hardwick v. Ault, 447 F. Supp. 116 (M.D. Ga. 1978).

[111]Cobb v. Aytch, *supra* note 103. *See also* Epps v. Levine, 457 F. Supp. 561, 564-67 (D. Md. 1978) (state law created due process right to court determination before detainee was transferred to prison).

[112]*See, e.g.,* Haymes v. Montayne, 547 F.2d 188 (2d Cir. 1976), *cert. denied,* 431 U.S. 967 (1977); Buise v. Hudkins, 584 F.2d 223 (7th Cir. 1978); Simmat v. Manson, 535 F. Supp. 1115 (D. Conn. 1982). See also Sec. C4d, *infra.*

[113]*See* Beshaw v. Fenton, 635 F.2d 239 (3d Cir. 1980); Rich v. Zitnay, 644 F.2d 41 (1st Cir. 1981); Colbeth v. Civiletti, 516 F. Supp. 73 (S.D. Ind. 1980).

[114]Dozier v. Hilton, 507 F. Supp. 1299 (D.N.J. 1981); *see* Ali v. Gibson, 631 F.2d 1126 (3d Cir. 1980).

transferred or during a transfer may be unlawful unless there is justification for it in a particular case.[115]

e. Programs and Classification

The courts have generally held that matters of classification and eligibility for programs do not implicate a liberty interest protected by due process.[116] An older line of cases held that classification of a federal prisoner as a "Central Monitoring Case" required procedural protections, but those cases have now been overruled.[117] If you can show that a statute or regulation creates a liberty interest, using the methods described in Sec. B1b, *supra,* you may be able to establish the right to some procedural protections.[118] However, programs and classification are considered by many judges to be the kind of prison "minutiae" with which the courts should not get involved.[119]

f. Parole and Temporary Release

Due process questions in the granting and revocation of parole are discussed in detail in Ch. VIII, *infra.* In summary, you have a constitutionally based liberty interest protected by due process when you are threatened with parole revocation; in the *granting* of parole, you do not have a liberty interest unless one is created by the relevant statutes and regulations.[120]

Due process analysis in work-release and furlough cases is generally similar to that in parole cases. Most courts have held that there is no constitutionally based liberty interest in *obtaining* temporary release, and that due process claims arising from denial of temporary release must be

---

[115]Hooker v. Arnold, 454 F. Supp. 527 (M.D. Pa. 1978); Leon v. Harris, 489 F. Supp. 221 (S.D.N.Y. 1980). See also Sec. C8, *infra.*

[116]*See, e.g.,* Moody v. Daggett, 429 U.S. 78, 88, note 9, 97 S.Ct. 274 (1976); Gibson v. McEvers, 631 F.2d 95, 98 (7th Cir. 1980); Altizer v. Padernick, 569 F.2d 821 (4th Cir. 1978).

[117]*See* Pugliese v. Nelson, 617 F.2d 916 (2d Cir. 1980); Makris v. United States Bureau of Prisons, 606 F.2d 575 (5th Cir. 1979).

[118]Raso v. Moran, 551 F. Supp. 294 (D.R.I. 1982) (state statute providing time off sentence for blood donations under certain circumstances created liberty interest protected by due process).

[119]Meachum v. Fano, *supra* note 100.

[120]*Compare* Morrissey v. Brewer, 408 U.S. 471, 92 S.Ct. 2593 (1972), *with* Greenholtz v. Inmates of the Nebraska Penal and Correctional Complex, 442 U.S. 1, 99 S.Ct. 2100 (1979).

based on governing statutes and regulations.[121] Some courts have held that there is a constitutionally based liberty interest in avoiding *revocation* of temporary release, since—like parole revocation—it involves a liberty that one already possesses.[122] Other courts have rejected this view or have confined their analysis to liberty interests created by statutes or regulations.[123] Be sure to research the law in your jurisdiction if you have a temporary release revocation issue.

The "process that is due" in temporary release revocation cases has generally been held to be more similar to the prison disciplinary requirements of *Wolff v. McDonnell* than the parole revocation requirements of *Morrissey v. Brewer.*[124]

g.   Correspondence, Reading Material, and Visiting

In activities related to communication and expression, you may have constitutionally based liberty interests protected by due process.

In *Procunier v. Martinez,*[125] the Supreme Court held that the First Amendment right to correspond is a liberty interest, and upheld the lower court's order that prisoners be notified when prison officials reject letters to or from them, that the author of the letter be given a "reasonable opportunity to protest," and that complaints be referred to someone other than the censor.[126]

---

[121]*See, e.g.,* Winsett v. McGinnes, 617 F.2d 996 (3d Cir. 1980) (en banc), *cert. denied sub nom.* Anderson v. Winsett, 449 U.S. 1093 (1981) (regulations containing definite standards create entitlement to decision on proper standards); Martino v. Gard, 526 F. Supp. 958 (E.D.N.Y. 1981); Young v. Hunt, 507 F. Supp. 785 (N.D. Ind. 1981).

[122]*See* United States ex rel. Flores v. Cuyler, 511 F. Supp. 386 (E.D. Pa. 1981); Wilson v. Loftus, 489 F. Supp. 996 (D. Del. 1980).

[123]*See* Durso v. Rowe, 579 F.2d 1365 (7th Cir. 1978); Gray v. Wisconsin Dept. of health and Social Services, 495 F. Supp. 321 (E.D. Wisc. 1980); Perrote v. Percy, 465 F. Supp. 112 (W.D. Wisc. 1979), *modified,* 489 F. Supp. 212 (E.D. Wisc. 1980.).

[124]*See* Perrote v. Percy, *id.;* People ex rel. Cunningham v. Metz, 61 A.D.2d 590, 403 N.Y.S.2d 330 (App. Div., 3d Dept. 1978); *contra,* United States ex rel. Flores v. Cuyler, 511 F. Supp. 386 (E.D. Pa. 1981) (witnesses and confrontation required).

[125]416 U.S. 396, 417-19, 94 S.Ct. 1800 (1974).

[126]*See also* Wheeler v. United States, 640 F.2d 1116 (9th Cir. 1981) (court order restricting prisoner's correspondence with witness and her relatives should have been based on notice and hearing absent "compelling" circumstances); Intersimone v. Carlson, 512 F. Supp. 526 (M.D. Pa. 1980) (restriction on correspondence with jurors required notice and opportunity to be heard); Hardwick

When prison officials undertake to censor reading material that is sent to prisoners, they must also observe basic procedural safeguards. (The substantive restrictions on such censorship are discussed in Sec. C1, *infra*.) At a minimum, you should receive notice and an opportunity to be heard, a meaningful statement of reasons for the censorship, a prompt decision, and the right to appeal to an official other than the censor.[127] Some courts have held also that the *sender* of literature should receive notice and an opportunity to be heard.[128]

In challenging prison censorship procedures, you should also be familiar with the Supreme Court cases on non-prison censorship, which have emphasized the need for adversary safeguards, prompt decisions, and other procedural protections.[129]

The law is not settled as to procedural protections related to visiting, probably because the courts have yet to agree on the constitutional basis for the right to visit, or even on whether there is a right to visit. (The substantive restrictions on visits are discussed in Sec. C1d, *infra*.) Some courts have flatly stated that there is no such right, either for the prisoner or the visitor, and therefore there is no liberty interest protected by due process.[130] Other courts have found a right to some visiting based on the First Amendment[131] or on other grounds.[132]

---

v. Ault, 447 F. Supp. 116, 129 (M.D. Ga. 1978) (*Procunier* requirements imposed); Laaman v. Helgemoe, 437 F. Supp. 269, 322 (D.N.H. 1977) (same).

[127] *See* Hopkins v. Collins, 548 F.2d 503, 504 (4th Cir. 1977); Jackson v. Ward, 458 F. Supp. 546, 565 (W.D.N.Y. 1978); Hardwick v. Ault, 447 F. Supp. 116, 131 (M.D. Ga. 1978); Cofone v. Manson, 409 F. Supp. 1033, 1041 (D. Conn. 1976); Aikens v. Lash, 390 F. Supp. 663, 672 (N.D. Ind. 1975), *aff'd as modified,* 547 F.2d 372 (7th Cir. 1976); The Luparar v. Stoneman, 382 F. Supp. 495, 502 (D. Vt. 1974), *appeal dismissed,* 517 F.2d 1395 (2d Cir. 1975); Battle v. Anderson, 376 F. Supp. 402, 426 (E.D. Okla. 1974); Laaman v. Hancock, 351 F. Supp. 1265, 1268 (D.N.H. 1972); Sostre v. Otis, 330 F. Supp. 941, 946 (S.D.N.Y. 1971).

[128] Hopkins v. Collins, *id.* at 504; Cofone v. Manson, *id.* at 1041. *See also* Vodicka v. Phelps, 624 F.2d 569 (5th Cir. 1980) (notice to sender could replace notice to prisoner under circumstances).

[129] *See, e.g.,* Southeastern Promotions, Ltd. v. Conrad, 420 U.S. 546, 95 S.Ct. 1239 (1975); Carroll v. President and Commissioners of Princess Anne, 393 U.S. 175, 89 S.Ct. 347 (1968); Freeman v. Maryland, 380 U.S. 51, 58-59, 85 S.Ct. 734 (1965); Bantam Books, Inc. v. Sullivan, 372 U.S. 58, 66, 83 S.Ct. 631 (1963).

[130] *See* Fennell v. Carlson, 466 F. Supp. 56, 59 (W.D. Okla. 1978); White v. Keller, 438 F. Supp. 110 (D. Md. 1977), *aff'd,* 588 F.2d 913 (4th Cir. 1979).

[131] Feeley v. Sampson, 570 F.2d 364, 372 (1st Cir. 1978).

[132] Lynott v. Henderson, 610 F.2d 340, 342-43 (5th Cir. 1980) (unspecified constitutional grounds); Cooper v. Morin, 399 N.E.2d 1188, 49 N.Y.2d 69, 424 N.Y.S.2d (1979) (state constitutional grounds).

Because the constitutional status of visiting is so unsettled, you should carefully research the law in your jurisdiction. You should also plead a liberty interest based on statutes or regulations if there is any basis for doing so, since the court may be willing to hear your case on this basis, even if it does not find a constitutional right to visit.[133]

One recent case held that the requirements of *Wolff v. McDonnell*[134] for prison disciplinary hearings would be required for the suspension of visits, although the court strictly limited its holding to the specific case before it.[135] Other courts have held that due process is satisfied by *"meaningful* written responses to the prisoner's request and an opportunity to seek review of a denial from an officer other than the one who initially denied the prisoner's request."[136] One decision held "poor conduct" to be too vague a standard to revoke a visiting privilege.[137]

h.   Erroneous Information

There is some authority upholding a limited due process right to have erroneous and derogatory information expunged from a prisoner's parole or institutional file. In *Paine v. Baker,*[138] the court held that to obtain judicial relief, a prisoner must show that the false information is in his/her file, that it is likely to be relied on in denying or revoking parole, good time, or another liberty interest, and that s/he has requested prison officials to correct the matter and has been refused.[139]

i.   Property

In *Parratt v. Taylor,*[140] the Supreme Court held that when prison officials negligently lose a prisoner's property, due process is not violated as long as state law provides an adequate means of redress. In other

---

[133]*See* Kozlowski v. Coughlin, 539 F. Supp. 852 (S.D.N.Y. 1982) (liberty interest in visiting created by state regulations and court decisions).

[134]418 U.S. 539, 94 S.Ct. 2963 (1974).

[135]Kozlowski v. Coughlin, supra note 133, at 858.

[136]Hamilton v. Saxbe, 428 F. Supp. 1101, 1110 (N.D. Ga. 1976) (emphasis in original), *aff'd sub nom.* Hamilton v. Bell, 551 F.2d 1056 (5th Cir. 1977), *accord,* Laaman v. Helgemoe, 437 F. Supp. 269, 321 (D.N.H. 1977).

[137]Laaman v. Helgemoe, *id.*

[138]595 F.2d 197 (4th Cir. 1979).

[139]*Accord,* Bukhari v. Hutto, 487 F. Supp. 1162 (E.D. Va. 1980); *see also* Doe v. United States Civil Service Commission, 483 F. Supp. 539, 567 (S.D.N.Y. 1980) (similar rule in non-prison case).

[140]451 U.S. 527, 101 S.Ct. 1908 (1981). *See* Begg v. Moffitt, 555 F. Supp. 1344 (N.D. Ill. 1983),for an extensive discussion of the meaning of *Parratt.*

words, the mere existence of the state remedy satisfies the requirements of due process. This means that if your property gets lost, you must take your claim to any state court or administrative body that will hear it, unless that body does not provide a fair procedure. The absence of punitive damages or trial by jury does not make the procedure inadequate; in *Parratt,* the Court asked only whether the remedy could provide full compensation for the value of the property. A procedure may be held adequate whether it is judicial or administrative in nature,[141] and whether it provides a remedy against a governmental body or against individual officers.[142] The *Parratt* rule has been held applicable to a suit for an injunction as well as to damage suits.[143]

The *Parratt* holding is not an "exhaustion of remedies" rule permitting you to resort to federal courts once the state proceedings are completed. If there is a state remedy, it is your *only* remedy unless you can show that it was inadequate. This will require some showing of unfairness or failure to deal with the merits of your claim; the fact that the state system ruled against you does not, by itself, make the remedy inadequate.[144]

The courts are divided as to whether *Parratt* applies to intentional deprivations of property such as confiscation during a search or destruction by guards.[145] One of the concurring opinions in *Parratt* stated that its holding should be restricted to negligent deprivations.[146]

---

[141]*See Parratt, id.* (judicial procedure); Steffen v. Housewright, 665 F.2d 245 (8th Cir. 1981) (administrative procedure); Al-Mustafa Irshad v. Spann, 543 F. Supp. 922 (E.D. Va. 1982) (administrative procedure).

[142]*Parratt, id.* at 543-44 (government body); Graham v. Mitchell, 529 F. Supp. 622 (E.D. Va. 1982) (individual officer).

[143]Shango v. Jurich, 681 F.2d 1091 (7th Cir. 1982).

[144]*See* Coleman v. Faulkner, 697 F.2d 1347 (10th Cir. 1982) (facially adequate remedy which prisoner was unable to use because of prison restrictions was inadequate); Williams v. Morris, 697 F.2d 1349 (10th Cir. 1982) (procedure that automatically denied compensation for items not listed in "property book" was probably inadequate); Loftin v. Thomas, 681 F.2d 364 (5th Cir. 1982) (if relief is denied by state for any reason other than lack of merit, §1983 action can be heard by federal court). State procedures were upheld as adequate in Steffen v. Housewright, 665 F.2d 245 (8th Cir. 1981); Hendrix v. Faulkner, 525 F. Supp. 435 (N.D. Ind. 1981); Al-Mustafa Irshad v. Spann, 543 F. Supp. 922 (E.D. Va. 1982).

[145]Cases holding *Parratt* applicable include Palmer v. Hudson, 697 F.2d 1220 (4th Cir. 1983); Engblom v. Carey, 667 F.2d 957 (2d Cir. 1982); Sheppard v. Moore, 514 F. Supp. 1372 (M.D.N.C. 1981); Whorley v. Karr, 534 F. Supp. 88 (W.D. Va. 1981).

[146]*Supra* note 140, at 545-46. *See also* Isaac v. Jones, 529 F. Supp. 175 (N.D.

Some cases decided before *Parratt* required that when prison officials intentionally take property, they must give the prisoner a receipt for the seized property, a statement of reasons for the seizure, the right to be heard in opposition to the seizure, and a decision with reasons if the seizure is upheld.[147] These cases are still good law if *Parratt* is restricted to negligent deprivations; they may not be if *Parratt* applies to intentional deprivations of property.

If your claim involves loss or destruction of property, you must carefully research the interpretation given *Parratt* by your federal circuit and district courts as well as any later decisions by the Supreme Court to determine if you can litigate those claims in federal court. You should also determine if the facts you allege support legal theories other than deprivation of property without due process of law. For example, even if you cannot recover on a due process theory when guards intentionally destroy your property, you may be able to recover on the same facts by asserting an unreasonably conducted search and seizure under the Fourth Amendment.[148] If the property was books or religious objects, you may have a First Amendment claim;[149] if legal papers were seized or destroyed, you could invoke the right of access to the courts;[150] if meaningful personal objects were maliciously destroyed, you might plead an Eighth Amendment violation for the "unnecessary and wanton infliction of pain."[151] You must also consider whether it is more prudent to go into state court in the first place, rather than take the risk of a federal court dismissal and having to start over in state court later.[152] If your main concern is simply obtaining compensation for the value of the property, going to state court may be the most prudent course of action.

Ill. 1981); Tarkowski v. Hoogasian, 532 F. Supp. 791 (N.D. Ill. 1982); Toins v. Ignash, 534 F. Supp. 452 (E.D. Mich. 1982); Peters v. Township of Hopewell, 534 F. Supp. 1324 (D.N.J. 1982); Parker v. Rockefeller, 521 F. Supp. 1013 (N.D. W. Va. 1981).

[147]United States ex rel. Wolfish v. Levi, 428 F. Supp. 333, 342, *supplemented,* 439 F. Supp. 114, 151 (S.D.N.Y. 1977), *aff'd in pertinent part,* 573 F. 2d 118, 131-32 n.29 (2d Cir. 1978), *rev'd on other grounds sub nom.* Bell v. Wolfish, 441 U.S. 520, 99 S.Ct. 1861 (1979); Steinberg v. Taylor, 500 F. Supp. 477 (D. Conn. 1980); *see* Thornton v. Redman, 435 F. Supp. 876, 881 (D. Del. 1977) (procedures not required during general shakedown).

[148]Palmer v. Hudson, 697 F.2d 1220(4th Cir. 1983); *accord,* Wolf-Lillie v. Sonquist, 699 F.2d 864 (7th Cir. 1983).

[149]See Secs. C1b and C7, *infra,* Publications and Religion, respectively.

[150]See Sec. C4, *infra,* Access to the Courts.

[151]Gregg v. Georgia, 428 U.S. 153, 173, 96 S.Ct. 2909 (1976).

[152]See Ch. IV, Sec. D, for a discussion of litigation in state court.

C. Substantive Constitutional Rights

1. Communication, Expression, and Association

Rights of communication, expression, and association are among those most jealously protected by the courts outside the prison context. In prison, however, these First Amendment rights, like other rights, are restricted to some degree. How much they can be restricted depends on exactly what kind of speech or conduct is at issue, on the circumstances surrounding it, and on the type of restriction that is imposed.

Four Supreme Court cases set the outlines of prison First Amendment analysis. In *Procunier v. Martinez*,[153] a challenge to prison mail censorship, the Court set out a two-pronged standard for evaluating prison restrictions on First Amendment rights:

(1) The regulation or practice in question must further an important or substantial governmental interest related to the suppression of expression; and

(2) the limitation of First Amendment freedoms must be no greater than is necessary or essential to the protection of the particular governmental interest involved.[154]

The first part of the test means that prison officials may not, for example, censor mail simply because a prisoner is complaining about prison conditions, or criticizing the prison administration, or even lying. Prison officials must show that the censorship furthers one or more of the substantial interests of security, order, and rehabilitation.

The second part of the test means that if the restrictions on your First Amendment rights do further an important or substantial interest of the prison administration, they will still be invalid if they are too broad. For example, a regulation that prohibited writing letters about prison revolution might be invalid because a regulation that provided that you could write about revolution in letters, but could not circulate such letters among other prisoners, would serve the same purpose; your revolutionary views would be confined to yourself and your outside correspondent and could not threaten the security of the institution, since you and your correspondent would be the only ones that are aware of what you were writing.

The same year, the Court decided *Pell v. Procunier*,[155] in which prisoners challenged a rule that prohibited media interviews with individual prisoners. This time, the Court stated that "a prison inmate

---

[153]416 U.S. 396, 94 S.Ct. 1800 (1974).

[154]*Id.* at 407-08.

[155]417 U.S. 817, 94 S.Ct. 2800 (1974).

retains those First Amendment rights that are not inconsistent with his status as a prisoner or with the legitimate penological objectives of the corrections system," *i.e.,* deterrence, rehabilitation, and security.[156] Because there were alternative means of communicating with the press (letters and visits by family, friends, and clergy), because of the security problems caused by outsiders entering the prison for face-to-face communication, and because the rule "operates in a neutral fashion, without regard to the content of the expression,"[157] the rule was upheld. The *Procunier v. Martinez* requirement that restrictions be as narrow as possible was not mentioned.

Later, in *Jones v. North Carolina Prisoners' Labor Union, Inc.,*[158] the Court upheld severe restrictions on prisoner union organizing activities, including a ban on all prisoner solicitation, all meetings of union members, and bulk mailings of union literature.[159] Citing *Pell v. Procunier,* the Court stated:

> Perhaps the most obvious of the First Amendment rights that are necessarily curtailed by confinement are those associational rights that the First Amendment protects outside of prison walls. The concept of incarceration itself entails a restriction on the freedom of inmates to associate with those outside of the penal institution. Equally as obvious, the inmate's "status as a prisoner" and the operational realities of a prison dictate restrictions on the associational rights among inmates.[160]

The Court went on to emphasize repeatedly that prison officials' decisions should be granted "deference";[161] it also emphasized, with regard to the bulk mailing of literature, that alternative sources of information (*i.e.,* individual mailings) were available, and that the increased cost and inconvenience of these did not "fundamentally implicate *free speech* values."[162]

In *Bell v. Wolfish,*[163] the Court upheld a modified "publisher only" rule which barred the receipt of hardcover books from anyone but the publisher, a book club, or a bookstore. The rule was designed to keep out contraband without requiring a careful search of every incoming

---

[156]*Id.* at 822-23.

[157]*Id.* at 923-28.

[158]433 U.S. 119, 97 S.Ct. 2532 (1977).

[159]*Id.* at 122.

[160]*Id.* at 125-26.

[161]*Id.* at 126 ("wide-ranging deference"); *id.* at 128 ("deference to [officials'] informed discretion"); *id.* at 136 ("full latitude of discretion").

[162]*Id.* at 130-31 (emphasis in original).

[163]441 U.S. 520, 99 S.Ct. 1861 (1979).

book.[164] The Court stressed the existence of alternative ways of getting books and noted that the rule was content-neutral, as in *Pell v. Procunier.*[165]

These varying statements of First Amendment standards do not reflect changes in the Supreme Court's view so much as they reflect the facts of each case. Your task as a litigant will often be to convince the court that you are entitled to the more liberal standard of *Procunier v. Martinez* and that the prison authorities are not entitled to the extreme deference granted in *Jones v. North Carolina Prisoners' Labor Union, Inc.* From the Supreme Court decisions, several principles can be gleaned which you can use in analyzing any question of prisoners' communication and expression rights.

1. The printed word is entitled to the greatest protection, and prison officials must show that their restrictions are justified and that they are no broader than necessary.

2. The entry of outside persons into the prison is entitled to less protection, and prison officials need only show that they are being reasonable.

3. Association and organization among prisoners is entitled to the least protection; courts must defer to prison officials' decisions unless you conclusively prove them wrong.

4. "Content-neutral" rules that restrict all shades of opinion equally are more likely to be upheld than restrictions on what may be said or written.

5. Rules that merely make it more difficult to communicate are more likely to be upheld than rules that completely bar particular types of communication.

a. Correspondence

The substantive standards for censorship of prisoners' mail are set out in *Procunier v. Martinez,* discussed in Sec. C1, *supra.* Under these standards, courts have disapproved censorship of mail considered unduly critical of prison conditions, profane, or obscene;[166] censorship of a letter which alleged that the mail censor, while reading the mail, "engaged in masturbation and 'had sex' with a cat,";[167] and punishment

---

[164]*Id.* at 550-51.

[165]*Id.* at 551-52.

[166]Hardwick v. Ault, 447 F. Supp. 116 (M.D. Ga. 1978). *See also* Milonas v. Williams, 691 F.2d 931 (10th Cir. 1982) (censorship to eliminate "negative thinking" and statements considered to be "untrue" enjoined).

[167]McNamara v. Moody, 606 F.2d 621 (5th Cir. 1979).

of a prisoner for letters criticizing prison officials' actions.[168] One court has held that refusal to deliver mail addressed to prisoners by their Muslim names violated the Constitution when the address was sufficient for prison officials to deliver it.[169] Censorship of mail on the ground that it would cause severe psychiatric or emotional disturbance cannot be done except by qualified psychiatric or psychological personnel.[170] Prison officials may not refuse to deliver mail because it is written in a language other than English.[171]

Obviously, prison officials cannot censor your mail without reading it, and courts have assumed that prisoner mail can be read without probable cause,[172] although some courts have restricted the reading of outgoing mail.[173] The most important restriction on reading of mail is the treatment of "privileged mail" such as attorney-client correspondence. Incoming privileged mail may not routinely be read; it may be opened and inspected for contraband, but only in the prisoner's presence.[174] Outgoing privileged mail may generally be sent sealed.[175] The status of privileged mail has been accorded not only to correspondence with attorneys and courts, but also in some cases to mail to and from legislators, Presidents, governors, probation and parole officers, agencies of federal, state, and local government, etc.[176] and the press.[177] Privileged mail may be held briefly to verify the identity of the addressee.[178]

---

[168]Cavey v. Levine, 435 F. Supp. 475 (D. Md. 1977).

[169]Masjid Muhammad-D.C.C. v. Keve, 479 F. Supp. 1311, 1326 (D. Del. 1979).

[170]Ramos v. Lamm, 639 F.2d 559, 581-82 (10th Cir. 1980).

[171]Id. at 581.

[172]Guajardo v. Estelle, 580 F.2d 748, 756-57 (5th Cir. 1978); Feeley v. Sampson, 570 F.2d 364, 374 (1st Cir. 1978); Smith v. Shimp, 562 F.2d 423, 426 (7th Cir. 1977); Sumlin v. State, 587 S.W.2d 571 (Sup.Ct. Ark. 1979).

[173]Wolfish v. Levi, 573 F.2d 118, 130 (2d Cir. 1978), rev'd in part on other grounds sub nom. Bell v. Wolfish, 441 U.S. 520, 99 S.Ct. 1861 (1979); State v. Sheriff, 619 P.2d 181 (Sup.Ct. Mont. 1980).

[174]Wolff v. McDonnell, supra note 40, at 577; Guajardo v. Estelle, supra note 172, at 757-59; Owen v. Schuler, 466 F. Supp. 5 (N.D. Ind. 1977), aff'd, 594 F.2d 867 (7th Cir. 1979); Ramos v. Lamm, 485 F. Supp. 122, 164 (D. Colo. 1979), modified on other grounds, 639 F.2d 559 (10th Cir. 1981).

[175]Davidson v. Scully, 694 F.2d 50 (2d Cir. 1982); Ramos v. Lamm, id., 639 F.2d at 582; Guajardo v. Estelle, supra note 172, at 759.

[176]Davidson v. Scully, id.; Guajardo v. Estelle, supra note 172, at 759.

[177]Guajardo v. Estelle, id.

[178]Id. at 758-59.

Restrictions on the number of letters you may send or receive have been held invalid.[179] Prison officials may forbid you to correspond with particular individuals if they have reasons meeting the *Procunier* standard, but they may not require you to obtain prior authorization before you can correspond with particular individuals[180] since people who do not want to receive mail from you can write prison officials and say so.[181] You may be prohibited from corresponding with witnesses or jurors in your criminal trial if the trial judge so orders.[182] Prison officials have substantial discretion to restrict correspondence between prisoners;[183] the courts have disagreed as to whether a prisoner may be prevented from corresponding with a "jailhouse lawyer" who has previously assisted him/her.[184] One court has struck down a rule forbidding prisoners to correspond with minors without their parents' consent, although the correspondence could be halted if the parents objected.[185] A prohibition on corresponding with a former correctional officer was struck down in *Stevens v. Ralston.*[186] Prisoners have been held entitled to correspond with their ministers[187] and with the Pope for religious purposes.[188] Prisoners may not be prohibited from (or punished for) corresponding with the press.[189]

Courts have not dealt consistently with the problem of mail being frequently delayed by prison officials. Some courts have held that there is a constitutional right to have mail promptly delivered or forwarded.[190]

---

[179]*Id.* at 756-57.

[180]*Id.* at 754-57 and n.4; Finney v. Arkansas Board of Corrections, 505 F.2d 194, 210-212 (8th Cir. 1974).

[181]Guajardo v. Estelle, *supra* note 172, at 755; Finney v. Arkansas Board of Corrections, *supra* note 180.

[182]Wheeler v. United States, 640 F.2d 1116 (9th Cir. 1981); Intersimone v. Carlson, 512 F. Supp. 526 (M.D. Pa. 1980).

[183]Schlobohm v. United States Attorney General, 479 F. Supp. 401 (M.D. Pa. 1979), and cases cited.

[184]*Compare* Watts v. Brewer, 588 F.2d 646 (8th Cir. 1978), *with* Storseth v. Spellman, 654 F.2d 1349 (9th Cir. 1981).

[185]Hearn v. Morris, 526 F. Supp. 267 (E.D. Cal. 1981).

[186]674 F.2d 759 (8th Cir. 1982).

[187]*See* Walker v. Blackwell, 411 F.2d 23, 24 (5th Cir. 1969). See also Sec. C7d3, *infra.*

[188]*See* Peek v. Ciccone, 288 F. Supp. 329, 333-34 (W.D. Mo. 1968).

[189]Guajardo v. Estelle, *supra* note 172, at 759 and cases cited; Cavey v. Levine, 435 F. Supp. 475 (D. Md. 1977).

[190]Nicholson v. Choctaw County, Ala., 498 F. Supp. 295 (S.D. Ala. 1980);

Others have held that there is no constitutional violation in mail delays.[191] Realistically, the courts know that mail is frequently mishandled outside prison, too, and they are not likely to hold prison officials liable for delays unless you can prove that they were intentional and unjustified and/or that you suffered some actual harm as a result (like missing a court deadline).

Under some circumstances, prison officials must provide you with procedural protections when they restrict your correspondence rights. (See Sec. B2g, *supra.*)

b. Publications

Most courts have held that prisoners' right to read publications of their choice is governed by the liberal *Procunier v. Martinez* standard discussed in Sec. C1, *supra.*[192] As one court put it, the *Procunier* standards "require a substantial factual showing by corrections officials that a publication poses a tangible threat to the order, security, or rehabilitative programs of the prison before they may bar the publication from the facility."[193] The idea of "deference" to prison officials is not applicable to restrictions on what you can read.[194]

Applying the standard, courts have ruled on various types of publications censored by prison officials. "Literature that criticizes police or corrections officials cannot be excluded . . . [without] a substantial showing that the publication does indeed pose a tangible threat to the order and security of the institution. . . ."[195] Material of a radical

---

Taylor v. Leidig, 484 F. Supp. 1330 (D. Colo. 1980); *see* Sherman v. McDougall, 656 F.2d 527 (9th Cir. 1981) (rule requiring delivery within 24 hours approved).

[191]Owen v. Schuler, 466 F. Supp. 5 (N.D. Ind. 1977), *aff'd,* 594 F.2d 867 (7th Cir. 1979) (delays not actionable unless "unreasonable"); Pickett v. Schaefer, 503 F. Supp. 27 (S.D.N.Y. 1980) (9½-day delay in sending legal mail permissible if no actual prejudice); Stinson v. Sheriff's Department of Sullivan County, 499 F. Supp. 259 (S.D.N.Y. 1980) (month delay in sending letter to minister not actionable).

[192]Pepperling v. Crist, 678 F.2d 787, 790 (9th Cir. 1982); Blue v. Hogan, 553 F.2d 960 (5th Cir. 1977); Hopkins v. Collins, 548 F.2d 503 (4th Cir. 1977); Aikens v. Jenkins, 534 F.2d 751, 753 (7th Cir. 1976); Morgan v. LaVallee, 526 F.2d 221, 224-25 (2d Cir. 1975); Jackson v. Ward, 458 F. Supp. 546, 558 (W.D.N.Y. 1978).

[193]Jackson v. Ward, *id.* at 559 (citations omitted); *accord,* Thibodeaux v. State of South Dakota, 553 F.2d 558 (8th Cir. 1977); Aikens v. Jenkins, *id.* at 755.

[194]Kincaid v. Rusk, 670 F.2d 737, 744-45 (7th Cir. 1982).

[195]Jackson v. Ward, *supra* note 192, at 563; *accord,* Vodicka v. Phelps, 624 F.2d 569 (5th Cir. 1980); Guajardo v. Estelle, *supra* note 172, at 760-61; Aikens v. Jenkins, *supra* note 192, at 757; Paka v. Manson, 387 F. Supp. 111, 127-28

or revolutionary political nature may not be censored solely because of the beliefs expressed;[196] it must pose some actual threat to security, order, or rehabilitation within the institution.[197] Prison union literature may not be categorically banned even if the unions are prohibited.[198] Some courts have stated that literature that advocates criminal activity *outside* the prison can only be banned if it presents a "clear and present danger" that such activity will actually occur.[199] Similarly, racial and religious literature may be censored only if it actually incites or encourages violence; mere statements expressing or supporting racial or religious antagonism cannot be suppressed.[200] Information concerning means of escape or the manufacture of explosives, weapons, or drugs may be excluded.[201] The courts have disagreed on the standard to be applied to sexual literature. Some courts have held that a publication must actually be obscene before it can be censored.[202] Others have upheld

---

(D. Conn. 1974); Epps v. Smith, 112 Misc.2d 724, 730 (N.Y. Sup. Ct. 1981); *see also* Procunier v. Martinez, *supra* note 153, at 413.

[196]United States ex rel. Larkins v. Oswald, 510 F.2d 583, 587-88 (2d Cir. 1975) ("revolutionary or militant rhetoric" improperly seized); Hardwick v. Ault, 447 F. Supp. 116, 130-31 (M.D. Ga. 1978) (books about communist doctrine improperly censored); Aikens v. Lash, 390 F. Supp. 663, 671-72 (N.D. Ind. 1975), *aff'd,* 534 F.2d 751 (7th Cir. 1976) (Mao Tse-Tung improperly excluded); Laaman v. Hancock, 351 F. Supp. 1265 (D.N.H. 1972) (*Guerilla Warfare and Marxism,* ed. Pomeroy, improperly censored).

[197]Cofone v. Manson, 409 F. Supp. 1033, 1040 (D. Conn. 1976); Jackson v. Ward, *supra* note 192, at 563; *see also* Procunier v. Martinez, *supra* note 153, at 416.

[198]Paka v. Manson, *supra* note 195, at 127-28; *see* Jones v. North Carolina Prisoners' Labor Union, *supra* note 158, at 130 (bulk mailings could be banned where prisoners could receive individual copies).

[199]Cofone v. Manson, *supra* note 197; Jackson v. Ward, *supra* note 192, at 563.

[200]Aikens v. Jenkins, *supra* note 192, at 756-57; Walker v. Blackwell, 411 F.2d 23, 28-29 (5th Cir. 1969); Jackson v. Godwin, 400 F.2d 529, 535 (5th Cir. 1968); Long v. Parker, 390 F.2d 816, 822 (3d Cir. 1968); Jackson v. Ward, *supra* note 192, at 562.

[201]Guajardo v. Estelle, *supra* note 172, at 761; Sherman v. McDougall, 656 F.2d 527 (9th Cir. 1981); Brown v. Hilton, 492 F. Supp. 771 (D.N.J. 1980); Nicholson v. Choctaw County, Ala., 498 F. Supp. 295 (S.D. Ala. 1980); Mayberry v. Robinson, 427 F. Supp. 297 (M.D. Pa. 1977) (Air Force Survival Manual excludable).

[202]Pepperling v. Crist, *supra* note 192, at 790; Jackson v. Ward, *supra* note 192, at 560.
The Supreme Court has stated the test for determining if a work is obscene as

broader restrictions on sexually explicit material.[203] One court has held that "preventing homosexual acts" is a legitimate rehabilitative and security interest and that literature that would encourage them can be excluded.[204] However, this holding was based in part on the fact that consensual homosexuality was illegal in the state in question, and it was directed at sexually explicit materials. If you are in a state where such acts are not illegal, and if the literature you seek to receive does not actually portray sexual acts (*e.g.,* gay newspapers), you should emphasize these facts in your papers.

The *Procunier v. Martinez* requirement that restrictions on First Amendment rights be no broader than necessary (see Sec. C1, *supra*) has additional corollaries. Prison officials may not impose a blanket ban on a periodical; they must review each issue individually.[205] Some courts have also held that only the objectionable *portions* of a publication may be excluded.[206]

Prison censors must be guided by "narrowly drawn regulation[s]";[207]

. . . (a) whether "the average person, applying contemporary community standards" would find that the work, taken as a whole, appeals to the prurient interest. . . ; (b) whether the work depicts or describes, in a patently offensive way, sexual conduct specifically defined by the applicable state law; and (c) whether the work, taken as a whole, lacks serious literary, artistic, political, or scientific value.

[*Miller v. California,* 413 U.S. 15, 24, 93 S.Ct. 2607 (1973) (citations omitted).]

Further comment on the obscenity standard is beyond the scope of this manual. However, it should be noted that the fact that a publication is readily available in adult bookstores does not mean that it is not obscene; it simply means that many local governments do not bother or are not able to enforce obscenity laws.

[203]Thibodeaux v. State of South Dakota, 553 F.2d 558 (8th Cir. 1977); Carpenter v. State of South Dakota, 536 F.2d 759 (8th Cir. 1976); Aikens v. Jenkins, *supra* note 197, at 756; Guajardo v. Estelle, *supra* note 172, at 762.

The courts are divided as to whether prisoners' receipt and possession of nude photographs can be restricted to commercial photographs as opposed to those of wives, lovers, etc. *Compare* Pepperling v. Crist, *supra* note 192, *with* Trapnell v. Riggsby, 622 F.2d 290 (7th Cir. 1980).

[204]Guajardo v. Estelle, *supra* note 172, at 762.

[205]Guajardo v. Estelle, *supra* note 172, at 762; Hardwick v. Ault, *supra* note 196, at 131; Cofone v. Manson, *supra* note 197, at 1041-42; McCleary v. Kelly, 376 F. Supp. 1186, 1190-91 (M.D. Pa. 1974); Laaman v. Hancock, *supra* note 196, at 1269; *contra,* Goodson v. United States, 472 F. Supp. 1211 (E.D. Mich. 1979).

[206]Guajardo v. Estelle, *supra* note 172, at 761; Pepperling v. Crist, *supra* note 192, at 791; Jackson v. Ward, *supra* note 192, at 564.

[207]Jackson v. Ward, *supra* note 192, at 563; *see* Procunier v. Martinez, *supra* note 153, at 416.

the absence of regulations is itself a constitutional violation.[208] The regulations must be capable of being understood and applied consistently;[209] denying publications to some prisoners and permitting them to others is unlawful.[210] Once regulations are promulgated, they must be followed.[211] You are also entitled to certain procedural rights when publications are censored. (See Sec. B2f, *supra*.)

Restrictions on reading matter that do not relate to the content of the publications are more often upheld by the courts. A prohibition on receiving hardcover books from anyone but the publisher, a book club, or a bookstore was upheld by the Supreme Court.[212] Broader "publisher only" rules have been upheld by lower courts,[213] though the Supreme Court's holding seems to suggest that such a rule could be invalidated if you showed that there were not sufficient alternatives for obtaining books. Even "content-neutral" regulations may be struck down if they are too sweeping.[214]

In some cases, courts have held that prison officials have an affirmative obligation to make reading material available to prisoners.[215]

The courts are divided on the proper treatment of prisoner-produced

---

[208]McMurry v. Phelps, 533 F. Supp. 742, 765-66 (W.D. La. 1982).

[209]Pepperling v. Crist, *supra* note 192, at 790; Craig v. Hocker, 405 F. Supp. 656 (D. Nev. 1975).

[210]Aikens v. Lash, 390 F. Supp. 663, 672 (N.D. Ind. 1975), *aff'd*, 534 F.2d 751 (7th Cir. 1976); Fortune Society v. McGinnis, 319 F. Supp. 901, 905 (S.D.N.Y. 1970).

[211]Thibodeaux v. State of South Dakota, *supra* note 193, at 560; Hardwick v. Ault, *supra* note 196, at 131.

[212]Bell v. Wolfish, 441 U.S. 520, 550-52, 99 S.Ct. 1861 (1979).

[213]Cotton v. Lockhart, 620 F.2d 670 (8th Cir. 1980); Rich v. Luther, 514 F. Supp. 481 (W.D.N.C. 1981); Ramos v. Lamm, 485 F. Supp. 122, 163 (D. Colo. 1979), *modified on other grounds*, 639 F.2d 559 (10th Cir. 1980).

[214]Kincaid v. Rusk, 670 F.2d 737 (7th Cir. 1982) (ban on pictorial magazines, newspapers, and hardcover books designed to prevent fires and protect plumbing unconstitutional); Parnell v. Waldrep, 511 F. Supp. 764 (W.D.N.C. 1981) (ban on magazines, newspapers, and paperbacks for same purpose unconstitutional); Hutchings v. Corum, 501 F. Supp. 1276 (W.D. Mo. 1980) (ban on newspapers struck down); Mitchell v. Untreiner, 421 F. Supp. 886 (N.D. Fla. 1976) (same); Manicone v. Corso, 365 F. Supp. 576 (E.D.N.Y. 1973) (same).

[215]Dawson v. Kendrick, 527 F. Supp. 1252 (S.D. W. Va. 1981); Barnes v. Government of Virgin Islands, 415 F. Supp. 1218 (D.V.I. 1976); *see also* Griffin v. Smith, 493 F. Supp. 129 (W.D.N.Y. 1980) (limit on books in segregation cells combined with inadequate library stated a claim); Giampetruzzi v. Malcolm, 406 F. Supp. 836 (S.D.N.Y. 1975) (greater library access required for prisoners in administrative segregation).

publications. Two cases have held that their censorship is governed by the *Procunier v. Martinez* standard applicable to literature received from outside, and that prison sponsorship and payment of publication costs did not give the authorities additional censorship powers.[216] A third decision[217] held that the controlling authority is *Jones v. North Carolina Prisoners' Labor Union, Inc.,*[218] which requires deference to the expertise of prison officials and places the burden of proof on the prisoners rather than the censors.

c.　Organizations, Protests, and Petitions

The courts have afforded very little legal protection to prisoners who oppose or criticize prison policies in any organized fashion. The Supreme Court in *Jones v. North Carolina Prisoners' Labor Union, Inc.* upheld prison officials' ban on prisoner solicitation for union membership, all union meetings, and bulk mailings of union literature for redistribution to prisoners, even though no strike or work stoppage was actually imminent.[219] The Court stressed that prisoners' status and the realities of prison life required restrictions on the right to associate, that prison officials' decisions should be granted deference, and that the prison environment could not be treated as a "public forum" open to all including groups that wished to pursue an "adversary relationship" with the prison administration.[220]

Recently, several courts have taken a similar negative view of prisoner petitions. In *Nickens v. White,*[221] the court upheld a regulation forbidding "mass protest petitions," noting that alternative methods of expressing grievances—correspondence and an internal grievance procedure—were available. Another court observed in dictum that a ban on petitions was permissible because the process of gathering signatures might lead to violence.[222] Some courts have pointed to the inflammatory

---

[216]Bailey v. Loggins, 156 Cal. Rptr. 654 (Ct. App. 1979); The Luparar v. Stoneman, 382 F. Supp. 495 (D. Vt. 1974), *appeal dismissed,* 517 F.2d 1395 (2d Cir. 1975).

[217]Pittman v. Hutto, 594 F.2d 407 (4th Cir. 1979).

[218]433 U.S. 119, 97 S.Ct. 2532 (1977). See discussion of this case in Sec. C1.

[219]*Id.*

[220]*Id.; see also* Preast v. Cox, 628 F.2d 292 (4th Cir. 1980) (prisoner groups could be required to receive official recognition before engaging in joint activities; denial of recognition would be virtually unreviewable by court).

[221]622 F.2d 967 (8th Cir. 1980).

[222]Edwards v. White, 501 F. Supp. 8 (M.D. Pa. 1979).

language that sometimes appears in petitions.[223] Other decisions, however, have recognized a right to petition.[224]

There is no constitutional requirement that prisons provide grievance procedures,[225] although some courts have approved or encouraged them or required their creation in order to protect other rights.[226] However, state law may create a right to a grievance procedure; under some circumstances, officials' failure to comply with such a state law mandate may state a constitutional claim.[227]

Courts have expressed different views about other forms of protest and criticism. Some take the view that complaints about jail conditions should not be cause for punishment unless they pose an actual danger to institutional security.[228] Others have held that certain critical statements are not protected by the First Amendment.[229] Realistically, prison First Amendment rulings will probably depend as much on the circumstances surrounding a statement as on the statement itself. Thus, if you believe a guard stole property during a cell search, and you accuse him/her of this

---

[223]Williams v. Stacy, 468 F. Supp. 1206 (E.D. Va. 1979) (petition describing guards as "Nazis" and "maniacs" and warning of "another Attica" could be suppressed, even if true).

[224]*See, e.g.,* Haymes v. Montanye, 547 F.2d 188, 191 (2d Cir. 1976); Stoval v. Bennett, 471 F. Supp. 1286 (M.D. Ala. 1979).

[225]Hutchings v. Corum, 501 F. Supp. 1276, 1298 (W.D. Mo. 1980), and cases cited. *But see* Canterino v. Wilson, 546 F. Supp. 174, 215-16 (W.D. Ky. 1982) (disparities in grievance procedures between men's and women's prisons violated equal protection). See also Ch. VI, Sec. D2, for a discussion of exhaustion of administrative remedies and the Civil Rights of Institutionalized Persons Act, 42 U.S.C. §1997e.

[226]Finney v. Mabry, 458 F. Supp. 720, 721 (E.D. Ark. 1978) (consent judgment containing grievance procedure approved); Miller v. Carson, 401 F. Supp. 835, 898-99 (M.D. Fla. 1975) (jail "Ombudsman" ordered); Laaman v. Helgemoe, 437 F. Supp. 269, 320 (D.N.H. 1977) (grievance procedure required to prevent abuse and mistreatment). *Contra,* Hoptowit v. Ray, 682 F.2d 1237, 1251 (9th Cir. 1982).

[227]Lucas v. Wasser, 425 F. Supp. 955, 961-62 (S.D.N.Y. 1976); *see also* Johnson v. Ward, 64 A.D.2d 186, 409 N.Y.S.2d 670 (App. Div. 1978) (state statute creating grievance procedure created liberty interest restricting transfers of grievance representatives).

[228]Collins v. Schoonfield, 344 F. Supp. 257 (D. Md. 1972).

[229]Pollard v. Baskerville, 481 F. Supp. 1157 (E.D. Va. 1979) (accusation that a guard brought in contraband not protected); Riggs v. Miller, 480 F. Supp. 799 (E.D. Va. 1979) ("bickering, argumentative conversation" not protected); Craig v. Franke, 478 F. Supp. 19 (E.D. Wisc. 1979) (accusation that officer was drunk not protected); Durkin v. Taylor, 444 F. Supp. 879 (E.D. Va. 1979) (statement that "I am tired of chickenshit rules" not protected).

in front of twenty or thirty other prisoners, your speech may not be protected because it presents a danger of violence or disruption. If you make the same statement privately to the guard or a superior officer or the warden, or in a letter to the press or a law enforcement agency, this danger is not present and there is no legitimate reason for your rights to be restricted.

d.   Visiting

The Supreme Court has never ruled broadly on prisoners' rights to visit with family and friends; its rulings have been confined to press interviews,[230] strip searches in connection with visits,[231] and visits by law students and paraprofessionals.[232] However, the Court has stated in connection with press interviews:

> [With respect to] the entry of people into the prisons for face-to-face communication with inmates, it is obvious that institutional considerations, such as security and related administrative problems, as well as the accepted and legitimate policy objectives of the corrections system itself, require that some limitation be placed on such visitations. So long as reasonable and effective means of communication remain open and no discrimination in terms of content is involved, we believe that, in drawing such lines, "prison officials must be accorded latitude."[233]

Thus, visiting requirements will generally be upheld unless you can show, by substantial evidence, that prison officials have exaggerated their response to a perceived problem; that their response is irrational; or that there is no real threat to security and order.[234]

The courts have yet to agree on whether there is a constitutional right to visit, and if so what it is based on.[235] You should therefore be sure to research the law in your particular jurisdiction, both federal and state,

---

[230]Pell v. Procunier, 417 U.S. 817, 94 S.Ct. 2800 (1974).

[231]Bell v. Wolfish, 441 U.S. 520, 558-60, 99 S.Ct. 1861 (1979).

[232]Procunier v. Martinez, 416 U.S. 396, 419-22, 94 S.Ct. 1800 (1974).

[233]Pell v. Procunier, *supra* note 230, at 826 (citation omitted).

[234]Bell v. Wolfish, *supra* note 231, at 555.

[235]*Compare* Fennell v. Carlson, 466 F. Supp. 56, 59 (W.D. Okla. 1978); White v. Keller, 438 F. Supp. 110 (D. Md. 1977), *aff'd,* 588 F.2d 913 (4th Cir. 1978) (no right to visit and no liberty interest protected by due process), *with* Feeley v. Sampson, 570 F.2d 364, 372 (1st Cir. 1978); McMurry v. Phelps, 533 F. Supp. 742, 764 (W.D. La. 1982) (right to visit protected by First Amendment); Lynott v. Henderson, 610 F.2d 340, 342-43 (5th Cir. 1980) (right to visit based on unspecified constitutional grounds); Laaman v. Helgemoe, 437 F. Supp. 269 (D.N.H. 1977) (unreasonable visiting restrictions violate Eighth Amendment); Hardwick v. Ault, 447 F. Supp. 116, 131 (M.D. Ga. 1978) (same).

before you bring a visiting case. State statutes, case law, and prison regulations may be more helpful to you than federal law.[236] Also, be aware that many older pretrial detention cases take a very liberal view toward visiting, but their holdings may not be valid after the Supreme Court's ruling in *Bell v. Wolfish*.[237]

Generally, courts uphold prison restrictions on visiting unless they are totally unreasonable or the prisoner is totally deprived of visits. However, several courts have struck down bans on visiting by children.[238] Refusal to permit visits between husband and wife states a constitutional claim,[239] and one court has required husband-wife visits when both were incarcerated;[240] however, even husband-wife visits, or visits with other close relatives, may be barred if there is good reason.[241] Greater restrictions on non-family than family visitors have been upheld,[242] as has the requirement of prior approval of visitors.[243] Refusal to permit visits based on race or religion is unlawful,[244] but courts have

---

[236]*See, e.g.,* Boudin v. Thomas, 533 F. Supp. 786 (S.D.N.Y. 1982) (federal prison regulation required contact visits); Cooper v. Morin, 399 N.E.2d 1188, 49 N.Y.2d 69 (N.Y. 1979) (state constitution required contact visits); Chambers v. Coughlin, 429 N.Y.S.2d 74 (Sup. Ct. 1980) (state regulation forbade visiting deprivations as punishments).

[237]*Supra* note 231. See Sec. E, *infra,* for a discussion of the effect of *Wolfish* on pretrial detention law.

[238]McMurry v. Phelps, 533 F. Supp. 742, 764 (W.D. La. 1982); Nicholson v. Choctaw County, Ala., 498 F. Supp. 295 (S.D. Ala. 1980); Valentine v. Englehardt, 474 F. Supp. 294 (D.N.J. 1979); Mitchell v. Untreiner, 421 F. Supp. 886, 901 (N.D. Fla. 1976).

[239]Massey v. Wilson, 484 F. Supp. 1332 (D. Colo. 1980).

[240]Perkins v. Wagner, 513 F. Supp. 904 (E.D. Pa. 1981) (inmates were detainees and co-defendants); *but see* Wallace v. Hutto, 80 F.R.D. 739 (W.D. Va. 1978) (husband-wife visits denied where both were convicts).

[241]Rowland v. Wolff, 336 F. Supp. 257 (D. Neb. 1971) (prisoner's half-sister had brought a gun into prison); Patterson v. Walters, 363 F. Supp. 486 (W.D. Pa. 1973) (wife had smuggled drugs).

[242]Ramos v. Lamm, 639 F.2d 559, 580 (10th Cir. 1980); Wilson v. Nevada Dept. of Prisons, 511 F. Supp. 750 (D. Nev. 1981); Hardwick v. Ault, 447 F. Supp. 116, 131 (M.D. Ga. 1978); Laaman v. Helgemoe, 437 F. Supp. 269, 320-22 (D.N.H. 1977).

[243]Ramos v. Lamm, *id.*

[244]Martin v. Wainwright, 526 F.2d 938 (5th Cir. 1976); Thomas v. Brierley, 481 F.2d 660, 661 (3d Cir. 1973); O'Malley v. Brierley, 477 F.2d 785 (3d Cir. 1973).

upheld the exclusion of unlicensed bondspersons[245] and released prisoners.[246]

Courts have generally upheld restrictions affecting the amount and conditions of visiting. It is not unlawful to place convicts in a prison so distant that it is difficult or impossible for them to receive visits.[247] Limits on the length and number of visits have been upheld in most recent cases,[248] as have distinctions in visiting conditions between general population prisoners and prisoners in segregation.[249] However, some courts have ordered expansion of visiting schedules.[250] Most recent decisions have held that contact visits are not constitutionally required,[251] nor are conjugal visits.[252] However, some have required that

---

[245]Carey v. Beans, 500 F. Supp. 580 (E.D. Pa. 1980).

[246]Alim v. Byrne, 521 F. Supp. 1039 (D.N.J. 1980); Farmer v. Loving, 392 F. Supp. 27 (W.D. Va. 1975).

[247]Ali v. Gibson, 631 F.2d 1126, 1134-35 (3d Cir. 1980); Dozier v. Hilton, 507 F. Supp. 1299 (D.N.J. 1981); Johnson v. Brelje, 482 F. Supp. 125 (N.D. Ill. 1979).

[248]Ramos v. Lamm, *supra* note 242, at 580 (five days or ten half-days a month upheld); Inmates, Washington County Jail v. England, 516 F. Supp. 132 (E.D. Tenn. 1980) (one 15-minute visit a week upheld); Walker v. Johnson, 544 F. Supp. 345 (E.D. Mich. 1982) (three hours a week enough); Tunnell v. Robinson, 486 F. Supp. 1265 (W.D. Pa. 1980) (limit of five visitors at one time upheld); Louis v. Ward, 444 F. Supp. 1107 (S.D.N.Y. 1978) (limits on number of visits and visitors upheld); Adams v. Aaron, 421 F. Supp. 430 (E.D. Ill. 1976) (limit on visits by particular individual upheld).

[249]Ramos v. Lamm, *supra* note 242, at 580 (denial of contact visits for segregated prisoner upheld); Bono v. Saxbe, 620 F.2d 609 (7th Cir. 1980) (same); Wilson v. Nevada Dept. of Prisoners, 511 F. Supp. 750 (D. Nev. 1981) (limits on non-family visitors for death row inmates upheld); Freeman v. Trudell, 497 F. Supp. 481 (E.D. Mich. 1980) (punitive segregation inmate could be handcuffed for visits); Wojtczak v. Cuyler, 480 F. Supp. 1288 (E.D. Pa. 1979) (restrictions on visits for protective custody inmates upheld). *But see* Hardwick v. Ault, 447 F. Supp. 116, 131 (M.D. Ga. 1978) (restrictions must be varied according to actual aggressiveness of inmate).

[250]McMurry v. Phelps, 533 F. Supp. 742, 764 (W.D. La. 1982) (30 minutes a week inadequate; hours accessible to working people required); Nicholson v. Choctaw County, Ala., 498 F. Supp. 295, 310 (S.D. Ala. 1980) (two sessions of two hours weekly inadequate; weekend, evening, and holiday visits required).

[251]Ramos v. Lamm, *supra* note 242, at 580; see also cases cited *infra,* Sec. E, at notes 636-640 and accompanying text.

[252]McCray v. Sullivan, 509 F.2d 1332 (5th Cir. 1975).

conditions of non-contact visiting be improved.[253] Strip searches of prisoners may generally be required in connection with contact visiting;[254] the courts have not agreed on the circumstances justifying strip searches of visitors.[255] (See Sec. C5, *infra,* for a fuller discussion of strip searches.)

When prison officials deprive you of visiting rights normally enjoyed in the prison, you may be entitled to procedural protections. (See Sec. B2g, *supra.*)

e. Communication With the Media

You have a constitutional right to communicate with the media. However, prison officials have substantial discretion to determine the time, place, and manner of that communication as long as adequate alternatives remain open. Thus, they may ban all interviews of particular prisoners by media representatives as long as prisoners are free to write the media or communicate through other visitors.[256] However, if officials choose to permit press conferences and interviews in some situations but not others, they must have non-discriminatory guidelines and fair procedures for granting or denying permission.[257] Prison officials may not restrict your right to write letters to the press or to write for publication unless they have substantial reasons.[258]

---

[253]McMurry v. Phelps, 533 F. Supp. 742, 764 (W.D. La. 1982) (lack of privacy and inability to talk and see condemned); Dawson v. Kendrick, 527 F. Supp. 1252, 1308 (S.D. W. Va. 1981) (conditions making it difficult to see and hear to be corrected).

[254]Bell v. Wolfish, *supra* note 231, at 558-60; *see also* Bono v. Saxbe, 527 F. Supp. 1182 (S.D. Ill. 1980) (strip searches before and after non-contact visits for segregated prisoners).

[255]Hunter v. Auger, 672 F.2d 668 (8th Cir. 1982) ("reasonable suspicion" required for strip search of visitor); Ybarra v. Nevada Board of State Prison Commissioners, 520 F. Supp. 1000 (D. Nev. 1981); Wool v. Hogan, 505 F. Supp. 928 (D. Vt. 1981) (strip searches as condition of visits not exaggerated response); State v. Custodio, 607 P.2d 1048 (Sup. Ct. Hawaii 1980) (strip search of visitor upheld); In re French, 164 Cal. Rptr. 800 (Ct. App. 1980) (barring visitor indefinitely for refusing strip search unreasonable).

[256]Pell v. Procunier, 417 U.S. 817, 94 S.Ct. 2800 (1974); *see also* Houchins v. KQED, Inc., 438 U.S. 1, 98 S.Ct. 2588 (1978) (reversing injunction granting television station access to jail; no majority opinion).

[257]Main Road v. Aytch, 565 F.2d 54 (3d Cir. 1977), previous opinion at 522 F.2d 1980, 1088-90 (3d Cir. 1975).

[258]Guajardo v. Estelle, 580 F.2d 748, 759 (5th Cir. 1978) (mail to press treated as privileged); Cavey v. Levine, 435 F. Supp. 475 (D. Md. 1977) (punishment of

2. Protection From Physical Abuse

In many prisons today, prisoners live in constant fear of being assaulted, physically or sexually, either by other prisoners or by prison guards. These assaults often occur as a result of prison officials' failure to properly classify prisoners or to take corrective actions when they become aware of assaults within their prison. These failures of prison officials have occurred despite their duty to protect prisoners from violence and the unreasonable fear of violence.[259]

a.   Protection From Other Prisoners

Prison officials are under a legal duty to protect you from assaults by other prisoners. However, they are not automatically liable for any assault committed by one prisoner upon another. Whether they are liable depends on what you can prove about their conduct and what legal theory you are relying on.

Under the Eighth Amendment ban on "cruel and unusual punishment," the courts have generally held that you must show that the defendants displayed "deliberate indifference," "callous indifference," "gross negligence," "egregious failure to act," or "reckless disregard" for your safety, and that this conduct caused the assault.[260] These phrases are generally used interchangeably, and they are defined in terms of "actual intent to deprive [an inmate] of his rights or . . . recklessness in ignoring known threats," "flagrant or remarkably bad failure to protect," "exceptional circumstances and conduct so grossly incompetent, inadequate, or excessive as to shock the conscience or to be intolerable to basic fairness."[261] "Mere negligence" (or "simple" or "ordinary" negligence), usually defined in terms of failure to exercise

---

prisoner for letters to newspapers unlawful); Tyler v. Ciccone, 299 F. Supp. 684, 688 (W.D. Mo. 1969) (restrictions on inmates' preparation of manuscripts struck down).

[259]Ruiz v. Estelle, 503 F. Supp. 1265, 1303 (S.D. Tex. 1980), *aff'd in part rev'd on other grounds,* 679 F.2d 1115 (5th Cir. 1982).

[260]*See, e.g.,* Wade v. Haynes, 663 F.2d 778 (8th Cir. 1981) (reckless disregard, gross negligence, callous indifference), *aff'd on other grounds sub nom.* Smith v. Wade, __U.S.__, 103 S.Ct. 1625 (1983); Branchcomb v. Brewer, 669 F.2d 1297 (8th Cir. 1982) (deliberate indifference); Doe v. Burwell, 537 F. Supp. 186 (S.D. Ohio 1982) (gross indifference); Holmes v. Goldin, 615 F.2d 83 (2d Cir. 1980) (deliberate indifference).

[261]Wade v. Haynes, *id.* at 781-82; Clappier v. Flynn, 605 F.2d 519, 533 (10th Cir. 1979).

the ordinary care a reasonable person would use, does not make prison officials liable for an assault committed by a prisoner.[262]

Under the deliberate indifference standard, you must usually show that the defendants knew or should have known of the risk of assault and that they took no action to prevent it. This can be done either by proving facts about the institution as a whole or proving facts about your particular case. (*E.g.,* prison officials, when presenting their budgetary requests to the legislative body for more guards, will often testify concerning how many assaults had occurred at the different prison facilities within the past year; this can be used to show that they had knowledge of the level of violence. If you have previously been assaulted by the same prisoner, you may be able to show that a directive was previously issued that the two of you were not to be confined at the same institution.)

To win on the basis of institutional conditions, you must show that there is a "constant threat of violence,"[263] or a "pervasive risk of harm" either prison-wide or to an identifiable group of prisoners,[264] and that prison authorities have not taken adequate steps to prevent or remedy the situation. (E.g., numerous assaults had occured in the gymnasium, yet prison officials never assigned a guard to the inside of the gym when it was open to use by prisoners. Among the facts that courts have cited as actionable are an extensive history of prior assaults,[265] a well-entrenched subculture of sexual violence and a failure to properly classify prisoners,[266] and overcrowding, understaffing, and/or underfunding which result in a significantly increased risk of assault.[267])

---

[262]In Parratt v. Taylor, 451 U.S. 527, 101 S.Ct. 1908 (1981), the Supreme Court indicated that negligence might violate the Constitution under some circumstances. It is unlikely that the federal courts will adopt a negligence standard in inmate assault cases and subject themselves to a potential flood of additional litigation. *See* Burr v. Duckworth, 547 F. Supp. 192 (N.D. Ind. 1982) (negligence standard rejected). See also Ch. VI, Sec. C3, for a further discussion of negligence and its application to the Federal Tort Claims Act.

[263]Ruiz v. Estelle, 679 F.2d 1115, 1140-42 (5th Cir. 1982); Ramos v. Lamm, 639 F.2d 559, 572 (10th Cir. 1980).

[264]Withers v. Levine, 615 F.2d 158, 161 (4th Cir. 1980).

[265]Stevens v. County of Dutchess, N.Y., 445 F. Supp. 89 (S.D.N.Y. 1977).

[266]Doe v. Lally, 467 F. Supp. 1339 (D. Md. 1979); Redmond v. Baxley, 475 F. Supp. 1111 (E.D. Mich. 1979).

[267]Ruiz v. Estelle, *supra* note 263, at 1140-42 (crowding and understaffing); Dawson v. Kendrick, 527 F. Supp. 1252, 1289 (S.D. W. Va. 1981) (understaffing); Finney v. Mabry, 534 F. Supp. 1026, 1039 (E.D. Ark. 1982) (crowding which made proper surveillance impossible); McKenna v. County of Nassau, 538

If you can prove such a "pervasive risk" or "constant threat," you are probably entitled to an injunction correcting the conditions that create the risk or threat.[268] If your object is to win damages for an assault you have suffered, you must also prove that your particular assault was caused by the practices of which you complain. For example, if you claim that lack of classification created a pervasive risk of harm, but you and your assailant would have received the same classification and been housed together under an improved classification system, the defendants will not be held liable for your assault. You must be prepared to make the connection between what the defendants did or failed to do and what happened to you.

You may also try to prevail based only on facts pertaining to your particular case. Courts have held that an Eighth Amendment claim was stated where prison officials failed to isolate prisoners who were obvious potential victims,[269] placed a prisoner in the same cell as a known rapist,[270] failed to separate two prisoners who had fought in the past,[271] or failed to act on a prisoner's prior warning of danger.[272] However, other courts have taken a very restrictive attitude toward these cases. One court held that where prison officials disregarded a judge's instructions to separate a prisoner from Native American prisoners, and the prisoner was assaulted, the claim was at most one for negligence and not a constitutional claim.[273]

Prisoner assault cases may also be pled as common law torts under the less difficult standard of simple negligence, which requires prison of-

---

F. Supp. 737 (E.D.N.Y. 1982) (crowding); Mayes v. Elrod, 470 F. Supp. 1188 (N.D. Ill. 1979) (underfunding).

[268]*See, e.g.,* Withers v. Levine, 449 F. Supp. 473 (D. Md. 1978), *aff'd,* 615 F.2d 158 (4th Cir. 1980) (procedures for safe placement to be promulgated); Doe v. Lally, 467 F. Supp. 1339 (D. Md. 1979) (revision of classification program ordered); Ruiz v. Estelle, *supra* note 263, at 1140-42 (overcrowding to be reduced).

[269]Gullatte v. Potts, 654 F.2d 1007 (5th Cir. 1981); Wade v. Haynes, *supra* note 260.

[270]McCaw v. Frame, 499 F. Supp. 424 (E.D. Pa. 1980).

[271]Holmes v. Goldin, 615 F.2d 83 (2d Cir. 1980).

[272]Mastrota v. Robinson, 534 F. Supp. 434 (E.D. Pa. 1982); West v. Rowe, 448 F. Supp. 58 (N.D. Ill. 1978).

[273]Cline v. United States Department of Justice, 525 F. Supp. 525 (D.S.D. 1981); *see also* Branchcomb v. Brewer, 683 F.2d 251 (8th Cir. 1982) (no liability where assailants had suggestive information in file but defendants did not know about it); Schaal v. Rowe, 460 F. Supp. 155 (S.D. Ill. 1978) (no liability where defendants investigated warnings but did not honor transfer request).

ficials "to exercise ordinary care for the prisoner's protection and to keep him safe and free from harm."[274] If your claim of negligence is against state or local officials, it can be brought either in a state court or as a pendent state claim (see Ch. VI, Sec. B3) to a federal §1983 action. If your claim is against federal officials, it can be brought under the Federal Tort Claims Act (see Ch. VI, Sec. C2).

The following discussion will give you an idea of the kinds of factual issues that will determine the outcome of prisoner assault cases. These cases were all decided under a negligence standard.

In *Williams v. United States*,[275] the prisoner was attacked by another prisoner, "F," in the early morning when he was asleep. F fire-bombed Williams' cell with gasoline. Williams alleged that prison officials were negligent because they should have known of existing hostilities between F and him, arising from an altercation two days before. He contended that, because of the altercation, prison officials should have taken some kind of "precautionary" measures to assure his safety (*e.g.*, locking F in segregation). Williams also alleged that prison officials were negligent because F was able to obtain gasoline.

The government contended that after the altercation both Williams and F assured them that their differences were settled and, therefore, there was no reason to believe that any hostility remained. The government also showed a policy statement requiring that all flammables be kept under lock and key and that prisoners not be allowed to use them unless they were closely supervised. Finally, the government contended that Williams, and not the government, was the "proximate cause" of his assault because he had sexually assaulted F the day before the incident, and Williams should have expected retaliation.

The court held that the government was not negligent in not segregating F, or in permitting F to obtain flammable liquid, and thus denied damages to Williams. This decision was based on the fact that prison officials had no reason to believe hostility still existed between the two prisoners, since they both assured officers that their "misunderstanding" was settled and there would be no more trouble. The court further found that Williams had not shown how F had obtained the flammable liquid and, therefore, could not say that the government was negligent in this respect. Finally, the court found that Williams was the "proximate cause" of his own injuries due to the fact that he had assaulted F and should have expected retaliation.

An opposite holding is found in a case with very similar facts where a prisoner was severely burned with gasoline. In *Bourgeois v. United*

---

[274]Cohen v. United States, 252 F. Supp. 679, 687 (N.D. Ga. 1966), *modified*, 389 F.2d 689 (5th Cir. 1967).

[275]384 F. Supp. 579 (D.D.C. 1974).

States,[276] a prisoner, "M," hurled a molotov cocktail into Bourgeois' cell after wiring the cell door closed when Bourgeois was asleep. A guard had observed M tampering with the deadlock system that locks the cell doors. Tampering with any lock was a violation of prison regulations. The guard took no precautionary or disciplinary action against M for tampering with the lock box.

The court held that the failure of the guard to take precautionary action against M was the proximate cause of Bourgeois' injuries. It further found that flammable liquid in the hands of prisoners without any supervision was contraband and that these liquids had been readily available to M, who had been able to "fish" them out through the bars of a locked cell with a broom handle. Because the court found that the government was negligent, it awarded Bourgeois $15,000 in damages for the burns he sustained in the fire.

Unlike the *Williams* case, *supra,* the prisoner in *Bourgeois* showed that: (1) notwithstanding the policy that required flammables to be kept locked, M had gained easy access to them; (2) the guard, in not taking disciplinary or precautionary action against M when he saw him tampering with the lock box, had not exercised "ordinary diligence" in performing his duties; and (3) the failure to provide adequate supervision in the cellblock where the fire occurred was negligence, since the government had a duty to care for and protect prisoners in its custody.

In *Garrett v. United States,*[277] the court held that it was negligent to release a prisoner with a long history of violent misconduct to general population shortly after his arrival, and awarded damages to the victim of his assault.[278] Another court held that an assault by someone "no worse than the general run of prison inmates" was not caused by negligent supervision.[279]

Whether you proceed on a constitutional claim or a negligence claim or both, be sure to specify *facts* supporting your claim in your complaint—not just that you were assaulted, but why it is prison officials' fault. Failure to spell this out has resulted in the dismissal of many cases.[280]

---

[276]375 F. Supp. 133 (N.D. Tex. 1974).

[277]501 F. Supp. 337 (N.D. Ga. 1980).

[278]For other cases finding negligence in prisoner assault cases, *see* Cohen v. United States, *supra* note 274; *See also* United States v. Muniz, 374 U.S. 150, 83 S.Ct. 1850 (1963).

[279]Cowart v. United States, 617 F.2d 112 (5th Cir. 1980); *see also* Guy v. United States, 492 F. Supp. 571 (N.D. Cal. 1980); Fleishour v. United States, 244 F. Supp. 762 (N.D. Ill. 1965), *aff'd,* 365 F.2d 126 (7th Cir.), *cert. denied,* 385 U.S. 987 (1966).

[280]*See, e.g.,* Cunningham v. Ray, 648 F.2d 1185 (8th Cir. 1981); Sturts v. City

Even if you believe you have a valid Eighth Amendment "deliberate indifference" claim, you should always state a negligence claim in addition. If you are suing under §1983, you can assert a state pendent claim for negligence;[281] if you are suing federal officials, you can join your constitutional *Bivens* claim with a claim under the Federal Tort Claims Act.[282]

Finally, if you have any means of getting a lawyer to handle your prisoner assault case, you should do so rather than handle it *pro se*. To prove a "pervasive risk" case, you will need to interview numerous present and former prisoners and conduct a lot of discovery (over prison officials' strong resistance) into institutional records and security practices. Even in a simpler case, you will have to go into the details of security practices (*e.g.*, what kind of investigation is conducted when a prisoner claims to be in danger). A prisoner will have great difficulty doing all these things *pro se*. It may be easier than usual to get an attorney to take such a case since courts have made substantial damage awards in cases involving serious injuries or sexual assaults.[283]

b.   Limits on Guards' Use of Force

Courts are agreed that the excessive or unnecessary use of force violates the Constitution, but they have not agreed on what provision it violates. Some have relied on the Eighth Amendment;[284] others have held that the ordinary prison guard assault is not cruel and unusual punish-

---

of Philadelphia, 529 F. Supp. 434 (E.D. Pa. 1982); Ballard v. Elsea, 502 F. Supp. 105 (W.D. Wisc. 1980). See also Ch. VII, Sec. B., for a discussion of dismissal or judgment on the pleadings.

[281]Clappier v. Flynn, 605 F.2d 519 (10th Cir. 1979); McCaw v. Frame, 499 F. Supp. 424 (E.D. Pa. 1980); Stevens v. County of Dutchess, N.Y., 445 F. Supp. 89 (S.D.N.Y. 1977).

[282]Norton v. United States, 581 F.2d 390 (4th Cir. 1978); Picariello v. Fenton, 491 F. Supp. 1020 (M.D. Pa. 1980). See Ch. VI, Sec. C3, for a discussion of how to combine FTCA and *Bivens* actions; Sec. C1, for a discussion of a *Bivens* action; and Sec. C2, for a discussion of the Federal Tort Claims Act.

[283]*See, e.g.,* Redmond v. Baxley, 475 F. Supp. 1111 (E.D. Mich. 1979); Cohen v. United States, 252 F. Supp. 679 (N.D. Ga. 1966), *modified,* 389 F.2d 689 (5th Cir. 1967).

[284]Furtado v. Bishop, 604 F.2d 80, 95-96 (1st Cir. 1979); Finney v. Arkansas Board of Correction, 505 F.2d 194, 205 (8th Cir. 1974); United States v. Georvassilis, 498 F.2d 883, 885 (6th Cir. 1974); Patmore v. Carlson, 392 F. Supp. 737, 739 (E.D. Ill. 1975); *see also* Ingraham v. Wright, 430 U.S. 651, 669, 97 S.Ct. 1401 (1977) (dictum), *quoting* 525 F.2d 909, 915 (5th Cir. 1976) ("Prison brutality . . . is 'part of the total punishment . . . and, as such, is a proper subject for Eighth Amendment scrutiny.'").

ment but instead is a due process violation;[285] other have avoided the question[286] or cited both the Eighth Amendment and the Due Process Clause.[287] As shown *infra,* the standards are the same no matter what amendment is cited; to be safe, cite both the Eighth Amendment and due process in your complaint. (Pretrial detainees cannot be punished at all, of course, so they should cite only the Due Process Clause. See Sec. E, *infra.*)

In *Johnson v. Glick,*[288] the court stated a legal standard for prison brutality claims:

> Not every push or shove, even if it may later seem unnecessary in the peace of a judge's chambers, violates a prisoner's constitutional rights. In determining whether the constitutional line has been crossed, a court must look to such factors as the need for the application of force, the relationship between the need and the amount of force that was used, the extent of injury inflicted, and whether force was applied in a good faith effort to maintain or restore discipline or maliciously and sadistically for the very purpose of causing harm.[289]

Although *Johnson* was a due process case, this standard has been widely adopted under the Eighth Amendment as well as the Due Process Clause.[290] Other standards that courts have used, such as "reasonable force under the circumstances,"[291] or "conduct that shocks the conscience,"[292] amount more or less to the same thing.[293]

The courts have generally required that you assert at least some

---

[285]George v. Evans, 633 F.2d 413 (5th Cir. 1980), previous opinion at 620 F.2d 495 (5th Cir. 1980); Johnson v. Glick, 481 F.2d 1028 (2d Cir.), *cert. denied,* 414 U.S. 1033 (1973); Lamb v. Hutto, 467 F. Supp. 562 (E.D. Va. 1979).

[286]Martinez v. Rosado, 614 F.2d 829 (2d Cir. 1980); United States v. Santos, 588 F.2d 1300 (9th Cir. 1979).

[287]Freeman v. Franzen, 695 F.2d 485 (7th Cir. 1982); King v. Blankenship, 636 F.2d 70 (4th Cir. 1980).

[288]*Supra* note 285.

[289]*Id.* 481 F.2d at 1033.

[290]*See, e.g.,* Putman v. Gerloff, 639 F.2d 415 (8th Cir. 1981); King v. Blankenship, 636 F.2d 70, 73 (4th Cir. 1980); Furtado v. Bishop, 604 F.2d 80, 95 (1st Cir. 1979); Henderson v. Counts, 544 F. Supp. 149 (E.D. Va. 1982).

[291]Ridley v. Leavitt, 631 F.2d 358, 360 (4th Cir. 1980).

[292]Black v. Stephens, 662 F.2d 181, 188 (3d Cir. 1981).

[293]In Johnson v. Glick, the court considered the above quoted standard as spelling out the "shocks the conscience" test. *Supra* note 285, 481 F.2d at 1033, *quoting* Rochin v. California, 342 U.S. 165, 172, 72 S.Ct. 205 (1952).

minimum amount of injury to state a constitutional claim.[294] However, the injury need not be crippling or life-threatening,[295] and one court has found that brandishing a loaded pistol at point-blank range was sufficient to "shock the conscience."[296] As a practical matter, if you suffered broken bones, cuts requiring stitches or bandaging, a concussion, or some other identifiable injury requiring medical treatment, you will probably state a constituional claim; if your injuries are limited to bruises, you may not.[297] Conversely, no matter how serious your injuries are, the defendants will not be held liable if their conduct was justified by the circumstances and they were not trying to harm you.[298]

You may sue for excessive use of force even if you were engaging in misconduct yourself at the time, although your actions may make it harder to win.[299] "While prison officials should be afforded broad discretion in maintaining order and discipline within the prison walls, we do not think that any amount of force is justified, especially if the threat of disorder or disobedience has subsided."[300]

If you were subjected to the excessive use of force, you may recover damages not only from the guard(s) who beat you but from other guards or supervisors who were actually present but did nothing to intervene.[301] (See Ch. VI, Sec. E2, for further discussion of supervisory liability.)

By itself, verbal abuse usually does not violate the Constitution.[302] The

---

[294]Bates v. Westervelt, 502 F. Supp. 94 (S.D.N.Y. 1980); Santiago v. Yarde, 487 F. Supp. 52 (S.D.N.Y. 1980); Patricia B. v. Jones, 454 F. Supp. 18 (W.D. Pa. 1978).

[295]Shillingford v. Holmes, 634 F.2d 263 (5th Cir. 1981).

[296]Black v. Stephens, 662 F.2d 181 (3d Cir. 1981).

[297]Peterson v. Davis, 551 F. Supp. 137 (D. Md. 1982); Santiago v. Yarde, 487 F. Supp. 52 (S.D.N.Y. 1980).

[298]Williams v. Kelley, 624 F.2d 695 (5th Cir. 1980) (officers were not liable where they accidentally strangled a prisoner while trying to subdue him).

[299]King v. Blankenship, 636 F.2d 70 (4th Cir. 1980); Martinez v. Rosado, 614 F.2d 829 (2d Cir. 1980); O'Connor v. Keller, 510 F. Supp. 1359 (D. Md. 1981).

[300]Ridley v. Leavitt, 631 F.2d 358, 360 (4th Cir. 1980).

[301]Bruner v. Dunaway, 684 F.2d 422 (6th Cir. 1982); Putman v. Gerloff, 639 F.2d 415 (8th Cir. 1981); Byrd v. Brishke, 466 F.2d 6, 11 (7th Cir. 1972); Harris v. Chancelor, 537 F.2d 203, 206 (5th Cir. 1976); Curtis v. Everette, 489 F.2d 516, 518 (3d Cir. 1973), cert. denied, 416 U.S. 995 (1974).

[302]Cumbey v. Meachum, 684 F.2d 712 (10th Cir. 1982); Franklin v. State of Oregon, 662 F.2d 1337 (9th Cir. 1981); Williams v. Pecchio, 543 F. Supp. 878 (W.D.N.Y. 1982); Freeman v. Trudell, 497 F. Supp. 481 (E.D. Mich. 1980).

courts will entertain claims of verbal abuse only when it is closely involved with physical abuse or violation of other rights.[303]

The unnecessary use of tear gas or other chemical agents has been held unlawful by a number of courts.[304] One court has limited their use to situations involving the imminent threat of bodily harm, or a riot or escape;[305] another held that tear gas may be used in "dangerous quantities" only when there is a threat of injury to persons or to "substantial amounts of valuable property."[306] The Seventh Circuit upheld the use of tear gas against prisoners locked in their cells who were "inciting a riot at a time of tremendous tension in the prison," but not to retrieve a metal tray or to make prisoners stop shouting and uttering threats.[307] Other courts have come to different conclusions about the use of chemical agents, depending on the facts involved.[308]

Claims of excessive force may also be litigated as common law torts (*i.e.,* as claims of assault and battery). Some courts assume there is a major difference between the legal standards involved. A leading case states that the common law action for battery "makes actionable any intentional and unpermitted contact with the plaintiff's person or anything attached to it," but that "[n]ot every push or shove" violates the Constitution.[309] You should not rely on this view of the tort of assault

---

[303]Hoptowit v. Ray, 682 F.2d 1237, 1249-51 (9th Cir. 1982) (physical and verbal abuse enjoined); Herrera v. Valentine, 653 F.2d 1220 (8th Cir. 1981) (threat of death in conjunction with physical abuse actionable); Hudspeth v. Figgins, 584 F.2d 1345 (4th Cir. 1978) (death threat to prisoner because of his litigation violated Constitution); Finney v. Mabry, 534 F. Supp. 1026, 1043 (E.D. Ark. 1982) (racial slurs to be eliminated as part of comprehensive remedial order).

[304]*See* Ruiz v. Estelle, 503 F. Supp. 1265, 1305 (S.D. Tex. 1980), *aff'd in part and rev'd in part on other grounds,* 679 F.2d 1115 (5th Cir. 1982), and cases cited.

[305]Battle v. Anderson, 376 F. Supp. 402 (E.D. Okla. 1974), *aff'd,* 564 F.2d 388 (10th Cir. 1977); *see also* Stringer v. Rowe, 616 F.2d 993 (7th Cir. 1980) (use of chemical agents against individuals should be restricted).

[306]Spain v. Procunier, 600 F.2d 189, 196 (9th Cir. 1979).

[307]Lock v. Jenkins, 641 F.2d 488 (7th Cir. 1981).

[308]*Compare* McCargo v. Mister, 462 F. Supp. 813 (D. Md. 1978) (damages awarded for use of tear gas on prisoners locked in cell), *with* Arroyo v. Schaefer, 548 F.2d 47, 49-50 (2d Cir. 1977); Clemmons v. Greggs, 509 F.2d 1338 (5th Cir. 1975), *cert. denied,* 423 U.S. 946 (1975); LeBlanc v. Foti, 487 F. Supp. 272 (E.D. La. 1980); Hendrix v. Faulkner, 525 F. Supp. 435 (N.D. Ind. 1981) (use of tear gas upheld in various situations).

[309]Johnson v. Glick, *supra* note 285, at 1033.

and battery. In a prison or jail, not every push or shove amounts to a tort since most states allow the use of necessary and reasonable force to maintain order.[310] Nevertheless, it is usually wise to plead an assault and battery claim as well as a constitutional claim in case you fall slightly short of proving a constitutional violation. (See Ch. VI, Sec. B3, for a discussion of pendent jurisdiction.)

3. Medical Care

In *Estelle v. Gamble*,[311] the Supreme Court held that "deliberate indifference to serious medical needs of prisoners constitutes the 'unnecessary and wanton infliction of pain' . . . proscribed by the Eighth Amendment."[312] However, a complaint of negligence or medical malpractice does not state an Eighth Amendment claim.[313] (See Sec. C2a, *supra,* notes 259-261 and accompanying text for a definition of "deliberate indifference.")

Under the "deliberate indifference" standard, courts will not get into a mere disagreement with medical personnel's idea of proper care.[314] As long as there has been an exercise of professional judgment—even a mistaken or incompetent one—the courts will hold that the Constitution has been satisfied.[315] What you must do, to prove a constitutional violation, is show that an exercise of professional judgment is *not* what you are complaining about. Among the factual allegations that may state a constitutional claim are:

(a) You had a serious medical problem, but you never got to see a doctor, or there was a long delay in your getting to a doctor.[316]

---

[310]*See, e.g.,* 3 N.Y. Jurisprudence, Assault and Battery, §11.

[311]429 U.S. 97, 97 S.Ct. 285 (1976).

[312]*Id.* at 104.

[313]*Id.* at 106.

[314]Perry v. Ralston, 635 F.2d 740 (8th Cir. 1980); McCracken v. Jones, 562 F.2d 22 (10th Cir. 1977); *see* McEachern v. Civiletti, 502 F. Supp. 532 (N.D. Ill. 1980) (prison officials not liable if they relied on doctors' reports).

[315]A few courts have suggested that there is a level of incompetence so bad that it violates the Eighth Amendment. Sturts v. City of Philadelphia, 529 F. Supp. 434 (E.D. Pa. 1982) (failure to remove stitches promptly to avoid scarring was treatment "so woefully inadequate as to amount to no treatment at all"); Joseph v. Brierton, 431 F. Supp. 50 (N.D. Ill. 1976) (fatal administration of contraindicated medication states claim). *See also* Tomarkin v. Ward, 534 F. Supp. 1224, 1230 (S.D.N.Y. 1982), and cases cited. Others have seemingly rejected this view. Mastrota v. Robinson, 534 F. Supp. 434 (E.D. Pa. 1982) (claim of failure to diagnose vertebral fracture and failure to insert drainage tube after surgery did not state Eighth Amendment violation).

[316]Robinson v. Moreland, 655 F.2d 887 (8th Cir. 1981) (weekend's delay in

(b) You were seen by medical personnel, but they were not qualified to exercise judgment about your problem (*e.g.,* you had a psychotic episode, but only got to see a general practitioner and not a psychiatrist; you are losing your vision but never got to an ophthalmologist; etc.)[317]

(c) You got to a doctor, but there were factors that interfered with his/her exercise of judgment (*e.g.,* the doctor did not actually examine you; the x-ray machine was broken; correction officers interfered with the examination; or the doctor did not look at your medical records).[318] In extreme cases, you may be able to show that a doctor exercised a judgment that was not medical in nature but reflected deliberate indifference.[319]

(d) The doctor exercised judgment, but his/her judgment was not carried out (*e.g.,* you didn't get the medication or therapy prescribed; you didn't get taken to the specialist the doctor referred you to; or the administration ignored a medical excuse from work).[320]

---

treating broken hand); Hurst v. Phelps, 579 F.2d 940 (5th Cir. 1978) (refusal to take prisoner to doctor's appointments); Tomarkin v. Ward, 534 F. Supp. 1224, 1232 (S.D.N.Y. 1982) (superintendent's knowing failure to see that prisoner received treatment); Isaac v. Jones, 529 F. Supp. 175 (N.D. Ill. 1981) (guards' delay in providing care).

Not every delay violates the Eighth Amendment. Mills v. Smith, 656 F.2d 337 (8th Cir. 1981) (1½-hour delay in hospitalizing prisoner with gunshot wound); Brown v. Commissioner of Cecil County Jail, 501 F. Supp. 1124 (D. Md. 1980) (delay of less than a week in treating gonorrhea); Morrison v. Washington County, Ala., 521 F. Supp. 947 (S.D. Ala. 1981) (small rural jail not required to have medical personnel on premises).

[317]Inmates of Allegheny County Jail v. Pierce, 612 F.2d 754, 762 (3d Cir. 1979) (inmates with psychiatric problems had right to be treated by qualified staff); West v. Keve, 571 F.2d 158, 162 (3d Cir. 1978) (post-operative patient had right to care by qualified doctor); Williams v. Edwards, 547 F.2d 1206, 1216-18 (5th Cir. 1977) (reliance on untrained personnel unconstitutional). *But see* Partee v. Lane, 528 F. Supp. 1254 (N.D. Ill. 1981) (medical technician's judgment that prisoner need not see a doctor was not deliberate indifference).

[318]Boyce v. Alizaduh, 595 F.2d 948 (4th Cir. 1979) (prison doctor ignored complaint of allergy to medication); Todaro v. Ward, 431 F. Supp. 1129, 1144 (S.D.N.Y.), *aff'd,* 565 F.2d 48 (2d Cir. 1977) (sick call conducted under conditions preventing meaningful evaluations).

[319]Williams v. Vincent, 508 F.2d 541, 543 (2d Cir. 1974).

[320]Layne v. Vinzant, 657 F.2d 468 (1st Cir. 1981) (no effort to obtain recommended physical therapy); Cummings v. Dunn, 630 F.2d 649 (8th Cir. 1980) (denial of prescribed medication); Jones v. Evans, 544 F. Supp. 769 (N.D. Ga. 1982) (confiscation of prescribed back brace); Goodman v. Wagner, 553 F. Supp. 255 (E.D. Pa. 1982) (failure to follow doctor's orders for treatment and denial of prescribed medication).

Some courts have held that denial or delay of prescribed medication does not violate the Eighth Amendment if the delay is short or the consequences are not

Even if the facts of your case reflect deliberate indifference, you must carefully figure out who was responsible for the deliberate indifference and make sure that person (or persons) is joined as a defendant(s). If it took you three days to see a doctor when you had a broken arm, the proper defendant may not be the doctor for not seeing you promptly. It may instead be the fault of guards or nurses for not having you taken to a doctor, or it may be the fault of the warden or medical administrator for making no plans for medical emergencies when no doctor is present. Often, you will not know where the fault lies when you file your complaint, so you may have to join everyone up and down the line as defendants: guards, nurses, doctors, wardens, and administrators. You should then be able to narrow the list of defendants as you obtain information during discovery. (See Ch. VII, Secs. A1 and E, for a discussion of filing your complaint and how to do discovery.)

The other half of the *Estelle v. Gamble* test requires that "serious medical needs" be involved. A serious medical need has been defined as "one that has been diagnosed by a physician as requiring treatment or one that is so obvious that a lay person would easily recognize the necessity for a doctor's attention."[321] Most courts consider any condition causing significant pain a serious medical condition.[322]

Particular areas in which the courts have made significant rulings under the *Estelle* standard include:

a. Psychiatric care

Denial of adequate psychiatric care may violate the Eighth Amendment.[323] Courts have condemned various aspects of psychiatric care and treatment of mentally ill prisoners, including lack of qualified staff,[324]

---

serious. Martin v. New York City Dept. of Corrections, 522 F. Supp. 169 (S.D.N.Y. 1981); Russell v. Eniser, 496 F. Supp. 320 (D.S.C. 1979), *aff'd,* 624 F.2d 1095 (4th Cir. 1980); Burrascano v. Levi, 452 F. Supp. 1066 (D. Md. 1978).

[321]Ramos v. Lamm, 639 F.2d 559, 575 (10th Cir. 1980), and cases cited.

  West v. Keve, 571 F.2d 158, 162 (3d Cir. 1978) (pain while awaiting a delayed operation was actionable); Case v. Bixler, 518 F. Supp. 1277 (S.D. Ohio 1981) (boil might be serious); *but see* Stinson v. Sheriff's Dept. of Sullivan County, 499 F. Supp. 259, 263 (S.D.N.Y. 1982) ("bruises and lacerations" serious, vague claims of head pain and pain and suffering from an "eye injury" were not); Butler v. Best, 478 F. Supp. 377 (E.D. Ark. 1979) (ten-day failure to give prescribed medication did not relate to serious medical needs).

[323]Ramos v. Lamm, *supra* note 321, at 574; Inmates of Allegheny County Jail v. Pierce, 612 F.2d 754, 761-63 (3d Cir. 1979); Cruz v. Ward, 558 F.2d 658, 662 (2d Cir. 1977); Robert E. v. Lane, 530 F. Supp. 930 (N.D. Ill. 1981); Griffin v. Smith, 493 F. Supp. 129 (W.D.N.Y. 1980).

[324]Inmates of Allegheny County Jail v. Pierce, *supra* note 317; Kendrick v.

absence of a separate facility for psychiatric care,[325] and the housing of the mentally ill in disciplinary segregation units.[326] Some courts have stated that psychiatric treatment may be "limited to that which may be provided upon a reasonable cost and time basis,"[327] and one court held that a prisoner's complaint of "depression" was not a serious medical need requiring psychiatric treatment.[328]

Sometimes it is as important to avoid psychiatric treatment (or "treatment") that you don't need as it is to get treatment that you do need. The Supreme Court has held that under the Due Process Clause you are entitled to notice and a hearing before being transferred to a mental hospital; the Court held that the stigma attached to psychiatric commitment and the possibility of involuntary subjection to psychiatric treatment constituted a deprivation of liberty requiring due process.[329] Based on this reasoning, it has been held that subjection of *all* prisoners to a behavior modification program without a showing of individual need also denied due process.[330] Similarly, if you have been involuntarily committed to a hospital for the criminally insane because you were not able to stand trial, officials have a duty to inform the committing court when you no longer require treatment.[331] Under the Eighth Amendment or the Due Process Clause, courts have also struck down the use of various types of psychiatric treatment for disciplinary purposes[332] and

---

Bland, 541 F. Supp. 21, 26 (W.D. Ky. 1981); D.B. v. Tewksbury, 545 F. Supp. 896 (D. Ore. 1982); Ruiz v. Estelle, 503 F. Supp. 1265, 1339 (S.D. Tex. 1980), *aff'd in part and rev'd in part on other grounds,* 679 F.2d 1115 (5th Cir. 1982).

[325]Finney v. Mabry, 534 F. Supp. 1026, 1036 (E.D. Ark. 1982).

[326]Kendrick v. Bland, *supra* note 324; Feliciano v. Barcelo, 497 F. Supp. 14, 35 (D.P.R. 1979).

[327]Bowring v. Godwin, 551 F.2d 44 (4th Cir. 1977); *accord,* Woodall v. Foti, 648 F.2d 268 (5th Cir. 1981). *See also* Grubbs v. Bradley, 552 F. Supp. 1052, 1129-30 (M.D. Tenn. 1982) (court upholds system that usually provided care to prisoners with "truly serious mental health needs," despite deficiencies).

[328]Partee v. Lane, 528 F. Supp. 1254 (N.D. Ill. 1981) ("No doubt most, if not all, prisoners are depressed some if not all the time.").

[329]Vitek v. Jones, 445 U.S. 480, 494-95, 100 S.Ct. 1254 (1980).

[330]Canterino v. Wilson, 546 F. Supp. 174, 208-09 (W.D. Ky. 1982).

[331]Stuebig v. Hammel, 446 F. Supp. 31 (M.D. Pa. 1977); *see* O'Connor v. Donaldson, 422 U.S. 563, 95 S.Ct. 2486 (1975) (unjustified confinement in civil mental hospital unconstitutional).

[332]Nelson v. Heyne, 491 F.2d 352, 357 (7th Cir. 1974) (tranquilizers could not be used to keep order); Knecht v. Gillman, 488 F.2d 1136 (8th Cir. 1973) (punitive use of drugs unlawful); Wheeler v. Glass, 473 F.2d 983 (7th Cir. 1973) (use of restraints for discipline violated Eighth Amendment); Wright v. Mc-

the psychiatric confinement or isolation of prisoners under degrading or excessively restrictive conditions.[333] The use of seclusion and physical restraints even for psychiatric purposes has also been restricted by the courts.[334]

Some courts have suggested that there is a limited right to refuse psychotropic medication, at least on the part of civilly committed patients.[335] The full extent of this right and its applicability to prisoners have not yet been worked out in the courts.

b.   Medical Diets

Several courts have held that prisons must provide medically required special diets to prisoners.[336]

Mann, 460 F.2d 126, 129 (2d Cir. 1972) (psychiatric isolation cells could not be used for disciplinary purposes); Negron v. Ward, 458 F. Supp. 748 (S.D.N.Y. 1978) (damages awarded for disciplinary placement on seclusion ward).

[333]Scott v. Plante, 641 F.2d 117 (3d Cir. 1981), *vacated and remanded for reconsideration without opinion,* 102 S.Ct. 3474 (1982), *on remand,* 691 F.2d 634 (3d Cir. 1982) (prisoners' confinement in psychiatric hospital under inhuman conditions stated Eighth Amendment claim); Johnson v. Levine, 588 F.2d 1378, 1381 (4th Cir. 1978) (psychiatric isolation cells similar to punitive segregation condemned); McCray v. Burrell, 622 F.2d 705 (4th Cir. 1980) (conditions of mental observation cell condemned); Flakes v. Percy, 511 F. Supp. 1325 (W.D. Wisc. 1981) (prisoners not to be locked in mental hospital cells without toilets for more than one hour); *but see* McMahon v. Beard, 583 F.2d 172 (5th Cir. 1978) (90 days' confinement in strip cell after suicide attempt upheld); Hawkins v. Hall, 644 F.2d 914 (1st Cir. 1981) (short confinement in strip cell with hole in floor for toilet did not violate Eighth Amendment).

[334]Campbell v. McGruder, 580 F.2d 521, 551 (D.C. Cir. 1978) (doctor's authorization, written records required for use of restraints); Burks v. Teasdale, 492 F. Supp. 650, 679 (W.D. Mo. 1980) (lack of policy for use of restraints and seclusion unconstitutional); Owens-El v. Robinson, 442 F. Supp. 1368, 1381 (M.D. Pa. 1978), *aff'd in part and rev'd in part on other grounds sub nom.* Inmates of Allegheny County Jail v. Pierce, 612 F.2d 754 (3d Cir. 1979) (use of restraints limited); Negron v. Preiser, 382 F. Supp. 535, 542-43 (S.D. N.Y. 1974) (records to be kept regarding justification for seclusion); *see also* Wyatt v. Stickney, 344 F. Supp. 387, 401 (M.D. Ala. 1972) (restraints to be used in civil mental hospital only to prevent injury).

[335]Rogers v. Okin, 634 F.2d 650 (1st Cir. 1980), *vacated and remanded on other grounds sub nom.* Mills v. Rogers, __U.S.__, 102 S.Ct. 2442 (1982); Rennie v. Klein, 653 F.2d 836 (3d Cir. 1981).

[336]Twyman v. Crisp, 584 F.2d 352 (10th Cir. 1978); French v. Owens, 538 F. Supp. 910, 928 (S.D. Ind. 1982); Johnson v. Harris, 479 F. Supp. 333 (S.D.N.Y. 1979).

c. Prison Assignments and Regulations

A prisoner may not be given a work assignment inconsistent with his/her medical condition.[337] However, no constitutional claim is stated where prison medical personnel have authorized the assignment.[338] Prison regulations may be enjoined in particular cases if they have adverse medical consequences.[339]

d. Handicapped Prisoners

The obligations of prison officials to accommodate the special problems of handicapped prisoners have not been fully explored by the courts. Prisoners may sue under the federal Rehabilitation Act of 1973,[340] which bars programs receiving federal funds from discriminating against persons on the basis of their handicaps.[341] Prisons may be obligated to seek appropriate treatment or placement in a more acceptable institution for severely handicapped prisoners.[342]

e. Dental Care

Several courts have held that dental care must be provided to prisoners,[343] although some have limited the services that must be provided.[344]

---

[337]Cotton v. Hutto, 540 F.2d 412, 415 (8th Cir. 1976); McDaniel v. Rhodes, 512 F. Supp. 117 (S.D. Ohio 1981); Speed v. Adams, 502 F. Supp. 426 (E.D. Ark. 1980); *see also* Roba v. United States, 604 F.2d 215 (2d Cir. 1979) (prisoner could not be transferred if medical condition prohibited it); Finney v. Mabry, 534 F. Supp. 1026, 1033 (E.D. Ark. 1982) (medical personnel must be consulted before prisoner is disciplined for medically-based refusal of assignment).

[338]Shepard v. Stidham, 502 F. Supp. 1275 (M.D. Ala. 1980).

[339]Monroe v. Bombard, 422 F. Supp. 211 (S.D.N.Y. 1976) ("no beard" rule could not be applied to prisoner with skin condition).

[340]29 U.S.C. §794.

[341]Journey v. Vitek, 685 F.2d 239 (8th Cir. 1982).

[342]Layne v. Vinzant, 657 F.2d 468 (1st Cir. 1981); Villa v. Franzen, 511 F. Supp. 231 (N.D. Ill. 1981); *but see* Journey v. Vitek, *id.* (paraplegic's claim rejected on facts); Rowe v. Fauver, 533 F. Supp. 1239 (D.N.J. 1982) (regulation barring all "medically disabled" prisoners from earning work credits similar to good time was not unconstitutional as applied to paralyzed prisoners).

[343]Ramos v. Lamm, 639 F.2d 559, 574 (10th Cir. 1980); Heitman v. Gabriel, 524 F. Supp. 622 (W.D. Mo. 1981) (preventive services required); Morgan v. Sproat, 432 F. Supp. 1130, 1157 (S.D. Miss. 1977) (non-emergency services

f. Medical Examinations

Some courts have held that medical examinations on intake, at least for the purpose of identifying persons with communicable diseases, are required.[345] However, prisons are generally not required to provide routine physical examinations.[346]

g. Prison Emergencies

Routine medical services may be curtailed during emergencies such as lockdowns.[347] However, essential medical care must be provided.[348]

h. Drug Dependency Treatment

Prisons and jails are required to provide some form of treatment for drug withdrawal, but recent cases hold that they need not provide methadone maintenance even for persons who were in methadone programs outside prison.[349] One court has held that alcoholism treatment programs are matters of rehabilitation rather than medical care and need not be provided.[350]

---

required). *But see* Grubbs v. Bradley, 552 F. Supp. 1052, 1129 (M.D. Tenn. 1982) (delays in access to non-emergency care not unconstitutional); Lucas v. Benton County Board of Commissioners, 531 F. Supp. 146 (N.D. Ind. 1982) (no constitutional claim for lack of dental care).

[344]Nicholson v. Choctaw County, Ala., 498 F. Supp. 295, 308 (S.D. Ala. 1980) (dentures need not be provided); Clifton v. Robinson, 500 F. Supp. 30 (E.D. Pa. 1980) (five-day delay in treatment of toothache acceptable during emergency); Stokes v. Hurdle, 393 F. Supp. 757 (D. Md. 1975) (services in punitive segregation could be restricted to emergencies).

[345]LaReau v. Manson, 651 F.2d 96, 109 (2d Cir. 1981); Heitman v. Gabriel, 524 F. Supp. 622 (W.D. Mo. 1981); *contra,* Lock v. Jenkins, 464 F. Supp. 541 (N.D. Ind. 1978), *aff'd in part and rev'd in part on other grounds,* 641 F.2d 488 (7th Cir. 1981).

[346]Tunnell v. Robinson, 486 F. Supp. 1265, 1271 (W.D. Pa. 1980).

[347]Clifton v. Robinson, 500 F. Supp. 30 (E.D. Pa. 1980); Gray v. Levine, 455 F. Supp. 267 (D. Md. 1978).

[348]LaBatt v. Twomey, 513 F.2d 641, 649 (7th Cir. 1975).

[349]Inmates of Allegheny County Jail v. Pierce, 612 F.2d 754 (3d Cir. 1979); United States ex rel. Walker v. Fayette County, Pa., 599 F.2d 573 (3d Cir. 1979); Palmigiano v. Garrahy, 443 F. Supp. 956, 989 (D.R.I. 1977); Holly v. Rapone, 476 F. Supp. 226 (E.D. Pa. 1979); *but see* Cudnik v. Kreiger, 392 F. Supp. 305 (N.D. Ohio 1974) (methadone required for prisoners who had previously received it).

[350]Pace v. Fauver, 479 F. Supp. 456 (D.N.J. 1979).

In medical care litigation, even more than other types of litigation, you must have a clear idea before you start of what you hope to accomplish. This is so because of the great importance of the rights involved and the great difficulty of some medical litigation. If you are trying to get some sort of care to which you are entitled and if the issues are straight-forward—*e.g.,* you were supposed to go to the oral surgeon and they never took you, or you have been waiting for months for eyeglasses, or correction officers took away your prescribed back brace—a *pro se* lawsuit may be a quick way of making prison officials pay attention to your problem. (It may also be a way to set yourself up for harassment and neglect by the medical staff; you should find out what other prisoners' experience in this respect has been.) If the issues are not straightforward, or if the care you seek has not actually been prescribed, proceeding *pro se* exposes you to the danger of a quick loss if the prison doctor files an affidavit claiming that s/he has exercised professional judgment in refusing the treatment you want. You may wish to make extra efforts to obtain counsel in this situation. The same considerations apply in damage cases; you may be able to win *pro se* in a simple case where the defendants didn't do what the doctor ordered, but in a more complex case the technical issues may overwhelm you. Particularly in a case where you have suffered painful or lasting injuries, you should attempt to obtain counsel; bear in mind that if there is a possibility of a large damage award for actual injuries, you may be able to interest a lawyer who does not usually take prison cases. Finally, if your concern is with the inadequacies of the whole medical system, you must obtain counsel, preferably counsel experienced in prison or similar litigation. To prevail, you will have to prove " 'a series of incidents closely related in time . . . disclos[ing] a pattern of conduct amounting to deliberate in-difference' . . . [or] systemic deficiencies in staffing, facilities, or procedures [which] make unnecessary suffering inevitable.' "[351] The complicated proof and discovery required in such medical class actions is beyond the resources of a *pro se* litigant.[352]

The choice of what court to sue in is also crucial in medical cases. As explained *supra,* the *Estelle v. Gamble* standard is very difficult to meet and the federal courts are very reluctant to entertain prison medical claims, probably because they know how bad prison medical care is and are afraid of being overwhelmed by cases. State prisoners should there-fore think very seriously about suing in state court (see Ch. IV, Sec. D2)

---

[351]Todaro v. Ward, 565 F.2d 48, 52 (2d Cir. 1977), *quoting* Bishop v. Stone-man, 508 F.2d 1224 (2d Cir. 1974).

[352]For descriptions of the proof in medical class actions, *see* Hendrix v. Faulk-ner, 525 F. Supp. 435 (N.D. Ind. 1981); Lightfoot v. Walker, 486 F. Supp. 504 (S.D. Ill. 1980); Todaro v. Ward, 431 F. Supp. 1129 (S.D.N.Y.), *aff'd,* 565 F.2d 48 (2d Cir. 1977).

and federal prisoners should think very seriously about suing under the Federal Tort Claims Act (see Ch. VI, Sec. C2) for negligence or medical malpractice. (Medical malpractice is generally defined as the failure to exercise the skill and learning commonly applied by the average prudent and reputable physician in the community.[353])

For state prisoners, if your deliberate indifference claim is a borderline case, or if part of your injury was caused by deliberate indifference and part by bad judgment on the part of medical personnel, you may have to litigate all or part of your case in state court; perhaps it is better to start out there rather than wasting months or years in federal court.[354] For federal prisoners, an Eighth Amendment claim and a Federal Tort Claims Act suit can be combined in the same complaint (see Ch. VI, Sec. C3); you should always assert both claims in medical cases.

4.   Access to the Courts

The Supreme Court has stated, "It is now established beyond doubt that prisoners have a constitutional right of access to the courts,"[355] and that access must be "adequate, effective, and meaningful."[356] Although early decisions referred to the "constitutionally and statutorily protected availability of the writ of habeas corpus,"[357] it is now acknowledged that the right extends to other types of legal proceedings.[358] "Regulations and practices that unjustifiably obstruct the availability of professional

---

[353]BLACK'S LAW DICTIONARY, 5th ed. (1979).

[354]You can assert a state malpractice claim along with your constitutional claim in a §1983 action under the doctrine of pendent jurisdiction (see Ch. VI, Sec. B3), but the judge does not have to accept it, and if your constitutional claim is dismissed before trial, your state law claim will also be dismissed and you will have to refile it in state court. See Ch. IV, Sec. D2, for a discussion of bringing a §1983 claim in state court.

[355]Bounds v. Smith, 430 U.S. 817, 821, 97 S.Ct. 1491 (1977). The courts have cited both the Due Process Clause and the First Amendment as a basis for the right. *Compare* Procunier v. Martinez, 416 U.S. 396, 419, 94 S.Ct. 1800 (1974), *with* Milhouse v. Carlson, 652 F.2d 371 (3d Cir. 1981).

[356]Bounds v. Smith, *id.* at 822.

[357]Johnson v. Avery, 393 U.S. 483, 489, 89 S.Ct. 747 (1969); *accord,* Ex parte Hull, 312 U.S. 546, 549, 61 S.Ct. 640 (1941).

[358]Bounds v. Smith, *supra* note 355, at 827 ("original actions seeking new trials, release from confinement, or vindication of fundamental rights"); Wolff v. McDonnell, 418 U.S. 539, 579, 94 S.Ct. 2963 (1974) (civil rights actions); Spates v. Manson, 644 F.2d 80, 84 (2d Cir. 1981) ("nonfrivolous claims"); Carter v. Mandel, 573 F.2d 172 (4th Cir. 1978) (legal assistance program excluding §1983 actions was inadequate).

representation or other aspects of the right of access to the courts are invalid.''[359]

The right of access to the courts involves a variety of issues, including access to a law library and to other necessary materials and services; the right to legal assistance, either state provided or from other prisoners; the right to confidential communication with the courts, attorneys, and public officials; and the right to exercise all of the foregoing rights without fear of punishment or retaliation.

Claims of denial of access to courts have been presented both as individual claims (usually for damages) and as challenges to a prison's whole system of providing access to courts (usually injunctive class actions). Generally, in individual cases the courts require proof that you were actually harmed, such as by having your case dismissed.[360] In broader challenges to the system, courts are usually satisfied with proof that the system cannot provide adequate access to all prisoners, without proof that individual cases have been dismissed or lost.[361] One court spelled this out, stating that in a class action, it would have found a 45-minute law library period inadequate, but that in plaintiff's individual case, it must be determined if his particular problem could be dealt with in 45 minutes.[362]

a.   Law Libraries and Services for *Pro Se* Litigants

The Supreme Court has held that prisoners have a right of access to an adequate law library *or* adequate assistance from persons trained in the law in order to have "a reasonably adequate opportunity to present claimed violations of fundamental constitutional rights to the courts.''[363] Most courts have held that if the state provides adequate legal assistance,

---

[359]Procunier v. Martinez, *supra* note 360, at 419.

[360]*See, e.g.,* Harrell v. Keohane, 621 F.2d 1059 (10th Cir. 1980); McDonald v. Hall, 610 F.2d 16 (1st Cir. 1979); United States v. Mayo, 646 F.2d 369 (9th Cir. 1981); Twyman v. Crisp, 584 F.2d 352, 357 (10th Cir. 1978); Isaac v. Jones, 529 F. Supp. 175 (N.D. Ill. 1981); Pickett v. Schaefer, 503 F. Supp. 27 (S.D.N.Y. 1980). *Contra,* Nees v. Bishop, 524 F. Supp. 1310 (D. Colo. 1981) (two-day delay in seeing public defender supported award of damages).

[361]Hooks v. Wainwright, 578 F.2d 1102 (5th Cir. 1978), *on remand,* 536 F. Supp. 1330 (M.D. Fla. 1982); Nadeau v. Helgemoe, 561 F.2d 411, 418 (1st Cir. 1977); Carter v. Mandel, 573 F.2d 172 (4th Cir. 1978); Cruz v. Hauck, 527 F.2d 710 (5th Cir. 1980); Battle v. Anderson, 614 F.2d 251, 254-56 (10th Cir. 1980). *But see* Hudson v. Robinson, 678 F.2d 462 (3d Cir. 1982) (showing of harm required in injunctive cases).

[362]Williams v. Leeke, 584 F.2d 1336, 1340 (4th Cir. 1978).

[363]Bounds v. Smith, *supra* note 355, at 827.

it need not provide you with a law library in addition, even if you are proceeding *pro se* in a criminal case.[364] If there is a legal assistance program that serves your prison, a court may find you have no right to a law library unless you show that your case has been rejected by the program, that the program does not cover the full range of prisoners' legal needs, or that its resources are inadequate to serve the prison population.[365]

A law library obviously must be "adequate."[366] Courts have reached various conclusions about what an adequate law library must contain;[367] a list of volumes recommended by the American Association of Law Libraries Committee on Law Library Services to Prisoners has been cited as relevant in some decisions.[368] (This list is reprinted in Appendix E.) Prisoners' access to the law library must also be adequate. While prison officials may place reasonable limits on the time, place, and manner of access,[369] restrictions that deny meaningful access to the law library will be struck down. Courts have condemned schedules that provided too

---

[364]United States v. Garza, 664 F.2d 135 (7th Cir. 1981); Almond v. Davis, 639 F.2d 1086 (4th Cir. 1981); Spates v. Manson, 644 F.2d 80, 85 (2d Cir. 1981); United States v. Blue Thunder, 604 F.2d 550 (8th Cir. 1979); Falzerano v. Collier, 535 F. Supp. 800 (D.N.J. 1982); Bell v. Hopper, 511 F. Supp. 452 (S.D. Ga. 1981).

[365]Spates v. Manson, *supra* note 358, at 84; Leeds v. Watson, 630 F.2d 674, 676 (9th Cir. 1980); Hooks v. Wainwright, 578 F.2d 1102 (5th Cir. 1978); Carter v. Mandel, 573 F.2d 172 (4th Cir. 1978). *But see* Kelsey v. State of Minnesota, 622 F.2d 956 (8th Cir. 1980) (program that excluded "lawsuits against public agencies or public officials to change social or public policy" adequate).

[366]Bounds v. Smith, *supra* note 355, at 828.

[367]*See, e.g.,* Wattson v. Olsen, 660 F.2d 358 (8th Cir. 1981); Cruz v. Hauck, 627 F.2d 710 (5th Cir. 1980); Hooks v. Wainwright, 536 F. Supp. 1330 (M.D. Fla. 1982); Hardwick v. Ault, 447 F. Supp. 116 (M.D. Ga. 1978); *see also* Rich v. Zitnay, 644 F.2d 41 (1st Cir. 1981) (Maine prisoner held in Kansas federal prison had right of access to Maine legal materials).

Courts have held that county jails may have smaller law libraries but that a complete denial of access to legal materials in jails is unlawful. Leeds v. Watson, 630 F.2d 674 (9th Cir. 1981); Parnell v. Waldrep, 511 F. Supp. 764 (W.D.N.C. 1981); Fluhr v. Roberts, 460 F. Supp. 536 (W.D. Ky. 1978). *But see* Williams v. Leeke, 584 F.2d 1336, 1340 (4th Cir. 1978) ("We should not be understood to say that every small jail must have a law library, but misdemeanants serving sentences of up to 12 months in local jails should not be left wholly without resources. . . .").

[368]Ramos v. Lamm, *supra* note 343, at 584; Bounds v. Smith, *supra* note 355, at 819-20 n.4.

[369]Twyman v. Crisp, 584 F.2d 352 (10th Cir. 1980); Collins v. Ward, 544 F. Supp. 408 (S.D.N.Y. 1982).

little time for meaningful legal research,[370] regulations which forbid actual physical access to the library,[371] and other restrictive practices.[372]

Some courts have held that establishment of a law library may by itself be inadequate to provide meaningful court access if prisoners lack the skill to use it, and have required that some legal assistance be provided by prisoners or attorneys.[373]

Prisoners in segregation units must be provided with some access to the law library. Most courts have upheld a system of cell delivery of law books instead of requiring physical access,[374] although some have emphasized that these prisoners also had access to some form of legal assistance.[375] Some courts have rejected challenges to delays and other inadequacies in the cell delivery system.[376] However, one recent case held that a protective custody prisoner must have "at least the equivalent of the opportunity [to do legal research] that is available to an inmate who is permitted to go personally to the prison law library."[377]

---

[370]Cruz v. Hauck, 627 F.2d 710, 720 (5th Cir. 1978) (two or three hours a week might be inadequate); Walker v. Johnson, 544 F. Supp. 345 (E.D. Mich. 1982) (four and a half hours a week required); Ramos v. Lamm, 485 F. Supp. 122, 166 (D. Colo. 1979), *aff'd in part and rev'd in part,* 639 F.2d 559 (10th Cir. 1980), *cert. denied,* 101 S.Ct. 1759 (1981) (three hours every four to six weeks inadequate).

[371]Leeds v. Watson, 630 F.2d 674 (9th Cir. 1980); Williams v. Leeke, 584 F.2d 1336, 1339 (4th Cir. 1978); United States ex rel. Wolfish v. Levi, 439 F. Supp. 114, 129 (S.D.N.Y. 1977), *aff'd in pertinent part sub nom.* Wolfish v. Levi, 573 F.2d 118 (2d Cir. 1978), *rev'd on other grounds sub nom.* Bell v. Wolfish, 441 U.S. 520, 99 S.Ct. 1861 (1979); Hooks v. Wainwright, 536 F. Supp. 1330 (M.D. Fla. 1982).

[372]Ruiz v. Estelle, 679 F.2d 1115, 1154 (5th Cir. 1982) (harassing strip searches at law library enjoined).

[373]Cruz v. Hauck, 627 F.2d 710, 721 (5th Cir. 1980); Battle v. Anderson, 614 F.2d 251 (10th Cir. 1980); Hooks v. Wainwright, 536 F. Supp. 1330 (M.D. Fla. 1982); Glover v. Johnson, 478 F. Supp. 1075 (E.D. Mich. 1979). *See also* Stewart v. Gates, 450 F. Supp. 583, 589 (C.D. Cal. 1978) ("runner" system upheld where inmates also had access to public defender).

[374]Dorrough v. Hogan, 563 F.2d 1259 (5th Cir. 1977); Arsberry v. Sielaff, 586 F.2d 37, 44 (7th Cir. 1978); Black v. Brown, 524 F. Supp. 856 (N.D. Ill. 1981); Johnson v. Anderson, 370 F. Supp. 1373, 1384-85 (D. Del. 1974); *see also* Rucker v. Grider, 526 F. Supp. 617 (W.D. Okla. 1980) (exclusion of reception center inmates, with exceptions for emergencies, upheld).

[375]Williams v. Leeke, 584 F.2d 1336, 1339 (4th Cir. 1978); Frazier v. Ward, 426 F. Supp. 1354, 1371 (N.D.N.Y. 1977).

[376]Griffin v. Smith, 493 F. Supp. 129 (W.D.N.Y. 1980); Evans v. Fogg, 466 F. Supp. 949 (S.D.N.Y. 1979).

[377]Wojtczak v. Cuyler, 480 F. Supp. 1288, 1301 (E.D. Pa. 1979).

Prison authorities may also have to provide *pro se* litigants with other services. The Supreme Court stated, "It is indisputable that indigent inmates must be provided at state expense with paper and pen to draft legal documents, with notarial services to authenticate them, and with stamps to mail them."[378] Restrictions on photocopying have drawn mixed responses from the courts.[379] Access to typewriters is generally not required.[380]

b. Legal Assistance

The Supreme Court has held that prison authorities may not prohibit prisoners from helping each other with legal matters unless they provide reasonable alternative forms of-assistance.[381] Conversely, "jailhouse lawyering" can be prohibited if adequate alternatives are provided.[382] Where jailhouse lawyers have the right to function, they may not be punished for their legal activities.[383] Restrictions on correspondence between jailhouse lawyers and their "clients" have drawn mixed responses from the courts.[384] Prison authorities may prohibit jailhouse lawyers

---

[378]Bounds v. Smith, *supra* note 355, at 824-25; *accord,* Ruiz v. Estelle, 503 F. Supp. 1265, 1371 n.206 (S.D. Tex. 1980), *aff'd in pertinent part, rev'd on other grounds,* 679 F.2d 1115, 1153-55 (5th Cir. 1982) (notarial services).
Despite the Supreme Court's observation in *Bounds,* some courts have demonstrated great reluctance to require provision of these services. Kershner v. Mazurkiewicz, 670 F.2d 440, 444 (3d Cir. 1982).

[379]Jones v. Franzen, 697 F.2d 801 (7th Cir. 1983) (restrictions upheld where no actual denial of court access was shown); Johnson v. Parke, 642 F.2d 377 (10th Cir. 1981) (refusal to make copies may be actionable if contrary to prison rules); Gibson v. McEvers, 631 F.2d 95 (7th Cir. 1980) (restrictions upheld); Harrell v. Keohane, 621 F.2d 1059 (10th Cir. 1980) (lack of free copying upheld); Ramos v. Lamm, 485 F. Supp. 122, 166 (D. Colo. 1979), *aff'd in pertinent part,* 639 F.2d 559 (10th Cir. 1980) (access to photocopier might be required in circumstances).

[380]Twyman v. Crisp, 584 F.2d 352, 358 (10th Cir. 1978); Wolfish v. Levi, 573 F.2d 118, 132 (2d Cir. 1978), *rev'd on other grounds sub nom.* Bell v. Wolfish, 441 U.S. 520, 99 S.Ct. 1861 (1979).

[381]Wolff v. McDonnell, 418 U.S. 539, 578-79, 94 S.Ct. 2963 (1974); Johnson v. Avery, *supra* note 357, at 490; *accord,* Cruz v. Hauck, 627 F.2d 710, 721 (5th Cir. 1980); Wade v. Kane, 448 F. Supp. 678 (E.D. Pa. 1978).

[382]Storseth v. Spellman, 654 F.2d 1349 (9th Cir. 1981); Graham v. Hutto, 437 F. Supp. 118 (E.D. Va. 1977).

[383]Buise v. Hudkins, 584 F.2d 223 (7th Cir. 1978); Vaughn v. Trotter, 516 F. Supp. 886 (M.D. Tenn. 1980); Wetmore v. Fields, 458 F. Supp. 1131 (W.D. Wisc. 1978).

[384]*Compare* Watts v. Brewer, 588 F.2d 646 (8th Cir. 1978), *with* Storseth v. Spellman, 654 F.2d 1349 (9th Cir. 1981).

from charging fees.[385] Courts may enjoin the activities of particular jailhouse lawyers if they abuse the judicial process.[386]

An adequate program of trained legal assistance will satisfy the requirements for meaningful court access and obviate any need for law libraries or jailhouse lawyering. (See Sec. C4a, *supra*.) Where such programs exist, courts have enjoined attempts to terminate or reduce them until such time as other adequate alternatives are provided.[387]

c. Communication With Attorneys, Courts, and Public Officials

Prisoners have a right to free and confidential correspondence with attorneys, courts, and public officials, and to confidential visits with attorneys and their assistants. These rights are discussed fully in Secs. C1a, Correspondence, and C1d, Visiting, *supra*.

d. Interference, Punishment, and Retaliation

It is unlawful to retaliate against or threaten a prisoner for exercising the right of access to courts, regardless of the form of the threat or retaliation.[388] Such actions may be remedied by an injunction, even if the practices are not formally part of official policy,[389] or by an award of damages.[390] Seizure of a prisoner's legal papers may also violate the Constitution.[391] However, actions taken for a legitimate purpose that

---

[385]Henderson v. Ricketts, 499 F. Supp. 1066 (D. Colo. 1980).

[386]Matter of Green, 586 F.2d 1247 (8th Cir. 1978).

[387]Hooks v. Wainwright, 578 F.2d 1102 (5th Cir. 1978); Wade v. Kane, 448 F. Supp. 678 (E.D. Pa. 1978).

[388]Milhouse v. Carlson, 652 F.2d 371 (3d Cir. 1981) (conspiratorially planned disciplinary actions); Courtney v. Reeves, 635 F.2d 326 (5th Cir. 1981) (mail interrupted, wife harassed); Ferranti v. Moran, 618 F.2d 888 (1st Cir. 1980) (denial of transfer and medical care); Cruz v. Beto, 603 F.2d 1178 (5th Cir. 1979) (placement of attorney's clients in segregated unit); Hudspeth v. Figgins, 584 F.2d 1345 (4th Cir. 1978) (death threat); Buise v. Hudkins, 584 F.2d 223 (7th Cir. 1978) (transfer); Carter v. Newburgh Police Dept., 523 F. Supp. 16 (S.D.N.Y. 1980) (threats and beatings); McDaniel v. Rhodes, 512 F. Supp. 117 (S.D. Ohio 1981) (threats of adverse parole action); Inmates of Nebraska Penal and Correctional Complex v. Greenholtz, 436 F. Supp. 432, 437 (D. Neb. 1976), *aff'd,* 567 F.2d 1381 (8th Cir. 1977), *cert. denied,* 439 U.S. 841 (1978) (refusal of parole consideration).

[389]Ruiz v. Estelle, 679 F.2d 1115, 1154 (5th Cir. 1982).

[390]Lamar v. Steele, 693 F.2d 559 (5th Cir. 1982), *on rehearing,* 698 F.2d 1286 (5th Cir. 1983); Cruz v. Beto, 603 F.2d 1178 (5th Cir. 1979).

[391]Franklin v. State of Oregon, 662 F.2d 1337 (9th Cir. 1981); Tyler v.

inadvertently obstruct court access are generally not unconstitutional.[392] (See also Ch. XI for a discussion of how to protect yourself from prison officials.)

5. Searches, Seizures, and Privacy

The Fourth Amendment ensures "the right of the people to be secure in their persons, houses, papers, and effects against unreasonable searches and seizures."[393] The Supreme Court has also recognized a constitutional right of personal privacy based on a variety of constitutional provisions.[394] An older Supreme Court case suggested that jails might be outside the scope of the Fourth Amendment.[395] However, more recently the Supreme Court has left the question open,[396] and most lower courts now hold that prisoners have at least limited Fourth Amendment and privacy rights.[397]

It is clear that prisoners' Fourth Amendment and privacy rights are drastically limited. Warrants are generally not required in prisons.[398]

Woodson, 597 F.2d 643 (8th Cir. 1979); Stringer v. Thompson, 537 F. Supp. 133 (N.D. Ill. 1982); Slie v. Bordenkircher, 526 F. Supp. 1264 (N.D. W. Va. 1981).

[392]United States v. Mayo, 646 F.2d 369 (9th Cir. 1981) (transfer and loss of papers); Mingo v. Patterson, 455 F. Supp. 1358 (D. Colo. 1978) (transfer).

[393]U.S. Const., Amend. IV.

[394]Roe v. Wade, 410 U.S. 113, 153, 93 S.Ct. 705 (1973).

[395]Lanza v. New York, 370 U.S. 139, 142-43, 82 S.Ct. 1218 (1962).

[396]Bell v. Wolfish, 441 U.S. 520, 556-58, 99 S.Ct. 1861 (1979); see also Wolff v. McDonnell, supra note 381, at 555-56 ("no iron curtain drawn between the Constitution and the prisons of this country"); Katz v. United States, 389 U.S. 347, 351, 88 S.Ct. 507 (1967) ("the Fourth Amendment protects people, not places").

[397]United States v. Chamorro, 687 F.2d 1, 4 (1st Cir. 1982); United States v. Hinckley, 672 F.2d 115, 129 n.99 (D.C. Cir. 1982), and cases cited.

[398]See Bell v. Wolfish, 441 U.S. 520, 555-57 and n.38, 99 S.Ct. 1861 (1979) (jail officials' policy of unannounced searches of inmate living areas at irregular intervals upheld); Olson v. Klecker, 642 F.2d 1115 (8th Cir. 1981) (search of prisoner's cell without warrant was constitutional); United States v. Lilly, 576 F.2d 1240, 1244-47 (5th Cir. 1978) (prison officials need neither a warrant nor probable cause to conduct a search or seizure); United States v. Miller, 526 F. Supp. 691 (W.D. Okla. 1981) (need to maintain prison discipline allows dispensing with the warrant and probable cause requirement in prison setting); Smith v. Marchewka, 519 F. Supp. 897 (N.D.N.Y. 1981) (room-search rule does not violate Fourth Amendment); Clifton v. Robinson, 500 F. Supp. 30, 35 (E.D. Pa. 1980). But see United States v. Bradley, 571 F.2d 787 (4th Cir. 1978) (unless established exception exists, parole officer must secure warrant prior to conducting search of parolee's residence).

"Shakedown" searches either of whole housing areas or of randomly selected prisoners' cells may be conducted without probable cause;[399] in fact, they may be required in order to protect prisoners' safety.[400] Searches of particular prisoners' cells, not pursuant to institutional routine, have been subjected to some limitations, such as a requirement of reasonable basis for believing that a prisoner possesses contraband.[401] Even searches conducted pursuant to a valid security procedure may be unreasonable if they go beyond legitimate security requirements (*e.g.*, if mail or diaries are read without good reason).[402] Searches which are motivated by a purpose unrelated to prison security may also be unreasonable.[403] Even a validly conducted search must be conducted in a reasonable manner;[404] a search that leaves a prisoner's cell in a shambles and his/her property damaged has been held unreasonable.[405]

With respect to searches of prisoners' persons, the Supreme Court has upheld a requirement that after every contact visit a prisoner strip and expose his/her anal and genital areas for visual inspection, without probable cause.[406] However, the Court noted that the "test of reasonableness . . . requires a balancing of the need for the particular search against the invasion of personal rights that the search entails."[407] Before and after *Bell v. Wolfish*, courts have scrutinized strip search requirements carefully and have often drawn fine lines in determining what is reasonable. Thus, courts have barred close visual inspection of anal and genital areas requiring prisoners to spread their buttocks, lift their

---

[399]Bell v. Wolfish, *supra* note 396, at 556-57; Montana v. Commissioners' Court, 659 F.2d 19 (5th Cir. 1981); Olson v. Klecker, 642 F.2d 1115 (8th Cir. 1981).

[400]Hamilton v. Landrieu, 351 F. Supp. 549, 551 (E.D. La. 1972).

[401]Palmer v. Hudson, 697 F.2d 1220 (4th Cir. 1983).

[402]United States v. Hinckley, *supra* note 397, at 128-32; Olson v. Klecker, 642 F.2d 1115 (8th Cir. 1981). *But see* DiGuiseppe v. Ward, 698 F.2d 602 (2d Cir. 1983) (reading of diary during post-riot search upheld); United States v. Vallez, 653 F.2d 403 (9th Cir. 1981) (officer's suspicion that letter might contain map or escape plans justified opening it); Gardner v. Johnson, 429 F. Supp. 432 (E.D. Mich. 1977) (diary could be seized where prisoner had used prison property to write in).

[403]Nakao v. Rushen, 542 F. Supp. 856, 859-61 (N.D. Cal. 1982) (warrantless search of cell for evidence in attempt to fire prisoner's correspondent from government job); Palmer v. Hudson, *supra* note 401 (search intended to harass prisoner).

[404]Bell v. Wolfish, *supra* note 396, at 559, 560.

[405]Brown v. Hilton, 492 F. Supp. 771, 775 (D.N.J. 1980).

[406]Bell v. Wolfish, *supra* note 396, at 558-60.

[407]*Id.* at 559; *see also* Frazier v. Ward, 528 F. Supp. 80, 81 (N.D.N.Y. 1981).

genitals, etc., while upholding the requirement that prisoners strip.[408] Some courts have held that certain strip search procedures were unnecessary for closely controlled segregation prisoners,[409] but others have held that these prisoners pose special dangers justifying more intrusive searches.[410] Courts have held that prisoners must be given notice that they may be subjected to body cavity searches on less than probable cause.[411] Strip searches may be found unreasonable because of the presence of guards of the opposite sex,[412] because they are conducted in a non-private setting,[413] or because they are accompanied by verbal abuse.[414] Strip searches without reasonable cause in connection with depositions, visits to the law library, transfers, and medical visits have been prohibited or limited.[415] Use of reasonable force to conduct an otherwise valid strip search is permissible.[416]

Prisoners have the right not to be unnecessarily viewed in the nude or while performing private bodily functions,[417] particularly by persons of

---

[408]Hurley v. Ward, 549 F. Supp. 174 (S.D.N.Y. 1982); Frazier v. Ward, 426 F. Supp. 1354, 1360-66 (N.D.N.Y. 1977); Hodges v. Klein, 412 F. Supp. 896 (D.N.J. 1976).

[409]Frazier v. Ward, *id.;* Hodges v. Klein, *id.*

[410]Arruda v. Fair, 547 F. Supp. 1324 (D. Mass. 1982); Bono v. Saxbe, 527 F. Supp. 1182 (S.D. Ill. 1980).

[411]United States v. Lilly, 576 F.2d 1240, 1246 (5th Cir. 1978).

[412]Franklin v. State of Oregon, 662 F.2d 1337 (9th Cir. 1981); Lee v. Downs, 641 F.2d 1117 (4th Cir. 1981); *see also* Smith v. Fairman, 678 F.2d 52 (7th Cir. 1982) (female guard may conduct pat search of inmate except in genital area).

[413]Iskander v. Village of Forest Park, 690 F.2d 126 (7th Cir. 1982); Estes-El v. State of New York, 552 F. Supp. 885 (S.D.N.Y. 1982).

[414]Bell v. Wolfish, *supra* note 396, at 560. Verbal abuse in searches will not support abolition of the entire search procedure. Arruda v. Fair, *supra* note 410.

[415]Hurley v. Ward, *supra* note 408, at 184-86 (visual inspection of anal and genital areas prohibited for transfers, medical visits, etc.); Ruiz v. Estelle, 679 F.2d 1115, 1154-55 (5th Cir. 1982) (strip searches of prisoners entering and leaving law library were "unwarranted harassment"); Sims v. Brierton, 500 F. Supp. 813 (N.D. Ill. 1980) (requirement of body cavity search before deposition struck down). *Contra,* Arruda v. Fair, *supra* note 410 (strip searches in connection with attorney visits and law library visits upheld for segregation inmates).

[416]Akili v. Ward, 547 F. Supp. 729 (N.D.N.Y. 1982); Hendrix v. Faulkner, 525 F. Supp. 435, 449-50 (N.D. Ind. 1981).

[417]Walker v. Johnson, 544 F. Supp. 345, 361 (E.D. Mich. 1982) (prisoners could not be required to walk to showers naked); *see also* D.B. v. Tewksbury, 545 F. Supp. 896, 905 (D. Ore. 1982) (absence of privacy while showering, using toilet, or maintaining feminine hygiene violated due process rights of juvenile detainees).

the opposite sex.[418] However, courts have not been willing to ban guards of the opposite sex from supervising prisoners; they have generally balanced prisoners' privacy rights against guards' rights to equal employment opportunity and have directed that the two be accommodated.[419]

With respect to family relationships, most privacy issues of concern to prisoners have to do with correspondence and visiting. (See Secs. C1a and C1d, *supra.*) The courts are divided as to prisoners' right to marry. The Supreme Court has summarily affirmed a decision upholding a New York statute barring prisoners serving life terms from marrying,[420] and many courts have upheld stringent restrictions on prisoner marriage.[421] However, a few recent decisions, relying on Supreme Court non-prison precedent, have held that marriage is a fundamental right which cannot be restricted except as necessary to serve a "compelling interest" of government.[422]

In general, prisoners have few rights to control their personal ap-

---

[418]Cumbey v. Meachum, 684 F.2d 712 (10th Cir. 1982); Dawson v. Kendrick, 527 F. Supp. 1252, 1316 (S.D. W. Va. 1981); Bowling v. Enomoto, 514 F. Supp. 201 (N.D. Cal. 1981); Hudson v. Goodlander, 494 F. Supp. 890 (D. Md. 1980).

[419]Smith v. Fairman, 678 F.2d 52 (7th Cir. 1982) (female guards may conduct pat down searches of male prisoners excluding the genital area); Forts v. Ward, 621 F.2d 1210 (2d Cir. 1980) (male guards need not be barred from night shift where officials would permit women prisoners to wear "satisfactory sleepwear" and to cover their cell windows for 15-minute periods); Gunther v. Iowa State Men's Reformatory, 612 F.2d 1079 (8th Cir. 1980) (female guards' duties can be arranged to protect male prisoners' privacy); Avery v. Perrin, 473 F. Supp. 90 (D.N.H. 1979) (use of female guard to deliver mail in men's prison upheld).

[420]Johnson v. Rockefeller, 365 F. Supp. 377 (S.D.N.Y. 1973), *aff'd sub nom.* Butler v. Wilson, 415 U.S. 953 (1974).

[421]Hudson v. Rhodes, 579 F.2d 46 (6th Cir. 1978), *cert. denied,* 440 U.S. 919 (1979) (unwritten ban on prisoner marriage upheld); Bradbury v. Wainwright, 538 F. Supp. 377 (M.D. Fla. 1982) (regulation barring prisoner marriage upheld); Wool v. Hogan, 505 F. Supp. 928, 932-33 (D. Vt. 1981) (individual request to marry could be denied); Holland v. Hutto, 450 F. Supp. 194 (W.D. Va. 1978) (rejection of prisoner request and upholding of requirement that prisoner show "need to be married"); Polmaskitch v. United States, 436 F. Supp. 527 (W.D. Okla. 1977) (denial of marriage discretionary and unreviewable); In re Goalen, 30 Utah 2d 27, 512 P.2d 1028 (1973), *appeal dismissed,* 414 U.S. 1148 (1974).

[422]Salisbury v. List, 501 F. Supp. 105 (D. Nev. 1980) (rule prohibiting marriage except for "strong, compelling reasons" unconstitutional); In re Carrafa, 143 Cal. Rptr. 848 (Ct. App. 1978); Vance v. Rice, 524 F. Supp. 1297 (S.D. Iowa 1981) (detainee could be prohibited from marrying material witness in his prosecution under compelling interest test where witness would then have been unable to testify against him).

pearance. Prison officials can require prisoners to wear institutional clothing[423] and to shave and cut their hair.[424] To win a personal appearance case, you will generally have to have some constitutional basis other than the right to privacy. For example, the right to a fair trial prevents you from being tried in prison garb over your objection;[425] you may be exempted from shaving if your medical condition so requires;[426] and prison officials may be required to respect religious rules regarding hair, beard, and attire.[427]

6. Property

Prisoners' most frequent property complaint is that their belongings have been improperly seized, destroyed, or lost. Prisoners' rights in these situations are discussed in the sections on Procedural Due Process (see Sec. B2i, *supra*); Searches, Seizures, and Privacy (see Sec. C5, *supra*).

Restrictions on prisoners' acquisition of property are generally upheld by the courts. In *Bell v. Wolfish*,[428] the Supreme Court held that jail officials could bar the receipt of all packages of food and other personal items.[429] Lesser restrictions are also likely to be upheld.[430] Prisoners may be prohibited from transferring property among themselves.[431]

---

[423]Wolfish v. Levi, 573 F.2d 118, 132-33 (2d Cir. 1978), *rev'd on other grounds sub nom.* Bell v. Wolfish, 441 U.S. 520, 99 S.Ct. 1861 (1979). *But see* Forts v. Malcolm, 426 F. Supp. 464 (S.D.N.Y. 1977) (female pretrial detainees could wear pants).

[424]Sloan v. Southampton Correctional Center, 476 F. Supp. 196 (E.D. Va. 1979); Poe v. Werner, 386 F. Supp. 1014 (M.D. Pa. 1974).

[425]Estelle v. Williams, 425 U.S. 501, 96 S.Ct. 1691 (1976).

[426]Shabazz v. Barnauskas, 598 F.2d 345 (5th Cir. 1979); Monroe v. Bombard, 422 F. Supp. 211 (S.D.N.Y. 1976); *contra,* Gamble v. Benton, 600 P.2d 328 (Sup. Ct. Okla. 1979).

[427]See Sec. C7d4, *infra,* for a discussion of personal appearance cases involving religious claims.

[428]441 U.S. 520, 99 S.Ct. 1861 (1979).

[429]*Id.* at 553-55; *accord,* Jensen v. Klecker, 643 F.2d 1179 (8th Cir. 1981).

[430]Tunnell v. Robinson, 486 F. Supp. 1265 (W.D. Pa. 1980) (restriction of mail orders to certain companies upheld); Vaughn v. Garrison, 534 F. Supp. 90 (E.D.N.C. 1981) (same); Griffin v. Smith, 493 F. Supp. 129 (W.D.N.Y. 1980) (limits on commissary purchases by segregated prisoners did not state a constitutional claim); Ward v. Johnson, 437 F. Supp. 1053 (E.D. Va. 1977) (transferred prisoner could be required to send property home and buy new items at receiving prison). *But see* Williams v. Manson, 499 F. Supp. 773 (D. Conn. 1980) (ban on prisoners' purchase of lottery tickets denied equal protection).

[431]Ford v. Schmidt, 577 F.2d 408 (7th Cir. 1978); Velarde v. Ricketts, 480 F. Supp. 261 (D. Colo. 1979).

Prisoners must be able to obtain, or be provided, certain types of property, such as books, writing materials, religious objects, clothing, and personal hygiene items, pursuant to other constitutional rights. (See Sec. C, subsecs. 1, 3, 4, and 7.) Most of these items, such as writing materials and personal hygiene items, you are entitled to receive from the state only if you are indigent.

Prison officials have substantial discretion in how prisoners' money is handled.[432] However, they may not simply appropriate a prisoner's funds for their own purposes.[433] Some courts have held that confiscated currency (which is contraband in most prisons) may be forfeited;[434] others have held that forfeiture must be authorized by statute or by court order.[435]

7. Religion

Under the First Amendment, all people have the absolute right to whatever religious beliefs they wish.[436] It is only when they attempt to practice their beliefs that the government may impose restrictions. Even in prison, however, "reasonable opportunities must be afforded to all prisoners to exercise the religious freedom guaranteed by the First and Fourteenth Amendments without fear of penalty."[437]

In deciding whether your religious rights are violated by a prison restriction, the court will first determine whether you in fact have a sincerely held belief that is religious in nature. If the court finds that this is the case, it will then apply the relevant constitutional standard to determine whether the restriction in question is constitutional.

The courts, in deciding whether a prisoner's beliefs are entitled to First Amendment protection, will determine whether the beliefs are (1) sincerely held, and (2) religious in nature.[438] If the court has found that your

---

[432]Tunnell v. Robinson, 486 F. Supp. 1265 (W.D. Pa. 1980) (various restrictions on bank accounts upheld); Henderson v. Ricketts, 499 F. Supp. 1066 (D. Colo. 1980) (ban on inter-prisoner fund transfers upheld); Gray v. Lee, 486 F. Supp. 41 (D. Md. 1980) (requirement that some money be kept in non-interest-bearing "reserve account" upheld); Jackson v. Cuyler, 432 F. Supp. 1296 (E.D. Pa. 1977).

[433]Randolph v. Dept. of Correctional Services, 289 N.W.2d 529 (Sup. Ct. Neb. 1980); *see also* Smith v. Robinson, 456 F. Supp. 449 (E.D. Pa. 1978) (prisoners entitled to complete account statement).

[434]Lowery v. Cuyler, 521 F. Supp. 430 (E.D. Pa. 1981).

[435]Hanvey v. Blankenship, 631 F.2d 296 (4th Cir. 1980); Sullivan v. Ford, 609 F.2d 197 (5th Cir. 1980); Sell v. Parratt, 548 F.2d 753 (8th Cir. 1977).

[436]Wisconsin v. Yoder, 406 U.S. 205, 219-20, 92 S.Ct. 1526 (1972).

[437]Cruz v. Beto, 405 U.S. 319, 322 n.2, 92 S.Ct. 1079 (1972).

[438]*See* United States v. Seeger, 380 U.S. 163, 185, 85 S.Ct. 850 (1965); Africa

beliefs are sincere and religious in nature, it will then determine to what constitutional protection you are entitled.[439]

a. Sincerity of Belief

In determining whether your religious beliefs are entitled to First Amendment protection, the first inquiry is the sincerity of these beliefs.[440] The court will ask whether your beliefs occupy a meaningful place in your life.[441] A number of factors may be considered: whether you have adhered to these beliefs in the face of threats of punishment by prison officials,[442] whether you adhered to them before you entered prison,[443] and whether your behavior in general is consistent with the beliefs you profess to hold.[444] (If prison officials try to show you are not sincere because you have used drugs, committed violent acts, or otherwise violated tenets of your religion, you should remind the court that no one is perfect and that being a sinner does not mean that you cannot be a sincere believer.[445])

---

v. Comm. of Pa., 662 F.2d 1025, 1030 (3d Cir. 1981); Callahan v. Woods, 658 F.2d 679 (9th Cir. 1981); Vaughn v. Garrison, 534 F. Supp. 90, 92 (E.D.N.C. 1981); Gallahan v. Hollyfield, 516 F. Supp. 1004 (E.D. Va. 1981), aff'd, 670 F.2d 1345 (4th Cir. 1982).

[439]See Subsec. c, infra, for a discussion of these tests.

[440]Jones v. Bradley, 590 F.2d 294 (9th Cir. 1979); Africa v. State of Pennsylvania, 520 F. Supp. 967 (E.D. Pa. 1981), aff'd, 662 F.2d 1025 (3d Cir. 1981); Gallahan v. Hollyfield, 516 F. Supp. 1004 (E.D. Va. 1981); Alim v. Byrne, 521 F. Supp. 1039, 1044 (D.N.J. 1980).

[441]See Childs v. Duckworth, 509 F. Supp. 1254, 1259 (N.D. Ind. 1980).

[442]Moskowitz v. Wilkinson, 432 F. Supp. 947 (D. Conn. 1977) (prisoner's sincerity demonstrated by fact that he had received four disciplinary tickets and had lost good time for refusing to cut his hair in violation of religious beliefs).

[443]Gallahan v. Hollyfield, 516 F. Supp. 1004 (E.D. Va. 1981), aff'd, 670 F.2d 1345 (4th Cir. 1982). Your beliefs may not be presumed to be insincere simply because you acquired them in prison, Maguire v. Wilkinson, 405 F. Supp. 637, 640 (D. Conn. 1975); see also Masjid Muhammad-D.C.C. v. Keve, 479 F. Supp. 1311, 1321-22 (D. Del. 1979) (relief granted to Muslims who changed their names after becoming Muslims in prison).

[444]Vaughn v. Garrison, 534 F. Supp. 90, 92 (E.D.N.C. 1981) (prison officials could limit Muslim prayer rugs to persons who had submitted request for the pork-free diet required by Muslim tenets).

[445]Luke 7:36-50, "Let him without sin cast the first stone;" see also Matthew 7:1-14.

b. Are the Beliefs Religious in Nature?

Whether particular beliefs are religious in nature has often perplexed the courts.[446] Religion has been defined as an individual's sincere belief, even though not theistic in nauture, "based upon a power or being, or upon a faith, to which all else is ultimately dependent."[447] Belief in the existence of a God is not critical to whether a particluar set of beliefs is a religion.[448] However, needless to say one does not have a right to devise a religion in order to obtain concessions from prison officials,[449] nor to use it to disrupt prison life.[450] The courts, in considering a claim involving a "non-traditional" religious belief or practice, will "look[ ] to the familiar religions as models in order to ascertain, by comparison, whether the new set of ideas or beliefs is confronting the

---

[446]*See* Thomas v. Review Board, Indiana Employment Security Division, 450 U.S. 707, 714, 101 S.Ct. 1425 (1981); Africa v. Comm. of Pa., 662 F.2d 1025, 1031 (3d Cir. 1981).

[447]United States v. Seeger, 380 U.S. 163, 176, 85 S.Ct. 850 (1965); Welsh II v. United States, 398 U.S. 333, 90 S.Ct. 1792 (1970). The following cases have held non-theistic beliefs are religions: United States v. Ballard, 322 U.S. 78, 64 S.Ct. 882 (1943) ("I Am"); Dreibelbis v. Marks, 675 F.2d 579 (3d Cir. 1982) (Church of Prophetic Meditation); Kennedy v. Meacham, 540 F.2d 1057 (10th Cir. 1976) (Satanism); Green v. White, 525 F. Supp. 81 (E.D. Mo. 1981) (Human Awareness Life Church); Williams v. Warden, Federal Correctional Inst., 470 F. Supp. 1123 (D. Conn. 1979) (Christian Adamic). *Compare* Church of the New Song v. Establishment of Religion, 620 F.2d 648 (7th Cir. 1980) (Church of the New Song not a religion), *with* Remmers v. Brewer, 361 F. Supp. 537 (S.D. Iowa 1973), *aff'd per curiam,* 494 F.2d 1277 (8th Cir.), *cert. denied,* 419 U.S. 1012 (1974), *and* Loney v. Scurr, 474 F. Supp. 1186 (S.D. Iowa 1979) (Church of the New Song is a religion). The following cases have held beliefs are not religions: Africa v. Comm. of Pa., 662 F.2d 1025 (3d Cir. 1981) (MOVE is not a religion); Brooks v. Wainwright, 428 F.2d 652 (5th Cir. 1970) (prisoner claimed he was a religion, not established religion); Brown v. Wainwright, 419 F.2d 1376 (5th Cir. 1970). *See also* Jones v. Bradley, 590 F.2d 294 (9th Cir. 1979) (court held it need not reach issue whether Universal Life Church is a religion).

[448]*See* Torcaso v. Watkins, 367 U.S. 488, 495 n.11, 81 S.Ct. 1680 (1961).

[449]Green v. White, 525 F. Supp. 81 (E.D. Mo. 1981) (prisoner demanded conjugal visits, banquets, and payment as a chaplain).

[450]*See* Theriault v. Silber, 391 F. Supp. 578, 582 (W.D. Tex. 1975) (purpose of Church of the New Song is to encourage disruption of established prison discipline), and 453 F. Supp. 254, 260 (W.D. Tex. 1978) ("Church of the New Song appears . . . a masquerade designed to obtain First Amendment protection. . . .").

same concerns, or serving the same purposes, as unquestioned and accepted 'religion.'"[451]

In determining whether a particular set of beliefs is a religion, a court is not authorized to examine the content of the particular beliefs to determine its truth or falsity but only to determine whether the beliefs asserted are, or are not, a religion.[452] The Third Circuit has used a three-pronged test in asking this question.[453] First, does the particular set of beliefs address fundamental and ultimate questions having to do with, among other things, life and death, right and wrong, and good and evil?[454] Second, is the particular set of beliefs comprehensive in nature or just a "number of isolated, unconnected ideas?"[455] Third, does the particular set of beliefs present certain formal and external signs?[456] Under the third prong, the court will examine your religion to determine whether it has a formal structure similar to a regular church, such as hierarchy of members, ministers, etc.;[457] whether it holds services or some type of ceremony; and whether the beliefs are in concrete form (like a Bible or some other religious book).[458]

The courts may not find your beliefs to be non-religious simply because they are not absolutely consistent with those of other members of the religion or with orthodox interpretations of it.[459] Thus, in

---

[451]Malnak v. Yogi, 592 F.2d 197, 207 (3d Cir. 1979) (Adams, J., concurring). *See also* Founding Church of Scientology v. United States, 409 F.2d 1146, 1160 (D.C. Cir. 1969); Alim v. Byrne, 521 F. Supp. 1039 (E.D.N.J. 1980); Remmers v. Brewer, 361 F. Supp. 537, 540 (S.D. Iowa 1973).

[452]Malnak v. Yogi, *id.,* 592 F.2d at 208. *See also* Thomas v. Review Board of Indiana Employment Sec., 450 U.S. 707, 101 S.Ct. 1425 (1981).

[453]Africa v. Comm. of Pa., 662 F.2d 1025 (3d Cir. 1981), *aff'd,* Africa v. State of Pennsylvania, 520 F. Supp. 967, 970 (E.D. Pa. 1981). *See also* Malnak v. Yogi, 592 F.2d 197 (3d Cir. 1979); Dreibelbis v. Marks, 675 F.2d 579, 582 (3d Cir. 1982).

[454]Africa v. Comm. of Pa., *id.* at 1032-33.

[455]*See* Wisconsin v. Yoder, 406 U.S. 205, 216, 92 S.Ct. 1526 (1972 (dictum).

[456]Africa v. Comm. of Pa., *supra* note 453, at 1035-36.

[457]Loney v. Scurr, 474 F. Supp. 1186, 1195-96 (S.D. Iowa 1979).

[458]Malnak v. Yogi, *supra* note 453, at 209. *See also* Stevens v. Berger, 428 F. Supp. 896, 900 (E.D.N.Y. 1977). These are signs of a religion but are not absolutely required for a set of ideas to be classified as a religion.

[459]Thomas v. Review Board, Indiana Employment Security Division, 450 U.S. 707, 715-16, 101 S.Ct. 1425 (1981) ("Intrafaith differences . . . are not uncommon among followers of a particular creed, and the judicial process is singularly ill equipped to resolve such differences in relation to the Religion

Moskowitz v. Wilkinson,[460] where a Jewish prisoner challenged a no-beard policy, the court held:

> It cannot be denied that different levels of observance exist among the world's Jews. But the fact that some Jews do not object to shaving, or that others accept the distinction between shaving and cutting, does not defeat the plaintiff's claim. It is his own religious belief that is asserted, not anyone else's. The Court need not and should not attempt to determine whether a religious tribunal would hold that the tenets of the Jewish religion do not require petitioner to adhere to his preferred level of observance. He need not show that his religious practice is absolutely mandated in order to receive constitutional protection.[461]

Nor are your beliefs non-religious because you are "struggling" with your position or because your beliefs "are not articulated with the clarity and precision that a more sophisticated person might employ."[462]

Once the court has determined that your beliefs are religious in nature, it will apply one of the constitutional tests to determine what protection you are entitled to.

c.   Legal Standards

In deciding religious restriction cases, the courts have stated the constitutional standard for the free exercise of religion in several ways. Most have stated that restrictions will be upheld "only when [they] serve an important governmental objective and 'the restraint on religious liberty is reasonably adapted to achieving that objective' ";[463] that restrictions must be "reasonably and substantially justified by considerations of prison discipline and order" and "in a form substantially warranted by the requirements of prison safety and order";[464] or that they "arise[] from a compelling state interest in prison security, discipline, or admin-

---

Clauses. . . . [T]he guarantee is not limited to beliefs which are shared by all of the members of a religious sect.").

[460]432 F. Supp. 947 (D. Conn. 1977).

[461]*Id.* at 949. *See also* Teterud v. Gillman, 385 F. Supp. 153 (S.D. Iowa 1974), *aff'd sub nom.* Teterud v. Burns, 522 F.2d 357 (8th Cir. 1974); Monroe v. Bombard, 422 F. Supp. 211, 215 n.4 (S.D.N.Y. 1976).

[462]Thomas v. Review Board, Indiana Employment Security Division, *supra* note 459, at 715.

[463]Moorish Science Temple of America, Inc. v. Smith, 693 F.2d 987, 990 (2d Cir. 1982) (citation omitted).

[464]Gallahan v. Hollyfield, 670 F.2d 1345, 1346 (4th Cir. 1982) (citation omitted).

istration and [are] among the least restrictive means reasonably available to prison officials."[465] However the standard is stated, it involves two aspects: balancing prison officials' interests against the prisoner's interest in freely practicing his/her religion, and determining whether the restriction is broader than necessary to serve those interests.

In *Sweet v. South Carolina Dept. of Corrections,*[466] a prisoner in segregation for his own protection sought to attend congregate chapel religious services. The court found that the prison's interest in security outweighed the prisoner's interest in attending congregate religious services.[467] In other cases, the courts have found that prisoners' religious interest in growing beards outweighed prison officials' alleged security interest in ease of identification,[468] and that Muslims' interest in being free of the requirement of using their "slave names" outweighed the interest in administrative convenience asserted by prison officials.[469]

Even if the prison officials have cited weighty correctional interests, the court will examine the methods they use to serve those interests and determine whether there exist any other methods not as restrictive. In *Weaver v. Jago,*[470] the court held that prison officials had to offer more than a conclusory statement that short hair was required to aid identification, security, hygiene, and safety of prisoners. The court found that the least restrictive alternative for prison officials was to require that long hair be kept clean, require that it be pulled back in a ponytail, and search the hair for contraband, as done in regular prisoner searches.

Some courts have recently taken a more restrictive view of prisoners' religious rights, holding that they must defer to prison officials' discretion whenever a conflict arises between religious interest and security. In *St. Claire v. Cuyler,*[471] the court held that prison officials' sincere belief that the wearing of a religious head piece in the dining area could cause security problems required the district court to defer to their judgment unless the prisoner could prove by "substantial evidence that the officials' security concerns are unreasonable or their response

---

[465]Chapman v. Pickett, 491 F. Supp. 967, 971 (C.D. Ill. 1980).

[466]529 F.2d 854 (4th Cir. 1975).

[467]*Id.* at 861.

[468]Wright v. Raines, 457 F. Supp. 1082 (D. Kan. 1978).

[469]Masjid Muhammad-D.C.C. v. Keve, 479 F. Supp. 1311, 1322-24 (D. Del. 1979).

[470]675 F.2d 116 (6th Cir. 1982). *Accord,* Gallahan v. Hollyfield, 670 F.2d 1345 (4th Cir. 1982).

[471]634 F.2d 109, 114 n.8 (3d Cir. 1980), *reh'g denied,* 643 F.2d 103 (3d Cir. 1980) (Adams, J., dissenting).

exaggerated.''[472] This approach does away with the balancing test and the requirement of the least restrictive alternative, and places the burden of proof on the prisoner as soon as prison officials produce any evidence that there is even a potential danger to security.[473] However, even under this standard, if prison officials have sought to restrict your religious interest for some other reason than security, such as discipline or rehabilitation, the court will still balance your religious interest against prison officials' concerns and look to the least restrictive alternative.[474]

You are entitled to equal protection of the law with respect to religious freedom. (See Sec. D, *infra,* for a more detailed discussion of equal protection.) In *Walker v. Blackwell,*[475] the court held that Muslims were entitled to receive religious publications "in the same manner that other newspapers are allowed to other inmates."[476] The court, in *Cochran v. Rowe,*[477] also held that different religions had to be treated similarly. It required that Muslim clergy be compensated as other clergy, and that prison funds allocated for religious purposes had to be distributed proportionately to all religious groups.[478]

There are limits to the requirement of equal treatment. The Supreme Court stated, "We do not suggest . . . that every religious sect or group within a prison—however few in number—must have identical facilities or personnel. A special chapel or place of worship need not be provided for every faith regardless of size, nor must a chaplain, priest, or minister be provided without regard to the extent of the demand."[479] However,

---

[472]*Id.* at 116.

[473]*Id.* at 114, 116. *See also* Rogers v. Scurr, 676 F.2d 1211, 1215 (8th Cir. 1982) (no balancing required when issue of security is raised by prison officials); Otey v. Best, 680 F.2d 1231 (8th Cir. 1982) (prison officials need only produce some evidence of a danger to prison security); Aziz v. LeFevre, 642 F.2d 1109, 1112 (2d Cir. 1981) (Meskill, J., concurring) (plaintiff has burden of showing restriction is unreasonable; prison officials need not show it is "least restrictive means"); Furqan v. Georgia State Board of Offender Rehabilitation, 554 F. Supp. 873 (N.D. Ga. 1982) (rational basis test, not least restrictive means, governs challenge to prohibition on beards).

[474]St. Claire v. Cuyler, *supra* note 471, 634 F.2d at 114 n.8.

[475]411 F.2d 23 (5th Cir. 1969).

[476]*Id.* at 29.

[477]438 F. Supp. 566 (N.D. Ill. 1977).

[478]*See also* Native American Council of Tribes v. Solem, 691 F.2d 382 (8th Cir. 1982) (claim that Christians were permitted to have guests at their religious ceremonies but Native Americans were not stated an equal protection violation).

[479]Cruz v. Beto, 405 U.S. 319, 322 n.2, 92 S.Ct. 1079 (1972).

any substantial inequality of treatment states a claim of denial of equal protection and will require prison officials to justify the inequality.[480]

d. Practices

The courts have ruled on a wide variety of religious practices. We discuss the major categories of decisions in this section.

1) Religious Services and Leaders

Religion has been recognized as serving a rehabilitative function for prisoners by providing "an area within which the inmate may reclaim his dignity and reassert his individuality."[481] Every religion need not be provided by prison officials with a special place to worship,[482] nor an individual chaplain, priest, or minister.[483] You only need to be provided a reasonable opportunity in a non-discriminatory manner to practice your beliefs comparably to fellow prisoners who adhere to conventional religions.[484] A prison will often have only one religious person in charge of the prison church in which s/he will serve the religious needs of as many religions as there are organized religious groups in the prison. In providing religious leaders for other religions, prison officials will either contract with outside organizations or seek volunteers.[485] However, a prison system that allocates funds for religious purposes must allocate these funds proportionately to the membership of each religious group.[486]

---

[480]Moorish Science Temple of America, Inc. v. Smith, 693 F.2d 987, 990 (2d Cir. 1982).

[481]Barnett v. Rodgers, 410 F.2d 995 (D.C. Cir. 1969); Cochran v. Rowe, 438 F. Supp. 566, 570 (N.D. Ill. 1977).

[482]Mathes v. Carlson, 534 F. Supp. 226, 227 (W.D. Mo. 1982), *quoting from* Cruz v. Beto, 405 U.S. 319, 322 n.2, 92 S.Ct. 1079 (1972). *See also* Jones v. Bradley, 590 F.2d 294 (9th Cir. 1979).

[483]Mathes v. Carlson, *id. See also* Glasshofer v. Thornburgh, 514 F. Supp. 1242 (E.D. Pa. 1981) (no Jewish Chaplain on staff).

[484]*See* Cruz v. Beto, 405 U.S. 319, 322 n.2, 92 S.Ct. 1079 (1972); Finney v. Hutto, 410 F. Supp. 251 (E.D. Ark. 1976). See also Sec. D, *infra,* for a discussion of equal protection.

[485]*See* St. Claire v. Cuyler, 481 F. Supp. 732, 736 n.5 (E.D. Pa. 1979), *rev'd on other grounds,* 634 F.2d 109 (3d Cir. 1980). *See also* Cochran v. Rowe, *supra* note 481 (Muslim clergy should be compensated in a like manner as other clergy); Northern v. Nelson, 315 F. Supp. 687, 688 (N.D. Cal. 1970), *aff'd,* 448 F.2d 1266 (9th Cir. 1971) (same).

[486]*See* Cochran v. Rowe, *id. See also* Pitts v. Knowles, 339 F. Supp. 1183 (W.D. Wisc. 1972), *aff'd,* 478 F.2d 1405 (7th Cir. 1973).

Prisoners confined in segregation do not have a right to attend religious services in a chapel.[487] While in segregation, you have a right to see an outside religious leader,[488] but not a prisoner religious leader.[489] Your First Amendment rights can also be violated if you are confined in segregation and prison officials allow a religious leader to enter segregation and preach so that all prisoners can hear it even if they do not want to.[490] Death row prisoners do not have a right to attend chapel services, but must be allowed visits with religious leaders, religious literature, and religious dietary meals.[491]

You have a right to correspond with an outside religious leader.[492] One court has implied that religious reports could not be the basis of a parole eligibility decision.[493] A prisoner may be the minister of a religious group, but this does not entitle him/her to perform marriages,[494] receive payment as a minister,[495] or to attend to the religious needs of those confined in segregation.[496] Prison officials may deny visits to a former prisoner who had been a religious leader while confined.[497] Congregate religious services may be curtailed during an emergency or lockdown.[498]

Native American prisoners have been allowed access to traditional spiritual leaders on a group or individual basis and access to religious paraphernalia, such as gourds, beads, feathers, drums, literature, and sweat lodge.[499] Other courts have split over whether a prisoner has a

---

[487]Sweet v. South Carolina Dept. of Corrections, 529 F.2d 854, 865 (4th Cir. 1975), and cases cited. See also St. Claire v. Cuyler, 634 F.2d 109 (3d Cir. 1980).

[488]See Wojtczak v. Cuyler, 480 F. Supp. 1288 (E.D. Pa. 1979); Finney v. Hutto, 410 F. Supp. 251, 281 (E.D. Ark. 1976), rev'd in part on other grounds, 548 F.2d 740 (8th Cir. 1977); Knuckles v. Prasse, 302 F. Supp. 1036 (E.D. Pa. 1969), aff'd, 435 F.2d 1255 (3d Cir. 1970), cert. denied, 403 U.S. 936 (1971).

[489]Sweet, supra note 487, at 865-66.

[490]Campbell v. Cauthron, 623 F.2d 503 (8th Cir. 1980).

[491]Otey v. Best, 680 F.2d 1231 (8th Cir. 1982).

[492]See Walker v. Blackwell, 411 F.2d 23 (5th Cir. 1969).

[493]Remmers v. Brewer, 494 F.2d 1277, 1278 (8th Cir. 1974), cert. denied, 419 U.S. 1012 (1974).

[494]See Jones v. Bradley, 590 F.2d 294 (9th Cir. 1979).

[495]See Green v. White, 525 F. Supp. 81 (E.D. Mo. 1981).

[496]See supra note 489.

[497]Alim v. Byrne, 521 F. Supp. 1039 (D.N.J. 1980).

[498]Id. See also Sec. C9, infra, for a discussion of prison emergencies and lockdowns.

[499]See Battle v. Anderson, 457 F. Supp. 719, 738 (E.D. Okla. 1978), aff'd on other grounds, 594 F.2d 786 (10th Cir. 1979).

religious right to have candles and incense for use in his/her cell.[500]

Prisoners have no First Amendment right to hold a banquet to celebrate their religion.[501] If prison officials allow one of the other religious groups to have a banquet but deny yours, the Equal Protection Clause may have been violated (see Sec. D, *infra*, for a discussion of equal protection). Some courts have upheld prison regulations precluding the wearing of religious head pieces outside of religious services.[502]

2) Dietary Needs

Prison officials must make reasonable accommodation to meet the dietary needs of its religious prisoners. The Bureau of Prisons is required to provide Orthodox Jews with kosher diets.[503] Muslims are also entitled to receive a no-pork diet.[504] They may be required to select from the regular prison menu if doing so, after rejecting pork items, will provide a nutritionally adequate diet; in such a case, they must be informed as to which items contain pork.[505] The utensils used in preparing non-pork diets need not be rigidly segregated from pork items as long as they are cleaned sufficiently before being used to cook items consumed by those who do not eat pork.[506]

---

[500]Compare Childs v. Duckworth, 509 F. Supp. 1254 (N.D. Ind. 1980) with Kennedy v. Meachum, 540 F.2d 1057 (10th Cir. 1976) (court remanded for hearing whether members of Satanic religion had right to possess candles, robes, incense, gong, etc., in cell).

[501]*See* Glasshofer v. Thornburgh, 514 F. Supp. 1242 (E.D. Pa. 1981).

[502]St. Claire v. Cuyler, 634 F.2d 109 (3d Cir. 1980). *But see* Burgin v. Henderson, 536 F.2d 501, 504 (2d Cir. 1976) (court held a factual record was necessary to determine "whether a rule barring all hats—of whatever size, style, or religious significance—is necessary to prevent hiding weapons").

[503]Kahane v. Carlson, 527 F.2d 492 (2d Cir. 1975). *See also* Schlesinger v. Carlson, 489 F. Supp. 612 (M.D. Pa. 1980) (Hasidic Jew entitled to special cooking facilities).

[504]Masjid Muhammad-D.C.C. v. Keve, 479 F. Supp. 1311, 1319 (D. Del. 1979). *See also* Ross v. Blackledge, 477 F.2d 616, 618-19 (4th Cir. 1972); Alim v. Byrne, 521 F. Supp. 1029 (D.N.J. 1980) (prison officials required to provide pork substitute at meals); Bryant v. McGinnis, 463 F. Supp. 373 (W.D.N.Y. 1978); United States ex rel. Wolfish v. Levi, *supra* note 147, 439 F. Supp. at 129.

[505]Battle v. Anderson, 376 F. Supp. 402 (E.D. Okla. 1974). *See also* Bryant v. McGinnis, 463 F. Supp. 373 (W.D.N.Y. 1978); Barnes v. Virgin Islands, 415 F. Supp. 1218 (D.V.I. 1976).

[506]Masjid Muhammad-D.C.C. v. Keve, *supra* note 504.

Prison officials cannot punish Muslim prisoners for refusing to handle pork items.[507]

3) Religious Literature

Prisoners have a constitutional right to receive religious materials from outside sources,[508] whether confined in general population or segregation.[509] You also have a right to communicate with your spiritual advisor on the outside; however, there is no right to communicate with a prisoner spiritual leader.[510]

4) Hair and Beards

If your religious tenets or beliefs require you to wear long hair or beard, you usually may do so.[511] Courts have generally rejected prison officials' arguments that a no-beard or long hair rule is required for effective identification and to ensure prison security and to facilitate apprehension of escape prisoners.[512]

Prison officials have a right to require that you be repeatedly photographed with any changes in the length of your hair and beard; submit to hair and beard searches; and, due to prison officials' claim of security, you may be required to cut your hair when you are first incarcerated so that a picture can be obtained of you with short hair.

---

[507]Chapman v. Pickett, 491 F. Supp. 967 (C.D. Ill. 1980). *See also* Kenner v. Phelps, 605 F.2d 850 (5th Cir. 1979) (per curiam) (reversed dismissal of complaint alleging punishment of Muslim prisoner for refusal to handle pork).

[508]*See* Africa v. State of Pennsylvania, 520 F. Supp. 967, 970 (E.D. Pa. 1981), *aff'd on other grounds,* 662 F.2d 1025 (3d Cir. 1981), *cert. denied,* 102 S.Ct. 1756 (1982); Parnell v. Waldrep, 511 F. Supp. 764 (W.D.N.C. 1981); Rowland v. Jones, 327 F. Supp. 821 (D. Neb. 1971), *aff'd,* 452 F.2d 1005 (8th Cir. 1971). See Sec. C1b, *supra,* for a general discussion of the right to receive publications.

[509]*See* Rudolph v. Locke, 594 F.2d 1076 (5th Cir. 1979).

[510]*See* Neal v. Georgia, 469 F.2d 446, 450 (5th Cir. 1972).

[511]Wright v. Raines, 457 F. Supp. 1082 (D. Kan. 1978); Moskowitz v. Wilkinson, 432 F. Supp. 947 (D. Conn. 1977). You have no constitutional right to grow long hair or a beard for reasons of personal appearance, see Sec. C5, *supra.*

[512]*See* Teterud v. Burns, 522 F.2d 357 (8th Cir. 1975); Gallahan v. Hollyfield, 516 F. Supp. 1004 (E.D. Va. 1981), *aff'd,* 670 F.2d 1345 (4th Cir. 1982); Moskowitz v. Wilkinson, *id.* at 950. *Contra,* Furqan v. Georgia State Board of Offender Rehabilitation, 554 F. Supp. 873 (N.D. Ga. 1982).

5) Name

A prisoner may adopt a religious name and prison officials may not require the prisoner to identify him/herself by a prior name.[513] Prison officials can not refuse to deliver mail addressed to you provided that you have notified the mailroom of your religious name change and your incoming mail has your prison number on it.[514] However, prison officials cannot be mandated to address you by your religious name, and they need not go through all your prison records and change these to reflect your religious name, such as court commitment papers.[515] If you refuse to obey an order given by a prison official when s/he has used your non-religious name, a disciplinary action taken against you for disobeying a direct order would be upheld by the courts.[516]

8.   Segregation: Punitive, Administrative, and Protective

Prison officials may place you in a segregated housing unit to punish you for misconduct (punitive segregation), to prevent you from committing future misconduct or otherwise threatening security (administrative segregation), or to protect you from harm by other prisoners (protective custody). The procedural requirements for placement in segregation are discussed in Sec. B2b and c, *supra*. The courts have also imposed some limits on the reasons for which prisoners may be segregated, the length of time they may be segregated, and the conditions of segregation units.

In *Hutto v. Finney*,[517] the Supreme Court upheld a 30-day limit on confinement in "isolation"; however, the Court did so largely because of the extremely bad conditions of confinement.[518] When conditions are not so bad, the courts have been unwilling to impose any set limit on time spent in segregation.[519] In a specific case, a court may find that a term of

---

[513]Barrett v. Commonwealth of Virginia, 689 F.2d 498 (4th Cir. 1982); Masjid Muhammad-D.C.C. v. Keve, 479 F. Supp. 1311 (D. Del. 1979).

[514]Masjid Muhammad-D.C.C. v. Keve, *supra* note 513, at 1322-24.

[515]Barrett v. Commonwealth of Virginia, *supra* note 513; Imam Ali Abdullah Adba v. Cannery, 634 F.2d 339 (6th Cir. 1980).

[516]Masjid Muhammad-D.C.C. v. Keve, *supra* note 513, at 1322-24.

[517]437 U.S. 678, 98 S.Ct. 2565 (1978).

[518]*Id.* at 686-87; *accord,* Pugh v. Locke, 406 F. Supp. 318, 327-28, 332-33 (M.D. Ala. 1976), *aff'd as modified sub nom.* Newman v. Alabama, 559 F.2d 283 (5th Cir. 1977), *cert. denied sub nom.* Alabama v. Pugh, 438 U.S. 913 (1978); Berch v. Stahl, 373 F. Supp. 412 (W.D.N.C. 1974).

[519]Sostre v. McGinnis, 442 F.2d 178, 192-93 (2d Cir. 1971), *cert. denied sub*

segregation is so disproportionate to the prisoner's offense that the Eighth Amendment is violated.[520] Disparities in punishment are generally not unlawful,[521] unless there is a pattern of them that is completely irrational.[522]

Some courts have placed limits on prison officials' discretion to place prisoners in administrative segregation.[523] However, a recent Supreme Court decision indicating that prison officials may rely on "rumor," "subjective evaluations," and "intuitive judgments" in segregating prisoners casts doubt on these cases.[524] Administrative segregation for indefinite periods of time is not unconstitutional as long as there is continuing justification for it.[525] Prison officials are subject to limited procedural requirements for demonstrating this continuing justification. (See Sec. B2c, *supra*.)

With respect to conditions in segregation units, courts have often condemned conditions that are unsanitary, degrading, or unhealthful. However, conditions that are merely boring or restrictive have generally been upheld; one court stated, "Inactivity, lack of companionship, and a

---

nom. Sostre v. Oswald, 404 U.S. 1049 (1972), and Oswald v. Sostre, 405 U.S. 978 (1972).

[520]Adams v. Carlson, 368 F. Supp. 1050 (E.D. Ill.), *on remand from* 488 F.2d 619 (7th Cir. 1973) (sixteen months excessive for involvement in work stoppage); Fulwood v. Clemmer, 206 F. Supp. 370 (D.D.C. 1962) (two years too much for disruptive preaching); Black v. Brown, 524 F. Supp. 856 (N.D. Ill. 1981) (eighteen months too much for running in yard); Hardwick v. Ault, 447 F. Supp. 116, 127 (M.D. Ga. 1978) (indefinite segregation per se disproportionate). *But see* Rhodes v. Robinson, 612 F.2d 766 (3d Cir. 1979) (one month for threatening to kill another prisoner upheld); Glouser v. Parratt, 605 F.2d 419 (8th Cir. 1979) (30 days for possessing marijuana upheld).

[521]Phillips v. Gathright, 468 F. Supp. 1211 (W.D. Va. 1979).

[522]McCray v. Bennett, 467 F. Supp. 187 (M.D. Ala. 1978).

[523]Boudin v. Thomas, 533 F. Supp. 786 (S.D.N.Y. 1982) (conclusory evidence of security threats and notoriety of inmate inadequate justification); Brown v. Neagle, 486 F. Supp. 364 (S.D. W. Va. 1979) (past associations with escapees not enough).

[524]Hewitt v. Helms, __U.S.__, 103 S.Ct. 864, 872-73 (1983). *See also* Jones v. Marquez, 526 F. Supp. 871 (D. Kan. 1981) (where there appeared to be hidden weapons in the prison and plaintiffs were prisoner leaders, segregation was not arbitrary); Bukhari v. Hutto, 487 F. Supp. 1162 (E.D. Va. 1980) (past associations and prior escape justified segregation).

[525]Hewitt v. Helms, *id.* at 874 n.9; Bono v. Saxbe, 620 F.2d 609, 619 (7th Cir. 1980); Morris v. Travisono, 549 F. Supp. 291 (D.R.I. 1982) (refusing to stand up in court and sleeping at wrong end of bed did not justify continuing segregation after eight and a half years); Brown v. Neagle, 486 F. Supp. 364 (S.D. W. Va. 1979).

low level of intellectual stimulation do not constitute cruel and unusual punishment even if they continue for an indefinite length of time."[526] (Some courts have taken a slightly more liberal view toward protective custody prisoners. See *infra*.)

The courts have most consistently ruled in prisoners' favor in cases of "strip cell" confinement involving deprivation of clothing, washing and toilet facilities, and proper bedding.[527] Some courts have held even these conditions permissible for short periods of time or based on strong justification.[528] Absence of light and ventilation and poor sanitation have been condemned.[529] At least minimal opportunities for exercise are required.[530] Segregated prisoners must receive adequate food,[531] although cold food or a monotonous diet do not violate the Constitution.[532]

The courts have been less consistently protective of other rights and amenities. Restrictions on reading matter and correspondence have met with varying judicial responses.[533] Restrictions on visiting that do not

---

[526]Bono v. Saxbe, *id.* at 614.

[527]Maxwell v. Mason, 668 F.2d 361 (8th Cir. 1981); McCray v. Burrell, 622 F.2d 705 (4th Cir. 1980); Kimbrough v. O'Neil, 523 F.2d 1057 (7th Cir. 1975); LaReau v. MacDougall, 473 F.2d 974, 978 n.7 (2d Cir. 1972), and cases cited; Wright v. McMann, 460 F.2d 126 (2d Cir. 1972); O'Connor v. Keller, 510 F. Supp. 1359 (D. Md. 1981); Flakes v. Percy, 511 F. Supp. 1325, 1329 (W.D. Wisc. 1981); Strachan v. Ashe, 548 F. Supp. 1193 (D. Mass. 1982).

[528]Hawkins v. Hall, 644 F.2d 914 (1st Cir. 1981); McMahon v. Beard, 583 F.2d 172 (5th Cir. 1978); Owen v. Heyne, 473 F. Supp. 345 (N.D. Ind. 1978).

[529]Hutto v. Finney, *supra* note 517, at 686-87; Bono v. Saxbe, *supra* note 525, at 615 (inadequate lighting); Kirby v. Blackledge, 530 F.2d 583 (4th Cir. 1976) (lack of sanitation and ventilation); Imprisoned Citizens Union v. Shapp, 451 F. Supp. 893 (E.D. Pa. 1978) (absence of light); Hancock v. Avery, 301 F. Supp. 786 (M.D. Tenn. 1969) (absence of light and ventilation).

[530]Spain v. Procunier, 600 F.2d 189 (9th Cir. 1979) (five hours a week for long-term segregated prisoners); Dorrough v. Hogan, 563 F.2d 1259 (5th Cir. 1977) (two hours a week); Grubbs v. Bradley, 552 F. Supp. 1052, 1130-31 (M.D. Tenn. 1982) (confinement without recreation limited to three days); Bono v. Saxbe, 462 F. Supp. 146 (E.D. Ill. 1978), *aff'd in part and remanded in part on other grounds,* 620 F.2d 609 (7th Cir. 1980) (seven hours a week); Frazier v. Ward, 426 F. Supp. 1354 (N.D.N.Y. 1977) (five hours a week).

[531]Hutto v. Finney, *supra* note 517, at 683, 686-87; Cunningham v. Jones, 567 F.2d 653 (6th Cir. 1977); Moss v. Ward, 450 F. Supp. 591 (W.D.N.Y. 1978).

[532]Bono v. Saxbe, *supra* note 525, at 613; Dorrough v. Hogan, *supra* note 530.

[533]*Compare* Hardwick v. Ault, 447 F. Supp. 116, 128-31 (M.D. Ga. 1978) (mail and reading matter restrictions unconstitutional), *with* Johnson v. Anderson, 370 F. Supp. 1373, 1391-94 (D. Del. 1974) (deprivation of reading matter permissible).

amount to a complete denial of visits are usually upheld.[534] Segregated prisoners generally need not be permitted to go to the law library as long as some other provision is made for their access to courts.[535] Physical restraints may be used when segregated prisoners are out of their cells,[536] though some courts have limited their use.[537] The courts have divided as to the religious rights of segregated prisoners; some have held that these prisoners need not be permitted to attend religious services,[538] while others have held that at least this decision must be made on a case-by-case basis.[539] Limits on possession of personal property are generally upheld.[540] The courts have differed as to the legality of intrusive search procedures in segregated units.[541] Lack of program opportunities in segregation does not violate the Constitution.[542]

In evaluating protective custody conditions, most courts have made rulings similar to those in administrative or punitive segregation cases.[543] Although courts have rejected the notion that a prisoner who enters protective custody by choice cannot complain of the conditions,[544] they have not required that protective custody prisoners be treated much better than prisoners who are being punished. However, one court has

---

[534]Bono v. Saxbe, *supra* note 525, at 613; Griffin v. Smith, 493 F. Supp. 129 (W.D.N.Y. 1980); Dorrough v. Mullikin, 563 F.2d 187 (5th Cir. 1977); *contra,* Hardwick v. Ault, *id.* at 131 (visiting must be adapted to individual circumstances).

[535]See Sec. C4a, *supra.*

[536]Fulford v. King, 692 F.2d 11 (5th Cir. 1982); Freeman v. Trudell, 497 F. Supp. 481 (E.D. Mich. 1980).

[537]Spain v. Procunier, 600 F.2d 189 (9th Cir. 1979); Hardwick v. Ault, *supra* note 533, at 127.

[538]St. Claire v. Cuyler, 634 F.2d 109 (3d Cir. 1980); McGruder v. Phelps, 608 F.2d 1023 (5th Cir. 1979); McDonald v. Hall, 579 F.2d 120 (1st Cir. 1978).

[539]Mawhinney v. Henderson, 542 F.2d 1 (2d Cir. 1976); Stewart v. Gates, 450 F. Supp. 583 (C.D. Cal. 1978).

[540]Bono v. Saxbe, *supra* note 525, at 613.

[541]See cases cited in note 409, *supra.*

[542]McGruder v. Phelps, 608 F.2d 1023 (5th Cir. 1979).

[543]Nadeau v. Helgemoe, 561 F.2d 411 (1st Cir. 1977); Little v. Walker, 552 F.2d 193 (7th Cir. 1977); Sweet v. South Carolina Dept. of Corrections, 529 F.2d 854 (4th Cir. 1975) (more exercise opportunities and showers might be required; escort to religious services not required); M.C.I. Concord Advisory Board v. Hall, 447 F. Supp. 398 (D. Mass. 1978); Battle v. Anderson, 457 F. Supp. 719, 738 (E.D. Okla. 1978).

[544]Little v. Walker, *id.* at 197; Rudolph v. Locke, 594 F.2d 1076, 1078 (5th Cir. 1979); M.C.I. Concord Advisory Board v. Hall, *id.* at 401.

held that excessive restrictions in protective custody can amount to "unconstitutional conditions" on the exercise of the Eighth Amendment right to be protected from harm.[545] The prison was therefore required to make the plaintiff's conditions of confinement more like those of the general population within the limits of security, by providing a chair and educational programs in his cell.[546]

State statutes and regulations may provide more favorable legal standards for protective custody and other segregated prisoners. These may be asserted in state court or via the pendent jurisdiction of the federal courts.[547]

9. Prison Emergencies and Lockdowns

Under the Eighth Amendment,

> [W]hen a genuine emergency exists, prison officials may be more restrictive than they otherwise may be, and certain services may be suspended temporarily. The more basic the particular need, the shorter the time it can be withheld. It is doubtful, for example, that any circumstance would permit a denial of access to emergency medical care. Less critical needs may be denied, however, for reasonable periods of time when disciplinary needs warrant.[548]

Thus, courts have generally upheld "lockdowns" and other emergency procedures involving major restrictions on religious activity, law library access, time limits on disciplinary proceedings, visiting, showers, exercise, laundry, routine medical services, programs, and sanitation.[549]

---

[545]Wojtczak v. Cuyler, 480 F. Supp. 1288, 1302-05 (E.D. Pa. 1979); *see also* Rudolph v. Locke, *id.* at 1078 ("It is the state's responsibility to protect prisoners, and while it may find it necessary to restrict their freedoms in certain ways in order to protect them, it cannot simply force them to choose between relinquishing their constitutional rights and jeopardizing their own lives.").

[546]Wojtczak v. Cuyler, *id.* at 1306-07.

[547]Williams v. Lane, 548 F. Supp. 927, 932 (N.D. Ill. 1982); Wojtczak v. Cuyler, *supra* note 545, at 1302. See Ch. VI, Sec. B3, for a discussion of pendent jurisdiction.

[548]Hoptowit v. Ray, 682 F.2d 1237, 1258 (9th Cir. 1982).

[549]Hayward v. Procunier, 629 F.2d 599 (9th Cir. 1980), *cert. denied,* 451 U.S. 937 (1981) (lockdown); Collins v. Ward, 544 F. Supp. 408 (S.D.N.Y. 1982) (mass transfers under restrictive conditions); Ponds v. Cuyler, 541 F. Supp. 291 (E.D. Pa. 1982) (suspension of time limits for disciplinary hearings); Jordan v. Robinson, 464 F. Supp. 223 (W.D. Pa. 1979) (lockup of all Muslim prisoners after conflicts among Muslims); Gray v. Levine, 455 F. Supp. 267 (D. Md. 1978) (lockdown). *But see* LaBatt v. Twomey, 513 F.2d 641, 649-51 (7th Cir. 1975) (allegation of denial of treatment of serious medical needs during "deadlock" should not have been dismissed).

The courts generally will not second-guess prison officials' decision that an emergency exists unless the officials are shown to have acted in bad faith or on a pretext.[550] However, prisoners have had some success in challenging the prolonged continuation of emergency measures. As one court stated, "[t]he unreviewable discretion of prison authorities in what they deem to be an emergency is not open-ended or time unlimited."[551] Thus, in *Preston v. Thompson*,[552] the court upheld a finding that three months after a riot, the emergency was over, and prison officials were required to provide showers and yard recreation.

One court has suggested that prisoners have due process rights to procedural protections if emergency restrictions continue for a long time.[553] Others have rejected this view.[554]

10. Physical Conditions and Restrictions

General living conditions for convicted prisoners are governed by the Eighth Amendment's prohibitions of "cruel and unusual punishments."[555] (Pretrial detainees may not be punished at all under the Due Process Clause;[556] while many pretrial cases are cited in this section, the standards governing detainees' rights are discussed in Sec. E, *infra*.)

The Supreme Court recently held that prison conditions *"alone or in combination,* may deprive inmates of the minimal civilized measure of life's necessities."[557] This and previous holdings[558] are consistent with the "totality of the circumstances" approach used in most large-scale, multi-issue prison litigation.[559]

---

[550]Collins v. Ward, *id.* at 412, and cases cited.

[551]Hoitt v. Vitek, 497 F.2d 598, 600 (1st Cir. 1974).

[552]589 F.2d 300 (7th Cir. 1978); *accord,* Jefferson v. Southworth, 447 F. Supp. 179 (D.R.I. 1978); Walker v. Johnson, 544 F. Supp. 345 (E.D. Mich. 1982); *contra,* Hayward v. Procunier, *supra* note 549.

[553]LaBatt v. Twomey, *supra* note 549, at 646-47.

[554]Hayward v. Procunier, *supra* note 549; Saunders v. Packel, 436 F. Supp. 618, 624-25 (E.D. Pa. 1977).

[555]U.S. Const., Amend. VIII.

[556]Bell v. Wolfish, 441 U.S. 520, 99 S.Ct. 1861 (1979).

[557]Rhodes v. Chapman, 452 U.S. 337, 101 S.Ct. 2392, 2399 (1981) (emphasis added).

[558]Hutto v. Finney, 437 U.S. 678, 687, 98 S.Ct. 2565 (1978) ("We find no error in the court's conclusion that *taken as a whole* conditions in the isolation cells continued to violate the prohibition against cruel and unusual punishment.") (emphasis supplied).

[559]*See, e.g.,* Ruiz v. Estelle, 679 F.2d 1115 (5th Cir. 1982); Ramos v. Lamm,

As a *pro se* litigant, you should not try to litigate a "totality of conditions" case unless it involves grotesquely and obviously bad conditions in a small part of the prison. Justice Brennan has stated that in a totality case, the trial court must

> examine the effect upon inmates of the condition of the physical plant (lighting, heat, plumbing, ventilation, living space, noise levels, recreation space); sanitation (control of vermin and insects, food preparation, medical facilities, lavatories and showers, clean places for eating, sleeping, and working); safety (protection from violent, deranged, or diseased inmates, fire protection, emergency evacuation); inmate needs and services (clothing, nutrition, bedding, medical, dental, and mental health care, visitation time, exercise and recreation, educational and rehabilitative programming); and staffing (trained and adequate guards and other staff, avoidance of placing inmates in positions of authority over other inmates).[560]

This is a task that requires massive proof, numerous expert witnesses, years of discovery, etc., which are beyond the capabilities of a *pro se* litigant. (In fact, all the major totality cases have required several attorneys.) If you file a totality case *pro se,* you should do so with the hope and intention of obtaining counsel.

The Eighth Amendment standard that is applied both in totality and in single-issue cases is a difficult one to meet. Prison conditions that are "restrictive and even harsh are part of the penalty that criminal offenders pay for their offenses against society."[561] To violate the Eighth Amendment, conditions must "involve the wanton and unnecessary infliction of pain" or be "grossly disproportionate to the severity of the crime warranting imprisonment."[562] One court held that the Eighth Amendment required only that the state provide "reasonably adequate food, clothing, shelter, sanitation, medical care, and personal safety."[563] In applying these standards, courts will take into account the length of time one is subjected to the challenged conditions.[564]

---

639 F.2d 559 (10th Cir. 1980), *cert. denied,* 450 U.S. 1041 (1981); French v. Owens, 538 F. Supp. 910 (S.D. Ind. 1982); Burks v. Walsh, 461 F. Supp. 454 (W.D. Mo. 1978), *aff'd sub nom.* Burks v. Teasdale, 603 F.2d 59 (8th Cir. 1979); Glover v. Johnson, 478 F. Supp. 1075 (E.D. Mich. 1979); Palmigiano v. Garrahy, 443 F. Supp. 956 (D.R.I. 1977); Laaman v. Helgemoe, 437 F. Supp. 269 (D.N.H. 1977). One federal circuit continues to reject this view of the law. Hoptowit v. Ray, 682 F.2d 1237, 1246 (9th Cir. 1982).

[560]Rhodes v. Chapman, *supra* note 558, 101 S.Ct. at 2408 (citations omitted).

[561]*Id.* at 2399.

[562]*Id.*

[563]Newman v. Alabama, 559 F.2d 283, 291 (5th Cir.), *cert denied sub nom.* Alabama v. Pugh, 438 U.S. 915 (1978).

[564]Hutto v. Finney, *supra* note 558, at 685-86.

a.   Crowding

In *Rhodes v. Chapman*,[565] the Supreme Court held that prison overcrowding—in that case, double-celling in 63-square foot cells designed for single occupancy—was not per se unconstitutional where the prison was a modern facility in good condition in which "the prisoners [were] adequately sheltered, fed, and protected, and . . . opportunities for education, work, and rehabilitation assistance [were] available."[566] Similarly, the Ninth Circuit held that overcrowding could not be enjoined based solely on square footage; the court must consider the consequences of crowding, such as violence and excessive in-cell time.[567] The Fifth Circuit upheld a finding of unconstitutional overcrowding because it was shown to be related to violence, understaffing, and in-cell time.[568] This approach is typical of recent overcrowding decisions.[569] The trade-off between space and in-cell time is made even clearer in *Hendrix v. Faulkner*,[570] which held that *single*-celling in 37-square-foot cells was unacceptable in connection with 23½ hours a day of lock-in time. (For a discussion of crowding in pretrial detention facilities, see Sec. E, *infra*.)

b.   Furnishings

The courts have had little to say about the furnishings of cells and dormitories. However, several courts have held that the use of mattresses on the floor for sleeping violates the Eighth Amendment or due process.[571] Courts have also limited the use of "strip cells." (See Sec. C8, *supra*, for a discussion of strip cells.)

---

[565]*Supra* note 557.

[566]*Id.* at 101 S.Ct. at 2409 (Brennan, J., concurring).

[567]Hoptowit v. Ray, 682 F.2d 1237, 1248-49 (9th Cir. 1982).

[568]Ruiz v. Estelle, 679 F.2d 1115, 1140-42 (5th Cir. 1982).

[569]*See, e.g.,* Campbell v. McGruder, 554 F. Supp. 562 (D.D.C. 1982); Grubbs v. Bradley, 552 F. Supp. 1052, 1125-27 (M.D. Tenn. 1982); Finney v. Mabry, 534 F. Supp. 1026 (E.D. Ark. 1982) (overcrowding in "barracks" unconstitutional because it made effective surveillance impossible).

[570]525 F. Supp. 435 (N.D. Ind. 1981). *See also* Campbell v. Cauthron, 623 F.2d 503 (8th Cir. 1980) (degree of crowding permitted depends on out-of-cell time); Lock v. Jenkins, 641 F.2d 488 (7th Cir. 1981) (for pretrial detainees held in state prison, 22 hours a day in 37-square foot cell constituted punishment; more out-of-cell time required). *But see* Smith v. Fairman, 690 F.2d 122 (7th Cir. 1982) (double celling upheld despite long lock-in periods).

[571]LaReau v. Manson, 651 F.2d 96 (2d Cir. 1981); Jones v. Diamond, 636 F.2d 1364 (5th Cir. 1981); Vazquez v. Gray, 523 F. Supp. 1359 (S.D.N.Y. 1981); Union County Jail Inmates v. Scanlon, 537 F. Supp. 993 (D.N.J. 1982).

c. Ventilation

Several courts have held that inadequate ventilation violates the Eighth Amendment or can contribute to a "totality" violation.[572] Others have rejected ventilation claims.[573]

d. Heating

Inadequate heating violates the Eighth Amendment,[574] although mere variations in temperature do not.[575]

e. Lighting

Inadequate lighting may violate the Eighth Amendment.[576]

f. Noise

Excessive noise may violate the Eighth Amendment.[577]

g. Dilapidation

Physical deterioration of the prison may violate the Eighth Amendment.[578]

---

[572]Blake v. Hall, 668 F.2d 52 (1st Cir. 1981); Jones v. Diamond, 636 F.2d 1364 (5th Cir. 1981); Jordan v. Arnold, 472 F. Supp. 265 (M.D. Pa. 1979); Ramos v. Lamm, 639 F.2d 559, 568 (10th Cir. 1980).

[573]Biancone v. Kramer, 513 F. Supp. 908 (E.D. Pa. 1981); Russell v. Eniser, 496 F. Supp. 320 (D.S.C. 1979); Nadeau v. Helgemoe, 423 F. Supp. 1250 (D.N.H. 1976).

[574]Smith v. Sullivan, 553 F.2d 373, 380-81 (5th Cir. 1977); Ramos v. Lamm, *supra* note 578, at 572; Bel v. Hall, 392 F. Supp. 274 (D. Mass. 1975).

[575]Burks v. Walsh, 461 F. Supp. 454 (W.D. Mo. 1978).

[576]Ramos v. Lamm, *supra* note 572, at 568; French v. Owens, 538 F. Supp. 910 (S.D. Ind. 1982); Battle v. Anderson, 447 F. Supp. 516, 524 (E.D. Okla. 1977); Baker v. Hamilton, 345 F. Supp. 345, 353 (W.D. Ky. 1972). *See also* Bono v. Saxbe, 620 F.2d 609 (7th Cir. 1980) (poor lighting condemned on due process theory); Rhem v. Malcolm, 371 F. Supp. 594, 627 (S.D. N.Y. 1974), *aff'd,* 507 F.2d 333 (2d Cir. 1974) (absence of transparent windows violated detainees' rights); Dillard v. Pitchess, 399 F. Supp. 1225, 1229, 1235 (C.D. Cal. 1975).

[577]Palmigiano v. Garrahy, 443 F. Supp. 956, 979 (D.R.I. 1977); Anderson v. Redman, 429 F. Supp. 1105, 1112 (D. Del 1977); *see also* Rhem v. Malcolm, *id.,* 371 F. Supp. at 627 (pretrial detention case).

[578]Grubbs v. Bradley, *supra* note 519, at 1125-27; Battle v. Anderson, 447 F.

h.   Fire Protection

Several courts have held that inadequate fire protection violates the Eighth Amendment.[579] One recent decision reversed an injunction concerning fire safety on the ground that no one had yet been killed or seriously injured by the defendants' practices.[580]

i.   Sanitation

Inadequate sanitation violates the Eighth Amendment, whether it involves defective plumbing,[581] infestation by vermin,[582] or lack of cleaning and garbage disposal.[583] It is no defense for prison officials to blame the conditions on the prisoners.[584] Failure to conform to non-prison standards is not necessarily unconstitutional.[585] However, you should consider asserting state or local sanitation code violations as pendent state claims.[586] (See Ch. VI, Sec. B3, for a discussion of pendent jurisdiction.)

j.   Programs

Courts have generally held that prisoners have no right to rehabili-

---

Supp. 516, 525 (E.D. Okla.), *aff'd,* 564 F.2d 388 (10th Cir. 1977); Gates v. Collier, 390 F. Supp. 482, 486, 489 (N.D. Miss. 1975).

[579]French v. Owens, 538 F. Supp. 910 (S.D. Ind. 1982); Battle v. Anderson, 447 F. Supp. 516 (E.D. Okla. 1977). *See also* Leeds v. Watson, 630 F.2d 674 (9th Cir. 1980); Watson v. McGee, 527 F. Supp. 234 (S.D. Ohio 1981); Dawson v. Kendrick, 527 F. Supp. 1252, 1292-94 (S.D. W. Va. 1981) (pretrial detention cases).

[580]Ruiz v. Estelle, *supra* note 568, at 1152-53. *Contra,* Dimarzo v. Cahill, 575 F.2d 15 (1st Cir. 1978) (pretrial detention case).

[581]Blake v. Hall, 668 F.2d 52 (1st Cir. 1981); Ramos v. Lamm, *supra* note 572, at 569; Brenneman v. Madigan, 343 F. Supp. 128, 133 (N.D. Cal. 1972).

[582]Palmigiano v. Garrahy, 443 F. Supp. 956, 961, 979 (D.R.I. 1977); Ramos v. Lamm, *supra* note 572, at 569; Tate v. Kassulke, 409 F. Supp. 651, 659 (W.D. Ky. 1976). *But see* Dailey v. Byrnes, 605 F.2d 858 (5th Cir. 1979) ("irremediable" infestation despite extermination efforts not unconstitutional).

[583]Ramos v. Lamm, *supra* note 572, at 569; Palmigiano v. Garrahy, *id.; see also* Dawson v. Kendrick, 527 F. Supp. 1252, 1289 (S.D. W. Va. 1981) (pretrial detention cases).

[584]Blake v. Hall, 668 F.2d 52 (1st Cir. 1981); *see also* Hutchings v. Corum, 501 F. Supp. 1276, 1281 (W.D. Mo. 1980).

[585]Ruiz v. Estelle, *supra* note 568, at 1159.

[586]Anderson v. Redman, 429 F. Supp. 1105, 1122-23 (D. Del. 1977).

tation[587] and have refused to get involved in matters relating to in-prison programs.[588] However, a number of courts have condemned enforced idleness and have required that prisoners be provided with some opportunity for meaningful activity.[589] Some courts have adopted the view that if overall conditions violate the Eighth Amendment, rehabilitative programs may be required as part of the remedy.[590]

k. Recreation

One program area which courts have been more willing to get involved in is recreation and exercise; numerous decisions have required some expansion of recreational opportunities.[591]

l. Classification

Courts rarely intervene in matters of individual prisoners'

---

[587]French v. Heyne, 547 F.2d 994, 1002 (7th Cir. 1976); McCray v. Sullivan, 590 F.2d 1332, 1335 (5th Cir. 1975); Miller v. Landon, 545 F. Supp. 81 (W.D. Va. 1982); Collins v. Ward, 544 F. Supp. 408 (S.D.N.Y. 1982).

[588]Sellers v. Ciccone, 530 F.2d 199 (8th Cir. 1976); United States ex rel. Silverman v. Commonwealth of Pa., 527 F. Supp. 742 (W.D. Pa. 1981); Gardner v. Benton, 452 F. Supp. 170 (E.D. Okla. 1977).

[589]Palmigiano v. Garrahy, *supra* note 582, at 980, and cases cited; *contra,* Hoptowit v. Ray, 682 F.2d 1237, 1254-55 (9th Cir. 1982); Bono v. Saxbe, 620 F.2d 609, 614 (7th Cir. 1980) (administrative segregation case).

[590]Newman v. State of Alabama, 559 F.2d 283, 291 (5th Cir. 1977); Finney v. Arkansas Board of Corrections, 505 F.2d 194, 209 (8th Cir. 1974); Palmigiano v. Garrahy, *supra* note 582, at 988; Miller v. Carson, 401 F. Supp. 835, 900 (M.D. Fla. 1975); Taylor v. Sterrett, 344 F. Supp. 411, 419 (N.D. Tex. 1972).

[591]Ruiz v. Estelle, *supra* note 568, at 1150-51 (one hour a day for administrative segregation); Franklin v. State of Oregon, 662 F.2d 1337 (9th Cir. 1981); Preston v. Thompson, 589 F.2d 300 (7th Cir. 1978) (one hour a day in yard); Walker v. Johnson, 544 F. Supp. 345, 359-65 (E.D. Mich. 1982) (two hours a day in yard); French v. Owens, 538 F. Supp. 910 (S.D. Ind. 1982) (90 minutes a day off housing unit, choice of indoors or outdoors); Hendrix v. Faulkner, 525 F. Supp. 435 (N.D. Ind. 1981); *see also* Campbell v. Cauthron, 623 F.2d 503 (8th Cir. 1980) (one hour a day for detainees subjected to 16-hour lock-in); Dawson v. Kendrick, 527 F. Supp. 1252, 1298 (S.D. W. Va. 1981) (some recreation required for detainees; details up to defendants); Heitman v. Gabriel, 524 F. Supp. 622 (W.D. Mo. 1981) (detainees entitled to one hour a day of meaningful exercise). *But see* Stewart v. Gates, 450 F. Supp. 583 (C.D. Cal. 1978) (two hours 20 minutes a week "barely sufficient"); Dailey v. Byrnes, 605 F.2d 858 (5th Cir. 1979) (lack of outdoor exercise upheld); Bukhari v. Hutto, 487 F. Supp. 1162 (E.D. Va. 1980) (three hours a week outdoors adequate).

classification.[592] However, if a classification system is grossly inadequate, and the result is danger of assault or other serious consequences, courts will sometimes require classification to be established or improved.[593] State statutes may also provide rights to classification beyond the requirements of the federal Constitution.

m. Work

The Thirteenth Amendment to the federal Constitution forbids "slavery [or] involuntary servitude, *except* as a punishment for crime whereof the party shall have been duly convicted. . . ."[594] Thus, convicted prisoners may be required to work in prison,[595] and may be disciplined for refusing to work.[596] Although pretrial detainees are protected by the Thirteenth Amendment prohibition,[597] they may be required to perform housekeeping chores in their living units.[598]

Generally, the courts have held that prison work assignments do not raise constitutional issues unless prisoners are required to do work that is medically inappropriate,[599] beyond their physical capabilities,[600] or contrary to their religious beliefs.[601] The Constitution is not violated by long hours,[602] low pay or no pay,[603] disparities in hours or rate of pay,[604]

---

[592]Peck v. Hoff, 660 F.2d 371 (8th Cir. 1981); McGruder v. Phelps, 608 F.2d 1023 (5th Cir. 1979); Reed v. Hadden, 473 F. Supp. 658 (D. Colo. 1979); Carter v. Carlson, 545 F. Supp. 1120 (S.D. W. Va. 1982); Jones v. Cummings, 528 F. Supp. 1078 (W.D.N.Y. 1981); Bukhari v. Hutto, *id.*

[593]Ruiz v. Estelle, *supra* note 568, at 1149; Withers v. Levine, 449 F. Supp. 473, 477 (D. Md. 1978), *aff'd,* 615 F.2d 158 (4th Cir. 1980); Pugh v. Locke, 406 F. Supp. 318, 330 (M.D. Ala. 1976). *See also* Dawson v. Kendrick, *supra* note 583, at 1294 (pretrial detainees entitled to some classification); Nicholson v. Choctaw County, Ala., 498 F. Supp. 295, 314 (S.D. Ala. 1980) (same). *Contra,* Hoptowit v. Ray, 682 F.2d 1237, 1255-56 (9th Cir. 1982); Ramos v. Lamm, *supra* note 572, at 566.

[594]U.S. Const., Amend. XIII (emphasis supplied).

[595]Omasta v. Wainwright, 696 F.2d 1304 (11th Cir. 1983), and cases cited.

[596]Mosby v. Mabry, 697 F.2d 213, 215 (8th Cir. 1982).

[597]Johnston v. Ciccone, 260 F. Supp. 553, 556 (W.D. Mo. 1966).

[598]Bijeol v. Nelson, 579 F.2d 423 (7th Cir. 1978).

[599]See Sec. C3c, *supra.*

[600]Ray v. Mabry, 556 F.2d 881 (8th Cir. 1977).

[601]*Id.;* Chapman v. Pickett, 491 F. Supp. 967 (C.D. Ill. 1980).

[602]Coxson v. Godwin, 405 F. Supp. 1099, 1101 (W.D. Va. 1975).

denial of work,[605] removal from a job, or reassignment, with or without a hearing.[606] The federal courts' attitude is summed up in one judge's observation that "The administration of prison work is best left to the reasoned discretion of prison officials."[607] However, state statutes and prison regulations may be enforceable in state court or via pendent jurisdiction,[608] and in some cases may create liberty or property interests protected by due process.[609]

Courts have also been reluctant to find constitutional violations in the area of safety in work assignments.[610] Workplace accidents and injuries have generally been treated as common-law torts, which state prisoners must pursue in state court.[611] (Federal prisoners must generally use the Federal Prison Industries' Inmate Accident Compensation System, described in Ch. VI, Sec. C5.)

Some courts have ordered that work opportunities be made available as part of a remedy for widespread idleness.[612]

n. Food

Prisoners are entitled to "nutritionally adequate food that is prepared and served under conditions which do not present an immediate danger to the health and well being of the inmates who consume it."[613]

---

[603]Omasta v. Wainwright, *supra* note 595; Manning v. Lockhart, 623 F.2d 536, 538 (8th Cir. 1980).

[604]Finney v. Mabry, 534 F. Supp. 1026, 1034 (E.D. Ark. 1982); Newell v. Davis, 437 F. Supp. 1059 (E.D. Va. 1977), *aff'd,* 563 F.2d 123 (4th Cir. 1977).

[605]Byrd v. Vitek, 689 F.2d 770 (8th Cir. 1982) (failure to provide prisoners with job opportunities does not violate the Eighth Amendment).

[606]Gibson v. McEvers, 631 F.2d 95 (7th Cir. 1980); Peck v. Hoff, 660 F.2d 371 (8th Cir. 1981); McMath v. Alexander, 486 F. Supp. 156 (M.D. Tenn. 1980).

[607]Sowell v. Israel, 500 F. Supp. 209, 211 (E.D. Wis. 1980).

[608]Wojtczak v. Cuyler, 480 F. Supp. 1288, 1302 (E.D. Pa. 1980); see Ch. VI, Sec. B3, for a discussion of pendent jurisdiction.

[609]*See, e.g.,* Johnson v. Duffy, 588 F.2d 740, 744-46 (9th Cir. 1978).

[610]Ruiz v. Estelle, 679 F.2d 1115, 1159 (5th Cir. 1982) (no requirement that prisons conform to standards of private industry).

[611]Peery v. Davis, 524 F. Supp. 107 (E.D. Va. 1981); *see* Stilley v. State, 376 So.2d 1007 (damages awarded in tort case arising from work assignment).

[612]*See, e.g.,* Palmigiano v. Garrahy, 443 F. Supp. 956, 988 (D.R.I. 1977). *But see* Newman v. Alabama, 559 F.2d 283 (5th Cir. 1977) (work opportunities not constitutionally required), *cert. denied sub nom.* Alabama v. Pugh, 438 U.S. 913 (1978).

Numerous courts have issued injunctions requiring improvements in prison food, usually in class action challenges to the entire system of food service and preparation.[614] Some courts have required that food handling and kitchen sanitation conform to "free world" standards.[615]

Courts have been less responsive to individual complaints about prison food[616] and to complaints about dining arrangements,[617] although relief may be granted in extreme cases.[618]

Prisoners have frequently prevailed in cases seeking medically required diets or diets prescribed by their religious beliefs. (See Sec. C3, Medical Care, and C7, Religion, *supra*.)

o.   Personal Hygiene

Prisoners are entitled to maintain personal cleanliness. Courts have required prison officials to provide reasonable access to showers,[619] clean clothing[620] and bedding,[621] and toilet articles such as soap, toothbrush and toothpaste, etc.[622] One court recently held that inmates could not be

[613]Ramos v. Lamm, *supra* note 572, at 570-71; *accord* Palmigiano v. Garrahy, *supra* note 582, at 981; Anderson v. Redman, 429 F. Supp. 1105, 1120-23 (D. Del. 1977).

[614]Ramos v. Lamm, *id.* at 571, and cases cited; Leeds v. Watson, 630 F.2d 674 (9th Cir. 1980) (use of TV dinners questioned); Nicholson v. Choctaw County, Ala., 498 F. Supp. 295, 313 (S.D. Ala. 1980) ("No meat from an animal killed on the highway or road . . . shall be served in the jail.").

[615]Ramos v. Lamm, *id.* at 571; French v. Owens, 538 F. Supp. 910, 927 (S.D. Ind. 1980); *contra,* Ruiz v. Estelle, *supra* note 568, at 1159.

[616]Freeman v. Trudell, 497 F. Supp. 481 (E.D. Mich. 1980); Tuggle v. Evans, 457 F. Supp. 1015 (D. Colo. 1978); Boston v. Stanton, 450 F. Supp. 1049 (W.D. Mo. 1978).

[617]Walker v. Johnson, 544 F. Supp. 345 (E.D. Mich. 1982); Merriweather v. Sherwood, 518 F. Supp. 355 (S.D.N.Y. 1981).

[618]Cunningham v. Jones, 567 F.2d 653 (6th Cir. 1977); Moss v. Ward, 450 F. Supp. 591 (W.D.N.Y. 1978); Rutherford v. Pitchess, 457 F. Supp. 104 (C.D. Cal. 1978).

[619]Walker v. Johnson, *supra* note 591, at 364; Lightfoot v. Walker, 486 F. Supp. 504, 528 (S.D. Ill. 1980); Jefferson v. Southworth, 447 F. Supp. 179, 191 (D.R.I. 1978).

[620]Tate v. Kassulke, 409 F. Supp. 651, 662 (W.D. Ky. 1976); Hamilton v. Landrieu, 351 F. Supp. 549, 553 (E.D. La. 1972).

[621]Lightfoot v. Walker, *supra* note 619, at 528.

[622]Feliciano v. Barcelo, 497 F. Supp. 14, 40 (D.P.R. 1979); Palmigiano v. Garrahy, *supra* note 612, at 987.

confined under a severe lock-in schedule in cells with no hot water for more than a week.[623] Some courts have treated prisoner complaints related to personal hygiene as frivolous, but they are in a minority.[624]

Prison officials may make less provision for personal cleanliness in segregation units than in general population,[625] but serious denials of personal hygiene in segregation violate the Eighth Amendment.[626]

D. Equal Protection of the Law

The Fourteenth Amendment forbids the states to "deny any person within [their] jurisdiction the equal protection of the laws."[627] There is no Equal Protection Clause restricting the federal government, but the courts have held that the Due Process Clause of the Fifth Amendment requires the federal government to obey the same equal protection standards as the states.[628]

The principle of equal protection does not require government to treat everyone alike in all circumstances; it forbids only discrimination or classification that is unjustified or "invidious."[629] Generally, a court, in

---

[623]Grubbs v. Bradley, 552 F. Supp. 1052, 1132 (M.D. Tenn. 1982).

[624]*See, e.g.,* Citro v. Zeek, 544 F. Supp. 829 (W.D.N.Y. 1982); Cassidy v. Superintendent, City Prison Farm, 392 F. Supp. 330 (W.D. Va. 1975).

[625]Wojtczak v. Cuyler, *supra* note 608, at 1307; Griffin v. Smith, 493 F. Supp. 129 (W.D.N.Y. 1980).

[626]See Sec. C8, *supra.*

[627]U.S. Const., Amend. XIV.

[628]Buckley v. Valeo, 424 U.S. 1, 93, 96 S.Ct. 612 (1976) ("Equal protection analysis in the Fifth Amendment area is the same as that under the Fourteenth Amendment"); Bolling v. Sharpe, 347 U.S. 497, 499, 74 S.Ct. 693 (1954).

[629]Ferguson v. Skrupa, 372 U.S. 726, 732, 83 S.Ct. 1028 (1963). The Supreme Court, in Lindsley v. Natural Carbonic Gas Co., 220 U.S. 61, 78-79, 31 S.Ct. 337 (1911), established the prevailing rule for distinguishing between permissible and invidious discrimination:

1. The Equal Protection Clause of the Fourteenth Amendment does not take from the State the power to classify in the adoption of police laws, but admits of the exercise of a wide scope of discretion in that regard, and avoids what is done only when it is without any reasonable basis and therefore is purely arbitrary.
2. A classification having some reasonable basis does not offend against that clause merely because it is not made with mathematical nicety or because in practice it results in some inequality.
3. When the classification in such a law is called in question, if any state of facts reasonably can be conceived that should sustain it, the existence of that state of facts at the time the law was enacted must be assumed.

reviewing an equal protection challenge, must first determine whether the government has "articulated a legitimate governmental purpose" for its classification, and second, whether the classification bears a "rational relation" to the government's legitimate purpose.[630]

In some cases, where a "fundamental right" or a "suspect classification" is at issue, the courts have required a higher standard of justification from government ("strict scrutiny").[631] However, this standard is generally not applied in prison cases. The Supreme Court, in *Jones v. North Carolina Prisoners' Labor Union, Inc.,*[632] noted that the district court in its equal protection analysis had improperly treated the case as if the prison environment was essentially a "public forum." The Court held that, even where the First Amendment was involved, prison officials "need only demonstrate a rational basis for their distinction between organizational groups."[633]

> It is precisely in matters such as this, the decision as to which of many groups should be allowed to operate within the prison walls, where, confronted with claims based on the Equal Protection Clause, *the courts should allow prison administrators the full latitude of discretion,* unless it can be firmly stated that the two groups are so similar that the discretion has been abused.[634]

As a practical matter, it is very hard to win an equal protection claim in a prison case, since prison officials can usually come up with some "rational basis" for their actions; even if the court disagrees with their reasoning, it will be obligated to uphold the challenged practice. For this reason, you should always look for other legal theories besides equal protection when you challenge prison practices.

The following are some areas that courts have held *do not* give rise to equal protection violations:

(a) Denial of access to temporary release programs when others with similar records are in the programs does not deny equal protection. In

---

4. One who assails the classification in such a law must carry the burden of showing that it does not rest upon any reasonable basis but is essentially arbitrary.

[630]*See, e.g.,* Shapiro v. Thompson, 394 U.S. 618, 89 S.Ct. 1322 (1969); Loving v. Virginia, 388 U.S. 1, 12-13, 87 S.Ct. 1817 (1967).

[631]Personnel Adm'n of Massachusetts v. Feeney, 442 U.S. 256, 99 S.Ct. 2282 (1979); Benson v. Arizona State Bd. of Dental Examiners, 673 F.2d 27 (9th Cir. 1982).

[632]433 U.S. 119, 97 S.Ct. 2532 (1977).

[633]*Id.* at 134.

[634]*Id.* at 136 (emphasis added).

Martino v. Gard,[635] the court held the plaintiff was not denied equal protection when his brother who was serving the same sentence for the same offense and had the same institutional record was granted early release, and he was not. In *Rowe v. Cuyler,*[636] the plaintiff was not denied equal protection of the law when others with as deplorable, or more deplorable, records were granted access to community programs, and he was not. In *Marciano v. Coughlin,*[637] prison officials' assignment of more correctional personnel to process community release applications at one prison than another failed to allege a violation of equal protection. In *Jamieson v. Robinson,*[638] the court held that prison officials' failure to establish a work release program in each prison in the state did not deny equal protection.

(b) The court, in *Leslie v. Wainwright,*[639] held that differences between visiting privileges of people on death row and those in general population did not violate the Equal Protection Clause.

(c) In *Beathan v. Manson,*[640] the court held that a pay differential between two different prisons was constitutional.

(d) The court, in *Sweet v. Department of Corrections,*[641] held that non-disciplinary prisoners confined to administrative segregation are not entitled to the same privileges afforded the general population.

Prisoners have been more successful in challenging racial and gender-based discrimination. Courts have held that state statutes which require segregation of races in prisons and jails,[642] and prison administrators' subjection of black or Hispanic prisoners to disparate and unequal treatment, violate the Fourteenth Amendment.[643] When confronted with the issue of sex discrimination within a prison, the court, in *Glover v.*

---

[635] 526 F. Supp. 958 (E.D.N.Y. 1981).

[636] 534 F. Supp. 297 (E.D. Pa. 1982).

[637] 510 F. Supp. 1034 (E.D.N.Y. 1981).

[638] 641 F.2d 138 (3d Cir. 1981).

[639] 511 F. Supp. 753 (D. Nev. 1981).

[640] 499 F. Supp. 773 (D. Conn. 1980).

[641] 529 F.2d 854 (4th Cir. 1975).

[642] Lee v. Washington, 263 F. Supp. 327 (M.D. Ala. 1966), *aff'd,* 390 U.S. 333, 88 S.Ct. 994 (1968).

[643] Ramos v. Lamm, 485 F. Supp. 122, 164 (D. Colo. 1979), *aff'd in pertinent part,* 639 F.2d 559, 581 (10th Cir. 1980); Gates v. Collier, 349 F. Supp. 881 (N.D. Miss. 1972), *aff'd,* 501 F.2d 1291 (5th Cir. 1974). *But see* Pabon v. McIntosh, 546 F. Supp. 1328 (E.D. Pa. 1982) (failure to provide Spanish language classes for non-English-speaking prisoners upheld).

Johnson,[644] applied a "parity of treatment" test.[645] The *Glover* court held that prison officials are required "to provide women inmates with treatment facilities that are substantially equivalent to those provided the men—*i.e.,* equivalent in substance, if not in form—unless their actions, though failing to do so, nonetheless bear a fair and substantial relationship to achievement of the State's correctional objectives."[646] Prison officials are not required to provide identical rehabilitation programs to male and female prisoners.[647]

E. Pretrial Detainees' Rights[648]

Pretrial detainees, persons who are held in jail on pending criminal charges but have not yet been convicted, stand on a different legal footing from convicts, at least in theory. While convicts may not be subjected to cruel and unusual punishment, detainees may not be punished at all.[649]

Many older cases held that because of the presumption of innocence, detainees could only be held under the least restrictive conditions possible, and that any restrictions placed on them had to be justified by a "compelling necessity."[650] However, the United States Supreme Court overruled these cases in *Bell v. Wolfish,*[651] which held that the presumption of innocence was merely a rule of evidence that had nothing to do with jail conditions. Although the Court agreed that under the Due Process Clause detainees cannot be subjected to punishment, it stated

---

[644]478 F. Supp. 1075 (E.D. Mich. 1979) (plaintiffs alleged that women prisoners were not receiving treatment programs commensurate with the men. Men had access to twenty-two vocational courses at the various prisons which could lead to marketable skills; women had access to only five vocational courses, which did not provide them with marketable skills.).

[645]*Id.* at 1079. *Accord,* Canterino v. Wilson, 546 F. Supp. 174 (W.D. Ky. 1982); Dawson v. Kendrick, 527 F. Supp. 1252, 1317 (S.D. W. Va. 1981).

[646]*Id.*

[647]*Id.* at 1101.

[648]Other sections in this chapter also cite cases involving detainees; to research a detainees' rights issue, read the section concerning the substantive issue (*e.g.,* Visiting, Medical Care), as well as this section.

[649]Ingraham v. Wright, 430 U.S. 651, 671-72 n.40, 97 S.Ct. 1401 (1977); Bell v. Wolfish, 441 U.S. 520, 535, 99 S.Ct. 1861 (1979).

[650]*See, e.g.,* Rhem v. Malcolm, 507 F.2d 333, 336 (2d Cir. 1974); Brenneman v. Madigan, 343 F. Supp. 128, 136-38 (N.D. Cal. 1972).

[651]441 U.S. 520, 531-33, 99 S.Ct. 1861 (1979).

that "[n]ot every disability imposed during pretrial detention amounts to 'punishment' in the constitutional sense. . . ."[652] The Court continued:

> A court must decide whether the disability is imposed for the purpose of punishment or whether it is but an incident of some other legitimate governmental purpose. . . . Absent a showing of an expressed intent to punish on the part of detention facility officials, that determination generally will turn on "whether an alternative purpose to which [the restriction] may rationally be connected is assignable for it, and whether it appears excessive in relation to the alternative purpose assigned [to it.]" . . . Thus, if a particular condition or restriction of pretrial detention is reasonably related to a legitimate governmental objective, it does not, without more, amount to "punishment." Conversely, if a restriction or condition is not reasonably related to a legitimate goal—if it is arbitrary or purposeless—a court permissibly may infer that the purpose of the governmental action is punishment that may not constitutionally be inflicted upon detainees *qua* detainees.[653]

Those legitimate goals include both ensuring that detainees are present for their trials and the effective management and security of the jail.[654] The Court emphasized that courts should "defer to [prison officials'] expert judgment in matters related to security unless there is 'substantial evidence in the record that the officials have exaggerated their response to these conditions.'"[655] Moreover, the *Wolfish* Court noted that when security practices were at issue, there was little basis for distinguishing between convicts and detainees.[656] Thus, the theoretical distinction between convicts and detainees may not always make a practical difference in the outcome of a case.

Applying these standards, the *Wolfish* Court upheld the "double-bunking" of detainees under the circumstances of the case, the "publisher only" restriction on inmates' receipt of publications, the prohibition on receipt of packages, the refusal to let inmates watch room searches, and the requirement that inmates submit to routine body cavity inspections after each contact visit. These holdings, and their implications, are discussed more fully in other sections of this manual. (See Secs. B2g, C1, C5, and C6.)

Aside from these specific holdings, the decision in *Wolfish* has significant implications for many areas of detainees' rights.

The major effect of *Wolfish* has been to restrict courts' scrutiny of

---

[652]*Id*. at 537.

[653]*Id*. at 538-39, *quoting* Kennedy v. Mendoza-Martinez, 372 U.S. 144, 168-69, 83 S.Ct. 554 (1963) (footnote and other citations omitted).

[654]*Id*. at 539-40.

[655]*Id*. at 548.

[656]*Id*. at 546 and n.28.

security-related jail practices. The clearest example of this is contact visits, whose constitutional status was not decided in *Wolfish*.[657] Before *Wolfish*, most courts held that the denial of contact visits violated detainees' constitutional rights.[658] After *Wolfish*, most courts have held that contact visits are not required by the federal Constitution,[659] although they may be required by state law or by jail regulations.[660] Nevertheless, the courts have continued to scrutinize the security defenses raised by prison officials to ensure that they have some basis in reality. As one court observed, "We do not read anything in *Wolfish* as requiring this court to grant automatic deference to ritual incantations by prison officials that their actions foster the goals of order and discipline."[661]

Another major effect of *Wolfish* has been to relax the standards applied to jail overcrowding. Under *Wolfish*, there is clearly no per se rule against double-bunking or the violation of "rated capacity" or "design capacity" of a jail. However, courts have continued to act when overcrowding reaches serious proportions, especially when it is imposed for long periods of time and accompanied by severe restrictions on recreation and out-of-cell time, by threats to safety, or by other aggravating conditions. This approach is well illustrated by the Second Circuit's decision in *LaReau v. Manson*,[662] in which the court held double-celling in 60 to 65 square foot cells to be unconstitutional for longer than 15 days, where dayrooms were overcrowded and movement was limited; however, the use of mattresses on the floor was held unlawful for any period of time.[663] A key factor in these decisions is that no

---

[657]*Id.* at 560 n.40.

[658]*See, e.g.,* Rhem v. Malcolm, 371 F. Supp. 594, 625-26 (S.D.N.Y. 1974), *aff'd*, 507 F.2d 333 (2d Cir 1974).

[659]*See, e.g.,* Inmates of Allegheny County Jail v. Pierce, 612 F.2d 749 (7th Cir. 1980); Dawson v. Kendrick, 527 F. Supp. 1252, 1308 (S.D. W. Va. 1981); McMurry v. Phelps, 533 F. Supp. 742 (W.D. La. 1982). *But see* Montana v. Commissioners Court, 659 F.2d 19 (5th Cir. 1981) (claim of denial of contact visits not frivolous); Jones v. Diamond, 636 F.2d 1364 (5th Cir. 1981) (evidentiary hearing needed to decide whether contact visits were required); Calloway v. Fauver, 544 F. Supp. 584 (D.N.J. 1982) (monthly contact visits required for long-term protective custody inmates).

[660]*See* Cooper v. Morin, 49 N.Y.2d 69, 424 N.Y.S.2d 168 (1979); Marcera v. Chinlund, 91 F.R.D. 579 (W.D.N.Y. 1981); Boudin v. Thomas, 533 F. Supp. 786 (S.D.N.Y. 1982).

[661]Lock v. Jenkins, 641 F.2d 488, 498 (7th Cir. 1981).

[662]651 F.2d 96 (2d Cir. 1981).

[663]*See also* Dawson v. Kendrick, 527 F. Supp. 1252, 1294 (S.D. W. Va. 1981) (some short-term crowding with dayroom access upheld; double-celling in 35-

security interest is served by providing inadequate space for detainees; therefore courts are not required to defer to correctional officials' judgment as to whether conditions are acceptable. Nor do courts accept the mere desire to save money as a legitimate reason to subject detainees to "genuine privations and hardship over any substantial period of time."[664]

After *Wolfish,* courts have not hesitated to intervene where the totality of jail conditions was found to be inhumane; inadequate plumbing, lighting, sanitation, ventilation, fire protection, recreation, food service, medical care, and personal safety may still be remedied through a comprehensive court order.[665]

Outside the areas discussed above, the courts have so far provided little guidance in how to apply the *Wolfish* "punishment" test in cases where jail officials do not admit that their intent is punitive. In *Gawreys v. D.C. General Hospital,*[666] where the plaintiff had been subjected without any justification to the use of uncomfortable metal restraints rather than the cloth or leather ones required by jail regulations, the court held that he had been punished. In *Boudin v. Thomas,*[667] the court held it was not punishment to hold a detainee reasonably perceived to be a security risk in a specially created unit in a state prison under restrictive conditions when she was placed there for security reasons. In *Inmates of Allegheny County Jail v. Pierce,*[668] the refusal to continue methadone treatment for detainees who had received it before their arrest was held not to be punishment where jail officials had a security interest in keeping all drugs out of the jail.

Medical care and protection from harm by other inmates are issues

---

square foot cells prohibited); Lock v. Jenkins, 641 F.2d 488 (7th Cir. 1981) (confinement in 37-square foot cells for 22 hours a day was punishment; either more space or more out-of-cell time required); Hutchings v. Corum, 501 F. Supp. 1276 (W.D. Mo. 1980) (population limits placed on cells of various sizes); Vazquez v. Gray, 523 F. Supp. 1359 (S.D.N.Y. 1981) (floor mattresses prohibited; use of dayrooms for sleeping limited; dormitory overpopulation upheld); McKenna v. County of Nassau, 538 F. Supp. 737 (E.D.N.Y. 1982) (damages awarded where inmate housed in unsafe location because of crowding).

[664]LaReau v. Manson, *supra* note 662, at 104.

[665]*See* Jones v. Diamond, 636 F.2d 1364 (5th Cir. 1981) (en banc); McMurry v. Phelps, 533 F. Supp. 742 (W.D. La. 1982); Dawson v. Kendrick, 527 F. Supp. 1252 (S.D. W. Va. 1981); Hutchings v. Corum, 501 F. Supp. 1276 (W.D. Mo. 1980); Heitman v. Gabriel, 524 F. Supp. 622 (W.D. Mo. 1981).

[666]480 F. Supp. 853, 855 (D.D.C. 1979).

[667]543 F. Supp. 686, 692-93 (S.D.N.Y. 1982).

[668]612 F.2d 754, 760-61 (3d Cir. 1979).

which were not dealt with in *Wolfish*. The courts have generally applied the same standards in pretrial detention cases as in cases involving convicts. A detainee claiming an assault by another inmate or a denial of adequate medical care must show that his or her injuries were caused by conduct amounting to "deliberate indifference" on the part of prison officials, or that conditions or practices are so dangerous that they amount to deliberate indifference.[669] For a more detailed discussion of the deliberate indifference standard, see Secs. C2, Protection From Physical Harm, and C3, Medical Care.

Some courts have held that when detainees are treated more harshly than convicts, the Equal Protection Clause is violated.[670] However, more recent cases have questioned this theory, holding that equal protection is not violated where institutions are operated by different agencies,[671] or that the length of stay or other aspects of confinement are sufficiently different in jails and prisons to justify differences in treatment.[672] Moreover, jail and prison officials are generally required only to show a "rational basis" for the distinctions made among prisoners.[673] For a more detailed discussion of the Equal Protection Clause in prison cases, see Sec. D, *supra*. Thus, while it is always helpful for detainees to show that convicts are treated better than persons still awaiting trial, that fact will not automatically win one's lawsuit.

Detainees, like convicts, should be careful to research state constitutions, statutes and regulations, and local laws and regulations which may provide a more favorable legal standard than the federal Constitution. These claims may be asserted in state court or in federal court under the doctrine of pendent jurisdiction (see Ch. VI, Sec. B3).

---

[669]*See, e.g.,* Holmes v. Goldin, 615 F.2d 83 (2d Cir. 1980) (deliberate indifference required in inmate assault case); Inmates of Allegheny County Jail v. Pierce, 612 F.2d 754, 762-63 (3d Cir. 1979) (inadequate psychiatric staff violated deliberate indifference standard); Robinson v. Moreland, 655 F.2d 887 (8th Cir. 1981) (deliberate indifference standard applied to detainees' medical claim).

[670]*See, e.g.,* Rhem v. Malcolm, 507 F.2d 333, 336 (2d Cir. 1974); Hamilton v. Love, 328 F. Supp. 1182, 1191 (E.D. Ark. 1971).

[671]Dawson v. Kendrick, 527 F. Supp. 1252, 1286 (S.D. W. Va. 1981).

[672]Feeley v. Sampson, 570 F.2d 364, 373 (1st Cir. 1978).

[673]McGinnis v. Royster, 410 U.S. 263, 93 S.Ct. 1055 (1973); Lock v. Jenkins, 641 F.2d 488, 497 (7th Cir. 1981).

VI
Actions, Remedies and Defenses

A. Introduction

This chapter deals with the causes of action a state or federal prisoner can bring against prison officials in the federal courts, the types of defenses prison officials can raise and how you can seek to defeat these defenses, and the type of remedies you may obtain (damages, injunctive relief, or a declaratory judgment). Since federal district courts normally dismiss immediately 97% of the *pro se* lawsuits filed, you should closely follow the advice in this chapter. State prisoners should read Sections B and D through H, while a federal prisoner should read Sections C through H. The material in this chapter deals almost entirely with legal actions against acts, policies, or practices of prison officials. Other chapters address challenges to criminal convictions (see Ch. IX), parole decisions (see Ch. VIII), and detainers (see Ch. X).

B. Actions by State Prisoners

1. 42 U.S.C. §1983: Civil Rights Actions Against State and Local Officials

Every person who, under color of any statute, ordinance, regulation, custom, or usage of any State, Territory or the District of Columbia, subjects, or causes to be subjected, any citizen of the United States or other person within the jurisdiction thereof to the deprivation of any rights, privileges, or immunities secured by the Constitution and laws shall be liable to the party injured in an action at law, suit in equity, or other proper proceeding for redress. For the purposes of this section, any Act of Congress applicable exclusively to the District of Columbia shall be considered to be a statute of the District of Columbia.[1]

---

[1] 42 U.S.C. §1983 (1980).

Section 1983 permits you to sue for "deprivation of any rights, privileges, or immunities secured by the Constitution and laws" caused by persons acting "under color of state law." There is no requirement that you allege or show the defendant was acting maliciously or with the specific intent to violate your rights.[2]

a.   Jurisdiction, 28 U.S.C. §1343(3)

The district court shall have original jurisdiction of any civil action authorized by law to be commenced by any person:

***

(3) To redress the deprivation, under color of any State law, statute, or-dinance, custom, or usage, of any right, privilege, or immunity secured by the Constitution of the United States or by an Act of Congress providing for equal rights of citizens or of all persons within the jurisdiction of the United States.

While §1983 provides the basis for the cause of action and remedy for your lawsuit, 28 U.S.C. §1343(3) provides the jurisdiction for the federal court to hear your case, and you should cite it in your complaint as the basis for federal court jurisdiction.

b.   Elements

To state a cause of action under §1983, you must allege two elements:

(1) . . . [T]he conduct complained of was committed by a person acting under color of state law; and
(2) . . . this conduct deprived a person [you] of rights, privileges, or im-munities secured by the Constitution and laws of the United States.[3]

"Persons" who may be sued under §1983 include not only actual persons, but also city and county governments and their agencies.[4] States and their agencies may not be sued under §1983 because they are immune under the Eleventh Amendment. (See Sec. E1a, *infra,* for a discussion of the Eleventh Amendment.) Whenever possible, you should sue in-dividual guards or officials as well as local governments because the standards for obtaining relief against a government are hard to meet.[5]

---

[2]Monroe v. Pape, 365 U.S. 167, 180, 81 S.Ct. 473 (1961). *See also* Gomez v. Toledo, 446 U.S. 635, 100 S.Ct. 1920 (1980) (plaintiff need not allege that of-ficials acted in bad faith).

[3]Parratt v. Taylor, 451 U.S. 527, 101 S.Ct. 1908, 1913 (1981).

[4]Monell v. Department of Social Services, 436 U.S. 658, 98 S.Ct. 2018 (1978).

[5]For the city, county, or municipality to be liable for a civil rights violation, the act alleged must involve "a policy statement, ordinance, regulation, or

Acting "under color of state law" means that a person is using or abusing power that is "possessed by virtue of state law and made possible only because the wrongdoer is clothed with the authority of state law. . . ."[6] Usually, it is sufficient in a prison case to state in the complaint that the defendants are prison personnel and that they were acting under color of state law.[7] Except in an extreme situation (*e.g.*, guards going to your family's home and harassing them while off duty), prison officials' acts are made possible by their official positions, so they are acting under color of state law even if they violate state law or regulations.[8]

In civil rights actions, the prison officials you sue not only must have acted "under color of state law" but must have had a personal involvement in the constitutional violation. Supervisory prison officials (warden, captain of the guards, etc.) who did not commit the unlawful acts or were not present when they occurred cannot be held liable unless you can show how they caused you to be subjected to a violation of federally protected rights (*e.g.*, by failure to train and supervise guards in the use of mace or restraints). A more detailed discussion on how to establish personal involvement of supervisory prison officials appears in Sec. E2a, *infra*. It is a *must* that you follow the advice in that section in drafting your §1983 complaint or responding to defendants' motion to dismiss or for summary judgment.

You must also allege in your complaint that you have been deprived of a right, privilege, or immunity secured by the Constitution and laws of the United States, and you must state what the violation was. (See Ch. V for a discussion of what your rights, privileges, or immunities are.)

c.   Other Requirements

You must have a copy of the summons and complaint served on each of the defendants. Service of the summons and complaint can be done by mail, a member of your family or a friend may serve the papers, or the U.S. Marshal can serve them if you have been granted leave to proceed as an indigent by the court (see Ch. VII, Sec. A2, for a fuller discussion of how to have the summons and complaint served).

In a lawsuit against prison officials, you must also obtain proper venue

---

decision officially adopted and promulgated by that body's officers." *Id.* at 701. See Sec. E2b, *infra,* for a discussion of §1983 actions against local governments.

[6]Monroe v. Pape, 365 U.S. 167, 184, 81 S.Ct. 473 (1961); *accord,* Brown v. Miller, 631 F.2d 408 (5th Cir. 1980).

[7]See Appendix B, Form 1a, for a sample complaint.

[8]Monroe v. Pape, *supra* note 6, at 172.

over them by filing where they reside or where the cause of action arose.[9] (*E.g.,* if your lawsuit is for damages against the warden that just transferred you from a prison in federal district A to a prison in federal district B, you would need to file your lawsuit in the federal district court in A.)

2.   §1983, Habeas Corpus, and Appeals

When you are challenging prison conditions or your treatment by prison officials, you will generally want to use §1983, rather than a petition for a writ of habeas corpus under 28 U.S.C. §§2241 *et seq.* Although some courts hold you *can* bring "conditions cases" under federal habeas corpus,[10] you have to take your habeas case to the state court first—that is, exhaust your state judicial remedies. You generally do not have to exhaust before using §1983. (See Ch. IX, Sec. B2, for a discussion of habeas exhaustion, and Sec. D, *infra,* for a general discussion of exhaustion of administrative and judicial remedies.)

When you are challenging your conviction, sentence, or confinement in prison, and when you are seeking release from custody or shortening of your sentence, you *must* use habeas corpus after exhausting state remedies.[11] This rule applies both to challenges to the court proceedings that sent you to prison and to cases about deprivation of good time or miscalculation of your release or parole eligibility date.[12]

The Supreme Court has indicated that in cases involving lost good time, if you are not actually asking for your good time back but are seeking only damages, an injunction, or a declaratory judgment, you can bring your case under §1983.[13] However, the lower federal courts have

---

[9]28 U.S.C. §1391(b). *See also* Daugherty v. Procunier, 456 F.2d 97 (9th Cir. 1972); Fox v. Harris, 488 F. Supp. 488 (D.D.C. 1980).

[10]Knell v. Bensinger, 522 F.2d 729, 726 n.7 (7th Cir. 1975); *contra,* Crawford v. Bell, 599 F.2d 890 (9th Cir. 1979). *See* Preiser v. Rodriguez, 411 U.S. 475, 499, 93 S.Ct. 1827 (1973).

[11]In Preiser v. Rodriguez, the Court stated:

[W]hen a state prisoner is challenging the very fact or duration of his physical imprisonment, and the relief he seeks is a determination that he is entitled to immediate release or a speedier release from that imprisonment, his sole remedy is a writ of habeas corpus.

Id. at 500.

[12]*Id.;* Thomas v. Dietz, 518 F. Supp. 794 (D.N.J. 1981); Ringenberg v. Coy, 524 F. Supp. 112 (E.D. Va. 1981).

[13]*See* Wolff v. McDonnell, 418 U.S. 539, 94 S.Ct. 2963 (1974). *See also* Williams v. Ward, 556 F.2d 1143 (2d Cir. 1977) (§1983 proper method to challenge manner of parole decisionmaking, rather than its outcome).

split in applying this holding. Some federal courts have assumed that they can grant any relief under §1983 except good time or earlier release.[14] Others have held that *no* relief can be granted under §1983 if it would require a ruling on whether good time was properly taken, though relief can be granted requiring proper procedures.[15] Other courts have held that no relief can be granted under §1983 on any individual claim where good time was taken; only broad challenges to the entire good time system can be heard without exhaustion of state remedies.[16] Until the Supreme Court settles this question, prisoners will have to research the law in their jurisdiction.

The federal courts are also divided on whether claims arising from removal or exclusion from temporary release programs can be raised under §1983 or must proceed under habeas corpus after exhaustion of state remedies.[17]

The federal courts are often suspicious of §1983 actions based on facts relating to state criminal convictions, because they think prisoners are using them to bypass normal appeals procedures, or because they want to avoid the possibility of a conflict between state and federal court decisions. It is well established that a federal court suit cannot be used as a substitute for a state court appeal.[18] The federal courts will apply in civil actions the principle of collateral estoppel to prevent relitigation of issues already decided in state criminal proceedings.[19] If there are still state appellate proceedings going on, the court may dismiss your civil

---

[14]Jacobson v. Coughlin, 523 F. Supp. 1247, 1255 (N.D.N.Y. 1981).

[15]Godbolt v. Comm'r of Dept. of Correctional Services, 527 F. Supp. 21 (S.D.N.Y. 1981); Carter v. Newburgh Police Dept., 523 F. Supp. 16, 19 (S.D.N.Y. 1980), and cases cited; Derrow v. Shields, 482 F. Supp. 1144 (W.D. Va. 1980).

[16]Keenan v. Bennett, 613 F.2d 127 (5th Cir. 1980); Johnson v. Hardy, 601 F.2d 172 (5th Cir. 1979).

[17]*Compare* Jamieson v. Robinson, 641 F.2d 138 (3d Cir. 1981); Wright v. Cuyler, 624 F.2d 455 (3d Cir. 1980); Marciano v. Coughlin, 510 F. Supp. 1034 (E.D.N.Y. 1981); Tunin v. Ward, 78 F.R.D. 59 (S.D.N.Y. 1977); Parson v. Keve, 413 F. Supp. 111 (D. Del. 1976) (habeas is proper remedy when seeking conditional release for furloughs and work or educational release programs), *with* United States ex rel. Williams v. Cuyler, 447 F. Supp. 540 (E.D. Pa. 1977); Joyce v. Gilligan, 383 F. Supp. 1028 (N.D. Ohio 1974).

[18]Atlantic Coastline R.R. v. Brotherhood of Locomotive Engineers, 398 U.S. 281, 296, 90 S.Ct. 1739 (1970); Rooker v. Fidelity Trust Co., 263 U.S. 413, 416, 44 S.Ct. 149 (1923); Tang v. Appellate Division of New York Supreme Court, First Dept., 487 F.2d 138 (2d Cir. 1973), *cert. denied*, 94 S.Ct. 1611 (1974).

[19]Allen v. McCurry, 449 U.S. 90, 101 S.Ct. 411 (1980). See Sec. E3, *infra,* for a discussion of collateral estoppel.

case under the "comity" doctrine of *Younger v. Harris,*[20] or may stay it until appellate proceedings are concluded. Despite this, you may need to bring your civil case before your state criminal appeals are concluded to comply with the statute of limitations. (See Sec. E4, *infra,* for a discussion of statute of limitations.) You may not sue the judge, prosecutor, or witnesses in your criminal case for damages; they are protected by the doctrine of absolute immunity under §1983. (See Sec. E1b, *infra,* for a discussion of absolute immunity.)

For all of these reasons, you should never give up your appeal rights in favor of a §1983 action, nor should you expect to be able to use §1983 in order to gain an advantage in the appellate process.

3. Pendent Jurisdiction

Pendent jurisdiction will allow a federal court to decide claims alleging violation of the state's common law, regulations, statutes, or constitution that are not of a federal constitutional nature, as long as you have a non-frivolous federal law claim as well arising from the same facts.[21] Often, when prison officials have violated your constitutional rights, they have also violated state law. For example, suppose a state statute requires prison officials to provide for your safety. There is a gang of prisoners who have been terrorizing the prison for six months and prison officials have taken no action. You are assaulted by this gang. If you bring a lawsuit against prison officials, you will allege that prison officials had knowledge of the activities of this gang of prisoners, and their failure to take corrective measures amounted to "deliberate indifference," violating your Eighth Amendment right to be free from cruel and unusual punishment (see Ch. V, Sec. C2a, for a discussion of this right). You could also allege pendent claims that the state statute and the common law were violated when prison officials were negligent in providing adequately for your safety.[22] The federal court would have at least three grounds for deciding your case: (1) a constitutional violation; (2) a violation of a statute; and (3) a common-law negligence theory.

To assert a state law claim in federal court, you should include in the jurisdictional paragraph of your complaint the statement, "Plaintiff also invokes the pendent jurisdiction of this court." You also need to say what your state law claims are elsewhere in the complaint. (See Appendix

---

[20]401 U.S. 37, 91 S.Ct. 746 (1971).

[21]Hagans v. Lavine, 415 U.S. 528, 545-57, 94 S.Ct. 1372 (1974).

[22]*See* D.C. Code, §24-442, "[T]he District of Columbia shall . . . be responsible for the safekeeping, care, protection . . . of all persons committed to [its prison]." *See also* Matthews v. District of Columbia, 387 A.2d 731 (D.C. Ct. App. 1978) (common-law tort case).

B, Form 1a, model complaint.) Failure to spell out your pendent claim may cause you trouble later.[23]

The constitutional and pendent claims must "derive from a common nucleus of operative fact"[24] (*i.e.,* approximately the same transaction or occurrence[25]) in order for a federal court to exercise pendent jurisdiction. See the example in the first paragraph of this section, in which all three legal theories are based on the same set of facts.

The court has the discretion to exercise pendent jurisdiction or not, and will seldom be reversed on appeal. Factors that may influence the court to decline to exercise pendent jurisdiction are the possibility of jury confusion, a predominance of state law issues in the case, and uncertainty in the state law to be applied.[26] Courts will not exercise pendent jurisdiction if they believe it is inconsistent with a statute of Congress; thus, one court has held that pendent jurisdiction may not be exercised in a habeas corpus case because it is contrary to congressional intent.[27]

Generally, if the court does assume pendent jurisdiction in a case involving a constitutional claim, the court will decide the state law issue and avoid the constitutional claim.[28] Federal courts usually will not hear a state law claim against a party unless there is also a federal claim against the party.[29]

When a court rules on a pendent state claim, it is bound by state rules of law that would apply in a state court. Thus, there may be defenses or other problems with a pendent state claim that do not apply to the §1983 claim.[30]

---

[23]*See* Ruiz v. Estelle, 679 F.2d 1115, 1156-59 (5th Cir. 1982) (court should not have exercised pendent jurisdiction where plaintiff did not plead it); J.P. v. De Santi, 653 F.2d 1080 (2d Cir. 1981) (court should not have decided state law claim which was not pled); Smith v. Sullivan, 611 F.2d 1039 (5th Cir. 1980) (where federal court found only state law violation, order vacated; pendent jurisdiction not invoked); United States ex rel. Flores v. Cuyler, 511 F. Supp. 386 (E.D. Pa. 1981) (pendent claim not considered where not raised in time).

[24]United Mine Workers v. Gibbs, 383 U.S. 715, 725, 86 S.Ct. 1130 (1966).

[25]Nilsen v. City of Moss Point, Miss., 674 F.2d 379 (5th Cir. 1982).

[26]Cancellier v. Federated Dept. Stores, 672 F.2d 1312 (9th Cir. 1982); Carrillo /. Illinois Bell Telephone Co., 538 F. Supp. 793, 799 (N.D. Ill. 1982).

[27]United States ex rel. Hoover v. Franzen, 669 F.2d 453 (7th Cir. 1982).

[28]Hagans v. Lavine, *supra* note 21, at 547; Anderson v. Redman, 429 F. Supp. 1105, 1122 (D. Del. 1977). *But see* Lightfoot v. Walker, 486 F. Supp. 504, 508-09 (E.D. Ill. 1980) (court rules on constitutional rather than pendent claims).

[29]Williams v. Bennett, 689 F.2d 1370, 1379-80 (11th Cir. 1982); Crowe v. Washington County Board of Prison Inspectors, 504 F. Supp. 412 (W.D. Pa. 1980); McCaw v. Frame, 499 F. Supp. 424 (E.D. Pa. 1980).

[30]Jones v. Diamond, 636 F.2d 1364, 1379 (5th Cir. 1981) (en banc) (pendent

Federal courts have exercised pendent jurisdiction in prison cases over a wide variety of state law claims ranging from common-law torts to state health codes and prison and jail regulations.[31]

4.   Other Civil Rights Statutes

There are several other federal civil rights statutes that are sometimes invoked by prisoners. In most cases, these add little to the legal remedies available to state prisoners under §1983.

Claims of racial discrimination are actionable under 42 U.S.C. §1981, which provides that all persons must have the same rights "to make and enforce contracts, to sue, be parties, give evidence, and to the full and equal benefit of all laws and proceedings for the security of persons and property as is enjoyed by white citizens." This statute, unlike §1983, can be used against conduct by private parties and is not limited to action taken under color of state law.[32] However, virtually all acts of prison officials are committed under color of state law, so resort to §1981 is not necessary.

Private conduct is also actionable under 42 U.S.C. §1985(3), which provides for damage actions against persons who "conspire . . . for the purpose of depriving . . . any person or class of persons of the equal protection of the laws, or of equal privileges and immunities under the laws," and 42 U.S.C. §1986, which provides for damage liability for anyone "who, having knowledge that [a §1985 conspiracy is] about to be

---

state claim governed by state law limiting liability); Hamilton v. Roth, 624 F.2d 1204, 1208-12 (3d Cir. 1980) (pendent malpractice claim subject to state requirement of administrative exhaustion); Albers v. Whitley, 546 F. Supp. 726 (D. Ore. 1982) (pendent claim barred by state immunity statute).

[31]Williams v. Thomas, 692 F.2d 1032 (5th Cir. 1982) (assault and battery); Clappier v. Flynn, 605 F.2d 519 (10th Cir. 1979) (assault and battery); Miller v. Carson, 563 F.2d 757 (5th Cir. 1977) (state requirement that jail standards be promulgated); McCaw v. Frame, 499 F. Supp. 424 (E.D. Pa. 1980) (negligence in homosexual rape case); Smith v. Jordan, 527 F. Supp. 167 (S.D. Ohio 1981) (state statute limiting strip searches); Marcera v. Chinlund, 91 F.R.D. 579 (W.D.N.Y. 1981) (state constitutional requirement of contact visits for detainees); French v. Owens, 538 F. Supp. 910 (S.D. Ind. 1982) (state statute governing treatment of juvenile inmates); Williams v. Lane, 548 F. Supp. 927 (N.D. Ill. 1982) (statute governing housing and programs in protective custody); Canterino v. Wilson, 546 F. Supp. 174, 216-17 (W.D. Ky. 1982) (state education release statute); Taylor v. Sterrett, 344 F. Supp. 411, 418 (N.D. Tex. 1972), aff'd as modified, 499 F.2d 367 (5th Cir. 1974), cert. denied, 420 U.S. 983 (1975) (state statute regarding food handlers); Anderson v. Redman, 429 F. Supp. 1105, 1122 (D. Del. 1977) (prison department rules).

[32]Runyon v. McCrary, 427 U.S. 160, 96 S.Ct. 2586 (1976); Johnson v. Railway Express Agency, 421 U.S. 454, 95 S.Ct. 1716 (1975).

committed, and having power to prevent or aid in preventing the commission of the same, neglects or refuses to do so. . . ."[33] However, under these statutes, there must be "some racial, or perhaps otherwise class-based, invidiously discriminatory animus behind the conspirators' action."[34] Failure to meet this requirement will result in the dismissal of prisoners' claims under these statutes.[35]

5.   State Court Actions

Prisoners may bring their legal claims in state courts under the relevant state laws. It is not possible for us to deal in detail with the laws of fifty different states. However, most states permit suit in their courts for violations of prisoners' constitutional and state law rights, either against individual officials or against the state itself. Some state courts will hear actions under 42 U.S.C. §1983.[36] (See Ch. IV, Sec. D2, for a further discussion of state courts hearing §1983 actions.)

C.   Actions by Federal Prisoners

1.   Federal Question Actions Against Federal Officials

There is no statute like §1983 providing for suits against federal officials who violate your rights.[37] However, the courts have always assumed they could grant injunctive relief against federal officials.[38] More recently, the Supreme Court has held that federal officials who violate constitutional rights may be sued for damages as well in federal court.[39] These suits are called "*Bivens* actions" after the first case that authorized them.[40] The lower federal courts have heard such damage

---

[33]Griffin v. Breckenridge, 403 U.S. 88, 91 S.Ct. 1790 (1971).

[34]*Id.,* 403 U.S. at 101.

[35]*See, e.g.,* Trapnell v. Riggsby, 622 F.2d 290 (7th Cir. 1980).

[36]Cooper v. Morin, 49 N.Y.2d 69, 73 (N.Y. 1979).

[37]Federal officials may not be sued under §1983 because they do not act under color of state law. Hampton v. Holmesburg Prison Officials, 546 F.2d 1077 (3d Cir. 1976).

[38]See cases cited in Bivens v. Six Unknown Federal Narcotics Agents, 403 U.S. 388, 404, 91 S.Ct. 1999 (1971).

[39]Davis v. Passman, 442 U.S. 228, 99 S.Ct. 2264 (1979) (*Bivens* remedy inferred from the equal protection component of the Due Process Clause of the Fifth Amendment).

[40]Bivens v. Six Unknown Federal Narcotics Agents, *supra* note 38.

suits based on a wide variety of fact situations,[41] and the Supreme Court has upheld a *Bivens* action in a prison context.[42] At this point, the *Bivens* action is generally regarded as the federal equivalent of the §1983 damage action, and most of the rules and defenses applicable under §1983 will also apply in a *Bivens* action.

a.   Jurisdiction, 28 U.S.C. §1331(a)

Federal court jurisdiction over allegations of constitutional or other federal law violations is authorized in 28 U.S.C. §1331(a), which provides:

> The district court shall have original jurisdiction of all civil actions under the Constitution, laws, or treaties of the United States.[43]

The former requirement that you allege an "amount in controversy" of over $10,000 was eliminated by a recent amendment to the statute.

b.   Elements

To state a claim against federal officials, you only need allege (1) that your constitutional or other federal law rights were violated[44] and (2) that they were violated by persons acting under color of federal law.[45] Wheth-

---

[41]*See* Micklus v. Carlson, 632 F.2d 227 (3d Cir. 1980) (a prisoner who had been sentenced under Youth Corrections Act and had been denied the benefits of the Act by federal prison officials without due process can maintain an action for damages directly under the Fifth Amendment); Miller v. Stanmore, 636 F.2d 986 (5th Cir. 1981) (action for denial of prison visit and loss of good time credit); Gillespie v. Civiletti, 629 F.2d 637 (9th Cir. 1980) (action against U.S. marshals for treatment received while in their custody); Ellis v. Blum, 643 F.2d 68 (2d Cir. 1981).

[42]Carlson v. Green, 446 U.S. 14, 100 S.Ct. 1468 (1980) (a prisoner's medical claims alleging infliction of cruel and unusual punishment gave rise to a claim for damages under *Bivens*).

[43]28 U.S.C.A. §1331(a), as amended December 1, 1980, by Public Law 96-486, 94 Stat. 2369.

[44]Some courts have held that validly issued administrative regulations may be treated as "laws of the United States" for establishing jurisdiction. Gonzales v. Chasen, 506 F. Supp. 990 (D.P.R. 1980). *See also* Einhorn v. DeWitt, 618 F.2d 347 (5th Cir. 1980); Westinghouse Elec. Corp. v. Schlesinger, 542 F.2d 1190 (4th Cir. 1976), *cert. denied,* 431 U.S. 924 (1977).

[45]The courts have not spelled this point out, but it seems to be the clear implication of cases like Carlson v. Green, *supra* note 42, at 18. See Appendix B, Form 1o.

er a person acted under color of law presumably is determined in the same way for federal officials as for state officials. (See Sec. B1a, *supra.*)

c.   Other Requirements

In an injunctive action, where the federal official is being sued in his/her official capacity, which amounts to a suit against the federal government, a copy of the summons and complaint must be served upon the local United States Attorney in the district in which the action is brought, a copy must be sent by registered or certified mail to the Attorney General of the United States, Washington, D.C., and a copy must be sent to the individually named defendants by registered or certified mail.[46] If you are suing prison officials in their individual capacities for money damages, you must serve them with a copy of the summons and complaint.[47] Under a recent amendment to the Federal Rules of Civil Procedure, this service can be attempted by mail, or you may wish to have a member of your family or a friend serve the papers. (See Ch. VII, Sec. A2, for a more detailed discussion of how to have the summons and complaint served.)

Proper venue for federal officials being sued in their official capacities for declaratory and injunctive relief is in the federal district where any defendant resides, the events leading to the lawsuit occurred, or (except in real property actions) the plaintiff resides.[48] When prison officials are sued for damages in their individual capacities, venue is proper only "in the judicial district where all the defendants reside, or in which the claim arose."[49]

In a suit for injunctive or declaratory relief against federal officials, prisoners must generally have exhausted their administrative remedies before going to court. In a *Bivens* suit for money damages, most courts do not require exhaustion of remedies, although if you combine injunctive and damage claims, you may be required to exhaust administrative remedies on the whole case. (See Sec. D, *infra,* for a discussion of exhaustion of remedies.)

A damage action may not be brought against federal officials if there are "special factors counseling hesitation in the absence of affirmative

---

[46]*See* Rule 4(d)(4) and (5), FRCP, as amended February 26, 1983.

[47]*See* Micklus v. Carlson, 632 F.2d 227, 240-41 (3d Cir. 1980); McKnight v. Civiletti, 497 F. Supp. 657, 659 (E.D. Pa. 1980), and cases cited (personal services against officials must be affected in accordance with Rule 4(d)(1), FRCP).

[48]Stafford v. Briggs, 444 U.S. 527, 543-45, 100 S.Ct. 774 (1980).

[49]28 U.S.C. §1391(b). *See also* Stafford v. Briggs, *id.* at 544; McKnight v. Civiletti, *supra* note 47, at 659-60.

action by Congress."[50] This rule should not be a problem in prison cases, since defendants have the burden of demonstrating such factors, and the Supreme Court has held that the fact that the defendants are prison officials is not such a "special factor."[51]

2.   Federal Tort Claims Act

The United States government cannot be sued unless it has specifically consented to be sued and has waived its sovereign immunity. In 1946, Congress passed the Federal Tort Claims Act (FTCA),[52] which waived, with certain specified exceptions,[53] the government's immunity for liability in tort.

a.   Liability Under the FTCA

The Federal Tort Claims Act makes the federal government liable under the doctrine of *respondeat superior* for acts that would be common law torts in the state where they occurred.[54] It does not make the government liable for constitutional violations.[55] Do not be confused by the term "constitutional tort"; if you wish to pursue a case under the FTCA, you must plead a state tort law claim, even if the facts also amount to a constitutional violation.[56]

A tort is a personal injury caused by the wrongful or negligent act of another person. The torts that prisoners are most often concerned with fall into two broad categories: intentional torts and negligence. Intentional torts include such acts as assault, battery, and false imprison-

---

[50]Bivens v. Six Unknown Federal Narcotics Agents, *supra* note 38 at 403.

[51]Carlson v. Green, *supra* note 42, at 18-19.

[52]28 U.S.C. §§1346(b), 2671-2680 (hereinafter cited as FTCA). The FTCA allows "damages for injury or loss of property or personal injury or death caused by negligent or wrongful act or omission of any employee . . . while acting within the scope of his office or employment under the circumstances where the United States, if a private person would be liable to the claimant in accordance with the law of the place where the act or omission occurred." *Id.* at §2675(a).

[53]*See* 28 U.S.C. §2680 for exceptions.

[54]Carlson v. Green, *supra* note 42, at 23; Norton v. Turner, 427 F. Supp. 138, 146-47 (E.D. Va. 1977), *rev'd on other grounds sub nom.* Norton v. United States, 581 F.2d 390 (4th Cir. 1978), *cert. denied,* 439 U.S. 1003 (1978).

[55]Carlson v. Green, *id.*

[56]See Sec. C3, *infra,* for a more detailed discussion of cases involving both tort claims and constitutional violations.

ment.[57] Negligence includes a broad range of acts or failures to act that result in injury, and is defined as "the failure to use such care as a reasonably prudent and careful person would use under similar circumstances."[58]

The main intentional torts that prisoner litigants are likely to be concerned with are assault and battery ("[a]ny unlawful touching of another which is without justification or excuse"),[59] false arrest ("arrest without proper legal authority"), false imprisonment ("unlawful detention of the person of another, for any length of time, whereby he is deprived of his personal liberty"), malicious prosecution ("[o]ne begun in malice without probable cause to believe the charges can be sustained"), and trespass ("unlawful interference with one's person, property, or rights").[60] (These definitions are very general; if you are planning to bring a suit alleging any of them, you must research the precise definition and elements of the tort under the law of the state where it happened.)

An action for negligence may be brought under the FTCA for virtually any non-work-related injury[61] to person or property that is arguably the fault of prison personnel.[62]

The basic elements of a prisoner's negligence claim are

---

[57]Certain intentional torts—libel, slander, misrepresentation, deceit, and interference with contract rights—are not actionable under the FTCA. Others, including assault, battery, false imprisonment, false arrest, abuse of process, and malicious prosecution, are actionable when committed by investigative or law enforcement officers. 28 U.S.C. §2680(h). (Federal correctional officers are included in the definition of investigative or law enforcement officers. Hernandez v. Lattimore, 454 F. Supp. 763, 769 (S.D.N.Y. 1978), *rev'd on other grounds,* 612 F.2d 61 (2d Cir. 1979).) Other intentional torts, such as trespass, may also be pursued under the FTCA. Norton v. Turner, *supra* note 54, at 144 n.5.

[58]BLACK'S LAW DICTIONARY at 930 (5th ed. 1979).

[59]Prisoners will sue for assault and battery under the FTCA where the assault and battery was committed by prison personnel. Where it was committed by another prisoner, the FTCA claim will be one for negligence by prison personnel in permitting the assault to happen. See Ch. V, Sec. C2a, for a discussion of prisoner-on-prisoner assaults, and Sec. C2b, for a discussion of assaults by guards.

[60]All definitions in this list are from BLACK'S LAW DICTIONARY (5th ed. 1979).

[61]Work-related injuries are governed by the Federal Prison Industries' Inmate Accident Compensation System, discussed in Sec. C5, *infra. See* Sturgeon v. Federal Prison Industries, 608 F.2d 1153 (8th Cir. 1979).

[62]28 U.S.C. §1346(b).

(1) a *duty* on the part of prison personnel to follow a certain standard of care to protect prisoners from unreasonable risks;

(2) a *failure* by prison personnel to perform that duty;

(3) *actual injury* caused (or "proximately caused")[63] by the failure to perform that duty.[64]

The Supreme Court has held that "the duty of care owed by the Bureau of Prisons to federal prisoners is fixed by 18 U.S.C. §4042, independent of an inconsistent state rule."[65] This statute requires the Bureau to:

(2) provide suitable quarters and provide for the safekeeping, care, and subsistence of all persons charged with or convicted of offenses against the United States, or held as witnesses or otherwise; (3) provide for the protection, instruction, and discipline of all persons charged with or convicted of offenses against the United States. . . . "[66]

(This rule is an exception to the general rule that state tort law governs FTCA cases.)

Almost any violation of this duty can give rise to liability under the FTCA. For example, you have a claim under the FTCA if you get food poisoning because of improper prison food handling procedures, if you trip over construction debris that should have been cleaned up, if you are injured because a prison employee drives recklessly and has an accident when transporting you, or if you are assaulted by another prisoner because of prison officials' failure to supervise or classify.[67]

---

[63] "Proximate cause" is a complicated legal concept which is designed to prevent tort liability for remote or unpredictable results of negligent acts. *See* PROSSER, LAW OF TORTS, Ch. 7 (4th ed. 1971). For example, if you were negligently taken to an outside medical appointment on the wrong day, and that day happened to be the one on which the doctor's office burned down, a court would probably find that your injuries from the fire were not proximately caused by the negligence in transporting you on the wrong day.

[64] This definition is adapted from PROSSER, LAW OF TORTS at 143 (4th ed. 1971). As previously stated, FTCA actions are governed by state law, and the way these elements are defined may vary from state to state. Use the terms and definitions of negligence cases from the state where the tort occurred.

[65] United States v. Muniz, 374 U.S. 150, 165, 83 S.Ct. 1850 (1963) (federal prisoner beaten by other prisoners sued federal prison officials for negligence in their failure to properly supervise and segregate prisoners while they were in the prison yard).

[66] 18 U.S.C. §4042.

[67] United States v. Muniz, *supra* note 65. These claims are often difficult to prove; an assault by itself is not proof of negligence. Johnson v. United States, 258 F. Supp. 372, 376 (E.D. Va. 1966). See Ch. V, Sec. C2a, for a more detailed discussion.

The government may defend an FTCA suit by claiming that the prison personnel who caused your injury were performing (or failing to perform) a "discretionary function or duty."[68] A court, in determining whether a "discretionary function or duty" existed, will first determine whether the decision is one made at the planning level (discretionary) or at the operational level (non-discretionary).[69] A duty is non-discretionary if it involves enforcement or administration of a mandatory duty at the operational level.[70] If the prison official in performing his/ her duties must act without reliance upon a fixed or readily ascertainable standard, the decision made is discretionary and you can not sue under the FTCA, even if that discretion is abused.[71] For example, the former federal parole board was sued pursuant to the FTCA for releasing a prisoner on parole in total disregard of extensive medical reports confirming he was a homicidal psychotic.[72] The court, in determining whether the parole board duties were discretionary or non-discretionary, examined the parole statute authorizing release of prisoners on parole.[73] The court held that the statute gave the board complete discretion whether to release someone on parole and whether to subject him/her to any terms and conditions of parole.[74] An FTCA action could not be maintained based on the parole decision.

If there exists a definite standard by which prison officials' action is measured, it is not a discretionary act.[75] For example, the Bureau of Prisons was sued for negligence in not providing the parole board with a copy of the prison records of a federal prisoner being considered for parole.[76] The court examined the statutes applicable to the Bureau of Prisons and parole board and determined that the Bureau of Prisons was

---

[68]28 U.S.C. §2680(a).

[69]Payton v. United States, 679 F.2d 475, 480 (5th Cir. 1982); Lindgren v. United States, 665 F.2d 978, 980 (9th Cir. 1982). *See also* Dalehite v. United States, 346 U.S. 15, 72 S.Ct. 956 (1953).

[70]Barton v. United States, 609 F.2d 977, 979 (10th Cir. 1979).

[71]*Id.* Estrada v. Hills, 401 F. Supp. 429, 436 (N.D. Ill. 1975).

[72]Payton v. United States, *supra* note 69 (while on parole, he killed three people).

[73]18 U.S.C. §4203(a).

[74]Payton v. United States, *supra* note 69, at 480-82. *See* 18 U.S.C. §4203(a) (the parole board may release "upon such terms and conditions . . . as the board shall prescribe. . . .").

[75]Barton v. United States, *supra* note 70, at 979.

[76]Payton v. United States, *supra* note 69.

required by 18 U.S.C. §4208(c) to provide the prison records of a prisoner being considered for parole to the parole board. Since the Bureau had a duty, there was no discretion involved and their failure to provide the records would state a claim under the FTCA.[77]

It has been held that the Federal Bureau of Prisons' provision of medical treatment is not a discretionary act and the Bureau can be sued pursuant under the FTCA for negligent medical treatment.[78]

If the government claims that the discretionary function rule applies, you should try to show, using the analysis of these and similar cases, why the action that injured you was not a discretionary function.

Whether the government can take advantage of the defense of qualified immunity[79] in an FTCA suit has not been settled.[80] Because that defense is intended to protect individual government officials from personal financial liability, the government should not be permitted to use it.

You may also have a claim under the FTCA for injuries you receive in a local jail, if you are placed there by federal officials. The United States has a duty to use reasonable care in providing for the safety of federal prisoners confined in state institutions and must discharge this duty in a non-negligent manner.[81] If you suffer an injury in a local jail, however, you will have to prove that it resulted from some negligence of federal officials. You may also wish to sue the officials of the jail or prison where you were injured. You cannot do this under the FTCA; you will have to sue state or local officials under 42 U.S.C. §1983.[82] (See Sec. C4, *infra,* for a discussion of liability under a contract theory for injuries received by federal prisoners in a local jail.)

---

[77]*Id. See also* Ross v. United States, 640 F.2d 511, 519 (5th Cir. 1981) (when government undertakes to perform services which are not required, it will be liable if these activities are performed negligently).

[78]Jackson v. Kelly, 557 F.2d 735 (10th Cir. 1977).

[79]See Sec. E1d, *infra,* for a discussion of qualified immunity.

[80]*Compare* Norton v. United States, 581 F.2d 390 (4th Cir. 1978), *cert. denied,* 439 U.S. 1003 (1978) (government could raise qualified immunity), *with* Crain v. Krehbiel, 443 F. Supp. 202, 216 (N.D. Cal. 1977) (qualified immunity not available under FTCA).

[81]Logue v. United States, 411 U.S. 521, 532-33, 93 S.Ct. 2215 (1973); Gillespie v. Civiletti, 629 F.2d 637 (9th Cir. 1980); Brown v. United States, 374 F. Supp. 723 (E.D. Ark. 1974).

[82]See Sec. B, *supra,* for a discussion of §1983 actions. *See also* Gillespie v. Civiletti, *id.* at 643.

b.   Procedures Under the FTCA

Before you can sue under the FTCA, you must exhaust administrative remedies,[83] which means filing a claim with the governmental agency responsible for the tort (usually the Bureau of Prisons). This claim must be filed with the regional office of the Bureau of Prisons in the region where the tort happened within two years after your claim accrues.[84] The regional counsel has the authority to offer you a settlement, if it does not exceed $500. If the proposed settlement is for a value over $500, the regional counsel will send it with other documents to the Office of the General Counsel, Central Office, Washington, D.C. The General Counsel can offer you a settlement not to exceed $2,500. Any claim over $2,500 must be approved by the Attorney General.[85]

Once the Bureau of Prisons provides you with a denial of your claim, a lawsuit must be filed within six months of the date of the mailing of the notice of denial.[86] If you do not receive the Bureau's denial until six months has passed from its issuance, you should still sue. If the Bureau defends the suit on the grounds that you did not file the lawsuit within six months of the denial, you should bring to the court's attention the actual date you received the denial and the reasons for receiving it late. If the Bureau of Prisons fails to act on your claim within six months after you have filed it with them, you may assume that their failure to act is a final denial and bring a lawsuit any time.[87]

When filing a claim, you should use the form provided by the Bureau of Prisons.[88] These forms can usually be obtained from a prison staff member.[89] If you are not able to obtain a form, you can present "other written notification," such as a letter.[90] The letter should contain all the information called for in the form. The form or other written notification can be received from you or your duly authorized agent or legal representative.

---

[83] 28 U.S.C. §2675(a); 28 CFR §543.13 (1981).

[84] 28 CFR §543.13(b).

[85] 28 CFR §§14.6 and 543.21 (1981).

[86] 28 U.S.C. §2401(b). This is true regardless of whether the six-month period expires before the two-year limitation period for filing the claim. *See* Childers v. United States, 442 F.2d 1299 (5th Cir.), *cert. denied,* 99 S.Ct. 106 (1978).

[87] 28 U.S.C. §2675(a); 28 CFR §543.31(h). *See* Kelly v. United States, 560 F.2d 259, 260 (2d Cir.), *cert. denied,* 99 S.Ct. 106 (1978).

[88] See Appendix B, Form 20, Standard Form 95.

[89] 28 CFR §543.31.

[90] 28 CFR §14.2(a).

The Bureau of Prisons must be provided with more than just notice of an accident. They must be given the appropriate information upon which to base a decision.[91] The warden of the institution where the basis for the claim occurred will appoint a staff member to investigate the matter.[92] The Bureau of Prisons may request additional information pertaining to your claim.[93] You should always answer such a request. Your failure to provide this additional or supplemental information needed to process your claim can be considered a failure to file a proper claim, and can result in dismissal of a subsequent lawsuit.[94] Once the investigation is completed, the warden will forward the investigative report with his/her recommendation to the regional counsel.[95]

In your administrative claim, you must state in your request for money damages a "sum certain."[96] Failure to state a sum certain is a failure to comply with the regulation, and a court can dismiss your lawsuit.[97] Since a valid administrative claim requires personal authorization and a sum certain, class action claims can not be filed.[98] The amount you state in your administrative claim is generally the maximum you may receive, unless the increased amount is based upon newly discovered evidence which was not reasonably discoverable at the time of presenting the claim, or unless you prove that additional damages are justified by facts occurring after your claim is filed.[99]

Once you have filed your claim, you may amend it before a final decision is made on it.[100] If your claim has been denied, you may request reconsideration within the six-month period after denial and before you

---

[91] 28 CFR §14.4. You must provide a detailed description of the incident resulting in your loss, injury, assault, or battery and request money damages of a specific amount.

[92] 28 CFR §543.31(c) and (d).

[93] *Supra* note 91.

[94] Cummings v. United States, 449 F. Supp. 40 (D. Mont. 1978); Rothman v. United States, 434 F. Supp. 13, 17 (C.D. Cal. 1977).

[95] 28 CFR §543.31(e).

[96] 28 U.S.C. §2675(a); 28 CFR §14.2(a).

[97] Allen v. United States, 517 F.2d 1328 (6th Cir. 1975); Fallon v. United States, 405 F. Supp. 1320 (D. Mont. 1976).

[98] Blain v. United States, 552 F.2d 289, 290 (9th Cir. 1977).

[99] 28 U.S.C. §2675(b). *See* Molinar v. United States, 515 F.2d 246 (5th Cir. 1975); Husovsky v. United States, 590 F.2d 944 (D.C. Cir. 1978); United States v. Alexander, 238 F.2d 314 (5th Cir. 1956).

[100] 28 CFR §14.2(c).

file a lawsuit.[101] A request for reconsideration will toll (suspend) the time limit for filing your lawsuit. Once the Bureau of Prisons has denied your request for reconsideration, another six-month period during which you can file a lawsuit begins to run from the date of the second denial letter.[102] You can only ask for one reconsideration.[103]

3.   *Bivens* Actions and the FTCA

In deciding whether to bring a *Bivens* action or an FTCA action, you should keep in mind the differences between them.[104]

(a) The FTCA provides a remedy only for common-law torts; a *Bivens* action can only be brought for constitutional violations.

(b) In an FTCA action, there is no right to a jury trial; in a *Bivens* action, either plaintiff or defendant can demand a jury trial.

(c) An FTCA judgment against the government bars any later recovery against individual officials. If you win a *Bivens* action, you can also bring a later suit against the government if you are unable to collect on the first judgment.

(d) Under the FTCA, you can recover only compensatory damages; in a *Bivens* action, you can also obtain punitive damages.[105]

(e) Under the FTCA, officials are immune if they were performing discretionary functions or acting pursuant to a statute or regulation. In a *Bivens* action, most officials are entitled only to qualified immunity.[106]

(f) You must exhaust administrative remedies before filing an FTCA suit. Most courts do not require administrative exhaustion before bringing a *Bivens* action.[107]

If the acts about which you wish to sue amount to a common-law tort *and* a constitutional violation, you can bring either an FTCA or a *Bivens* action, or both. The Supreme Court has held that the FTCA and *Bivens* actions are separate remedies and that the existence of one does not keep you from using the other.[108] You can join both claims in the same lawsuit

---

[101]28 CFR §14.9(b). Your request for reconsideration will be filed with the person who had initially denied your request.

[102]*Id.*

[103]*Id.*

[104]See Secs. C1 and C2, *supra,* for more detailed discussions of each point.

[105]See Sec. F, *infra,* for a discussion of damages.

[106]See Sec. E1d, *infra,* for a discussion of qualified immunity.

[107]See Sec. D, *infra,* for a discussion of exhaustion.

[108]Carlson v. Green, 446 U.S. 14, 100 S.Ct. 1468 (1980).

if you wish.[109] However, the various differences in the two remedies apply, even if you join them in one lawsuit. Thus, you might wind up presenting one claim to a jury and one claim to the judge at the same time.[110]

4.   Contract Actions By Federal Prisoners Injured in Local Jails

Federal prisoners may be entitled to recover for injuries suffered in state or local facilities under the general principles of contract law as third-party beneficiaries.[111] The defendants in such a case would be the city, county, and/or the local jail officials responsible for carrying out the contract. You will need to look at the contract that existed between the two agencies (federal government and either the county or the jail) to determine what rights and protections you as a third party are entitled to by it.[112] The contract may require that the jail provide for your safety. If the jail has become overcrowded and you are assaulted as a result,[113] you would allege that your rights as a third-party beneficiary of the contract were violated.

To show a violation of your rights as a third-party beneficiary, you will need to allege:

(1) the existence of a contract between the federal government and the local county or sheriff;

(2) that the contract contains a provision providing benefits to you, such as that jail officials would provide for your safety; and either

(3) that this provision of the contract was breached by the U.S. government in their failure to inspect and make sure that jail officials were providing for your safety; or

(4) that jail officials breached the contract (*e.g.,* by allowing their jail to become so overcrowded that the danger of assault was unreasonably increased).

5.   Federal Prison Industries' Inmate Accident Compensation System

The Federal Prison Industries' Inmate Accident Compensation System

---

[109]Norton v. United States, *supra* note 80.

[110]*See* Picariello v. Fenton, 491 F. Supp. 1020 (M.D. Pa. 1980).

[111]Owens v. Haas, 601 F.2d 1242 (2d Cir. 1979) (federal prisoners sued county and jail officers for beating while confined in their jail under §1983); Hampton v. Holmesburg Prison Officials, 546 F.2d 1077 (3d Cir. 1976).

[112]Hampton v. Holmesburg Prison Officials, *id.*

[113]*See* McKenna v. County of Nassau, 538 F. Supp. 737 (E.D.N.Y. 1982) (assault found to have been caused by overcrowding).

(hereinafter IACS), 18 U.S.C. §4126, provides compensation to federal prisoners who are injured during the course of their employment in a federal prison. The Federal Prison Industries may pay "compensation to inmates or their dependents for injuries suffered in any industry or in any work activity in connection with the maintenance or operation of the institution where confined."[114] In *United States v. Demko,*[115] the Court held that the "prison compensation law" in 18 U.S.C. §4126 is the exclusive remedy against the government for a federal prisoner injured while working; the Federal Tort Claims Act may not be used.[116] Furthermore, a work-related injury that is aggravated by improper medical treatment cannot be the basis of a claim under the FTCA.[117] This Act, §4126, does not preclude you from bringing an action against a prison official in his/her individual capacity for injuries sustained from a work-related accident when s/he has performed or failed to perform acts of a non-discretionary nature.[118]

The statute does not establish guidelines or criteria for compensating prisoners for their work-related injuries. The guidelines and criteria are promulgated as rules by the Bureau of Prisons and will be found at 28 CFR §§301 *et seq.* (1980). These rules do not provide for compensation for your injury until you are released from prison. While you are incarcerated, you may receive compensation for lost prison wages for work-related injuries.[119] You may also receive lost-time wages and compensation for occupational disease or illness "proximately caused by the conditions of [your] work assignment."[120] You will be provided compensation if you lost in excess of three consecutive scheduled workdays. If you are not contributing to the support of dependents, you will receive only 66⅔ percent of the standard hourly rate, and if you are contributing to the support of dependents, you will receive 76 percent of the standard hourly wage. (See 28 CFR §301.10(c) for a definition of "providing support to dependents.") If you disagree with the deter-

---

[114]18 U.S.C. §4216. *See also* 28 CFR §301.9 (injuries resulting from voluntary work approved by staff in the operation or maintenance of the institution may be compensated).

[115]385 U.S. 149, 87 S.Ct. 382 (1966).

[116]Aston v. United States, 625 F.2d 1210 (5th Cir. 1980) (cause of injury is irrelevant so long as the injury itself occurred while prisoner was on job); Byrd v. Warden, 376 F. Supp. 37 (S.D.N.Y. 1974).

[117]*Byrd, id.* at 38-9, and cases cited therein.

[118]*Id.* at 41; Thompson v. United States, 492 F.2d 1082 (5th Cir. 1974). *See also* Carlson v. Green, 446 U.S. 14, 100 S.Ct. 1468 (1980).

[119]28 CFR §301.10.

[120]28 CFR §301(c).

mination made under this section, you may appeal it through the administrative appeal process. (See 28 CFR §301.10.)

You may receive compensation for injuries resulting from voluntary work approved by staff in the operation and/or maintenance of the institution. Compensation is not paid for injuries received while going to or leaving work, or going to or coming from lunch. Injuries resulting from participation in institutional programs are not compensable; nor are injuries received from willful violations of rules and regulations concerning a job assignment. (See 28 CFR §301.9.)

Compensation to be paid, aside from lost prison wages, will be based on the permanency and severity of the injury in terms of temporary and permanent impairment. The minimum wage prescribed by the Fair Labor Standards Act at the time of each periodic payment will be the basis in determining compensation. The provisions of the Federal Employees' Compensation Act, 18 U.S.C. §§4121 *et seq.,* shall be followed when practicable in determining disability and payment. (See 28 CFR §301.21.)

The following procedures are the steps that must be taken if you are to be compensated for your work-related injuries.

1. You must report all injuries, regardless of how trivial the injuries may appear, immediately to your supervisor so that proper medical treatment may be secured for you. Your refusal to accept such treatment may cause you to forfeit any valid claim you might otherwise have for compensation. (See 28 CFR §301.2.)

2. Your supervisor will secure a report of the cause, nature, and exact extent of your injury and *shall* make sure that you submit, within 48 hours, an Administrative Form 19, Injury Report (Inmate). The names and testimony of all witnesses shall be secured. (See 28 CFR §301.3.)

3. Form 19 shall contain a signed statement by the prisoner on how the accident occurred. An original and copies will be sent to the Institution Safety Manager for a review as to its completeness; the injured prisoner shall be provided with a copy. The Safety Manager shall ensure that a detailed medical description of the injury was included in Form 19, and that Administrative Form 19A (Injury—Lost-Time Follow-Up Report) is completed for all reported work injuries which result in lost time from the work assignment. If the Safety Manager thinks that an injury will result in time lost from the work assignment, s/he shall refer Forms 19 and 19A to the Institution Safety Committee so that they may make a determination whether the injury was actually work-related and whether the injured prisoner should receive lost-time wages. (See 28 CFR §301.4.)

4. If your prison work-related injury will affect your future earning potential, you may be entitled to compensation. Before your transfer to a community treatment center, or as soon as you obtain a release date, prison officials will give you an FPI Form 43, Inmate Claim for Com-

pensation on Account of Work Injury, and they shall inform you of your right to receive compensation after release. Prison officials will also provide you assistance in filling out and filing FPI Form 43. Your claim for compensation, if not made in prison, must be made within 60 days following release, and for "reasonable cause shown" you may file up to one year after release.

If you have made a claim pursuant to FPI Form 43, before your release from prison you shall be given a medical examination. A refusal to submit to a final medical examination shall result in the "forfeiture of all rights to compensation and to future medical treatment." The institution is to take pictures of all visible impairment, disfigurement, or loss of member. The FPI Form 43, after completion by the prisoner and physician, shall be forwarded to the Claims Examiner, Federal Prison Industries, Inc., Washington, DC 20534. (See 28 CFR §301.5.)

5. Your claim for accident compensation will be determined after your release. The amount paid for prior medical or surgical treatments or lost-time wages will not be subtracted from any amount awarded. The amount you shall receive after release will be determined by a single claims examiner appointed by the Commissioner of the Federal Prison Industries. S/he will consider all available evidence. You will be provided with a written decision, informing you of the reasons for the decision. You will be informed of the right to appeal the decision to the Inmate Accident Compensation Committee, Federal Bureau of Prisons, Washington, DC 20534. (See 28 CFR §§301.11 and .12.)

6. If you are not satisfied with the decision of the claims examiner, you must make a written request for a hearing or reconsideration to the Committee within 30 days after the date of the decision, or a longer period for "good cause shown." The Committee shall send you a copy of the information upon which the claims examiner based his/her determination to your last known address. (See 28 CFR §301.13.)

7. If you have requested a hearing or reconsideration of the claims examiner's decision, you may submit additional evidence which the Committee will consider along with the original record. The hearing or reconsideration by the Committee shall be held within 60 days of your request, but may be postponed by the Committee or at your request for good cause. You will be given sufficient notice of the hearing so that you may attend. The hearing is to be conducted at the Central Office of the Bureau of Prisons, Washington, DC 20534. Your failure to appear at the hearing or to show within 10 days "good cause" for that failure to appear will result in a determination that you have abandoned your claim. (See 28 CFR §§301.14 and .15.)

8. You may be represented at the hearing by the person of your choice, as long as s/he is not then in prison. At the hearing, the regular rules of evidence do not apply. The Committee has authority to conduct the hearing in the manner it determines is best for soliciting all the in-

formation. If you desire to present witnesses at the hearing, you must provide the Committee with a list of their names and an outline of their proposed testimony. The Committee does not have the power to compel the attendance of witnesses, and incarcerated witnesses may not appear, but their testimony can be received in written form. The hearing shall be recorded and a copy of the transcript may be provided to you if such a request is made within 90 days following the hearing. A decision by the Committee will normally be rendered within 30 days of the hearing. (See 28 CFR §§301.16, .17, .18, and .19.)

9. If you are not satisfied with the decision of the Committee, you may file a written appeal within 90 days from the day of the Committee's decision, or later when "good cause" is shown, to the Associate Commissioner of Federal Prison Industries, Inc., Washington, DC 20534. The Associate Commissioner will respond to a notice of appeal within 90 days after receipt by affirming or amending the Committee's decision. (See 28 CFR §301.20.)

10. If additional medical, hospital, or any other related treatment is needed after your release from prison, you will need to receive the claims examiner's *prior* approval for each such treatment or the Bureau of Prisons will not pay. (See 28 CFR §301.23.)

6.　Federal Question Actions, Federal Post-Conviction Relief, and Appeals

In federal courts, the major kinds of legal actions available to federal prisoners are the federal question actions described in Sec. C1 of this chapter; a motion to vacate, set aside, or correct a sentence under 28 U.S.C. §2255; a petition for a writ of habeas corpus under 28 U.S.C. §2241; and a motion for correction or reduction of sentence under Federal Rules of Criminal Procedure, Rule 35. (See also Ch. IX, Sec. H, for a further discussion of Rule 35 and §2255 proceedings.)

An action for an injunction against federal prison practices or conditions should generally be brought as a federal question action.[121] In some jurisdictions, you can also bring such a case as a petition for a writ of habeas corpus under 28 U.S.C. §2241.[122] In either case, you will probably be required to exhaust administrative remedies first.[123] An action for damages based on the acts or omissions of federal prison personnel may be brought as a federal question action, under the Federal

---

[121]See Sec. C1, *supra.*

[122]Wolfish v. Levi, 573 F.2d 118, 122 (2d Cir. 1978), *rev'd on other grounds,* 441 U.S. 520 (1975); *contra,* Crawford v. Bell, 599 F.2d 890 (9th Cir. 1979).

[123]See Sec. D1, *infra,* for a discussion of exhaustion of remedies by federal prisoners.

Tort Claims Act, or under the Federal Prison Industries' Inmate Accident Compensation System, depending on the facts involved.[124] Damages may not be awarded under the habeas corpus statutes.

If you believe your federal court conviction was unlawfully obtained, or your sentence was unlawfully imposed, you *must* appeal, and you *must* raise all issues in your appeal that you ever wish to present to a court. Courts are increasingly reluctant to consider issues in later proceedings that could have been, but were not, presented on direct appeal.[125]

If you appeal your federal conviction or sentence and lose, you may bring a post-conviction proceeding. Federal prisoners are ordinarily required to proceed by motion to vacate, set aside, or correct the sentence pursuant to 28 U.S.C. §2255, filed in the court where the sentence and conviction were obtained, rather than by writ of habeas corpus under §2241. You are limited in this collateral attack to raising claims alleging that the trial court lacked jurisdiction or that some error of a fundamental nature was committed which resulted in a miscarriage of justice[126] (*e.g.*, the sentencing court unconstitutionally used an uncounseled conviction as the basis for enhanced punishment).[127]

Challenges to the way your sentence is being carried out should be brought by writ of habeas corpus under §2241 and filed in the district where the prisoner is confined. Challenges to parole procedures, sentence computation, or loss of good time should be brought under this statute.[128]

If you are not challenging your conviction, but only the sentence imposed, you should file a motion under Rule 35 of the Federal Rules of Criminal Procedure. A Rule 35 motion is a challenge to the legality of your sentence and not to the underlying conviction[129] or a plea to the sentencing court for leniency because of factors that were either not before the court at sentencing or events that have occurred since sentenc-

---

[124]See Secs. C.1-C.3, *supra*.

[125]*See* United States v. Addonizio, 442 U.S. 178, 190, 99 S.Ct. 2236 (1979); United States v. Capua, 656 F.2d 1033 (5th Cir. 1981). See also Ch. IX, Post-Conviction Remedies.

[126]*See* Davis v. United States, 417 U.S. 333, 94 S.Ct. 2298 (1973) (after defendant was sentenced, legislature made conduct leading to his conviction legal; sentence was vacated).

[127]Burgett v. Texas, 398 U.S. 109, 115, 88 S.Ct. 258 (1967).

[128]Green v. Nelson, 442 F. Supp. 1047 (D. Conn. 1977); Lepore v. Anderson, 448 F. Supp. 716 (M.D. Pa. 1978).

[129]*See* United States v. Faust, 680 F.2d 540 (8th Cir. 1982) (ambiguity in sentence); United States v. Mooney, 654 F.2d 482 (7th Cir. 1981) (plea bargain for recommended sentence).

ing (e.g., since being sentenced, it has been determined that your wife will die of cancer within six months and you have six children under the age of 18 who only have you to support and care for them and you are requesting a reduction of sentence). (See also Ch. IX, Sec. H, for a further discussion.) The Supreme Court recently held that the sentencing court must decide a motion filed under Rule 35 within 120 days of imposition of sentence or issuance of a final decision in regards to your criminal appeal as of right,[130] so you must move quickly.

What you may not do is try to attack your conviction through a federal question action for an injunction or damages. As long as your criminal conviction stands, it bars any relitigation of the factual and legal issues which were decided in the criminal case. You must attack the criminal conviction through the appellate process followed by the post-conviction remedies provided by 28 U.S.C. §§2241 and 2255.

D. Exhaustion of Remedies

Sometimes courts require that, before you bring your case to them, you first present it to another court or to an administrative agency or use a grievance system or a claims procedure. This process is called the "exhaustion" of administrative or judicial remedies. Depending on your situation, a federal court may require that you exhaust your state judicial remedies before it will hear your case, and either a state or federal court may require you to exhaust your prison administrative remedies such as a grievance system or a claims procedure. In this section, we explain the various exhaustion requirements you may encounter.

1. Federal Prisoners in Federal Court

If you are suing a federal agency or agency official, including the Federal Bureau of Prisons or its employees, for an injunction, you are generally required to exhaust any administrative remedies that the agency makes available.[131] Sometimes you can avoid this exhaustion requirement by showing that your case falls into one of the recognized exceptions to the rule. Some courts have permitted exhaustion to be by-passed when it appeared that exhaustion would be futile,[132] that the ad-

---

[130]See United States v. Addonizio, supra note 125, at 190. See also Rule 35(b), FRCrP.

[131]See, e.g., Hardwick v. Ault, 517 F.2d 295, 296 (5th Cir. 1975); Willis v. Ciccone, 506 F.2d 1011, 1015 (8th Cir. 1974), and cases cited; Buckley v. United States, 494 F. Supp. 1000 (E.D. Ky. 1980); Payne v. Day, 440 F. Supp. 785 (W.D. Okla. 1977), and cases cited.

[132]Smith v. Carlson, 447 F. Supp. 422, 425 (N.D. Pa. 1978) (court held exhaustion would be futile since Bureau of Prisons claimed that the transfer of

ministrative remedies were inadequate, that "exigent circumstances" existed or "irreparable injury" would be suffered before the remedy could be effective,[133] or that the case involves legal issues that the agency cannot or will not decide.[134] The courts have often been very conservative and very unpredictable in applying these exceptions, so be very cautious and study the case law in your jurisdiction carefully before bypassing administrative remedies. Most prisoners, in making a "futility" or "inadequacy" argument to the courts for their having bypassed administrative procedures, will allege that prison officials are biased and unfair. Even if you are right, you should not use these arguments, since it is unlikely that you can come up with enough concrete proof to satisfy a federal judge.

If you are suing federal officials individually to obtain damages for a constitutional violation, you generally do not have to exhaust administrative remedies, since the Bureau of Prisons' remedies do not provide for damages.[135] One federal circuit, the Tenth, has held that you do have to exhaust administrative remedies, but the reasoning of this case is not persuasive, and it will probably not be followed outside the Tenth Circuit.[136]

If you are suing the government under the Federal Tort Claims Act, you are required to file an administrative claim first. This procedure is discussed *supra,* Sec. C2b.

---

the prisoner was not pursuant to their policy but that of the District of Columbia's Department of Corrections. *Cf.* Antonelli v. Ralston, 609 F.2d 340 (8th Cir. 1979) (court questioned whether adequate administrative relief at local prison was possible when what prisoner was requesting would conflict with national written prison policy).

[133]Miller v. Stanmore, 636 F.2d 986, 991 n.8 (5th Cir. 1981) (since prisoners had alleged that the administrative exhaustion procedures violated their due process rights, exhaustion of these procedures may not be required); Green v. Nelson, 442 F. Supp. 1047, 1052 (D. Conn. 1977) (since U.S. Parole Commission had continuously failed to adopt constitutionally mandated parole rescission hearing procedures, exhaustion was not required since the likelihood of relief through the Commission's appellate procedure was nil); Downes v. Morton, 360 F. Supp. 1151, 1152 n.1 (D. Conn. 1973) (since both prisoners were scheduled to be released with days of court hearing if good time was restored, requiring exhaustion would be futile).

[134]Green v. Nelson, *id.;* Brown v. Carlson, 431 F. Supp. 755, 763 (W.D. Wisc. 1977) (if the issue in question in a case is purely legal and not factual, the requirement of exhaustion is inappropriate).

[135]*See, e.g.,* Abdul-Khabir v. Lichtenberger, 518 F. Supp. 673, 675 (E.D. Va. 1981).

[136]Brice v. Day, 604 F.2d 664 (10th Cir. 1979) (use of administrative procedures is not to resolve constitutional issues or to consider damages, but to establish a record for the court to consider).

2.   State Prisoners in Federal Court

If you are challenging the fact or the duration of your conviction, rather than the conditions of your confinement, you must bring your case under the federal habeas corpus statutes, and you must first exhaust your state judicial remedies. This exhaustion requirement is discussed in more detail in Ch. IX, Sec. B2, and in Sec. B2 of this chapter.

If you are challenging the conditions of your confinement or acts by prison officials that do not affect the length of your confinement, you may proceed under 42 U.S.C. §1983. You do not have to exhaust state judicial remedies,[137] and ordinarily you do not have to exhaust your state administrative remedies before using §1983.[138] However, Congress passed a statute in 1980 called the Civil Rights of Institutionalized Persons Act,[139] which sets up a limited exhaustion requirement in certain circumstances. The Attorney General was required to promulgate minimum standards for "plain, speedy, and effective" administrative remedies. If the Attorney General has certified a state's remedies as acceptable, or if the court finds that they meet the statutory requirements, the judge may "continue" (stay) your lawsuit for a period of 90 days. Also, the court must find it would be "appropriate" and "in the interests of justice" to require exhaustion.

In order for the Attorney General to certify an administrative grievance system, or for the court to find it acceptable, it must meet a number of statutory requirements. Employees and prisoners must have an advisory role in the formulation, implementation, and operation of the grievance system. Specific time limits for written replies to grievances, with reasons at each decisional level, are required. There must be a provision for expediting grievances of an emergency nature, especially where delay would subject the grievance to a substantial risk of personal injury or other danger. The grievance procedure must include safeguards to avoid reprisal against any grievant or participant in the resolution of the grievance. Finally, the procedure must provide for independent review of the disposition of the grievance, including claims of reprisal, by a person not under the direct supervision or control of the institution.

In addition to these statutory requirements, the Attorney General has promulgated minimum standards for state prison grievance procedures which must be met in order for you to be required to exhaust these remedies. These minimum standards require that inmates be notified

---

[137]Monroe v. Pape, 365 U.S. 167, 183, 81 S.Ct. 473 (1961).

[138]Patsy v. Board of Regents of State of Florida, __U.S.__, 102 S.Ct. 2557 (1982).

[139]42 U.S.C. §1997e (1976 ed., Supp. IV).

orally and in writing about the procedure, that it be available to all inmates, regardless of their disciplinary or other classification, that it cover a broad range of complaints and make clear what is covered and what is excluded, that it provide a reasonable range of remedies, that the grievance process be completed within 90 days of initiation, and that there be an expedited procedure for emergency grievances.

This complicated discussion resolves into a few simple rules for state prisoners considering litigation:

(a) If the Attorney General has certified your state's grievance system, you must use it before going to federal court, unless your problem is not covered by the system or the remedy you seek (*e.g.,* money damages) is not available. To determine whether your state's grievance system has been certified, you should write either the director of the prison system or the chief judge of the federal district court in your state.

(b) If the grievance system has not been certified by the Attorney General but seems to meet the statutory requirements and minimum standards described above, the court will probably find that you have to exhaust the prison grievance procedure. Even if you think you have a good argument that the procedures do not meet the standards, you should exhaust anyway. If the defendants raise the exhaustion requirement, it may take 90 days for the court to decide whether exhaustion is required, and you may as well avoid this additional delay. (Another course is to file your administrative grievance and then file your lawsuit as quickly as possible afterward. Ideally, you can use part of the 90-day period of waiting for the grievance decision to work on your papers, and the court can deal with your in forma pauperis application during this period.)

(c) If the grievance procedure clearly does not meet the standards, or if your problem is not one that the grievance procedure is designed to deal with, you will not be required to exhaust.

There are a couple of rules you should know about which are similar to exhaustion requirements. Several courts have held that before you can challenge inaccurate information in your prison file under §1983, you must first request prison authorities to correct the misinformation.[140] The courts have held it is not the misinformation that violates due process; it is prison officials' refusal to correct it when you notify them of their mistake. Second, the Supreme Court has held that negligent property loss by prison officials only amounts to a constitutional violation if the state does not provide a remedy.[141] If they provide a

---

[140]Paine v. Baker, 595 F.2d 197 (4th Cir. 1979); Doe v. United States Civil Service Commission, 483 F. Supp. 539 (S.D.N.Y. 1980) (same rule in government employment case).

[141]Parratt v. Taylor, 451 U.S. 527, 101 S.Ct. 1908 (1981).

compensation procedure—administrative or judicial—they have done all the Constitution requires, and your *only* option is to use the state remedy. (For a fuller discussion of this holding, see Ch. V, Secs. B2a and C6.)

3.   State Prisoners in State Court

If you are suing in state court, you are bound by state law doctrines of exhaustion. We cannot review state procedures in detail here, but many states have exhaustion requirements. Frequently, state courts hold that you must exhaust your administrative remedies before a court will consider a challenge to prison policy or practices. Also, many states have "notice of claim" requirements applicable to money damage actions against the state or a county or city. In New York, for example, you must either bring the lawsuit or file a notice of claim within ninety days after the incident for which you seek damages in order to sue a state, county, or municipality.[142] You should research the law in your state on these questions. Notice of claim requirements are frequently considered part of a statute of limitations rather than an exhaustion requirement.

4.   Advantages of Exhausting Administrative Remedies

The obvious disadvantage of exhausting administrative remedies is that it delays getting your case before a court. However, there are some significant advantages to exhausting them even if you are not required to do so.

(a) *Exhausting remedies may save you a lot of argument about whether you have to exhaust them.* As noted earlier, the time you save by going directly to court may be lost if the defendants file a motion to stay or dismiss your case because you have not exhausted. Even if they are completely wrong and you win, it may take the court a long time to get around to deciding that issue. If you go ahead and exhaust your remedies, that is one less issue in the way of a court decision on the merits.

(b) *You might win the grievance.* Even a bad grievance system sometimes makes the right decision, and it is usually a lot easier and faster to file an adequate grievance than an adequate lawsuit.

(c) *You may look better in court.* Some judges believe that most prisoner claims do not really belong in court and that some prisoners use the courts to annoy and disrupt. You may get a more sympathetic reception if you can show that you tried to work out your problem in-

---

[142]New York Court of Claim Act, §10(3) (1963); New York General Municipal Law, §50(e) (1977, Supp. 1981).

house; for example, a judge may be more likely to believe your story in a credibility contest if s/he thinks you are a reasonable and orderly person and not a troublemaker.

(d) *Even if your grievance is denied, you can sometimes get information or statements that are useful in a later lawsuit.* For example, if the prison administration tells you in response to a grievance that they will not change a rule because it would cost too much, it will help you to rebut a claim they might make in court that the rule is necessary for security.

This last purpose—getting helpful information—can sometimes be served equally well by a simple letter to the superintendent or other responsible prison official, either from the prisoner or from his or her family or friends. We know of instances where officials admitted in responses to letters that a transfer was motivated by a prisoner's articles in a newspaper, that confinement in a psychiatric seclusion ward was disciplinary in intent, and that the use of physical restraints on segregated prisoners was a blanket policy, even though each prisoner received an individual notice about it. The first two admissions later helped win lawsuits, and the third one may do so. Prison officials are often more candid in these informal situations than they are in court, and you should be prepared to take advantage of that fact.

E.   Defenses in Civil Rights and Federal Question Actions

State and federal prison officials who are sued for constitutional violations in federal courts may take advantage of several special defenses, in addition to the usual defenses that your claim is not true, or that your allegations do not state a claim for constitutional violation, even if they are true.[143]

1.   Immunities

a.   The Eleventh Amendment and Sovereign Immunity

The Eleventh Amendment states that the federal courts do not have power to hear suits against a state by citizens of another state.[144] The

---

[143]See Ch. VII, Sec. B, for a discussion of motions to dismiss or judgment on the pleadings. See also Sec. D, *supra,* for a discussion of the requirements of exhaustion of administrative remedies.

[144]U.S. Const., Amend. VI. The actual language of the amendment is: "The judicial power of the United States shall not be construed to extend to any suit in law or equity, commenced or prosecuted against one of the United States by citizens of another state, or by citizens or subject of any foreign state."

federal courts have always interpreted the amendment as also barring
suits by citizens of the same state,[145] consistent with the ancient doctrine
of sovereign immunity. This rule applies to injunctive cases as well as
suits for damages,[146] and to suits against particular state agencies as well
as the state itself.[147]

The Eleventh Amendment does *not* bar either injunctive or damage
suits against individual officials or prison employees.[148] When suing, if
you name as defendants the governor, the commissioner of corrections,
or the prison warden instead of the state, the Department of Corrections,
or the prison itself, you will usually defeat the defense of Eleventh
Amendment immunity. Also, use the magic words "in his/her *individual*
(or personal) capacity" whenever you are suing for damages.[149] Finally,
do not waste a lot of time trying to make sense out of this area of the law.
As one court stated, "Any step through the looking glass of the Eleventh
Amendment leads to a wonderland of judicially created and perpetrated
fiction and paradox."[150] Just learn the rules and follow them.

In some cases, even suing an official in his/her individual capacity will
not defeat the Eleventh Amendment defense. If you are seeking an award
of damages which "will to a virtual certainty be paid from state funds,
and not from the pockets of the individual state officials who were the
defendants," the Eleventh Amendment bar applies.[151] What this means
is not totally clear. The case just quoted dealt with retroactive payments
of welfare benefits. By contrast, the courts have held that the Eleventh
Amendment does not bar ordinary awards of damages for constitutional
violations,[152] injunctions that will require future spending from state
funds,[153] or damage awards against individuals that will be reimbursed

---

[145]Edelman v. Jordan, 415 U.S. 651, 663, 94 S.Ct. 1374 (1974).

[146]Alabama v. Pugh, 438 U.S. 781, 98 S.Ct. 3057 (1978) (per curiam).

[147]Ruiz v. Estelle, 679 F.2d 1115, 1136-37 (5th Cir. 1982); Anderson v. New
York State Division of Parole, 546 F. Supp. 816 (S.D.N.Y. 1982); Provet v.
State of New York, 546 F. Supp. 492 (S.D.N.Y. 1982); Batton v. State Govern-
ment of North Carolina, 501 F. Supp. 1173 (E.D.N.C. 1980).

[148]Spicer v. Hilton, 618 F.2d 232, 237 (3d Cir. 1980).

[149]Owen v. Lash, 682 F.2d 648, 654-57 (7th Cir. 1982) (damage award against
warden in *official* capacity barred); Jacobson v. Coughlin, 523 F. Supp. 1247,
1248-49 (N.D.N.Y. 1981). See also Appendix B, Form 1o, sample complaint.

[150]Spicer v. Hilton, *supra* note 148, at 235.

[151]Edelman v. Jordan, *supra* note 145, at 668.

[152]Scheuer v. Rhodes, 416 U.S. 232, 238, 94 S.Ct. 1683 (1974); Spicer v.
Hilton, *supra* note 148, at 236.

[153]Edelman v. Jordan, *supra* note 145, at 667-68.

by the state under an indemnity statute.[154] In a prison context, you are probably safe in assuming that only an award of back wages or other monetary benefits that were wrongfully kept from you will be barred by the Eleventh Amendment. Such cases should probably be taken to state court.

A state may waive its Eleventh Amendment immunity to permit itself to be sued in federal court.[155] Most states have not, and the federal courts will not find a waiver of Eleventh Amendment protection unless it is spelled out very clearly in state law.[156]

Local governments (counties, cities, municipalities) and their agencies are not protected by the state's Eleventh Amendment immunity and may be sued under §1983.[157] A suit against local jail officials in their official capacities may be treated as a claim against the local government.[158]

The federal government is not protected by the Eleventh Amendment, but the doctrine of sovereign immunity prevents any suit against the United States government or its agencies except when the government gives its consent.[159] The government has consented to be sued for a variety of torts in the Federal Tort Claims Act.[160] Federal officials may be sued for damages or injunctive relief in their individual capacities.[161] Whenever you sue federal officials, you should sue them in both their individual and official capacities.[162]

State governments generally may be sued in state courts only if they have waived their sovereign immunity, as many have.[163]

---

[154]Downing v. Williams, 624 F.2d 612 (5th Cir. 1980); Ware v. Percy, 468 F. Supp. 1266 (E.D. Wisc. 1979).

[155]Marrapese v. State of Rhode Island, 500 F. Supp. 1207 (D.R.I. 1980).

[156]Edelman v. Jordan, *supra* note 145, at 673; Williams v. Bennett, 689 F.2d 1370, 1377 (11th Cir. 1982); West v. Keve, 541 F. Supp. 534 (D. Del. 1982).

[157]Monell v. New York City Department of Social Services, 436 U.S. 658, 98 S.Ct. 2018 (1978).

[158]Kincaid v. Rusk, 670 F.2d 737 (7th Cir. 1982).

[159]United States v. Testan, 424 U.S. 392, 399, 96 S.Ct. 948 (1976).

[160]See Sec. C2, *supra.*

[161]Carlson v. Green, 446 U.S. 14, 100 S.Ct. 1468 (1980).

[162]*But see* McKnight v. Civiletti, 497 F. Supp. 657 (E.D. Pa. 1980).

[163]*See, e.g.,* New Jersey Tort Claims Act, N.J.S.A., §§59-1 through 59-12 (1975 Supp.); Claims and Actions Against Public Entities and Public Employees, West's Calif. Annotated Government Code, §§810 *et seq.;* Iowa Tort Claims Act, Iowa Code Annotated, §§25A.1 *et seq.* (1975).

b. Absolute Immunity of Judges, Prosecutors, Witnesses, and Legislators

Judges are "absolutely immune" from damage awards for acts taken in their judicial capacities.[164] To defeat judicial immunity, you must show that an act was taken in the "clear absence of all jurisdiction."[165] Showing that the judge was wrong is not enough; you must show a complete departure from the judicial role.[166] Similarly, prosecutors are absolutely immune for all acts taken in "initiating a prosecution and presenting the state's case."[167] However, other acts by prosecutors may not be cloaked in absolute immunity.[168]

The Supreme Court has just recently held that police officers and other witnesses enjoy absolute immunity from damages under §1983 for their testimony and other participation in the judicial proceedings.[169]

Some courts have held that prison officials involved in prosecuting or deciding disciplinary charges are also absolutely immune from damages because of their "quasi-judicial" functions.[170] However, the Supreme

---

[164]Stump v. Sparkman, 435 U.S. 349, 98 S.Ct. 1099 (1978).

[165]*Id.* at 356-57.

[166]For examples of the extreme behavior required to permit a damage award against a judge, *see* Harper v. Merckle, 638 F.2d 848 (5th Cir. 1981) (when plaintiff went to judge's chambers for information, judge demanded that he be sworn, chased him down the hall, had him pursued and arrested, and held him in contempt without an attorney); Zarcone v. Perry, 572 F.2d 52 (2d Cir. 1978) (judge had coffee vendor brought into chambers in handcuffs to abuse him for low quality of coffee). *Compare* Figueroa v. Kapelman, 526 F. Supp. 681 (S.D.N.Y. 1981) (order to transfer inmate to prevent boycott of courts covered by immunity).

[167]Imbler v. Pachtman, 424 U.S. 409, 430-31, 96 S.Ct. 984 (1975).

[168]Price v. Moody, 677 F.2d 676 (8th Cir. 1982); Henderson v. Fisher, 631 F.2d 1115, 1120 (3d Cir. 1980); Briggs v. Goodwin, 569 F.2d 10 (D.C. Cir. 1977), *cert. denied,* 437 U.S. 904 (1978); Doe v. Russotti, 503 F. Supp. 942 (S.D.N.Y. 1980); Redcross v. County of Rensselaer, 511 F. Supp. 364 (N.D.N.Y. 1981).

[169]Briscoe v. LaHue, __U.S.__, 103 S.Ct. 1108 (1983).

[170]Ward v. Johnson, 690 F.2d 1098 (4th Cir. 1982) (en banc) (chairperson of disciplinary hearing granted absolute immunity in regard to denying request by prisoner to call witnesses. The court limited its holding by stating that "every case in which immunity is claimed for members of . . . [Disciplinary Committees] should be considered on its own facts and with reference to the particular procedure under which the disciplinary hearing is held." *Id.* at 1109.). *See also* Anderson v. Luther, 521 F. Supp. 91, 97 (N.D. Ill. 1981); Breedlove v. Cripe, 511 F. Supp. 467, 469-70 (N.D. Tex. 1981). Several courts have similarly

Court case which originated this doctrine of "quasi-judicial" immunity is easily distinguishable. In *Butz v. Economou*,[171] federal administrative law judges were held to be absolutely immune, largely because the federal administrative process contains many of the same safeguards as the judicial process.[172] By contrast, prisoners are *not* entitled to the full range of adversary safeguards. (See Ch. V, Sec. B2b, for a discussion of your procedural rights at a disciplinary hearing.) For that reason, absolute immunity is not appropriate in most prison disciplinary cases.[173] In arguing against absolute immunity, you should emphasize the differences between the process described in *Butz v. Economou* and the procedures involved in your disciplinary conviction. This approach is consistent with *Ward v. Johnson*,[174] where the court found that absolute immunity was proper because the Virginia procedures providing for assistance by counsel or counsel substitute, confrontation and cross-examination, and other safeguards were sufficiently "judicial" in character to fall under the rule of *Butz v. Economou*.

Legislators are generally held to be immune for their legislative acts.[175] However, local governments themselves may be liable under §1983 for acts of their legislative bodies.[176]

As a practical matter, absolute immunity will generally be asserted by defendants in a motion to dismiss or for summary judgment. If the court determines that the defendant was acting in a legislative, judicial, or prosecutorial capacity, damage claims against him/her will be dismissed before trial.

The absolute immunity of legislators extends to injunctive as well as damage suits.[177] Most courts have held that judicial and prosecutorial

---

held parole board members and other officials to be absolutely immune from damages. United States v. Irving, 684 F.2d 494 (7th Cir. 1982); Sellars v. Procunier, 641 F.2d 1295 (9th Cir. 1981); Franklin v. Shields, 569 F.2d 784 (4th Cir. 1977).

[171]438 U.S. 478, 98 S.Ct. 2894 (1978).

[172]*Id.* at 511-17.

[173]Hilliard v. Scully, 537 F. Supp. 1084, 1088-89 (S.D.N.Y. 1982); *accord,* Jihaad v. O'Brien, 645 F.2d 556, 561 (6th Cir. 1981); Mary and Crystal v. Ramsden, 635 F.2d 590 (7th Cir. 1980).

[174]690 F.2d 1098 (4th Cir. 1982) (en banc).

[175]Supreme Court of Virginia v. Consumers Union, 446 U.S. 719, 100 S.Ct. 1967 (1980); Hernandez v. City of Lafayette, 643 F.2d 1188 (5th Cir. 1981); Bruce v. Riddle, 631 F.2d 272 (4th Cir. 1980).

[176]Monell v. New York City Department of Social Services, 436 U.S. 658, 98 S.Ct. 2018 (1978).

[177]Supreme Court of Virginia v. Consumers Union, *supra* note 175, at 732-33.

immunity do not bar injunctive relief, although the Supreme Court views this as an open question.[178] Federal courts have often declined on other grounds to enter injunctions that intruded into the activities of state courts,[179] although some such injunctions have been issued.[180]

c. Absolute Immunity of Federal Officials For Common-Law Torts

Federal officials exercising discretion within the scope of their official duties are generally held to be entitled to absolute immunity from liability for common-law torts.[181] If the federal official is immune from tort liability for exercising discretion, the government is immune under the Federal Tort Claims Act.[182] What is discretionary and what is within the scope of official duty is not always clear. (See Sec. C2, *supra,* for a discussion of discretion.) As a practical matter, most prisoners with claims against federal officials can assert them in a *Bivens* action as constitutional violations, for which only qualified immunity is available.[183]

d. Qualified Immunity

Most government officials and employees, including prison personnel, are entitled to only "qualified immunity," sometimes known as "good-faith immunity,"[184] in damage suits. (Qualified immunity is not available in injunctive actions.[185])

Under the doctrine of qualified immunity, officials are liable only if they "knew or should have known" that they were violating your

---

[178]*Id.* at 735.

[179]Newman v. Alabama, 683 F.2d 1312, 1320 (11th Cir. 1982); Wallace v. Kern, 520 F.2d 400 (2d Cir. 1975), *cert. denied,* 424 U.S. 12 (1976).

[180]Gerstein v. Pugh, 420 U.S. 103, 95 S.Ct. 854 (1975), *on remand sub nom.* Pugh v. Rainwater, 422 F. Supp. 498 (S.D. Fla. 1976).

[181]Granger v. Marek, 583 F.2d 781 (6th Cir. 1978), and cases cited.

[182]Dalehite v. United States, 346 U.S. 15, 73 S.Ct. 956 (1953) (discretionary function exception includes "determination made by executives or administrators. . . ."). *See also* Payton v. United States, 679 F.2d 475 (5th Cir. 1982); United States v. Faneca, 332 F.2d 872 (5th Cir. 1964), *cert. denied,* 380 U.S. 971 (1965).

[183]See Sec. C13, *supra,* for a discussion of alleging constitutional violations.

[184]Harlow v. Fitzgerald, __U.S.__, 102 S.Ct. 2727, 2737 (1982); Butz v. Economou, 438 U.S. 478, 98 S.Ct. 2894 (1978).

[185]National Treasury Employees Union v. Nixon, 492 F.2d 587 (D.C. Cir. 1974); Knell v. Bensinger, 522 F.2d 720 (7th Cir. 1975).

rights—that is, if they were violating "clearly established constitutional or statutory rights of which a reasonable person would have known" at the time the acts were committed.[186] Persons occupying "responsible public office[s]" are expected to have "knowledge of the basic, unquestioned constitutional rights of [their] charges."[187] However, officials are not required "to be aware of a constitutional right that has not yet been declared."[188]

Previously, officials could also be held liable if they acted "with malicious intention to cause a deprivation of constitutional rights or other injury. . .," regardless of whether the rights were clearly established.[189] This part of the qualified immunity defense has now been abolished; the only issue is whether the defendant knew or should have known s/he was violating your rights.[190]

Whether a right is clearly established and whether the defendants knew or should have known they were violating it is not always clear. Obviously, if prison officials have acted in direct violation of a judgment against them,[191] or contrary to the specific holding of a previously decided case in the Supreme Court or in the local state or federal courts,[192] they are not entitled to qualified immunity.[193] In a less clear-cut case, the courts will look to several factors.

------

[186]Harlow v. Fitzgerald, *supra* note 184, at 2738.

[187]Wood v. Strickland, 420 U.S. 308, 321-22, 95 S.Ct. 992 (1975).

[188]Procunier v. Navarette, 434 U.S. 555, 565, 98 S.Ct. 855 (1978) (officials not immune where Supreme Court and their federal circuit had not ruled and where other courts were in disagreement); *see also* Cox v. Cook, 420 U.S. 734, 95 S.Ct. 1237 (1975) (damages barred for denial of notice and hearing in disciplinary case arising before Supreme Court decision on subject).

[189]Procunier v. Navarette, *id.* at 565.

[190]Harlow v. Fitzgerald, *supra* note 184, at 2737-39. If a right is clearly established, prison officials know or should know whether their acts violate it except in "extraordinary circumstances." Trejo v. Perez, 693 F.2d 482, 485 (5th Cir. 1982).

[191]Williams v. Bennett, 689 F.2d 1370, 1385-86 (11th Cir. 1982); Powell v. Ward, 643 F.2d 924, 934 n.13 (2d Cir. 1981).

[192]Chavis v. Rowe, 643 F.2d 1281 (7th Cir. 1981); Ware v. Heyne, 575 F.2d 593 (7th Cir. 1978); Bryant v. McGinnis, 463 F. Supp. 373 (W.D.N.Y. 1978).

[193]It cannot be said that prison officials "should have known" of a right if they had no opportunity to find out about it. Thus, an "unpublished" court opinion—one that a court makes available only to the parties to the case—cannot "clearly establish" a right. Ward v. Johnson, 690 F.2d 1098, 1111 (4th Cir. 1982) (en banc). However, where an opinion is made publicly available, officials are charged with knowledge of it, even before it is reported in the advance sheets. Ware v. Heyne, 575 F.2d 593 (7th Cir. 1978).

—How extreme or sweeping was the denial of rights? Especially in Eighth Amendment cases, courts have refused to grant qualified immunity when the violations were "of such a shocking nature that no reasonable man could have believed that they were constitutional."[194]

—If a constitutional *standard* is clearly established, damages may be awarded for conduct that violates the standard even if there is no prior "case in point." Thus, where prison officials refused to deliver mail addressed to prisoners in their Muslim names, one court held that the clearly established standards governing mail restrictions had been violated and therefore rejected qualified immunity, even though there was no case law on mail and Muslim names.[195] As one court stated, officials

> cannot hide behind a claim that the particular factual tableau in question has never appeared *in haec verba* [in those words] in a reported opinion. If the application of settled principles to this factual tableau would inexorably lead to a conclusion of unconstitutionality, a prison official may not take solace in ostrichism.[196]

—Violation of statutes by officials will defeat qualified immunity;[197] violation of prison regulations may also weigh against immunity.[198] However, a defendant who followed relevant statutes and regulations may be immune even if the statute or regulation is unconstitutional.[199]

---

[194]Landman v. Royster, 354 F. Supp. 1292, 1318 (E.D. Va. 1973). *See also* Layne v. Vinzant, 657 F.2d 468 (1st Cir. 1981) (officials required to follow "evolving standards of decency" as to medical care, even before court decision on subject); Doe v. Renfrow, 631 F.2d 91 (7th Cir. 1980) (qualified immunity not available where "simple common sense" suggested search was unreasonable); Chapman v. Pickett, 586 F.2d 22 (7th Cir. 1980) (qualified immunity may not be available in Eighth Amendment disproportionality case).

[195]Masjid Muhammad-D.C.C. v. Keve, 479 F. Supp. 1311, 1326 (D. Del. 1979). *See also* Mary and Crystal v. Ramsden, 635 F.2d 590 (7th Cir. 1980) (general instructions as to Eighth Amendment standard supported damage award without case in point).

[196]Little v. Walker, 552 F.2d 193, 198 (7th Cir. 1977). *Accord,* Picha v. Wielgas, 410 F. Supp. 1214, 1219 (N.D. Ill. 1976) ("There is a limitation to the notion that school officials can have one 'free' constitutional violation before they are liable for ignoring constitutional rights that arise in each unique factual setting.").

[197]Harlow v. Fitzgerald, *supra* note 184, at 2739; Scott v. Plante, 691 F.2d 634 (3d Cir. 1982); Williams v. Treen, 671 F.2d 892 (5th Cir. 1982).

[198]McCray v. Burrell, 622 F.2d 705 (4th Cir. 1980); Strachan v. Ashe, 548 F. Supp. 1193, 1205 (D. Mass. 1982); O'Connor v. Keller, 510 F. Supp. 1359 (D. Md. 1981).

[199]Green v. White, 693 F.2d 45 (8th Cir. 1982); Taylor v. Carlson, 671 F.2d

When a regulation is involved, you should therefore sue the higher-ups who promulgated the regulation as well as the lower-level personnel who followed it.

For qualified immunity purposes, supervisory officials will generally be held to a higher standard of knowledge of the law than lower-level employees such as guards.[200]

Qualified immunity is an affirmative defense which defendants must plead in order to rely on.[201] If they do not raise it in their answer or in a pretrial motion, they should not be permitted to argue it at trial.[202] The courts have not made up their minds as to who bears the burden of proof regarding qualified immunity.[203] Until the Supreme Court rules on the question, you should assume that you have the burden. This means that you must demonstrate to the court that there were prior cases, statutes, or regulations establishing your rights at the time the defendants violated them. You should also ask in discovery what statute, rule, or case law the defendants relied upon in believing their actions to be lawful.

Sometimes officials will be granted qualified immunity even when they violate clearly established rights because they did not and could not know that their acts would violate those rights. For example, officials who hold a prisoner past his/her release date are not liable where they reasonably rely on someone else's erroneous calculation of time owed.[204]

Qualified immunity is available only to individual officials. Local governments sued under §1983 are not entitled to it.[205]

Qualified immunity, like absolute immunity, is likely to be asserted in a motion to dismiss or a summary judgment motion.[206]

2. Lack of Personal Involvement

Supervisory prison officials (wardens, captains of the guard, etc.)

---

137 (5th Cir. 1982); Jihaad v. O'Brien, 645 F.2d 556 (6th Cir. 1981); Ayler v. Hopper, 532 F. Supp. 198 (M.D. Ala. 1981).

[200]Wood v. Strickland, *supra* note 187, at 321-22.

[201]Gomez v. Toledo, 446 U.S. 635, 100 S.Ct. 1920 (1980).

[202]Boyd v. Carroll, 624 F.2d 730 (5th Cir. 1980).

[203]*See* Crowder v. Lash, 687 F.2d 996, 1003 (7th Cir. 1982); Saldana v. Garza, 684 F.2d 1159 (5th Cir. 1982); Wolfel v. Sanborn, 666 F.2d 1005 (6th Cir. 1982); Jihaad v. O'Brien, 645 F.2d 556 (6th Cir. 1981).

[204]Johnson v. Shaw, 609 F.2d 124 (5th Cir. 1980); Williams v. Anderson, 599 F.2d 923 (10th Cir. 1979). *See also* West v. Keve, 541 F. Supp. 534 (D. Del. 1982); La Plante v. Southworth, 484 F. Supp. 115 (D.R.I. 1980).

[205]Owen v. City of Independence, Mo., 445 U.S. 622, 100 S.Ct. 1398 (1980).

[206]*See* Harlow v. Fitzgerald, *supra* note 184, at 2737-38.

when sued usually will defend by alleging that they had no personal involvement in the injury that occurred to you. If you fail to allege sufficient facts in your complaint showing that supervisory prison officials subjected, or caused you to be subjected, to a violation of federally protected rights, the court will dismiss those parties. The mere fact that an individual holds the position of warden or commissioner of a corrections department does not make him/her liable for all unlawful acts committed by prison employees. The doctrine of *respondeat superior*—an employer's automatic responsibility for the torts of employees—is not applicable in civil rights actions.[207] You must prove that a particular defendant was personally involved in the deprivation of your rights.[208]

This principle applies both in damage actions and in injunctive actions. Courts often do not look as closely at personal involvement in injunctive actions, but the Supreme Court has warned that an injunction against higher officials cannot be based solely on acts of their subordinates.[209] Those few cases which approve of *respondeat superior* liability under §1983 in injunctive cases[210] should not be relied upon, and you should not mention this doctrine in your §1983 papers.

a.   Establishing Personal Involvement

Where a particular prison official beat you up, suspended your visits, or signed an order placing you in segregation, proving personal involvement is easy. You may also be able to prove liability based on less direct involvement, or on the failure to act. "Acts of omission are actionable in this context to the same extent as acts of commission."[211]

---

[207]Parratt v. Taylor, 451 U.S. 527, 101 S.Ct. 1908, 1913 n.3 (1981); Monell v. New York City Department of Social Services, 436 U.S. 658, 98 S.Ct. 2018 (1978).

[208]Johnson v. Glick, 481 F.2d 1028, 1034 (2d Cir. 1973).

[209]Rizzo v. Goode, 423 U.S. 362, 370-71, 96 S.Ct. 598 (1976); *see also* Ruiz v. Estelle, 679 F.2d 1115, 1154-55 (5th Cir. 1982) (system-wide injunction must be based on institutional practices, not isolated misconduct).

[210]*See* Isaac v. Jones, 529 F. Supp. 175 (N.D. Ill. 1981); Ganguly v. New York State Dept. of Mental Hygiene, 511 F. Supp. 420, 424 (S.D.N.Y. 1981). Several older cases which held that state *respondeat superior* doctrines could be used under §1983 have been overruled. Baskin v. Parker, 602 F.2d 1205 (5th Cir. 1979).

[211]Smith v. Ross, 482 F.2d 33, 36 (6th Cir. 1978). *Accord,* Estelle v. Gamble, 429 U.S. 97, 106, 97 S.Ct. 285 (1976) (claim of denial of medical care may be based on "acts or omissions"); Bogard v. Cook, 586 F.2d 399 (5th Cir. 1978) ("nonfeasance as well as misfeasance" actionable).

Here are some of the ways that §1983 liability may be established against persons who were passively or indirectly involved in violating your rights.

—*Knowledge and acquiescence.* If prison officials know of violations of your rights, are in a position to correct them, and fail to do so, they may be liable. Officers who are present at a beating and fail to intervene may be liable.[212] Higher officials who are aware of unconstitutional living conditions may be liable to persons confined under them,[213] unless they have no power to alter them.[214] Knowledge and acquiescence in other constitutional violations has been held sufficient to establish liability in damages.[215] Of course, to be liable under this theory, an official must know enough to be on notice of the illegal conduct.[216]

Knowledge and acquiescence may be inferred by a court where (1) a high official would normally exercise reasonably close supervision over a subordinate, and (2) the subordinate actually inflicting constitutional deprivations was not doing so in a secret or isolated manner.[217]

One way to show knowledge and acquiescence is to create it yourself. If you file grievances or write letters of complaint about beatings by guards or other misconduct, you can put officials on notice and they can be held liable for later events if they do not correct the problem.[218]

---

[212]Bruner v. Dunaway, 684 F.2d 422 (6th Cir. 1982); Harris v. Chanclor, 537 F.2d 203, 206 (5th Cir. 1976); Curtis v. Everette, 489 F.2d 516, 518 (3d Cir. 1973), *cert. denied,* 416 U.S. 995 (1974); Byrd v. Brishke, 466 F.2d 6, 11 (7th Cir. 1972). Some courts have restricted this liability to officers superior in rank to those doing the beating. McCoy v. McCoy, 528 F. Supp. 712 (N.D. W. Va. 1981).

[213]Villanueva v. George, 659 F.2d 851 (8th Cir. 1981) (en banc); Holland v. Connors, 491 F.2d 539 (5th Cir. 1974); Wright v. McMann, 460 F.2d 126, 134-35 (2d Cir. 1972); Strachan v. Ashe, 548 F. Supp. 1193 (D. Mass. 1982).

[214]Williams v. Bennett, 689 F.2d 1370, 1388 (11th Cir. 1982).

[215]Vaughn v. Franzen, 549 F. Supp. 426 (N.D. Ill. 1982) (inadequate disciplinary procedures); King v. Cuyler, 541 F. Supp. 1230 (E.D. Pa. 1982) (disciplinary frame-up); Vaughn v. Trotter, 516 F. Supp. 886 (M.D. Tenn. 1980) (interference with access to courts).

[216]Orpiano v. Johnson, 632 F.2d 1096 (4th Cir. 1982) (single prior incident not enough to show acquiescence in beating); Russ v. Ratliff, 538 F.2d 799 (5th Cir. 1976), *cert. denied,* 429 U.S. 1041 (1977) (distant rumors too vague to prompt action by reasonable person, or information reasonably believed to lack credibility, inadequate to establish liability); King v. Cuyler, 541 F. Supp. 1230 (E.D. Pa. 1982) (superintendent not liable when disciplinary papers he reviewed did not contain evidence of unlawful conduct).

[217]McClelland v. Facteau, 610 F.2d 693 (10th Cir. 1979).

[218]Strachan v. Ashe, 548 F. Supp. 1193 (D. Mass. 1982).

—*Promulgation of policy.* Officials who set policy or write regulations may be liable if they are not directly involved in enforcing the policy or regulations against you.[219] In fact, where prison employees act pursuant to policy or regulation, the policymaker may be the *only* person who can be held liable.[220] The policy need not be formal or written to serve as the basis for liability.[221]

Regulations or policy may also serve as a defense for higher officials. If the unlawful acts were in violation of the policy they set, the policymakers cannot be held liable,[222] except in those rare instances when a court views the violation of rules as showing a failure to train or supervise.[223]

—*Absence of policy or procedures.* If higher officials have failed to establish ways of dealing with problems that they knew or should have known about, they may be liable for the consequences.[224]

—*Responsibility imposed by statute or regulation.* Where a statute or regulation imposes a duty on someone, failure to perform it may make that person liable even if s/he does not know about the resulting constitutional violation.[225] If the statute is extremely general, however, it may not serve as a basis for liability by itself.[226] If a statute imposes liability on one person, the result may be to excuse others from liability.[227]

---

[219]Black v. Stephens, 662 F.2d 181 (3d Cir. 1981); Wanger v. Bonner, 621 F.2d 675 (5th Cir. 1980); DuChesne v. Sugarman, 566 F.2d 817 (2d Cir. 1977); Anderson v. New York State Division of Parole, 546 F. Supp. 816 (S.D.N.Y. 1982); Hearn v. Morris, 526 F. Supp. 267 (E.D. Cal. 1981).

[220]Wanger v. Bonner, 621 F.2d 675 (5th Cir. 1980).

[221]Smith v. Jordan, 527 F. Supp. 167 (S.D. Ohio 1981); Ruiz v. Estelle, 679 F.2d 1115, 1154-55 (5th Cir. 1982).

[222]Fisher v. Washington Metropolitan Area Transit Authority, 690 F.2d 1133 (4th Cir. 1982); Carwile v. Ray, 481 F. Supp. 33 (E.D. Wash. 1979).

[223]O'Connor v. Keller, 510 F. Supp. 1359 (D. Md. 1982).

[224]Murray v. City of Chicago, 634 F.2d 365 (7th Cir. 1980); Fowler v. Cross, 635 F.2d 476 (5th Cir. 1981); Williams v. Heard, 533 F. Supp. 1153 (S.D. Tex. 1982); Doe v. Burwell, 537 F. Supp. 186 (S.D. Ohio 1982); Redmond v. Baxley, 475 F. Supp. 1111 (E.D. Mich. 1979); Bryant v. McGinnis, 463 F. Supp. 373 (W.D.N.Y. 1978).

[225]Tatum v. Hooser, 642 F.2d 253 (8th Cir. 1981); Doe v. New York City Dept. of Social Services, 649 F.2d 134 (2d Cir. 1981); Johnson v. Duffy, 588 F.2d 740 (9th Cir. 1978); United States ex rel. Larkins v. Oswald, 510 F.2d 583, 589 (2d Cir. 1975).

[226]DuChesne v. Sugarman, 566 F.2d 817 (2d Cir. 1977).

[227]Polk v. Montgomery County, Md., 548 F. Supp. 613 (D. Md. 1982).

—*Failure to train and supervise.* The failure of higher officials to train or supervise their subordinates may establish the higher-ups' liability.[228] Most courts have held that a failure to train or supervise must be so serious as to constitute "deliberate indifference" before supervisors will be liable on this basis.[229] The mere fact that prison guards have violated your rights does not prove that their superiors failed to train or supervise them.

When you bring a §1983 or federal question action, you may not know at first exactly who was at fault. You should be sure to include as defendants all those persons up and down the chain of command who might be said to have "caused you to be subjected" to a violation of law. Thus, if you come back from the yard and find that your cell has been ransacked by guards, you may wish to sue the guards who conducted the unreasonable search; the watch commander or other supervisor who decided that your cell was to be searched; the superintendent who failed to have his guards trained to conduct searches without tearing inmates' cells apart; and the commissioner who promulgated a cell search regulation that does not safeguard prisoners' belongings. As the litigation progresses and you learn more about what happened, you may drop some of these defendants and you may add others.

b.   Local Government Liability

In *Monell v. New York City Department of Social Services,*[230] the Supreme Court held that local governments and their agencies can be sued under §1983 for constitutional violations arising from "a policy statement, ordinance, regulation, or decision officially adapted and promulgated by that body's officers."[231] "Customs," as well as formal policies, may also result in *Monell* liability.[232] However, the mere fact that a constitutional violation was committed by an employee of the local government does not make that government liable; *respondeat superior* does not apply.[233] Thus, proving *Monell* liability is a variation of demonstrating personal involvement.

---

[228]Jones v. Evans, 544 F. Supp. 769 (N.D. Ga. 1982); O'Connor v. Keller, 510 F. Supp. 1359 (D. Md. 1981).

[229]Owens v. Haas, 601 F.2d 1242 (2d Cir. 1979); Jones v. Denton, 527 F. Supp. 106 (S.D. Ohio 1981). See Ch. V, Sec. F, for a discussion of the deliberate indifference standard.

[230]436 U.S. 658, 98 S.Ct. 2018 (1978).

[231]*Id.* at 690.

[232]*Id.* at 690-91.

[233]*Id.* at 691-94.

For prisoners, the main significance of *Monell* is that city and county jail prisoners can sue the city or county for unconstitutional jail conditions or practices or for police misconduct resulting from government policy or custom.[234] The connection between the constitutional violation and government policy or custom can be shown in several ways.

—*Decision or formal policy*. As *Monell* indicates, a policy statement, ordinance, or regulation may make the local government liable for a constitutional violation. Failure to provide enough funds to operate in a lawful manner may also be a basis for *Monell* liability,[235] as may a decision by the head of an agency of local government.[236]

—*Custom*. Practices which are shown to be widespread and well-known may constitute a "custom" for which a local government can be held liable.[237]

—*Inadequate training, supervision, or procedures*. Where constitutional violations are caused by a local government's inadequate procedures, the local government may be liable.[238] Inadequate training and supervision of police or corrections officers may also make a city or county liable for damages.[239] However, mere failure to respond to a few complaints or to give all the training that could have been provided will not make the local government liable.[240] The mere fact that you were mistreated by police or correctional officers does not by itself prove that they were inadequately trained and supervised.

---

[234]Herrera v. Valentine, 753 F.2d 1220 (8th Cir. 1981); McKenna v. County of Nassau, 538 F. Supp. 637 (E.D.N.Y. 1982).

[235]Parnell v. Waldrep, 538 F. Supp. 1203 (W.D.N.C. 1982); Mayes v. Elrod, 470 F. Supp. 1188 (N.D. Ill. 1979).

[236]Black v. Stephens, 662 F.2d 181 (3d Cir. 1981) (police chief's regulations and policy); Schneider v. City of Atlanta, 628 F.2d 915 (5th Cir. 1980) (personnel decision of director of corrections).

[237]Webster v. City of Houston, 689 F.2d 1220, 1225-27 (5th Cir. 1982). *Accord*, Monell v. Dept. of Social Services, Mo., *supra* note 230, at 690-91. One court has defined "custom" as "the deeply imbedded traditional way of carrying out . . . policy." Knight v. Carlson, 478 F. Supp. 55 (E.D. Cal. 1979).

[238]Powe v. City of Chicago, 664 F.2d 639 (7th Cir. 1981) (procedures for preparation of warrants); Watson v. McGee, 527 F. Supp. 234 (S.D. Ohio 1981) (inadequate fire safety procedures in jail).

[239]Herrera v. Valentine, 653 F.2d 1220 (8th Cir. 1981); Owens v. Haas, 601 F.2d 1242 (2d Cir. 1979), *cert. denied sub nom.* County of Nassau v. Owens, 444 U.S. 980, 100 S.Ct. 483 (1979); Popow v. City of Margate, 476 F. Supp. 1237 (D.N.J. 1979).

[240]Turpin v. Mailet, 619 F.2d 196 (2d Cir.), *cert. denied sub nom.* Turpin v. West Haven, 449 U.S. 1016, 101 S.Ct. 577 (1980); Cattan v. City of New York, 523 F. Supp. 598 (S.D.N.Y. 1981); Harlee v. Hagen, 538 F. Supp. 389 (E.D.N.Y. 1982).

Local governments are not entitled to the defense of qualified immunity.[241] However, punitive damages may not be assessed against them.[242]

3. Res Judicata and Collateral Estoppel

A basic principle of our legal system is that once something is decided, it should stay decided; the same parties are not permitted to litigate the same issues over and over. To prevent this, the legal system developed the doctrines of res judicata and collateral estoppel, which apply in virtually all types of legal actions. These doctrines are sometimes referred to as "claim preclusion" and "issue preclusion," respectively.

Before going into the details of these doctrines, we should state the bottom line very clearly: if you get an adverse court decision, you must deal with it directly by appealing it[243] or by making a motion to modify, amend, or vacate the judgment.[244] If you do not do this, you are probably stuck with the judgment,[245] and you cannot get around it by bringing a different lawsuit, even if you go to a different court or call your suit by a different name. If you bring a lawsuit and then for some reason you cannot pursue it at that time, you should consider taking a voluntary dismissal.[246] Otherwise, if the defendants get the case dismissed because you do not respond to a motion, the decision will be final, even though you might have had a valid response, and you will not be able to reinstate the case at some later point.

Res judicata (Latin for "thing decided") means that you cannot bring a lawsuit if there has already been a judgment on the merits by a court of competent jurisdiction in a prior suit involving the same parties or their privies.[247] If any of these conditions does not exist, then res judicata does not apply and the second suit is not barred.

—*Judgment on the merits.* In a civil case, a judgment is "on the

---

[241]Owen v. City of Independence, 445 U.S. 622, 100 S.Ct. 1398 (1980).

[242]City of Newport v. Fact Concerts, Inc., 453 U.S. 247, 101 S.Ct. 2748 (1981).

[243]For a discussion of the procedures to appeal an adverse decision in a civil action, see Ch. VII, Sec. P, and to appeal a denial of a writ of habeas corpus, see Ch. IX, Sec. F.

[244]See Ch. VII, Sec. O, for a discussion of how to file a motion to modify, amend, or vacate the judgment.

[245]Redwood v. Council of the District of Columbia, 679 F.2d 931 (D.C. Cir. 1982); Pearl v. Dobbs, 649 F.2d 608 (8th Cir. 1982).

[246]*See* Rule 41(a)(1), FRCP.

[247]Lawlor v. National Screen Service, 349 U.S. 322, 326, 75 S.Ct. 865 (1954); Williams v. Codd, 459 F. Supp. 804, 811-16 (S.D.N.Y. 1978).

merits" if it decides the question of whether the plaintiff's legal rights
were violated by the defendant(s). A judgment is not on the merits if the
court holds it does not have jurisdiction, that the case is moot, or anything else unrelated to the legal claim concerning the case. A voluntary
dismissal pursuant to Rule 41(a), FRCP, is not a judgment on the merits.

—*Court of competent jurisdiction.* A court of competent jurisdiction
is one that has jurisdiction of the parties and the subject matter. If you
sue state prison officials in federal court for a common-law tort and
nothing else, and the case is dismissed, res judicata will not apply, even if
the federal court claims to be ruling on the merits of your case, because
the federal court generally lacks jurisdiction over common-law torts
unless they are "pendent" to federal law claims. (See Sec. B3, *supra,* for
a discussion of pendent jurisdiction.) You will thus be able to bring a second lawsuit in the state court on the tort claim.

—*The same parties or their privies.* "Privity" is an old and confusing
legal concept which has little application in prison cases.

—*The same cause of action.* The meaning of "cause of action" is not
precise, but as a practical matter, any significant difference between the
factual issues in the first and second lawsuits may mean they are not the
same cause of action.[248] Different legal claims arising out of the same
facts may still amount to the same cause of action. Thus, if you are
beaten up on two occasions, you should be able to bring two lawsuits.
However, if you are beaten up on one occasion and want to bring two
legal claims, for assault and battery and violation of constitutional
rights, you may have to bring them in the same lawsuit or risk having a
second lawsuit barred by res judicata. Some courts have made an exception where a state law claim is brought in state court and a federal law
claim based on the same facts is brought later in a §1983 suit.[249] Be sure
that this is the law in your jurisdiction before you assume that you can
proceed this way. Other courts have held that, even in this situation, all
claims that could have been brought in the prior suit are barred by res
judicata.[250]

Collateral estoppel is the principle that you cannot relitigate factual or
legal issues which were actually litigated and decided in a prior suit involving you, regardless of whether the same cause of action was
previously litigated.[251] For example, the Supreme Court has held that a
decision in a suppression motion in a criminal case holding that evidence

---

[248]Landrigan v. City of Warwick, 628 F.2d 736, 741 (1st Cir. 1980).

[249]Williams v. Codd, *supra* note 247, at 812.

[250]*See, e.g.,* Castorr v. Brundage, 674 F.2d 531, 536 (6th Cir. 1982). The Supreme Court has not decided this question. Allen v. McCurry, 449 U.S. 90, 97
n.10, 101 S.Ct. 411 (1980).

[251]Lawlor v. National Screen Service, *supra* note 247, at 326.

was not seized in violation of the Fourth Amendment prevented a prisoner from later bringing a damage action alleging an unreasonable search and seizure.[252] The criminal case and the suit for damages were not the same cause of action, but the factual and legal issues were the same. If the issues were different, you will not be collaterally estopped. For example, the fact that you were convicted of a crime does not determine the legal and factual issue of whether the police used excessive force in arresting you; if you plead guilty to a crime without having lost a suppression motion, you are not barred from bringing a later civil suit claiming an illegal search.[253] Also, if it is impossible to tell what was litigated and decided in the prior action, collateral estoppel cannot apply.[254] The party asserting collateral estoppel has the burden of proof as to what was litigated and decided.[255]

Collateral estoppel also cannot apply unless the prior judgment was based on a full and fair opportunity to litigate.[256] Circumstances that may violate this requirement are lack of competent representation,[257] lack of any representation at all, unfair limits on what issues could be pursued or what evidence could be presented, or your failure to receive adequate notice of the hearing or motion upon which the court based its decision.

Collateral estoppel also cannot apply if an issue was previously decided but the ruling on that issue was not necessary to the decision in the prior case—*i.e.,* if it was "dicta."[258]

Since collateral estoppel applies between federal civil rights suits and state or federal criminal proceedings, you cannot challenge your criminal conviction in a civil lawsuit or bring a §1983 suit for damages based matters which were determined adverse to you in the criminal case. First, you have to get your conviction reversed, either through the appellate process or through habeas corpus or another post-conviction proceeding. (See Ch. IX.)

Most courts hold that if the plaintiffs win a class action for injunctive relief, res judicata will not bar a later damage action by a member of the class based on the same constitutional violations unless the person bringing the damage action received notice that such damage claims had to be

---

[252]Allen v. McCurry, *supra* note 250.

[253]Haring v. Prosise, __U.S.__, 103 S.Ct. 2368 (1983); Hernandez v. City of Los Angeles, 624 F.2d 935, 938 (9th Cir. 1980).

[254]Russell v. Place, 94 U.S. 606 (1876).

[255]Hernandez v. City of Los Angeles, *supra* note 253, at 937.

[256]Allen v. McCurry, *supra* note 250, at 104.

[257]Cerbone v. County of Westchester, 508 F. Supp. 780 (S.D.N.Y. 1981).

[258]Hyman v. Regenstein, 258 F.2d 502, 510-11 (5th Cir. 1958).

litigated as part of the class action.[259] (If the court rules *against* the plaintiffs, an individual suit based on the same alleged constitutional violations would be barred.) In addition, when a court has already found constitutional violations, defendants should be collaterally estopped by the previous judgment from disputing that conditions are unconstitutional, although other issues not determined in the previous action will still have to be litigated. Thus, where a court found in a class action for an injunction that conditions in certain housing units were unconstitutionally dangerous, a prisoner bringing a damage suit based on an assault in one of the housing units did not have to prove again that conditions were unconstitutional. However, he still had to prove that his injuries were caused by those conditions and that the defendants he sued were personally responsible for them.[260]

4.   Statutes of Limitations

Statutes of limitations are time limits on how long you can wait before filing a lawsuit. If you wait too long, your lawsuit will be "time-barred." Different kinds of lawsuits involve different statutes of limitations. Generally, statutes of limitations are most relevant to damage claims; however, some states also have limitations for injunctive-type actions.

Suits based on state law are governed by state statutes of limitations, which generally spell out fairly clearly what types of suits they cover. Suits under 42 U.S.C. §1983 are also governed by the "appropriate" state statute of limitations.[261] Unfortunately, the Supreme Court has not spelled out how to decide what is the appropriate statute to apply, and (except in those states which have adopted special statutes of limitations for §1983)[262] the result has been confusing, with different federal courts reaching different conclusions.

Thus, in New York, the federal courts have adopted a simple rule that all §1983 suits are governed by the state statute of limitations for liabilities created or imposed by statute.[263] Some states do not have such

---

[259]Crowder v. Lash, 687 F.2d 996 (7th Cir. 1982); Jones-Bey v. Caso, 535 F.2d 1360 (2d Cir. 1976). *Contra,* Jackson v. Hayakawa, 605 F.2d 1121, 1125 (9th Cir. 1979).

[260]Williams v. Bennett, 689 F.2d 1370 (11th Cir. 1982).

[261]Board of Regents of University of State of New York v. Tomanio, 446 U.S. 478, 100 S.Ct. 1790 (1980), *quoting* Johnson v. Railway Express Agency, Inc., 421 U.S. 454, 462, 95 S.Ct. 1716 (1975).

[262]Statutes of limitations specifically governing §1983 have been passed in some states. *See* Wright v. State of Tennessee, 628 F.2d 949 (6th Cir. 1980); Kosikowski v. Bourne, 659 F.2d 105, 107 (9th Cir. 1981).

[263]Pauk v. Board of Trustees of City University of New York, 654 F.2d 856

a statute, and the federal courts have had to use a different kind of state statute.[264] Other courts have held that no single statute applies to all §1983 actions and have tried to find the right statute of limitations by determining what kind of state law case (malicious prosecution, slander, assault and battery, etc.) was most like the §1983 action before them.[265] In some cases, this results in different statutes of limitations applying to different parts of the same case.[266]

Until the Supreme Court deals with this question, the only way to be sure what statute of limitations applies in a §1983 case is to find the relevant federal cases from the state involved. Fortunately, this is easy if you have an adequate law library, since the Modern Federal Practice Digest has a single key number (Civil Rights 13.10) covering §1983 statute of limitations cases. If the courts have not yet made a clear ruling for your state, look at all the state statutes that could possibly apply and comply with the shortest one.

A state statute of limitations may not be applied in federal court if it "evidences hostility or discrimination toward a federal cause of action."[267] However, courts have generally upheld very short statutes of limitations in §1983 cases.[268]

In a federal civil rights case, the statute of limitations begins to run when the cause of action accrues or commences; this occurs when the plaintiff knows or has reason to know of the injury upon which the action is based.[269] Where the injury took place over a period of time (a "continuing wrong"), the statute may not start to run until the end of that period of wrong.[270] However, what constitutes a continuing wrong may not always be clear, and a court may break your claim up into parts (*e.g.,* your placement in segregation without notice or an opportunity to

---

(2d Cir. 1981), *cert. denied,* 102 S.Ct. 1631 (1982); Singleton v. City of New York, 632 F.2d 185 (2d Cir. 1980), *cert. denied,* 450 U.S. 920 (1981).

[264]Movement for Opportunity and Equality v. General Motors, 622 F.2d 1235 (7th Cir. 1980).

[265]Kilgore v. City of Mansfield, Ohio, 679 F.2d 632 (6th Cir. 1982).

[266]McNeil v. McDonough, 515 F. Supp. 113, 120 (D.N.J. 1980), *aff'd,* 648 F.2d 178 (3d Cir. 1981); Wilkinson v. Ellis, 484 F. Supp. 1072, 1078 (E.D. Pa. 1980).

[267]Johnson v. Davis, 582 F.2d 1316 (4th Cir. 1978) (rejecting one-year statute of limitations for §1983).

[268]Burns v. Sullivan, 619 F.2d 99 (1st Cir. 1980) (six months); Wright v. State of Tennessee, *supra* note 262 (one year).

[269]Drayden v. Needville Independent School District, 642 F.2d 129, 132 (5th Cir. 1981); Phillips v. Purdy, 617 F.2d 139 (5th Cir. 1980).

[270]Stuebig v. Hammel, 446 F. Supp. 31 (M.D. Pa. 1977).

comment may be treated as separate from your confinement in segregation past the date on which you were supposed to be released). The
early parts of your claim might be barred by the statute of limitations if
this happens. Play it safe and bring your suit early enough so that everything that has happened is within the statute of limitations.

In federal court, you need only file your complaint before the statute
of limitations has run. The date of filing is considered to be the date the
clerk receives your complaint in cases where actual filing is delayed while
the court processes your in forma pauperis motion.[271] In state court, you
may need to serve process as well; be sure you know what state law
requires.

Sometimes a statute of limitations may be "tolled," *i.e.,* may not start
to run for a time after your cause of action has accrued. Some state
statutes provide that the limitations period is tolled while a person is
incarcerated.[272] However, some federal courts have refused to apply
these statutes where the prisoner was in fact able to bring suit.[273] If you
have delayed bringing suit because of misrepresentation by the defendants, the statute may be tolled until the time that the misrepresentation
was discovered.[274] In *Leigh v. McGuire,* one court held that a statute of
limitations on a §1983 damage claim was tolled while state criminal
appeals on the same issues were pending.[275] However, a recent Supreme
Court case rejected this theory when a state *civil* proceeding is pending,
so it is not clear whether *Leigh v. McGuire* is valid law.[276]

Your suit must be commenced within the statute of limitations against
all the defendants; your claim is time-barred against any defendant not
joined by name within the limitation period. There is an exception to this
in Rule 15(c), FRCP, which states that an amended complaint adding
parties "relates back" to the time of filing of the original complaint if
the two complaints deal with the same subject matter and if certain
notice requirements are met. However, the courts have reached mixed
conclusions in applying this rule.[277] You should always attempt to join

---

[271]Rosenberg v. Martin, 478 F.2d 520, 522 (2d Cir.), *cert. denied,* 414 U.S. 872
(1973); Allah v. Commissioner of Dept. of Correctional Services, 448 F. Supp.
1123 (N.D.N.Y. 1978).

[272]Miller v. Smith, 625 F.2d 43 (5th Cir. 1980); Brown v. Bigger, 622 F.2d 1025
(10th Cir. 1980).

[273]Campbell v. Guy, 520 F. Supp. 53 (E.D. Mich. 1981).

[274]Swietlowich v. County of Bucks, 610 F.2d 1157 (3d Cir. 1979).

[275]613 F.2d 380 (2d Cir. 1979).

[276]Board of Regents of the University of the State of New York v. Tomanio,
supra note 261, at 490-91.

[277]*See* McCurry v. Allen, 688 F.2d 581, 584-85 (8th Cir. 1981); Wood v.

all defendants and to name all "John Doe" defendants before the statute of limitations has run. (See Ch. VII, Sec. C, for a fuller discussion of amending a complaint.)

F. Damages

The law recognizes three different types of damage awards: compensatory, nominal, and punitive.[278] All of these may be available, whether the defendants are state or federal prison officials.[279]

1. Compensatory Damages

Compensatory damages are meant to place the plaintiff back in the position s/he was in before the injury occurred. The concept of "making the victim whole" means that the wrongdoer (prison official) is liable for all the necessary or natural consequences of his/her unlawful acts.[280] These consequences include both those which result in actual dollars-and-cents losses to you (doctor bill, loss of earning capacity, value of property) and those which do not (pain and suffering, emotional distress, humiliation).[281] The dollars-and-cents type of injury is called "special damages"; the more abstract injuries are called "general damages."

When you show that your substantive rights have been violated, compensatory damages are usually appropriate. However, the courts are divided as to whether it is the constitutional deprivation itself, or only the injuries that are caused by that violation, that justified the damages.[282] Most courts hold that mental and emotional distress is an injury for which damages can be awarded.[283] However, without proof of such

---

Woracheck, 618 F.2d 1225, 1229-30 (7th Cir. 1980); Florence v. Krasucki, 533 F. Supp. 1047, 1052-54 (W.D.N.Y. 1982); Davis v. Krause, 93 F.R.D. 580 (E.D.N.Y. 1982).

[278]*See* Koren, "Criteria for the Decision To Bring a Lawsuit for Damages: A Guide for Practitioners and Prisoners," 1 PLM 283 (May 1979).

[279]Carey v. Piphus, 435 U.S. 247, 266, 98 S.Ct. 1042 (1978); Carlson v. Green, 446 U.S. 14, 22, 100 S.Ct. 1468 (1980); Paton v. LaPrade, 524 F.2d 862, 871-72 (3d Cir. 1975).

[280]*See* Aumiller v. University of Delaware, 434 F. Supp. 1273, 1309-13 (D. Del. 1977), for a discussion of compensatory and punitive damages.

[281]*Id.*

[282]*See* Owen v. Lash, 682 F.2d 648, 657-59 (7th Cir. 1982), and cases cited; Corriz v. Naranjo, 667 F.2d 892, 897 (10th Cir. 1981).

[283]Mary and Crystal v. Ramsden, 635 F.2d 590, 600 (7th Cir. 1980); Rhodes v. Robinson, 612 F.2d 766 (3d Cir. 1979); Baskin v. Parker, 602 F.2d 1205, 1209 (5th Cir. 1979).

injury, some courts have awarded only nominal damages even when substantive rights were violated.[284] Therefore, in a damage case, you had better be prepared to show how a constitutional deprivation affected your life, even if this amounts only to telling the court how terrible you felt when you saw prison guards throw your family pictures on the floor during a cell search.

When your claim is for denial of procedural due process, you *must* prove that the denial of rights caused you an actual injury.[285] For example, if you claim that you were put in segregation without adequate notice and a hearing, you cannot recover damages for being in segregation unless the court finds that you would *not* have been put there even if you had received proper notice and hearing. If you can show that you suffered some injury, such as emotional distress, from the absence of proper procedures, and not from being in segregation, you can recover for that injury regardless of what the outcome of a proper hearing would have been.[286]

2. Nominal Damages

If you show that your procedural rights were violated but do not show any actual injury, you can recover "nominal damages" of only one dollar.[287] Some courts have applied the same rule to substantive constitutional rights.[288] Even in this situation, you may be entitled to punitive damages. (See Subsec. 3, *infra*.)

3. Punitive Damages

Punitive or exemplary damages are awarded for the purpose of punishing the defendants for their conduct or deterring them and others from committing similar acts in the future. They are available whether or not you have proven actual damages.[289] To obtain them, you must show

---

[284]Kincaid v. Rusk, 670 F.2d 737, 745-46 (7th Cir. 1982); McNamara v. Moody, 606 F.2d 621, 626 (5th Cir. 1979).

[285]Carey v. Piphus, *supra* note 279; Seaton v. Sky Realty Co., 491 F.2d 634 (7th Cir. 1974); Powell v. Ward, 540 F. Supp. 515, 517 (S.D.N.Y. 1982).

[286]Carey v. Piphus, *id.* at 262-64.

[287]Carey v. Piphus, *supra* note 279; United States ex rel. Tyrrell v. Speaker, 535 F.2d 823 (3d Cir. 1976) (nominal damages awarded for placement in segregation since it was less restricted than institution from which transferred); Magnett v. Pelletier, 488 F.2d 33 (1st Cir. 1973); Thompson v. Burke, 556 F.2d 231 (3d Cir. 1977).

[288]See cases cited in notes 282-284, *supra*.

[289]Spence v. Staras, 507 F.2d 554, 558 (7th Cir. 1974); Basista v. Weir, 340 F.2d 74, 86-88 (3d Cir. 1965).

that the prison official exhibits a reckless indifference to the rights of others, ill will, a desire to injure, or malice.[290] A municipality is immune from punitive damages under 42 U.S.C. §1983.[291]

The judge or jury is never required to award punitive damages.[292] The amount of punitive damages is also left to the discretion of the trier of fact. "The allowance of such damages inherently involves an evaluation of the nature of the conduct in question, the wisdom of some form of pecuniary [money] punishment, and the advisability of a deterrent."[293] An example of jury instructions on punitive damages appears in *Parker v. Shonfeld.*[294] Evidence relating to the prison official's income or net worth is admissible if substantial punitive damages are sought.[295] An award of punitive damages may not be disturbed on appeal unless it is "grossly excessive" or "shocking to the conscience."[296]

Punitive damages are rarely granted, even in cases where the court awards compensatory damages. As one court stated,

> Since such damages are punitory and are assessed as an example and warning to others, they are not a favorite in law and are to be allowed only with caution and within narrow limits.[297]

4. Amounts of Damages

In deciding what amount of damages to request, you should remember that most damage awards in prison cases are fairly small. Large awards tend to be reserved for cases involving serious bodily harm or shockingly bad treatment.[298] Awards for beatings not involving serious or per-

---

[290]Smith v. Wade, __U.S.__, 103 S.Ct. 1625 (1983); Silver v. Cormier, 529 F.2d 161, 163 (10th Cir. 1976); *see also* Stengel v. Belcher, 522 F.2d 438 (6th Cir. 1975), *cert. denied,* 429 U.S. 118 (1976).

[291]City of Newport v. Fact Concerts, Inc., 453 U.S. 247, 101 S.Ct. 2748 (1981).

[292]Smith v. Wade, *supra* note 290.

[293]Gill v. Manuel, 488 F.2d 799, 801 (9th Cir. 1973).

[294]409 F. Supp. 876, 881 n.6 (N.D. Cal. 1976). *See also* Fountila v. Carter, 571 F.2d 487, 492-94 (8th Cir. 1978), for a discussion of punitive damages and a jury instruction on the issue of punitive damages.

[295]Zarcone v. Perry, 572 F.2d 52, 56 (2d Cir. 1978), *cert. denied,* 439 U.S. 1072 (1979) (defendant has the burden of showing his modest means to minimize an award of punitive damages).

[296]*See id.* at 54-57.

[297]Simpson v. Weeks, 570 F.2d 240, 243 (8th Cir. 1978), *quoting from* Lee v. Southern Home Sites Corp., 429 F.2d 290, 294 (5th Cir. 1970).

[298]*See, e.g.,* Herrera v. Valentine, 653 F.2d 1220 (8th Cir. 1981) ($300,000

manent injury are usually much lower.[299] Damages for improper confinement in segregation are often in the range of $25 or $30 a day,[300] with larger sums for unconstitutionally bad conditions.[301] Damages for other violations are often modest as well.[302]

You should be realistic in the amount of damages you request in your complaint. Asking for enormous sums of money may satisfy your anger, but it will not help win your case. In fact, it may hurt. Judges may be antagonized or refuse to take you seriously,[303] and defendants may be unwilling to offer you a settlement if they think you are totally unreasonable.

G. Injunctive Relief

An injunction is a court order prohibiting a party from a specific course of action or requiring a party to perform some action. Injunctive relief can consist of a "temporary restraining order," a "preliminary injunction," or a "permanent injunction."

1. Temporary Restraining Order

The temporary restraining order (TRO) is used where immediate relief is necessary to prevent you from suffering irreparable injury (*e.g.,* if you have been placed in segregation improperly, or under inhuman conditions, you could request that a court speedily consider your request for relief pursuant to Federal Rules of Civil Procedure, Rule 65(b)). A TRO is very

---

upheld where pregnant woman was kicked in stomach and lost child, denied medical care, arrested, threatened with death, jailed, and denied counsel); Spicer v. Hilton, 618 F.2d 232, 235 (3d Cir. 1980) ($50,000 for amputation of foot); Redmond v. Baxley, 475 F. Supp. 1111 (E.D. Mich. 1979) ($130,000 for homosexual rape, beating, and psychological damage).

[299]Orpiano v. Johnson, 632 F.2d 1096 (4th Cir. 1980) ($10,000); Stanley v. Henderson, 597 F.2d 651 (8th Cir. 1979) ($1,000 compensatory and $2,500 punitive).

[300]Riley v. Johnson, 528 F. Supp. 333 (E.D. Mich. 1981); Pitts v. Kee, 511 F. Supp. 497 (D. Del. 1981).

[301]Maxwell v. Mason, 668 F.2d 261 (8th Cir. 1981); O'Connor v. Keller, 510 F. Supp. 1359 (D. Md. 1981).

[302]Steinberg v. Taylor, 500 F. Supp. 477 (D. Conn. 1980) ($475 for seizure of legal papers); Brooks v. Shipman, 503 F. Supp. 40 (W.D. Pa. 1980) ($100 compensatory and $50 punitive for improper search); Vaughn v. Trotter, 516 F. Supp. 886 (M.D. Tenn. 1980) ($2,040 for harassment of jailhouse lawyer).

[303]*See, e.g.,* Sloan v. Southhampton Correctional Center, 476 F. Supp. 196 (E.D. Va. 1979).

difficult for a *pro se* prisoner to obtain. The major reason it is hard for a *pro se* prisoner to obtain a TRO is because it is considered extraordinary and requires a great deal of persuasion. Technically, you should appear at court for the hearings if you are proceeding *pro se*. This is very hard to accomplish since you are incarcerated.

Even though judges are authorized to issue a TRO without notice to the defendant, they seldom do in prison cases. The date and time of the TRO hearing must be obtained from the clerk of the court so that information can be provided to the adverse parties when you serve them with copies of the pleadings. You must provide the defendant and, if you can, his/her attorney with a copy of the above documents.

A court will grant a TRO or a preliminary injunction only if you can demonstrate: (a) an immediate and irreparable injury in the absence of injunctive relief; (b) little or no adverse impact upon the defendant; (c) injunctive relief would serve the public interest; and (d) your likelihood of success on the merits.[304] Remember, as with any other phase of a lawsuit, a TRO or preliminary injunction motion will be won or lost on the *FACTS*. The facts are to be established by affidavits, oral testimony, or both.[305] A denial of a TRO is not appealable as of right to the court of appeals.

a. Irreparable Injury

The key factor in obtaining a TRO or preliminary injunction is showing that you will suffer irreparably during the pendency of the lawsuit if the relief requested is not granted.[306] The courts are to balance the hardships that will be suffered by the parties. A strong showing of irreparable injuries by you will make up for a weak showing in other areas.[307] You need to allege that there is "no adequate remedy at law," future compensation in damages will be an insufficient remedy, and that your injuries now are actual and of serious consequences to you. A

---

[304]*See* Williams v. Barry, 490 F. Supp. 941, 943 (D.D.C. 1980), *citing* Virginia Petroleum Jobbers Association v. F.P.C., 259 F.2d 921, 925 (D.C. Cir. 1958). *See also* National Prisoners Reform Assoc. v. Sharkey, 347 F. Supp. 1234 (D.R.I. 1972).

[305]You should attach affidavits of other prisoners who know first-hand of the facts of your case.

[306]*See* Crandall v. Cole, 230 F. Supp. 705 (E.D. Pa. 1964).

[307]Inmates of Attica Correctional Facility v. Rockefeller, 453 F.2d 12 (2d Cir. 1972); Securities v. Exchange Comm. v. World Radio Mission, Inc., 544 F.2d 535, 540-42 (1st Cir. 1976). *See* Jackson Dairy, Inc. v. H.P. Hood & Sons, Inc., 596 F.2d 70, 72 (2d Cir. 1979).

showing that your constitutional rights have been violated is sufficient to establish irreparable harm.[308]

b.   Balancing of the Interests

If you cannot show a probability of success on the merits and some irreparable injury, you should argue that a balancing of the hardships entitles you to the TRO or preliminary injunction.[309] You can either cite similar factual cases or, if similar cases are not available, you will need to convince the court that if relief is denied *you will suffer more than prison officials*. This argument is very similar to the one made that you will suffer irreparable injury. You should stress to the court the differences in the conditions in segregation and general population. Also, make the court aware that if you later lose the case on the merits, prison officials can have you serve time in segregation. But, if you serve your segregation time now and win on the merits later, you can never regain the loss of privileges general population offers.

c.   Public Interest

You need to show the court that it is in the public interest to grant you a TRO or preliminary injunction.[310] If you are alleging that prison officials have violated their own rules and regulations, a statute, or the Constitution, it is always in the public interest that governmental officials act in a lawful manner. The Supreme Court has stated that injunctive relief should be "conditioned by the necessities of the public interest which [the rules, regulations, or laws] . . . sought to protect."[311] The intent of the government in passing its laws and requiring prison officials to comply with the laws "is a public interest aspect which cannot be ignored."[312]

d.   Likelihood of Success on the Merits

The courts have held that if the first three factors are compelling, the

---

[308]Elrod v. Burns, 427 U.S. 347, 96 S.Ct. 2673 (1976); Deerfield Med. Ctr. v. City of Deerfield Beach, 661 F.2d 328, 338 (5th Cir. 1981); Johnson v. Bergland, 586 F.2d 993, 995 (4th Cir. 1978).

[309]Inmates of Attica Correctional Facility v. Rockefeller, *supra* note 307, at 20; Bay Ridge Diagnostic Laboratory, Inc. v. Dumpson, 400 F. Supp. 1104, 1108-09 (E.D.N.Y. 1975); Pride v. Community Sch. Bd. of Brooklyn, N.Y. Sch. D. #18, 482 F.2d 257, 264, 270-71 (2d Cir. 1973).

[310]Walling v. Brookland Braids, Co., 152 F.2d 938, 940 (2d Cir. 1945).

[311]Hecht Co. v. Bowles, 321 U.S. 321, 330, 64 S.Ct. 587 (1944).

[312]*Id.* at 339-40.

likelihood of success need not constitute a mathematical probability.[313] If you can show the court that the level of irreparable injury, the balance of equities, and public policy strongly favor the injunctive relief you are seeking, the court may grant an injunction even though your chances of winning your case on the ultimate merits is narrow.[314]

If the first three factors are not compelling, you will need to persuade the court that your case law is stronger than the law supporting the defendant. Most of this persuasion should have been set forth in the other three factors and you should only need to summarize your earlier presentation.

2. Preliminary Injunction

The above four criteria also govern whenever you seek a preliminary injunction. You can seek a preliminary injunction without first having sought a TRO. A preliminary injunction can be used to secure fast relief, but not as immediate as relief under a TRO. If the court denies your motion for a preliminary injunction, it is appealable as of right under 28 U.S.C. §1292(a)(1).[315]

3. Security for a TRO or Preliminary Injunction

A court may require the person obtaining a TRO or preliminary injunction to post security.[316] You should not be required to post security since a TRO or preliminary injunction in a *pro se* case seldom will require ⌐rison officials to expend money. A requirement that you post security is especially inappropriate if you are proceeding in forma pauperis.[317]

4. Permanent Injunction

A permanent injunction is not issued by a court until the claims of the litigation have been resolved, either by trial, consent decree, or motion for summary judgment.

---

[313]Washington Metropolitan Area Transit Commission v. Holiday Tours, Inc., 559 F.2d 841, 843 (D.C. Cir. 1977); Williams v. Barry, 490 F. Supp. 941, 943 (D.D.C. 1980).

[314]Williams v. Barry, *id.* at 944-47.

[315]The denial of a preliminary injunction is reviewable by the court of appeals under an abuse of discretion standard.

[316]Fed. R. Civ. P. 65(c).

[317]*See* J.L. v. Parham, 412 F. Supp. 112 (D. Ga. 1976), *rev'd on other grounds,* 442 U.S. 584, 99 S.Ct. 2493 (1979).

5. Documents To File When Seeking a TRO or Preliminary Injunction

The documents you must file when seeking a TRO or preliminary injunction under Fed. R. Civ. P. 65 are:[318]

1) A complaint. In the relief section of your complaint, you will ask the court to grant you (a) a temporary restraining order, and/or (b) a preliminary injunction.

2) A "Motion for a Temporary Restraining Order and/or Preliminary Injunction."

3) Affidavit. You will need at least your own affidavit in support of the motion. If you can obtain affidavits from other prisoners based on their first-hand knowledge to factually support your case, you should do so.

4) A brief in support of your request for TRO or Preliminary Injunction. This brief should list the four criterion, state the facts supporting each criteria, and cite case law, statutes, regulations, etc., supporting your contention.

5) You should draft a proposed order granting you the relief requested in your TRO.[319]

6) A proof of service. Since you will not be able to deliver personally to the defendant a copy of all the above documents, you will mail a copy of these documents to the defendant and his/her attorney, which is usually the Attorney General of your state, and you will send the court an affidavit stating that you have done so.

Examples of these documents can be found in Appendix B.

If you wish to proceed without payment of fees, you will need to file a motion to proceed as an indigent and an affidavit in support. (See Ch. VII, Sec. A3, for a discussion of indigency.)

H. Declaratory Judgment

A declaratory judgment is a means by which you may obtain a binding declaration regarding your legal rights.[320] The Federal Declaratory Judgment Act provides that in a case of "actual controversy within its jurisdiction," a federal court "may declare the rights and other legal relations of any interested party seeking such declaration, whether or not further relief is or could be sought."[321] Declaratory judgments have been

---

[318]See Appendix B for a sample of most of these documents.

[319]See Ch. III, Sec. C, concerning drafting of orders.

[320]28 U.S.C. §§2201-2202 (1976); Fed. R. Civ. P. 57.

[321]28 U.S.C. §2201. *See also* Geraghty v. United States Parole Commission, 579 F.2d 238 (3d Cir. 1978), *vacated on other grounds,* 100 S.Ct. 1202 (1980).

sought by prisoners when challenging the constitutionality of a statute or governmental regulation which seeks to interpret that statute, or rules and regulations promulgated by the prison system.[322]

Declaratory judgments are usually requested along with an injunction and money damages. The declaratory judgment is not an order mandating that someone act or refrain from acting. It only declares whether a legal right or obligation exists between prison officials and you. The court assumes that the parties to a declaratory judgment will adhere to and respect the court's adjudication without further orders. If you have been granted a declaratory judgment concerning the prison disciplinary rules and prison officials ignore the court's declaration, the court can exercise its broad remedial power under the Federal Declaratory Judgment Act, 28 U.S.C. §§2201-2202, and grant you an injunction requiring them to obey the declaration.[323] If prison officials refuse to obey the injunction, the court can use its contempt powers to obtain compliance.

A court can not be compelled to render a declaratory judgment. The court should exercise its discretion in a liberal manner to achieve the remedial purpose of the Declaratory Judgment Act. Since declaratory judgments are not considered extraordinary remedies, you are not required to show irreparable harm or inadequate remedies at law, as is required for issuance of an injunction.[324] (See Sec. G, *supra,* for a discussion on injunction.) You also need not have suffered the infliction of an injury to obtain a declaratory judgment.[325]

You should examine your state statues concerning declaratory relief and the applicable court rules. Your state may not have a statute concerning declaratory judgment, but should have a court rule authorizing issuance of a declaratory judgment. Once you have found your state statute and/or court rule concerning declaratory judgment, you should "shepardize" them and then read the cases that have interpreted them. For instructions on how to shepardize, see Ch. II, Sec. C4.

---

[322]*See* Morris v. Travisono, 373 F. Supp. 177, 182 (D.R.I. 1974), *modified,* 495 F.2d 562 (1974), *aff'd,* 509 F.2d 1358 (1st Cir. 1975) (declaratory judgment regarding prison disciplinary rules); Karr v. Bay, 413 F. Supp. 579 (N.D. Ohio 1976) (declaration regarding incarceration of indigent prisoners for non-payment of fines).

[323]Morris v. Travisono, *id.*

[324]Fed. R. Civ. P. 57; Aetna Life Ins. Co. v. Haworth, 300 U.S. 227, 241, 56 S.Ct. 461 (1937); Diaz v. Stathis, 576 F.2d 9 (1st Cir. 1978).

[325]*See* N.Y. State Association for Retarded Children, Inc. v. Carey, 466 F. Supp. 479, 482 (E.D.N.Y. 1978).

VII
How to Litigate in Federal Court

This chapter is about procedures you must follow in litigating a lawsuit. Because we cannot deal with the court rules of the 50 different state court systems, we focus on the Federal Rules of Civil Procedure (FRCP),[1] which apply in federal district courts. Many states have modeled their systems after the federal rules. However, whether you are in federal or state court, you must learn and obey the rules of the court where you are litigating.

The Federal Rules of Civil Procedure govern civil cases in federal court. In a habeas corpus or other federal post-conviction proceeding, the FRCP apply,[2] unless they conflict with the rules governing these cases.[3] Additional procedural requirements in federal post-conviction proceedings are discussed in Ch. IX.

You should also be aware that federal district courts have local rules with which you must comply. These rules can be obtained from the clerk of your local court. (The courts will usually charge you one or two dollars for a copy of their rules.) Particular state courts may also have local rules you should obtain and study if you are litigating in those courts.

---

[1]These rules, with annotations, may be found at the end of Title 28 of the U.S. Code. The rules are also published separately in various editions. You can obtain copies of the federal rules of civil, criminal and appellate procedures and evidence by writing the U.S. House of Representatives, Committee on Judiciary, Washington, D.C. 20515.

[2]*See* United States v. Frady, __U.S.__, 102 S.Ct. 1584, 1594 n.15 (1982), for a discussion of the application of the FRCP to habeas proceedings under §§2254 and 2255.

[3]See Appendix C, Sec. 2, Rule 11, and Sec. 3, Rule 12.

A. Starting Your Lawsuit

1. General Requirements of a Complaint/Petition

A lawsuit starts with a complaint or a petition. Examples of what a complaint and petition should look like are given in Appendices B and C, respectively. Your complaint/petition should be separated into numbered paragraphs.[4] Each paragraph should express one idea. The complaint should contain the following information:

(1) A short and plain statement of the basis of the court's jurisdiction.[5]

(2) The name and address of the plaintiff, usually you, and where you are incarcerated.

(3) The name of each defendant and his/her official position, duties, and any statutes, rules, or policy directives explaining those duties.

(4) A short and plain statement of your factual allegations, in chronological order, showing that your legal rights have been violated and how each named defendant is connected to those legal violations. Each numbered paragraph should contain only one factual allegation and should generally not be longer than four lines.

(5) A separate paragraph stating which of your legal rights were violated.

(6) A demand for the relief to which you are entitled. You may demand relief in the alternative or of several different types.[6]

Pro se complaints are held to less stringent standards than formal pleadings drafted by lawyers.[7] However, "Complaints based on civil rights statutes must do more than state simple conclusions [*e.g.,* the warden violated my right of access to the courts]; they must at least outline the facts constituting the alleged violation [*e.g.,* when the warden entered my cell and took my legal papers and tore them into many pieces, he violated my right of access to the courts]."[8]

---

[4]See also Rule 10, FRCP, Form of Pleadings and Ch. III, "Legal Writing."

[5]When a state prisoner is filing a civil rights action in federal court, s/he will allege the court has jurisdiction pursuant to 28 U.S.C. §1343. See also Ch. VI, Sec. B1a. A federal prisoner will allege the court has jurisdiction pursuant to 28 U.S.C. §1331. See also Ch. VI, Sec. C1a.

[6]In your relief section, you may request a declaratory judgment, injunctive relief, and/or money damages, and you will always include the following: "Any other relief this court deems just." See Ch. VI, for a discussion of the different types of relief you may request.

[7]Haines v. Kerner, 404 U.S. 519, 92 S.Ct. 594 (1972), *cited in* Hughes v. Rowe, 449 U.S. 5, 101 S.Ct. 173, 176 (1980).

[8]Dougherty v. Harper's Magazine Co., 537 F.2d 758, 761 (3d Cir. 1976). *See*

Some federal district courts require that, when filing *pro se,* you use a standardized form provided by the court instead of filing a complaint you drafted. (See Appendix B, Form 1e, for a sample of the standardized complaint.)

2. Requirements of Filing and Service

Once you have prepared your complaint, you must file it with the court and "serve process" on each defendant—that is, you must see that every defendant is provided with a copy of the complaint and the summons,[9] which informs the defendant that s/he has been sued and must respond. Until proper service of process is made on a defendant, the court does not have "personal jurisdiction" over the defendant and cannot take any action against him/her. The requirements for proper service of process are set forth in Rule 4, FRCP, as amended February 26, 1983.

You must provide the clerk of the court with the proper number of legal documents for filing. The clerk should receive the original of the summons and complaint/petition,[10] a copy of each for each named defendant,[11] and an extra copy to be date stamped and returned to you. You only need to send the original and one copy of the motion to proceed in forma pauperis (as an indigent, without payment of fees and costs) with the affidavit and the request for counsel.[12]

If you are seeking to proceed in forma pauperis, once the clerk has received your papers, they will be assigned to a judge for a determination whether you should be allowed to proceed without payment of filing fees and costs. Except in an emergency, you should allow the court approximately two months to act on your papers before writing to inquire about any delay. If the court does grant you leave to proceed as an indigent, your case will then be assigned to a judge, who will usually remain on the case throughout any further proceedings in district court. The second

---

also Pavilonis v. King, 626 F.2d 1075 (1st Cir. 1980); Durso v. Rowe, 579 F.2d 1365, 1371 (7th Cir. 1978).

[9]See Appendix B, Form 4, for an example of a summons.

[10]The original or all motions, briefs, discovery requests, etc. must be filed with the court.

[11]If you have listed "John Doe" defendants, you do not need to send their copies of the complaint and summons to the court at the time of filing of the case. When you have discovered who the John Does are during discovery, you will then ask the court to issue summons in the name of these people and you will need to serve each with a copy of the amended complaint and summons. See Appendix B, Form 1b.

[12]See Appendix B, Form 2, for sample in forma pauperis pleadings and Sec. A3a, "In Forma Pauperis," *infra.*

judge is usually the one who will determine whether you will be assigned counsel. If the court denies you leave to proceed in forma pauperis, you can either pay the filing fee, if you have it, or appeal the denial of in forma pauperis status.[13]

Exactly how you file and serve your summons and complaint may depend on how big a hurry you are in and what kind of help you can get from people on the outside. If time is not of the essence—for example, in a damage case—you will file the summons and complaint along with a motion to proceed as an indigent; the court, when it grants the motion, will return to you the extra copies of the complaint and summons. You can either have a copy of the complaint and summons served on each defendant by any non-party 18 years old or more, have them served by the U.S. Marshal if you have been granted in forma pauperis status, or mail a copy of the summons and complaint to the defendant with two copies of a "Notice and Acknowledgment of Receipt of Summons and Complaint" form[14] and a self-addressed prepaid envelope.[15] The defendant has 20 days after you mail the request for acknowledgment to sign and return it to you. If s/he does not return the acknowledgments signed under oath within 20 days, you can then ask the court either to appoint a special process server, such as a friend or family member, or to order the U.S. Marshal to serve process on the defendant.[16]

These steps can involve significant delay. If you are seeking a temporary restraining order[17] or an injunction to remedy some immediate serious problem, you may wish to expedite matters by paying the filing fee, have a friend or family member file and serve the summons and complaint immediately, and file for in forma pauperis status later. You should only do this if you can have the service of process done by a trustworthy and competent person who you are confident can follow instructions and deal with court and prison bureaucracies. S/he will have to take the pleadings to the office of the court clerk to be filed and stamped, take the stamped copies to the prison or home or office of the defendant, and give them to the proper person. (Alternatively, if you or your family can afford it, you could have it done by a professional process server.)

The summons and complaint must be served within 120 days after the

---

[13]See Sec. P, *infra*, Appeals.

[14]See Appendix B, Form 4a.

[15]See Rule 4(c)(2)(C)(ii), as amended February 26, 1983. The service must be by first-class mail, postage prepaid. You should always send it by certified or registered mail requesting return receipt.

[16]*Id.*

[17]See Ch. VI, Sec. G1, for a discussion of the requirements for a temporary restraining order.

filing of the complaint.[18] If you cannot show good cause why you were not able to serve a defendant within 120 days,[19] the court will dismiss the action without prejudice as to that defendant. If the court did dismiss an action against one of the defendants, you would have to file a motion to add a party and a motion to amend the complaint if you wanted the dismissed defendant to be a part of the original lawsuit. See Sec. C, *infra,* for a discussion of amending complaints and adding parties.

Once the summons has been served, proof of service[20] to show when, where, and on whom it was served must be filed with the court by the person serving the documents.[21]

3.   Indigency and Appointment of Counsel

a.   In Forma Pauperis

To file a lawsuit, you must ordinarily pay a filing fee of $60; for a petition for writ of habeas corpus, the fee is $5.[22] Additional fees and costs that may be required at successive stages of litigation are: marshal's fees for service of process and subpoenas, witness fees, docket fees, appeal fees, judgment and execution fees, cost for production of transcripts (preliminary injunction and trial), appeal and security bond, etc.[23] A court, when presented with the proper documents, may permit a prisoner who is "unable to pay such costs or give security" to commence or defend a civil or criminal action in forma pauperis (without payment of fees and costs).[24]

If you are filing your legal action in federal court, you will request,

---

[18]See Rule 4(i), FRCP, as amended February 26, 1983.

[19]Example of good cause for failing to serve the summons within 120 days might be that you had mailed a copy of the summons and complaint with the acknowledgments and defendant never responded; that you had a friend, pursuant to the local state rule, try to serve a guard at the prison but no one would accept service; or that the U.S. Marshals were ordered to serve your papers and they did not do so within the 120 days.

[20]See Appendix B, Form 17.

[21]See Rule 4(g), FRCP, as amended February 26, 1983.

[22]28 U.S.C. §1914.

[23]*See* 28 U.S.C. §§1821, 1913, 1914, 1917, 1920-23.

[24]28 U.S.C. §1915. *But see* Morrow v. Igleburger, 584 F.2d 767, 772 n.7 (6th Cir. 1978), *cert. denied,* 439 U.S. 1118 (1979) (court said that it possessed, but would not exercise, authority to use in forma pauperis status to cover witness fees).

pursuant to 28 U.S.C. §1915, leave to proceed in forma pauperis.[25] Section 1915, titled "Proceedings in forma pauperis," provides:

(a) Any court of the United States may authorize the commencement, prosecution, or defense of any suit, action or proceeding, civil or criminal, or appeal therein, without prepayment of fees and costs or security therefor, by a person who makes affidavit that he is unable to pay such costs or give security therefor. Such affidavit shall state the nature of the action, defense, or appeal and affiant's belief that he is entitled to redress.

An appeal may not be taken in forma pauperis if the trial court certifies in writing that it is not taken in good faith.

(b) Upon the filing of an affidavit in accordance with subsection (a) of this section, the court may direct payment by the United States of the expenses of (1) printing of the record on appeal in any civil or criminal case, if such printing is required by the appellate court; (2) preparing a transcript of proceedings before a United States magistrate in any civil or criminal case, if such transcript is required by the district court, in the case of proceedings conducted under §636(b) of this title or under §3401(b) of Title 18, United State Code; and (3) printing the record on appeal if such printing is required by the appellate court, in the case of proceedings conducted pursuant to §636(c) of this title. Such expenses shall be paid when authorized by the Director of the Administrative Office of the United States Courts.

(c) The officers of the court shall issue and serve all process, and perform all duties in such cases. Witnesses shall attend as in other cases, and the same remedies shall be available as are provided for by law in other cases.

(d) The court may request an attorney to represent any such person unable to employ counsel and may dismiss the case if the allegation of poverty is untrue, or if satisfied that the action is frivolous or malicious.

(e) Judgment may be rendered for costs at the conclusion of the suit or action as in other cases, but the United States shall not be liable for any of the costs thus incurred. If the United States has paid the cost of a stenographic transcript or printed record for the prevailing party, the same shall be taxed in favor of the United States.

You will submit to the clerk of the court, along with your complaint and summons. a "Motion To Proceed In Forma Pauperis," affidavit in support, and a proposed order granting leave to proceed without payment of fees and costs.[26] The affidavit is the most important of these documents. Your affidavit should be simple and contain the language of the statute, such as, you are "unable to pay such costs or give security."[27] This statement must be supported with *facts* informing the clerk and the judge of your financial situation within the prison, any bank accounts or property owned by you, and any money that you

---

[25]State prisoners filing in state court should examine state statutes and court rules for similar provisions.

[26]See Appendix B, Form 2.

[27]28 U.S.C. §1915(a).

receive weekly or monthly from outside sources. The clerk will present your initial pleading and the motion to proceed in forma pauperis to the judge. The decision should be based solely on your financial considerations, not on the merits of your claims.[28]

The Supreme Court, in *Adkins v. Dupont,*[29] recognized that litigants need not give up their "last dollar . . . and thus make themselves and their dependents wholly destitute"[30] to be granted in forma pauperis status. In *Souder v. McGuire,*[31] the *Adkins* standard was applied to a habeas corpus action and the court held that:

> [W]e do not think that prisoners must totally deprive themselves of these small amenities of life which they are permitted to acquire in a prison or mental hospital beyond the food, clothing, and lodging already furnished by the state. An account of $50.07 would not purchase many such amenities, perhaps cigarettes and some occasional reading material. These need not be surrendered in order for a prisoner or a mental patient to litigate in forma pauperis in the district court.[32]

Some courts have required prisoners with as little as $50 in their prison accounts to pay filing fees.[33] The district court in *Braden v. Estelle*[34] reached a middle ground between non-payment and full payment when it required a prisoner to pay a portion of the costs.

> As emphasized throughout this Order, the purpose of the "partial payment" requirement is to curb the indiscriminate filing of prisoner civil rights actions by prompting inmates to "confront the initial dilemma which faces most other potential civil litigants: is the merit of the claim worth the cost of pursuing it?"[35]

Because different courts have used different approaches to defining indigency, you should look for cases from your federal district and circuit. You should also see if there are any special requirements for in forma pauperis status in the local rules of the court.

---

[28]Forester v. California Adult Authority, 510 F.2d 58, 60 (8th Cir. 1975); Sinwell v. Shapp, 536 F.2d 15, 18-19 (3d Cir. 1976).

[29]335 U.S. 331, 69 S.Ct. 85 (1948).

[30]*Id.* at 339.

[31]516 F.2d 820 (3d Cir. 1975).

[32]*Id.* at 824; *see also* In re Smith, 600 F.2d 714 (8th Cir. 1979).

[33]*See* Ward v. Werner, 61 F.R.D. 639 (M.D. Pa. 1974) (prisoners with accounts of $50 and $65 were not entitled to proceed in forma pauperis); Shimabuka v. Britton, 357 F. Supp. 825 (D. Kan. 1973), *aff'd,* 504 F.2d 38 (10th Cir. 1974).

[34]428 F. Supp. 595 (S.D. Tex. 1977).

[35]*Id.* at 596. (Citation omitted.).

A judge may grant you leave to proceed without payment of fees and costs and then summarily dismiss your lawsuit as being "frivolous or malicious."[36] However, a *pro se* complaint is held to "less stringent standards than formal pleadings drafted by lawyers,"[37] and should not be dismissed unless your claims clearly do not state a legal violation or are not supported by factual allegations.[38]

Courts have stated the test of whether a *pro se* complaint is frivolous and should be dismissed in various ways. The court in *Bennett v. Passic*[39] held that the test for frivolousness is "whether the plaintiff can make a rational argument on the law or facts in support of his claim."[40] Some courts have stated that a complaint "without arguable merit, both in law and fact, can be dismissed as frivolous."[41] Other courts have held that a complaint is frivolous and should be dismissed when plaintiff's "realistic chances of success are slight."[42]

The courts have emphasized that a prisoner's complaint alleging facts supporting a civil rights violation should not be dismissed before the complaint is served on the defendants and they reply to it.[43] Section 1915(d) does not provide for "cursory treatment of meritorious com-

---

[36]28 U.S.C. §1915(d). *See* Watson v. Ault, 525 F.2d 886 (5th Cir. 1976); Taylor v. Gibson, 529 F.2d 707, 709 (5th Cir. 1976); Collins v. Hladky, 603 F.2d 824 (10th Cir. 1979); French v. Butterworth, 614 F.2d 23 (1st Cir.), *cert. denied,* 446 U.S. 942 (1980).

[37]Haines v. Kerner, 404 U.S. 519, 92 S.Ct. 594 (1972); *accord,* Hughes v. Rowe, 449 U.S. 5, 101 S.Ct. 173 (1980); 3 PLM 91 (April 1981).

[38]Slavin v. Curry, 574 F.2d 1256, 1260 (5th Cir. 1978) (The personal view of a judge that the "allegations of a *pro se* complaint are implausible [cannot] temper his duty to appraise such pleadings liberally.").

[39]Bennett v. Passic, 545 F.2d 1260, 1261 (10th Cir. 1976).

[40]*Id.; accord,* Collins v. Hladky, *supra* note 36.

[41]Watson v. Ault, *supra* note 36, at 892, adopting the test for frivolous criminal appeals defined in Anders v. California, 386 U.S. 738, 744, 87 S.Ct. 1396 (1967). *See also* Scellato v. Dept. of Corrections, 438 F. Supp. 1206 (W.D. Va. 1977); Boyce v. Alizaduh, 595 F.2d 948 (4th Cir. 1979).

[42]Sims v. Zolango, 481 F. Supp. 388 (S.D.N.Y. 1979); Harvey v. Clay County Sheriff's Dept., 473 F. Supp. 741 (W.D. Mo. 1979); Boston v. Stanton, 450 F. Supp. 1049 (W.D. Mo. 1978); Clark v. Zimmerman, 394 F. Supp. 1166 (M.D. Pa. 1975). *See also* Anderson v. Coughlin, 700 F.2d 87 (2d Cir. 1982) (standard for dismissal as frivolous broader than standard for dismissal under FRCP).

[43]Bayron v. Trudeau, 702 F.2d 43 (2d Cir. 1983); Fries v. Barnes, 618 F.2d 988 (2d Cir. 1980). *See also* Cline v. Herman, 601 F.2d 374 (8th Cir. 1979); United States ex rel. Walker v. Fayette County, 599 F.2d 573 (3d Cir. 1979); Ibarra v. Olivarri, 587 F.2d 677 (5th Cir. 1979).

plaints.''[44] The discretion of district courts to dismiss your legal pleadings "may not be exercised arbitrarily and is limited . . . in every case by the language of the statute itself which restricts its application to complaints found to be 'frivolous or malicious.' ''[45]

> [J]udges must balance their misgivings and skepticism about the usual §1983 prisoner suit against the cold knowledge that in certain instances injustices to prisoners occur in jails and prisons, some of which violate constitutional mandates. . . . [I]t is the responsibility of the courts to be sensitive to possible abuses in order to ensure that prisoner complaints, particularly *pro se* complaints, are not dismissed prematurely, however unlikely the set of facts postulated.[46]

If you have been denied leave to proceed in forma pauperis or have had your pleading dismissed as "frivolous or malicious" by the district court, you have three options. If you think the judge was simply wrong, you can appeal. If you appeal, you may move to proceed in forma pauperis in the appellate court. (See Sec. P1, *infra,* for a discussion of appeals to the appellate court.) If you think the district court missed or misunderstood something in your papers, you can file a motion within 10 days of the entry of the order to alter the judgment. This motion should point out what you think the judge missed, or should cite some other ground besides what you said in your original motion.[47] (See Sec. O1, *infra,* for a discussion of these motions.) If the judge dismisses your complaint for some reason which can be corrected, such as suing the right party, you can file an amended complaint. (See Sec. C, *infra,* on amending complaints.)

The fact that you are granted in forma pauperis status does not mean that you will never be liable for fees or costs. If you lose your case, an award of costs may be made against you.[48] Some courts have restricted these awards to cases where "there is 'a complete absence of merit, coupled with the intent to use the court as a vehicle for harassment. . . .' ''[49] (We do not know whether and under what circumstances these awards are actually enforced.)

---

[44]McTeague v. Sosnowski, 617 F.2d 1016, 1019 (3d Cir. 1980).

[45]Boyce v. Alizadah, *supra* note 41, at 951.

[46]Taylor v. Gibson, *supra* note 36, at 713.

[47]*See* Ali v. Cuyler, 547 F. Supp. 129 (E.D. Pa. 1982) (prisoner with $450 in savings account would not be granted in forma pauperis status but would be permitted to show that the money had by this time been exhausted).

[48]*See* Rule 54(d), FRCP.

[49]Marks v. Calendine, 80 F.R.D. 24, 31 (N.D. Va. 1978).

b.   Appointment of Counsel

Even though you do not have a constitutional right to have counsel appointed in a civil action,[50] it is recommended that all *pro se* litigants seek appointment of counsel. As one court put it, counsel can

> . . . explain the applicable legal principles to the complainant and . . . limit litigation to potentially meritorious issues. In addition, appointment of a lawyer provides the unlettered inmate with an opportunity to obtain representation equally qualified with the professional counsel usually provided by the state for the defendants.[51]

Even if you are not "unlettered," counsel can generally do a better job than a prisoner at conducting discovery, negotiating a settlement of meritorious claims, and the other difficult tasks of litigation, by virtue of experience and of not being locked up in the defendants' custody.

When you file your motion for leave to proceed in forma pauperis, you should file a motion for appointment of counsel pursuant to 28 U.S.C. §1915(d).[52] The court has the discretion to "request that an attorney represent . . . [a] person unable to employ counsel. . . ."[53] If you are granted leave to proceed as an indigent and your complaint is not dismissed as frivolous, the court will consider requesting counsel to represent you.[54] However, the court has no authority to order an attorney to represent you, or—more important—to pay an attorney to represent you.[55]

---

[50]Hardwick v. Ault, 517 F.2d 295, 298 (5th Cir. 1975); Matter of Nine Applications for Appointment, 475 F. Supp. 87 (N.D. Ala. 1979); Johnson v. Teasdale, 456 F. Supp. 1083, 1089 (W.D. Mo. 1978); Peterson v. Nadler, 452 F.2d 754 (8th Cir. 1971).

[51]Wright v. Dallas County Sheriff's Dept., 660 F.2d 623 (5th Cir. 1981), *quoting* Knighton v. Watkins, 616 F.2d 795 (5th Cir. 1980); Stringer v. Rowe, 616 F.2d 993, 1001 (7th Cir. 1980).

[52]See Appendix B, Form 18, Motion for Appointment of Counsel and Brief in Support.

[53]28 U.S.C. §1915(d).

[54]*See* Bounds v. Smith, 430 U.S. 817, 97 S.Ct. 1491 (1977). *See also* Gordon v. Leeke, 574 F.2d 1147, 1153 and n.3 (4th Cir. 1978) (court should appoint counsel where *pro se* litigant has a colorable claim); Aldabe v. Aldabe, 616 F.2d 1089, 1093 (9th Cir. 1980) (court should appoint counsel only when exceptional circumstances exist), and cases cited; Lamb v. Hutto, 467 F. Supp. 562 (E.D. Va. 1979). If you have filed an action in state court invoking the state court's concurrent jurisdiction to hear a civil rights action, you should request that counsel be appointed to represent you based on the reasons in this section. See Ch. IV, Sec. D2, for a discussion of use of state courts for litigating civil rights actions.

[55]An attorney who wins a civil rights case for you is ordinarily entitled to a fee:

The following are some of the factors that a district court will consider in determining whether to request counsel to represent you. *First,* the court will consider whether you have much chance of success.[56] *Second,* is whether you are in a position to investigate the crucial facts needed to prove your claims.[57] *Third,* is whether there are facts in dispute and whether the disputes are complicated or substantial; if not, the court usually will not appoint counsel.[58] *Fourth,* is the complexity of the legal issues raised by the complaint. Where the law is not clear, the court should appoint counsel.[59] *Finally,* the court should consider the capability of the indigent to present the case.[60] If you have demonstrated by your pleadings, discovery requests, and briefs a knowledge of the legal process, the court may require you to represent yourself.

If you are petitioning for a writ of habeas corpus or other post-conviction relief, the court's authority to appoint and pay counsel is somewhat broader. (See Ch. IX, Sec. E5, for a discussion of appointment of counsel in post-conviction proceedings.) This may be a reason to

---

to be determined by the court and paid by the defendants. 42 U.S.C. §1988. *See* Hensley v. Eckerhart, __U.S.__, 103 S.Ct. 933 (1983).

[56]Mosby v. Mabry, 697 F.2d 213 (8th Cir. 1982). *See also* Ligare v. Harries, 128 F.2d 582, 583 (7th Cir. 1942) (counsel not appointed on appeal where law is clearly settled); Spears v. United States, 266 F. Supp. 22, 25-26 (S.D. W. Va. 1967) (court must determine whether claim has some merit in fact and law before counsel is appointed); Miller v. Pleasure, 296 F.2d 283 (2d Cir. 1961), *cert. denied,* 270 U.S. 964 (1962).

[57]Slavin v. Curry, 690 F.2d 446 (5th Cir. 1982); Stringer v. Rowe, *supra* note 51; Shields v. Jackson, 570 F.2d 284, 285 (8th Cir. 1978) (indigent prisoner in no position to investigate his case when he has sued arresting officer for confiscating personal property); Maclin v. Freake, 650 F.2d 885 (7th Cir. 1981). *See also* Murrell v. Bennett, 615 F.2d 306, 311 (5th Cir. 1980) (district court should have appointed counsel to aid plaintiff with his discovery).

[58]Lopez v. Reyes, 692 F.2d 15 (5th Cir. 1982); Manning v. Lockhart, 623 F.2d 536 (8th Cir. 1980) (counsel should have been appointed where a question of credibility of witnesses and serious allegations of fact existed); U.S. ex rel. Robinson v. Meyers, 222 F. Supp. 845, 848 (E.D. Pa. 1963), *aff'd,* 326 F.2d 972 (3d Cir. 1963).

[59]Merritt v. Faulkner, 697 F.2d 761 (7th Cir. 1983); Ligare v. Harries, *supra* note 56; Rhodes v. Houston, 258 F. Supp. 546, 579 (D. Neb. 1966), *cert. denied,* 397 U.S. 1049 (1970).

[60]*See* Gordon v. Leeke, *supra* note 54; Drone v. Natto, 565 F.2d 543 (8th Cir. 1977) (counsel should be appointed where record indicated plaintiff suffered from mental disease); Davis v. United States, 214 F.2d 594 (7th Cir. 1954); Spears v. United States, *supra* note 56 (indigent's working knowledge of legal process demonstrated by pleadings filed with court).

use the habeas corpus statute if you are bringing a challenge to prison conditions or practices.[61] (See Ch. VI, Sec. B2, for a discussion of use of habeas corpus in conditions cases.)

Ways to try to get counsel on your own are discussed in Ch. I, Sec. D.

4. Joinder of Claims

Rule 18, FRCP, sets no limitation on the number and kind of claims you can bring against a single defendant. You are not required to bring all your claims against one defendant at the same time. But, if these claims arise out of the same factual situation and you fail to bring them all at the same time, the rule of res judicata may preclude you from raising the other claims later.[62]

5. Answer

The defendant is required to respond to your complaint within 20 days (60 days for federal government defendants)[63] after a copy of the complaint and summons has been served by either filing an answer or filing one of the motions permitted under Rule 12, FRCP.[64] An answer is a reply to your complaint, either admitting or denying each statement contained in the paragraphs of the complaint, or stating that the defendant does not know whether a particular statement is true, which has the same effect as a denial of your allegation.[65] Whenever the defendant has filed an answer and has not replied to one of the factual paragraphs in the complaint, that paragraph is taken as admitted.[66] If the defendant fails to file a response to the complaint within the time period, you should consider seeking a default judgment. (See Sec. H, *infra,* for a discussion of default judgments.)

---

[61]One judicial study group has disapproved the use of habeas corpus for this purpose. Federal Judicial Center, *Recommended Procedures for Handling Prisoner Civil Rights Cases in the Federal Courts,* at 43 (1980).

[62]See Ch. VI, Sec. E3, for a discussion of res judicata.

[63]If you are suing the federal government, one of its agencies (such as the Federal Bureau of Prisons), or a federal employee, they have 60 days to respond after service upon the U.S. Attorney. FRCP 12(a). See also Rule 4(d)(4) and (5) for the proper parties to serve when suing the United States, its agencies, or its employees.

[64]The defendants could file a motion to dismiss (see Sec. C, *infra*), for a more definite statement (Rule 12(e)), for an extension of time to answer, etc.

[65]Rule 8(b), FRCP..

[66]Rule 5(d), FRCP.

A defendant may file an answer that contains a counterclaim against you.[67] A counterclaim is a claim for relief (usually damages) filed by the defendant against the plaintiff. (*E.g.,* you sue officer "X" for assaulting you and he counterclaims against you, alleging you injured him while he was properly performing his duties. Or, you sue prison officials for destroying your property and they counterclaim against you, alleging you destroyed the sink and commode in your cell.) If an answer contains a counterclaim, you *must* file a reply to the counterclaim.[68] Failure to do so can result in a default judgment being granted against you.

Defendants often do not file responses within the time period allowed. They will usually ask for an extension of time to respond to your complaint.[69] Whenever a defendant asks for more time to respond, unless you are seeking a temporary restraining order or trying to deal with an immediate serious problem, such as being in segregation, you should agree to the time extension. Courts are very generous in allowing extra time for responding, so it will do you little good, and possible some harm, to refuse defendant's request for more time. After all, you may need an extension of time yourself at some point.

B.   Motion To Dismiss or for Judgment on the Pleadings

Instead of filing an answer within the time allowed, the defendant may file a motion raising certain defenses. The seven different defenses a defendant may raise are listed in Rule 12(b). The most common Rule 12 motion made by prison officials is a motion to dismiss your complaint for failure to state a claim upon which relief can be granted. It is commonly called a 12(b)(6) motion. If this kind of motion is filed after the defendants have answered, it is called a motion for judgment on the pleadings.[70]

In this kind of motion, the court must accept as true the clear, factual allegations of the complaint.[71] "[A] complaint should not be dismissed for failure to state a claim unless it appears beyond doubt that the plaintiff can prove no set of facts in support of his claims which would entitle him to relief."[72]

---

[67]Rule 13, FRCP.

[68]Rule 12(a), FRCP.

[69]Rule 6(b), FRCP.

[70]Rule 12(c), FRCP.

[71]*See* Cruz v. Beto, 405 U.S. 319, 322, 92 S.Ct. 1079 (1972), *cited in* Hughes v. Rowe, *supra* note 37, at 176; Jamieson v. Robinson, 641 F.2d 138, 141 (3d Cir. 1981).

[72]Conley v. Gibson, 355 U.S. 41, 78 S.Ct. 99 (1957); *see also* Scheyer v. Rhodes, 416 U.S. 232, 236, 94 S.Ct. 1683 (1974).

If defendant's motion is supported by an affidavit or by other matters outside the pleadings, then Rule 12(b) requires that the motion be treated as a motion for summary judgment.[73] However, you are entitled to notice and an opportunity to respond whenever a court converts a 12(b) motion to a motion for summary judgment.[74]

A court has the discretion to dismiss a *pro se* complaint filed in forma pauperis on its own initiative without a motion from the defendant. But, before the court may dismiss a *pro se* complaint on its own initiative, the court must give you notice and an opportunity to respond.[75]

If you receive a motion to dismiss from the defendants or a notice from the court that it is considering dismissing your complaint, you must either oppose dismissal with a brief explaining why your complaint should not be dismissed or file an amended complaint correcting the defects noted by the court or the defendants. (See Sec. C, *infra,* for a discussion of amending your complaint.) However, not every motion to dismiss can be met by amending your complaint. For example, if you forgot to explain that the warden ordered you confined in segregation, and the warden moves to dismiss because you have not alleged his/her personal involvement, amending to add the facts about the warden's involvement is sufficient. If the warden claims instead that it was not unlawful to place you in segregation, you must respond with arguments showing why the conduct was illegal.

C.   Changing, Expanding, or Contracting Your Lawsuit

Under Rule 15(a), FRCP, you can amend your complaint once without permission from the court if the defendant has not filed an answer. If the defendant has filed an answer or a challenge to your complaint, you must request permission from the court to amend the complaint. Permission to amend a complaint should be, and usually is, freely given. The Supreme Court, in *Foman v. Davis,*[76] stated:

> In the absence of any apparent or declared reason—such as undue delay, bad faith, or dilatory motive on the part of the movant, repeated failure to cure deficiencies by amendments previously allowed, undue prejudice to the opposing party by virtue of allowance of the amendment, futility of amendment, etc.—the leave sought should, as the rules require, be "freely given."[77]

---

[73]Sprague v. Fitzpatrick, 546 F.2d 560, 563 (3d Cir. 1976). See Sec. G, *infra,* for a discussion of summary judgment.

[74]Winfrey v. Brewer, 570 F.2d 761, 764 (8th Cir. 1978).

[75]Pavilonis v. King, 626 F.2d 1075, 1028 n.6 (1st Cir. 1980).

[76]371 U.S. 178, 83 S.Ct. 227 (1962).

[77]*Id.* at 182-83.

The party opposing your amendment has the burden of showing s/he will be prejudiced by it.[78]

An amendment of a pleading containing a new claim or defense may "relate back" to the time of the initial filing of the case when it relates to the facts alleged in the original pleading. This may be important when you wish to amend your complaint after the statute of limitation[79] has run. Usually, when the statute of limitation has run on a cause of action or against a party, you will not be able to sue. But the amended complaint relating back to the original pleading may save the lawsuit since it is incorporated into the original pleading as if it had been filed with it.

All amendments of a complaint should be done as early as possible. However, Rule 15(b), FRCP, provides that "issues not raised by the pleadings [may be] tried by express or implied consent of the parties, [and if so,] they shall be treated in all respects as if . . . raised in the pleadings." This means that evidence on a new issue is presented at trial and the opposing party does not object, the court will act as if the new issue had been raised in an amended complaint.

You must be sure you have named the proper defendants in the complaint. (See Ch. VI, Sec. E2, for a discussion of proper defendants under §1983.) If you do not have the names of the prison officials who have harmed you, you will name them as "John Doe defendants" in your complaint[80] until you have had an opportunity during discovery to determine their names. Once you have determined their names, you will amend your complaint adding their names to the heading and body of the complaint.[81] (You must read Rules 12(c) and 21, FRCP, closely before you amend to add parties.) You will then have a copy of the complaint and summons served on each added defendant.

Because an amendment adding new parties may not relate back to the time the original complaint was filed, you should be sure to name and serve all defendants, including "John Does," before the statute of limitations runs.[82]

An amended complaint deals with things that happened before the original complaint was filed. A supplemental complaint deals with events that have occurred since you filed your original complaint. You may file

---

[78]Beeck v. Aquaslide 'N' Dive Corp., 562 F.2d 537 (8th Cir. 1977).

[79]See Ch. VI, Sec. E4, for a discussion of statutes of limitations.

[80]See Appendix B, Form 1a, for an example of a complaint.

[81]See Appendix B, Form 1b, for an example of an amended complaint.

[82]Some courts have permitted claims against "John Does" to relate back under certain circumstances. See Davis v. Krauss, 93 F.R.D. 580 (E.D.N.Y. 1982); Campbell v. Bergeron, 486 F. Supp. 1246 (M.D. La. 1980); see also Wood v. Woracheck, 618 F.2d 1225 (7th Cir. 1980). However, you should not rely on this possibility if you can avoid it.

a supplemental complaint[83] only with the permission of the court. The court, in determining whether to grant you leave to file a supplemental complaint, will examine how it relates to the original complaint, possible unexcused delay, the effect on a prompt disposition of the already pending action, and the wisdom of trying the matters together.[84]

To file a supplemental complaint, or to file an amended complaint after an answer has been filed, you must make a motion to the court and attach a copy of the proposed new complaint. Send the original and a copy to the court and a copy to each of the defendants. If you are adding a new party, you will also have to serve him/her with a copy of the new complaint and summons.

D. Class Actions

Even though many major prison conditions cases have been class actions and courts favor them, there are few reported cases where a *pro se* litigant has been granted permission to represent a class.[85] Most courts have refused permission to *pro se* litigants to represent a class because of the belief that they could not "fairly and adequately protect the interests of the class."[86] One court cited "the built-in disadvantage which a

---

[83]See Appendix B, Form 1c, for an example of a supplemental complaint.

[84]*See* 6 Wright & Miller, Federal Practice and Procedure, §1510; Wisconsin Heritages, Inc. v. Harris, 490 F. Supp. 1334, 1338 (E.D. Wisc. 1980) (15 months too long a delay for the filing of a supplemental complaint). *But see* Fidenas AG v. Honeywell, Inc., 501 F. Supp. 1029, 1032-33 (S.D.N.Y. 1980) (no specific prejudice was shown by defendants; supplemental complaint allowed).

[85]*See, e.g.,* Dorrough v. Hogan, 563 F.2d 1259 (5th Cir. 1977) (class representation granted since federal prisoner met requirements of Rule 23(a) and (b), and the government did not object).

[86]Wallace v. Hutto, 80 F.R.D. 739, 740 (W.D. Va. 1978), *aff'd*, 601 F.2d 583 (4th Cir. 1979) ("It is plain error to permit an imprisoned litigant, who is unassisted by counsel, to represent fellow inmates in a class action. . . . The competence of a prisoner representing himself is too limited to allow him to represent the rights of others as well." (cite omitted)); Oxendine v. Williams, 509 F.2d 1405, 1407 (4th Cir. 1977) ("[A]bility to protect the interests of the class depends in part on the quality of counsel, and we consider the competence of a layman representing himself to be clearly too limited to allow him to risk the rights of others." (cite omitted)); Inmates, Washington Cty. Jail v. England, 516 F. Supp. 132, 144 (E.D. Tenn. 1980) (*pro se* plaintiffs failed to show prerequisites to a Rule 23 action); Jeffery v. Malcolm, 353 F. Supp. 395, 397 (S.D.N.Y. 1973) ("The ordinary layman will generally not possess the requisite training, expertise, and experience to be able to adequately serve the interests of a proposed class. The plaintiff has not asserted or evidenced any special

layman, presumably unfamiliar with various substantive and procedural aspects of the law applicable to his case, must face in attempting to prove that case, on behalf of a class against experienced counsel for the government," and wondered "whether plaintiff could adequately represent the varying interests of the broad proposed class if those interests came into conflict with his own."[87] If you are going to try and represent a class, you must deal with these concerns in your motion and brief for class certification.

Some courts, when denying permission for a *pro se* litigant to represent a class, have held that class certification was not necessary because any declaratory or injunctive relief granted would benefit all prisoners in the same situation anyway.[88]

. The above discussion is not meant to discourage you from bringing a lawsuit that seeks class certification. It is only to make you aware of the pitfalls when bringing a class action and to urge you to request that the court appoint counsel to assist you.

If your lawsuit is to qualify for class certification, you will need to demonstrate to the court that:

> (1) the class is so numerous that joinder of all members [those prisoners similarly situated] is impracticable,
> (2) there are questions of law or fact [contained in your complaint] common to the class,
> (3) the claims or defenses of the representative parties [you and any other named plaintiffs] are typical of the claims or defenses of the class, and
> (4) the representative parties will fairly and adequately protect the interest of the class.[89]

The first requirement, "numerosity," means that you must show in your complaint or your class certification motion that as a practical matter all the people who would be affected by the outcome of the lawsuit cannot be joined as plaintiffs. This number does not have to be enormous.[90] You do not have to prove the size of the class with precision

---

qualifications which might justify maintenance by him, *pro se,* of a class action").

[87]Martin v. United States, 420 F. Supp. 779, 781 (D.C.C. 1976).

[88]Griffin v. Smith, 493 F. Supp. 129 (W.D.N.Y. 1980) ("Plaintiffs requested declaratory and injunctive relief to remedy their claims. If plaintiffs prevail on non-frivolous claims, the relief provided may sufficiently nullify any need to go forward as a class." *Id.* at 132.); Inmates, Washington Cty. Jail v. England, *supra* note 86. See Ch. VI, Secs. G and H, for a discussion of injunctive relief and declaratory judgments, respectively.

[89]Rule 23(a), FRCP.

[90]Ballard v. Blue Shield of Southern W. Va., Inc., 543 F.2d 1075, 1080 (4th

as long as you furnish a factual basis for determining how large it is.[91] The fact that a class is "fluid"—*i.e.,* that its membership changes, as is the case with most prisons and jails—weighs in favor of class certification.[92] The fact that many class members are poorly educated or have little access to lawyers also weighs in favor of class certification.[93]

The second requirement is met if there is one or more common issue of law or fact as to all the class members.[94] The existence of some factual variations does not defeat class certification.[95] Thus, if you challenge a prison's failure to provide a prompt sick call procedure, which affects all prisoners, the fact that some prisoners are healthier than others will not defeat class certification.

The third requirement of "typicality" of the named plaintiffs' claims means only that they involve a "common element of fact or law"[96] or "the same legal or remedial theory" as the other class members' claims.[97] The fact that some class members might choose not to assert their rights does not mean that the named plaintiffs do not meet the typicality requirement, nor does the existence of other factual variations.[98]

Cir. 1976), *cert. denied,* 430 U.S. 922 (1977) (class of 45); Cypress v. Newport News General & Nonsectarian Hospital Assn., 375 F.2d 648 (4th Cir. 1976) (class of 18); Fidelis Corp. v. Litton Industries, 293 F. Supp. 164, 170 (S.D.N.Y. 1968) (class of 35 to 70).

[91]*See* Sims v. Parke Davis & Co., 334 F. Supp. 774 (E.D. Mich. 1971), *cert. denied,* 405 U.S. 978 (1972) (plaintiff need not establish a class size with precision; it is sufficient if he presents some information from which the number of class members can be approximated). *See also* Tolbert v. Western Electric Co., 56 F.R.D. 108, 113 (N.D. Ga. 1972) (plaintiff must make a positive showing that joinder is impracticable); Kinsey v. Legg, Mason & Co., Inc., 60 F.R.D. 91 (D.D.C. 1973) (bare allegations of numerosity nor speculation as to the number of parties will suffice).

[92]Gerstein v. Pugh, 420 U.S. 103, 110-11 n.11, 95 S.Ct. 854 (1975); Powell v. Ward, 487 F. Supp. 917, 921-22 (S.D.N.Y. 1980), *aff'd,* 643 F.2d 924 (2d Cir. 1981); Santiago v. City of Philadelphia, 72 F.R.D. 619, 624 (E.D. Pa. 1976).

[93]United States ex rel. Sero v. Preiser, 506 F.2d 1115, 1126 (2d Cir. 1974).

[94]Stewart v. Winter, 669 F.2d 328, 335 (5th Cir. 1982); McCoy v. Ithaca Housing Authority, 559 F. Supp. 1351, 1355 (N.D.N.Y. 1983); In re Federal Skywalk Cases, 93 F.R.D. 415, 421 (W.D. Mo. 1982).

[95]Like v. Carter, 448 F.2d 798, 802 (8th Cir. 1971); Escalera v. New York City Housing Authority, 425 F.2d 853, 867 (2d Cir. 1970).

[96]Senter v. General Motors Corp., 532 F.2d 511, 525 (6th Cir. 1976).

[97]Penn v. San Juan Hospital, Inc., 528 F.2d 1181, 1189 (10th Cir. 1976).

[98]3B MOORE'S FEDERAL PRACTICE, ¶23.06.2, at 23-327 (1977), *citing* Norwalk CORE v. Norwalk Redevelopment Agency, 395 F.2d 920, 937 (2d Cir. 1968); *see*

The fourth requirement of class certification, that the *pro se* litigant be able to fairly and adequately represent the interests of other class members, is the biggest barrier. This is very difficult to meet if you do not have a lawyer. If you wish to proceed *pro se* anyway, you should consider requesting that the court appoint counsel for the class[99] while permitting you and any other named plaintiffs to proceed *pro se*.

In addition to the counsel issue, a court will consider whether you have any conflicts of interest with other class members indicating whether you can represent a class.[100]

Once you have met the requisites of Rule 23(a), you must then meet one of the three standards of Rule 23(b):

(1) the prosecution of separate actions by or against individual members of the class would create a risk of

(A) inconsistent or varying adjudications with respect to individual members of the class which would establish incompatible standards of conduct for the party opposing the class, or

(B) adjudications with respect to individual members of the class which would as a practical matter be dispositive of the interests of the other members not parties to the adjudications or substantially impair or impede their ability to protect their interests; or

(2) the party opposing the class has acted or refused to act on grounds generally applicable to the class, thereby making appropriate final injunctive relief or corresponding declaratory relief with respect to the class as a whole; or

(3) the court finds that the questions of law or fact common to the members of the class predominate over any questions affecting only individual members, and that a class action is superior to other available methods for the fair and efficient adjudication of the controversy.

If the relief you are seeking in your lawsuit is either a declaratory judgment and/or injunctive relief, you should seek class certification pursuant to Rule 23(b)(2). You should allege that the defendants/prison officials have acted "on grounds generally applicable to the class" (*e.g.,* before placement in administrative segregation, prison officials do not inform prisoners of the reason(s); prison officials allow prisoners access to the law library only one hour per week; etc.). Whenever you request monetary damages, your suit must fit either Rule 23(b)(1) or (b)(3).

---

also Green v. Wolf Corp., 406 F.2d 291, 299 (2d Cir. 1968); Lucas v. Wasser, 73 F.R.D. 361, 362 (S.D.N.Y. 1976).

[99]E.G. Armstrong v. O'Connell, 416 F. Supp. 1325, 1340-42 (E.D. Wisc. 1976); Amos v. Board of School Directors of City of Milwaukee, 408 F. Supp. 765, 775 (E.D. Wisc.), *aff'd sub nom.* Armstrong v. Brennan, 539 F.2d 625 (7th Cir. 1976). *See* Gonzales v. Cassidy, 474 F.2d 67, 75-76 (5th Cir. 1973).

[100]Martin v. United States, *supra* note 87, at 781 n.1.

Decisions to certify a class or not cannot be appealed until final judgment has been entered in the case.[101]

E. Preparing Your Factual Case

1. Gathering Evidence

In most *pro se* cases, the most important proof will be the plaintiff's own testimony, documents in the plaintiff's possession, and witnesses previously known to the plaintiff. You may obtain helpful evidence from the defendants in discovery, but be sure to use the resources already available to you.

If there are prisoner witnesses (or cooperative prison employees), interview them and get them to sign statements. These should be notarized or otherwise sworn to.[102] Obtaining these statements serves three purposes. They will help you keep track of what you can prove; the statements can be submitted in response to defendants' summary judgment motion, or in support of yours;[103] and they may help you convince a reluctant judge that the witnesses should be produced for trial.[104]

If your state has a freedom of information act or public record act and the opposing party is a state agency, make a request of that agency to obtain copies of regulations, policy directives, and other information that would be helpful to your litigation.[105] It may also be helpful to use the grievance procedure, or just write a letter (or have a friend or family member write it) seeking information—for example, why you were transferred or put in segregation.

You should also determine what information you will need to prove your allegations. You should list each cause of action and each element of that cause of action. Under each individual element, you should include not only the information you will need to prove your case, but also the possible defenses the opposing party will raise and what information or documents you will need to defeat these defenses.

2. Discovery

The general rules concerning discovery are contained in Rules 26-37,

---

[101]Cooper v. Lybrand & Livesay, 437 U.S. 463, 98 S.Ct. 2454 (1982).

[102]*See* 28 U.S.C. §1746 (procedure for swearing to documents without a notary).

[103]See Sec. G, *infra,* for a discussion of summary judgment.

[104]See Sec. M, *infra,* for a discussion of getting your witnesses produced.

[105]*See* Manville, "Freedom of Information Act," 2 PLM 180 (Jan. 1980).

FRCP. You should also obtain a copy of the local federal district court rules since some of the federal rules have been expanded or limited through local rules.[106] The discovery devices available are: Depositions (Rules 27, 30, 31); Interrogatories to Parties (Rule 33); Production of Documents and Things and Entry Onto Land (Rule 34); Physical and Mental Examination of Persons (Rule 35); and Requests for Admissions (Rule 36).

a.   Nature and Objectives of Discovery

Discovery is just what the word implies. It is a way to discover or uncover facts, documents, and relevant information about your case to help you present a complete picture to the court. Its primary use is to narrow and clarify the issues and claims of each party before trial. Accordingly, discovery rules are given broad and liberal treatment.[107]

One of the big advantages of discovery is that it allows you to get the statements of certain people while their stories are still fresh, and frequently before their attorneys have a full understanding of how they want to develop their case. This minimizes attempts by witnesses, and especially defendants, to change their testimony or statements halfway through the case. You can solidify the record through discovery and hold the parties to what they say during it, making it difficult for them to change their earlier statements. Using discovery effectively will let you know exactly what you will have to prove and disprove in order to win your case. During discovery, you will accumulate information that will raise questions and lead to other information. Further discovery will lead to more information. Pursuing leads is what discovery is all about.

b.   Scope of Discovery: Relevance, Privileges, and Practical Considerations

The usual scope of discovery is set forth in Rule 26(b):

Parties may obtain discovery *regarding any matter not privileged, which is relevant to the subject matter* involved in the pending action, whether it relates to the claim or defense of the party seeking discovery or to the claim or defense of any other party, including the existence, description, nature, custody, condition and location of any books, documents, or other tangible things, and the *identity* and *location* of persons having knowledge of any

---

[106]*See* Cohen, "Federal Discovery: A Survey of Local Rules and Practices in View of Proposed Changes to the Federal Rules," 63 Minn. L. Rev. 253 (1979).

[107]Oppenheimer Fund, Inc. v. Sanders, 437 U.S. 340, 98 S.Ct. 2380 (1978); Schlagenhuf v. Holden, 379 U.S. 104, 114, 85 S.Ct. 234 (1964); Hickman v. Taylor, 329 U.S. 495, 501, 67 S.Ct. 428 (1947).

discoverable matter. *It is not ground for objection that the information sought will be inadmissible at the trial if the information sought appears reasonably calculated to lead to the discovery of admissible evidence.* [Emphasis added.]

Your discovery request of prison officials must only be "relevant to the subject matter involved in the pending litigation." The Supreme Court, in *Oppenheimer Fund, Inc. v. Sanders,* construed this phrase "broadly to encompass any matter that bears on, or that reasonably could lead to other matter that could bear on, any issue that is or may be in the case."[108] Your request for discovery should be permitted "unless it is clear that the information sought can have no possible bearing upon the subject matter of the action.[109]

Recently, Rule 26 was amended to permit the district court to set limits to avoid discovery that is "cumulative or duplicative," more readily available from another source, or unduly burdensome or expensive. An attorney or *pro se* litigant is now required to certify that any discovery request or objection is lawful, not improperly motivated, and not unreasonably burdensome or expensive.[110]

Rule 26 exempts from discovery information which is privileged. The same rules of privilege applied at trial are applicable to discovery.[111] There are a variety of privileges that may be asserted by a party opposing discovery: the attorney-client privilege, the physician-patient privilege, the priest-penitent privilege, the husband-wife privilege, the privilege against self-incrimination, etc. Most of these will rarely arise in prisoners' cases.

The most frequently raised privileges in prison cases are the governmental or official information privilege (often referred to as "executive privilege") and the related privileges protecting ongoing criminal investigations and the identity of informers. The governmental privilege does not cover everything that officials may want to keep secret; it is designed to protect "deliberative and decisionmaking processes of government officials" and "investigative reports of an administrative agency to the extent that they reflect advisory rather than factual material."[112] Thus, even if prison officials can keep their decisionmaking processes secret, they must disclose purely factual matter relating to their

---

[108]Oppenheimer Fund, Inc. v. Sanders, *id* at 351 (footnote omitted).

[109]La Chemise Lacoste v. Alligator Co., Inc., 60 F.R.D. 164, 171 (D. Del. 1973).

[110]Rule 26(g), FRCP, as amended April 28, 1983.

[111]*See* Federal Rules of Evidence, Rule 501; United States v. Reynolds, 345 U.S. 1, 6, 73 S.Ct. 528 (1953).

[112]Kinoy v. Mitchell, 67 F.R.D. 1, 10-11 (S.D.N.Y. 1975).

decisions.[113] Moreover, a litigant can obtain "deliberative" or "advisory" materials when the litigant's need for the materials outweighs the policies favoring secrecy.[114] For example, if prison officials put a lot of prisoners into segregation without notice or hearing, the prisoners' need to find out if prison officials really believed there was an emergency might outweigh any interest the defendants had in keeping their deliberations secret; if so, you could discover their internal memos on the subject.

The governmental privilege is also subject to procedural requirements: it must be formally asserted and supported with specific factual allegations.[115] "An improperly asserted claim of privilege is no claim of privilege."[116]

There is also a privilege for "attorney work product," which is exempted from discovery pursuant to Rule 26(b)(3).[117] This phrase has been defined broadly to include any materials "prepared in anticipation of litigation or for trial by or for another party or by or for that other party's representative (including his attorney, consultant, surety, indemnitor, insurer, or agent). . . ."[118] But it does not include the documents and information compiled in the ordinary course of running the prison, such as disciplinary reports, grievances, prison rules, etc.

Despite the work product rule, a party or another person can obtain his/her own statement from counsel, and the opinions of experts who will testify[119] at trial may be obtained.

There are several other important principles concerning privileges which you should be aware of.

(a) In federal court, privileges are governed by federal law except when a state law claim (for example, a pendent claim) is in question.[120] A state law forbidding disclosure does not create a privilege in federal court and will not be enforced if it is inconsistent with the federal law of

---

[113]Environmental Protection Agency v. Mink, 410 U.S. 72, 86-87, 93 S.Ct. 827 (1974); Ernest and Mary Hayward Weir Foundation v. United States, 508 F.2d 894, 895 n.2 (2d Cir. 1974).

[114]Kinoy v. Mitchell, *supra* note 112, at 11.

[115]*See* United States v. Nixon, 418 U.S. 683, 94 S.Ct. 3090 (1974); United States v. Reynolds, *supra* note 111, at 7-8; Carter v. Colson, 56 F.R.D. 9, 11 (D.D.C. 1972).

[116]Black v. Sheraton Corp. of America, 371 F. Supp. 97, 101 (D.D.C. 1974).

[117]*See* Hickman v. Taylor, *supra* note 107.

[118]Rule 26(b)(3), FRCP.

[119]Rule 26(b)(3), (4), FRCP.

[120]Rule 501, Federal Rules of Evidence.

privileges,[121] although state law may be considered in interpreting the scope of federal court privileges.

(b) The mere assertion that information is "confidential" establishes no privilege enforceable in federal court.[122]

(c) A privilege cannot be used to protect information about something that the litigant has him/herself put in issue.[123] If a litigant claims to have been injured, s/he cannot invoke the physician-patient privilege to withhold information about subsequent medical treatment or examinations; similarly, if prison officials claim they did something on the advice of counsel, they cannot rely on the attorney-client privilege to keep the advice secret.[124] This principle cuts both ways; if you sue about an event, you cannot then refuse to answer questions about your own conduct during it on the grounds of the privilege against self-incrimination.[125]

(d) Privileges may not be asserted in a generalized fashion; documents or information claimed to be privileged must be specifically designated and described.[126]

(e) Litigants cannot assert that information is privileged if they have released it to other persons. A privilege "should not be regarded as a right which can be disclosed to some and withheld from others."[127] Thus, if you can show that information you need is or can be released to others (prison employees, their lawyers, insurance companies, etc.), defendants should not be able to deny it to you. If there are laws or regulations governing release of information—for example, a state freedom of information law—see if it has disclosure provisions that are inconsistent with defendants' claims that they must keep the information secret.

In addition to privilege claims, prison officials may assert that the

---

[121]Kerr v. United States District Court, 503 F.2d 192, 197 (9th Cir. 1975), aff'd, 426 U.S. 394, 96 S.Ct. 2119 (1976); Patterson v. Norfolk and Western Railway Co., 489 F.2d 303 (6th Cir. 1973); Colton v. United States, 306 F.2d 633, 636 (2d Cir. 1962).

[122]Nguyen Da Yen v. Kissinger, 528 F.2d 1194, 1205 (9th Cir. 1975); Mackey v. United States, 351 F.2d 794, 795 (D.C. Cir. 1965); Luey v. Sterling Drug, Inc., 240 F. Supp. 632, 636 (W.D. Mich. 1965).

[123]Anderson v. Nixon, 444 F. Supp. 1195, 1199-1200 (D.D.C. 1978).

[124]Hearn v. Rhay, 68 F.R.D. 574, 580-81 (E.D. Wash. 1974).

[125]Communications Specialities, Inc. v. Hess, 65 F.R.D. 510 (E.D. Pa. 1975); Brown v. Ames, 346 F. Supp. 1176 (D. Minn. 1972).

[126]Kerr v. United States District Court, supra note 121; Black v. Sheraton Corp. of America, supra note 116.

[127]In re Natta, 48 F.R.D. 319, 322 (D. Del. 1969); see also Bergman v. Kemp, 97 F.R.D. 413, 416 (W.D. Mich. 1983).

discovery you seek will involve undue burden or expense. However, even burdensome or expensive discovery may be required if it is relevant to the case.[128] A mere general objection that discovery is burdensome raises no issue; there must be a specific showing of reasons why discovery should not be required.[129] Also, if discovery will be burdensome only because of the way defendants keep their records, defendants will not be permitted to evade discovery.[130] You can also respond to claims of burdensomeness by being flexible; for example, you could agree that if prison officials let you look through the relevant files, you will identify the particular documents you need.

Recent amendments to the FRCP require you to certify that your discovery requests are not unduly burdensome.[131]

As a practical matter, despite these favorable legal rules, discovery disputes can seriously bog down your case even if you ultimately win. Also, courts are sometimes inclined to resolve these disputes according to their own ideas of what is reasonable rather than to follow the letter of existing case law. Because federal discovery decisions are generally not appealable until a final judgment has been entered in the case,[132] you are stuck with whatever the district court decides. For these reasons, you should follow some simple rules to keep discovery disputes to a minimum and get what you need promptly.

- *Keep it short.* The less you ask for, the more likely you are to get it quickly and without an argument. You should never use discovery just to make the defendants or their lawyer work; this tactic will almost certainly backfire, and it is prohibited by the rules.

- *Spell it out.* Make it as clear as possible exactly what you want; if you can describe the precise documents or information you want in the terminology used by prison officials (*e.g.,* "unusual incident reports" or "Administrative Bulletin No. 66"), do so. The defendants' attorney may

---

[128]Krantz v. United States, 56 F.R.D. 555 (W.D. Va. 1972); King v. Georgia Power Co., 50 F.R.D. 134 (N.D. Ga. 1970); 4A MOORE'S FEDERAL PRACTICE, ¶33.20 (1975).

[129]Leumi Financial Corp. v. Hartford Accident and Indemnity Co., 295 F. Supp. 539, 544 (S.D.N.Y. 1969); 4A MOORE'S FEDERAL PRACTICE, ¶33.20 (1975).

[130]Kozlowski v. Sears Roebuck & Co., 73 F.R.D. 73, 76 (D. Mass. 1976). *See also* NLRB v. Sears Roebuck & Co., 421 U.S. 142, 95 S.Ct. 1504 (1974) (agency required to provide records covering a five-year period).

[131]Rule 26(g), FRCP, as amended April 28, 1983.

[132]*See* Branch v. Phillips Petroleum Co., 638 F.2d 873 (5th Cir. 1981) (production of documents); United States v. Johnson, 467 F.2d 630 (2d Cir. 1972) (interrogatories). *See also* Cogen v. United States, 278 U.S. 221, 223-24, 49 S.Ct. 118 (1929).

know less than you do about prison policies and recordkeeping, and the easier you make his/her job, the more likely it is that you will get the information rather than a hard time. Also, the more specific you are, the harder it is for the defendants to pretend not to understand your request. A good tactic is to make a general request and then add specifics: for example, "any and all documents and reports concerning a disturbance in H Block on January 4, 1983, including, but not limited to, unusual incident reports, use of force reports, disciplinary charges, statements of witnesses, findings and conclusions of disciplinary hearings, etc."

- *Know why you want the information.* If defendants refuse to give you something and you go to court to make them give it to you,[133] you will have to explain to the court why the information is relevant. You should think this through *before* you file your discovery request.

- *Establish priorities.* You should think about what information is most important to you and what will be easiest to get; you may want to seek discovery in stages rather than all at once. For example, if you are beaten by guards, you will want the defendants' reports of the incident. You may also want records of any prior complaints or disciplinary actions against the guards in order to show that their superiors should have been aware of their violent natures. Since prison officials rarely relinquish personnel records of any sort without a fight, you may wish to postpone requesting them until you receive the other documents; if you ask for everything at once, the defendants may refuse to produce anything without a court order.

- *Be reasonable.* If defendants offer you a compromise that will give you what is most important to you, consider it seriously. If they ask for more time to produce the information, agree to it as long as you are not dealing with an emergency and the time they ask for is not unreasonably long. One thirty-day extension is routinely granted by courteous litigators, and defendants will probably be able to get it from the court even if you do not consent.[134] By being reasonable, you may be able to get what you need without a long court fight, and even if you do have to go to court, the judge may be more willing to exercise his/her discretion in your favor.

c. Depositions

Oral depositions are very difficult for a prisoner to use. Also, they are normally very expensive. However, since depositions are the only

---

[133]See Subsec. g, *infra,* for a discussion of motion to compel discovery.

[134]Actually, extensions of time must always be authorized by the court. *See* Rules 29, 33(a), 34(b), and 36(a), FRCP. The common practice in many jurisdictions is for the parties to sign a stipulation and submit it to the judge for approval.

discovery device available to obtain information from non-parties (persons not named as defendants), you may need to use them.

You must specifically follow the procedural steps contained in Rule 30, FRCP. A party does not need to be subpoenaed, but a non-party must be subpoenaed to appear at the deposition.[135] You must always give the other party's attorney and the person being deposed reasonable notice of the scheduled deposition.

Normally, depositions are taken stenographically by a court reporter. Few, if any, prisoners can afford to depose by this method. If you can get access to a tape recorder, you should first seek permission from the opposing party to record depositions by other than stenographic means.[136] If the other party will not stipulate to allow deposition by tape recording with a copy of the tape to be filed with the court, you must file a motion with the court requesting permission.[137] If you want a transcript of a taped deposition, you will have to pay for it. Alternatively, you could transcribe it yourself and try to obtain the defendant's agreement that the transcript is accurate, or serve a request for admissions to that effect. (See Sec. E2f, *infra,* for a discussion of requests for admissions.)

If you are going to use oral depositions and have obtained a stipulation or court permission to depose by tape recording, you may be limited to deposing only those prison officials or prisoners at your local prison. Having someone serve the subpoena on a person not at the local prison and arranging with prison officials for use of a room to depose someone subpoenaed from outside the local prison walls are just a few of the problems associated with oral depositions.

The purpose of a deposition is to obtain a clear, comprehensive statement of the facts. You should be friendly and business-like and not antagonistic. You should have basic questions written out before the deposition and try to anticipate the information you will receive. Your questions to the deponent should be open-ended, and you should let the witness speak freely even if s/he is not directly responding to your question. (You can always repeat the question if necessary.) As the person is being deposed, take notes concerning areas of his/her statement about which you will want to ask more specific questions. Counsel for the other side may object to some of your questions. You should note the objections for the record and then obtain an answer from the deponent. As long as the information sought is relevant and not privileged, the fact that it may be objectionable at trial does not permit refusal to answer.

---

[135]You will obtain the subpoena from the clerk of the court. The subpoena may be served by the U.S. Marshals or by a non-party over 18 years of age. Rule 45(c), (d), FRCP.

[136]Rule 30(b)(4), FRCP.

[137]*Id.*

Depositions of defendants and their agents[138] may be introduced in a court proceeding consistent with the rules of evidence.[139] You may prove official policy or practice of the agency by the use of that deposition without calling a witness.[140] This is just one of many uses of a deposition. Read Rule 31 and shepardize it to find cases explaining its other uses.

You must obtain leave of the court to do an oral deposition of anyone in prison.[141] This requirement applies to the defendants, too, if they wish to take your deposition. If they notice your deposition without obtaining leave of court, you may object in writing immediately.[142] However, if you are the one who brought the lawsuit, courts will assume there is nothing unfair about your deposition being taken; if a controversy arises, they will grant permission and not suppress a deposition taken in violation of the rule.[143] You should not refuse to take part in the deposition based on the defendants' failure to get leave of the court.

Courts will not always allow a prisoner/plaintiff to attend his/her civil rights trial or to have prisoner witnesses brought to the courthouse to testify.[144] Since prison officials may transfer your witnesses to another prison or a prisoner may be paroled, you may wish to take the oral deposition of these witnesses as early as possible after you have filed your lawsuit. You are allowed to introduce depositions of persons incarcerated instead of them being brought from prison to the courts to testify.[145] On the other hand, if you think you can keep track of the witnesses and are very concerned that they appear personally, you may prefer to avoid taking their depositions so the judge will have more reason to have them produced.

---

[138]*E.g.,* if you sue the warden, a captain or a guard will generally be the warden's agent.

[139]See Sec. N4d, *infra,* for a discussion of putting depositions into evidence.

[140]Suppose you are suing concerning the procedures used in placing you in administrative segregation. As part of discovery, you depose the sergeant in charge of administrative segregation. If during the deposition you obtained information that the procedures used to place you in administrative segregation are not the standard procedures, you could introduce the deposition instead of subpoenaing the sergeant to testify.

[141]Rule 30(a), FRCP. *See also* Kendrick v. Schnorbus, 655 F.2d 727 (6th Cir. 1981).

[142]Rule 32(d)(1), FRCP.

[143]*See* Kendrick v. Schnorbus, 655 F.2d 727 (6th Cir. 1981).

[144]See Sec. M, *infra,* for a discussion of court appearance.

[145]Rule 32(a)(3)(C). *See also* Charles v. Wade, 665 F.2d 661 (5th Cir. 1982)

d. Interrogatories[146]

Interrogatories can be used to obtain information only from named parties or their agents. They consist of written questions submitted to the defendant for an answer. The defendant, within 30 days of service of interrogatories, must, under oath, answer or object to your questions. If a party objects and refuses to answer an interrogatory, the reasons must be stated.[147]

The federal rules provide no limit on the number of interrogatories or questions you may ask.[148] The local district court rules sometimes impose a limitation, however, so remember to get a copy of the local district court rules. The original copy of each set of interrogatories must be filed with the court.

Interrogatories can be used to obtain answers to "why" type questions. But be aware that defendant and his/her counsel have considerable time to formulate an answer that may be harmful to you. Therefore, you should not rely solely on interrogatories for answers to these questions; you should get relevant documents first, if you can. If defendants must turn over a document that says you were transferred because the warden was tired of your lawsuits, they will not be able to claim in their answer to the interrogatories that they did it for program reasons. Your interrogatories should also try to identify witnesses and other people with information, determine the location of documents,[149] and obtain information as to defenses and evidence or legal theories supporting them.

e. Request for Production of Documents[150]

Requests for production of documents can generally only be served upon named parties of the lawsuit or persons under their control. Rule 34 authorizes a party to request any other party

(1) to produce and permit the party making the request, or someone acting on his behalf, to inspect and copy any designated documents (including

---

[146]Rule 33, FRCP; see also Appendix B, Form 5, for sample interrogatories.

[147]Dollar v. Long Mfg., N.C., Inc., 561 F.2d 613 (5th Cir. 1977), *cert. denied,* 435 U.S. 996 (1978). See Appendix B, Form 6.

[148]Crown Center Redevelopment Corp. v. Westinghouse Elec. Corp, 82 F.R.D. 108 (W.D. Mo. 1979).

[149]Roesberg v. Johns-Manville Corp., 85 F.R.D. 292 (E.D. Pa. 1980).

[150]See Appendix B, Form 7, for an example of a request for production of documents.

writings, drawings, graphs, charts, photographs, phono-records, and other data compilations from which information can be obtained, translated if necessary, by the respondent through detection devices into reasonably usable form), or to inspect and copy, test, or sample any tangible things which constitute or contain matters within the scope of Rule 26(b) and which are in the possession, custody, or control of the party upon whom the request is served. . . .[151]

You must state with reasonable specificity the items you want prison officials to permit you to inspect and possibly copy.[152] You should include a reasonable time, place, and manner for making the requested inspection.[153] (For convenience, in many cases the defendants will simply make copies and send them to you.)

Your request for production should be specific *and* general to ensure that you obtain everything you need.[154] The general request may turn up information you did not know existed. It is very helpful to combine a request for documents with interrogatories so that non-production of the documents will force the defendant to state why they were not produced.[155]

f.   Admissions[156]

Admissions are among the most useful tools of discovery. Once a party has admitted facts under Rule 36, FRCP, they are absolutely binding upon him/her. This binding effect of an admission eliminates your having to prove factual issues at summary judgment or at trial.

Requests for admissions can be used to establish (1) facts,[157] (2) the

---

[151]Rule 34(a), FRCP.

[152]You should inspect all documents requested and then determine which of them need to be copied.

[153]If you wish to review prison records kept in a different city, prison officials may allege the records cannot leave that city without disrupting their orderly office. You can suggest the examination of the records take place on a weekend at the prison where you are incarcerated while a deputy warden or an officer is on duty. This should create no inconvenience to any of the parties.

[154]A general request typically begins with the phrase "Any and all" and would include reference to "manuals, rules, and policy directives governing prison disciplinary proceedings." A specific request is "A copy of disciplinary report dated May 11, 1982, pertaining to Daniel E. Manville," or "A copy of prison policy directive PD-BCF-41.101."

[155]See Appendix B, Form 7, for an example of a request for production of documents..

[156]See Appendix B, Form 8, for an example of a request for admissions.

[157]Admissions can be used in connection with interrogatories for this purpose.

genuineness of documents, and (3) the application of law to facts. Requests for admissions as to questions of law alone are not appropriate.

The request for admissions should contain simple, straightforward, and neutral language. Do not ask for an admission that "Plaintiff was subjected to outrageous physical abuse by defendants"; say instead, "Plaintiff was struck in the face [or kicked, or thrown down the stairs] by guards." In many cases, you will not expect the defendants to admit the fact that they mistreated you; you may want to follow up an admission like the example just stated with a series of admissions that will pinpoint exactly how far the defendants are willing to go. For example, you might ask for the following admissions:

(1) Prison guards X and Y escorted plaintiff from his cell on the fourth tier to the control center.

(2) Plaintiff's hands were handcuffed behind his back.

(3) The guards were walking behind plaintiff as he went down the stairs.

(4) The stairs plaintiff was walking down were not defective.

(5) Plaintiff, while being escorted by guards X and Y, fell down the stairs.

(6) There were no other witnesses to plaintiff's falling down the stairs except for the two guards and plaintiff.

(7) Plaintiff was not on medication at the time he fell down the stairs.

(8) Plaintiff has lived on the fourth tier for over one year.

(9) Plaintiff is required to walk down these stairs at least three times a day if he wishes to eat the meals served at the mess hall.

(10) There are no reports of prisoners falling down these stairs unless escorted by prison guards.

Each separate admission should contain only one idea. If there are a number of different points you want admitted, put each one into a separate, numbered item.

Requests for admissions can be used any time during litigation. The original is filed with the court and a copy is sent to the defendant's attorney. Once requests for admissions are served, the opposing party has thirty (30) days to answer or to object. If no response is made, the request is deemed admitted. If objection is made to a request, it must specifically state the reasons for the objection. Prison officials cannot rely on an objection, such as lack of knowledge, unless they state what reasonable efforts have been made to ascertain the answer and these steps have left them without sufficient information to admit or deny the request.

If prison officials deny the truthfulness of facts set forth in a request

---

For example, a typical interrogatory would ask: "If the foregoing admission is denied in whole or in part, state [which policy directive is applicable; which rules apply; what report was written, etc. (be specific)]."

for an admission which are later proven to be true, they become liable for all of the costs which were incurred in proving the facts they earlier denied.[158]

g.   Compelling Discovery and Sanctions[159]

The discovery process is intended to work without the need for court intervention. However, if a party has refused to comply with a discovery request, the opposing party may file a motion pursuant to Rule 37(a), FRCP, for an order compelling discovery. The party against whom the motion is filed will have a chance to answer the motion. The other side can then file a reply. The court then decides whether an order compelling discovery should be issued.

Often, when you file a motion to compel answers to your discovery request, prison officials will provide the answers immediately to avoid annoying the judge. However, they may claim that the information you want is privileged, or that it would be embarrassing, oppressive, or unduly burdensome or expensive to produce it.[160] (They may not wait for your motion to compel to make these claims; these arguments may also be raised by them in a motion for a protective order, provided for in Rule 26(c), FRCP.) You must counter these arguments; ways of doing this are discussed in Sec. F2b, *supra.*

An issue that you may be able to exploit in making a motion to compel is the timeliness of defendant's objections. As noted, interrogatories and document requests must be answered within 30 days unless an extension of time has been granted by the court. There is ample case law that objections are waived if they are not made in a timely fashion,[161] even if the objections are based on a claim of privilege.[162] Thus, you should be sure to point out any failure to comply with time limits when you move to compel discovery. (You should, of course, always comply with these time limits yourself when defendants seek discovery from you.)

---

[158]Rule 37(c), FRCP.

[159]See Appendix B, Form 6. If you fail to comply with a discovery request of the defendants, they may also seek an order compelling your response. Remember, the discovery process is a two-way street and whatever you can do, they can do too. See Sec. E2h, *infra,* for a discussion of your responses to the defendants' discovery requests.

[160]Rule 26(c), FRCP.

[161]Davis v. Romney, 53 F.R.D. 247, 248 (E.D. Pa. 1971); Cephas v. Busch, 47 F.R.D. 371, 373 (E.D. Pa. 1969); Sturdevant v. Sears, Roebuck & Co., 32 F.R.D. 426 (W.D. Mo. 1963).

[162]United States v. 58.16 Acres of Land, More or Less, 66 F.R.D. 570, 572 (E.D. Ill. 1975); Baxter v. Vick, 25 F.R.D. 229 (E.D. Pa. 1960); Cardox Corp. v. Olin Matthiesen Chemical Corp., 23 F.R.D. 27 (S.D. Ill. 1958).

Be sure to consult local court rules before filing a motion to compel. Many courts have rules requiring you to contact your adversary and seek to settle discovery disputes before bringing them into court. (You should do this, in writing, even if the local rules do not require it.) Some courts also have specific requirements as to what the motion to compel must contain, such as copies of the discovery requests themselves and evidence of your efforts to settle the matter out of court.[163]

If an order compelling discovery has been granted and the party refuses to comply with the order, Rule 37(b) provides sanctions.

> [A court may issue an order] striking out pleadings or parts thereof, or staying further proceedings until the order is obeyed, or dismissing the action or proceeding or any part thereof, or rendering a judgment by default against the disobedient party. . . .[164]

These sanctions will only be used if the court finds that the party has willfully refused to comply with an order compelling discovery. This could include the dismissal of your complaint with prejudice if you fail to comply with a discovery order.[165]

h.   Responding to Discovery Requests

You are under the same obligation to respond to discovery requests as the defendants, and you must follow the same rules discussed in the preceding sections. In general, you should answer questions that are put to you, whether at a deposition, in interrogatories, document requests, or requests for admissions, as long as they have something to do with the case. Answering a question does not mean the answer automatically can go into evidence; you can still object at trial.[166] Defendants will be permitted to ask about your background, including your criminal records and your prison disciplinary record.[167] You may not assert your

---

[163]*See, e.g.,* Rules of the United States District Court for the Southern District of New York, Civil Rule 3(e), (f).

[164]*See* Patterson v. C.I.T. Corp., 352 F.2d 333 (10th Cir. 1965); In re Anthracite Coal Antitrust Litigation, 82 F.R.D. 364 (M.D. Pa. 1979) (default judgment for failure to comply with discovery order where a party has acted repeatedly and in bad faith). *See also* Epstein, "An Update on Rule 37 Sanctions After *National Hockey League v. Metropolitan Clubs, Inc.*," 84 F.D.R. 145 (1979); Gutman, "Combatting Defendants' Obstructionism in the Discovery Process," 55 Journal of Urban Law, 983 (1978).

[165]*See* National Hockey League v. Metropolitan Hockey Club, Inc., 427 U.S. 639, 643, 96 S.Ct. 2778 (1975); Jones v. Louisiana State Bar Ass'n, 602 F.2d 94 (5th Cir. 1979).

[166]Rule 32(b), FRCP.

[167]Christy v. United States, 68 F.R.D. 375, 377-78 (N.D. Tex. 1975); *see also*

Fifth Amendment privilege against self-incrimination about matters that you have put into issue by bringing the lawsuit,[168] although you can do so with respect to unrelated criminal acts for which you have not been prosecuted. You may have to answer questions about other prisoners if they are relevant to the events you are suing about. If a question appears *completely* irrelevant, you may refuse to answer it, but even then you should state that you will answer it if the other side will explain its relevance.

You should not treat defendants' discovery as a confrontation. This is especially true at depositions, where defendants' lawyer may try to get you angry or upset so you will say something that hurts your case. You should answer the questions as honestly and as briefly as possible. If you do not understand a question, ask for an explanation.

When a party takes a deposition, the other party has the right to ask questions at the end. At your deposition, if you feel that the defendants have managed to confuse you and get you to say damaging things, you should be able to give additional testimony to set the record straight. Do not do this unless there was some genuine confusion earlier in the deposition.

F.   Subpoena[169]

If your trial is scheduled, you should make sure each of your witnesses receive a subpoena at least two weeks prior to trial date requiring their presence. To obtain witness subpoenas, you would write the clerk of the court and ask for some blank witness subpoenas. Once you have obtained the subpoenas you will complete them[170] If you have been granted in forma pauperis status, you can send your completed subpoenas to the U.S. Marshal, along with a copy of the order granting in forma pauperis status, requesting them to serve the subpoenas. The fastest method of having your subpoenas served whether proceeding as an indigent or paying the costs of litigation is to have friend 18 years or older serve them for you.[171] If some of the witnesses you need to testify at trial are pris-

---

Hickman v. Taylor, *supra* note 107, 329 U.S. at 511 (discovery for purposes of impeachment permitted).

[168]*See supra* note 125.

[169]You should read Rule 45 closely since it concerns issuance of subpoenas for attendance at trial and depositions.

[170]Rule 45(a), FRCP.

[171]Rule 45(c), FRCP. If you have not been granted in forma pauperis status, you must present a witness a subpoena fee for one day's trial attendance and mileage. These fees are set forth in 28 U.S.C. §1821. You will probably have to check with the court clerk to determine mileage rates in effect.

oners, you will need to file a petition for a writ of habeas corpus *ad testificandum* to have these prisoners brought to the courtroom.[172]

If the defendants or non-parties have in their possession documents you will need at trial, you can obtain subpoenas *duces tecum* signed and sealed from the clerk. You will fill in the name of the person and the documents they have that you need produced at trial.[173] These subpoenas should be served by a U.S. Marshal or by a person not a party to the suit who is 18 years or older. You should try to obtain copies of all documents you will need through discovery; if you do this, you should not need to subpoena the originals at trial.

G. Summary Judgment

A motion for summary judgment is filed by one of the parties who feels there is no genuine issue as to any material fact and the moving party is entitled to judgment as a matter of law.[174] If the court finds there is no dispute as to any material fact, there is no reason for a jury trial to consider the issue. The court will only look to the law then to determine if the undisputed facts justify a legal ruling in the moving party's favor. If they do, the court will grant summary judgment. Summary judgment should not be granted if there is a dispute as to any of the major facts. "Any doubt as to the existence of a genuine issue of fact is to be resolved against the moving party [for summary judgment]."[175] Summary judgment may be requested as to some of the issues in the case (partial summary judgment) or all of them.

To obtain summary judgment, you must file a motion, a brief, and documents establishing the facts.[176] The factual matter will usually consist of one or more affidavits (made by you or by other witnesses), accompanied by any prison documents, admissions obtained from the defendants, or other material that supports your claim. For example, if you claim that you were placed in punitive segregation with inadequate notice, without being allowed to speak at your hearing, and without receiving a meaningful statement of reasons, you would write an affidavit describing the hearing and attach the inadequate notice and state-

---

[172]See Appendix B, Form 4, for an example of a summons.

[173]Rule 45(a), FRCP.

[174]Rule 56(c), FRCP. *See* United States ex rel. Jones v. Rundle, 453 F.2d 147, 150 (3d Cir. 1971). *See also* Adickes v. S.H. Kress & Co., 398 U.S. 144, 90 S.Ct. 1598 (1970); Augustin v. Quern, 611 F.2d 206 (7th Cir. 1979) (an issue of law is no barrier to summary judgment).

[175]United States ex rel. Jones v. Rundle, *id.* at 150.

[176]See Appendix B, Form 11, for an example of summary judgment papers.

ment of reasons to the affidavit as exhibits. If you claimed defendants violated their own regulations in doing this, you would also attach the regulations as an exhibit and your affidavit would describe the particular actions that violated the regulations. In your brief, you would refer to these factual submissions and explain how they proved your rights were violated. If the defendants did not dispute your factual allegations, the judge would then decide the case on those facts; if the defendants did dispute them, summary judgment would be denied and the facts would be determined at trial.

Affidavits must be based on personal knowledge, not hearsay.[177] If you claim that Officer X took property from your cell based on what inmate Y told you, you will need inmate Y's affidavit as well as your own.

You can respond to a motion for summary judgment in one of three ways: dispute the facts, concede the facts and cross-move for summary judgment yourself, or request that the motion be denied or stayed until you have had an opportunity to obtain discovery.

If the defendants' factual allegations are not correct or are incomplete, you *must* file an affidavit in response stating which facts alleged by the defendants you dispute, or which material facts the defendants left out, and how you know these facts. If the facts are demonstrated by documents, attach copies of the documents as exhibits to your affidavit. You *cannot* simply rely on the allegations in your complaint; if you do, the court will rule against you.[178]

If you agree that the defendants' factual allegations are true and complete, but still think you are in the right, you should cross-move for summary judgment, explaining why the facts as alleged by the defendants show that you are legally correct and entitled to judgment.

If you have not had an opportunity to complete discovery or the defendants have not yet complied with your discovery requests, you should request that the court deny, or at least stay, the defendants' motion until you have obtained the necessary information.[179] "[W]here the facts are in the possession of the moving party, a continuance of a

---

[177]Rule 56(a), FRCP. *See* Scharf v. United States Atty. Gen., 597 F.2d 1240 (9th Cir. 1979); Broadway v. City of Montgomery, Alabama, 530 F.2d 657, 661 (5th Cir. 1976) (hearsay evidence not admissible at trial cannot be used to avoid summary judgment); Paton v. LaPrade, 524 F.2d 862 (3d Cir. 1975) (opinion evidence admissible at trial can be submitted by affidavit); Kauffman v. Johnson, 454 F.2d 264 (3d Cir. 1972) (statements by counsel in briefs cannot be bases of summary judgment). See Sec. N2, *infra,* on hearsay.

[178]Rule 56(e), FRCP.

[179]*See* Costlow v. United States, 552 F.2d 560, 564 (3d Cir. 1977); Madyun v. Thompson, 484 F. Supp. 619 (C.D. Ill. 1980).

motion for summary judgment should be granted as a matter of course."[180]

If there is more than one issue involved in the summary judgment motion, you may wish to adopt more than one of these strategies. For example, if you brought suit because you were beaten up and then given a disciplinary hearing without adequate notice or statement of reasons, defendants might move for summary judgment claiming you were not beaten, the notice and reasons were sufficient, and the superintendent was not liable because he had no personal involvement in the case. You might respond to this motion (a) that you claim that you were beaten and that this factual dispute prevents summary judgment on the beating; (b) that there is no factual dispute about the notice and reasons, and that you are the one who is entitled to summary judgment on that issue; and (c) the defendants have not yet turned over their rules which spell out the superintendent's involvement in disciplinary hearings, so the summary judgment motion should be denied or stayed until you obtain these regulations.

In *Murrell v. Bennett,*[181] the court of appeals reversed the district court's grant of summary judgment to the defendants. Plaintiff had filed a *pro se* complaint alleging numerous deprivations of medical care. Defendants moved alternatively for dismissal and summary judgment, supporting their motion with affidavits. Prisoner Murrell filed a request for *subpoenas duces tecum,*[182] subpoenas to produce witnesses,[183] a response to defendants' motion outlining the factual disputes that existed, and a request for appointment of counsel. The district court, adopting the magistrate's recommendation, denied Murrell's requests for subpoenas and failed to mention the request for counsel.

The court of appeals found that "[t]he absence of documents for Murrell is the very injustice of this case. Indigent prisoners are hampered in their access to the proof necessary to ward off summary judgment."[184] The court also found that Murrell did not have sufficient time to

---

[180]Costlow v. United States, *id.* at 564. *See also* National Life Insurance Co. v. Solomon, 529 F.2d 61 (2d Cir. 1976) (per curiam) (courts are particularly reluctant to grant summary judgment where there has been no opportunity for pretrial discovery).

[181]615 F.2d 306 (5th Cir. 1980).

[182]The subpoenas were requested for discovery of the time of Murrell's arrival at the hospital, the amount of blood he received, the type of ambulance used, and what, if any, substitute medicine was prescribed. *Id.* at 310.

[183]These witnesses would have testified about the type of diet provided at the prison.

[184]*Supra* note 181, at 310.

complete discovery since his case was "nipped in the bud only thirty-two days after the complaint was filed."[185]

The court of appeals held that given the claims and requests in this case, the lower court should have done more before granting summary judgment to defendants. Some of the options suggested by the court were: 1) the appointment of counsel; 2) issuance of the subpoenas requested; 3) granting of a continuance pursuant to Rule 56(a) pending discovery; or 4) denial of summary judgment and the holding of an evidentiary hearing.

A *pro se* plaintiff should be advised by the court of his/her right under Rule 56 to file opposing affidavits to defeat a motion for summary judgment.[186]

> We hold that before entering summary judgment against appellant, the district court, as a bare minimum, should have provided him with fair notice of the requirements of the summary judgment rule. We stress the need for a form of notice sufficiently understandable to one in appellant's circumstances fairly to apprise him of what is required.[187]

H. Default Judgment

A default judgment can be entered against a defendant when s/he has failed to file an answer within the time prescribed by law, failed to bring a motion raising a 12(b) defense within that time,[188] and failed to request an extension of time to file an answer. You should not seek a default judgment on the 21st day after the service of the summons and complaint since courts will seldom grant a permanent default judgment unless the time for answering has long since passed. A default judgment, even when entered, can be set aside if prison officials show good cause for their failure to file the answer within the time period and raise a meritorious defense.[189]

To obtain a default judgment, you must first submit a request to the clerk of the court for entry of a default with an affidavit in support.[190] After the clerk has entered a default, you will submit a request for default judgment to either the clerk (if the amount you have requested is

---

[185]*Id.*

[186]Madyun v. Thompson, 657 F.2d 868, 877 (6th Cir. 1981); Gordon v. Leeke, *supra* note 54, at 1151.

[187]Hudson v. Hardy, 412 F.2d 1091, 1094 (D.C. Cir. 1968).

[188]See Rule 12, FRCP; see also Secs. A5, B, *supra*.

[189]*See* Thorpe v. Thorpe, 364 F.2d 692 (D.C. Cir. 1966); Bonaventure v. Butler, 593 F.2d 625 (5th Cir. 1979).

[190]See Rule 55(a), FRCP; Appendix B, Form 10a.

a sum certain)[191] or the judge (if the amount is not a sum certain).[192] If the sum is certain, you will submit to the clerk with your request for default judgment an affidavit that defendant is not in the military service, and a judgment for the clerk to sign.[193] If the sum is not certain, you will submit to the court a motion for default judgment, notice of motion for judgment that must be sent to the defendant you are seeking default against, affidavit that defendant is not in the military service, and a judgment for the court to sign.[194] A hearing will then be held and you will be given an opportunity to present evidence concerning the damages you feel you are entitled to. The defendant will be allowed to produce only evidence opposing your proof of damages.

I.   Pretrial Conference and Proceedings

A pretrial conference is often scheduled 4-8 weeks prior to the trial date. The pretrial conference is a hearing held by the court, usually in the judge's chambers, with the attorneys for the parties to plan and/or restrict the events that will occur at the trial. Rule 16, FRCP, permits, but does not require, a federal district court to hold a pretrial conference; local rules may, so you must ask the clerk of the court for a copy of the local rules.[195]

Because of your confinement and the problems with transporting you from the prison to the court and back, a pretrial conference will not normally be held in a *pro se* case. If you feel that a pretrial conference is necessary in your case, you should write the judge or magistrate, sending a copy to opposing counsel, requesting that it be held. In your letter, you may request that the pretrial conference be held at the prison, if necessary.[196] If your case has not yet been assigned to a magistrate, you

---

[191]*Id.,* at Form 10b. *See also* SEC v. Wencke, 557 F.2d 619 (9th Cir. 1978), *cert. denied,* 99 S.Ct. 451 (1979); National Discount Corp. v. O'Mell, 194 F.2d 452 (6th Cir. 1952).

[192]See Appendix B, Form 10c.

[193]*Id.,* at Form 10b2, 3, and 4. See also Rule 55(a) (if entitlement to default "is made to appear by affidavit or otherwise, the clerk shall enter his default."); Davis v. Mercier-Freres, 368 F. Supp. 498 (E.D. Wisc. 1973).

[194]See Appendix B, Form 10c1, 2, 3, 4, and 5; Rule 55(b), FRCP.

[195]The local court may charge a couple of dollars for a copy of their local rules.

[196]For a brief discussion of the statutory basis and the reasons for holding court proceedings at the prison, see Bagwell, "Procedural Aspects of Prisoners' §1983 and §2254 Cases in the Fifth and Eleventh Circuits," 95 F.R.D. 435, 450-51 (1982).

may also ask that a magistrate be appointed to conduct the pretrial conference at the prison.

Even when you request that a pretrial conference be held at the prison, a court generally will not hold the conference if your case is straight-forward (*e.g.*, there is only one issue, such as whether you received prop-er notice before your disciplinary hearing, you will be your only witness, and very limited discovery was done in the case). But, if your case in-volves numerous alleged constitutional violations (*e.g.*, you have alleged violations of your right to access to the courts, excessive use of mace, physical assault by guards, and denial of adequate medical care), you have done extensive discovery, and you plan on calling a large number of prisoners and experts to testify, the court will, in all likelihood, wish to hold a pretrial conference.

At the pretrial conference, the judge or magistrate will simplify the issues to be tried; seek additional admissions of facts and documents beyond what has already been obtained by the parties; seek to limit the number of witnesses a *pro se* plaintiff wants brought to the court-house;[197] and so forth. The parties may also raise procedural issues, such as continuation of discovery for a reasonable period of time, post-ponement of trial, issuance of writs of habeas corpus *ad testificandum* so your prisoner witnesses can be brought to the trial. You may also need to get an order from the court allowing you to talk to your witnesses or, if they have been transferred since the incident that is the basis of your lawsuit, to write them and have them respond without prison officials' opening the letter outside the addressees' presence. In some cases, the pretrial conference may become a forum for settling a case or resolving a problem through administrative action.[198]

At the end of the pretrial conference, the court will issue a pretrial order reflecting the events that occurred; this order will then control the subsequent events unless modified by the court. If the parties are granted additional time to do discovery or for presenting motions, the court will establish a pretrial calendar that must be followed.

Sometimes courts try to accomplish the above described task without actually holding a pretrial conference. The parties may be required to submit an agreed pretrial order in writing. (If this happens, and if the court does not supply you with an outline or sample, you may wish to ask the court for an example of an acceptable pretrial order.) A magistrate may be requested to prepare the pretrial order after reviewing the file.[199]

---

[197]See Sec. M, *infra,* for a discussion of whether a plaintiff/prisoner has a right to be present at a civil trial and have prisoner/witnesses present.

[198]*See* Johnson v. Teasdale, 456 F. Supp. 1083, 1086 (W.D. Mo. 1978).

[199]Federal Judicial Center, *Recommended Procedures for Handling Prisoner Civil Rights Cases in the Federal Court,* at 83 (1980).

The court may also ask you to state in writing what each of your witnesses will testify to so it can decide if any of them are "cumulative," or repetitive, and not necessary to call.[200]

Since a court may restrict the number of witnesses that can be brought to the courthouse to testify, you should consider whether to ask to have your trial occur at the prison. If the trial is before a judge or magistrate and not a jury, there should be little hesitancy on your part to have the trial at the prison. A judge or magistrate will not be as uptight about being in a prison as jurors might. Since jurors may be adversely affected by entering a prison, you must weigh the benefit gained (probably having all your witnesses testify) against the adverse effect the prison may have on the jurors.

J.   Preparation for Trial

After the pretrial conference and before the trial, there are certain things you must do. First, you will want to draft the questions that will be asked each witness including yourself. Your witnesses should not ramble while testifying, and you can prevent this by organizing your questions logically. Second, you need to talk to your witnesses, or write them if they have been transferred, to ensure that they are still willing to testify. The witnesses that are still at your prison should be questioned in the manner you will question them at trial. If possible, someone else should cross-examine them as you think opposing counsel will. Third, you need to draft proposed jury instructions regarding each of your claims to submit them at the beginning of the trial.[201] Fourth, you should mark all the documents that you want admitted at trial in the order you will introduce them (*e.g.,* Plaintiff's Proposed Exhibit No. 1, Plaintiff's Proposed Exhibit No. 2, etc.). Fifth, if the trial is to occur at the courthouse, you must make sure the court has issued writs of habeas corpus *ad testificandum* to have your prisoner/witnesses brought to the courthouse. Sixth, if you will have a trial by jury, you should ask the clerk of the court for a list of the jury pool and their background information. This will assist you in drafting proposed *voir dire* questions. Seventh, if you are going to have a jury trial and the judge will conduct the *voir dire,* you should submit your proposed *voir dire* questions prior to trial. (See Sec. K3.) Eighth, you should make a motion *in limine* (to restrict the evidence that defendants can introduce at trial concerning your conviction or your prison record), if one is appropriate. (See Sec. N6.)

---

[200]*Id.* at 77.

[201]See Sec. K12, *infra,* for a discussion of jury instructions.

K. Trials

This section will introduce the basics of trial practice. It sticks to the basics because a full treatment of trial practice would fill another long book.[202] However, we hope to provide the information you will need to present your case correctly and clearly to a judge or jury.

1. What Happens at a Trial

The purpose of a trial is to decide facts that are in dispute. If there is no factual dispute, there is no need for a trial, and the judge can decide the case without one. There may be some variation in the way trials are conducted, but most civil trials adhere to the following order of events.

A trial begins with the selection of a jury, if the parties have asked for a jury trial. If they have not asked (or if the case is one where there is no right to a jury), the judge will decide the case. (A trial without a jury is called a "bench trial.")

Next, the plaintiff makes an opening statement, telling the judge or jury what s/he expects to prove. The defendant then may make an opening statement or may wait until after the plaintiff's evidence has been presented.

After opening statements, the plaintiff will present his/her evidence. At the close of the plaintiff's case, the defendant may move for a directed verdict (in a jury trial) or move to dismiss the case (in a bench trial) on the ground that the evidence, even if believed, does not establish a violation of law.

If the judge denies the defendant's motion, the defendant presents his/her evidence. If new issues are raised in defendant's evidence, the plaintiff may then present rebuttal evidence; if more new issues are introduced, the defendant may present "surrebuttal" evidence.

After all the evidence is in, in a jury trial, the defendant may again move for a directed verdict, and the plaintiff may also move for a directed verdict, claiming that the defendant's proof would not establish a defense even if believed.

Next, the parties make their closing arguments. In a bench trial, the case is ready for decision after closing argument; in a jury trial, the judge will then charge, or instruct, the jury as to what its duties are and what the parties must have proved in order to win. The jury will then deliberate and return with a verdict; in a bench trial, the judge will either issue an oral decision at that time or a written decision later.

After the verdict or decision, the losing party may make a motion for judgment notwithstanding the verdict or for a new trial.

---

[202]*See, e.g.,* Hunter, *Federal Trial Handbook* (Lawyers Co-Operative Publishing Co., 1974); Keaton, *Trial Tactics and Methods* (Little, Brown & Co., 2d ed., 1973).

2. The Right to Trial by Jury

In a damage suit against prison officials in federal court, you have the right to a jury trial.[203] You do not have the right to a jury trial when you are seeking an injunction[204] or when you are suing the federal government under the Federal Tort Claims Act.[205] If you are in a state court, your right to a jury trial in a civil case is governed by state law; the states are not bound by the Seventh Amendment provision regarding jury trials in civil cases.[206]

To get a jury trial, you have to ask for it. The best time and place to do this is in the complaint.[207] You must ask for a jury trial within ten days of the service of the last pleading directed to the issue you want a jury trial on.[208] This generally means ten days after the defendants serve their answer. If you do not ask for a jury trial in time, you have waived the right; however, the court has discretion to give you a jury trial anyway.[209] Either party can ask for a jury trial, and a party may not withdraw a jury demand without the other side's consent.[210]

Whether to ask for a jury trial is a major decision. You should consider how sympathetic the judge might be if you do not have a jury, what the attitude of people in the community toward prisoners is, whether you have a claim that lay people will easily understand (*e.g.,* they beat you up and broke your arm), or one that is more technical (*e.g.,* they did not give you a timely disciplinary hearing and the statement of reasons is inadequate), how long it takes to get a jury trial (usually longer than a bench trial in most jurisdictions), and whether the factual issues are more complicated than a jury will understand. A jury trial is also harder to conduct than a bench trial, and you should consider whether your skills are adequate. Expert trial lawyers often believe that juries are more likely to be moved by sympathetic appeals than judges,[211] and that judges are

---

[203]U.S. Const., Amend. VII; Dolence v. Flynn, 628 F.2d 1280, 1282 (10th Cir. 1980).

[204]Johnson v. Teasdale, *supra* note 198, at 1089. If you seek damages *and* an injunction, you have the right to a jury trial on the damages portion of the trial.

[205]Birnbaum v. United States, 588 F.2d 319, 335 (2d Cir. 1978). See Ch. VI, Sec. C2, for a discussion of the Federal Tort Claims Act.

[206]Melancon v. McKeithen, 345 F. Supp. 1025 (E.D. La.), *aff'd sub nom.* Hill v. McKeithen, 99 S.Ct. 290 (1972).

[207]See Appendix B, Form 1a, for a sample complaint with a jury demand.

[208]Rule 38(b), FRCP.

[209]Rule 38(d), FRCP; United States v. Unum, Inc., 658 F.2d 300, 303 (5th Cir. 1981).

[210]Rule 38(d), FRCP.

[211]Keaton, *Trial Tactics and Methods, supra* note 202, at §7.2.

more likely to stick strictly to the facts and the law. Which way this cuts obviously depends on the facts of the case, including facts about you, such as what crimes you have been convicted of[212] and whether you come across as a dangerous or dishonest person or as someone who is less threatening to the kinds of people who show up on juries.[213]

In a jury trial, the jury decides the facts; the court retains power to decide all legal questions that arise. You are thus entitled to a jury trial only if your case presents a factual issue that, if decided your way, would entitle you to win. If a judge decides that your factual claims would not legally entitle you to win even if they were all true, or that there is no factual issue to be resolved, the judge may decide the case on that basis without violating your right to a jury trial.[214]

3.   Selecting a Jury

In a civil case, the usual number of jurors is six.[215] One or more alternate jurors may also be selected in case one of the regular jurors gets sick and cannot hear all the evidence; the alternate juror will then replace that juror.[216] Alternates are more likely to be selected for longer trials.

You have the right to an impartial jury. Impaneling an impartial jury has two main parts. First, a number of prospective jurors (an "array") will be called to the courtroom. Second, the judge will supervise the selection of specific jurors through a *voir dire* examination.

By statute, people must be called for jury duty on a random basis, and anyone is deemed to be qualified for jury service if s/he is a United States citizen at least twenty-one years old who has lived for a year in the judicial district, can speak English, can fill out the required forms, is physically and mentally able to serve, and does not have a conviction or a pending charge of a serious crime.[217]

The *voir dire* examination consists of asking the prospective juror a number of questions designed to find out if s/he can decide the case fairly. In federal court, the *voir dire* may be conducted either by the judge or by counsel.[218] Usually, the judge does it because it is faster;

---

[212]This evidence may be excluded from the trial; see Sec. N5a, *infra.*

[213]See Sec. K3, *infra,* for a discussion of this subject.

[214]Manaia v. Potomac Electric Power Co., 268 F.2d 793, 798-99 (4th Cir.), *cert. denied,* 361 U.S. 913 (1959).

[215]Rule 27, FRCP.

[216]Rule 47(b), FRCP. An alternate juror who is not designated to replace a regular juror will be dismissed before the jury retires to consider a verdict. Alternates are selected in the same way as regular jurors.

[217]28 U.S.C. §§1863, 1865.

check the local court rules to see if there is a prescribed practice in your jurisdiction. Sometimes the judge will permit counsel to ask additional questions after s/he has finished. The judge has broad discretion in conducting *voir dire.*[219]

Voir dire questions should be designed to learn if there are any reasons why a particular juror cannot decide the case fairly based on the evidence.[220] If a juror has preconceived ideas about the case; prejudices based on race, religion, your status as a prisoner, or some other factor; prior knowledge of the case which might influence his/her decision; or personal or business relationships with parties to the case or their relatives, that juror should not sit on your case. Your *voir dire* questions should focus on these issues.[221] You should submit proposed *voir dire* questions to the court in advance of the trial.

If a juror's answers reveal some bias about the case, you may challenge that juror for cause.[222] The judge will then either excuse the juror or overrule your challenge and refuse to excuse the juror. Often, federal judges will respond to a challenge for cause by asking the juror if s/he can set aside feelings or personal relationships and be fair; if the juror says yes, the challenge may be overruled.

If your challenge for cause is overruled, or if you think a juror may be biased but you can not cite a specific reason, you may exercise a "peremptory challenge" and have that juror removed. Ordinarily, each party is limited to three peremptory challenges.[223] If there are multiple plaintiffs or defendants, the judge will decide whether each of them gets three peremptory challenges or whether they are restricted to a total of three among them.[224] Be sure to ask the court to restrict the other side to a total of three if you have sued a number of defendants.

After the *voir dire,* the judge will swear in the jury. If you have any objections to the way the jury was selected, you must make them before the jury is sworn or you will waive the objection.[225]

Before jury selection starts, you should ask the judge to explain to you exactly how s/he intends to proceed. Practices may vary from place to

---

[218]Rule 47(a), FRCP.

[219]Blake v. Cich, 79 F.R.D. 398 (D. Minn. 1978).

[220]*See* Darbin v. Nourse, 664 F.2d 1109 (9th Cir. 1981).

[221]See Appendix B, Form 23, for a sample list of possible *voir dire* questions.

[222]*Supra* note 220, at 1113.

[223]28 U.S.C. §1870.

[224]John Long Trucking, Inc. v. Greear, 421 F.2d 125, 127-28 (10th Cir. 1970).

[225]Hunter, *Federal Trial Handbook,* at §24.27 (1974).

place and from judge to judge, and it is easy to get confused about
things such as when and how to make peremptory challenges.

You should understand that you do not have a right to a "jury of your
peers" in the sense of people who come from similar social or racial
backgrounds. The purpose of jury selection is to provide a cross-section
of the community, and if your trial is taking place in a white, middle-
class or rural area, you will get a white, middle-class or rural jury.
Moreover, juries in general tend to underrepresent minorities and low-
income people (in part because jury rolls are made up from voter lists,
and these groups have low voter registration rates), and to overrepresent
people who will receive their full salaries while serving (like many government employees) and people who do not have to work or take care
of children (like retired people). Many people simply cannot afford to sit
on juries and lose time from work, or are subject to family obligations
that prevent them from serving; the judge is likely to excuse these people.
Also, prospective jurors who appear to be more sympathetic to
prisoners, minority group members, or poor people are likely to be
removed from the jury by the defendant's peremptory challenges. These
facts should be kept in mind in deciding whether to ask for a jury trial.

4.   Starting the Trial

To begin the trial, the court normally only introduces counsel and then
asks plaintiff's counsel whether s/he is ready to proceed. If the parties to
the lawsuit have stipulated to certain facts that need not be proved at
trial, these stipulated facts should probably be read to the jury before the
first witness testifies.

5.   Opening Statement

Both parties are entitled to present opening statements. The plaintiff
will present his/her opening statement first, and the defendant can either
present his/her opening statement immediately after the plaintiff or
reserve opening statement until after all the plaintiff's witnesses have
testified.

Opening statements are intended to tell the court or jury the issues that
will be presented and the facts that will be proved. They should not be
argumentative. Opening statements are not evidence. If you assert a fact
in your opening statement, you must later put that fact into evidence or
the judge or jury will not be able to consider it. Also, if you make a claim
and then fail to back it up with evidence, your credibility will be
damaged.

There are two things you will try to accomplish in your opening statement. One is to give the judge or jury a preview of the evidence you will
be presenting so they will know what to expect and be able to understand

it better. This is particularly important if you will have several witnesses whose testimony will cover various times and places. You may also wish to explain some things about the prison setting with which a judge or jury may be unfamiliar. The other purpose of an opening statement is to introduce yourself as well as your case. The judge or jury will be assessing you as a person and judging your credibility, and the opening statement will be your first chance to try to make a favorable impression. Be respectful and calm and avoid rhetoric and name-calling. You should also try to tell the jurors something about yourself so they can begin to see you as a human being and not just as a convict. (This should be kept brief. The judge will probably allow you some latitude as a *pro se* litigant, but do not try to tell your life story.) If your criminal record is going to be brought out in the trial,[226] you should be the one to do it.

We have drafted a sample opening statement to illustrate these points.

> Good morning. My name is Dan Manville. I am 32 years old and I am an inmate at the State Prison of Southern Michigan, Jackson, where I am serving a sentence for manslaughter. Until the events that you are going to hear about, I had a job in the prison tailor shop and I was studying for my high school equivalency certificate.
>
> On the morning of January 19, 1983, I was placed in handcuffs in my cell, maced, and then beaten with an axe handle while I was being taken to the hole. (The "hole" is a term used for a special unit the prison uses for solitary confinement and segregation of prisoners they say broke the rules.) I was handcuffed during this entire period and was not fighting back.
>
> You will hear my testimony about how I was locked in my cell for the noon count (a prison procedure for determining whether anyone has escaped) when Lieutenant Smith and Officer Jones approached my cell and Lieutenant Smith told me to place my hands between the bars so I could be handcuffed. I will tell you how Officer Jones, pursuant to an order from Lieutenant Smith, maced me even though I was locked in my cell in handcuffs, and how Officer Brown later beat me with an axe handle as we walked to the hole.
>
> You will hear testimony of prisoner Ronald Lev that his cell is directly across from mine and that he saw Officer Jones mace me without provocation while I was handcuffed. Prisoner Stuart Steinberg will testify that as I was being led out of the cell block, he saw Officer Brown strike me on the head and shoulders with an axe handle.
>
> You will see the prison medical records that verify that I had severe bruises on my shoulders and neck and lumps on my head after all this happened, and I will testify about the pain and suffering that I experienced from the beating, including dizziness and blurred vision for a period of a week and being unable to take any exercise for three or four weeks.

---

[226]Whether your criminal record can be referred to should be established before trial through a motion *in limine*. See Sec. N6 for a discussion of this motion.

6.   Plaintiff's Evidence[227]

You, as the plaintiff, will present your case first: all the witnesses and all the documents that you think help show that your rights were violated. You should not try to surprise the defendants by holding back a crucial piece of evidence until after they have presented their case. It is your burden to present a prima facie case[228] at the beginning, and if you fail to do this the judge may dismiss your case or direct a verdict against you. Also, rebuttal is restricted to answering new issues raised by the defendants, and if they do not handle their case as you expect, you may not be permitted to put in certain rebuttal evidence.

When you put on witnesses to support your case, you will get their testimony on the record by asking them questions. Since they are your witnesses, you will be conducting direct examination. After they have responded to your questions, the other side can ask them questions too; this is called cross-examination. The rules governing direct and cross-examination are discussed later in Sec. N3.

Your main witness may be yourself. Since it would be silly to ask yourself questions, you should prepare your testimony in the form of a narrative or story which you will tell from the witness stand. You may wish to write out an outline to help you remember everything. However, the other side will be permitted to examine any notes you refer to while on the witness stand.[229] You should be familiar enough with what you want to say that you can do it without notes if you have to. If you keep referring to notes, it will not help your credibility.

While the case is being presented, you or the defendant's lawyer may believe that an improper question has been asked. (What questions are improper is discussed in Sec. N3b, *infra*.) In that case, you or the other lawyer will make an objection. To make an objection, you say, "Objection" or "I object." If you can state the grounds of the objection in a word or two, you should do so—*e.g.*, "Objection, hearsay," or "Objection, leading question." Then you should stop talking and wait for the judge to rule; courts generally do not have time for extended argument on objections. If the other side makes an objection to one of your questions, do not respond or continue asking questions; wait until the judge rules. An objection should always be treated as a "stop light" in the trial; until the judge gives you the green light by ruling on the objection, do not proceed.

If you have more than one witness or a large number of documents,

---

[227]This section deals with the sequence of events at trial. For a discussion of the rules of evidence, see Sec. N, *infra*.

[228]See N1f, *infra*, for a discussion of what is a prima facie case.

[229]Rule 612, Federal Rules of Evidence.

you will have to decide in what order to present your evidence. You want your case to be as forceful as possible and as clear as possible. To be forceful, you will generally want to present your strongest witness (usually yourself) first; to be clear, you will usually want to present witnesses in chronological order. Sometimes these two considerations are in conflict. You can put documents into evidence at any point in your case. (See Sec. N4, *infra,* for a discussion of putting documents into evidence.) When you will want to do this depends on what the documents are and how many of them there are. It is often very effective to put documents in as their subject matter comes up in testimony. For example, if you claim that an officer beat you because you had earlier filed a complaint against him, you could put that complaint into evidence when you mention it at the beginning of your testimony; you could put medical records showing your injuries into evidence later, after you describe the beating. You should also consider how you want the documents communicated to the jury. The judge has discretion to read them to the jury or let you read them, or to give them to the jury to read. Reading them to the jury is advantageous if the documents are long and hard to read or understand; letting the jury read them for themselves may be better if the documents are short and clear.

7. Motions After the Plaintiff's Evidence

After you have presented your case, the defendant has the right to make a motion to dismiss (in a bench trial) or for a directed verdict (in a jury trial).[230] In either case, the defendant will be claiming that your evidence, even if it is believed, does not show that your rights were violated—that is, you have failed to prove a prima facie case.[231] If you fail to produce some evidence as to every element of your legal claim, you will have failed to make a prima facie case.

There are two things you can do in responding to such a motion. First, you can show the judge that you *have* produced some evidence in support of each element of your claim. (It is useful for this purpose to keep a checklist of what you have to prove and check off each fact as it is put into evidence.) The defendants may also claim that you have failed to prove something that you are not legally required to prove. For example, they may say you did not prove that a particular officer actually struck you during a beating; however, if you proved that the officer did stand by while other officers beat you, you should tell the judge this and remind the judge that this is legally sufficient to hold that officer liable.[232] Second, if it turns out that you have accidentally left something

---

[230]Rules 41(b), 50(a), FRCP.

[231]*Supra* note 228.

[232]See Ch. VI, Sec. E2a.

out of your proof, you can ask to reopen the case and put in the missing evidence. Whether to permit this is in the judge's discretion.[233]

8.   Defendant's Evidence

If you have proved a prima facie case, the defendant will be required to present his/her evidence. During the defendant's case, the defendant's lawyer will conduct the direct examination of witnesses, and you will cross-examine them. The defendant will introduce whatever documents support his/her case.

9.   Rebuttal and Surrebuttal

After the defendant's case has been presented, the plaintiff may present rebuttal evidence to counter evidence presented by the defendant.[234] Rebuttal evidence usually is limited to new issues raised by the defendant; evidence that could logically have been presented as part of the plaintiff's original evidence (or "case-in-chief") may not be permitted on rebuttal, although the district court has discretion to relax this rule. The defendant may be permitted "surrebuttal" to respond to the plaintiff's rebuttal evidence.[235]

As mentioned earlier, you should *not* hold back evidence that supports your legal claim in order to present it on rebuttal. If you think it is important and helpful, present it in the first place.

10.   Motions After the Evidence is Closed

Once the evidence is closed, both you and the defendant may make motions for a directed verdict if the case is being tried before a jury.[236] The defendant will argue that you have not proved a prima facie case (see Sec. K7, *supra*); you will argue that the evidence provided by the defendant does not establish a defense even if it is true, and therefore there is nothing for the jury to decide. For example, if you show that prison guards waited for four days before sending you to a doctor for your broken arm, and the defendants prove only that they provided adequate medical care once you got to the doctor, that fact does not provide a defense for the original delay, and you could move for a directed verdict against the guards responsible for it.

---

[233]*Supra* note 225, at §27.5.

[234]*Id.* at §27.3.

[235]*Id.* at §27.4.

[236]Rule 50, FRCP.

11. Closing Arguments

After all the evidence is in, you and the defendant's lawyer will be permitted to make closing arguments to the jury or to the judge concerning what the evidence shows and why you should win the case. Generally, the plaintiff argues first, followed by the defendant, and the plaintiff is then permitted rebuttal. Some judges may vary this procedure; you should ask the judge at the beginning of the trial so you can prepare properly.

Closing arguments should be limited to the issues in the case and the evidence that has been presented.[237] Facts which are not supported by evidence in the record may not be argued, although you may argue reasonable inferences from facts that are in the record. (*E.g.,* if three officers' reports of an incident contradict your version and are identically worded, you can suggest to the jury or judge that they probably got together to concoct their story.) It is improper to appeal to the jury's sympathy, prejudice, or passion, for example, by relying on racial, religious, or political biases. You should not ask the jury if they would wish themselves or members of their family to undergo what happened to you. (You can probably make your point by just describing what happened in detail.) Statements based on evidence which the court ruled inadmissible are improper, as are statements about your personal beliefs or experiences. It is improper to mention any settlement offers that were made. Personal attacks on opposing parties or witnesses are inappropriate; comments about them should be restricted to what the evidence will support. Criticisms of opposing counsel must not be abusive; counsel should not be accused of suppressing facts unless you have evidence to show that this happened. These rules apply both to you and to defendant's counsel.

In a civil case, it is proper to comment on the fact that a party has failed to call a witness who could be expected to testify favorably to that party or failed to produce documents that would be expected to help the party's case. You can argue that the evidence was probably not produced because it would not have been favorable. For example, if the warden who reviews all disciplinary convictions claims that s/he actually passed this work on to a subordinate in your case, and if the subordinate does not testify, you can argue that the jury should infer that the subordinate would not have supported the warden's story.

It is also proper to comment on the credibility of witnesses. However, these comments should be based on their testimony and demeanor at the trial and on other evidence in the case. If you know that a particular

---

[237]A more extensive discussion of this subject appears in Hunter, *Federal Trial Handbook,* Ch. 86 (1974).

guard is a notorious liar, it is not proper for you to say so in argument unless you have produced evidence to that effect.

You should not argue the law extensively to a jury. It is the judge's job to instruct them as to the law. You should restrict your comments on the law to simple statements of legal standards and you should do this as a way of commenting on the evidence. For example, in a brutality case you might say, "Under our Constitution, prison guards are permitted to use reasonable force to keep order, prevent escapes, etc., but they are not permitted to use excessive force or to use force for the purpose of harming or injuring prisoners. The evidence shows that the force used against me was far in excess of anything required to keep order and that the guards beat me because they were mad at me and wanted to hurt me." Then you would discuss the actual evidence that proved this statement, without further comment on the law pertaining to guards' use of force.

In your closing argument, you will have three goals. First, you want to make sure that the judge or jury understands your case. To do this, you should go over each element of your legal claim and summarize the evidence that was produced in support of each one. Second, you want to persuade the judge or jury that you are right on those issues where there is a factual dispute. You should be sure to emphasize any reason supported by the record for finding your evidence more credible than the other side's. For example, if a guard's testimony about an altercation with you is inconsistent with the guard's written report, with the kind of injuries you received, or with some other evidence in the case, cite that fact as a reason why the guard's testimony should not be believed in any respect. Third, you want to convince the judge or jury that you are a worthwhile human being and that they should not be prejudiced against you simply because you are a prisoner. The best way to do this is to conduct yourself in a dignified and businesslike manner during your argument.

In a damage case, you will have to deal with the amount of damages you are entitled to.[238] This can be very difficult in cases which involve intangible constitutional rights. How do you translate the denial of a meaningful statement of reasons or confinement for a week in a substandard disciplinary cell into dollars and cents? We do not have any magic answers to this question, but we suggest the following approach. Break down what happened to you into as many separate elements as you can think of, and ask the jury to consider each one. For example, in a case of improper disciplinary segregation, you might say:

> In deciding how much I am entitled to in damages, I want you to think about my spending a month locked in a steel box five feet wide by eight feet long. I want you to think about my being deprived of all my personal property—my books, my clean clothing, my personal letters and pictures, my

---

[238]See Ch. VI, Sec. F, for a discussion of damages.

drawing and painting materials. I want you to think about my sitting there for 24 hours a day with nothing to do. I want you to think about my not having a mop or any disinfectant to clean my cell. I want you to think about the lack of hot water for washing, and the fact that I only got one shower a week, and that I had to wear the same clothes for a week at a time.

In a bench trial, particularly a complicated one, the judge may want you to write a post-trial brief in place of giving closing arguments. You should find out before the trial (at the pretrial conference, if there is one) what the judge's preference is; if you have a preference, you should state it at that time. If you make a closing argument on the spot, the judge is more likely to decide on the spot or very soon; if you are afraid that the evidence was confusing or that the judge may miss something that is very important, writing a brief may be more advantageous. If you are not a great writer, you may be better off taking your chances with the spoken word.

12. Jury Instructions

In a jury trial, the judge will instruct the jury about the law before the jury decides the case. These jury instructions (or "charge" to the jury) will generally come after the closing arguments.

Parts of the jury instructions will be standard instructions, such as the fact that the plaintiff in a civil case has the burden of proof, that all people have equal rights under the law, etc. These instructions are often taken from published sets of "pattern" instructions.[239]

Other parts of the jury instructions will be tailored to the issues in your case. For example, in any §1983 case, the defendant must be shown to be acting "under color of state law," so the judge will instruct the jury as to the meaning of that phrase.[240] The judge will explain to the jury what is involved in proving whatever legal claim you have made. For example, if you claim that your correspondence was illegally interfered with, the judge will explain to the jury what your legal rights are with respect to correspondence.[241] Jury instructions should not be given as to issues which are not actually in the case. For example, if the defendant has violated a right which is clearly established, the court should not instruct the jury as to the defense of qualified immunity or "good faith."[242] If

---

[239]*See, e.g.,* Devitt and Blackmar, *Federal Jury Practice and Instructions* (3d ed. 1977).

[240]See Ch. VI, Sec. B1b, for a definition of "under color of state law."

[241]See Ch. V, Secs. B2g, C1a, for a discussion of your procedural and substantive rights regarding correspondence.

[242]See Ch. VI, Sec. E1d, for a discussion of the qualified immunity defense.

there is no evidence of reckless or malicious conduct, no instruction should be given about punitive damages.[243]

The parties should submit proposed jury instructions to the court before the trial.[244] A *pro se* litigant should probably not worry about standard matters like the burden of proof, how to weigh evidence, etc. You will have too many other things to take care of. However, you should submit proposed instructions on those issues which are likely to be most controversial. These will generally include the explanation of the legal right you claim was violated, the qualified immunity defense,[245] the personal responsibility of supervisory officials,[246] and the measure of damages.[247] The best way to write proposed jury instructions is to find one or more cases in the Supreme Court or your federal circuit dealing with the issue you are concerned with, and take language out of these cases. For example, if your claim is one for deprivation of medical care, you might modify the Supreme Court's language in *Estelle v. Gamble*[248] and write: "Deliberate indifference to serious medical needs of prisoners constitutes cruel and unusual punishment. This is true whether the indifference is manifested by prison doctors in their response to the prisoner's needs or by prison guards in intentionally denying or delaying access to medical care or intentionally interfering with the treatment once prescribed." You should tell the court where you got this language. You may also wish to add a more specific statement relating to the facts of your case, such as, "If you find that Dr. Smith prescribed a back brace for the plaintiff but that Officer Jones took it away from her, you may find that Officer Jones was deliberately indifferent to the plaintiff's serious medical needs."

If you submit proposed jury instructions in advance, the court should tell you how it has decided to charge the jury before closing arguments.[249] If you feel that the judge has made a mistake, you may be able to argue the point at this "charge conference." If you wish to appeal the case based on faulty jury instruction, you *must* object to the instruction before the jury actually retires to decide the case.[250]

---

[243]See Ch. VI, Sec. E3, for a discussion of punitive damages.

[244]*See* Rule 51, FRCP.

[245]*Supra* note 242.

[246]See Ch. VI, Sec. E2a, for a discussion of establishing personal responsibility of supervisory officials.

[247]See Ch. VI, Sec. F, for a discussion of damages.

[248]429 U.S. 97, 104-05, 97 S.Ct. 285 (1976). The language used is not a precise quotation.

[249]Rule 51, FRCP.

[250]*Id.*

13. Verdict or Decision

In a jury trial, the jury will retire to consider the case after the judge has instructed it. The jury may ask to have particular portions of the record read back to it, to have exhibits brought into the jury room, or to receive further instruction from the judge. You should be permitted to be present when this is being done.

When the jury returns with a verdict, it will be read by the foreperson or the court clerk. The jury may be polled (asked individually if they agree with the verdict). In most cases, the jury will return only a "general verdict"—*i.e.,* a finding for the plaintiff or the defendant, with an amount of damages if the plaintiff wins. At the court's discretion, the jury may be required to return a "special verdict" by making written findings of fact as to the basic issues.[251]

In a bench trial, the judge may rule orally from the bench or may issue a written decision later.

14. Motions After the Verdict or Decision

There are three kinds of motions that are often made by the losing party in the district court immediately after the decision.

a. Motion for Judgment Notwithstanding the Verdict[252]

If a party has moved for a directed verdict during the trial and the judge does not grant it, that party may move within ten days after the verdict (decision) to have it set aside on the same grounds that were raised for a directed verdict. This motion is only available to a party who moved for a directed verdict at trial, and is designed for situations where there were no real issues to go to the jury.

b. Motion for a New Trial[253]

Within ten days after the entry of judgment, a motion for a new trial can be made. This motion may be based on a claim that the verdict was against the weight of the evidence, that the damages were excessive or inadequate, that evidence was improperly admitted or rejected, that the jury instructions were erroneous, or that other errors were made in the conduct of the trial.[254] New trials are rarely granted unless there are gross

---

[251]Rule 49(a), FRCP.

[252]Rule 50, FRCP.

[253]Rule 59, FRCP.

[254]*See* 6A Moore's Federal Practice, §59.08[1] (1983).

errors in the way the trial was conducted or there is significant newly discovered evidence. If you claim newly discovered evidence, you should submit an affidavit explaining why the evidence was not available before or during trial.

c.   Motion To Alter or Amend the Judgment[255]

This motion must also be filed within ten days; it is appropriate for correcting simple mistakes such as typographical errors, omission of issues on which the court obviously intended to rule, or provisions of the judgment/order that are inconsistent.

Other motions aimed at modifying or overturning a judgment are discussed in Sec. O, *infra*. Appeals are discussed in Sec. P, *infra*.

L.   Magistrates

Most United States district courts use magistrates to ease the heavy workload of district judges. Magistrates are judicial officers who are assigned their duties by the district court. The district court may refer certain matters in civil or criminal cases[256] to magistrates for a recommendation or decision, and civil trials may be held before magistrates with the consent of the parties. Some courts have adopted a policy of routinely referring prisoner cases to a magistrate.[257]

Magistrates exercise their power in several ways. The most important are as follows.

1. A district judge may refer most pretrial matters to a magistrate for a hearing and decision without consent of the parties. Pretrial matters which may *not* be referred to a magistrate for a decision include motions for injunctive relief, for judgment on the pleadings, for summary judgment, to dismiss or to permit maintenance of a class action, to dismiss for failure to state a claim upon which relief can be granted, and to involuntarily dismiss an action.[258] The magistrate can decide a motion to compel discovery, for extension of time, etc. These decisions of pretrial matters may be reconsidered by the district court only if they are "clearly

---

[255]Rule 59(e), FRCP.

[256]See Ch. IX, Sec. G, for a discussion of use of magistrates in criminal and habeas corpus proceedings.

[257]*See, e.g.,* Johnson v. Teasdale, 456 F. Supp. 1083 (W.D. Mo. 1978); Rule (44)(E), General Rules, United States District Court for the Northern District of New York.

[258]*See* 28 U.S.C. §636(b)(1)(A) for a listing of criminal matters that a magistrate may not hear or make a final determination upon.

erroneous or contrary to law.''[259] If you do not wish a pretrial matter decided by the magistrate, you must file objections with the court at the time of referral or soon thereafter.[260]

2. The district court may also ask a magistrate to conduct hearings in certain other matters and make proposed findings of fact and recommendations for disposition.[261] The matters subject to this procedure include the pretrial matters mentioned above which magistrates may not actually decide (motions for injunctive relief, for judgment on the pleadings, etc.),[262] applications for post-conviction relief, and prisoners' petitions challenging conditions of confinement[263]—in short, most cases brought by prisoners.[264] The important distinction between this procedure and the one described in the previous paragraph is that the judge is required to make a completely new (de novo) determination of any part of the findings and recommendations of the magistrate that either party finds objectionable.[265]

Once the magistrate has made his/her proposed findings and recommendations, a copy will be filed with the court and copies will be mailed to all parties.[266] The magistrate must inform you that objections are to be filed within ten days,[267] and that failure to file objections is a

---

[259]Hill v. Duriron, 656 F.2d 1208 (6th Cir. 1981); Merritt v. International Bro. of Boilermakers, 649 F.2d 1013 (1st Cir. 1981); Pascale v. G.D. Searle & Co., 90 F.R.D. 55 (D.R.I. 1981) (discovery order); Citicorp v. Interbank Card Ass'n, 87 F.R.D. 43 (S.D.N.Y. 1980); Princiotta v. New England Tel. & Tel. Co., Inc., 532 F. Supp. 1009 (D. Mass. 1982).

[260]Hill v. Duriron, *id.* at 1213 and cases cited. *See also* Piper v. Hauck, 532 F.2d 1016 (5th Cir. 1976).

[261]28 U.S.C. §636(b)(1)(B); Taylor v. Oxford, 575 F.2d 152 (7th Cir. 1978).

[262]Neal v. Miller, 542 F. Supp. 79 (S.D. Ill. 1982); Turner v. Steward, 497 F. Supp. 557 (E.D. Ky. 1980).

[263]28 U.S.C. §636(b)(1)(B).

[264]*But see* Hill v. Jenkins, 603 F.2d 1256, 1260 (7th Cir. 1979) (concurring opinion) (not all prisoner complaints referable to magistrate).

[265]Nettles v. Wainwright, 677 F.2d 404, 410 (5th Cir. 1982); United States v. Lee Wood Contracting, Inc., 529 F. Supp. 119 (E.D. Mich. 1982); Chamblee v. Schweiker, 518 F. Supp. 519 (N.D. Ga. 1981).

[266]28 U.S.C. §636(b)(1)(C).

[267]*Id.* When you receive by mail a document from the court or a party that you must file a response with within a certain time period, you can add three days to the time required for responding (*e.g.*, to file objections to a magistrate's recommendation, you would have 13 days from the day after it was mailed to you). See Rule 66(e), FRCP. If due to your incarceration you did not receive the

waiver of your right to appeal the district court's order adopting the magistrate's recommendation.[268] If the magistrate has failed to inform you of these rights, you do not waive them.[269] Your objections must specifically identify the findings that are objectionable.[270]

If you have timely filed objections, the judge who referred your matter to the magistrate must make a de novo determination of those portions of the report or specified proposed findings or recommendations you found objectionable.[271] The court may accept, reject, or modify, in whole or in part, the findings and recommendations of the magistrate.[272] The court, in conducting a careful and complete review of the objectionable portions, may hold its own hearing[273] or may remand the matter to the magistrate for further proceedings.[274]

If the parties have not filed objections to the magistrate's recommendations, the court, in deciding whether to adopt these recommendations, will only review them to see if they are clearly erroneous.[275]

The statute does not make clear whether a jury case can be referred to a magistrate for trial without the parties' consent. One court has held that a magistrate may conduct a jury trial subject to de novo review by the district judge.[276] There are strong arguments against this conclusion.

---

magistrate's recommendations until 6 or 7 days after it was mailed and you do not think you can file your objections within the time left, you should file with the court a motion asking for an extension of time for filing your objections. *See* Consorcio Construction Impregilo v. Mack Trucks, Inc., 497 F. Supp. 591 (E.D. Pa. 1980).

[268]Nettles v. Wainwright, *supra* note 265, at 408; United States v. Walters, 638 F.2d 947, 949-50 (6th Cir. 1981).

[269]United States v. Walters, *id.*

[270]Nettles v. Wainwright, *supra* note 265, at 410.

[271]*Id.;* United States v. Lee Contracting, Inc., *supra* note 265; Chamblee v. Schweiker, *supra* note 265.

[272]28 U.S.C. §636(b)(1)(C); Nettles v. Wainwright, *supra* note 265; Hill v. Duriron, *supra* note 259, at 1215.

[273]Spaulding v. Univ. of Washington, 676 F.2d 1232 (9th Cir. 1982) (calling of witnesses); United States v. Marshall, 609 F.2d 152 (5th Cir. 1980) (credibility of witnesses).

[274]McDonnell Douglas Corp. v. Commodore Business Machines, Inc., 656 F.2d 1309 (9th Cir. 1981), *cert. denied,* 102 S.Ct. 1277 (1981); Federal Deposit Ins. Corp. v. United States, 527 F. Supp. 942 (S.D. W. Va. 1981).

[275]Chamblee v. Schweiker, *supra* note 265.

[276]Coleman v. Hutto, 500 F. Supp. 586 (E.D. Va. 1980); *see also* Bagwell, "Procedural Aspects of Prisoner §1983 and §2254 Cases in the Fifth and Eleventh Circuits," 95 F.R.D. 435, 446-48 (1982).

First, one can argue that having a jury verdict reduced to the status of a magistrate's recommendation which is subject to de novo review by a judge is contrary to the deference ordinarily given to jury verdicts and may therefore violate the Seventh Amendment.[277] Second, the statute pertaining to magistrates specifically provides that they may conduct "all proceedings in a jury or non-jury civil matter" when the parties consent.[278] The provisions pertaining to prisoner cases do not contain any reference to jury trials.[279] Therefore, it is arguable that Congress's failure to say anything about jury trials in the prisoner case section means that it did not intend for magistrates to conduct them without consent.

3. The parties may consent to a magistrate hearing "any and all" civil matters, including jury and non-jury proceedings, and entering final judgment in them.[280] The parties could consent to the magistrate holding a trial with an appeal to the district court,[281] or a direct appeal to the court of appeals.[282] Whether you have consented to an appeal to the district court or directly to the court of appeals, you must file your notice of appeal within 30 days from entry of judgment.[283]

Although magistrates are not full judges, they are officers of the court and you should not feel you are getting second rate justice if you must appear before one. Some of the factors you should keep in mind when determining whether to consent or object to a magistrate handling your case are the following: (1) both sides are entitled to a review of the magistrate's recommendation or decision; (2) it may be easier to have a magistrate come to the prison to hold an evidentiary hearing or trial than a judge; and (3) what you know, or can find out, concerning how s/he has ruled in other prisoner actions.

---

[277]Dunn v. Sears Roebuck & Co., 639 F.2d 1171, 1174-75 (5th Cir. 1981), *corrected on other grounds,* 645 F.2d 511 (5th Cir. 1982).

[278]28 U.S.C. §636(c)(1).

[279]28 U.S.C. §636(b)(1)(B).

[280]28 U.S.C. §636(b)(3), (c)(1); Coleman v. Hutto, *supra* note 276.

[281]28 U.S.C. §636(c)(4); Loewen-America, Inc. v. Advance Distributing Co., Inc., 673 F.2d 219 (8th Cir. 1982). If you choose to appeal to the district court and not directly to the court of appeals from a decision of the magistrate, you can only take an appeal to the court of appeals by discretionary leave to appeal. See 28 U.S.C. §636(c)(5).

[282]28 U.S.C. §636(c)(3); Alaniz v. Calif. Processors, Inc., 690 F.2d 717 (9th Cir. 1982).

[283]Gregg v. Manno, 667 F.2d 1116 (4th Cir. 1981).

M. Court Appearance

The federal district courts have the authority to issue a writ of habeas corpus *ad testificandum*[284] for your production, or the production of your witnesses, at civil proceedings,[285] from anywhere in the country.[286] However, an incarcerated prisoner has no constitutional right to appear personally at a hearing or at a trial in a civil suit s/he has filed. The U.S. Supreme Court, in *Price v. Johnson,*[287] stated:

> Lawful incarceration brings about the necessary withdrawal or limitation of many privileges and rights, a retraction justified by the considerations underlying our penal system. Among those so limited is the otherwise unqualified right given by §272 of the Judicial Code, 28 U.S.C. §294 [now 28 U.S.C. §1651] to parties in all courts of the United States to "plead and manage their own cases personally."[288]

You do have a constitutional right to be present as a defendant in a criminal trial.[289]

The trial court cannot automatically refuse to produce the plaintiff/prisoner or his/her incarcerated witnesses for a civil trial.[290] The Seventh Circuit, quoting from *Price v. Johnson,*[291] found that a district court has the discretion to order a prisoner brought before it in a civil matter.[292]

---

[284]*See* 28 U.S.C. §2241(c)(5); *see also* 28 U.S.C. §1651(a).

[285]*See also* Jerry v. Francisco, 632 F.2d 252 (3d Cir. 1980); Holt v. Pitts, 619 F.2d 558 (5th Cir. 1980)

[286]Stone v. Morris, 546 F.2d 730, 737 (7th Cir. 1976) (*citing* 28 U.S.C. §2241(d)(5)).

[287]334 U.S. 266, 68 S.Ct. 1049 (1948) (held that appeals court had the power to order prisoner brought before it to present oral argument in habeas case).

[288]*Id.* at 285-86. *See also* Wolff v. McDonnell, 418 U.S. 539, 576, 94 S.Ct. 2963 (1974); Clark v. Hendrix, 397 F. Supp. 966, 969 (N.D. Ga. 1975).

[289]*See* Illinois v. Allen, 397 U.S. 337, 90 S.Ct. 1057 (1970); Snyder v. Massachusetts, 291 U.S. 97, 54 S.Ct. 330 (1934).

[290]*See* Spears v. Chandler, 672 F.2d 834 (11th Cir. 1982) (reversed district court holding that it lacked the authority to order prisoner produced for civil trial); Holt v. Pitts, *supra* note 285 (prisoner should be produced at trial where "physical presence will contribute significantly to a fair judgment of his claims." *Id.* at 561). *See also* Jerry v. Francisco, *supra* note 285 (same considerations should be weighed in determining whether incarcerated nonparty should be brought to courthouse).

[291]*Supra* note 287.

[292]Stone v. Morris, *supra* note 286.

[T]his discretion is to be exercised with the best interests of both the prisoner and the government in mind. If it is apparent that the request of the prisoner to argue personally reflects something more than a mere desire to be freed temporarily from the confines of the prison, that he is capable of conducting an intelligent and responsible argument and that his presence in the courtroom may be secured without undue inconvenience or danger, the court would be justified in issuing the writ. But if any of those factors were found to be negative, the court might well decline to order the prisoner to be produced.[293]

Some of the factors that a trial court should consider in determining whether a prisoner or his/her incarcerated witnesses should be allowed to attend a civil proceeding (such as a trial or a habeas corpus evidentiary hearing)[294] include the following:[295]

1. The costs and convenience to the government in transporting these prisoners from their places of incarceration to the courtroom.[296]

2. Any potential danger or security risk that the prisoner would pose. Courts have considered the length of the sentence and the crime of conviction in making this determination.[297]

3. The substantiality of the matter being tried and the chances of plaintiff winning. This should not be a big factor when you request issuance of writs of habeas corpus *ad testificandum* immediately before trial since your case should have already been reviewed for its merits through motions for dismissal and summary judgment.

4. Whether there is a great need for an early determination of the matter. There is a great need for early determination of an injunctive case, whereas a damage case does not have the same urgency.

---

[293]*Supra* note 286, at 735.

[294]See Ch. IX, Sec. E6, for a discussion of a habeas evidentiary hearing.

[295]See the following cases for a discussion of these factors: Heidelberg v. Hammer, 577 F.2d 429, 431 (7th Cir. 1978); Stone v. Morris, *supra* note 286, at 735-36; Matter of Warden of Wisconsin State Prison, 541 F.2d 177, 181 (7th Cir. 1976); *see also* Mitchum v. Purvis, 650 F.2d 647 (5th Cir. 1981); Bonner v. City of Prichard, Ala., 661 F.2d 1206 (11th Cir. 1981); Ball v. Woods, 402 F. Supp. 803 (N.D. Ga. 1975), *aff'd without opinion sub nom.* Ball v. Shambler, 529 F.2d 520 (5th Cir. 1976).

[296]Holt v. Pitts, *supra* note 285 (court of appeals held that the district court did not abuse its discretion when it denied the *pro se* plaintiff's request for a writ to transport him from a federal penitentiary in California to a pretrial conference in Tennessee based on costs and inconvenience).

[297]*See* Ball v. Woods, *supra* note 295, 402 F. Supp. at 809 (the court denied issuance of the writ to a *pro se* prisoner based on his dangerousness and his prsent inability to conduct a meaningful case).

5. The interest of the prisoner in testifying in person compared to his/her testimony being presented through deposition. If the case depends on credibility of the parties, you have a strong argument that the jury should see and hear you testify so it can evaluate your demeanor.

6. Whether the prisoner is represented or is proceeding *pro se,* and if *pro se,* whether his/her presence is necessary to present the case. When you have an attorney and credibility is not a big issue, the court may find your testimony can be received by a reading of the deposition of your testimony. If you are proceeding *pro se,* you have a stronger argument that you are needed at trial so the evidence in your case can be presented to the jury and you can cross-examine the defendants and their witnesses. A court may seek to force counsel upon you. You will have to decide then whether to oppose the appointment or agree to counsel if s/he will consult you in the preparation of your case for trial. A court can not dismiss your case with prejudice if you refuse appointment of counsel.

7. Defendant's interest in an early adjudication of the claims against him/her.[298]

8. If the trial is by judge and not jury, whether it can be held at the prison.

You need not be produced in court for pretrial proceedings, especially if doing so would be expensive or difficult. However, the court cannot then dismiss your case for failure to prosecute because you do not appear at a pretrial conference.[299]

In *Jerry v. Francisco,*[300] it was held that a district court, in deciding whether an incarcerated non-party (usually a witness) needed to be brought to the courthouse, is to rely upon the same considerations as for a *pro se* plaintiff. It has also been held that the *pro se* plaintiff "must demonstrate to the court the nature and materiality of the testimony" of the requested prisoner.[301]

A court may decide that your testimony, or that of your witnesses, can be adequately presented through a deposition without producing you or your witnesses in court. You should probably object to this procedure. If you are not permitted to attend your trial, you will not be able to respond to the evidence and argument presented by the defendant or to cross-examine defendant or his/her witnesses. Having your witnesses testify by

---

[298]Ball v. Woods, *supra* note 295, 402 F. Supp. at 812.

[299]Holt v. Pitts, *supra* note 285; *see also* Camps v. C & P Tel. Co., 692 F.2d 120, 124 and n.41 (D.C. Cir. 1982).

[300]*Supra* note 285.

[301]Cook v. Bounds, 518 F.2d 779 (4th Cir. 1975) (ten of the witnesses Cook had sought had previously escaped and now were scattered at different prisons in Tennessee).

deposition should also be objectionable, since you will not be able to call them for rebuttal purposes if that appears necessary. More important, the judge or jury will not be able to observe your demeanor or your witnesses and are less likely to have any feeling for you as a human being.

If a court wishes to arrange for depositions at which you can present your testimony the way you want it, this may be barely acceptable. If the court proposes to rely on depositions previously taken by the defendant's lawyer, you should vigorously object, since these depositions will have been controlled by your adversary and will reflect the other side's interests rather than yours.

N. Evidence

This section identifies the basic concepts of the law of evidence that you must be familiar with and the most common evidentiary problems you will encounter as a *pro se* prisoner. The section focuses on the Federal Rules of Evidence (FRE), which govern proceedings in federal courts. State rules of evidence will often be similar to the Federal Rules of Evidence, but if you are litigating in state court, you must find out what the state rules are.

The rules of evidence have been the subject of many long books,[302] and we can only scratch the surface of the subject here. If you want to pursue the subject further, you should obtain one of the short guides to evidence prepared for lawyers and law students.[303] Also, many editions of the Federal Rules of Evidence contain the Notes of Advisory Committee on Proposed Rules, which provide useful background information about the rules.

One important evidentiary subject, privileges, is discussed separately in Sec. E2b, *supra.*

1. Basic Concepts

a. Direct evidence

Direct evidence is evidence of the precise fact in issue (*e.g.,* whether guard X hit you with an axe handle) and is generally received from witnesses who saw the act done (*e.g.,* prisoners A and B testify they saw guard X hit you with an axe handle) or heard the words spoken, or through documents prepared by these witnesses.

---

[302]For example, see Wigmore, Evidence (10 volumes, various editions and dates); Weinstein's Evidence (5 volumes, 1982).

[303]The following books can be obtained from West Publishing Co.: Smith's *Review on Evidence;* Rothstein's *Evidence in a Nutshell.*

b.   Circumstantial Evidence

Circumstantial evidence is evidence of facts from which one can reasonably infer a fact in issue. For example, suppose two prisoners testify they saw guard X carrying an axe handle take you shackled into a closed-off room five minutes before you were found unconscious and bloody, with your hands still shackled, lying next to a bloody axe handle. It is reasonable to infer (1) that guard X struck you with the axe handle, and (2) that his statement that you attacked him with a knife is not true (since when you were found unconscious your hands were still shackled). Circumstantial evidence is legally as valid as direct evidence.

c.   Relevance and Materiality

Generally, all evidence that is relevant is admissible. Relevant evidence is defined by Rule 401, FRE, as "evidence having any tendency to make the existence of any fact that is of consequence to the determination of the action more probable or less probable than it would be without the evidence." In other words, evidence is relevant if it helps prove or disprove a fact that is an issue in the lawsuit.

The court may exclude evidence which is relevant "if its probative [proof] value is substantially outweighed by the danger of unfair prejudice, confusion of the issues, or misleading the jury, or by considerations of undue delay, waste of time, or needless presentation of cumulative evidence."

In the past, it was generally said that evidence had to be "material" as well as relevant. Material evidence was defined as evidence tending to prove a fact in dispute. The difference between relevance and materiality was never very clear, and the Federal Rules of Evidence have dropped the concept of materiality and adopted a broad definition of relevance instead.[304] Evidence that is relevant under the above quoted definition can be assumed to be material as well.

d.   Inferences and Presumptions

An inference is a process of reasoning by which a fact or proposition you are trying to prove may be deduced as a logical consequence from other facts already proved or admitted. Inferences are generally made from circumstantial evidence. For example, suppose a jar of flammable liquid was thrown by prisoner B on you while you slept. At a civil trial against prison officials, evidence is presented that this flammable liquid is stored in a locked enclosed building and is only dispensed to guards. The jury can, but does not have to, infer that prisoner B would not have

---

[304]Rule 401, FRE, Notes of Advisory Committee on Proposed Rules.

obtained any of the flammable liquid unless a guard was negligent in the handling of some of the flammable liquid.

If the court *requires* the jury to infer a fact from some other facts, this is called a presumption.[305] A presumption may be rebutted if the opposing party presents some evidence to the contrary. For example, it is presumed that two people living together as man and wife are lawfully married until evidence is shown to the contrary.

e.   Judicial Notice

Courts may take "judicial notice" of facts which are "not subject to reasonable dispute" because they are either "(1) generally known within the territorial jurisdiction of the trial court or . . . (2) capable of accurate and ready determination by resort to sources whose accuracy cannot reasonably be questioned."[306] Judicial notice will rarely be useful in a prison case. Many facts which you may believe are not subject to reasonable dispute (*e.g.,* that most prison guards are racists) will be viewed as very debatable in court, and matters pertaining to prison practices and conditions are seldom "generally known" outside the prison. "Sources whose accuracy cannot reasonably be questioned" will probably be limited to dictionaries, encyclopedias, technical books, maps, charts, etc. Typical matters that courts may take judicial notice of might be the fact that there is usually heavy traffic in New York City at rush hour, or the time the sun rises and sets on a particular day.

f.   Burden of Proof and Prima Facie Case

The burden of proof is the requirement that a party produce a certain amount of evidence in order to establish that something is true. The burden of proof on most issues is on the plaintiff in a civil case. However, there may be certain issues (often called affirmative defenses) on which the defendants have the burden of proof. For example, if the defendants claim that your lawsuit is barred by res judicata or collateral estoppel, they have the burden of proof on that question.[307] However, if they claim that they were not personally involved in the unlawful acts you are complaining about, the burden of proof will still be on you to prove that a particular defendant violated your rights. The courts have not agreed on who bears the burden of proof as to qualified immunity.[308]

---

[305]*See* Rule 301, FRE.

[306]Rule 201(b), FRE.

[307]Hayles v. Randall Motor Co., 455 F.2d 169 (10th Cir. 1972). See Ch. VI, Sec. E3, for a discussion of res judicata and collateral estoppel.

[308]*See* Gomez v. Toledo, 446 U.S. 635, 100 S.Ct. 1920 (1980). See also Ch. VI, Sec. E1d, for a discussion of qualified immunity.

In civil cases, the party with the burden of proof must prove the facts by a "preponderance of the evidence." A fact is proved by a preponderance of the evidence if you show that it is more likely true than not true. The preponderance of the evidence is not determined by the number of witnesses on either side, but by the credibility of the evidence; one credible witness may carry more weight than ten incredible ones.

The party with the burden of proof on an issue also has the burden of going forward with the evidence. That is, s/he must establish a prima facie case. This is done by producing enough evidence to justify a finding in the party's favor unless the evidence is explained or discredited by the other side. Once a party has made a prima facie case, the burden of going forward with the evidence shifts to the other side. The burden of proof does not shift.

You can probably understand this better with an example. Suppose you sue a guard for beating you up. You have the burden of proof and the burden of going forward. If you testify that you were minding your own business and the guard suddenly slugged you, you have met your burden of going forward, and that burden shifts to the guard. If the guard then testifies that you were slashing someone with a knife when s/he slugged you, the guard has met his/her burden of going forward. At that point, the judge or jury will decide if you have proved your case by a preponderance of the evidence. If your story is more credible, you win; if the guard's story is more credible, the guard wins; if the stories are equally credible, the guard also wins, because the burden of proof is on you.

The best way to understand the burden of proof in a particular case is to read other cases involving similar facts and issues and see what the courts have required the parties to prove.

Procedurally, the burden of going forward will become an issue if the defendant makes a motion to dismiss at trial after you have presented your evidence. (See Sec. K7, *supra,* for a discussion of how to respond.) The burden of proof will be an issue at the end of the trial, and you will address it in your closing argument or post-trial brief. (See Sec. K11, *supra,* for a discussion of closing argument.)

2.   Hearsay and Admissions

The Federal Rules of Evidence provide that "[h]earsay is not admissible except as provided by these rules" or by other properly enacted rules.[309] To understand what this means, you first have to understand what is and is not hearsay.

Hearsay is defined as "a statement, other than one made by the de-

---

[309]Rule 802, FRE.

clarant while testifying at the trial or hearing, offered in evidence to prove the truth of the matter asserted.''[310] In other words, you cannot introduce a statement made by a person at some other time and place if the purpose of putting the statement into evidence is to prove what the statement says. Thus, if you sue guard A for beating you up, and if prisoner B tells you, ''I saw guard A hitting you while you were handcuffed,'' you cannot testify in court as to what prisoner B told you to prove that guard A beat you. It is hearsay. The only way to get this evidence before the court is to get prisoner B to testify personally as to what s/he saw.

Written evidence is often hearsay also. Thus, if prisoner B in the above example wrote that he saw guard A beat you, that statement still could not come in as evidence, even if it were notarized, witnessed, etc. (See Sec. N4, *infra,* for more information on written and documentary evidence.)

A statement is not hearsay if it is not placed in evidence to prove the truth of what the statement says. For example, if you wrote a statement and sent it to the warden complaining that guard A beat you up, it would be hearsay in court if you were trying to prove that guard A beat you up. However, if you were trying to prove something else—for example, that you were transferred in retaliation for your complaints to the warden— your complaint could be admitted for the purpose of showing that you had made complaints.

A statement is also not hearsay if it is a prior statement by a witness at the trial and it is used to impeach the witness's credibility or restore the witness's credibility after it is attacked.[311] (The use of prior statements by witnesses is discussed in more detail in Sec. N3c, 4d, *infra.*)

A statement is also not hearsay if it is an ''admission by a party-opponent.'' This is one of the most important aspects of the hearsay rule, because it permits you to use past statements made by the defendants and their agents, employees, etc. The full definition of an admission by a party-opponent is:

> The statement is offered against a party and is (A) his own statement, in either his individual or a representative capacity, or (B) a statement of which he has manifested his adoption or belief in its truth, or (C) a statement by a person authorized by him to make a statement concerning the subject, or (D) a statement by his agent or servant concerning a matter within the scope of his agency or employment, made during the existence of the relationship, or (E) a statement by a co-conspirator of a party during the course and in the furtherance of the conspiracy.[312]

---

[310]Rule 801(c), FRE.

[311]Rule 801(d)(1), FRE.

[312]Rule 801(d)(2), FRE.

Thus, if the warden says to you, "I'm having you transferred because I am sick of your complaining," you can testify that s/he said this in a suit against the warden claiming a retaliatory transfer. Also, if a transfer order is written by a prison employee stating, "Prisoner to be transferred at the Warden's authorization because of constant complaints," that document could be admitted into evidence against the warden as an admission "by a person authorized by him to make a statement concerning the subject" or "by his agent or servant concerning a matter within the scope of his agency or employment."[313] In general, any written or oral statement by a prison employee that helps you in your lawsuit is likely to be an admission and therefore to be admissible in evidence despite the hearsay rule.

There are also many exceptions to the hearsay rule—that is, types of statements that are admissible even though they are hearsay. These are listed in Rule 803, FRE. Among the most important are the "present sense impression" and "excited utterance" exceptions, which admit as evidence statements "describing or explaining an event or condition made while the declarant was perceiving the event or condition, or immediately thereafter," or "relating to a startling event or condition made while the declarant was under the stress of excitement caused by the event or condition."[314] Thus, if you are beaten by guards and then brought into the view of a group of inmates, and the inmates look at you and say things like, "Good God, he's half dead!", those statements made on the scene should be admissible to show what your physical condition was at the time, but not that you were beaten by those guards. Another important exception admits statements reflecting "then existing mental, emotional, or physical condition,"[315] which may permit a witness to testify that s/he heard you screaming "Stop! You're killing me!" while guards were in your cell beating you, because it reflects the pain you were suffering at the time. Statements made for purposes of medical diagnosis or treatment[316] are also admissible. In addition, there are various exceptions pertaining to documentary evidence,[317] which will be discussed in more detail in Sec. N4, *infra*.

---

[313]*Id.*

[314]Rule 803(1), (2), FRE.

[315]Rule 803(3), FRE.

[316]Rule 803(4), FRE.

[317]Rule 803(5), (6), (7), (8), FRE.

3. Testimonial Evidence

a. Competency

Every person, including children and insane persons, is presumed competent to testify until challenged.[318] A person will be held competent if s/he is willing to take an oath or affirmation,[319] has personal knowledge of which s/he will testify,[320] and can communicate that knowledge. Unless you can demonstrate that a witness does not have personal knowledge, was under the influence of drugs or alcohol so that s/he could not have observed, or is incapable of recollection now, that person is competent to testify.

b. Direct Examination

Direct examination of a witness is done by the party calling the witness. You will conduct direct examination of your witnesses, and defendants will conduct direct examination of theirs. Direct examination is usually limited to "non-leading" questions. What constitutes a leading question is hard to explain, and judges may differ in their rulings.[321] The basic idea is that a leading question is one which suggests to the witness what the answer is. For example, if you are trying to establish that guard X was carrying an axe handle at a particular time, you cannot ask on direct examination, "Did guard X have an axe handle in his hands?" because it is a leading question. It is probably a leading question to ask, "What did guard X have in his hand?" It is probably *not* a leading question to ask, "Did guard X have anything in his hand?" and *then* ask, "What did he have in his hand?" It is definitely not a leading

---

[318]Rule 601, FRE.

[319]Rule 603, FRE.

[320]Rule 602, FRE.

[321]One writer states:

A leading question is one that suggests to the witness the answer that is desired. That is, it puts words into the witness's mouth. It may assume to be proved a fact which has not been proved. If it meets that test, it may be leading even though it is put into the alternative. A question that may be answered by a simple yes or no may or may not be leading, but is not leading where it is no more suggestive of one answer than the other. On the other hand, a leading question may be one that calls for something more than a yes or no answer. Questions that are intended to call attention to a subject or subjects about which testimony is desired, but not in themselves suggesting the answers expected, are not leading.

Hunter, *Federal Trial Handbook* at §40.3 (1974).

question to ask "Did you observe anything unusual about guard X?" As a *pro se* litigant, you will probably not be held to as strict a standard in this respect as an attorney would be. However, you should do your best to avoid leading questions on direct examination.

The rules about leading questions apply to defendant's lawyer too. If your adversary asks a leading question of a defense witness, you may object. You are allowed to use leading questions on direct examination under certain limited circumstances, such as when you call a hostile witness, an adverse party, or a witness identified with an adverse party.[322] You may also use leading questions "as may be necessary to develop [the witness's] testimony."[323] This provision includes establishing preliminary matters which are not disputed, such as the witness's presence at a particular time and place, dealing with witnesses who have difficulty testifying because of age or mental or physical condition, and helping to get a confused witness back on the track. (If your witness does get confused, you should ask the court's permission to ask a leading question to overcome the witness's problem.)

The purpose of direct examination for you is to establish your claim, and your questions should be designed to prove your case and not to disprove something you think the other side may try to show later. For example, if you think the defendants will try to show that you have threatened your witness to make him/her testify, do not ask the witness on direct examination if s/he has been threatened; save it for redirect examination or your rebuttal case.[324]

Whenever possible, you should go over the testimony of each of your witnesses a day or so before trial. You should have all the questions that you are going to ask written out and go through them with the witness.

c. Cross-Examination

Cross-examination is conducted by the party who did not call the witness. It takes place after direct examination and is generally limited to the subjects that were covered in direct examination and matters relating to the witness's credibility.[325]

On cross-examination, leading questions are permitted;[326] in fact, they are generally preferred by most lawyers, because they permit the

---

[322]*See* Rule 611, FRE.

[323]*Id.*

[324]See Sec. N3d, *infra,* for a discussion of redirect; see also Sec. K9, *supra,* for a discussion of rebuttal.

[325]*See* Rule 611(b), FRE.

[326]Rule 611(c), FRE.

questioner to keep greater control over the situation. Thus, on cross-examination, you would be permitted to ask, "Did guard X have an axe handle in his hand?" For that matter, you could ask, "Guard X had an axe handle in his hand, didn't he?" What you are not permitted to do is argue with the witness or badger the witness. The other side is subject to the same limitations when cross-examining you or your witnesses.

Cross-examination is probably the trickiest part of a trial and the one where you must think the most quickly and clearly. When you are on the stand being cross-examined, remember that your adversary is trying to do two things: to discredit your testimony, and to discredit you as a person. In order to do the latter, the opposing lawyer will probably try to make you angry, hostile, or confused on the witness stand so s/he can make you look undeserving or take advantage of the jury's or judge's stereotypes about prisoners. Remember this, and do not lash out at the opposing attorney. Keep your dignity, answer the questions, do not try to argue, and if you do not understand the question, ask to have it repeated. If the attorney badgers you or shouts at you, you can ask the judge to tell him/her to stop; if the judge does not do this, accept it and do not argue with the judge. By keeping your dignity on the stand, you will keep the case focused on the issues in the case and not on the personalities.

When the defendants present their case, you will have an opportunity to cross-examine their witnesses. The most important aspect of cross-examination is having a clear idea of what it is that you want to accomplish. It is a big mistake simply to get up and ask a lot of questions that result only in repetition of the witness's story; this only bolsters the witness's testimony. Instead, you should focus on particular points where you can help your case or hurt the other side's case through cross-examination. Some of the ways to do this are as follows.

—*Establishing the witness's bias, prejudice, or interest.* A witness's testimony can be attacked by showing that the witness has some reason to lie. For example, if several guards are buttressing each other's false testimony to cover up the misconduct of one of them, you might try to bring out the fact that they work together, see each other every day, rely on each other in tight spots, hang out together after work, etc. If you previously complained about a prison employee who is testifying, that fact might indicate a motivation to testify falsely against you. If an employee violated prison rules and would be subject to discipline if s/he were found out, another motive to testify falsely is shown. Generally, you can ask the witness about these subjects on cross-examination; if you have evidence to prove something the witness denies, you can put it into evidence on rebuttal.

These same tactics can and will be used by the defense against you.

Cross-examination on the basis of bias, prejudice, or interest is one of several forms of "impeachment" of a witness's credibility.

—*Testing the witness's opportunity to observe.* Sometimes witnesses will testify to things it is doubtful they had an opportunity to see or hear. If a guard testifies that s/he saw you strike the first blow in an altercation, but you know s/he was at the other end of a long gallery and you were surrounded by other inmates at the time, you can bring these facts out with appropriate questions.

—*Limiting the witness's testimony.* Sometimes a witness will help the other side in some small respect but will not be able to testify at all about some other major aspect of the case. Sometimes it is helpful to emphasize this on cross-examination. For example, if a guard testified that you walked out of a housing unit with two other guards peacefully and in good physical condition, and you claim that you were beaten in a stairwell, you might ask, "You didn't see me after we left the housing unit, did you? You couldn't see into the stairwell, could you? So if they beat me in the stairwell, you couldn't see it, could you?" Also, a prison official may testify as to certain prison practices without knowing whether the practices were followed in your case. You might ask, for example, "You don't have any idea, do you, whether I actually received notice of charges in advance of the hearing, do you?"

—*Highlighting helpful parts of the testimony.* Sometimes an adverse witness will give some testimony that is helpful to you. Often, this testimony will consist of something that contradicts another defense witness. You can make this clear to the judge or jury by asking questions about the testimony that helped your case. For example, if two guards claim that you assaulted one of them and had to be removed from the housing unit by force, and a third guard testifies that you did commit the assault but that you left the housing unit peacefully, on cross-examination you can ask the third guard, "You testified, didn't you, that you saw me leaving the housing unit peacefully?" This testimony may help undermine the testimony of the other guards.

—*Stating your case again.* Sometimes it is effective to state your case again through accusatory leading questions. You have to be careful to avoid getting into an argument with the witness, and you have to keep it short and punchy. After all, since the witness will presumably deny everything, you are looking for dramatic effect rather than information. For example, you might ask at the end of a cross-examination, "Isn't it true that you hit me in the face while I was handcuffed? Isn't it true that you stood by while Officer Smith hit me in the head with an axe handle? Isn't it true that you walked out of my cell leaving me handcuffed and bleeding? Isn't it true that you ignored me when I called for medical help?" Since the answer to each of these questions will probably be a loud "No," you should probably avoid this tactic with a self-confident witness whose credibility has not been successfully attacked. You run the risk of bolstering defendants' case. If the witness is not self-confident, or if you have successfully impeached his/her credibility, an accusatory cross-examination may be more effective.

—*Impeachment by use of prior inconsistent statements.* If a witness testifies in a way that is inconsistent with a prior statement s/he made, you can cross-examine the witness about the statement. There is an accepted way of doing this properly and effectively. First, get the witness to repeat the inconsistent testimony. Then, ask the witness if s/he made the other statement, giving the time and place it was made. For example:

> Q: You testified, didn't you, that the only officer present when you took me to segregation was Officer Smith?
> Q: Do you recall giving a deposition at the prison on January 11 of this year?
> Q: And were you under oath?
> Q: And were you asked these questions, and did you give these answers? [Read inconsistent testimony.]

Use a similar sequence of questions if the prior inconsistent statement was made in an official report, in conversation, or some other form.

If the witness denies making the statement, you may offer the statement into evidence as long as "the witness is afforded an opportunity to explain or deny the [statement] and the opposite party is afforded an opportunity to interrogate him thereon. . . ."[327] If you do not confront the witness with the prior inconsistent statement on cross-examination, you may lose the chance to put it in evidence.

You should be very sure that the prior statement is actually inconsistent with the witness's present testimony, or your attempt to impeach the witness may actually bolster his/her testimony. However, a prior statement does not have to be flatly contradictory to be inconsistent. A serious omission in the prior statement may also be inconsistent. For example, if you were charged with assaulting an officer, and at trial a witness accused you of assaulting the officer with a broomstick, you could impeach the witness with an initial report in which the broomstick was not mentioned.

A prior *consistent* statement may be put into evidence if the witness has been subjected to an "express or implied charge against him of recent fabrication or improper influence or motive."[328] If your credibility is attacked and if you have prior statements—for example, a complaint to the warden or a letter to your family—which show you have been telling the same story all along, you may be able to place these prior statements on the record.

---

[327]Rule 613(b), FRE.

[328]Rule 801(d)(1)(B).

Do not use every possible inconsistency you find in the record. Be selective and choose the ones that make the most dramatic points.

—*Impeachment by reference to criminal convictions, prior bad acts, character, etc.* This subject is dealt with in detail in Sec. N5, *infra*.

d. Redirect Examination

Redirect examination is available to the party calling the witness once the cross-examination has been completed. Leading questions are generally prohibited on redirect examination. If your witness has given harmful or confusing testimony on cross-examination, you may seek to cure the harm or confusion on redirect examination. On redirect, you are limited to the subjects covered during cross-examination. You can not introduce new evidence during redirect that you should have introduced on direct examination but forgot.

After redirect examination, recross will be permitted, limited to the subjects covered in the redirect.

4. Documentary Evidence

In most cases, documents you will want to use at trial will fall into one of several categories: documents created by prison personnel in the course of their duties, documents created by you or by other prisoners such as lists of lost property, grievances, or eyewitness accounts of events, or prior testimony at depositions or court proceedings. We have focused on these types of documents. The rules cited in this section will be your starting point if you have a problem involving a different kind of document.

a. Authentication of Documents.

The party offering a document into evidence must demonstrate its authenticity—that is, that the document is what it claims to be and not a fake. However, if there is no actual dispute that the document is authentic, no proof is necessary. There will rarely be a dispute as to records created by prison personnel. If the record was created by someone else, such as yourself, the testimony of the person who created it is the best way to authenticate it. The technical requirements of authentication are discussed in Rules 901 and 902, FRE.

b. Best Evidence

The "best evidence" rule is an old rule which provides that to prove what a document says, you must introduce the document. Testimony about the document or references to it in another document are not good enough. The rule does not apply if the document itself is lost, destroyed, or otherwise unavailable, or if the other side has it, knows it will be an issue, and fails to produce it.[329] The "best evidence" rule once limited the admissibility of copies, but the Federal Rules of Evidence now provide that duplicates are admissible unless there is a genuine question as to their authenticity or some other circumstance making it unfair to use the duplicate.[330]

c.   Hearsay Problems

Any document may appear to be hearsay.[331] You should be prepared to explain why any document you wish to introduce either is not hearsay or falls into an exception to the hearsay rule. This is not difficult when the document is part of the regular prison recordkeeping system. Often, a prison document will be a statement by one of the defendants or by an agent of one of the defendants, and can therefore come in as an admission by a party-opponent.[332] In almost all cases, prison documents will be admissible as "records of regularly conducted activity" (often termed "business records") or "public records and reports." These terms are defined in Rule 803(6), (8), FRE.

Documents qualifying as records of regularly conducted activity or as public records and reports may not be admitted "if the sources of information or other circumstances indicate lack of trustworthiness."[333] One court has held that reports made by prison guards concerning events for which they are being sued are "dripping with motivations to misrepresent" and for that reason are not trustworthy enough to be admitted.[334] You should think twice before you try to keep such records out of evidence, however. If the defendants' lawyer wishes to put the documents in to avoid calling certain witnesses, keeping the document out may mean that more witnesses will be called to testify against you. This can be good or bad, depending on who the witnesses are and how impressive they are likely to be. Also, if the documents are not very credible, or if they are inconsistent with each other or with the testimony, you may be better off having them in the record.

Documents which are not written by defendants or their agents and

---

[329]Rule 1004, FRE.

[330]*See* Rule 1003, FRE.

[331]See Sec. N2, *supra,* for a discussion of hearsay.

[332]*See* Rule 801(d)(2), FRE; see Sec. N2, *supra,* for further discussion of admissions.

[333]Rule 803(6), (8) FRE.

[334]*See* Bracey v. Herringa, 466 F.2d 702, 704-05 (7th Cir. 1972).

which are not part of regular prison practice are harder to get into evidence. Generally, written statements that you obtain from witnesses will not be admissible at trial, even if they are sworn to. You should plan on calling the witnesses to testify if you need their evidence. Even if a witness is unavailable, a prior statement is inadmissible unless it is prior testimony in court or at a deposition or is a statement under belief of impending death, a statement against interest, or a statement of personal or family history.[335] The court has discretion to admit a hearsay statement of an unavailable witness if the statement appears to be trustworthy and a number of other requirements are met,[336] but you should not expect this to happen in a factually contested prison case.

Where a witness's credibility has been attacked in certain ways, documents containing prior consistent statements by the witness may be admissible. (See Sec. N5c, *infra*.)

Sometimes you or one of your witnesses will have written something down when it happened but will not be able to testify from memory by the time of trial. For example, you might make a list of your lost property right after it was lost, or make a list of volumes missing from the law library while working there. You cannot place this document into evidence; however, you can testify that the document was written when the matter was fresh in your mind and that it was accurate when you wrote it, and then read it into the record.[337]

d.   Depositions and Prior Testimony.

Depositions and testimony from prior court proceedings are always admissible to impeach the testimony of a witness.[338] Depositions may be used as a substitute for live testimony if the witness is dead, more than 100 miles from the court, or unavailable because of age, illness, infirmity, or imprisonment.[339] Under this rule, a court may be tempted to refuse to produce you or your witnesses for trial if the defendants have taken depositions.[340] You should argue vigorously that it is unfair for you to have to present your case through depositions which were taken by the other side to prepare their case and that these depositions do not adequately reflect the nature of your case.

Deposition testimony can be excluded if it would not be admissible

---

[335]*See* Rule 804(b), FRE.

[336]*Id.*

[337]*See* Rule 803(5), FRE.

[338]Rule 32(a)(1), FRCP; Rule 801(d)(1), FRE.

[339]Rule 32(a)(3), FRCP.

[340]See Sec. M, *supra,* for a discussion of court appearance.

from a witness on the stand.[341] For example, if a witness gives hearsay testimony in a deposition, that part of the deposition should not be admissible at trial, if you timely object to its admission as being hearsay, unless it falls within one of the exceptions to the hearsay prohibition. However, the rules also provide that if a party offers part of a deposition, other parts may also be introduced;[342] often, the result is that the whole deposition goes into evidence.

e.   Handling Documentary Evidence

Federal courts generally try to streamline the use of documents; they have little patience with technical disputes at trial, particularly about subjects like authenticity or whether a document is a business or public record. You should therefore try to work these problems out before trial. One way to do this with your documents is to file a request for admissions[343] that the documents you wish to introduce are authentic, that they are admissible as business or public records, etc.[344] If you want to keep certain documents out of evidence, file a motion *in limine* explaining the reasons well before trial. (See Sec. 6, *infra,* for a discussion of these motions.) If you do not do either of these things but the court has a pretrial conference,[345] bring the documents to it that you wish to introduce and ask the other side to stipulate that they are authentic and admissible, and inform the court at that time of any evidence you know of that you think should be excluded.

Do not make notes, underlines, or other marks on documents you wish to put into evidence. Since your notes and marks are not admissible, you may wind up in a long argument about whether the whole document has to be excluded, or there may be a delay while the parties search for a clean copy of the document.

When you wish to put a document into evidence at trial, use the following procedure. State on the record what the document is and hand it to the court reporter to be marked as an exhibit. (You should have

---

[341]*See* Rule 32(b), FRCP.

[342]*See* Rule 32(c)(4), FRCP.

[343]See Sec. E2f, *supra,* for a discussion of request for admissions.

[344]For example, you could ask defendants to admit that:

(1) The attached document, dated February 19, 1983, and headed "Adjustment Committee Notice," is a true copy of the disciplinary change taken against the plaintiff.
(2) The attached document headed "Adjustment Committee Notice," dated February 19, 1983, is a public record setting forth the actions of a public agency.

[345]See Sec. I for a discussion of pretrial conference.

marked the documents prior to trial.) At that point, it will be given a number or letter and deemed "marked for identification." Next, give it to the lawyer for the other side to inspect. Tell the judge if there is an admission or stipulation as to its authenticity or admissibility. If not, you may have to "lay a foundation" by testifying, having a witness testify, or producing other evidence that the document is authentic, that it is a business record, etc. After this has been done, offer the document into evidence. The other side will have a chance to object, and the judge will rule.

You should keep a list of all the exhibits, noting which ones are only marked for identification and which ones are actually admitted into evidence. Before you close your case, you should be sure that all the documents you want in the record have been admitted into evidence. If the judge has delayed a ruling on any of the documents, request the judge to rule before the taking of the evidence is closed.

5. Prior Records of Plaintiff and Defendant

The rules of evidence place limits on when and how evidence of prior crimes and other misconduct can be used in litigation.

a. Criminal Convictions

Under Rule 609, FRE, a witness's prior convictions can be put into evidence if the crime

(1) was punishable by death or imprisonment in excess of one year under the law under which he was convicted, and the court determines that the probative value of admitting this evidence outweighs its prejudicial effect to the defendant, or (2) involved dishonesty or false statement, regardless of the punishment.[346]

The use of convictions which occurred more than ten years previously is strictly limited by the rule; however, if you went to prison for the crime, the ten years is calculated from the date you were released from prison, not the date of the conviction.[347] Thus, if your prior conviction (or your witness's) is old enough, or if the longest sentence you could have received was a year or less and the crime did not involve dishonesty or false statement, you may be able to get the conviction excluded from evidence.

You may be able to get other crimes excluded as well. Rule 609 also provides that unless the crime "involved dishonesty or false statement," the court must determine before it can admit the crime into evidence

---

[346]Rule 609(a), FRE.

[347]Rule 609(b), FRE.

"that the probative value of admitting this evidence outweighs its prejudicial effect to the defendant. . . ."[348] Some federal courts have held that this provision only applies to criminal defendants and cannot be used to exclude convictions in civil cases.[349] Others have used it to exclude criminal convictions in civil cases.[350] Still others have held that Rule 403, FRE,[351] permits them to exclude criminal convictions even if Rule 609 does not.[352] Depending on your judge's view of the law, you may be able to get more recent, serious convictions excluded from evidence if they do not have much to do with credibility and if there is a likelihood that they would prejudice a jury against you.[353]

Prior convictions are generally used only to impeach the credibility of a party or witness.[354] They are not supposed to be used to show that you are a bad person and ought to lose your lawsuit, or that because you did something in the past (like assault an officer) that you probably did it again in the case before the court.[355] However, you prior convictions may be admitted if there is some other reason they may be relevant, for example, to prove "motive, opportunity, intent, preparation, plan, knowledge, identify, or absence of mistake or accident."[356]

Generally, prior convictions are brought out through cross-examination, and if the witness denies the conviction, the record of conviction may be admitted. The details of the crime usually are not admitted.

If your criminal record, or that of one of your witnesses, is going to come in, you should probably bring it out yourself at the beginning of the testimony ("pull its teeth," as trial lawyers say). In order to know

---

[348]Rule 609(a), FRE.

[349]See Garnett v. Kepner, 541 F. Supp. 241, 244-45 (M.D. Pa. 1982).

[350]See Howard v. Gonzales, 658 F.2d 352, 358-59 (5th Cir. 1981).

[351]This rule states in part, "Although relevant evidence may be excluded if its probative value is substantially outweighed by the danger of unfair prejudice, confusion of the issues, or misleading the jury. . . ."

[352]Rozier v. Ford Motor Co., 573 F.2d 1332 (5th Cir. 1978).

[353]See, e.g., United States v. Alberti, 470 F.2d 878, 882 (2d Cir. 1972) (assault conviction "does not relate to truthfulness or untruthfulness"); United States v. Puco, 453 F.2d 539, 542 (2d Cir. 1971) (". . . we do not believe that a narcotics conviction is particularly relevant to in-court veracity").

[354]Rule 609(a), FRE.

[355]Rule 404(b), FRE, states, "Evidence of other crimes . . . is not admissible to prove the character of a person in order to show that he acted in conformity therewith."

[356]Id.

whether to do this, you obviously need a prior ruling as to whether your convictions will be admitted. This ruling can be obtained through a motion *in limine,* discussed in Sec. N6, *infra.*

b.   Prior bad acts

Rule 404(b), FRE, provides that "Evidence of other crimes, wrongs, or acts is not admissible to prove the character of a person in order to show that he acted in conformity therewith. It may, however, be admissible for other purposes, such as proof of motive, opportunity, intent, preparation, plan, knowledge, identity, or absence of mistake or accident." This means, for example, that prison officials should not be able to show that you have prior disciplinary convictions for assaulting officers in order to prove that you started an altercation about which you are suing. It also means that you cannot show that an officer beat up ten other prisoners in order to show that s/he beat you up too. However, if you or your adversary can think of some other reason for the evidence to come in, it may be admitted. For example, you might argue that an officer's prior assaults show a motive (hostility to prisoners) or an intent (to harm prisoners who are outspoken), which would be relevant to whether the officer used excessive force against you. This kind of argument can also be used against you; your disciplinary record may reveal your motive, intent, etc. Whether the judge will admit this kind of evidence should depend on whether its value as proof outweighs the danger of unfair prejudice.[357]

c.   Character Evidence

Evidence of a person's character is admissible only under strictly limited circumstances set forth in Rules 404, 405, and 608, FRE. Character evidence is restricted because it is likely to be a distraction from the main factual issues in the case.[358] You will generally not be able to put in favorable evidence from your institutional record or the testimony of counselors, ministers, etc., in order to show that you are a good person. This kind of evidence will generally not be admitted unless you can think of another reason why it is relevant. For example, if you claim that you were put in administrative segregation in retaliation for legal action, evidence of a good institutional record would be relevant to show that the defendants lied when they claimed you were a danger to security.

---

[357]*See* Stengel v. Belcher, 522 F.2d 438, 442-43 (6th Cir. 1975), *cert. denied,* 429 U.S. 118 (1976).

[358]Rule 404(a), FRE, Notes of Advisory Committee on Proposed Rules.

6.   Pretrial Rulings on Evidence: The Motion *In Limine*

Most decisions on whether to admit evidence come during the trial when an objection is made. The problem with this procedure is that the evidence may come out before the objection can be made, or the jury may get an idea of what it is while the objection is being argued. Also, sometimes you need to know before the trial what is coming in so you can plan your case.

If you know there will be an important evidentiary issue, you can request a pretrial ruling through a motion *in limine* (Latin for "at the beginning"). The best way to make this motion is in writing at least several weeks (preferably longer) before the trial. You can also make the motion orally at a pretrial conference or just before the trial begins. In your motion, you should tell the court what the evidence is and why you think it should be kept out or let in.

In some cases, the judge may be reluctant to rule before trial because s/he may feel that hearing other evidence will make it easier to make the right ruling. In that case, you should stress to the court any reason why you need a ruling to prepare your case—for example, to know if you should mention your criminal record at the beginning of your testimony.

O.   Procedures After a Decision

1.   Relief From Judgment or Order

Rule 60, Fed.R.Civ.P., permits a judgment or order to be corrected or vacated under certain circumstances. This rule does not provide a substitute for an appeal.[359] However, it may be useful in certain limited circumstances. Clerical errors in judgments, orders, or other parts of the record may be corrected at any time.[360] A party may obtain relief from a judgment within one year on a showing of "mistake, inadvertence, surprise, or excusable neglect,"[361] newly discovered evidence, or fraud or misrepresentation by an adverse party.[362] (You cannot accuse the other

---

[359]Eutectic Corp. v. Metco, Inc., 597 F.2d 32 (2d Cir. 1979). *But see* D.C. Federation of Civic Associations v. Volpe, 520 F.2d 451 (D.C. Cir. 1975) (party may move trial court to correct its own error before time for appeal has run).

[360]See Rule 60(a). *See also* In re Merry Queen Transfer Corp., 266 F. Supp. 605, 607 (S.D.N.Y. 1967); Bershad v. McDonough, 469 F.2d 1333 (7th Cir. 1972).

[361]*See* Kenniar Corp. v. Crawford Door Sales Co., 49 F.R.D. 3 (D.S.C. 1970) (not being represented by counsel has been taken into consideration); Marshall v. Monroe & Sons, Inc., 615 F.2d 1156 (6th cir. 1980).

[362]*See* Armour & Co. v. Nard, 56 F.R.D. 610 (D. Iowa 1972) (fraud under

side of fraud or misrepresentation just because they have opposed your claims and won; you must have some concrete evidence of fraud besides what you presented unsuccessfully at trial.) A party may also use Rule 60(b) to obtain relief from a judgment which is void, which has been satisfied or which, for some reason, should not continue to be effective, or for "any other reason justifying relief from the operation of the judgment." This portion of Rule 60 may be useful where your case has been dismissed and you were not aware that a motion was pending (e.g., you were recently transferred and your mail took a long time to catch up with you), or the court granted summary judgment to defendants without informing you that you should file an affidavit in opposition.[363]

2. Enforcement and Modification of Judgments

Winning a judgment does not always mean that you have succeeded in vindicating your rights. Sometimes you have to take further action to enforce or execute[364] the judgment. In some major prison reform cases, enforcement efforts have continued for many years because of the refusal or inability of prison officials to obey court orders.[365] Unfortunately, if prison officials choose not to obey a judgment you have obtained, it may take a lot of additional time and effort actually to obtain your rights. Sometimes you will need to give the defendant numerous opportunities to comply with the judgment before seeking enforcement of it. Also, courts are often *very* reluctant to hold governmental officials in contempt for not obeying judgments.

A judgment is not automatically enforceable the moment it is signed. The losing party has ten days to file a motion for new trial or a motion for judgment notwithstanding the verdict, during which time the prevailing party cannot seek an execution of a money judgment.[366] If the

---

60(b)(3) reaches only that by an adverse party, whereas fraud by a third party may be cognizable under 60(b)(6)). *See also* Clarkson Co., Ltd v. Shaheen, 544 F.2d 624, 631 (2d Cir. 1976) (must be established by clear and convincing evidence).

[363]*See* Gordon v. Leeke, 574 F.2d 1147, 1151 (4th Cir. 1978), *cert. denied sub nom.* Leeke v. Gordon, 439 U.S. 970 (1978).

[364] Obtaining compliance with a court order is called "enforcement"; this term is most frequently used in connection with injunctive orders. Enforcement of a money judgment is often referred to as "execution" of the judgment.

[365]*See* Palmigiano v. Garrahy, 448 F. Supp. 659 (D.R.I. 1978) (contempt granted against prison officials); Newman v. State of Alabama, 466 F. Supp. 628 (M.D. Ala. 1979) (appointment of receiver over state prison system).

[366]*See* Rule 62(a), FRCP. An injunction can be enforced from the moment it is issued unless the losing party has obtained a stay. *See also* Gross v. JFD Mfg., Inc., 31 F.R.D. 250 (E.D.N.Y. 1962).

losing party files one of these motions within the ten days after entry of judgment, the court has the discretion to continue to stay enforcement of the judgment until the motion before it is decided.[367]

You are allowed discovery in aid of execution of a money judgment. The scope of discovery is very broad under the federal discovery rules;[368] in state courts, the rules vary.

a.   Collecting a Money Judgment

If you have obtained a money judgment against the defendants and they have not filed an appeal and either obtained a stay of the judgment or posted a security bond, you need to discuss with defendants' attorney how long it will take the state or other governmental agency to issue a check if defendant was found officially liable, or how long it will take the defendant to pay if s/he was held personally liable.[369] It normally takes a state 30-60 days to issue a check. A court will probably not order the defendants to issue the check any faster than this unless you can show they are acting in bad faith, which is very hard to show.

When a defendant, either the state when it is officially liable or the prison official when s/he is personally liable, has failed to pay a money judgment within 120 days and you have communicated to no avail with defendant's attorney on numerous occasions to resolve this nonpayment, you should consider seeking a writ of execution. A writ of execution is the only means provided by Rule 69, FRCP,[370] for collection of a money judgment from a defendant held personally liable. If the defendant has been held officially liable, you can either seek a writ of execution or mandamus action against the state. Since issuance of a writ of execution is to be in accordance with the practice and procedures of the state in which the district court is located, you must examine your state law as to procedures for issuance of this writ.[371]

----

[367]Rule 62(b), FRCP. *See also* Ohio-Sealy Mattress Mfg. Co. v. Sealy, Inc., 585 F.2d 821 (7th Cir. 1978).

[368]Rule 69(a), FRCP. *See also* G-Fours, Inc. v. Miele, 496 F.2d 809 (2d Cir. 1974). For a discussion of the discovery procedures, see Sec. E2, *supra*.

[369]Sometimes the state or municipal government will pay the judgment against an individual officer under an "indemnity statute." *See, e.g.,* N.Y. Public Officers' Law, §17 (Supp. 1982-83). Be sure to find out if your state or locality has this type of statute.

[370]*See* Gabovitch v. Lundy, 584 F.2d 559 (1st Cir. 1978).

[371]*See* Traveler's Insurance Co. v. Lawrence, 509 F.2d 84 (9th Cir. 1974) (Rule 69 makes availability and effect of federal process subject to state law). *See also* First National Bank of Boston v. Antonio Santisteban & Co., Inc., 285 F.2d 855 (1st Cir. 1961) (federal writ of execution does not reach unearned wages of a

You should also allege in your motion for enforcement of the money judgment that a former action was commenced by you and that a judgment was rendered on your behalf. You should then list the name of the court, the type of cause of action, the time and place of judgment, the amount of the judgment, the person in whose favor and against whom it was rendered, and that the amount has not been paid.[372] If you can, you should also attach a copy of the judgment to your motion.

b.   Enforcing or Modifying an Injunctive Order

An injunctive order may be enforced through a motion for a finding of contempt or through a motion that may be called a "motion to enforce" or a "motion for further relief." It is not totally clear which approach is best. On the one hand, courts are notoriously reluctant to hold public officials in contempt; on the other, one court has held that a judgment of contempt is the *only* proper way to deal with noncompliance problems.[373] The safest approach is probably to ask for the relief you need and rely on both the contempt power and the court's equitable and statutory power to enforce its order.

1) Contempt

There are two types of contempt—criminal and civil. We are not interested in criminal contempt since it is aimed at vindicating the dignity of the court.[374] It is not the dignity of the court you will be seeking to

---

Puerto Rican judgment debtor because Puerto Rico law gives no effect to such a writ); United States ex rel. Marcus v. Lord Elec. Co., 43 F. Supp. 12 (W.D. Pa. 1942) (bank deposits affected by writ of execution because state law so provided). However, there is some authority that state laws preventing execution of a judgment may not be applied to bar enforcement of a federal statute. Collins v. Thomas, 649 F.2d 1203 (5th Cir. 1981).

[372]Bower v. Cassanave, 44 F. Supp. 501 (S.D.N.Y. 1941); see also Rule 9(e), FRCP.

[373]Newman v. State of Alabama, 683 F.2d 1312 (11th Cir. 1982), *cert. denied,* 103 S.Ct. 1773 (1983).

[374]Criminal contempts are "those prosecuted to preserve the power and vindicate the dignity of the courts, and to punish for disobedience of their orders. . . . [They] are punitive in their nature and the government, the courts, and the people are interested in their prosecution." In re Nevitt, 117 F. 448, 458 (8th Cir. 1902); *cf.* United States v. United Mine Workers, 330 U.S. 258, 302, 67 S.Ct. 677 (1947). Thus, the court, not an adverse party, may institute criminal contempt proceedings upon its own motion. Rule 42(b), FRCrP, when a violation of its orders constitutes an affront to its dignity and warrants punishment. *See also* Clark v. Boynton, 362 F.2d 992 (5th Cir. 1966), for a discussion of the differences between civil and criminal contempts.

vindicate, but your right to have a judgment that was rendered favorably to you enforced. Civil contempt serves

> to preserve and enforce the rights of private parties to suits, and to compel obedience to orders and decrees made to enforce the rights and administer the remedies to which the court has found them to be entitled . . . [they] are civil, remedial, and coercive in their nature, and the parties chiefly interested in their conduct and prosecution are the individuals whose private rights and remedies they were instituted to protect or enforce. . . .[375]

Civil contempt can be instituted only by a party seeking to enforce the court's judgment.[376]

Civil contempt has a two-fold purpose: (1) to compensate the prevailing parties for losses or damages caused by the other's noncompliance, and (2) to coerce the derelict person into compliance with the original order.[377] As part of the relief of a civil contempt order, a court could order a governmental official to be incarcerated.[378] But the character and purpose of the incarceration must be demonstrated to be remedial: "[t]he decree in such cases is that the defendant stand committed unless and until he performs the affirmative act required by the court's order."[379] To this end, courts may use "wide discretion in fashioning a remedy,"[380] and may order a "variety of acts" designed to meet "the requirements of full remedial relief."[381] Courts may also impose a fine as a penalty for civil contempt against prison officials. This fine can either be paid to the injured party or to the federal government. Other actions a court might take based on a contempt finding include appointing a master or monitor to supervise compliance;[382] requiring inspections, recordkeeping, or reports to the courts; or any other action that makes sense as a way of ensuring compliance.

---

[375]United States v. United Mine Workers, *id.* at 303-04. *See also* Shillitani v. United States, 384 U.S. 364, 370, 86 S.Ct. 1531 (1966) ("There can be no question that courts have inherent power to enforce compliance with their lawful orders through civil contempt.").

[376]MacNeil v. United States, 236 F.2d 149, 153 (1st Cir. 1956).

[377]McComb v. Jacksonville Paper Co., 336 U.S. 187, 191, 69 S.Ct. 38 (1949); United Mine Workers, *supra* note 374, 330 U.S. at 304-05.

[378]Newman v. State of Alabama, *supra* note 373, at 1318.

[379]Gompers v. Buck's Stove & Range Co., 221 U.S. 418, 442, 31 S.Ct. 492 (1911).

[380]Vuitton et Fils, S.A. v. Carousel Handbags, 592 F.2d 126, 130 (2d Cir. 1979).

[381]McComb v. Jacksonville Paper Co., *supra* note 377, at 193.

[382]Powell v. Ward, 487 F. Supp. 917, 935 (S.D.N.Y. 1980); Jones v. Wittenberg, 73 F.R.D. 82, 85 (N.D. Ohio 1976).

A court may hold a party in contempt whenever s/he has failed or refuse to comply with a valid order of which s/he had notice and the ability to obey.[383] The party against whom civil contempt sanctions are sought need not have failed to have complied with the whole order.[384] The party need only have failed to comply with some substantial portion of the court order. You also need not prove that the defendant's actions were intentional, since willfulness is not an element of civil contempt.[385]

Courts, in determining whether a party should be held in civil contempt, have used different standards. One court considered whether the "defendants have been reasonably diligent and energetic in attempting to accomplish what was ordered."[386] (*E.g.,* if the court has ordered all prisoners to be reclassified, it will consider whether the defendants have used the resources they have available to comply.) Another court asked whether the defendants had taken "all the reasonable steps within their power to ensure compliance with the orders."[387] (*E.g.,* if you had only named prison officials in your lawsuit and you have obtained a judgment requiring state funds to be spent, the court will probably not hold the defendants in civil contempt if the legislature will not appropriate the funds.)

The party seeking civil contempt sanctions has the burden of proving the noncompliance by "clear and convincing" evidence. You need not show that the other party has the capacity to comply with the judgment.[388] The burden is on them to show the court that they do not have the capacity.[389]

A person must have had knowledge of a court order before being held in contempt of it. However, an employee or an agent of a party who has knowledge may be held in contempt of the order.[390] Thus, once the

---

[383]Danielson v. United Seafood Workers, 405 F. Supp. 396 (S.D.N.Y. 1975).

[384]Aspira of New York v. Bd. of Education of City of New York, 423 F. Supp. 627, 654 (S.D.N.Y. 1976).

[385]McComb v. Jacksonville Paper Co., *supra* note 377, at 191; Thompson v. Johnson, 410 F. Supp. 633, 640 (E.D. Pa. 1976); Landman v. Royster, 354 F. Supp. 292 (E.D. Va. 1973).

[386]*Supra* note 384, at 654.

[387]Sekaquaptewa v. MacDonald, 544 F.2d 396, 406 (9th Cir. 1976).

[388]United States v. Rizzo, 539 F.2d 458, 465 (5th Cir. 1976).

[389]NLRB v. Trans Ocean Export Packing, Inc., 473 F.2d 612, 616 (9th Cir. 1973); Aspira of New York v. Bd. of Education of City of New York, *supra* note 384, at 654.

[390]Rule 65(d), FRCP. *See also* Shakman v. Democratic Organization of Cook Cty., 533 F.2d 344, 352 (7th Cir. 1976) (Rule 68(d) does not require that an employee of a party have actual knowledge of an injunction before s/he can be bound by it).

warden of a prison is informed of a court order, the guards and other employees may be subject to contempt if they violate it. The warden may also be subject to contempt if s/he does not make sure that prison employees obey it.[391] No one can be held in contempt of an order unless it is specific enough that they can understand it and unless the acts they committed are clearly in violation of the order.[392]

Once you have filed your motion, affidavits, and other supporting documents, the court will hold a hearing in accordance with Rule 43(a), FRCP. The court, at the contempt hearing, must make findings of fact and conclusion of law as required by Rule 52(a), FRCP.[393] The party against whom contempt is sought can raise the defenses of substantial compliance and/or inability to comply.[394] During discovery in seeking enforcement of your judgment, you should seek information from the other party to persuade the court that they have not substantially complied and that they could comply.[395]

A civil contempt order or denial of a request for one is appealable as a formal order if the merits of your case have already been resolved.[396] If your case has not been decided on the merits, a contempt motion granted or denied is not a final and appealable order.[397]

2) Motions To Enforce or for Further Relief

A court has the inherent equitable power to make additional orders where a judgment has not achieved its purpose.[398] This power is further supported by Rule 60(b), which provides for the modification of orders "upon such terms as are just," and by the All Writs Act, which permits federal courts to "issue all writs necessary or appropriate in aid of their

---

[391]Jordan v. Arnold, 472 F. Supp. 265, 289 (M.D. Pa. 1979).

[392]Rinehart v. Brewer, 483 F. Supp. 165 (S.D. Iowa 1980); Jordan v. Arnold, *supra* note 391.

[393]*See* Lander v. Morton, 518 F.2d 1084 (D.C. Cir. 1975), for an indication of some issues that will be considered by a court at a civil contempt hearing.

[394]Washington Metropolitan Area Transit Auth. v. Amalgamated Transit Union, 531 F.2d 617 (D.C. Cir. 1976).

[395]See Sec. E2, *supra,* for a discussion of discovery procedures.

[396]9 Moore's Federal Practice, §110.12(4) n.29 and text accompanying (1982); *see also* Doyle v. London Guar. & Acc. Co., 204 U.S. 599, 27 S.Ct. 313 (1901).

[397]*See* International Business Machines Corp. v. United States, 493 F.2d 112 (2d Cir. 1973); Hodgson v. Mahoney, 460 F.2d 326 (1st Cir. 1972).

[398]United States v. United Shoe Machinery Corp., 391 U.S. 244, 248-49, 88 S.Ct. 1496 (1968); King-Seeley Thermos Co. v. Aladdin Industries, Inc., 418 F.2d 31, 35 (2d Cir. 1971).

respective jurisdictions,''[399] including orders "necessary or appropriate to effectuate and prevent the frustration of orders [the court] has previously issued.''[400] You should probably invoke all three of these powers in asking the court to enforce its prior orders. Based on these powers, you can ask the court to make the same type of order that it could enter after a finding of contempt (except for incarceration).

3) Modification of Judgments

Under the court's equitable powers and Rule 60(b), FRCP, a court may modify its prior orders as well as enforce them.[401] (The distinction between modification and enforcement is sometimes a subtle one.) Thus, a court may respond to new problems that arise after it enters an injunction. For example, suppose you won an order permitting some religious activities in administrative segregation, but the prison officials scheduled them in conflict with recreation periods. You might file a motion requesting that the judgment be modified to prohibit this practice so you would not have to choose between your religious rights and physical exercise.

Defendants, too, can apply for modification of an injunction. However, the standards are more stringent for defendants than for plaintiffs. A plaintiff need only show that the existing order has not accomplished its purpose.[402] A defendant seeking to escape the terms of an injunction generally must show "grievous wrong,"[403] "oppressive hardship,"[404] or "exceptional circumstances."[405] Some courts have refused to hold prison officials to this strict a standard.[406] However, prison officials have been denied modification of judgments in a number of cases.[407]

---

[399]28 U.S.C. §1651(a).

[400]United States v. New York Telephone Co., 434 U.S. 159, 172, 98 S.Ct. 364 (1977).

[401]System Federation v. Wright, 364 U.S. 642, 647-48, 81 S.Ct. 368 (1966).

[402]United States v. United Shoe Machinery Corp., *supra* note 398, at 248-49; King-Seeley Thermos Co. v. Aladdin Industries, Inc., *supra* note 398; English v. Cunningham, 269 F.2d 517, 523 (D.C. Cir. 1959).

[403]United States v. Swift & Co., 286 U.S. 106, 119, 52 S.Ct. 460 (1932).

[404]Humble Oil Refining Co. v. American Oil Co., 405 F.2d 803 (8th Cir. 1969).

[405]Mayberry v. Maroney, 529 F.2d 332, 335 (3d Cir. 1976) (prison case).

[406]Nelson v. Collins, 659 F.2d 420 (4th Cir. 1981) (en banc); *see also* New York State Association for Retarded Children v. Carey, 706 F.2d 956 (2d Cir. 1983).

[407]*See, e.g.,* Union County Jail Inmates v. Scanlon, 537 F. Supp. 993 (D.N.J.

c. Declaratory Relief[408]

Once you have obtained declaratory relief against the other party, you may need to seek enforcement of it. In *Morris v. Travisono,*[409] prison officials, after a disturbance, had suspended regulations regarding disciplinary classification and mail procedures which had been established by a declaratory judgment. The court, under its broad remedial power contained in the Federal Declaratory Judgment Act,[410] issued a permanent injunction.[411] Once a court has issued an injunction to enforce a declaratory judgment, the injunction may be enforced through the court's contempt power.

P. Appeals

1. Court of Appeals

If you lose your case in the district court and you believe the district court was wrong, you should consider appealing to the court of appeals for the federal circuit where you are confined.[412] You may appeal from an adverse decision on the merits of your case, from a dismissal of an in forma pauperis case as frivolous or malicious,[413] or from a refusal to permit you to proceed in forma pauperis.[414]

If you have won in the district court, the defendants can appeal to the court of appeals. If this happens, and if the district court had granted you only partial relief, you can file a notice of appeal (often called a "cross-appeal") on the issues you lost.

Appeals in federal courts are governed by the Federal Rules of Appellate Procedure (FRAP).[415] Courts of appeals also have local rules, which you can obtain from the court clerk; sometimes the clerk will charge a few dollars for them.

The party who files the notice of appeal is called the "appellant," and

---

1982); Benjamin v. Malcolm, 528 F. Supp. 925 (S.D.N.Y. 1981); Frazier v. Ward, 528 F. Supp. 80 (N.D.N.Y. 1981).

[408]See Ch. VI, Sec. H, for a discussion of how to obtain a declaratory judgment.

[409]373 F. Supp. 177 (D.R.I. 1974).

[410]28 U.S.C. §§2201-2201.

[411]*Supra* note 409, at 182-83 and cases cited therein; *see also supra* note 408.

[412]See Appendix A for a listing of the addresses of the courts of appeals.

[413]See Sec. A3a, *supra,* for a discussion of these dismissals.

[414]See Sec. A3a, *supra,* for a discussion of in forma pauperis standards.

[415]*See* 28 U.S.C., Federal Rules of Appellate Procedure.

the other party is called the "appellee." If there is a cross-appeal, the person who filed it is sometimes called the "cross-appellant," and the other party is the "cross-appellee." This can get pretty confusing, so the rules provide that you can use the terms "plaintiff" and "defendant" as you did in the district court, or other clear terms.[416]

a.   What Can Be Appealed

Not every decision of a district court can be appealed at the time it is made. The relevant statutes are designed to prevent "piecemeal appeals" and to ensure that all issues are combined in one appeal at the end of the case whenever possible.[417] Federal appellate review is generally limited to "final decisions" of a district court[418] and to orders granting, modifying, or continuing an injunction or refusing to do so.[419] Most "interlocutory" (interim) orders such as class certification, discovery, and evidentiary rulings are not appealable until final judgment on the whole case is entered.[420] The courts have disagreed as to whether the refusal to appoint counsel is appealable before a final judgment is entered.[421]

---

[416]Rule 28(d), FRAP.

[417]Firestone Tire and Rubber Co. v. Risjord, 449 U.S. 368, 373-74, 101 S.Ct. 669 (1981).

[418]28 U.S.C. §1291. A "final decision" is one "which ends the litigation on the merits and leaves nothing for the court to do but execute the judgment." Catlin v. United States, 324 U.S. 229, 233, 65 S.Ct. 631 (1945).

[419]28 U.S.C. §1291(a)(1). This statute contains several other rules about appealability which you should read.

[420]See Coopers v. Lybrand & Livesay, 437 U.S. 463, 98 S.Ct. 2454 (1978) (class certification denial not appealable); Matter of Fischel, 557 F.2d 209, 213 (9th Cir. 1977) (evidentiary ruling not appealable); Eastern Maico Distributors, Inc. v. Maico-Fahrzeugfabrik, G.m.b.H., 658 F.2d 944 (3d Cir. 1981) (discovery orders not appealable). There are two exceptions to this rule. If you obtain special permission from the district court and the court of appeals, you can appeal an interlocutory order. 28 U.S.C. §1292(b). Also, if the order is a "collateral order," it can be appealed. See Firestone Tire and Rubber Co. v. Risjord supra note 47, for a discussion of collateral orders. See also National Life Insurance Co. v. Hartford Accident & Indemnity Co., 615 F.2d 595, 597 (3d Cir. 1980) (discovery order appealable under circumstances); Southern Methodist University Association of Women Law Students v. Wynne & Jaffe, 599 F.2d 707, 711-712 (5th Cir. 1979) (same).

[421]Compare Ivey v. Board of Regents of University of Alaska, 673 F.2d 266, 269 (9th Cir. 1982); Ray v. Robinson, 640 F.2d 474, 477 (3d Cir. 1981), and cases cited (refusal to appoint counsel immediately appealable), with Cotner v. Mason, 657 F.2d 1390 (10th Cir. 1981) (refusal to appoint counsel not appealable until final judgment).

If you have sued multiple parties or raised multiple legal claims, and the court makes a decision concerning only part of the case, that order is not final unless the court expressly finds there is no reason to delay and directs the entry of final judgment.[422] Thus, if the court dismisses the warden from your lawsuit but leaves the guards as defendants, or if it grants summary judgment on your medical care claim but not on your procedural due process claim, the order is not final and appealable unless the court says so.

b.   Notice of Appeal

The basic step that anyone must take to appeal is the filing of a notice of appeal.[423] This notice should be filed with the clerk of the district court.[424] Usually this is done within 30 days of the decision you are appealing; however, if one of the parties is the United States, its officers, or one of its agencies, the time is 60 days.[425] If a notice of appeal is mistakenly filed with the court of appeals, its clerk will write on the notice the day of receipt, which will be considered the date the notice was filed, and send it to the district court clerk.[426] Once a party has filed a notice of appeal, the opposing party has 14 days to file his/her cross notice of appeal.[427] The notice of appeal must specify the party taking the appeal; the judgment, order, or part thereof appealed from; and the court to which the appeal is taken.[428]

The time for filing the notice of appeal begins to run when the judgment or order is entered by the clerk in the civil docket book and not necessarily from the oral announcement of the decision in the courtroom.[429] If you have filed a timely motion (1) for a judgment notwithstanding the verdict, (2) requesting that the judgment be amended or additional finding of facts be made, or (3) for a new trial or that the

---

[422]Rule 54(g), FRCP.

[423]*See* Rules 3 and 4, FRAP.

[424]Rule 3(a), FRAP. See Appendix B, Form 19, for a sample notice of appeal.

[425]Rule 4(a)(1), FRAP.

[426]*Id.*

[427]Rule 4(a)(3), FRAP. If a defendant has filed a notice of appeal concerning a partial judgment granted you, unless you file a notice of appeal concerning the portion of the judgment you lost you can not brief and argue on appeal the losing issues.

[428]Rule 3(c), FRAP. See Appendix B, Form 19, for a sample notice of appeal.

[429]*See* Rules 4(a)(6), FRAP; 58 and 79(a), FRCP. This is usually the same date contained on the copy of the written judgment order you will receive.

judgment be altered,[430] the time period for filing the notice of appeal will be tolled (suspended) until the clerk enters an order denying a new trial or granting or denying any other of the motions.[431]

If you have not filed or can not file your notice of appeal within the 30-day time period, you may obtain, from the *district* court, an extension for filing it of up to 30 days if you can show excusable neglect or good cause for your delay.[432] If your request for an extension is filed before the original time period expires, you can file an ex parte motion,[433] but if the time period expires, you will need to serve a copy of the motion on the other side.[434] The court can not grant an extension for longer than 30 days or 10 days from the date of entry of the order granting you an extension for filing the notice, whichever occurs later.[435]

c. In Forma Pauperis

If you were previously granted permission to proceed in forma pauperis (IFP) in the district court, you need not file any further papers on that subject unless the district court certifies that the appeal is not taken in good faith or that you are no longer entitled to proceed IFP.[436] If you were not already proceeding IFP, you must file *in the district court* a motion for leave to do so,[437] which includes a statement of the issues which you intend to present on appeal, and an affidavit in support.[438] If the district court denies your motion, or has certified that the appeal is not taken in good faith or that you are not longer entitled to proceed IFP, you may file *in the court of appeals* another motion for leave to

---

[430]See Sec. O1, *supra,* for discussions of these matters. Each must be filed within 10 days of entry of the judgment or order.

[431]Rule 4(a)(4), FRAP.

[432]Rule 4(a)(5). You would submit a motion containing an affidavit explaining why you need the extension. If you had not received the judgment/order until the 25th day of the 30 days to file your notice of appeal had passed because prison officials had transferred you, this should be excusable neglect or good cause.

[433]An ex parte motion is one that can be filed with the court without serving the other side before the court has made its decision. You should send the defendants a copy of your motion and affidavit for their files.

[434]Rule 4(a)(5), FRAP.

[435]*Id.*

[436]Rule 24(2), FRAP.

[437]See Appendix B, Form 2a, for a sample motion to proceed IFP.

[438]See Appendix B, Form 2b, for a sample affidavit in support of IFP motion. See also Sec. A3a, *supra,* for a discussion of IFP.

proceed IFP.[439] This motion should be similar to the one filed in the district court but would include the district court's statement of reasons for denying you IFP privileges and your response.[440] The motion should be filed within 30 days after the district court's action denying you IFP privileges.[441]

As noted above, you may appeal a district court decision to dismiss your case as frivolous or malicious or a decision to deny you leave to proceed IFP in the district court. The district court should have provided you with a statement of reasons for dismissing your legal pleadings, unless the reason is clear on the face of your complaint. If it did not, you should emphasize this fact to the court of appeals. As one court stated:

> To deny the right to file a petition . . . is an exercise of power so great in its impact on a petitioner that an appellate court must be able to ascertain the grounds for denial in order to fulfill its responsibility of review. It is therefore imperative that denial of leave to file the petition . . . be accompanied by an expression of the reasons for the denial either by informal memorandum, by recitals in an order, or by findings.[442]

The statement of reasons ensures that the district court has fully considered your legal pleadings and the applicable law, that the court of appeals and you are informed of the reasons for the dismissal, and that you are allowed to prepare an appeal properly. "Such a requirement is not onerous if the matter was dealt with in a conscientious manner in passing on the merits."[443]

d.   Stay of the Lower Court Decision

If the losing party wishes to appeal, it may apply for a stay pending appeal.[444] Normally, a court will require the party requesting the stay to file a bond (a sum of money designed to compensate the party opposing the stay for any losses caused by it).[445] If you are appealing a judgment

---

[439]Rule 24, FRAP.

[440]*Supra* notes 437 and 438.

[441]Rule 24(a), FRAP.

[442]Tatem v. United States, 275 F.2d 894, 896 (D.C. Cir. 1960) (Burger, J.) (habeas corpus); *see also* Collins v. Cundy, 603 F.2d 825, 828 (10th Cir. 1979).

[443]Davis v. Clark, 404 F.2d 1356, 1358 (D.C. Cir. 1968) (Judge Tamm, separate opinion) ("if the finding rests on considerations of fact, appropriate record citations might be given. If it rests on a matter of law, the general reasoning and relevant cases should be indicated.").

[444]*See* Rule 62, FRCP; Rule 8, FRAP.

[445]*See* Rule 62(d), FRCP; Rules 7, 8(b), FRAP. *See also* United States v. Neve, 80 F.R.D. 461 (E.D. La. 1978); Moore v. Townsend, 577 F.2d 424 (7th Cir. 1978).

against you and want a stay of the judgment, you must file a motion with the district court asking for the stay. If you had previously been granted leave to proceed as an indigent, you should bring this to the court's attention when requesting that you not be required to file a bond as part of the stay.

e.   Transmission of the District Court's Record

The appellant is responsible for ensuring that the record of the case is prepared and transmitted to the court of appeals and for preparing an appendix containing the relevant parts of the record.[446] If you are the appellant and have been granted leave to proceed without payment of fees and costs on appeal, you should file a motion requesting that the appeal be heard on the full record from the court below.[447] If you do not receive permission to proceed in forma pauperis on appeal, you will need to obtain portions or all of the transcript for the appeal;[448] obtain copies of documents in the file needed for the appeal; and have your brief printed so that the court receives 25 copies and each opposing counsel gets two copies.[449]

The court, in *Stanley v. Henderson*,[450] required that a prisoner who won in the trial court be provided with a copy of the transcript of the proceedings in district court, at government expense, when defending the district court judgment on appeal.

> [T]o us, it seems unreasonable and incongruous to permit a person who has been permitted to proceed in the district court in forma pauperis and who has lost his case and has appealed to be provided with a transcript at government expense, while denying a copy of the transcript for appellate use to an indigent who has won his case.[451]

If you are the appellee, your opponent will be responsible for preparing the appendix. You have a right to ask that parts of the record you consider relevant be included. However, if they are left out of the appendix, you can still refer to them in your brief.[452]

---

[446]*See* Rules 10, 11, and 30, FRAP.

[447]Rule 24(c), FRAP.

[448]Rule 10, FRAP.

[449]Rule 31(b), FRAP.

[450]590 F.2d 752 (8th Cir. 1979).

[451]*Id.* at 753-54. See also the Court Reporter Act, 28 U.S.C. §753(f) ("Fees for transcripts furnished in other proceedings to persons permitted to appeal in forma pauperis shall also be paid by the United States if the trial judge or a circuit judge certifies that the appeal is not frivolous (but presents a substantial question).").

[452]Rule 30, FRAP.

f.   Appellate Briefs

Once the district court's record has been received by the clerk of the court of appeals, the clerk shall notify all parties of the date on which it was filed.[453] The appellant has 40 days after the record is filed with the clerk of the court of appeals to serve and file his/her brief.[454] The appellee then has 30 days after service of appellant's brief to serve and file his/her brief.[455] A reply brief may be filed by the appellant within 14 days after service of the appellee's brief.[456] The court of appeals may set a different time schedule for filing briefs.[457]

If you cannot prepare you brief and have it filed within the time period allowed, you should file a motion with the court, alleging good cause, for an enlargement of time to prepare and file your brief.[458] If prison officials have only allowed you access to the prison law library for three hours a week, or you are confined in segregation and you can only get one law book at a time, this information should be included in an affidavit attached to your motion showing good cause for not meeting the briefing schedule deadline. Failure to file your brief in time or to request an enlargement of time can result in your appeal being dismissed if you are the appellant, or oral argument being denied to you if you are the appellee.[459]

The appellate court rules are very exact in regard to what the briefs will contain and their length;[460] you should also obtain a copy of the local appellate court rules, which may contain additional requirements. The principal briefs will not exceed 50 pages, and the reply brief will not exceed 25 pages, exclusive of the table of contents, tables of citations, and any appendix or exhibits.[461]

---

[453]Rule 12(b), FRAP.

[454]Rule 31(a), FRAP. Rule 26(c), FRAP, allows you an extra three days to perform an act that is required when the paper informing you of that requirement was served on you by mail. For example, if the clerk of the court of appeals has mailed you the notice that the record has been filed, you would have 43 days to file and serve your brief from the date the record was filed.

[455]Rule 31(a), FRAP.

[456]*Id.*

[457]*Id.*

[458]Rule 26(b), FRAP.

[459]Rule 31(c), FRAP.

[460]Rule 28, FRAP.

[461]Rule 28(h), FRAP.

The brief should consist of the following:[462]

(1) A *table of contents,* with page references, and a *table of authorities,* an alphabetical listing of the cases, statutes, and other authorities you have cited, listing the pages of the brief where they are cited.

(2) A *statement of issues.* You will list the issues you have briefed (*e.g.,* "whether defendants' macing of the plaintiff while he was handcuffed and confined in his cell violated the cruel and unusual punishment clause of the Eighth Amendment").

(3) A *statement of the case.* This will consist of two parts: (a) Statement of Proceedings, and (b) Statement of Facts. The Statement of Proceedings explains the procedural history of the case, and the Statement of Facts contains the relevant facts of the case.

(4) An *argument.*[463] This will contain your contentions with respect to the issues you listed in the "statement of issues," the reasons, and citations to cases, statutes, prison rules, or parts of the record.

(5) *Relief Requested.* This will contain a short conclusion stating the precise relief sought.

The appellee's brief will contain everything in (1)-(4) above.[464]

In your brief, when you are referring to the parties, you will use the terms used in the lower court (*e.g.,* the appellant will be either the plaintiff, the prisoner, the injured person, etc.; appellees would be the warden or defendant Jones, correctional officer or defendant Smith, etc.).[465] If in your brief you are referring to part of the record of the appeal that is not attached to your brief, you should clearly say so.[466]

If you have been granted leave to proceed in forma pauperis on appeal, you may file your brief, appendices, and other papers in typewritten form.[467] All typewritten legal documents filed in the federal court should be double spaced on 8½ by 11 white paper.[468] You must file an original and three copies with the court and send one copy to counsel for defendants.[469]

---

[462]*See* Rule 28(a), FRAP. See also Appendix B, Form 12, for a sample appellate brief; see Ch. III, Sec. E, for a discussion of preparation of a brief.

[463]See Ch. III, Sec. E, for examples of types of arguments you can make.

[464]Rule 28(b), FRAP.

[465]Rule 28(d), FRAP.

[466]Rules 28(e), 30, FRAP.

[467]Rule 24(d), FRAP.

[468]Rule 32, FRAP.

[469]Rule 31(b), FRAP.

g. Oral Argument

Even though Rule 34, FRCP, provides that oral argument normally should be allowed unless a panel of three judges are of the unanimous opinion that oral argument is not needed,[470] few courts of appeals will allow an incarcerated person to present oral argument. You should request by motion that you be allowed to present oral argument (see Sec. M, *supra,* for a discussion of court appearance).[471] You may also wish to request that if you are not permitted to argue orally, the other side should not be permitted to do so either.

If oral argument is permitted, the appellant will present his/her argument first and can reserve some of the time allocated to respond to appellee's argument.[472] The court will normally grant each party 15 to 30 minutes for oral argument. The appellant should include a fair and short statement of the facts and history of the case at the beginning of his/her argument. You should not read at length from your brief, the record, or other authorities.[473] The court is interested in learning more about the facts of your case and why the court below was wrong or right. You should expect the court to ask you questions and you should be prepared to answer them. You should study the other side's brief and be prepared to respond to any statement or argument in it. You should be able to answer questions about the facts and to tell the court where in the record it can find any fact that you wish to emphasize.

h. Rehearing or Rehearing En Banc

Once the court has issued a decision, you will be mailed a copy of it.[474] You may file a motion for rehearing[475] or rehearing en banc[476] within 14 days after entry of the judgment of the court of appeals.[477] Rehearings

---

[470]Rule 34(a), FRAP.

[471]*See* Rule 27, FRAP, for a discussion of motions in the court of appeals. The court's power to issue a writ of habeas corpus for your production in court is discussed in Price v. Johnson, 334 U.S. 266, 68 S.Ct. 1049 (1948).

[472]Rule 34(c), FRAP.

[473]*Id.*

[474]Rule 36, FRAP.

[475]Rule 40, FRAP.

[476]Rule 35, FRAP. A rehearing en banc is a rehearing by all the active judges of the court rather than by a three-judge panel.

[477]Rules 40(a), 35(c). You need only file one motion, designating it as a "Motion for Rehearing With Suggestion of Rehearing En Banc." Since the decision in the case will have been mailed to you, you will have 17 days (14 days

and rehearings en banc are very seldom granted. You must state in your petition with particularity the points of law or facts which you feel the court has overlookded or misapprehended and provide argument in support of them.[478] (You should consult the local rules of the court of appeals for any special requirements pertaining to rehearings.) The winning party need not respond to the petition for rehearing or rehearing en banc unless the court has so requested.

i. Appointment of Counsel

You do not have an absolute right to appointment of counsel when appealing a civil action. The courts of appeals are authorized, pursuant to 28 U.S.C. §1915(d), to request counsel to represent you (see Sec. A3b for a further discussion of appointment of counsel). It is recommended that you seek appointment of counsel.[479] Even if the district court refused to appoint counsel, the court of appeals may take a different view, and it is often easier to find a lawyer to take a case in a prestigious appellate court than it is in the district court.

2. Supreme Court

If you lose your case in the court of appeals and you believe the court of appeals was wrong, you may consider petitioning for review in the United States Supreme Court.[480]

a. Jurisdiction and Role of the Supreme Court

The Supreme Court takes very few cases and selects them carefully. In recent years, it has consistently rejected over 90% of the petitions for review it has received. The Supreme Court has the power to review virtually any decision of a federal court of appeals;[481] it has more limited powers to review decisions of the highest court of a state.[482] It is required to hear a particular case only under extremely limited circumstances.[483]

---

by Rule 40(a) or 35(c), and 3 days by Rule 26(c)) to file your petition for rehearing.

[478]Rule 40(a), FRAP.

[479]See Appendix B, Form 18, for a sample motion and brief regarding appointment of counsel.

[480]See Appendix A for the address of the Supreme Court.

[481]28 U.S.C. §1254(1).

[482]28 U.S.C. §1257.

[483]For a more detailed understanding of the jurisdiction of the Supreme Court, read 28 U.S.C. §§1251-1258 and cases interpreting these statutes.

The Supreme Court generally restricts itself to cases that present issues of importance to the federal judicial system or to the nation, not just to the people involved in the case.[484] Usually, it takes cases involving important and unsettled issues of federal constitutional or statutory law, conflicts with an earlier Supreme Court decision, or conflicts in decisions between federal courts of appeals or state and federal courts.[485] Unless the issue you present has caused a division in the courts or has implications far beyond the facts and parties in your case, the Supreme Court will not be interested. It is not in the business of correcting every mistake that the lower courts make.

Proceedings in the Supreme Court are governed by the Rules of the Supreme Court of the United States.[486]

b.   Petition for Writ of Certiorari

To apply for Supreme Court review, you must, in almost all cases, file a petition for writ of certiorari[487] within 90 days after entry of the judgment or decree in the court of appeals.[488]

A petition for writ of certiorari is a minature brief which should consist of the following:[489]

(1) *Questions presented.* These questions will be short and concise and not argumentative or repetitious. Since the Court will only consider questions set forth in the petition, you must specifically list the questions you feel the Court should consider.

(2) *List of parties.* You should list, either in the caption or in one of the footnotes, the names of all the plaintiffs and defendants.

(3) *Table of authorities.* This will contain an alphabetical listing of the cases, constitutional provisions, statutes, textbooks, etc., with reference to the pages where they were cited in the petition.

(4) *Jurisdictional grounds.* This will contain the date of the entry of the decision you are appealing; the date of entry of any order concerning a

---

[484]*See* Stern and Gressman, *Supreme Court Practice* (Bureau of National Affairs, Washington, DC, 1978).

[485]For a fuller statement of these criteria, see Rule 17, Supreme Court Rules.

[486]*See* 28 U.S.C., Rules, Supreme Court. You may also wish to write the Clerk of the Supreme Court to obtain a copy of its rules with the latest amendments.

[487]We restrict the discussion to the Court's certiorari jurisdiction because its appeal jurisdiction will rarely be invoked by prisoners. See 28 U.S.C. §§1252, 1254, and 1257; Rules 10-16, Supreme Court Rules, concerning appeal jurisdiction.

[488]28 U.S.C. §2101(c); Rule 20.2, Supreme Court Rules.

[489]*See* Rule 21.1, Supreme Court Rules. See also Appendix B, Form 21, for a sample petition for writ of certiorari.

request for rehearing; date and terms of an order granting an extension of time for filing a petition for certiorari; and the statutory provision conferring jurisdiction on the Supreme Court.

(5) *Constitutional provisions, statutes, ordinances, and regulations relied on.* If these are not too lengthy, you should list them as part of your brief; if lengthy, include them in the appendix.

(6) *Statement of the case.* This will contain the facts material to the questions presented. You will also list the jurisdictional basis used by the federal court of appeals to hear your case.

(7) *Argument.*[490] This will contain a direct and concise argument why the Supreme Court should grant your petition for certiorari.

(8) *Appendix.* This will contain a copy of any orders, decisions, etc. you received from the lower courts which you wish reviewed and any other documents you wish the Supreme Court to consider.

The petition for certiorari may not exceed 30 pages, including the table of authorities, any verbatim quotations, and the appendix.[491] It is to be typed double spaced, except for quotations, on 8½ by 13 inches white paper and bound at the upper left-hand corner.[492]

A copy of the petition for certiorari and the motion to proceed IFP with the affidavit must be served on counsel for the other side and a proof of service filed with the Clerk of the Supreme Court.[493] Service of these documents can be done by mail.[494] If you are suing the United States or any department, office, or agency (*e.g.,* Bureau of Prisons), officer (*e.g.,* Director Carlson in his official capacity), or employee (*e.g.,* the warden or a prison guard in his/her official capacity), you must serve a copy on the person being sued and send a copy to the Solicitor General, Department of Justice, Washington, DC 20530.[495]

The purpose of a petition for certiorari is not to convince the Supreme Court that you have been mistreated, but to convince it that your case is important enough to justify devoting the Court's limited time to it. In your statement of questions presented and in your argument, you should emphasize the importance of the issues, the lack of guidance from the Supreme Court to the lower court, and any conflicts on the issue in the lower courts. For example, if your visits are suspended for a year without a hearing, do not waste words on how severe the deprivation is or how prison officials' reasons were mistaken. Emphasize that the Supreme

---

[490]See Ch. III, Sec. E, for examples of types of arguments you can make.

[491]Rule 21.4, Supreme Court Rules.

[492]Rule 39.1, Supreme Court Rules.

[493]Rule 28.5, Supreme Court Rules.

[494]Rule 28.3, Supreme Court Rules.

[495]Rule 28.4(a), Supreme Court Rules.

Court has never ruled broadly on visiting rights, that the lower courts are in serious disagreement about what rights prisoners have with respect to visiting, and that the refusal to give you a hearing presents an undecided question whether visiting rights constitute a liberty interest requiring due process.[496]

c.   In Forma Pauperis

If you wish to proceed in the Supreme Court without payment of fees and costs and the typographic printing of a large number of copies of each document filed there, you will need to submit a motion to proceed IFP and a supporting affidavit.[497] The motion shall state the grounds why you should be allowed to proceed IFP and whether or not leave to proceed IFP was sought in the lower courts and, if so, whether it was granted.[498] The affidavit need not contain a listing of the issues you are presenting in your petition for certiorari but should be similar to the one filed in the lower court.[499] With your motion and affidavit, you are to file one copy of your petition for certiorari in typewritten form[500] and a proof of service showing that the attorney for the other side was mailed a copy of the petition and other documents. Once the clerk of the Court has received these documents, the petition for certiorari will be filed and placed on the docket.[501]

d.   Obtaining the Record

You may request that the record from your case in the lower court be sent by that court to the Supreme Court before or immediately after you file your petition for writ of certiorari. These requests are not encouraged before the granting of certiorari.[502] If you do request that your record from the lower court be sent to the Supreme Court, you will need to send a copy of the request to counsel for the other side and a copy to the Supreme Court, with a proof of service that you sent a copy to opposing counsel.[503]

---

[496]See Ch. V, Sec. C1d, for a discussion of these issues.

[497]Rule 46.1, Supreme Court Rules. See also Appendix B, Forms 2a, b, for sample motion and affidavit to proceed IFP.

[498]Rule 46.1, Supreme Court Rules.

[499]See Appendix B, Form 2b, for a sample affidavit to proceed IFP.

[500]Rules 21.2, 39, and 46, Supreme Court Rules.

[501]Rule 46.4, Supreme Court Rules.

[502]Rule 19.1, Supreme Court Rules.

[503]*Id.* See Appendix B, Form 22, Certification of Record to the Supreme Court

e.   Counsel

If the Supreme Court grants your petition for writ of certiorari, it will, upon a timely motion or request, appoint counsel to handle your case. If this motion or request is not included in the in forma pauperis motion or the petition for certiorari, it should be made within 20 days of the granting of the petition for certiorari.[504]

Since no prisoner will be permitted to proceed *pro se* in the Supreme Court, our discussion of Supreme Court practice will not be extended.[505]

Q.   Attorneys Fees

An attorney who wins a civil rights case is ordinarily entitled to a fee determined by the court and paid by the defendants.[506] Attorneys fees may be awarded to a civil rights plaintiff who obtains relief through settlement rather than through litigation in all but special circumstances.[507] One whose rights, either in part or in whole, have been vindicated "through a consent judgment or without formally obtaining relief" is a prevailing party.[508] Attorneys fees may be awarded to a civil rights plaintiff who obtains relief on a wholly non-civil-rights claim.[509]

---

[504]*See* Stern and Gressman, *Supreme Court Practice,* §8.12 (Bureau of National Affairs, Washington, DC, 1978).

[505]See the Supreme Court Rules and Stern and Gressman, *Supreme Court Practice, supra,* for further information on this subject.

[506]42 U.S.C. §1988. *See also* Hensley v. Eckerhart, __U.S.__, 103 S.Ct. 1933 (1983); Maine v. Thiboutot, 448 U.S. 1, 100 S.Ct. 2502 (1980); Maher v. Gagne, 448 U.S. 122, 100 S.Ct. 2570 (1980). *See generally,* Larson, *Federal Court Awards of Attorneys Fees* (Harcourt Brace Jovanovich, Publishers, 1981).

[507]*See* Knighton v. Watkins, 616 F.2d 795, 798 (5th Cir. 1980); Wallace v. King, 650 F.2d 529, 531 (4th Cir. 1980); Universal Amusement Co., Inc. v. Hofheinz, 616 F.2d 202, 204-05 (5th Cir. 1980), *modified on other grounds,* 646 F.2d 996 (5th Cir. 1981); Chicano Police Officer's Association v. Stover, 624 F.2d 127, 130 (10th Cir. 1980). The Supreme Court has made essentially the same holding in cases arising under Title VII of the Civil Rights Act of 1964. New York Gaslight Club, Inc. v. Carey, 447 U.S. 125, 100 S.Ct. 2024, 2033 (1980); Christianburg Garment Co. v. Equal Employment Opportunity Commission, 434 U.S. 412, 98 S.Ct. 694, 698 (1978).

[508]S. Rep. No. 94-1011, 94th Cong., 2d Sess., 5 (1976). Plaintiff may be deemed to have prevailed not only through final judgment but also through settlements and consent decrees, through voluntary compliance by defendants where the plaintiff's lawsuit can fairly be viewed as having provided the catalyst for defendants' actions, and even through post- and sometimes pre-lawsuit administrative proceedings. Larson, "Attorneys Fees—Major Issues," *Representing Prisoners,* p. 930 (Practising Law Institute, 1981). *See also* Hensley v. Eckerhart, *supra* note 506; Knighton v. Watkins,*id.* at 798-99, and cases cited.

Most courts have denied fees to *pro se* litigants on the grounds that fee awards were never intended to provide a windfall to *pro se* litigants.[510]

---

[509]Maher v. Gagne, *supra* note 506. *See also* Oldham v. Ehrlich, 617 F.2d 163 (8th Cir. 1980); McNanama v. Lukhard, 616 F.2d 727 (4th Cir. 1980); Holley v. Lavine, 605 F.2d 638 (2d Cir. 1979); Kimbrough v. Arkansas Activities Association, 574 F.2d 423 (8th Cir. 1978).

[510]Owens-El v. Robinson, 694 F.2d 941 (3d Cir. 1982); Pitts v. Vaughn, 679 F.2d 311 (3d Cir. 1982); Crooker v. U.S. Department of Justice, 632 F.2d 916 (1st Cir. 1980) (FOIA); Davis v. Parratt, 608 F.2d 717 (8th Cir. 1979); Hannon v. Security National Bank, 537 F.2d 327 (9th Cir. 1976) (Truth in Lending Act); Porter v. Windham, 550 F. Supp. 687 (W.D. Okla. 1981). *Contra,* Cox v. U.S. Department of Justice, 601 F.2d 1 (D.C. Cir. 1979) (FOIA). Several courts have allowed fees to *pro se* litigants who not only acted as their own attorneys but in fact were attorneys. *See* Ellis v. Cassidy, 625 F.2d 227 (9th Cir. 1980) (bad faith theory and §1928); Cuneo v. Rumsfeld, 553 F.2d 1360 (D.C. Cir. 1977) (FOIA).

VIII
Parole

A. Parole Release

Although in 1972 the Supreme Court required due process protections in parole revocation,[1] until 1979, the lower federal courts were split in their holdings as to whether a prisoner had a liberty interest entitled to constitutional protection in the granting of parole. The Supreme Court that year decided *Greenholtz v. Inmates of Nebraska Penal and Correctional Complex.*[2] The Court held that "[t]here is no constitutional or inherent right of a convicted person to be conditionally released before the expiration of a valid sentence."[3]

The Supreme Court quickly dispensed with the argument that parole release and parole revocation decisions affect the same interest and should be accorded the same constitutional protection. The Court found two crucial distinctions between prisoners seeking parole release and those already on parole.[4] The first is that prisoners being considered for parole are confined and subject to the necessary restraints of a prison,[5] unlike a parolee or probationer who is at liberty and may "be gainfully employed and [is] free to be with family and friends and to form the

---

[1]Morrissey v. Brewer, 408 U.S. 471, 92 S.Ct. 2593 (1972) (release on parole created "conditional liberty" interest entitling prisoner to certain procedural due process before parole could be revoked). *See also* Gagnon v. Scarpelli, 411 U.S. 778, 93 S.Ct. 1756 (1973) (probation revocation requires same procedural safeguards as parole revocation). For a general discussion of liberty interests, see Ch. V, Sec. B; for a general discussion of procedural due process, see Ch. V, Sec. C.

[2]442 U.S. 1, 99 S.Ct. 2100 (1979).

[3]*Id.* at 7.

[4]*Supra* note 2, at 9 (emphasis added).

[5]*See* Meachum v. Fano, 427 U.S. 215, 224, 96 S.Ct. 2532 (1976) ("[Under] a valid conviction, the criminal defendant has been constitutionally deprived of his liberty.").

other enduring attachments of normal life.''[6] The other major distinction, according to the Supreme Court, ''lies in the nature of the decision that must be made in each case.''[7] The Court held that a parole release decision is necessarily subjective in part and predictive in part.[8]

> The [parole] decision turns on a "discretionary assessment of a multiplicity of imponderables, entailing primarily what a man is and what he may become rather than simply what he has done.[9]

The parole or probation revocation decision is necessarily first a *factual question* to determine whether a condition of the release has been violated.

The Court held that ''the *possibility* of parole provided no more than a mere hope that the benefit [would] be obtained.''[10] The Court viewed a prisoner's interest in parole release as being no more substantial than his/her interest in not being transferred to another prison.[11] Thus, no constitutionally protected ''conditional liberty'' interest is created by the mere existence of a parole system.

Nevertheless, the plaintiffs had also alleged, and the court of appeals had found, that the statutory language created a protectible expectation of parole. Plaintiffs had argued that the use of the word ''shall'' in the statute created a presumption that a prisoner would be paroled ''unless'' one of the four designated reasons were found to exist. The Nebraska statute provided:

> Whenever the Board of Parole considers the release of a committed offender who is eligible for release on parole, it *shall* order his release *unless* it is of the opinion that his release should be deferred because:
>   (a) There is a substantial risk that he will not conform to the conditions of parole;
>   (b) His release would depreciate the seriousness of his crime or promote disrespect for law;
>   (c) His release would have a substantially adverse effect on institutional discipline; or
>   (d) His continued correctional treatment, medical care, or vocational or

---

[6]*Supra* note 2, at 9 (cite omitted).

[7]*Id.* at 9.

[8]The Court found that ''[u]nlike the revocation decision [which first involves a retrospective factual question whether one or more conditions of parole have been violated], there is no set of facts which, if shown, mandate a [parole] decision favorable to the individual.'' *Id.* at 10.

[9]*Supra* note 2, at 10 (cite omitted).

[10]*Id.* at 11 (emphasis in original).

[11]*See supra* note 5, at 225. See also Ch. V, Sec. B2d, B2f, for a further discussion of procedural rights in transfer and parole.

other training in the facility will substantially enhance his capacity to lead a law-abiding life when released at a later date.[12]

The Supreme Court held that a prisoner being considered for Nebraska parole is "entitled to some measure of constitutional protection"[13] since the statute created an expectation of release on parole "unless" the statutory reasons for parole denials are found. The Court emphasized that "this statute has unique structure and language and thus *whether any other state provides a protectible entitlement must be decided on a case-by-case basis.*"[14] In its analysis of what procedures must be provided, the Supreme Court stated that the procedural protections established in *Morrissey,*[15] *Gagnon,*[16] and *Wolff*[17] were not appropriate to a Nebraska parole release hearing.[18]

The Supreme Court found that the requirements of a formal hearing in all cases "provide at best a negligible decrease in the risk of error."[19] Since the prisoner is allowed to appear before the Board at an informal interview, s/he has the opportunity then to ensure that the Board is considering his/her record and to present any special factors meriting consideration. The Court found the "procedure [provided by the Board] adequately safeguards against serious risks of error"[20] and thus a formal hearing is not required to satisfy due process.

The Court further found that the present procedure of the Parole Board informing prisoners of the reasons for denial and not the evidence relied on "affords the process that is due under these circumstances."[21] Somehow the Court found that the prisoners had not claimed that the "timing of the notice or its substance prejudice their ability to adequately

---

[12]Nebraska Rev. Stat. §82-1,114(1) (1976) (emphasis added).

[13]*Supra* note 2, at 12.

[14]*Supra* note 2, at 12 (emphasis added). See discussion of cases decided since *Greenholtz* by the lower federal courts, *infra.*

[15]Morrissey v. Brewer, 408 U.S. 471, 92 S.Ct. 2593 (1972).

[16]Gagnon v. Scarpelli, 411 U.S. 778, 93 S.Ct. 1756 (1973).

[17]Wolff v. McDonnell, 418 U.S. 529, 94 S.Ct. 2963 (1974).

[18]The Court did not hold that the procedural requirements in *Wolff, Morrissey,* or *Gagnon* would never be applicable to a parole release hearing, but that based on the Nebraska statute in this case, they do not apply. See Ch. V, Sec. B2, for a further discussion of the procedural protections established by these cases.

[19]*Supra* note 2, at 14 (cite omitted).

[20]*Id.* at 15 (cite omitted).

[21]*Id.* at 16.

prepare for the [parole] hearing."[22] How a prisoner receiving notice on the day of a hearing is to have time to notify his/her attorney and witnesses and have them at the prison that day is not explained by the Court.[23]

1. State Parole

The federal courts, following *Greenholtz,* have looked closely at the language of each state parole statute, and its interpretation by state courts,[24] to determine if a protectible parole release interest is created.[25] The courts have looked at state statutes for the "shall . . . unless" directive that, in *Greenholtz,* the Supreme Court found created an expectation of parole release. Most post-*Greenholtz* decisions have failed to find the necessary formulation required to establish due process entitlement.[26]

In *Staton v. Wainwright,*[27] the Fifth Circuit held that the Florida parole release statute did not create a protectible interest in a timely initial hearing. The Florida statute provided that an initial parole hearing would take place within a certain specified time after incarceration. Based upon this initial interview, a "presumptive parole release"[28] date would be established. At least sixty days prior to this presumptive parole release date, a hearing is held to establish the actual release date.[29]

---

[22]*Id.* at 14 n.6.

[23]See the dissent, Marshall, J., *id., at 38-39.*

[24]*See* U.S. ex rel. Scott v. Illinois Parole and Pardon Bd., 669 F.2d 1185, 1189 (7th Cir. 1982).

[25]*See Greenholtz, supra,* note 2, 442 U.S. at 11-17.

[26]*See* Staton v. Wainwright, 665 F.2d 686 (5th Cir. 1982) (Florida); Williams v. Briscoe, 641 F.2d 274 (5th Cir. 1981) (Texas); Candelaria v. Griffin, 641 F.2d 868 (10th Cir. 1981) (New Mexico); Schuemann v. Colorado State Board of Parole, 624 F.2d 172, 175 (10th Cir. 1980) (Colorado); Averhart v. Tutsie, 618 F.2d 479, 481-82 (7th Cir. 1980) (Indiana); Sharp v. Leonard, 611 F.2d 136 (6th Cir. 1979) (Ohio); Wagner v. Gilligan, 609 F.2d 866 (6th Cir. 1979) (Ohio); Jackson v. Reese, 608 F.2d 159 (5th Cir. 1979) (Georgia); Boothe v. Hammock, 605 F.2d 661 (2d Cir. 1979) (New York); Shirley v. Chestnut, 603 F.2d 805, 807 (10th Cir. 1979) (Oklahoma).

[27]665 F.2d 686 (5th Cir. 1982). *But see* James v. Florida Parole and Probation Commission, 395 So.2d 197 (Fla. App. 1981) (Commission mandated to establish binding presumptive parole release date within statutory period despite lack of presentence report).

[28]This tentative parole release date is determined by parole guidelines.

[29]This determination is based on the presumptive parole release date, satisfactory institutional conduct, and an acceptable parole release plan.

The court found that, even though the Florida statute provided objective means for determining and establishing parole dates,[30] the Parole Commission had retained wide discretion in granting parole.[31] Until the Commission approved the prisoner's parole release plan, there existed no effective parole release date. Also, the guidelines used to set a presumptive parole release date allowed the Commission initially to go beyond the matrix range.[32]

In *Shirley v. Chestnut*,[33] the prisoner had requested access to adverse matters in his files, the right to subpoena witnesses to the hearing, and a written reason for denial of parole. The Tenth Circuit held that the Oklahoma parole statute did no more than create a parole system; it did not establish a liberty interest protected by due process.

In two cases from the Sixth Circuit, *Sharp v. Leonard*[34] and *Wagner v. Gilligan*,[35] the prisoners had asked for reasonable advance notice of the criteria for possible denial of parole, a right to submit documentary evidence, and a statement of the essential evidentiary factors on which the denial was based. The court found that the Ohio parole statutes did not create a protectible statutory entitlement to parole. The Parole Board had complete discretion in the granting or denying of parole and did not need to provide the prisoners with any of the procedures they requested.[36]

The New York federal district courts have also found that the New York Parole Board has wide discretion in granting parole.[37] In *Lott v. Dalsheim*,[38] the district court found that *Greenholtz* granted the discretion to a parole board to deny parole because a prisoner spent too much time in legal pursuits rather than in preparation to return to the community. In another case, *Cicero v. Olgiati*,[39] the New York parole release statute was challenged as being unconstitutionally vague. The

---

[30]Fla. Stat. §947.002.

[31]Fla. Stat. §947.18.

[32]*See* Baker v. Florida Parole and Probation Commission, 384 So.2d 746 (Fla. App. 1980).

[33]603 F.2d 805 (10th Cir. 1979).

[34]611 F.2d 136 (6th Cir. 1979).

[35]609 F.2d 866 (6th Cir. 1979).

[36]*See also* Bowles v. Tennant, 613 F.2d 776 (9th Cir. 1980) (prisoner has no constitutional right to be advised of the factors the board would consider).

[37]*See* Boothe v. Hammock, 605 F.2d 661 (2d Cir. 1979) (N.Y. state parole statute creates no protectible interest).

[38]474 F. Supp. 897 (S.D.N.Y. 1979).

[39]473 F. Supp. 653 (S.D.N.Y. 1979).

district court stated that *Greenholtz* allows a state parole statute to be either broadly worded or specific.

A small number of federal courts have found that state parole statutes do create a liberty interest entitled to some due process protection. In *United States ex rel. Scott v. Illinois Parole and Pardon Board,*[40] the court found that the Illinois parole statute created a "negative" inference that parole "shall" be granted "unless" one of the conditions is found.[41] The court also looked at the Rules of the Illinois Prisoner Review Board and found additional evidence that a protectible interest was created.

> In light of these rules, it appears that the Board itself has interpreted §1003-3-5(c) as requiring a finding that one of the statutory criteria exist before it can deny an eligible inmate his parole.[42]

Once it was determined that the Illinois parole statute created a protectible interest, the court then addressed the prisoner's contention that the Board's use of "boiler plate" reasons to deny his parole was constitutionally inadequate. The Seventh Circuit, citing its earlier adoption[43] of the test used in *United States ex rel. Johnson v. Chairman of N.Y. State Bd. of Parole,*[44] again held that a denial of parole must contain "what in [the prisoner's] record was felt by the Board to warrant his denial and why."[45]

> To satisfy minimum due process requirements, a statement of reasons should be sufficient to enable a reviewing body to determine whether parole has been denied for an impermissible reason or for no reason at all. For this essential purpose, detailed findings of fact are not required, provided the Board's decision is based upon consideration of all relevant factors and it

---

[40]669 F.2d 1185 (7th Cir. 1982).

[41]The court of appeals stated in its opinion, at 1188 n.3, that the district court finding in United States ex rel. McCalvin v. Irving, 504 F. Supp. 368 (C.D. Ill. 1980), holding that the Illinois parole statute did not create a liberty interest, was a too narrow a reading of *Greenholtz.*

[42]*Supra* note 40, at 1190 n.6.

[43]United States ex rel. Richerson v. Wolff, 525 F.2d 797 (7th Cir. 1975), *cert. denied,* 425 U.S. 914 (1976).

[44]500 F.2d 925 (2d Cir.), *vacated as moot,* 419 U.S. 1015 (1974).

[45]*Supra* note 40, at 1191. The court did not require a summary of the evidence relied upon. The court cited two cases as examples of the type of reasons required. *See Richerson, supra,* note 43 and Garcia v. United States Board of Parole, 557 F.2d 100 (7th Cir. 1979), where "the parole board had indicated that it had *considered* the *inmate's specific conduct,* and not just the statutory offense for which he had been found criminally liable." *Scott, supra,* note 40, at 1191 (emphasis added).

furnishes to the inmate both the grounds for the decision . . . and the essential facts upon which the Board's inferences are based.[46]

Recently, the Eighth Circuit, in *Williams v. Missouri Board of Probation and Parole,*[47] upon remand from the Supreme Court,[48] re-affirmed its earlier holding that the Missouri parole statute created a liberty interest entitled to protection. The court then considered the issue of whether prisoners had a right of access to adverse information contained in their parole files.[49]

Even though the Missouri statute does not preclude prisoners from access to information contained in their parole files, the Board's policy was not to disclose any information in the file to the prisoner, whether adverse or not. The court reaffirmed its earlier ruling which held:

> We are convinced that as a minimum due process requires that an inmate in Missouri seeking parole be advised of adverse information in his file. In order for an inmate to have a meaningful consideration of his application for parole, it is essential that he be apprised of such adverse information and given an opportunity to rebut or explain the parts he believes are incorrect. . . .[50]

The court found further support for its holding in *Greenholtz,* where the Court found that inaccurate information in the file that remains un-verified or unrebutted increased the risk of erroneous decision and could flaw the decisionmaking process.[51] The Board is required to inform a prisoner of any adverse information in his file that might lead to an unfavorable decision. The prisoner is to be given an opportunity to provide mitigating information.

State courts, relying on the federal constitution or on their own statutes and regulations, have come to different conclusions as to due process requirements in granting parole. The following state cases have held that you are entitled to some protection in the parole process: *Application of Trantino,* 177 N.J. Super. 499, 427 A.2d 91 (1981)

---

[46]*Supra* note 44, at 934.

[47]661 F.2d 697 (8th Cir. 1981).

[48]*See* Williams v. Missouri Board of Probation and Parole, 585 F.2d 922 (8th Cir. 1978), *vacated and remanded,* 442 U.S. 926, 99 S.Ct. 2853 (1979), for reconsideration in light of the decision in *Greenholtz.*

[49]The parole file contains the presentence report; psychiatric and psychological reports, if available; pre-review and progress reports; and information concerning prior juvenile proceedings, arrests, confinements, probation, parole, and other miscellaneous information. See also Ch. V, Sec. B2g, for a discussion of the due process right to challenge adverse information.

[50]585 F.2d at 925.

[51]442 U.S. at 13.

(legislature is obligated by state constitution to provide for parole); *Young v. Duckworth,* 394 N.E.2d 123 (Ind. 1979) (due process required under Indiana law in parole consideration); *Matter of Sinka,* 599 P.2d 1275 (Wash. 1979) (state parole statute requires due process); *Moore v. Florida Parole and Probation Commission,* 289 So.2d 719 (Fla. App. 1974) (though there is no absolute right to parole, there is a right to proper consideration, and eligibility for parole cannot be determined on illegal or improper grounds); *James v. Florida Parole and Probation Commission,* 395 So.2d 197 (Fla. App. 1981) (Commission mandated to establish binding presumptive parole release date within statutory period despite lack of presentence report). *Contrary* cases are: *State v. Wright,* 309 N.W.2d 891 (Iowa 1981) (prisoners do not have a constitutional right to parole); *Wainwright v. Bordenkircher,* 276 S.E.2d 205 (W.Va. 1981) (no automatic right to parole once prisoner reaches minimum sentence); *Sneed v. Cox,* 74 N.M. 659, 397 P.2d 308 (1964) (parole is a matter of grace and not a right); *Severance v. Armstrong,* 624 P.2d 1004 (Nev. 1981) (state statute did not create liberty interest in obtaining parole); *White v. Commonwealth of Ky.,* 611 S.W.2d 529 (Ky. App. 1980) (probation and parole are legislative clemencies granted as a matter of grace); *Redding v. Meeknia,* 306 N.W.2d 664 (Wisc. 1981) (parole and probation are matters of grace).

2. Federal Parole

Federal prisoners sentenced under 18 U.S.C. §4205(a) to a definite term of more than one year are *eligible* for release on parole after serving one-third of their sentence, or if sentenced to life or to a term over thirty years, are *eligible* for parole after ten years. A prisoner sentenced under 18 U.S.C. §4205(b)(2) is *only eligible* for consideration for release before serving one-third of the sentence.

Recently, in *Evans v. Dillahunty,*[52] the Eighth Circuit considered whether federal parole statutes[53] created a liberty interest entitled to due process protection.[54] The court of appeals stated:

[R]esolution of the question whether a federal prisoner has a limited right

---

[52]662 F.2d 522 (8th Cir. 1981).

[53]18 U.S.C. §§4201-4218. *See also* Title 28, Code of Federal Regulations (CFR) §2.1-.59.

[54]*See* Greenholtz v. Inmates of Nebraska Penal and Correctional Complex, 442 U.S. 1, 99 S.Ct. 2100 (1979) (though there is no inherent right in the Constitution to parole, a limited right may be provided by mandatory language contained in the parole statutes). *See also Williams, supra,* note 52 (whether a limited right to parole exists must be determined by the language of the parole statute and regulations governing parole).

to parole protected by the Due Process Clause necessarily involves an analysis of the relevant federal parole statutes. . . . [W]hen one can show that the decisionmaker is required to base its decision on specific defined criteria, a protectible interest is created that is entitled to some degree of due process protection.[55]

In comparing the federal parole statute, 18 U.S.C. §4206(a), and the Nebraska statute considered by the Supreme Court in *Greenholtz,* the court found the language very similar. 18 U.S.C. §4206(a) provides:

> *If* an eligible prisoner has substantially observed the rules of the institution . . . and *if* the Commission . . . determines: (1) that release would not depreciate the seriousness of his offense or promote disrespect for the law; and (2) that release would not jeopardize the public welfare; [then] subject to the . . . guidelines promulgated by the Commission . . . , such prisoner *shall* be released. [Emphasis added.]

The Nebraska statute provided that a prisoner "shall" be paroled "unless" certain conditions were found to exist. Based on this "shall . . . unless" directive, the Supreme Court found a protectible liberty interest in *Greenholtz.* Since the federal parole statute contained a "shall . . . if" directive, the Eighth Circuit held that a protectible liberty interest was created.

The court also found additional support for its holding when examining the guidelines promulgated by the United States Parole Commission pursuant to 18 U.S.C. §4203(a)(1).[56] These guidelines further limited what the Federal Parole Commission could consider in its determination whether "good cause" existed for deviating from the recommended time contained in .the guidelines matrix.[57] These limitations imposed on the Federal Parole Commission created for a prisoner a substantial expectancy of parole entitled to due process protection.[58]

The Fifth Circuit is the only other circuit to address the issue of whether the federal parole statute creates a protectible liberty interest. In

---

[55]*Supra* note 52, at 525 (footnote and cite omitted). *See also* Connecticut Board of Pardons v. Dumschat, 452 U.S. 458, 101 S.Ct. 2460 (1981) (prisoner had no right to pardon when statute did not contain prescribed grounds for granting of pardon).

[56]The Supreme Court, in *Greenholtz, supra* note 54, did not comment extensively on the parole guidelines of the Nebraska Parole Board. See Ch. V, Sec. B1, for a full discussion concerning the creation of a liberty interest entitled to due process protection by rules and regulations.

[57]28 CFR §2.1-.59.

[58]18 U.S.C. §4206(c). *See also* 28 CFR §2.20. The Nebraska Parole Board was free to consider any other factor it deemed relevant. *Greenholtz, supra,* 442 U.S. at 18.

Page v. United States Parole Commission,[59] they held that the federal parole statute does *not* create a protectible liberty interest. In support of its conclusion, the Fifth Circuit cited a case decided under the now repealed federal parole statute which contained provisions very different than those now in effect.[60] This conflict between federal court decisions will probably be resolved by the Supreme Court.

Another method of challenging denial of parole is by demonstrating that the Parole Commission violated a statute, regulation, or other restrictions.[61] This review is limited since Congress has committed to the Parole Commission an unreviewable discretion to grant or deny parole.[62] The court, in *Luther v. Molina,*[63] held that Congress clearly intended to commit parole release or denial *decisions* to the absolute discretion of the Parole Commission. You can avoid this problem by challenging the method by which the decision is made, not the decision to grant or deny parole.

> Where the controlling statute indicates that particular agency action is committed to agency discretion, *a court may review the action if there is a claim that the agency has violated constitutional, statutory, regulatory, or other restrictions, but may not review agency action where the challenge is to the decision itself.*[64]

You would be alleging that the Parole Commission acted outside the scope of the discretion granted them by the statute and contained in the guidelines.[65]

---

[59]651 F.2d 1083 (5th Cir. 1981).

[60]*See* Evans v. Dillahunty, *supra* note 52, at 525 n.5,

[61]*See, e.g.,* Edwards v. United States, 574 F.2d 937 (8th Cir. 1978) (actions of Parole Commission, though consistent with guidelines, reviewable by habeas corpus if that decision was exercised in an arbitrary or capricious manner); Page v. United States Parole Commission, 651 F.2d 1083 (5th Cir. 1981) (Parole Commission may not act in a flagrant, unwarranted, or unauthorized manner).

[62]18 U.S.C. §4218(d) provides: "Actions of the Commission pursuant to ¶¶(1), (2), and (3) of §4203(b) shall be considered actions committed to agency discretion for purposes of §701(a)(2) of Title 5, United States Code."

[63]627 F.2d 71, 75-76 (7th Cir. 1980). *See also* Smaldone v. United States, 458 F. Supp. 1000, 1004 (D. Kan. 1978).

[64]Garcia v. Neagle, 660 F.2d 983, 988 (4th Cir. 1981) (emphasis added; cites omitted).

[65]*See, e.g.,* Parness v. United States Parole Commission, 488 F. Supp. 102 (S.D.N.Y. 1980) (National Commission exceeded authority of 28 CFR §2.23 when plaintiff was designated as original jurisdiction case and referred for 28 CFR §2.17 hearing).

a.   Procedural Outline for Federal Parole—Administrative Remedies[66]

The Parole Commission promulgated rules and regulations[67] pursuant to the authority granted them by Congress[68] and established the Parole Guidelines.[69] The Parole Commission also was given the authority to establish Regional Parole Commissioners and hearing examiners to be used in the determination of parole decisions.[70]

(1) Initial Parole Hearing

Once you are incarcerated, you may request an initial parole release hearing to determine your earliest parole release date.[71] This hearing is usually held within 120 days of incarceration.[72] You may waive/postpone the holding of this initial hearing until a future time.[73] At least thirty days prior to your hearing, you must receive notice of the time and place, be informed of your right to review the documents the Parole Commission will consider, and be provided with a background statement to be completed by you.[74]

This initial parole hearing is to establish a presumptive parole release date that you will receive, barring any institutional problems or de-

---

[66]*See* 18 U.S.C. §§4201-4218; 28 CFR §§28.1-28.59.

[67]*See* 28 CFR §§28.1-28.59.

[68]18 U.S.C. §4203(a)(1).

[69]*See* 28 CFR §28.20 for a listing of these guidelines. *See* Rifai v. United States Parole Commission, 586 F.2d 695 (9th Cir. 1978) (parole guidelines are merely procedural guidelines without the force of law), *application for stay denied sub nom,* Portley v. Grossman, 444 U.S. 331 (1980); Kirby v. United States, 463 F. Supp. 703 (D. Minn. 1979) (ex post facto provision does not apply to administrative guidelines, such as Parole Commission guidelines). *See also* Priore v. Nelson, 626 F.2d 211 (2d Cir. 1980) (guidelines based mostly on severity of offense is rational and in accordance with statutory criteria and intent of Congress). *Cf.* Dobbert v. Florida, 432 U.S. 282, 293, 97 S.Ct. 2290 (1977) (procedural changes even though to disadvantage of defendant are not ex post facto).

[70]*See* 18 U.S.C. §4203(c)(1) and (2).

[71]*See* 28 CFR §2.11.

[72]18 U.S.C. §4208(a); 28 CFR §2.11a.

[73]*Id.* at 2.11(b). If you waive or postpone your initial hearing, you must give the Parole Commission at least 45 days' notice in order to get your hearing later.

[74]28 CFR §2.11(d). *See also* 28 CFR §2.25 and 18 U.S.C. §4208(b) and (c).

privation of good time.[75] At this hearing, two parole hearing examiners and, usually, your caseworker will be present. Your case is reviewed and special attention is focused on the presentence report offense section. Numerous questions are usually asked of you concerning your activity and level of responsibility in the crime.[76]

The hearing examiners, after obtaining the information they determine is relevant, will use the parole guidelines to determine a presumptive parole release date. The guidelines consist of two scales: one is the "salient factor score," which measures the risk of allowing you to be released on parole;[77] and the second is the "offense severity rating."[78] Once these scores have been determined, they are placed on a matrix or grid and a customary total time to be served before release is calculated.[79]

The major factors considered by the Parole Commission in establishing its parole policy were "the nature and circumstances of the offense and the history and characteristics of the prisoner."[80] The Parole Commission is not required to base its parole release decision on the sentence the judge imposed on you.

> We find no indication in the language of the Parole Act or in the legislative history that Congress intended the sentence to be the central framework for parole decision. It serves to define the outer limits of parole eligibility, but offense severity and offender characteristics are the touchstones for parole consideration.[81]

---

[75]28 CFR §2.12(d).

[76]When you review the materials the Parole Commission will consider, if there are any errors you feel could have an adverse impact on setting your parole release date, you should consider postponing your hearing until you can obtain the documentation to correct these errors.

[77]This score is determined by considering prior convictions and employment history. See 28 CFR §2.20. A scale rating from 1 to 11 is used, with the higher number indicating a better parole risk.

[78]The Parole Commission has placed the criminal offenses into seven security levels—low, low moderate, moderate, high, very high, greatest 1, and greatest 11. See 28 CFR §2.20.

[79]The Commission may give a sentence above or below the matrix guidelines when aggravating or mitigating circumstances are present. See 28 CFR §2.20(c) and (d). See also Stroud v. United States Parole Commission, 668 F.2d 843 (5th Cir. 1982) (pattern of fraudulent activity resulted in decision outside guidelines); Staege v. United States Parole Commission, 671 F.2d 266 (8th Cir. 1982) (reclassification to high category is authorized based on additional facts).

[80]18 U.S.C. §4206(a).

[81]Garcia v. Neagle, 660 F.2d 983, 991 (4th Cir. 1981) (cite omitted). See also United States v. Addonizio, 442 U.S. 178, 188-89, 99 S.Ct. 2235 (1979).

The Parole Commission is allowed to use the same information that a judge would when sentencing you.[82] The courts have held that the Parole Commission may use all the information contained in a presentence report, including charges dismissed, as part of the plea agreement and allegations of other crimes not charged.[83] The weight that is given such information contained in the presentence report or other materials is left to the discretion of the Parole Commission.[84]

The Parole Commission is authorized to consider recommendations received from sentencing judges, defense attorneys, prosecutors, and others.[85] For these recommendations to be helpful, they must contain the underlying factual basis and reasoning in support of such recommendations.[86] You must remember that a recommendation, either from the sentencing judge or prosecutor, is not binding upon the Parole Commission to grant or deny parole.[87] "[The sentencing] judge may select an early parole eligibility date, but that guarantees only that the defendant will be considered at that time by the Parole Commission. . . ."[88]

The courts have also held that your institutional adjustment is not a major factor in the determination of parole release.[89] In *Moore v. Nelson*,[90] the court stated that since the enactment of the Parole Commission and Reorganization Act of 1976,[91] sentencing judges are aware that "rehabilitation plays a minor part in the Commission's decision to parole a prisoner, and has no special significance for . . . prisoners."[92]

In *Allen v. United States Parole Commission*,[93] the plaintiff had

---

[82]*See* 18 U.S.C. §4207(2) and (3); 28 CFR §2.19.

[83]*See* Billiteri v. United States Bd. of Parole, 541 F.2d 938, 944 (2d Cir. 1976); Payton v. Thomas, 486 F. Supp. 64 (S.D.N.Y. 1980).

[84]Billiteri v. United States Bd. of Parole, *id* at 944-45.

[85]*See* 28 CFR §2.19(d).

[86]*Id.*

[87]*See* United States ex rel. Goldberg v. Warden, Allenwood Fed., 622 F.2d 60 (3d Cir. 1980); Shoult v. Fields, 514 F. Supp. 900, 905 (W.D. Wisc. 1981).

[88]United States v. Addonizio, 442 U.S. 178, 189, 99 S.Ct. 2235 (1979).

[89]Staege v. United States Parole Commission, 671 F.2d 266 (8th Cir. 1982); Stroud v. United States Parole Commission, 668 F.2d 843 (5th Cir. 1982).

[90]611 F.2d 434 (2d Cir. 1979).

[91]18 U.S.C. §§4201-4218.

[92]Moore v. Nelson, *supra* note 90, at 438.

[93]671 F.2d 322 (9th Cir. 1982).

appealed his denial of parole, alleging that the Parole Commission acted arbitrarily and capriciously when it did not consider he had received a certificate from a drug rehabilitation program.[94] The statute under which plaintiff was sentenced required completion of at least six months in a drug rehabilitation program before one could be considered for parole release. Plaintiff argued that since he had received a certificate of completion of the NARA drug rehabilitation program, he should have been paroled.

The court of appeals held that there was no requirement that the Parole Commission " 'actively' consider a certificate of completion or provide specific reasons why it feels that a certification [of drug rehabilitation] is insufficient to warrant release."[95] 18 U.S.C. §4207 provides wide discretion to the Parole Commission as to the weight to be given a particular factor in the parole release process, such as completion of a drug rehabilitation program.[96] The statute under which plaintiff was sentenced, 18 U.S.C. §4253(a), only provides that until the prisoner has completed six months of a drug rehabilitation program s/he can not be considered for parole. There is nothing contained in that statute mandating the release of a prisoner after completion of a drug rehabilitation program.

Prisoners sentenced under 18 U.S.C. §4205(b)(2),[97] though they are eligible for parole consideration at any point in their sentence, are not entitled to earlier release than other prisoners; the guidelines are equally applicable. The statute only provides that they are eligible for *consideration* for release before the one-third point.[98] The Parole Commission retains the discretion to release a prisoner sentenced under §4205(b)(2) "at such time as [it] may determine."

In *Wilden v. Fields,*[99] the prisoner had argued that since he was sentenced under §4205(b)(2), the Parole Commission could not apply the

---

[94]Plaintiff had been sentenced to an indeterminate sentence not to exceed ten years pursuant to 18 U.S.C. §4253(a).

[95]*Supra* note 93, at 324. *See also* United States v. Wallerlatum, 600 F.2d 1261 (9th Cir. 1979) (prisoner's rehabilitation is not primary criteria for parole release); Shoult v. Fields, 514 F. Supp. 900 (W.D. Wisc. 1981) (Parole Commission may deny parole, even though institutional record is superb).

[96]*See* Payton v. Thomas, 486 F. Supp. 64 (S.D.N.Y. 1980).

[97]18 U.S.C. §4205(b)(2) provides: "the court may fix the maximum sentence of imprisonment to be served in which event the court may specify that the *prisoner may be released on parole at such time as the Commission may determine.*" (Emphasis added.)

[98]*See* Shahid v. Crawford, 599 F.2d 666 (5th Cir. 1979).

[99]510 F. Supp. 1295 (W.D. Wisc. 1981).

guidelines to his parole release determination. The court, quoting from *Christopher v. United States Bd. of Parole,*[100] held:

> Even if [§4205(b)(2)] requires special review hearings for indeterminate sentences, it does not require that prisoners sentenced under that statute be considered for parole under any different criteria than other prisoners. . . . The existence of a serious criminal background is clearly a proper basis for parole denial. . . .[101]

(2) Regional Appeal

Once the hearing examiners have made a recommendation concerning your presumptive parole or parole release date, it is then forwarded to the Regional Office of the Parole Commission in the area in which you are incarcerated.[102] The Regional Commissioner has twenty-one days to either refer the hearing examiners' recommendation to the National Commissioners,[103] modify it,[104] or adopt it.

If the Regional Commissioner has adopted or modified the hearing examiner's recommendation and you are not satisfied, you have thirty days from the date of entry of the decision to appeal to the Regional Commissioner on Form I-22, which is provided at your institution.[105] This appeal form lists seven items upon which you may base your appeal. These include:

(1) [ ] The guidelines were incorrectly applied in my case as to any or all of the following:

(A) [ ] Offense severity rating;

(B) [ ] Salient factor score item(s)____;

(C) [ ] Time in custody.

(2) [ ] A decision outside the guidelines was not supported by the reasons or the facts as stated in the Notice of Action;

(3) [ ] Especially mitigating circumstances justify a different decision;

(4) [ ] The decision was based on erroneous information and the actual facts justify a different decision;

(5) [ ] The Commission did not follow correct procedure in deciding my case, and a different decision would have resulted if the error had not occurred;

---

[100]589 F.2d 924, 932 (7th Cir. 1978).

[101]*Supra* note 99, at 1307 (cites omitted).

[102]*See* 28 CFR §2.23.

[103]*See* 28 CFR §2.24(a).

[104]*Id.* at 2.24(b).

[105]*See* 28 CFR §2.25(a). This does not cover cases designated as "original jurisdiction."

(6) [   ] There was significant information in existence but not known at the time of the hearing;

(7) [   ] There are compelling reasons why a more lenient decision should be rendered on grounds of compassion.[106]

The Regional Commissioner has thirty days to decide your appeal. Once a decision is rendered, you then have another thirty days to appeal to the National Appeals Board.[107]

(3) National Appeal

The appeal to the National Appeals Board must be taken on the form provided (different from I-22) within thirty days of the Regional Commissioner's decision. You can not raise an issue before this Board that has not been presented to the Regional Commissioner. A decision must be rendered within sixty days of receipt of your appeal. Failure of the Board to render a decision within sixty days does not mean they must grant your appeal, unless you can allege, and prove, prejudice that resulted from the delay.[108]

(4) Reopening Your Case

The Regional Commissioner may reopen a case on his/her own motion whenever new information of "substantial significance" favorable to the prisoner becomes available.[109] If you have obtained new information that is of "substantial significance," you should write a letter to the Regional Commissioner and provide him/her with this information. A case classified as "original jurisdiction" may also be reopened pursuant to 28 CFR §2.17. If your parole date has already been established and you have received disciplinary infractions or new criminal charges, the Regional Commissioner is supposed to reconsider your release date.[110]

---

[106]Marking item 7 and listing compassion as your ground for leniency is not enough. You must spell out facts in support of your claims. For example, if there is a *severe* medical problem within your family (immediate only, such as parents, spouse, or children), this can be the basis of a compassion decision. Your medical problem(s) should be significantly documented before being presented to the Commissioner.

[107]See 28 CFR §2.26.

[108]See Page v. United States Parole Commission, 651 F.2d 1083, 1087 (5th Cir. 1981).

[109]See 28 CFR §2.28.

[110]See 28 CFR §2.14 (cases where prisoners have presumptive parole date) and §2.24 (cases where prisoners have effective date of parole).

B. Parole Revocation

Once the parole authority releases you from incarceration,[111] you will then be required to spend a period of time on parole.[112] While on parole, you are required to comply with a number of conditions.[113] If you obey the law and the rules of parole, you should successfully complete your parole and be discharged from the intitial criminal sentence. If you violate any of the conditions of parole or commit a new crime, you may have your parole revoked and be returned to prison.[114]

The Supreme Court, in *Morrissey v. Brewer*,[115] held that a parolee enjoys a "conditional liberty" entitled to the protection of the Due Process Clause of the Fifth and Fourteenth Amendments.

> The liberty of a parolee enables him to do a wide range of things open to persons who have never been convicted of any crime. The parolee has been released from prison based on an evaluation that he shows reasonable promise of being able to return to society and function as a reasonable, self-reliant person. Subject to the conditions of his parole, he can be gainfully employed and is free to be with family and friends and to form the other enduring attachments of normal life.[116]

The Court held that a parolee is entitled to two types of hearing: (1) a "preliminary" hearing to determine whether there is probable cause or

---

[111]You will not be required to do time on parole if you have served your maximum sentence authorized by law.

[112]Almost every state provides for parole, and a period of time on parole before you can be discharged from your initial criminal sentence. California, Indiana, and Maine are presently the only states that do not provide for parole.

[113]These conditions can consist of staying out of bars; not associating with other persons known to have a criminal record; regular employment; no assaultive or abusive behavior; not using drugs or being in the presence of others using or having drugs in their possession; not leaving the state without permission of your parole officer; etc.

[114]Even though the parolee is convicted of a new crime, s/he is generally afforded an opportunity to present mitigating evidence at a parole revocation hearing. *See* Pope v. Chew, 521 F.2d 400 (4th Cir. 1975); Preston v. Piggman, 496 F.2d 270 (6th Cir. 1974); Johnson v. Matthews, 425 F. Supp. 794 (E.D. Wisc. 1977). Look also to your state case law and statutes to determine whether they require a hearing before revocation after conviction on a new crime.

[115]408 U.S. 471, 92 S.Ct. 2593 (1971). Prior to *Morrissey,* most state and federal courts had held that revocation of parole did not implicate any federal or state constitutional rights. *See generally* Menechino v. Oswald, 430 F.2d 403 (2d Cir. 1970); Hyser v. Reed, 318 F.2d 225 (D.C. Cir. 1963).

[116]*Morrissey, id.* at 482.

reasonable grounds to believe that the parolee has violated the terms of parole, and (2) a "final" revocation hearing before the parole board for a final evaluation of any contested relevant facts and consideration of whether the facts as determined warrant revocation.[117]

At the "preliminary" hearing, you are minimally entitled to: (1) a hearing conducted by one not involved in initiating the revocation charges;[118] (2) notice of the facts upon which the revocation charges are based; (3) the right to be present and to be heard on your behalf;[119] (4) a written summary of the evidence and arguments presented; (5) a written decision containing the facts and reasoning for finding probable cause; and (6) the right to confront those providing adverse information unless the hearing officer determines that the informant would be subjected to risk of harm if his/her identity was disclosed.

If probable cause to believe you have violated your parole conditions has been found to exist at the "preliminary" hearing, you will be scheduled for a "final" hearing. You are entitled to more procedural safeguards at this "final" hearing since the parole board must determine whether to cancel your parole and reincarcerate you. At this hearing, you are minimally entitled to: (1) a hearing before a neutral and detached body, usually the parole board; (2) written notice listing your alleged parole violations; (3) disclosure of all the evidence to be used against you; (4) an opportunity to speak to the parole board to state why your parole should not be revoked, including an opportunity to present witnesses and documentary evidence; (5) an opportunity to confront and cross-examine adverse witnesses unless the parole board specifically finds good cause why you should not be allowed to; (6) a written decision stating the facts and the reasoning upon which your parole was revoked; and (7) a reasonably prompt hearing.[120]

The issue of a parolee's right to counsel was not resolved in *Morrissey*. The Supreme Court addressed this issue in *Gagnon v. Scarpelli*,[121] where it held that a parolee/probationer had a qualified right to counsel if a

---

[117]*Id.* at 485-88.

[118]The government is not required to establish a special hearing officer; the hearing officer may be a parole officer not involved in bringing the charges against you. *Id.* at 486.

[119]The parolee may present "letters, documents, or individuals who can give relevant information to the hearing officer." *Id.* at 487.

[120]A period of two months was found to be a reasonable period in which to hold both the preliminary and final revocation hearings. This was based on the assumption that the parolee would remain in custody from the time of his arrest on parole violation charges until the final hearing. *Morrissey*, 408 U.S. at 487-88.

[121]411 U.S. 778, 93 S.Ct. 1756 (1973).

substantial issue as to whether parole or probation was actually violated is raised, or if the issues to be raised in mitigation of any violations are so complex that the parolee/probationer is not capable of handling them effectively.

> Presumptively, it may be said that counsel should be provided in cases where, after being informed of his right to request counsel, the probationer or parolee makes such a request, based on a timely and colorable claim (i) that he has not committed the alleged violation of the conditions upon which he is at liberty; or (ii) that, even if the violation is a matter of public record or is uncontested, there are substantial reasons which justified or mitigated the violation and make revocation inappropriate, and that the reasons are complex or otherwise difficult to develop or present. In passing on a request for the appointment of counsel, the responsible agency also should consider, especially in doubtful cases, whether the probationer appears to be capable of speaking effectively for himself. In every case in which a request for counsel at a preliminary or final hearing is refused, the grounds for refusal should be stated succinctly in the record.[122]

You should be informed by the parole revocation hearing officer that you have a right to appointment of counsel under the limited circumstances described above.[123] It is then your responsibility to make a timely request for appointed counsel and to state why counsel is needed.[124] If the parolee facing revocation has a low mental capacity or suffers from a mental disorder which would impair his/her ability to defend, counsel should be appointed.[125] Your counsel should be allowed to examine and cross-examine the witnesses and to present such evidence and arguments as are relevant.

The Supreme Court, in *Morrissey,* held that your preliminary hearing must be conducted at, or reasonably near, the place of the alleged parole violation or arrest.[126] This will allow you to present witnesses and other

---

[122]*Id.* at 790-91.

[123]Federal prisoners are entitled to appointment of counsel, if indigent, upon request. 18 U.S.C. §4214; 28 CFR §2.48(b); Baldwin v. Benson, 584 F.2d 953 (10th Cir. 1978). *See also* Barton v. Malley, 626 F.2d 151 (10th Cir. 1980) (counsel not needed where state prisoner had admitted violation and he was found adequately capable of speaking in his behalf); Butenhoff v. Oberquell, 603 P.2d 1277 (Ct. App. Wash. 1979) (reversed parole revocation for failure to appoint counsel despite requests until two days before the hearing).

[124]United States ex rel. Vitoratos v. Campbell, 410 F. Supp. 1208 (N.D. Ohio 1976).

[125]*Cf.* United States ex rel. Ross v. Warden, 428 F. Supp. 443 (E.D. Ill. 1977) (counsel at disciplinary hearing required where prisoner mentally unable to prepare defense).

[126]*See* Mack v. McCune, 551 F.2d 251 (10th Cir. 1977) (parolee and counsel waived local hearing); Kartman v. Parratt, 535 F.2d 450 (8th Cir. 1976).

evidence at this hearing which you might not otherwise be allowed to present at the final hearing a great distance away. Since most states do not provide the parole board, or their hearing officers, with the power to compel witnesses to attend revocation hearings, your witnesses may not have the money or time to travel great distances to testify at a hearing if it is held at the prison.[127]

If one is convicted of a new criminal offense, a preliminary hearing is not required since probable cause that you have violated your parole will exist at the moment of conviction.[128] The courts have held that, even though you are acquitted of a criminal charge, parole revocation is permissible.[129] Only if, as a matter of law, the dismissal of state charges removes all factual support from revocation can a parolee be successful on this ground.[130]

The issue of the timeliness of the preliminary and final revocation proceedings when based on a criminal conviction was considered in *Moody v. Daggett.*[131] The Supreme Court, in its earlier decision of *Morrissey,* had held that a period of two months was a reasonable period in which to hold both the preliminary and final revocation hearings. In *Moody,* the federal parolee had pled guilty and was sentenced. The federal parole board had issued, but did not execute, a parole violation warrant which was lodged as a detainer.[132] The prisoner had requested that the parole board execute the detainer, but they stated it would not be executed until he was released from the sentence he was presently serving. This meant that he lost the opportunity to serve the new sentence and the remainder of his old sentence concurrently. The Court upheld the parole board's refusal to execute the warrant. "With only a prospect of future incarceration, which is far from certain, we cannot say that the parole violation warrant has any present or inevitable effect upon the

---

[127]*Supra* note 115, 408 U.S. at 485 (a preliminary hearing should be conducted when the "information is fresh and the sources are available").

[128]Moody v. Daggett, 429 U.S. 78, 86 n.7, 97 S.Ct. 274 (1976) (subsequent conviction gives the parole authority probable cause).

[129]Standlee v. Rhay, 557 F.2d 1303, 1307 (9th Cir. 1977). *See also* United States v. Manuszak, 532 F.2d 311 (3d Cir. 1976) (probation revocation permissible, even though acquitted of criminal charges).

[130]Robinson v. Benson, 570 F.2d 920, 923 (10th Cir. 1978). *See also* Mack v. McCune, 551 F.2d 251 (10th Cir. 1977) (reversal of state conviction that was basis of parole violation did not affect revocation unless the acquittal removed all factual support from the parole revocation); United States ex rel. Carrasquilla v. Thomas, 527 F. Supp. 1105 (S.D.N.Y. 1981) (collateral estoppel or res judicata do not apply to non-legal civil proceedings such as parole revocation).

[131]429 U.S. 78, 97 S.Ct. 274 (1976).

[132]See Ch. XI for a discussion concerning detainers.

liberty interests which *Morrissey* sought to protect."[133] The Court noted that a parole board, upon execution of the parole warrant, might either not revoke parole, or, if parole is revoked, grant credit for time served.[134] The U.S. Parole Commission's policy now is that unless "substantial circumstances" are shown, the parole violation term of a parolee convicted of a new crime is to run consecutively to the new sentence imposed.[135]

The prisoner in *Moody* also raised the issue that evidence mitigating the parole violation charge would be lost if the hearing is not held promptly. The Court found that the prisoner had not alleged what additional evidence would be lost if the hearing was not held immediately. Had the prisoner made such an allegation, the Parole Commission could have conducted an immediate hearing.[136]

Federal courts have similarly held that a state prisoner is not entitled to an immediate violation hearing when a federal detainer is lodged with the state prison officials alleging violation of federal parole due to a state felony conviction.[137] The same result has been reached when a state parole violation warrant was lodged as a detainer with prison officials of another state.[138]

State prisoners must look closely at their state case law to determine how the local courts have interpreted the requirements of *Morrissey* and *Gagnon* in relation to parole revocation proceedings.

---

[133]*Supra* note 131, 429 U.S. at 87. *See also* Heath v. United States Parole Commission, 526 F. Supp. 584 (W.D.N.Y. 1981) (Commission may hold in abeyance an issued warrant until disposition of outstanding charges).

[134]*Moody, supra* note 128, at 87.

[135]*See* 28 CFR §2.74(c).

[136]*Supra* note 128, at 88 n.9. *See also* United States ex rel. Caruso v. United States Board of Parole, 570 F.2d 1150, 1154 n.9 (3d Cir. 1978) (under certain circumstances, parolee can force Commission to place mitigation evidence on record preserving it for subsequent revocation hearing).

[137]*See* United States ex rel. Hahn v. Revis, 560 F.2d 264 (7th Cir. 1977); Hicks v. Board of Parole, 550 F.2d 401 (8th Cir. 1977).

[138]*See* Larson v. McKenzie, 554 F.2d 131 (4th Cir. 1977) (per curiam); Gaddy v. Michael, 519 F.2d 669 (4th Cir. 1975).

IX
Federal Post-Conviction Remedies

By Jack Guttenberg*

Federal post-conviction relief is available in federal court to both state and federal prisoners once the normal appellate process has been completed. This form of relief, being very limited in nature, should be viewed as a last resort and not as an alternative to normal appellate procedures. Because the procedures for obtaining federal post-conviction relief are different from most other prison litigation, it is very important that you read this chapter before proceeding with your case.

The rules governing federal post-conviction relief are somewhat different for state and federal prisoners. These differences are discussed at length in this chapter. At the outset, your should understand that state prisoners will in all cases be seeking a writ of habeas corpus pursuant to 28 U.S.C. §2254. Federal prisoners, however, will usually make a motion to "vacate, set aside or correct [their] sentence" pursuant to 28 U.S.C. §2255 when they wish to challenge a federal criminal conviction or sentence. This procedure is intended to provide federal prisoners with the same protections as the writ of habeas corpus;[1] the major difference is that §2255 required the motion to be filed in the federal district court which imposed the sentence, not the court in the district where the petitioner is incarcerated. Federal prisoners may only seek a writ of habeas corpus pursuant to 28 U.S.C. §2241 in a case which is not covered by §2255[2] or

---

*Assistant Professor Law, Cleveland-Marshall College of Law, Cleveland State University

[1]United States v. Hayman, 342 U.S. 205, 72 S. Ct. 263 (1952).

[2]The statute covers cases where you are "claiming the right to be released upon the ground that the sentence was imposed in violation of the Constitution or laws of the United States, or that the court was without jurisdiction to impose such sentence, or that the sentence was in excess of the maximum authorized by law, or is otherwise subject to collateral attack . . . ." 28 U.S.C. §2255.

in which the §2255 remedy is "inadequate or ineffective to test the legality of his detention."[3]

This chapter also discusses the right of federal prisoners to move to correct or reduce their sentences pursuant to Rule 35 of the Federal Rules of Criminal Procedure. (See Sec. H, at the end of this chapter.)

A. General and Miscellaneous Information

1. Statutes and Court Rules

Federal post-conviction relief is governed by statute and by rules that govern the statutes. The sections in the United States Code which deal with federal post-conviction relief are found in volume 28 of the United States Code, §§2241 through 2255.[4] these sections should be read very carefully, along with the rules governing §§2254[5] and 2255.[6]

2. Uses of Federal Post-Conviction Relief

There are essentially two uses of federal post-conviction relief: attacking a state or federal conviction or sentence, and challenging the conditions of your confinement. When challenging your conviction or sentence, you are alleging that they were obtained in violation of the federal Constitution or laws, and therefore you are being confined illegally. This is the primary use of federal post-conviction relief, and is the main focus of this chapter.

As just indicated, federal post-conviction relief can also be used to challenge the conditions of your confinement.[7] Generally, challenges to the conditions of your confinement should be brought under 42 U.S.C. §1983, instead of relying on federal post-conviction remedies, due to the exhaustion[8] requirements of the federal post-conviction procedures and various other limitations. However, when the conditions of which you are complaining affect the length or duration of your confinement, you must rely on the federal post-conviction procedures and cannot use

---

[3]See McGhee v. Hanberry, 604 F.2d 9 (5th Cir. 1979); Application of Galante, 437 F.2d 1164, 1165 (3d Cir. 1971).

[4]See Appendix C, Sec. 1, 28 U.S.C. §§2241-2245.

[5]See Appendix C, Sec. 2, "Rules Governing Proceedings Under 28 U.S.C. §2254."

[6]See Appendix C, Sec. 3, "Rules Governing Proceedings Under 28 U.S.C. §2255."

[7]See cases, *infra,* Sec. I1.

[8]See cases, *infra,* Sec. I2. See also Ch. VI, Sec. D, for a further discussion of exhaustion.

§1983.[9] This will occur when you are claiming that you were wrongfully deprived of good time credits, held beyond your release date, given more time, or any other situation which either increases your time in prison, affects your release date, or prevents you from getting out when you should.[10] When any of these occur, you must follow the prerequisites and procedures stated in this chapter to get relief in federal court. When in doubt, contact an attorney or a prisoners' rights organization.[11]

B.   Prerequisites to Filing for Post-Conviction Relief

In order to grant relief in a federal post-conviction proceeding, the court must find that certain prerequisites for granting relief are present. If these prerequisites are not met, the court will dismiss the petition. For both state and federal prisoners seeking relief under 28 U.S.C. §§2241, 2254 and 2255 the court must find that the petitioner is in "custody" of state or federal authorities. For state prisoners, the court must find that the petitioner has exhausted the remedies available to him or her in state court; federal prisoners are required to use the ordinary appeals procedure before resorting to post-conviction remedies. Finally, both state and federal prisoners must show that they did not waive or forfeit the right to present an issue by failing to follow the trial court's rules for preserving issues for appeal. In general this means that the petitioner or his/her lawyer must have objected at trial concerning the issue presented in the petition.

In brief, then, in order to prevail in a post-conviction proceeding, you must be able to show that the issues in the petition were raised at trial, argued on appeal or in some other state court proceeding, and that you are still in custody. These requirements are explained in detail below.

1.   Custody

28 U.S.C. §§2254 and 2255 require that both state and federal prisoners be in custody at the time they seek post-conviction relief.[12] All that is required is that the person be in custody at the time the petition is filed; a later outright release will not prevent the granting of the petition.[13] A case should not be abandoned either in the district court or on appeal simply because the petitioner has completed his/her term of imprisonment.

---

[9]Preiser v. Rodriguez, 411 U.S. 475, 93 S.Ct. 1827 (1973).

[10]*See supra* note 7.

[11]See Ch. XI and list of organizations at the end of that chapter.

[12]See cases, *infra,* Sec. I3.

[13]Carafas v. LaVallee, 391 U.S. 234, 88 S. Ct. 1560 (1968) (prisoner, while on parole, challenged disqualification from voting or serving as a union official).

Custody includes imprisonment or incarceration, release on parole or probation,[14] and release on bail before the start of the sentence.[15] A person serving consecutive sentences for multiple convictions should attack those convictions at the earliest possible time. One does not have to wait until starting to serve the second sentence to pursue post-conviction remedies on the second sentence, even if the convictions are in different jurisdictions.[16] The same applies to those being held on detainers to start serving sentences in other jurisdictions.

2.   Exhaustion

The second and perhaps the most important of the prerequisites to bringing a federal post conviction proceeding is that a state prisoner must exhaust state remedies with respect to *every* issue raised in the petition.[17] What "exhaustion of state remedies" means is that the issues presented in the petition have been previously presented to the state courts. Usually this means that the same issues were raised on direct appeal after the conviction, but remedies may also be exhausted by being raised in a state post-conviction proceeding.[18] In general, if you are raising in your federal habeas proceeding issues that have already been raised in the briefs in the state courts, the exhaustion requirement will pose no problems. But if any one of the issues presented was not briefed in the state courts, the federal court must dismiss the petition. Thus, to have any chance of success in a post conviction proceeding, *all* the issues you present must have been in the briefs presented to the state court, either on appeal or in a state post conviction proceeding.

To have presented a claim to the state court sufficiently to exhaust state remedies, the petitioner must have raised the issue at every level at which it could have been raised. Thus, if after conviction there were appeals to the intermediate appellate court and then the highest court in a state, the issue must have been raised in both appeals to have been exhausted. If, however, there was no appeal to the highest court because that court refused to hear it, the appeal to the intermediate court would be sufficient to exhaust the claim, since the appellant presented it to every court where the appeal was allowed. To have exhausted remedies as to a claim does not require that the state court actually decide the issue.

---

[14]Jones v. Cunningham, 371 U.S. 236, 83 S.Ct. 373 (1963).

[15]Hensley v. Municipal Court, 411 U.S. 345, 93 S.Ct. 1571 (1973).

[16]Peyton v. Rowe, 391 U.S. 54, 88 S.Ct. 1549 (1968).

[17]Rose v. Lundy, 455 U.S. 509, 519-20, 102 S.Ct. 1198 (1982).

[18]Humphrey v. Cady, 405 U.S. 504, 516, 92 S.Ct. 1048 (1972); Wade v. Mayo, 334 U.S. 672, 677, 68 S.Ct. 1270 (1948).

All that is necessary is that the court be given a fair opportunity to decide it.[19] And the state courts need be given that opportunity only once; if the issue has been presented to the state courts on direct appeal after conviction, it need not be subsequently pursued in state post-conviction proceedings.[20] Also, you are not required to file an appeal or petition for a writ of certiorari to the United States Supreme Court after losing in the state's highest court in order to exhaust state remedies.[21]

It is important that the *same* issue be presented to the state and federal court.[22] Sometimes issues that look the same are in fact different. For example, the identical facts may be the basis of a claim that a confession should be suppressed because no *Miranda* warnings were given or a claim that the confession was coerced. If only the *Miranda* issue was presented to the state court, then that is the only issue on which remedies have been exhausted. Similarly, the same facts may underlie both a state law claim and a federal constitutional claim. For example, the admission of certain evidence may violate the confrontation clause of the Sixth Amendment as well as state law hearsay rules. If only the state law hearsay issue has been raised in the state court, however, remedies have not been exhausted on the Sixth Amendment issue. For this reason, you must have presented *both* the same facts and the same legal arguments to the state courts in order to have exhausted state remedies.[23]

It is very important to be able to identify which claims satisfy the exhaustion requirement, since under a recent Supreme Court decision, any petition that contains an unexhausted issue must be dismissed even if it also contains issues on which remedies have been exhausted. The Court wrote that its rule "provides a simple and clear instruction to potential litigants: before you bring any claims to federal court, be sure that you first have taken each one to state court. Just as pro se petitioners have managed to use the federal habeas machinery, so too should they be able to master this straightforward exhaustion requirement."[24]

It may occur, of course, that a court decides that some issues in the pe-

---

[19]Smith v. Digmon, 434 U.S. 332, 333-34, 98 S.Ct. 597 (1978); Francisco v. Gathright, 419 U.S. 59, 95 S.Ct. 257 (1974).

[20]Brown v. Allen, 344 U.S. 443, 447-50, 73 S.Ct. 397 (1953).

[21]Fay v. Noia, 372 U.S. 391, 435-38, 83 S.Ct. 822 (1963); County Court of Ulster County v. Allen, 442 U.S. 140, 149 n.7, 99 S.Ct. 2213 (1979).

[22]Anderson v. Harless, ____U.S.____, 103 S.Ct. 276 (1983); Picard v. Connor, 404 U.S. 270, 92 S.Ct. 509 (1971); Daye v. Attorney General, 696 F.2d 186 (2d Cir. 1982) (en banc); Gayle v. LeFevre, 613 F.2d 21, 22-23 (2d Cir. 1980); Johnson v. Metz, 609 F.2d 1052 (5th Cir. 1979).

[23]Anderson v. Harless, *id.,* 103 S.Ct. at 277.

[24]Rose v. Lundy, *supra* note 17, at 520.

tition you thought had been exhausted had not been and dismisses the entire petition. Or you may know that you have a number of issues, some exhausted and some not, and have to decide how to proceed. In either case, you have the choice of filing a petition immediately containing only issues as to which remedies have been exhausted, or of going back to state court post-conviction proceedings to exhaust remedies on your unexhausted claims.

The first option, filing a petition immediately, has some advantages and some risks. Since state court proceedings may be lengthy and complicated, filing a federal petition with exhausted claims immediately has the advantage of getting your case to court more quickly. In addition, the exhausted issues, which were raised in state court by trial and appellate lawyers, are probably the best issues in the case, and should be presented as soon as possible. The risk in doing this is that if the first petition is dismissed by the court and you then want to exhaust and raise the remaining issues, the court may refuse to hear them. Four Justices of the Supreme Court have stated that a district court may dismiss subsequent petitions if it finds that "the failure of the prisoner to assert those new grounds in a prior petition constituted an abuse of the writ."[25] Of course, this rule was not supported by a majority of the Supreme Court and accordingly is not necessarily binding on the district court, but it does suggest that issues not presented in the first petition might later be lost. You must decide in each case whether the advantage of proceeding immediately on what may be the best issues in the case is worth the risk of losing the remaining, unexhausted, issues. If you feel that the unexhausted issues are good ones, you should take them to state court first, and then file a petition with all issues.

Exhaustion of *state* remedies has no application to federal prisoners. However, federal prisoners should try to exhaust their federal appellate remedies with respect to all claims they wish to raise concerning their conviction. Many courts have held that a §2255 or habeas corpus proceeding is not a substitute for an appeal.[26] The Supreme Court has stated that relief on constitutional grounds is not barred solely by the failure to raise the issue on appeal.[27] However, the other side of the coin is that nonconstitutional issues will be barred by a failure to raise them on appeal.[28] Some cases have excused failure to raise nonconstitutional issues

---

[25]*Id.* at 520-21.

[26]Sosa v. United States, 550 F.2d 244, 246 (5th Cir. 1977); United States v. Cox, 567 F.2d 930, 932 (10th Cir. 1977), *cert. denied,* 435 U.S. 927, 98 S.Ct. 1496 (1978); DiPiazza v. United States, 471 F.2d 719 (6th Cir. 1973).

[27]Kaufman v. United States, 394 U.S. 217, 223 (1969).

[28]United States v. Cox, *supra* note 26, at 931-32.

on appeal on various grounds.[29] Also, some issues are difficult or impossible to raise on appeal, often because they concern matters not in the trial record.[30] The basic rule you should follow is: if you can appeal it, do so; there is nothing to be gained by waiting for a post-conviction proceeding. Even a constitutional claim may be barred if the court finds that you "deliberately bypassed" your appeal remedy or that their was no excuse for your failure to appeal.[31]

Federal prisoners are also required to use §2255 and not the habeas corpus procedure to raise any claim that is covered by §2255, unless it is shown that §2255 is "inadequate or ineffective to test the legality of [their] detention."[32]

Federal prisoners using habeas corpus pursuant to 28 U.S.C. §2241 for issues separate from their original conviction and sentence (prison conditions, parole and good time problems, etc.) are required to exhaust any available and adequate administrative remedies.[33]

3. Procedural Forfeitures

The final prerequisite for seeking post-conviction relief is that there have been no "procedural forfeiture" of an issue in the trial court. A procedural forfeiture occurs if, in a criminal trial, the defendant fails to follow state court rules to insure that the state courts will review an issue on direct appeal. In general, the state court rules require that the defendant *object at the time an issue arises* in order to be entitled later to raise that issue on appeal. When the defendant or his/her lawyer has not made a

---

[29]United States v. McDonald, 611 F.2d 1291 (10th Cir. 1980); Sosa v. United States, *supra* note 26; Natarelli v. United States, 516 F.2d 149 (2d Cir. 1975).

[30]*See* United States v. Gray, 464 F.2d 632, 634 n.1 (8th Cir. 1972) (claim of inadequate counsel should be heard under §2255 after development of factual record, not on direct appeal).

[31]Jones v. United States, 580 F.2d 349 (8th Cir. 1978), *cert. denied,* 439 U.S. 985, 99 S.Ct. 578 (1970); Houser v. United States, 508 F.2d 509, 518 (8th Cir. 1974); Kaufman v. United States, *supra* note 27, at 227, n.8.

[32]This standard is met "only if it can be shown that some limitation of scope or procedure would prevent a Section 2255 proceeding from affording the prisoner a full hearing and adjudication of his claim of wrongful detention." Application of Galante, 437 F.2d 1164, 1165 (3d Cir. 1971), *quoting* United States ex rel. Leguillou v. Davis, 212 F.2d 681, 684 (3d Cir. 1954). The fact that you expect to lose in a §2255 motion before the sentencing court does not meet this standard. *Id.*

[33]Wingo v. Ciccone, 506 F.2d 1011 (8th Cir. 1974); Talerico v. Warden, United States Penitentiary, 391 F. Supp. 193 (M.D.Pa. 1975). *But see* Coppola v. United States Attorney General, 455 F. Supp. 15 (D.Conn. 1977).

timely objection at trial concerning an issue, a procedural forfeiture has usually occurred.[34]

When there has been a procedural forfeiture on an issue on which post-conviction relief is being sought, the court must usually dismiss the petition with respect to that claim.[35] There are, however, two exceptions to this rule.

The first, and probably the most important, exception is that even where a forfeiture has occurred in the criminal trial, the federal court will hear the issue if the state appellate courts have considered the issue on its merits.[36] For example, if no objection was made to the admission of particular evidence at the criminal trial, the defendant has technically forfeited his/her right to complain on direct appeal and in post-conviction proceedings that the evidence should not have been admitted. However, if the state appellate court deals with the issue in its opinion anyway, the federal court can also consider it in a post-conviction proceeding. However, if the appellate court rejects the claim because no objection was made at trial, rather than dealing with the substance of the issue, then the federal court will find that a procedural forfeiture has occurred.

The second exception to the rule requiring dismissal of issues where a procedural default occurred at trial is that such claims will be considered if the petitioner can show "cause" for failing to follow the court rules requiring him to object at trial and "actual prejudice" resulting from the issue the petitioner alleges.[37] The Supreme Court has not, as of this writing, completely defined cause and actual prejudice, but two recent cases shed some light on the terms. In the first, *Engle v. Isaac,*[38] the defendants had failed to comply with an Ohio court rule requiring that all objections to jury instructions be made before the jury retires to deliberate, or they are forfeited. The trial judge had instructed the jury that the defendants

---

[34]You can usually tell this is a problem if the prosecutor argued on appeal that there was no objection at trial. *See* County Court of Ulster County v. Allen, 442 U.S. 140, 152, 99 S.Ct. 2213 (1979). If the prosecutor is correct that no objection was made at the appropriate time, you must argue that one of the exceptions to the rule of procedural forfeiture applies.

[35]Wainwright v. Sykes, 433 U.S. 72, 87, 97 S.Ct. 2497 (1977).

[36]County Court of Ulster County v. Allen, *supra* 34, at 154; Warden v. Hayden, 387, U.S. 294, 297 n.3, 87 S.Ct. 1642 (1967); *see also* Henderson v. Kibbe, 431 U.S. 145, 97 S.Ct. 1730 (1977) (federal courts reviewed jury instruction issue in habeas proceeding despite lack of any objection at trial where state appellate court had reviewed merits).

[37]Wainwright v. Sykes, *supra* note 35, at 90-91; Francis v. Henderson, 425 U.S. 536, 96 S.Ct. 1708 (1976); Davis v. United States, 411 U.S. 233, 93 S.Ct. 1577 (1973).

[38]____U.S.____, 102 S.Ct. 1558 (1982).

had the burden of proving an affirmative defense, that of self-defense. The Supreme Court rejected the defendants' first allegation of cause—that the Ohio courts had consistently upheld the constitutionality of the burden shifting instruction and any state court litigation on the issue would be useless—with a finding that the "futility of presenting an objection to the state court cannot *alone* constitute cause for the failure to object at trial."[39] It is now clear that all your federal claims must be litigated in the state courts, even if those courts have consistently rejected the claim and do not offer any evidence of changing their position.

The second allegation of cause offered by the *Isaac* defendants was that at the time of their trial the state of the law was so undeveloped that they could not have known that the jury instruction complained of raised constitutional questions. The Court found that it did not have to decide whether the undeveloped state of the law could ever constitute cause, because at the time of the *Isaac* defendants' trials, the "tools to construct" the constitutional claims existed and other attorneys around the country were raising similar issues.[40] The Court further implied that, while not every astute attorney would have recognized the constitutional issue, the failure to do so did not deprive the *Isaac* defendants of competent counsel or a fair trial. Finally, the Supreme Court in *Isaac* restated that the post-conviction petitioner must prove *both* cause and actual prejudice, and not one or the other.[41]

In *United States v. Frady,*[42] a federal prisoner post-conviction proceeding, the Court dealt with the term "actual prejudice." Before defining actual prejudice, the Court specifically stated that the plain error rule of Rule 52(b), FRCrP, was only to be used on direct appeal, and not in a §2255 proceeding.[43] The same applies to state prisoners as well.[44] Prior to *Frady,* the Court had rejected the use of presumed prejudice arising from the nature of the constitutional violation.[45] *Frady*

---

[39]*Id.* at 1573-74 (emphasis in original).

[40]*Id.* at 1574.

[41]*Id.* at 1675 n.43.

[42]___U.S.___, 102 S.Ct. 1584 (1982).

[43]*Id.* at 1592-94. *See also* Rule 52(b), FRCrP. Plain error has been defined as error which is "both obvious and substantial. . . ." It is invoked "only in exceptional circumstances [where necessary] to avoid a miscarriage of justice." *See, e.g.,* United States v. Gerald, 624 F.2d 1291, 1299 (5th Cir. 1980), *cert denied,* 450 U.S. 920 (1981); United States v. DiBenedetto, 542 F.2d 490, 494 (8th Cir. 1976).

[44]*See* Engle v. Isaac, *supra* note 38, at 1575 n.44.

[45]Davis v. United States, *supra* note 37, at 244-45.

involved a constitutional challenge to jury instructions on the meaning of malice, and the Court concluded that actual prejudice would exist where it could be shown that "the ailing instruction by itself so infected the entire trial that the resulting conviction violates due process."[46] This standard requires the reviewing court to evaluate the jury instructions in the total context of the trial to determine if sufficient harm occurred. In *Frady,* the Court found that overwhelming evidence of malice, uncontradicted at trial, prevented a finding of actual prejudice. Interestingly, the Court did state that if Frady had brought before the district court affirmative evidence that he had been wrongly convicted of a crime of which he was innocent, the case would be different.[47]

After *Isaac,* it appears that cause might be limited to instances where the defendant can show that the state prevented the discovery of the necessary facts needed to raise the constitutional issues;[48] that the state of the law was so undeveloped that counsel did not have the tools to develop the argument;[49] or where the procedural forfeiture resulted from the ineffective assistance of counsel.[50] *Frady* indicates that only a strong showing of actual harm, or possibly a colorable claim of innocence, will permit a finding of prejudice.

Finally, in *Sykes, Isaac,* and *Frady,* the forfeitures occurred at or before trial. The Supreme Court has not specifically indicated whether cause and prejudice apply to appellate forfeitures. Appellate forfeitures occur in one of two ways: the failure to take a timely appeal, or the failure to include certain issues when there is an appeal. In the first situation, the federal courts of appeals have generally applied the "deliberate bypass" test, which only bars federal post-conviction review where the defendant himself knowingly and intentionally decided not to

---

[46]*Supra* note 42, at 1595.

[47]*Id.* at 1596 (although the Court does not state how the case would have been different).

[48]*See* Thompson v. White, 680 F.2d 1173 (8th Cir.), *on remand from the Supreme Court,* 102 S.Ct. 2003 (1982) (fact that county sheriff had personally selected entire petit jury panel in a police murder case kept from defendant until after trial).

[49]*See* Ross v. Reed, 704 F.2d 205 (4th Cir. 1983), *on remand from the Supreme Court,* 102 S.Ct. 1063 (1982) (burden shifting jury instruction prior to 1970).

[50]*See, e.g.,* United States v. Hearst, 638 F.2d 1190 (9th Cir. 1980); Indiviglio v. United States, 612 F.2d 624 (2d Cir. 1979); Sincox v. United States, 571 F.2d 876 (5th Cir. 1978).

take an appeal.[51] Where certain issues are left out of an appeal, the courts have generally applied the cause and actual prejudice test.[52]

As is readily apparent, none of the above definitions are very clear or readily applicable to the facts of a given case. If you have a procedural forfeiture problem, where the courts have refused to hear your constitutional claims because your attorney failed to properly preserve them at trial or on appeal, you will have to research the issue in your given circuit, until the Supreme Court finally resolves the issue.

C. Grounds for Relief - State and Federal Prisoners*

In this section the grounds for claiming federal post-conviction relief will be discussed. As a general rule, state prisoners can only attack their convictions or sentences in federal court on the basis of *federal* constitutional violations. You *cannot* allege violations of state laws, rules, or procedures unless you can claim that such a violation also violates the federal Constitution. For example, if a judge takes a guilty plea and fails to follow the proper state procedures, but has done enough to comply with federal constitutional requirements, a federal court may not grant relief based on the state law violation.

The following is a list of areas which can be pursued in attacking the constitutional validity of your conviction or sentence. This list does not cover everything, and is only given as a starting point. If you have an issue not covered below, be sure to research it, as it may prove to be a good claim. Furthermore, because this list was compiled before this manual was published, it will need updating from time to time.

1. Grounds for Attacking Your Conviction and Sentence

a. Defects in the Charge, Indictment, or Information[53]

(1) Convicted under an unconstitutional statute.
(2) Tried twice for the same offense—double jeopardy.

---

[51]*See* Crick v. Smith, 650 F.2d 860 (6th Cir. 1981); Boyer v. Patton, 579 F.2d 284 (3d Cir. 1978); Jones v. Shell, 572 F.2d 1278 (8th Cir. 1978).

[52]Ford v. Strickland, 686 F.2d 434 (11th Cir. 1982); Matias v. Oshiro, 683 F.2d 318 (9th Cir. 1982); Forman v. Smith, 633 F.2d 634 (2d Cir. 1980); Cole v. Stevenson, 620 F.2d 1055 (4th Cir. 1980; Sincox v. United States, *supra* note 50.

*All footnotes in this section refer to cases at the end of this chapter, Sec. I4, Grounds for Relief.

[53]See cases, *infra,* Sec. I4a.

(3) Tried for an offense for which you were not charged.

(4) Statute of limitations had run out at time you were charged with the offense (federal prisoners only).

(5) The grand jury was unconstitutionally selected.

(6) The indictment shows no offense on its face, or offense charged is not illegal under any statute.

b. Pretrial Issues[54]

(1) Denial of the right to counsel, either by not being warned of right to court-appointed counsel in cases of indigency, or by not being provided with counsel at all stages in the criminal proceedings.

(2) Improper waiver of right to counsel at pretrial, during trial, or at sentencing.

(3) Unconstitutional confessions, violative of *Miranda* or taken involuntarily.

(4) Unconstitutional pretrial identification procedures.

(5) Denial of right to speedy trial.

(6) Prejudicial pretrial publicity.

c. Trial Issues[55]

(1) Denial of right to counsel.

(2) Denial of the effective assistance of counsel.

(3) Mental incompetency at any point in the criminal proceedings, but not at time of offense.

(4) Denial of right to jury trial.

(5) Denial of right to be present at trial.

(6) Denial of or unconstitutional comment on right to remain silent.

(7) Denial of right to cross-examine the witness against you.

(8) Prosecution's use of false testimony or lies s/he knew or had reason to believe was false.

(9) Prosecution withheld favorable evidence from you.

(10) The verdict was against the weight of the evidence.

---

[54]See cases, *infra,* Sec. I4b.

[55]See cases, *infra,* Sec. I4c.

d.   Guilty Pleas[56]

(1) Failure of the trial court and defense counsel to inform you of your right to a trial by jury or the court, to confront the witnesses against you, and of your privilege against compulsory self-incrimination.[57]

(2) Persuaded to plead guilty by promises which were not kept.

(3) Persuaded to plead guilty by threats from a judge, lawyers, police, or other persons.

(4) Never informed of the charge to which you were pleading guilty.

(5) Guilty plea was otherwise not knowingly and voluntarily given.

e.   Sentencing[58]

(1) Judge pronounced sentence without your attorney being present.

(2) Judge or jury failed to fix the degree of the offense.

(3) Sentence, or part of sentence, was excessive because:

(a) Sentenced for same offense more than once.

(b) Sentence was influenced by an earlier conviction which was not valid (unconstitutionally obtained or otherwise).

(c) Sentence not authorized by statute.

(4) Sentenced for an offense you were not charged with committing.

f.   Appeals[59]

(1) Failure of trial attorney to perfect appeal, either by failing to inform you of your right to appeal and the necessary procedures to be followed, or by failing to comply with the procedures for processing your appeal.

(2) Denial of the effective assistance of counsel on appeal.

---

[56]See cases, *infra,* Sec. I4d.

[57]Failure to inform you of all of these rights will be grounds for relief; a failure to inform you of one or more may not, depending on the rest of the plea.

[58]See cases, *infra,* Sec. I4e.

[59]See cases, *infra,* Sec. I4f.

(3) Denial of an attorney, all documents necessary for the appeal, including transcripts, and waiver of fees in cases of indigency.

2.   Fourth Amendment, Search and Seizure Issues - State Prisoners

In 1976, the United States Supreme Court effectively cut off the use of federal post-conviction relief for most state prisoners claiming a violation of their Fourth Amendment rights involving unlawful searches and seizures.[60]

In *Stone v. Powell,* the Court ruled that if the habeas petitioner claiming a Fourth Amendment violation was given the opportunity for a full and fair hearing in the state courts, the federal court would not hear the Fourth Amendment issues. The question under *Powell* is not whether you actually had such a hearing, but whether the state courts provided you with an *opportunity* for such a hearing, even if you or your attorney never actually asked for the hearing.[61] If the state courts prevented you from raising your Fourth Amendment claim, or did not provide a procedure for you to raise your claim, then you can raise this issue in federal court; otherwise, the court will not decide the Fourth Amendment issues.[62] Again, when in doubt, raise the issue![63]

D.   Relief Available - State and Federal Prisoners

If you prevail on the merits of your case, the district court will usually issue an order requiring your release from custody, unless the state or federal government wishes to retry you within a stated period of time, usually 90 to 120 days. If you are going to be retried, you will not be released from custody, but should be sent back to the place of your original trial, and you will be eligible to post bond for your release pending trial, just as was the case prior to your first trial. The order will usually include a provision preventing your release if the state or federal government appeals the district court's decision. In this event, you will not be released until the completion of the appeal. Generally, the court will not grant you bond for your release pending appeal, but it never hurts to try.

---

[60]Stone v. Powell, 428 U.S. 465, 96 S.Ct. 3037 (1976).

[61]*Id.,* at 494.

[62]Doescher v. Estelle, 616 F.2d 205 (5th Cir. 1980); Curry v. Garrison, 423 F. Supp. 109 (W.D.N.C. 1976).

[63]*See* Riley v. Gray, 674 F.2d 522 (6th Cir.), *cert. denied,* 102 S.Ct. 266 (1982) (state must provide opportunity in theory and in practice); see also cases, *infra,* Sec. I5.

If you have successfully challenged your sentence or conviction, the district court will order your release unless you are resentenced or you are granted a new appeal within a specified time period.

E.   Procedures and Process of Petitioning for Post-Conviction Relief

Federal post-conviction proceedings are started by the prisoner when s/he files a petition for post-conviction relief in the United States District Court. This section will describe the process from the filing of the petition through appeal.

1.   When To File

There is no advantage in delaying before you file your federal post-conviction petition. Once state remedies have been exhausted, the petition should be filed as soon as possible. Since you must still be in custody (as defined earlier) to file the petition, do not delay. In addition, any delay may be taken as an abuse of the writ and be grounds for dismissing the petition.

2.   Where To File

Federal prisoners must file their post-conviction petitions in the federal district court where they were convicted. *See* 28 U.S.C. §2255. State prisoners have the option of filing their petitions in the district court of the district where they are incarcerated or where they were convicted. *See* 28 U.S.C. §2241(d).

3.   How To File

a.   The Petition

The easiest and best way to file a petition for post-conviction relief is to use the forms supplied by the district court.[64] These forms can be obtained from any district court free of cost.[65]

When filling out these forms, you should follow the instructions exactly. Certain information is required in every petition, whether using the form or not. This includes the petitioner's name; place of confinement; the name of the warden of the prison where you are being

---

[64]See Appendix C, Forms 3, 4, and 7, for Petition for Habeas Corpus and Brief in Support.

[65]See Appendix A, Federal Court Directory.

confined;[66] and the trial court, judge, sentence, date of conviction, and offense from which you are seeking relief. To resolve the exhaustion issue, you should list the courts, dates, and results of all appeals and state post-conviction proceedings with regards to the conviction from which you are seeking relief.

If you are attacking two or more separate convictions arising out of the same court, you do not need to use separate petitions, but if you are challenging different convictions arising out of different state courts, or state and federal courts, a separate petition must be used for each court.

In addition to the above, you must state the grounds upon which relief should be granted.[67] When stating the grounds for relief, you must state the facts which you believe support your claims as clearly and simply as possible. Do not state conclusions of law without first stating the facts that support the conclusions of law. Example: If you are claiming that your guilty plea was involuntary because you were not warned of the constitutional rights you waived by pleading guilty, *do not* just state that your guilty plea was involuntarily taken. State the facts which support this conclusion: that when you pled guilty the judge and your attorney never told you that in pleading guilty you were waiving your right to trial by jury, the right to confront witnesses against you, your privilege against compulsory self-incrimination, and that you had no knowledge that you were waiving these rights. Likewise, if you are claiming ineffective assistance of counsel, state why counsel was ineffective: s/he failed to investigate defenses by not talking to the witnesses; s/he failed to follow discovery procedures; s/he failed to file a timely notice of alibi; and so on. It is very important that you *clearly* and *simply* state the factual basis for the grounds you are asserting. It is also important to state all the issues in your petition and not to state just a few, for the issues you leave out may represent your best claims!

b.   In Forma Pauperis Affidavit

Along with your petition, you should include a motion and an affidavit to proceed in forma pauperis.[68] These forms can also be obtained from the district court. They are very important because if and when in forma pauperis status is granted, it permits you to proceed as an indigent, waiving all filing fees, court costs, transcript fees, and service of

---

[66]For state prisoners, the person you are suing is always the warden of the prison, if you are incarcerated, or the head of the parole board, if you are on parole. For federal prisoners, the opposing party will be the United States.

[67]*See supra* notes 53-59 and accompanying text.

[68]See Appendix C, Forms 9 and 10. See also Ch. VII, Sec. A3a, for a general discussion of criteria for proceeding in forma pauperis.

process fees and makes you eligible for appointment of counsel at government expense.[69] Without the granting of your motion to proceed in forma pauperis, you will have to pay filing fees and all other expenses involved in your case.

c.   After Completing Petition

After completing the petition and the motion and affidavit to proceed in forma pauperis, send the original and two copies of each to the appropriate district court clerk's office.[70]

4.   Preliminary Review of Petition

Once the petition is filed with the district court, it is assigned to a specific district judge who will conduct an initial review of the petition. In some districts and with some judges, your petition will be referred to a magistrate who will handle the petition much in the same way as the judge would. If your case is assigned to a magistrate or you get a magistrate's recommendation, it is very important that you read the section on magistrates, Sec. G, *infra*.[71] Initially, the district judge has three options: to grant summary dismissal, to order the petition be amended, or to order the respondent to show cause why the petition should not be granted.

a.   Summary Dismissal

Upon complete review of the petition, the district court should only dismiss the petition at this point in the proceedings if the petition has been properly drafted, the claims are clearly stated, and based on those claims the petitioner is not entitled to relief. If this is so, the judge should issue an order dismissing the petition, which should include the reasons for such dismissal. In reality, many petitions are hastily dismissed because they are improperly drafted. If your petition has been dismissed because it was improperly or insufficiently drafted, you should file a new or amended petition, clearly explaining why the first one was dismissed and what you have done to remedy its shortcomings. Otherwise, you should consider an appeal. (See Secs. F and G, *infra,* on Appeals and

---

[69]See Appendix C, Form 12, "Request for Counsel."

[70]*Id.,* Form 8, "Habeas Cover Letter." See Appendix A for mailing addresses of the district courts.

[71]*See also* 28 U.S.C. §636 (1979); United States v. Raddatz, 447 U.S. 667, 100 S.Ct. 2406 (1980), for a discussion of the use of U.S. magistrates. For a discussion of the use of magistrates in civil rights actions, see Ch. VII, Sec. L.

Magistrates, respectively.) In any event, the court should state its reasons for dismissing the petition, and if it does not, you should file a motion for clarification immediately with the court requesting a written opinion as to why your case was dismissed.

b.   Order To Amend Petition.

If your petition has been improperly or incompletely drafted, the district court should return the petition to you with an order requiring you to amend your petition. If your petition is returned with an order for you to amend, follow the order, making the needed corrections or additions, and return the amended petition to the district court.

c.   Order To Show Cause

If you state an arguable case in your petition, the court will normally order the respondent to show cause why the writ of habeas corpus should not be granted. The order will be addressed to the respondent, but s/he will not personally file an answer or return; this is usually done by the state or federal attorney general's office which represents the respondent. The answer should address all of the allegations in your petition, in addition to stating whether you have exhausted state remedies. The court may also require the respondent to submit all transcripts and other documents necessary to decide your case (which includes transcripts, appellate court decisions, or any other documents related to your case).

5.   Review After Respondent's Return Filed and Appointment of Counsel

Once the respondent has filed his/her return (the answer to the petition), the court will again review the petition in light of the respondent's return and determine if the petitioner has made an arguable claim for relief. If s/he has not, the petition will be dismissed; however, if the court determines that an arguable claim for relief still exists, the court may appoint counsel to represent the petitioner.[72] The Supreme Court has not held that an indigent petitioner has the right to appointed counsel in post-conviction cases, but it is clearly within the discretion of the district court to appoint counsel for the indigent petitioner. *In every case, the petitioner should ask the court to appoint counsel to represent him/her.*[73] The petitioner should point out to the court in his/her request for appointed counsel the complexity of the legal issues involved, petitioner's lack of legal training and education, and that the appointment of counsel is necessary to insure the adequate presentation of

---

[72]Norris v. Wainwright, 588 F.2d 130 (5th Cir.), *cert. denied,* 444 U.S. 846.

[73]*Supra* note 69.

petitioner's case and is in the best interest of justice. The district court's failure to appoint counsel should always be considered as one of the issues to be raised if the court dismisses the petition and an appeal is taken.

6.   Evidentiary Hearing

If no evidentiary hearing is to be held, see Sec. 7, *infra*.

a.   When Should the Court Order an Evidentiary Hearing?

At this point, the petitioner and his/her attorney, if one has been appointed, must determine whether to request an evidentiary hearing. The district court is required to hold an evidentiary hearing only if there are disputed questions of fact and the petitioner did not receive a full and fair evidentiary hearing in the state courts.[74] However, if the petitioner had a full and fair evidentiary hearing in the state courts on the same facts in issue in the federal proceeding and the state court, trial or appellate, made a written finding of fact, or if its legal conclusions involved certain findings of fact, those determinations are presumed to be correct, and the petitioner has the heavy burden of establishing by convincing evidence that the factual determination by the state court was incorrect.[75] However, if petitioner can show one of the following situations, this will remove the presumption of correctness from the state court finding of fact, enabling the petitioner to get an evidentiary hearing in federal court:

(1) The merits of the factual dispute were not resolved in the state court hearing;

(2) the factfinding procedure employed by the state court was not adequate to afford a full and fair hearing;

---

[74]Cuyler v. Sullivan, 446 U.S. 335, 100 S.Ct. 1708 (1980); 3 PLM 35 (Feb. 1981) (state court findings concerning multiple representation is a question of law and fact, which is not entitled to presumption of correctness); Brewer v. Williams, 430 U.S. 387, 97 S.Ct. 1232 (1977) (district court, in habeas case alleging non-waiver of counsel, is not bound by state court's finding, since waiver of right to counsel is a question of law, not fact); Ellis v. Mabry, 601 F.2d 363 (8th Cir. 1979) (per curiam) (district court must hold evidentiary hearing to make specific findings, if dismissal of petition is based on grounds of prejudice to the state from delay and abuse of writ); Bolius v. Wainwright, 597 F.2d 986 (5th Cir. 1979) (federal court can make an independent assessment of facts relating to petitioner's competency to make guilty plea).

[75]28 U.S.C. §2254(d); Summer v. Mata, 449 U.S. 539, 101 S.Ct. 764 (1981); Summer v. Mata (II), ___U.S.___, 102 S.Ct. 1303 (1982); Marshall v. Lanberger, ___U.S.___, 103 S.Ct. 843 (1983).

(3) the material facts were not adequately developed at the state court hearing;

(4) the state court lacked jurisdiction of the subject matter or over the person;

(5) the state court, in deprivation of his constitutional right, failed to appoint counsel to represent him [indigent applicant] in the state court proceeding;

(6) the applicant did not receive a full, fair, and adequate hearing in the state court

(7) applicant was otherwise denied due process of law in the state court proceeding;

(8) that part of the record of the state court proceeding in which the determination of such factual issue was made . . . is produced . . . and the federal court . . . concludes that such factual determination is not fairly supported by the record. . . .[76]

These conditions are set forth in 28 U.S.C. §§2254(d).[77] Due to the inherent problems involved in overcoming a state court determination of fact, petitioner should always seek the appointment of counsel to assist him/her.[78]

b.   Conducting the Hearing

Prior to holding an evidentiary hearing, petitioner should request the appointment of counsel to aid in the gathering of evidence, an activity that petitioner's confinement will prevent him/her from doing, and to aid in conducting the hearing itself.

The petitioner should be careful to see that all the relevant factual evidence is presented to the court concerning his/her case. This should include any and all witnesses who can shed light on the situation, and all documentary and tangible evidence related to the case. A complete job should be done at this stage, as another opportunity may not present itself.

c.   Presence at Evidentiary Hearing

If there are substantial factual issues to be decided, the prisoner

---

[76]28 U.S.C. §2254(d).

[77]When the federal post-conviction court makes a determination of fact contrary to the findings of fact made in the state courts, the federal court must state its reasons for doing so with specific reference to the applicable sections of 28 U.S.C. §2254(d). Summer v. Mata, *supra* note 75.

[78]*Supra* note 74; Brewer v. Williams, 430 U.S. 387, 403-4, 97 S.Ct. 1232 (1977); Neil v. Biggers, 409 U.S. 188, 193 n.3, S.Ct. 375, 379 n.3 (1972).

generally has the right to be present at the hearing.[79] A prisoner may not be entitled to be present when only legal issues are to be decided[80] or the disputed facts are not within the prisoner's knowledge.[81]

d. Ordering a Transcript

Upon completion of the evidentiary hearing, the petitioner must decide if further pleadings or briefs are going to be filed, or if an appeal will follow a decision against him/her. If the answer to any of the above is yes, or if in doubt, you should order a copy of the hearing transcript. Your in forma pauperis status entitles you to a free transcript.

7. Motion for Summary Judgment or Post-Hearing Briefs

If there are no factual issues in dispute, the petitioner, immediately upon receipt of the respondent's return, should move the court for time to file a motion for summary judgment with accompanying brief. Such a motion and brief should be filed as soon as practical thereafter. The motion should just state that there are no existing disputed facts and on the law the petitioner is entitled to relief. The brief should contain a statement of all the relevant facts and the law as it applies to those facts. Petitioner's brief should be straightforward, short, and accurate. Remember, the courts generally dislike *pro se* pleadings and long pleadings, so say what you have to, but try to do it in as few words as possible.

If an evidentiary hearing has been held, at the conclusion of the hearing petitioner should inform the court that s/he wishes to file a brief incorporating the facts as resolved at the hearing and the applicable law to show that petitioner is entitled to relief.

Once all briefs have been filed, the court will be in a position to decide the case.

---

[79]Walker v. Johnston, 312 U.S. 275, 61 S.Ct. 574 (1941); United States ex rel. Griffin v. McMann, 310 F. Supp. 72 (E.D.N.Y. 1970); United States v. Hayman, 342 U.S. 205, 222-23, 72 S.Ct. 263 (1952).

[80]Foster v. Barbour, 613 F.2d 59 (4th Cir. 1980); *see also* Price v. Johnson, 334 U.S. 266, 68 S.Ct. 1049 (1948) (no right to appear at appellate argument in habeas case).

[81]Sanders v. United States, 373 U.S. 1, 20-21 (1963); Machibroda v. United States, 368 U.S. 487, 495-96 (1962); United States v. Boggs, 612 F.2d 991 (5th Cir. 1980) (per curiam); United States v. Missio, 597 F.2d 60 (5th Cir. 1979) (per curiam).

8.   Order of Court Granting or Denying Relief

a.   Order Granting Relief

If the court deems that the petitioner is entitled to post-conviction relief, it will issue an order so stating. Generally, such an order will state the reasons why the petition should be granted, the relief petitioner is entitled to, and that if the state desires to retry the petitioner, it must do so within a given period of time, usually 90 to 120 days, or the petitioner will be released. Should the respondent wish to appeal, this will stay the execution of the order during the appeal.

b.   Order Denying Relief

If the court believes that the petition should not be granted, it will issue an order and opinion so stating. The opinion should state exactly why the petition is not being granted. If the court just issues an order without an opinion, the petitioner should request that the court issue an opinion stating its reasons for denying the petition. This is done by filing a motion for clarification immediately with the court requesting a written opinion as to why your case was dismissed.

F.   Appeals

An appeal may be taken by either the petitioner or respondent from a final order of the district court granting or denying relief. You should appeal when there is *any* chance of success on appeal. The initial appeals process requires you to file a notice of appeal and to obtain a certificate of probable cause. Once this has been done, your appeal is handled just like any other appeal. Because of the time limits for filing a notice of appeal, act immediately and do not delay.

1.   Notice of Appeal

An appeal is started by filing a notice of appeal with the clerk of the district court. You have 30 days from the entry of the judgment or order of the district court to file the notice of appeal. (See Rule 4(a), Federal Rules of Appellate Procedure.) The notice of appeal must state the party taking the appeal, that is, the petitioner; the order being appealed, that being the denial of the petition for post-conviction relief; and the court to which the appeal is being taken, the United States Court of Appeals for the circuit where the district court is located.[82] The clerk of the district court will send a copy of the notice of appeal to the proper court

---

[82]See Appendix C, Form 6.

of appeals. The petitioner must make sure that the proper forms are filed ordering a transcript (if there was an evidentiary hearing in the district court and the transcript is not already part of the record) and transferring the district court record to the court of appeals. Since prisoners have 30 days after the district court issues its final order, they should file the notice of appeal before obtaining the certificate of probable cause.

2.   Certificate of Probable Cause[83] - State Prisoners

A state prisoner seeking an appeal from the district court ruling must obtain a certificate of probable cause before the appeal can be heard. Federal prisoners and the state or federal government do not need to obtain a certificate of probable cause.

The prisoner, immediately upon receiving a decision against him/her, should apply to the district court for a certificate of probable cause. This is done by filing a motion in the district court requesting the certificate. The motion should state the reason why an appeal is meritorious. The standard for issuing a certificate of probable cause varies, from an appeal presenting a "substantial question" to an appeal which is not "plainly frivolous." What this means is very hard to determine.

If the district court issues the certificate of probable cause, the court of appeals must hear the appeal and decide the issues presented. If the district court refuses to issue the certificate of probable cause, the prisoner can and *should* request that the court of appeals issue the certificate. The court of appeals is required to give "weighty consideration" to the district court's denial; however, this should not stop one from proceeding to seek a certificate of probable cause in the court of appeals, as it may be granted there.

Once the certificate of probable cause has been issued, the appeal proceeds just as any other appeal of right. The prisoner should request that the court appeals appoint counsel to represent him/her.[84]

3.   In Forma Pauperis[85]

An indigent prisoner who wishes to appeal a denial of his/her petition for post-conviction relief must obtain in forma pauperis status to avoid the cost of the appeal and be eligible for appointment of counsel. If the petitioner has already been granted in forma pauperis status by the district court s/he needs no further authorization to appeal in that status, unless the district court certifies in writing "that the appeal is not taken

---

[83]See Appendix C, Form 13, "Motion for Certificate of Probable Cause."

[84]See Appendix C, Form 12.

[85]See Ch. VII, Sec. A3a, for a general discussion of in forma pauperis.

in good faith,'' or that the appellant "is otherwise not entitled to so proceed,'' both of which are unlikely. (See also Ch. VII, Sec. P, for a general discussion of appeals taken in forma pauperis.)

However, if in forma pauperis status was not obtained prior to seeking an appeal, the prisoner must petition the district court for such status,[86] which will usually be granted unless the district judge certifies that the appeal is not taken in good faith, the allegations of poverty are not true, or the appeal is frivolous or malicious. If the district judge denies such a petition, the reasons must be stated in writing. Upon such a denial, the petitioner can and should seek such status from the court of appeals, which will give great weight to the district court's decision.[87]

G. Magistrates

Most United States District Courts make use of magistrates.[88] Magistrates are merely judicial officers who are appointed by the district court. In post-conviction cases, the district court will refer the petition to the magistrate to make findings of fact and conclusions of law. Once a case is referred to a magistrate, s/he will handle it in much the same manner as would the district court judge, the primary difference being that the final order deciding the outcome of the case must be made by the district judge.

Once the magistrate has made a final recommendation on the case, the parties have *ten days* to file objections to the magistrate's recommendations with the district court.[89] The district judge will then review the magistrate's recommendations, along with the objections filed by the parties, and give a final decision. If objections have been filed to the magistrate's report, the district court order adopting the magistrate's report and recommendation must specifically indicate that the district judge has reviewed the entire record of the case *de novo* (on his/her own).[90] If the order does not state this, a motion should be filed immediately with the district court requesting the judge to review the record, and if s/he refuses, this should be raised as an issue on appeal. It is very important that if you do not completely agree with the magistrate and intend to appeal the district court's decision if it adopts the magistrate's recommen-

---

[86]See Appendix C, Forms 9 and 10.

[87]*Supra* note 85.

[88]See Ch. VII, Sec. L, for a discussion of use of magistrates in civil action.

[89]28 U.S.C. §636(b)(1)(C).

[90]*See* 28 U.S.C. §§2254, Rule 8(b)(4); §2255, Rule 8(b)(4); Nettles v. Wainwright, 677 F.2d 404 (5th Cir. 1982); United States v. Walters, 638 F.2d 947, 949 (6th Cir. 1981).

dation, you promptly file objections to the magistrate's report, or you may be precluded from raising the issues on appeal.[91]

In addition, upon agreement of both parties, the magistrate can act as the district judge and issue final appealable orders, with the parties having the choice, agreed to ahead of time, to appeal directly to the district court or the court of appeals. When given this choice, it would be best to choose to appeal directly to the court of appeals. If you choose to appeal to the district court, you can only take an appeal to the court of appeals by discretionary leave to appeal.[92]

H. Federal Prisoner's Motion to Correct or Reduce Sentence

The final form of post-conviction relief we will discuss is available only to federal prisoners as a means of correcting or reducing their sentences. It is a completely distinct procedure from the forms or relief we have discussed above, and may be pursued only in the manner described in this section.

Rule 35 of the Federal Rules of Criminal Procedure (FRCrP) provides that a federal court may correct an illegal federal sentence at any time.[93] The rule also allows a federal court, within 120 days of sentence being imposed or the appeal process as of right being completed,[94] to correct a sentence imposed in an illegal manner, reduce the sentence, or place the prisoner on probation.[95] Note that this 120-day limit applies to the *court,* not to persons making the motion. Thus, you should submit your Rule 35 motion well before the 120 days have passed so the court will have time to consider and decide it before the 120 days expire. Any proceeding under Rule 35 is a continuation of the original criminal prosecution,[96] and therefore an indigent prisoner has the right to appointed counsel.

An illegal sentence is one that is in excess of the statutory time

---

[91]*See* United States v. Walters, *id.*

[92]*See* 28 U.S.C. §636(c)(5).

[93]As to time limits, *see* United States v. De Meir, 671 F.2d 1200 (8th Cir. 1983); United States v. Herrick, 627 F.2d 1007 (9th Cir. 1980); United States v. Mendoza, 565 F.2d 1285 (5th Cir. 1978).

[94]Rule 35(b), FRCrP. *See also* United States v. Addonizio, 442 U.,S. 178, 190, 99 S.Ct. 2235 (1979).

[95]*See* United States v. Sparrow, 673 F.2d 862 (5th Cir. 1982); United States v. Smith, 650 F.2d 206 (9th Cir. 1981); United States v. Calvin, 644 F.2d 703 (8th Cir. 1981); United States v. Cumbie, 569 F.2d 173 (5th Cir. 1978).

[96]Heflin v. United States, 358 U.S. 415, 79 S.Ct. 451 (1959); Semet v. United States, 422 F.2d 1269 (10th Cir. 1970).

provisions or otherwise contrary to the applicable statute.[97] A sentence imposed in an illegal manner is one which would otherwise be valid but for the procedures used before or at the time the court imposed the sentence. This would include a denial of the defendant's right to allocution, bias on the part of the trial judge, denial of the right to counsel at sentencing, failure to disclose the presentence report upon request, etc.

A motion to reduce a federal prisoner's sentence on grounds other than illegality is addressed to the discretion of the trial court.

Rule 35 is limited to correcting a sentence and does not apply to any errors which occurred at trial or other proceedings prior to the imposition of the sentence.[98] There is some overlap between Rule 35 and §2255 proceedings with respect to excessive sentences and sentences imposed in an unconstitutional manner.[99] When the time limits of Rule 35 have expired, relief may only be obtained under §2255.[100] If possible, you should file a Rule 35 motion rather than waiting and filing a §2255 petition, since you will get your case back before the sentencing judge while it is still fresh in his/her mind.

I.   Cases

1.   Conditions of Confinement

a.   General

Preiser v. Rodriguez, 411 U.S. 475, 93 S.Ct. 1827 (1973) (a prisoner is unlawfully subjected to physical restraint where a statute under which s/he was sentenced is unconstitutional, is imprisoned prior to trial on account of a defective indictment, is unlawfully confined in wrong institution, was denied constitutional rights at trial, gave invalid guilty plea, or where his/her parole was unlawfully revoked resulting in reincarceration).

Crawford v. Bell, 599 F.2d 890 (9th Cir. 1979) (habeas corpus is limited to attacks upon legality or duration of confinement).

Cook v. Hanberry, 596 F.2d 658 (9th Cir. 1979), *cert. denied,* 442 U.S. 932 (1978) (prisoner's allegation of mistreatment by prison officials demonstrating cruel and unusual punishment is not cognizable by habeas

---

[97]United States v. Risenhoover, 92 F.R.D. 741 (D. Okla. 1979); United States v. Becker, 536 F.2d 471 (1st Cir. 1976); United States v. Huss, 520 F.2d 598 (2d Cir. 1975).

[98]Hill v. United States, 368 U.S. 424, 82 S.Ct. 468 (1962).

[99]United States v. McDonald, 611 F.2d 1291 (9th Cir. 1980).

[100]United States v. De Lutro, 617 F.2d 316 (2d Cir. 1980).

corpus where appropriate remedy is an injunction requiring prison official to correct conditions).

United States v. Sisneros, 599 F.2d 946 (10th Cir. 1979) (habeas corpus proceeding is not proper remedy for allegations of inadequate medical treatment).

Brown v. Carlson, 431 F. Supp. 755 (D. Wisc. 1977) (federal prison officials' violations of the provisions of the Youth Corrections Act relating to place of confinement and classification are cognizable in a habeas corpus proceeding).

Smith v. United States, 577 F.2d 1025 (5th Cir. 1978) (for a delay in the holding of a final parole revocation hearing to be cognizable, the parolee must show (1) that, considering all the circumstances, the delay was unreasonable, and (2) that the delay was prejudicial). *See also Northington v. U.S. Parole Commission,* 587 F.2d 2 (6th Cir. 1978).

Ross v. Mebane, 536 F.2d 1199 (7th Cir. 1976) (challenges affecting the fact or duration of a prisoner's confinement are cognizable by habeas corpus).

Mason v. Ciccone, 517 F.2d 73 (8th Cir. 1975) (habeas corpus relief is prospective).

Wilwording v. Swenson, 404 U.S. 249, 92 S.Ct. 407 (1971) (prisoner's request for relief from certain living conditions and disciplinary measures at state prison was cognizable in federal habeas corpus proceeding). *See also Armstrong v. Cardwell,* 457 F.2d 34 (6th Cir. 1972).

b.   Release From Sentence/Community Placement

Drollinger v. Milligan, 552 F.2d 1220 (7th Cir. 1977) (habeas corpus is appropriate remedy for a defendant seeking release from custody or expansion of the perimeters of his/her confinement).

Eskridge v. Casson, 471 F. Supp. 98 (D. Del. 1979) (sole remedy for state prisoner seeking release from prison is habeas corpus, and not Civil Rights Act, 42 U.S.C. §1983).

Riggs v. Warden, Federal Correctional Inst., 476 F. Supp. 465 (D. Va. 1979) (federal prisoner could challenge by habeas corpus his/her denial of transfer to community treatment center since it directly concerns prisoner's custody status).

Thomas v. Cuyler, 467 F. Supp. 1000 (D. Pa. 1979) (challenge to standard used in denial of request for furlough is challenge of fact or duration of confinement and habeas corpus is proper remedy).

c.   Segregation/Transfer

Beck v. Wilkes, 589 F.2d 901 (5th Cir. 1979), *cert. denied,* 100 S.Ct. 90 (1979) (Lorton prisoner transferred to prison in Atlanta for administrative reasons by the authority of U.S. Attorney General could not challenge transfer in habeas corpus proceeding).

James v. McColley, 404 F. Supp. 350 (D. Md. 1975) (prisoner alleging s/he was entitled to a transfer to a prison camp or minimum security prison is not cognizable by habeas corpus in absence of a showing that action by prison officials was arbitrary or capricious or designed to punish the prisoner).

Knell v. Bensinger, 522 F.2d 720 (7th Cir. 1975) (habeas corpus remedy proper to challenge increased confinement to isolation).

Streeter v. Hooper, 618 F.2d 1178 (5th Cir. 1980) (prisoner's complaint seeking release from administrative segregation for denial of due process would be dismissed for failure to exhaust state remedies).

d. Good Time

Zaczek v. Huber, 437 F. Supp. 402 (D. Va. 1977), *aff'd,* 570 F.2d 346 (4th Cir. 1978) (appropriate remedy for restoration of good conduct credit is habeas corpus, not civil rights action).

Quarls v. State of Missouri, 337 F. Supp. 1025 (D. Mo. 1972) (habeas corpus is proper method to challenge "good time" deprivation).

2. Exhaustion

Wiley v. U.S. Board of Parole, 380 F. Supp. 1194 (D. Pa. 1974) (federal prisoner may not challenge his/her conviction by means of habeas corpus until all the ordinary remedies in the circuit wherein s/he was convicted have been exhausted). *See also Ghee v. Hanberry,* 604 F.2d 9 (5th Cir. 1979) (a motion to vacate sentence is primary method of collateral attack for federal prisoner on imposed sentence. Writ of habeas corpus is not a suitable substitute for motion to vacate sentence.).

Brown v. United States, 610 F.2d 672 (9th Cir. 1980) (federal prisoner challenging government's right to use a state conviction in imposing federal sentence is not per se required to exhaust state remedies). *But see Stead v. Linck,* 540 F.2d 923 (9th Cir. 1976) (federal prisoner's motion to vacate sentence based on prior invalid state conviction requires exhaustion of state remedies).

Coppola v. United States, 455 F. Supp. 15 (D. Conn. 1975) (federal prisoner alleging that prison officials violated his/her constitutional due process rights was not required to exhaust administrative remedies).

United States ex rel. Jacoby v. Arnold, 442 F. Supp. 144 (D. Pa. 1977) (federal prisoner alleging that Parole Commission had not followed sentencing recommendation was required to seek from the sentencing judge a vacating or correcting of sentence before filing habeas corpus proceeding).

Talerico v. Warden, U.S. Penitentiary, 391 F. Supp. 193 (D. Pa. 1975) (federal prisoner must exhaust administrative remedies from adverse decision of the U.S. Parole Commission before seeking habeas corpus relief).

Baxter v. Estelle, 614 F.2d 1030, *rehearing denied,* 622 F.2d 1043 (5th Cir. 1980) (state prisoner must exhaust established administrative remedies when challenging disciplinary hearing). *See also Lerma v. Estelle,* 585 F.2d 1297 (5th Cir. 1978), *cert. denied,* 444 U.S. 848 (1979).

Hoffman v. Edwards, 269 S.E.2d 311 (N.C. App. 1980) (state trial court did not have jurisdiction to hear habeas corpus action challenging disciplinary imposed punishment when s/he failed to exhaust administrative remedies).

McLallen v. Wyrick, 494 F. Supp. 138 (D. Mo. 1980) (to exhaust state remedies, a habeas petitioner must give the state courts a full and fair opportunity to decide and apply federal law to the claims raised, regardless of whether the state court actually decides federal questions).

Conley v. White, 470 F. Supp. 1 (D. Mo. 1979) (state petitioner must give the state an opportunity to pass upon and correct alleged constitutional violations before seeking federal habeas corpus relief). *See also Klimas v. Marly,* 599 F.2d 842 (8th Cir. 1979); *Johnson v. Hall,* 465 F. Supp. 516 (D. Mass. 1979), *aff'd,* 605 F.2d 577 (1st Cir. 1979).

Pitchess v. Davis, 421 U.S. 482, 95 S.Ct. 1748 (1975) (for federal courts to consider a claim presented by habeas corpus petition, each claim sought to be presented must have been presented to the state courts).

Carothers v. Rhay, 594 F.2d 225 (9th Cir. 1979) (prisoner's failure to exhaust state remedies as to all claims presented to federal courts requires dismissal without prejudice of habeas corpus petition). *See also Connor v. Auger,* 595 F.2d 407 (8th Cir. 1979), *cert. denied,* 444 U.S. 851 (1979). *But see Canet v. Turner,* 606 F.2d 89 (5th Cir. 1979) (a prisoner's failure to exhaust state remedies relating to all claims presented to federal court does not preclude consideration of claims exhausted).

United States ex rel. Cunningham v. Cuyler, 479 F. Supp. 765 (D. Pa. 1979) (purpose of exhaustion doctrine is to enable state courts to correct any mistakes which may have occurred in the criminal process).

3. Custody

Rose v. Morris, 619 F.2d 42 (9th Cir. 1980) (state detainer warrant against a federal prisoner is sufficient custody to confer habeas corpus jurisdiction). *See also Lublin v. Arnold,* 442 F. Supp. 54 (E.D.N.Y. 1977).

Newman v. Missouri, 394 F. Supp. 83 (D. Mo. 1974) ("custody" requirement of federal habeas corpus is measured at time of filing of petition by state prisoner).

Lewis v. Delaware State Hospital, 490 F. Supp. 177 (D. Del. 1980); 3 PLM 64 (March 1981) (if the state prisoner is in custody at the time of the filing of the petition, a subsequent escape does not destroy that custody).

Application of Cochran, 434 F. Supp. 1207 (D. Neb. 1977) (a prisoner released on bond is still in custody so s/he can bring a habeas corpus action).

Edwards v. Oklahoma, 429 F. Supp. 668 (D. Okla. 1976), *rev'd on other grounds,* 577 F.2d 1119 (10th Cir. 1978) (prisoner released on parole or probation who is subject to incarceration for failure to pay a fine or follow certain conditions is in custody).

Pueschel v. Leuba, 383 F. Supp. 576 (D. Conn. 1974) (a fine, without possible incarceration for non-payment, does not establish "custody"). *See also Wright v. Bailey,* 544 F.2d 737 (4th Cir. 1976).

Harrison v. Indiana, 597 F.2d 115 (7th Cir. 1979) (a conviction which sentence has been served can be the basis of a habeas action where such conviction delayed the start of a present sentence and thus delayed release).

Jones v. Cunningham, 371 U.S. 236, 240, 83 S.Ct. 373 (1963) (parole conditions constitute custody for habeas corpus purposes).

Hensley v. Municipal Court, 411 U.S. 345, 351, 93 S.Ct. 1571 (1973) (prisoner released on own recognizance pending execution of sentence satisfies custody requirement of habeas).

Warren v. Cardwell, 621 F.2d 319 (9th Cir. 1980) (federal prisoner freed on bond pending appeal of federal conviction was transferred to state prison to serve state sentence. Court held he was not entitled to habeas relief as a federal prisoner because he was exclusively within the custody of the state, and that he was also ineligible for federal habeas as a state prisoner because he had not exhausted state remedies).

4.   Grounds for Relief

a.   Defects in the Charge, Indictment, or Information

Application of Berkowitz, 3 Kan. App.2d 726, 602 P.2d 99 (1979) (trial court pretrial denial of claim of double jeopardy is challengeable by habeas corpus).

Crowell v. Zahradnick, 571 F.2d 1257 (4th Cir.), *cert. denied,* 439 U.S. 956 (1977) (an illegal arrest normally presents no grounds for habeas relief for a convicted defendant, unless it alleges denial of a fair trial due to introduction of evidence which came from the illegal arrest).

Martley v. Douglas, 463 F. Supp. 4 (D. Okla. 1977) (normally a state indictment is not subject to habeas relief, unless a material element of the offense is missing). *Francis v. Henderson,* 425 U.S. 536, 96 S.Ct. 1708 (1976) (a prisoner challenging the composition of the grand jury in a habeas proceeding must show cause for failure to object to the composition before trial and actual prejudice). *See also Evans v. Maggio,* 557 F.2d 430 (5th Cir. 1977).

Baker v. Metcalfe, 489 F. Supp. 930 (N.D. Tex. 1980) (prosecutorial misconduct that resulted in mistrial barred re-prosecution). *See also United States ex rel. Van Pelt v. Warden,* 461 F. Supp. 618 (N.D. Ill. 1978) (mistrial declared without explaining to prisoner why, barred from retrial); *Tipton v. Baker,* 432 F.2d 245 (10th Cir. 1970) (prisoner's sentence nullified at his own request allowed state judge to impose higher sentence).

United States ex rel. Rock v. Pinkey, 430 F. Supp. 176 (N.D. Ill. 1977), *aff'd,* 582 F.2d 1282 (8th Cir. 1977) (federal court will not strike down a state law because the court finds the law unwise or improvident).

Burrows v. Engle, 545 F.2d 552 (6th Cir. 1976) (to obtain federal habeas relief, one must allege more than a technical defect in the indictment).

James v. Reise, 546 F.2d 325 (9th Cir. 1976) (the Fifth Amendment requirement that one be indicted by a grand jury does not apply to the states).

Rose v. Mitchell, 443 U.S. 545, 99 S.Ct. 2993 (1979) (a constitutionally obtained criminal conviction can be challenged in a habeas proceeding alleging racial discrimination in the selection of a grand jury).

b. Pretrial Issues

United States v. Brown, 557 F.2d 541 (6th Cir. 1977) (federal courts must make independent determination on ultimate issue of voluntariness of confession). *See also Cannistrace v. Smith,* 470 F. Supp. 586 (S.D.N.Y. 1979).

Thompson v. Wainwright, 601 F.2d 768 (5th Cir. 1979) (once criminal defendant requests counsel, police officers cannot argue that counsel may not be in defendant's best interest or that counsel, when present, would tell defendant to act in a particular manner).

Davis v. Hudson, 436 F. Supp. 1210 (D.S.C. 1977) (to present a claim in a habeas petition for *Miranda* violation, one must present facts to support this allegation).

Bonaparte v. Smith, 362 F. Supp. 1315 (D. Ga. 1973) (failure to give a habeas petitioner *Miranda* warnings is not grounds for habeas, since no confession was given or used at trial).

Martin v. Indiana, 438 F. Supp. 234 (D. Ind. 1977), *aff'd without opinion,* 577 F.2d 749 (7th Cir.), *cert. denied,* 439 U.S. 900 (1978) (given pretrial lineup where only two black men present, one short and the other tall, and only the tall black man was wearing prison clothes and required to speak, habeas relief would be appropriate under totality of circumstances). *But see Bellew v. Gunn,* 424 F. Supp. 31 (D. Cal. 1976).

United States ex rel. Weger v. Brierton, 414 F. Supp. 1150 (D. Ill. 1976) (petition for habeas relief alleging pretrial publicity was denied since defendant had waived any objection by not moving for change of venue or continuance, and by not exhausting preemptory challenges during jury selection).

Potts v. Estelle, 529 F.2d 450 (5th Cir. 1976) (every reasonable presumption against waiver of counsel must be indulged in by habeas courts; the state has the burden to demonstrate appropriate waiver).

c.   Trial Issues

Cuyler v. Sullivan, 446 U.S. 335, 100 S.Ct. 1708 (1980) (petitioner seeking habeas relief on grounds of ineffective assistance of counsel must show actual conflict of interest, not merely possibility that conflicts exist).

Jackson v. Virginia, 443 U.S. 307, 99 S.Ct. 2781 (1979) (approving federal post-conviction review of a claim that the evidence presented at trial was insufficient to prove all of the essential elements beyond a reasonable doubt).

Davison v. Oklahoma, 428 F. Supp. 34 (W.D. Okla. 1976) (there is a heavy burden on petitioner to establish claim of ineffective assistance of counsel, and neither hindsight nor success is measured).

Willis v. Lane, 469 F. Supp. 318 (E.D. Tenn. 1978) (state trial court was not required to hold mental competency hearing based only on petitioner's allegation that he was mentally incompetent). *See also United States ex rel. Trantino v. Hatrack,* 563 F.2d 86 (3d Cir. 1977).

Davis v. Alabama, 596 F.2d 1214 (5th Cir. 1979) (habeas relief will be granted where trial counsel failed to investigate or develop evidence as to insanity defense where defendant had history of mental illness and insanity was the only possible defense).

Leon v. Kuhlman, 443 F. Supp. 50 (S.D.N.Y. 1977) (habeas relief will not be granted where evidence presented is overwhelming as to defendant's guilt and prosecutor's statement as to defendant's silence did not amount to egregious misconduct). *See also Zeming v. Solem,* 438 F. Supp. 455 (D.S.D. 1977); *Cook v. Bordenkircher,* 602 F. 2d 117 (6th Cir. 1979).

Henderson v. Kibbe, 431 U.S. 145, 97 S.Ct. 1730 (1977) (a petitioner, to be entitled to habeas relief based on erroneous jury instruction, must demonstrate that the instructions infected the entire trial resulting in conviction and violation of due process). *See Wright v. Smith,* 569 F.2d 1188 (2d Cir. 1978).

Reid v. Riddle, 550 F.2d 1003 (4th Cir. 1977) (court refusal to instruct the jury that they could not consider defendant's silence as evidence, after prosecutor in his closing made reference to it, could not be considered harmless error, and the writ should be issued).

Thurgood v. Tedford, 473 F. Supp. 339 (D. Conn. 1978) (where there has been a denial of the constitutional right of confrontation under the Sixth and Fourteenth Amendments, the defendant need not demonstrate that he was prejudiced).

United States ex rel. Moore v. Brierton, 560 F.2d 288 (7th Cir. 1977), *cert. denied,* 434 U.S. 1088 (1978) (habeas relief is not available where evidence the prosecutor failed to turn over to the defendant at trial did not raise a reasonable doubt as to guilt).

Castlebury v. Crisp, 414 F. Supp. 945 (D. Okla. 1976) (if defendant's counsel had independent knowledge of and access to exculpatory evidence that the prosecutor failed to provide to defendant, habeas relief is not proper).

Hawkins v. Robinson, 367 F. Supp. 1025 (D. Conn. 1973) (when identity of informant was highly relevant to identification and alibi defense of defendant, failure to reveal identity of informant was a denial of due process). *But see Carver v. England,* 470 F. Supp. 900 (E.D. Tenn. 1978), *aff'd without opinion,* 599 F.2d 1055 (6th Cir. 1979); *Pena v. Lefevre,* 419 F. Supp. 112 (E.D.N.Y. 1976).

Greenwood v. Massey, 469 F. Supp. 935 (S.D. Fla. 1979), *aff'd without opinion,* 614 F.2d 1295 (5th Cir. 1980) (unless defense counsel requests investigative reports from the prosecutor, the prosecutor is constitutionally required to voluntarily disclose only such evidence as is exculpatory). *See also Sims v. Brown,* 567 F.2d 752 (8th Cir. 1977).

Dustin v. Coiner, 367 F. Supp. 396 (D. W.Va. 1973) (admissibility of evidence is generally a matter of state law and procedure and is not cognizable in a habeas corpus proceeding).

d.   Guilty Pleas

Williams v. Wainwright, 604 F.2d 404 (5th Cir. 1979) (nolo contendere plea was voluntary where district court had ample basis for finding plea was voluntarily and intelligently made and state court advised defendant he would be waiving certain constitutional rights by pleading guilty).

Bonner v. Wyrick, 462 F. Supp. 1205 (D. Mo. 1976), *aff'd,* 563 F.2d 1293 (8th Cir.), *cert. denied,* 439 U.S. 913 (1977) (defendant's allegation that his guilty plea was involuntarily made because at time of pleas the alternative of jury trial was unlawfully chilled did not specify factual context and nature of legal premises).

Hunter v. Fogg, 470 F. Supp. 1041 (S.D.N.Y. 1979), *rev'd on other grounds,* 616 F.2d 55 (2d Cir. 1980) (test for determining constitutional validity of state court's guilty plea as to sentencing information is whether defendant was aware of actual sentencing possibilities and, if not, whether accurate information would have made any difference in the decision to plead guilty).

Blackledge v. Allison, 431 U.S. 63, 97 S.Ct. 1621 (1977) (federal courts may not adopt per se rule excluding all possibility that federal defendant's representations at the time of his/her guilty plea was accepted were the products of such factors as misunderstanding, duress, or misrepresentation by others as to make the guilty plea an unconstitutional basis for imprisonment).

Bergman v. Lefkowitz, 569 F.2d 705 (2d Cir. 1977) (plea bargain will not be set aside because of lack of forcefulness by the prosecutor when recommending sentence).

Santos v. Laurie, 443 F. Supp. 195 (D.R.I. 1977) (a defendant whose plea agreement was not kept has the choice of withdrawing the plea or specific enforcement).

U.S. v. Timmreck, 441 U.S. 780, 99 S.Ct. 2085 (1979), *on remand,* 600 F.2d 1228 (6th Cir. 1980) (a formal violation of Rule 11 without an allegation of prejudice to defendant is not entitled to §2255 relief). *See also Schriever v. United States,* 553 F.2d 1152 (8th Cir. 1977).

United States v. Goodman, 590 F.2d 705 (8th Cir. 1979), *cert. denied,* 440 U.S. 985 (1979) (a federal prisoner alleging that s/he pled guilty as a result of fear and coercion must show that s/he was subjected to threats or promises or illegitimate action and feared a greater sentence).

e. Sentencing

Williams v. Illinois, 399 U.S. 235, 90 S.Ct. 2018 (1970) (sentencing judges are vested with wide discretion in determining appropriate punishment, and are not required by the Constitution to give identical sentences to co-defendants).

United States v. Washington, 578 F.2d 256 (9th Cir. 1978) (sentence which is within limits set by valid statute may not be overturned on appeal as cruel and unusual).

Rummel v. Estelle, 445 U.S. 263, 100 S.Ct. 1133 (1980) (courts are reluctant to review legislatively mandated terms of imprisonment).

Hart v. Coiner, 483 F.2d 136 (4th Cir. 1973) (if the sentence imposed is within that authorized by the legislature, absent extraordinary and special circumstances that would shock human sensibilities, it is permissible). *See United States v. Wooter,* 503 F.2d 65 (4th Cir. 1974).

Brown v. Wainwright, 574 F.2d 200 (5th Cir. 1978) (life sentence for $71 robbery was not excessive when considering Florida's liberal provisions for parole eligibility).

U.S. v. McClintic, 606 F.2d 827 (8th Cir. 1979) (per curiam) (a defendant has the right to be present at resentencing if the sentence is made more onerous, or if the entire sentence is set aside and the cause remanded for resentencing, but not if the sentence is reduced under Rule 35).

United States v. Bacheler, 611 F.2d 443 (3d Cir. 1979) (explanation for sentence not required but would eliminate issue on appeal). *But see United States v. Beecroft,* 608 F.2d 753, 761-62 (9th Cir. 1979) (explanation of sentences required when court gives disparate sentences to co-defendants, although formal statement of reasons not necessary).

United States v. Main, 598 F.2d 1086, 1094 (7th Cir. 1979), *cert. denied,* 444 U.S. 943 (1979) (weight to be given various sentencing factors matter of discretion with which appellate court will not interfere). *But see Yates v. United States,* 356 U.S. 363, 78 S.Ct. 766 (1968) (per curiam) (failure of judge to properly exercise sentencing discretion requires imposition of new sentence).

Brown v. United States, 610 F.2d 672 (9th Cir. 1980) (failure to object before sentencing to inaccuracies in the presentence report after reviewing report generally precludes appellate or collateral relief).

Roberts v. United States, 445 U.S. 552, 100 S.Ct. 1358 (1980) (Supreme Court upheld a trial judge's discretion to consider a defendant's refusal to cooperate with the government as relevant to sentencing).

United States v. Tucker, 404 U.S. 443, 92 S.Ct. 589 (1972) (due process prevents the use of prior uncounseled convictions for sentencing purposes).

Baldasar v. Illinois, 446 U.S. 222, 100 S.Ct. 1585 (1980) (per curiam)

Benites v. U.S. Parole Commission, 597 F.2d 115 (7th Cir. 1979) (habeas corpus is appropriate remedy for attack on execution of federal sentence).

Duldulago v. U.S. Parole Commission, 461 F. Supp. 1138 (D. Fla. 1978) (allegation that sentencing judge's intentions were frustrated by Parole Commission's action is not cognizable injury for habeas corpus).

Coates v. State of Maryland, 436 F. Supp. 226 (D. Md. 1977) (trial court imposition of maximum sentence authorized by statute does not violate any federal right of state prisoner).

Peyton v. Rowe, 391 U.S. 54, 88 S.Ct. 1549 (1968) (federal district court may consider second sentence not yet being served on consecutive sentences if prisoner claims it was constitutionally invalid).

f.   Appeals

Abney v. United States, 431 U.S. 651, 97 S.Ct. 2034 (1977) (a denial of motion to dismiss indictment on double jeopardy grounds is a final determination of a collateral issue and is immediately appealable).

Browder v. Director, Dep't of Corrections of Ill., 434 U.S. 257, 98 S.Ct. 556 (1978) (a state prisoner must comply with the 30-day time limit for appeal from district court).

Sailer v. Gunn, 548 F.2d 271 (9th Cir. 1977) (appellate court will apply a "clearly erroneous" standard in reviewing the district court's disposition of a habeas petition).

Taylor v. Lombard, 606 F.2d 371 (2d Cir. 1979), *cert. denied,* 445 U.S. 946 (1980) (appellate court may make an independent factual determination of district court's disposition of a habeas petition when district court based its findings solely on the state court record).

Lucas v. Wainwright, 604 F.2d 373 (5th Cir. 1979) (per curiam) (petitioner abandons claims s/he fails to reassert on appeal from denial of habeas petition).

5.   Fourth Amendment—Search and Seizure Issues

Stone v. Powell, 428 U.S. 465, 96 S.Ct. 3037 (1976) ("where the state has provided an opportunity for full and fair litigation of a Fourth Amendment claim, a state prisoner may not be granted federal habeas corpus relief on the ground that evidence obtained in an unconstitutional search or seizure was introduced at the trial." 428 U.S. at 494).

O'Berry v. Wainwright, 546 F.2d 1204 (5th Cir. 1977) (*Stone* applies even if state court decision directly counter to ruling in an earlier Supreme Court case).

Jarrell v. Stahl, 446 F. Supp. 395 (W.D.N.C. 1977) (police observation of defendants in public toilet, even though a violation of reasonable expectation of privacy, is still foreclosed by *Stone*).

Caver v. Alabama, 577 F.2d 1188 (5th Cir. 1978) (where pretext arrest for vagrancy led to line-up at which voice identification was made, no claim of illegal arrest made in state court, federal court could not consider the matter).

Simmons v. Clemente, 552 F.2d 65 (2d Cir. 1977) (identity of witness and her later trial testimony following alleged illegal arrest cannot be reconsidered after state courts passed on claim).

United States ex rel. Sanders v. Rowe, 460 F. Supp. 1128 (N.D. Ill. 1978) (federal courts still free to consider Fifth and Sixth Amendment claims in habeas petition after *Stone*).

Walker v. Wilmot, 603 F.2d 1038 (2d Cir. 1979) (federal courts will still consider *Miranda* claims without citing *Stone*).

Berg v. Morris, 483 F. Supp. 179 (E.D. Cal. 1980) (*Stone* does not apply to due process violations affecting integrity of the factfinding process).

Fasano v. Hall, 615 F.2d 555 (1st Cir. 1980) (*Stone* principle held to apply to alleged violations of Interstate Agreement on Detainers). *But compare United States v. Williams,* 615 F.2d 585 (3d Cir. 1980) (IAD violation is cognizable in §2255 proceeding for federal prisoner).

Gamble v. Oklahoma, 583 F.2d 1160 (10th Cir. 1978) (*Stone* contemplates colorable application of correct law).

White v. Finkbeiner, 687 F.2d 885 (7th Cir. 1982) (detailing courts' failure to extend *Stone* beyond Fourth Amendment claims).

Williams v. Brown, 609 F.2d 216 (5th Cir. 1980) (absent showing that state routinely and systematically prevents Fourth Amendment litigation, *Stone* precludes federal post-conviction collateral review).

Sallie v. North Carolina, 587 F.2d 636 (4th Cir. 1978) (*Stone* does not preclude ineffective assistance of counsel claim based on counsel's failure to litigate Fourth Amendment claims). *Contra, LePuma v. Dept. of Corrections,* 560 F.2d 84, 93 n.6 (2d Cir. 1977).

Lenza v. Wyrick, 665 F.2d 804 (8th Cir. 1981); *United States ex rel. Maxey v. Morris,* 591 F.2d 386 (7th Cir. 1979); *Swicegood v. Alabama,* 577 F.2d 1322 (5th Cir. 1978) (all three hold that state court errors of law in Fourth Amendment cases do not permit federal post-conviction collateral review).

6. Delayed Petitions

Laches—such delay in enforcing one's rights as works disadvantage to another. 30A, C.J.S. Equity, §112, p. 19.

Mayola v. State of Ala., 623 F.2d 992 (5th Cir. 1980) (petition for habeas corpus may be dismissed under Rule 9 governing §2254 when prisoner has delayed unreasonably in filing his/her petition, and if the state can demonstrate it has suffered actual prejudice from the delay in its ability to respond to claims raised in petition). *See also Baxter v. Estelle,* 614 F.2d 1030 (5th Cir. 1980) (15-year delay under circumstances unreasonable); *Silva v. Zahradnick,* 445 F.Supp. 331 (D. Va. 1978) (delay of 21 years, where counsel had died 16 years earlier, unreasonable); *but see Sutton v. Lash,* 576 F.2d 738 (7th Cir. 1978) (21 years since trial not unreasonable); *Hawkins v. Bennett,* 423 F.2d 948 (8th Cir. 1970) (delay of 44 years did not bar habeas corpus proceeding).

Sanders v. United States, 373 U.S. 1, 83 S.Ct. 1068 (1963) ("nothing in the traditions of habeas corpus requires the federal courts to tolerate needless piecemeal litigation, [or] to entertain collateral proceedings whose only purpose is to vex, harass, or delay").

Price v. Johnson, 334 U.S. 266, 68 S.Ct. 1049 (1948) (if the government alleges the petitioner has abused the writ of habeas corpus, it is required to show with particularity the alleged abuse).

Paprskar v. Estelle, 612 F.2d 1003 (5th Cir.), *cert. denied,* 101 S.Ct. 239 (1980) (a second writ is not an abuse of the writ requiring dismissal where, at the time of the first writ, the state had not finally acted upon the issues raised in the second writ).

Cody v. Missouri Board of Probation and Parole, 468 F. Supp. 431 (W.D. Mo. 1979) (a petitioner who withholds claims from consideration by the state courts until after his first federal habeas has been determined has abused the writ and the claims later raised should be dismissed).

Johnson v. Copinger, 420 F.2d 395 (4th Cir. 1969) (before habeas petition can be dismissed as an abuse of the writ, the petitioner must be given an opportunity to explain the omissions from his/her earlier petition). *See also Patton v. Fenton,* 491 F. Supp. 156 (D. Pa. 1979) (before court may dismiss second habeas petition as an abuse of the writ, the court must determine whether same issues raised in both petitions were determined in the first petition adversely to petitioner and on the merits).

Harlow v. Murray, 443 F. Supp. 1327 (D. Va. 1978), *aff'd,* 588 F.2d 1348 (4th Cir. 1978) (petitioner misinterpreted state court decision, but this would not prevent filing of second habeas petition raising identical grounds).

Irons v. Montanye, 520 F.2d 646 (2d Cir. 1975) (in a second habeas petition presenting previously raised issues not afforded an evidentiary hearing, justice requires a hearing on the issues raised).

7. Applicable Laws

Townsend v. Sain, 372 U.S. 293, 83 S.Ct. 745 (1963) (federal district court must apply applicable federal law to state court factfindings independently of state court's finding of law).

Toler v. Wyrick, 563 F.2d 372 (8th Cir. 1977), *cert. denied,* 435 U.S. 907 (1978) (in determining whether an evidentiary hearing is required in a habeas corpus proceeding, the federal court must apply federal constitutional law; it may apply that law to facts found by a state court).

Harrell v. Israel, 478 F. Supp. 752 (E.D. Wis. 1979) (federal courts are bound by interpretation by state's highest court of state statute). *See Wartlitner v. Weatherholtz,* 447 F. Supp. 82 (W.D. Va. 1977), *dismissed,* 598 F.2d 617 (4th Cir. 1979) (federal courts bound by Virginia Supreme Court's interpretation of Virginia law as it relates to the existence of malice in a homicide case); *Brewer v. Overberg,* 624 F.2d 51 (6th Cir. 1980) (federal courts bound by state court's interpretation of its own court's procedural rules). *But see Rinehart v. Brewer,* 561 F.2d 126 (8th Cir. 1977) (federal courts not bound by state court's interpretation of its procedural rules that defendant had waived all his federal claims).

8. Res Judicata/Collateral Estoppel

Fay v. Noia, 372 U.S. 391, 83 S. Ct. 822 (1963) (res judicata does not fully apply to habeas corpus proceedings).

Troy v. State of New York, 483 F. Supp. 235 (S.D.N.Y. 1980) (a prior state court judgment will collaterally estop a subsequent civil action based upon the same issues. Collateral estoppel does not bar a subsequent habeas corpus action based on those same issues.).

Wilwording v. Swenson, 502 F.2d 844 (8th Cir. 1974), *cert. denied,* 420 U.S. 912 (1975) (a prisoner's prior voluntary dismissal of certain claims, even with prejudice, will not prevent him/her from raising the same issues later in a habeas action. Collateral estoppel only precludes a new hearing on issues actually litigated and determined in a prior suit.).

X

Detainers

By George N. Brezna*

Prisoners are frequently wanted in other jurisdictions because of an outstanding criminal charge, sentence, or parole/probation violation. If the jurisdiction where such charges are pending decides to prosecute you, it will initiate detainer or extradition proceedings against you. You have different rights relative to each proceeding, so it is important for you to protect yourself by pursuing the proper procedures.

Detainers are the primary focus of this chapter and will be examined in detail. A brief discussion of extradition is also presented, however, in Sec. E, *infra*. Important relationships between detainer and extradition proceedings are noted when appropriate.

A. Effects of a Detainer

A detainer is a written request from the prosecuting authority of another jurisdiction. It is sent to your warden and informs him/her of criminal matters pending against you in the other jurisdiction. It also asks your warden to hold you at the end of your sentence to permit that jurisdiction to take custody of you.

Generally, if a detainer is lodged against you, you will be released to the custody of the demanding jurisdiction to dispose of the outstanding criminal matters either during your present term of imprisonment or upon your release from prison. Normally, prison officials mark your prison file to indicate that a detainer has been lodged against you. Thereafter, they will usually tell you a detainer is present in your prison file. They should also advise you of your right to demand prompt disposition of the criminal matters underlying the detainer.

Prisoners are commonly faced with one of three possible detainers:

1. the detainer based on an outstanding, untried charge;
2. the detainer based on a parole or probation violation; or

---

* J.D., Antioch School of Law, 1982; M.A., Univ. of Dayton, 1974; member of the Maryland bar.

3. the detainer based on an outstanding sentence.

Of the three, the detainer based on an outstanding, untried charge is the most common. Most of the discussion in this chapter will concern this type. Detainers based on parole or probation violations are discussed in Sec. C, *infra*. Disposing of a detainer based on an outstanding sentence is usually a losing proposition, but the discussion in this chapter concerning negotiation may help you remove this kind of detainer from your prison file.

A detainer and delay in the disposition of the charges underlying it can adversely affect you in the following ways:

1. You may be confined under increased security measures to prevent your possible escape;

2. You may be excluded from institutional opportunities for rehabilitation, such as educational and work-release programs or parole;

3. You may be unable to make a good defense to the charges underlying the detainer because you cannot keep track of witnesses and do not have the ready availability of counsel while imprisoned;

4. You may be prevented from receiving a sentence for the charges underlying the detainer early enough to be at least partially concurrent with your present sentence; and

5. You may suffer extreme psychological pressures from the uncertainties presented by a detainer and its underlying charges pending against you.[1]

Prisoners have generally not been very successful in challenging the effects of detainers on their status in prison. The Supreme Court has held that restrictions on classification and program opportunities caused by detainers do not require procedural due process protections.[2] Courts have generally considered the question as the type of classification matter with which they will not interfere.[3] The major exception is the decision in

---

[1]Smith v. Hooey, 393 U.S. 374, 378-80, 89 S.Ct. 575 (1969). *See* Abramson, *Criminal Detainers,* (Ballinger Publishing Co., 1979), for an excellent survey of the law concerning detainers; Burns, "The Dangling Sword: Detainers and the Rights of Prisoners Under the Interstate Agreement on Detainers," 1 PLM 116 (Oct. 1978); Note, 77 YALE L.J. 767 (1968); Note, 18 RUTGERS L. REV. 828 (1964); Bennett, "The Last Full Ounce," 23 FED. PROB. 20 (June 1969). *See also* H.R. Rep. No. 1018, 91st Con., 2d Sess. at 3 (1970); S. Rep. No. 1356, 91st Con., 2d Sess. at 3 (1970), *reprinted in* [1970] U.S.C.C.A.N.

[2]Moody v. Daggett, 429 U.S. 78, 88, 97 S.Ct. 274 n.9 (1977).

[3]*See* Stevens v. Heard, 674 F.2d 320, 324 (5th Cir. 1982); Rinaldi v. United States, 484 F. Supp. 916 (S.D.N.Y. 1977); Harness v. Day, 428 F. Supp. 18 (W.D. Okla. 1976) See also Ch. V, Secs. B3e, C10L for discussions of classification.

Reddin v. Israel,[4] in which the court rejected the plaintiff's procedural due process attack on the prison's reliance on a detainer to keep him in a restrictive classification, but held that the prison's per se exclusion of prisoners with detainers from certain classifications and programs denied equal protection and substantive due process. The court observed that prisoners facing short terms pursuant to detainers were subject to more restrictions than persons facing much longer terms without detainers, and that this distinction was arbitrary and irrational.[5]

B. Detainer Strategies

There are five ways to deal with a detainer:

1. inaction;
2. negotiation;
3. Interstate Agreement on Detainers (IAD) or intrastate detainer laws;
4. constitutional speedy trial arguments; and
5. statutory speedy trial arguments.

When deciding which course to take, you should first consider exactly *how harmful* is this detainer: will it cause me to be deprived of prison privileges, such as educational and work-release programs, furloughs, and other prison activities enjoyed by other prisoners; will demanding final disposition of the charges underlying the detainer lead to another conviction and additional prison time; will the demanding jurisdiction's case against me be weakened by passage of time and loss of witnesses and other evidence, possibly resulting in dismissal of the prosecutor's case; will my defenses to the charges underlying the detainer be weakened by the passage of time. If there is a high probability that you will be convicted at an early trial on the charges, a "wait and see" attitude may be appropriate.

1. Inaction

Certain benefits may actually accrue to you by not demanding a speedy trial of the charges underlying the detainer. For example, the demanding jurisdiction might decide to summarily dismiss the charges

---

[4]455 F. Supp. 1215 (E.D. Wisc. 1978).

[5]*Id.* at 1221. *Accord,* Holt v. Moore, 357 F. Supp. 1102 (W.D.N.C. 1973), *rev'd on other grounds,* 541 F.2d 460 (4th Cir. 1976). See Ch. V, Sec. D, for a discussion of equal protection. Generally, a classification will be upheld if it bears a rational relationship to a legitimate governmental objective or purpose, in this case, security, punishment, deterrence, or rehabilitation.

simply because you are presently serving a substantial prison sentence. The prosecutor of the demanding jurisdiction might also decide that the cost of bringing you to trial is more trouble and expense than a possible new conviction and short sentence is worth. If a substantial period of time has elapsed since the underlying charge was filed against you, the prosecutor might decide that the detainer is ineffective since you have a high probability of avoiding the underlying charge on speedy trial grounds or because witnesses and evidence are unavailable.

There are three primary benefits from a "wait and see" approach to the detainer lodged against you. First, you have time to develop a sound and coherent strategy for dealing with the detainer and its underlying charges. Second, you leave open the possibility that the prosecutor's case will fall into disrepair. Third, you avoid the additional prison time which may result from a hasty decision to seek a trial of the charges underlying the detainer.

Of course, if the demanding jurisdiction is actively seeking custody of you for trial on the charges underlying its detainer, you might not have much time to wait and see what develops. In that case, you should at least take the time to develop a strategy for dealing with the detainer and its underlying charges. The following discussion should help you formulate that strategy.

2. Negotiation With Prosecutor

It may be possible for you to remove the detainer from your prison files through active negotiation with the proper authorities of the demanding jurisdiction. However, you should at least consider two items before proceeding with any negotiation. First, realize that any negotiation requires an appropriate negotiator and delicateness of negotiation style. Second, realize that the facts and circumstances of your case and the nature of the detainer are crucial to the outcome of any negotiation.

The proper authority with whom the negotiations should be conducted is usually the district attorney for the jurisdiction in which the charge is pending. As you already know, apart from plea bargaining sessions and the like, district attorneys dislike extra-trial contact with the accused or prisoners. Consequently, negotiation with them is best conducted by an attorney. In some cases, however, a caseworker or other intermediary could also successfully conduct the negotiations.

You should *exercise extreme caution* when attempting to negotiate dismissal of a detainer. One mistake can mean additional prison time and the loss of a good defense or strategy. You are not relieved of legal responsibilities simply because negotiations are in progress. For example, you still have a duty to make a request for final disposition of the detainer under the Interstate Agreement on Detainers (IAD), even though negotiations are proceeding between your counsel and prosecuting authorities.[6] Hastily instituting negotiation may cause the prosecutor to accelerate prosecution of the charges underlying the detainer when s/he might very well have let the case fall into disrepair due to inattention. More important, any statements made during the course of negotiation sessions might assist the prosecuting authority with his/her prosecution of the charge if a decision is ultimately made to keep both the charge and the detainer intact.

It is important for you to examine certain factors when debating whether to attempt removal of a detainer through negotiation with the prosecuting authority of the demanding jurisdiction. You should consider the following factors:

a. seriousness of outstanding charge(s) underlying the detainer;
b. length of present sentence;
c. prison record and behavior;
d. adverse impact of detainer on conditions of confinement;
e. distance of demanding state from holding state;
f. your willingness to make restitution;
g. legal arguments to support dismissing the detainer; and
h. benefit to the prosecutor if the detainer is dismissed.

You should also consider the negotiation strategies illustrated by the case examples appearing after the discussion of these factors. You may then be able to determine (1) whether negotiation is appropriate in your case; (2) what negotiation strategy is appropriate, and (3) what factors should be emphasized in negotiation with the prosecuting authority of the demanding jurisdiction.

a. Seriousness of Outstanding Charge(s) Underlying the Detainer

The easiest detainers to negotiate away are those based on minor charges related to property, including petit larceny, malicious destruction of property, auto theft, worthless checks, and forgery. Detainers based on crimes of violence to persons, including murder, rape, and aggravated battery, on the other hand, are extremely difficult to negotiate away. As a rule of thumb, consider that the more serious the outstanding charge, the less likely your success with negotiation. If the detainer is based on more than one underlying charge, it will also be more difficult for you to successfully negotiate the dismissal of the detainer.

---

[6] *See, e.g.,* Edmond v. Michigan Department of Corrections, 78 Mich. App. 196, 259 N.W.2d 423 (1977). *See also infra,* note 26 (a prisoner's rights under the IAD attach only after there has been full compliance with its provisions).

b. Length of Present Sentence

The length of your present sentence is also an important consideration. If you are serving a relatively long prison term, the prosecutor of the demanding jurisdiction might be persuaded to dismiss the detainer because it would be in society's, and your, best interest. You should emphasize that you are presently off the streets and may still be rehabilitated during your remaining term of imprisonment *if* the detainer and its underlying charges are dismissed.

If you are serving a relatively short prison term, it will probably be more difficult to persuade the prosecutor of the demanding jurisdiction to dismiss the detainer and its underlying charges. You should emphasize that you will be under the supervision of parole authorities, an employer, or others upon release from prison. But you should not emphasize how quickly you can achieve liberty after the detainer and its underlying charges are dismissed.

c. Prison Record and Behavior

Your institutional record is perhaps the most persuasive argument to use in negotiation with the prosecutor. Evidence of rehabilitation can cause an otherwise skeptical prosecutor to consider dismissing the detainer. You should emphasize that prison has been a positive rehabilitation experience in your life.

Certain factors present in your prison record reflect a positive approach and successful rehabilitation. For example, lack of write-ups, absence of segregation status, receipt of meritorious good time, trustee status, acquired job skills, high school equivalency diploma, college classes, and psychological therapy can be presented as positive negotiation points. Recommendations from the warden, a caseworker, psychologist, teacher, or job supervisor are also important to show that you are a model of successful rehabilitation. The more positive your behavior while in prison, the easier it will be to use this factor effectively.

d. Adverse Impact of Detainer on Conditions of Confinement

While prisoners without a detainer in their prison file can enjoy some benefits of prison life, such as work release, honor farm status, academic classes, and job training, the prisoner with a detainer in his/her prison file is usually excluded from these rehabilitative programs. The adverse impact of a detainer on the conditions of your confinement can be persuasively emphasized during negotiation with prosecuting authorities of the demanding jurisdiction.

If it appears that the prosecuting authorities are not aware of the hardships that arise when a detainer is present in a prisoner's file, you should compile a list of those hardships and present them to the prosecutor during negotiation. The list should highlight the differences in treatment of those prisoners who have no detainer lodged against them and those who do. You should try to compile the list in such a way that the prosecuting authorities of the demanding jurisdiction will be convinced that the likelihood of your rehabilitation while in prison will be enhanced if the detainer is dismissed.

e.   Distance of Demanding State From Holding State

The mere fact that the demanding state is far removed from the holding state may cause the prosecutor of the damanding state to cease prosecution of a detainer. The prosecutor may be reluctant to pursue the detainer because of problems connected with coordination of your transfer and the expenses associated with transporting you from one jurisdiction to another. Also, if it seems unlikely that you will return to the demanding state after your release, the prosecutor may not be so interested in making you serve more time.

f.   Your Willingness To Make Restitution

If you show sincere remorse for your offense and are willing to make amends to the injured party, your negotiation posture is enhanced. Although restitution cannot usually be employed in cases of violence to a person, it is possible that the prosecutor will consider your remorse and willingness to make amends in deciding whether to dismiss a detainer based on a charge of such alleged violence. No matter what the alleged offense, however, you should exercise great care when using this factor in negotiation since remorse or restitution generally go hand in hand with an admission of criminal conduct.

g.   Legal Arguments To Support Dismissing a Detainer

Before you employ legal arguments in negotiation, you should consider three items. First, even though sound legal arguments against the detainer are present in your case, there is great reluctance on the part of prosecuting authorities to negotiate away a detainer, even when you present good cause for its dismissal. The prosecuting authority of the demanding jurisdiction might even decide to prosecute a detainer that is a losing proposition. Second, in most cases, you are not an attorney or trained in legal argument. Even if you have a sound legal argument for dismissal of the detainer, you might not be able to effectively utilize it in negotiation. Third, it may be unwise to disclose your arguments to prosecuting authorities if your case involves a serious crime or if there is little likelihood that the prosecuting authorities will dismiss your case.

After considering whether the circumstances of your case make it a suitable course of action, you should consider whether it is appropriate to make arguments during negotiation based on speedy trial guarantees, the provisions of the Interstate Agreement on Detainers (IAD), or arguments based on both. Although we will consider the IAD and speedy trial guarantees in more detail later, their relevance to negotiation strategy can be illustrated by two examples.

If the IAD governs the detainer lodged against you, a favorable negotiation posture is presented by the following conditions. First, you have requested final disposition of the charges underlying the detainer as provided in Article III of the IAD. Second, the 180-day period therein provided has run without your transfer to the demanding jurisdiction. The "threat" of legal action at this point can be persuasively emphasized as good cause for dismissing the detainer because the IAD has been violated.

If the IAD is inapplicable to your case, you may be able to use a similar "threat" of legal action based on speedy trial arguments to successfully negotiate the detainer away. As in the previous example, however, certain conditions must be present before a favorable negotiation posture is presented. First, you must have made a demand for a speedy trial of the charges underlying the detainer. Second, an excessive and unreasonable period of time must have passed since your request was made. Negotiation on this ground may then be successful. These points will be fully developed in Sec. 3 of this chapter.

Although you can make strong legal arguments in support of dismissing the detainer, you should first emphasize the six previous considerations when negotiating. Extensive and formal pleading of your legal arguments should not be necessary. But you should attach a brief summary of your legal arguments when communicating with the prosecuting authority of the demanding jurisdiction concerning your negotiations.

h.   Benefit to Prosecutor

Although a prisoner benefits most from dismissal of the detainer, the prosecuting authority of the demanding jurisdiction also benefits. It is important to emphasize exactly how the prosecutor can benefit from dismissal of the detainer because the more a prosecutor will gain from dismissal of the detainer and its underlying charges, the more likely it is that s/he will negotiate them away.

In this negotiation strategy, you should emphasize first those factors illustrated in the seven previous sections. You should concentrate on those aspects of your prison life that indicate rehabilitation, continuing penal or parole supervision, and the uselessness of prosecuting the detainer. You should also emphasize that the prosecutor's crowded docket will be cleared of old warrants, files, and cases and that time and effort will be saved if the detainer and its underlying charges are dismissed. If given any reasonable justification for dismissing the detainer, the prosecutor of the demanding jurisdiction might dismiss it simply because s/he has enough to do without pursuing a prisoner who is already serving a prison term. If, however, the prosecutor perceives you as being particularly dangerous, the prosecutor will probably decide to prosecute the detainer in any event.

i.   Illustration and Analysis of Negotiation Strategies*

Case 1: Prisoner A is paroled from his latest conviction in state X to a detainer based on an untried stolen check indictment in state Y.[7] The conviction in the holding state (X) is a one- to five-year sentence for a stolen check. The stolen checks for both offenses were passed at approximately the same time. Prisoner A is presently awaiting extradition to the demanding state (Y) and it is only a matter of a few days before he is taken there. If convicted in the demanding jurisdiction of the charge underlying the detainer, he will probably serve substantial time in prison because of its habitual offender statute.

Analysis: It is too late to employ the Interstate Agreement on Detainers (IAD) or speedy trial arguments in this case since it is only a matter of a few days before Prisoner A is extradited to the demanding jurisdiction. It is necessary therefore to employ rapid negotiation to avoid probable conviction on the charge and additional time in prison.

Prisoner A consults his attorney and they develop a negotiation strategy which is tailored to the particular facts and circumstances of the case. The attorney contacts the district attorney of the demanding jurisdiction and stresses the following factors on Prisoner A's behalf:

1. The outstanding charge is not serious. It is a property crime.

2. If the indictment and detainer are dismissed, the prisoner would become a parolee. He would be subject to the supervision of the parole authorities of state Y.

3. The current conviction is similar to the outstanding charge underlying the detainer and occurred at or near the time of the alleged conduct contained in the untried indictment.

---

* These examples have been adapted from those presented in Fleischman, *A Practical Guide to Detainers,"* 2 PLM 262 (April 1980).

[7] Any similarity between the case examples and actual cases is, of course, purely coincidental. Although reference in these examples is made to state X and state Y, the examples apply equally well to situations in which the prisoner is imprisoned in federal jurisdiction X and is faced with a detainer lodged by federal jurisdiction Y.

4. Prisoner A's prison record and behavior have been excellent. He received a high school equivalency diploma while in prison. He received meritorious good time and is a trustee. He has excellent recommendations from the chaplain and his caseworker. If the detainer was dismissed, he could find a good job on the outside which would employ skills he developed in prison.

5.Prisoner A stands ready to make restitution on the stolen check as soon as he gets the money. (It may be possible to make this a condition of parole in state Y to give the prosecutor in state X some concrete reassurances on this point.)

Case 2: Prisoner B is imprisoned in state X on a motor vehicle offense which carries a one- to five-year sentence. She has been sent to the honor farm and has been placed on work release. A detainer based on an untried stolen motor vehicle charge is then lodged against her by state Y. As soon as state Y lodged the detainer, Prisoner B was returned to a maximum security prison where she was placed on idle status.

Analysis: Prisoner B consults her attorney and they consider whether to pursue negotiation, the Interstate Agreement on Detainers (IAD), or speedy trial arguments to remove the detainer. They decide that negotiation is the best approach because of the risk, work, and time involved in pursuing the other alternatives, even though the other approaches might also ultimately remove the detainer from Prisoner B's prison files.

The attorney contacts the district attorney of the demanding state (Y) and indicates that the detainer lodged against Prisoner B should be dismissed for the following reasons:

1. The outstanding charge is not serious. It is a property crime.

2. The present conviction is similar to and occurred at or near the time of the alleged conduct contained in the untried indictment.

3. Prisoner B has a good institutional record and has lost a job because of the detainer. Until the detainer was lodged, she was being rehabilitated by the prison system. Now, with the detainer in her prison file, she suffers with idle status at a maximum security prison. If the detainer was dismissed, she would go back to a satellite facility where she could continue her program of rehabilitation and contribution to society.

4. Prisoner B has an arguable statutory speedy trial claim since the demanding state (Y) has failed to follow its own statutory speedy trial provisions.

Case 3: Prisoner C is serving a two- to ten-year sentence and a one- to five-year sentence which are to run consecutively. A detainer is lodged against her based on three untried indictments in state Y. She fills out a Request for Final Disposition pursuant to Article III of the Interstate Agreement on Detainers (IAD), and gives it to the warden where she is being held. The 180-day period provided for in the IAD runs and no action is taken by the demanding state (Y) to try Prisoner C.

Analysis: Prisoner C is in an excellent position to negotiate away the detainer and its underlying charges for several reasons. First, the demanding state (Y) violated its statutory speedy trial guarantees by failing to promptly bring Prisoner C to trial on the outstanding charges. Second, the explicit terms of the IAD were violated when the prosecuting authority of the demanding state failed to bring Prisoner C to trial within the statutory period therein provided.

Prisoner C decides to consult her attorney since her case involves complex litigation. They decide that negotiation would be the best strategy to employ to remove the detainer. The attorney contacts the prosecutor of state Y and presents the following reasons why the detainer against Prisoner C should be dismissed:

1. She will be imprisoned in state X for many years because of the consecutive sentences.

2. She has a good prison record.

3. She may succeed on the merits of her case since strong legal arguments against the detainer based on the IAD and speedy trial guarantees exist.

4. The prosecutor is facing a losing battle and can save time and effort by dismissing the detainer.

Case 4: Prisoner D is imprisoned for aggravated battery with a firearm in state X. For most of his sentence, he has been administratively segregated because he is a constant source of trouble. He has approximately six years left of his present sentence, but will not make parole or honor farm status because of his bad prison record. State Y lodges three detainers against Prisoner D. One is for murder. The others are based on kidnapping and attempted murder. All of the alleged offenses involved the use of a firearm.

Analysis: The facts presented by this example indicate a situation in which it will be extremely difficult for the prisoner to negotiate the detainer away. Prisoner D has been violent while living in society *and* while in prison. The presence of the detainers would have no practical adverse impact on the quality of Prisoner D's confinement since he is usually segregated from the prison community. In addition, Prisoner D is presently imprisoned for a violent crime to a person, while the detainers are also based upon charges of alleged violence to a person. Finally, both the crime for which Prisoner D was convicted and the crimes which he allegedly committed involved firearms. That fact alone will certainly make the prosecuting authority of the demanding jurisdiction less willing to negotiate dismissal of the detainers than if they were based on weaponless crimes.

Since Prisoner D cannot negotiate the detainers away, he must employ one of the alternative methods for removing them. Although he can demand a speedy trial of the charges underlying the detainers or initiate a Request for Final Disposition under Article III of the IAD, if it applies in his situation, he should act with caution when making these demands since they might yield a much longer sentence than that which he is presently serving. The best approach for Prisoner D is inaction. He should wait and do little to instigate any matter concerning the detainers in the hope that the demanding state will violate its speedy trial provisions or that the prosecutor's case will fall into great disrepair with the passage of time.

As the previous illustrations suggest, your success will depend on a combination of the right factors occurring at the right time, facilitated by the right negotiator.

If you do not have a good case for negotiation, you should completely avoid it. You already carry a heavy burden because the presumption is usually against you and in favor of the prosecutor in detainer and negotiation proceedings. You should be wary of establishing contact with prosecuting authorities of the demanding jurisdiction since they may thereupon decide to initiate an extradition proceeding, a proceeding on Writ of Habeas Corpus Ad Prosequendum, or an Interstate Agreement on Detainers (IAD) Article IV request for temporary custody of you for trial of the outstanding charges underlying the detainer.

Before starting negotiation, you should be well prepared in terms of the facts and law of your case to ensure that the negotiations will follow the strategy you have outlined. It might help to discuss your strategy with a trusted friend, especially an attorney.

3. Litigation

If you determine that negotiation will probably fail to remove the detainer or that it is inappropriate in your case, there are two alternative procedures available for removing a detainer based on an untried charge. Both of them are related to the guarantee of speedy trial contained in the Sixth Amendment to the Constitution of the United States insofar as they protect similar interests. Generally, they both protect your interests (1) in avoiding prolonged imprisonment prior to trial; (2) in avoiding prolonged psychological pressure and public suspicion while charges are pending against you; and (3) in disposing of your case before your defense is lost.

The first procedure is contained in the Interstate Agreement on Detainers (IAD),[8] a compact entered into by a majority of states.[9] Under

---

[8]Pub. L. 91-538, 84 Stat. 1397. See Appendix D, Sec. 1, for a copy of the IAD. See also Appendix D, Sec. 2, for a list of the states that have adopted the IAD.

the IAD, you have clearly defined rights to a speedy disposition of charges underlying a detainer request from prosecutors of *another compact state,* regardless of whether you or the prosecutor requests a final disposition or trial of the outstanding criminal charges. If you are not afforded those rights by the demanding state, the detainer must be dismissed. Specific details of the IAD will be discussed in detail later.

The second procedure for removing a detainer based on an untried charge is a conventional demand for speedy trial of the charge underlying the detainer. This right can be derived from federal or state constitutional or statutory guarantees. You should review pertinent constitutional and/or statutory provisions, local court rules, and case law applicable to speedy trial guarantees before finally deciding to litigate dismissal of the charges underlying the detainer. More detail concerning speedy trial guarantees and arguments will be presented later in this chapter.

a.   Interstate Agreement on Detainers Act (IAD)

The IAD is a compact between forty-seven states, the District of Columbia, and the federal government.[10] It was passed in 1970 to answer the problems that arise when you are imprisoned in one jurisdiction and are wanted for trial *on an outstanding charge* in another jurisdiction.[11]

---

[9]*See* Cuyler v. Adams, 449 U.S. 433, 101 S.Ct. 703 (1981) (interpretation of the IAD presents a question of federal law).

[10]Under IAD, Art. II(a), the United States or federal government is *one* jurisdiction. *See* United States v. Krohn, 558 F.2d 390, 392 (8th Cir. 1977); United States v. Cappucci, 342 F. Supp. 790, 793 (E.D. Pa. 1972); State v. Wiggins, 425 So.2d 621 (Fla. App. 1983). As a result, the IAD has no effect on the transfer of a defendant-prisoner from one federal district to another, a situation analogous to that presented by an intrastate detainer. *See* IAD, Art. II(a); United States v. Bryant, 612 F.2d 806, 810 (4th Cir. 1979) (when a federal district court obtains a state prisoner for trial under circumstances invoking the IAD, only that district is deemed a state within the contemplation of the Act). See Appendix D, Sec. 2, for a list of applicable state statutes. The IAD also has no application in states that have not adopted it. *See* State v. McCabe, 420 So.2d 955 (La. 1983) (indictment not quashed because Louisiana is not a party to the IAD).

[11]See discussion of Pub. L. 91-538, 84 Stat. 1397, contained in H.R. Rep. No. 91-1018 (1970) and S. Rep. 91-1356, *reprinted in* [1970] U.S.C.C.A.N. *See also* 116 Cong. Rec. 13997-14000, 38840-38842 (1970); Note, "The Interstate Agreement on Detainers: Defining the Federal Role," 31 Vanderbilt L. Rev. 1017 (1978).

Detainers based on untried indictments, information, and complaints are the only detainer-types covered by the IAD. *See* IAD, Art. I. *See* United States v. Dobson, 585 F.2d 55 (3d Cir. 1978), *cert. denied,* 99 S.Ct. 264 (1978) (a parolee

Under the nine separate articles of the IAD, found in the statutory law of the party states and the federal government, "[a] prisoner can force the expeditious disposition of outstanding detainers and their underlying charges. Similarly, prosecutors can more easily obtain prisoners for trial; judges and prison and parole authorities can more rationally administer punishment and rehabilitation."[12] Generally, before seeking relief through court action, you should request final disposition of the outstanding charges under the IAD because the IAD provisions present a simple, orderly, efficient, and uniform method for dealing with detainers involving party jurisdictions or states.[13]

Provisions of the IAD entitle you to prompt notice from your warden of any detainer lodged against you and its source.[14] You must also be

---

confined awaiting a parole revocation hearing is not "serving a term of imprisonment" within the intendment of the IAD. Provisions of the IAD are therefore inapplicable); Argiz v. United States, 704 F.2d 384 (7th Cir. 1983) (INS charges in deportation proceedings are not untried indictments, informations, or criminal complaints within meaning of IAD). *See also* United States v. Roberts, 548 F.2d 665, 670-71 (6th Cir. 1977); United States v. Harris, 566 F.2d 610 (8th Cir. 1977); United States v. Evans, 423 F. Supp. 528, 531 (S.D.N.Y. 1976), *aff'd,* 556 F.2d 561 (2d Cir. 1977). The House and Senate reports explain that "[a] detainer is a notification filed with the institution in which a prisoner is serving a sentence, advising that he is wanted to face pending criminal charges in another jurisdiction." [1970] U.S.C.C.A.N., p. 4865. A detainer may be lodged against you by a prosecutor or law enforcement official. United States v. Mauro, 436 U.S. 340, 98 S.Ct. 1834 (1978). Filing a detainer is an informal process that generally can be done by any person who has authority to take a prisoner into custody. United States v. Dixon, 592 F.2d 329 (6th Cir. 1979), *cert. denied,* 441 U.S. 951 (1979). *But see* United States v. Woods, 465 F. Supp. 89 (E.D. Ky. 1979) (filing of detainer by U.S. Marshal for Western District for charge not associated with present charge in Eastern District did not trigger IAD).

[12]United States v. Ford, 550 F.2d 732, 741 (2d Cir. 1977), *aff'd,* 436 U.S. 340 (1978). *See also* People v. Squitieri, 91 Misc.2d 290, 397 N.Y.S.2d 888 (1977).

[13]Consider the discussion in Grant v. Hogan, 505 F.2d 1220, 1224 (3d Cir. 1974). See discussion under subsection "Obtaining Relief for Violations of the IAD," *infra.*

[14]IAD, Art. III(c). The IAD, however, does *not* provide for any sanction against prison authorities for failure to timely notify a prisoner of the filing of a detainer. Such failure on the part of prison officials "cannot be condoned," Baity v. Ciccone, 379 F. Supp. 552, 560 (W.D. Mo.), *appeal dismissed,* 507 F.2d 717 (8th Cir. 1974), but the prisoner may have to resort to constitutional speedy trial arguments for redress. *But see* People v. Gonzales, 601 P.2d 644 (Colo. App. 1979); People v. Lincoln, 601 P.2d 644 (Colo. App. 1979) (adverse consequences, such as dismissal of charges, from failure of warden to notify prisoner). *See also* Watson v. Ralston, 419 F. Supp. 536, 541 (W.D. Wisc. 1976) (responsibility of warden).

advised of your right to request a final disposition of the charges underlying the detainer.[15]

(1) Prisoner's Request for Final Disposition Under IAD, Article III

Before requesting a final disposition of the charges underlying a detainer, you should review subsections B1 and 2, Inaction and Negotiation, regarding the possibility that you may be better off *not* requesting a final disposition.[16] You should also consider and keep in mind the following considerations concerning the nature of the IAD, its procedures, and certain precautions:

1. The IAD applies only to interstate detainers based on untried indictments, information, and complaints. Requests for final disposition of charges underlying probation, parole, conviction, and intrastate (or intrajurisdictional) detainers *cannot* be processed under the provisions of the IAD.

2. Your request for final disposition under IAD, Art. III must be *in writing*.

3. Your request for final disposition under IAD, Art. III should be made on the proper form and presented to your warden or other authorized prison official. Even though the IAD provisions may not require strict compliance with each particular of the notice requirement, a request addressed to the *proper authority,* in the *proper form,* and accompanied by the *proper documents* will avoid a later charge of the prosecuting authorities that your request is invalid.[17]

4. Your written request for final disposition should be *dated, notarized,* and *made in duplicate.* Your copies should be kept in a safe place, preferably outside the prison.

5. You should allow a reasonable period of time to pass before initiating further legal action. For example, although you have made a

---

[15]IAD, Art. III(c).

[16]Under IAD, Art. III(a), when the prisoner requests final disposition, the demanding jurisdiction has 180 days in which to bring the prisoner to trial on the charges underlying the detainer. Under IAD, Art. IV(a), when the prosecuting authorities of the demanding jurisdiction make the request, the demanding jurisdiction has 120 days after the prisoner's *arrival* in which to bring the prisoner to trial. See Appendix D, Sec. 1.

[17]*See, e.g.,* Williams v. Maryland, 445 F. Supp. 1216, 1220 (D. Md. 1978) (request for final disposition requires more than merely addressing request to one of the individuals required by statute to be notified). *See also* People v. Uplinger, 69 Ill.2d 181, 370 N.E.2d 1054 (1977) (requests for information are not demands for final disposition).

proper request for final disposition and the 180-day period for bringing
you to trial has passed, the dismissal sanction under IAD, Art. V(c) may
not be available[18] because under IAD, Art. III(a), a continuance of the
time period may have been granted to the demanding jurisdiction by the
court having jurisdiction over the matter.[19]

The actual request for final disposition of the charges underlying the
detainer is a relatively simple process. You provide your warden,
commissioner of corrections, or other official of the holding state
designated to receive the request for final disposition with your written
request.[20] Although you can draft your own request for final disposition,
it is better practice to use a standardized form which can usually be
obtained from the prison or your caseworker.[21]

When you properly request final disposition of the charges underlying
the detainer, your rights under the IAD take effect. Your warden or other prison authorities must promptly forward your request for final
disposition to the appropriate prosecuting official and court of the
detainer or demanding jurisdiction.[22] They must also send a certificate of

---

[18]This is also true of the requests of prosecuting authorities under IAD, Art.
IV(a).

[19]*See infra*, note 31. If any continuance is granted, your warden will be
notified and s/he should notify you.

[20]*See, e.g*, People v. Wolever, 43 Ill. App.3d 25, 356 N.E.2d 611 (1976) (letter
to governor asking for denial of another state's request for custody is not proper
request); State v. Brockington, 215 A.2d 362 (N.J. Super. 1965) (letter mailed
directly to prosecutor is not proper request); Williams v. State, 445 F. Supp.
1216 (D. Md. 1978) (letter mailed directly to court clerk is not proper request).
See also Beebe v. State, 346 A.2d 169 (Del. Supr. 1975); People v. Daily, 46 Ill.
App.3d 195, 360 N.E.2d 1131 (1977); State v. Savage, 522 S.W.2d 144 (Mo.
App. 1975). *But see* McQueen v. Wyrick, 543 S.W.2d 778, 784 (Mo. 1976)
(Seiler, J. concurring) (written request sent directly to records officer complies
with IAD); Rainey v. Michigan Dept. of Corrections, 41 Mich. App. 313, 199
N.W.2d 829 (1972) (letter to district attorney requesting a bill of particulars and
referring to right to speedy trial is sufficient) (holding limited to instant case).

[21]*See, e.g.,* People v. Uplinger, *supra,* 370 N.E.2d 1054 (1977) (requests for
information concerning the handling of a detainer are not requests for final
disposition); People v. Beamon, 83 Mich. App. 121, 268 N.W.2d 310 (1978)
(motion for speedy trial is not a proper request). *See also* People v. Butcher, 46
Mich. App. 40, 207 N.W.2d 430 (1973); State v. Cox, 505 P.2d 360, 363 (Ore.
App. 1973) (language in demand letter did not contain information required by
IAD, Art. III, nor had defendant entered upon "a term of imprisonment" as
required). See Appendix D, Sec. 7, for model forms.

[22]IAD, Art. III(b). *See, e.g.,* People v. Wilson, 69 Cal. App.3d 631, 138 Cal.
Rptr. 259 (1977); Bursque v. Moore, 26 Conn. Sup. 469, 227 A.2d 255 (1966).
But see Rhodes v. Schoen, 574 F.2d 968 (8th Cir. 1978) (delay in forwarding

inmate status which states the length of sentence you have already served, your good time earned, the date of your parole eligibility, and any decisions of state parole authorities concerning you.[23]

Your request for final disposition of the charges underlying the detainer "will operate as a request for final disposition of all untried indictments, information, or complaints [existing against you] in the demanding state."[24] Your request for final disposition will also operate as a waiver of your extradition rights.[25] Consequently, you are *not* entitled to a pre-transfer hearing when *you* initiate the transfer (disposition) procedure of Article III.

After you have sent a written request for final disposition of the charges underlying the detainer to the appropriate prison official and he/she has forwarded it with the proper accompanying certificate to the prosecuting authorities and court of the demanding or detainer jurisdiction, you must be brought to trial on the charges within 180 days.[26] If a trial is not held within that statutory period, the charges *must*

---

request was permissible since trial began 180 days after the request was made). *See also* Scrivener v. State, 441 N.E.2d 954 (Ind. 1982) (180-day time period begins to run when request delivered to court and prosecutor). Even though it is possible for you to file your request directly with the prosecutor and court of the demanding jurisdiction, it is not recommended. *See, e.g.,* State v. Wells, 453 A.2d 236 (N.J. Super. 1982).

[23]IAD, Art. III(a). *See, e.g.,* Isaacs v. State, 31 Md. App. 604, 358 A.2d 273, 278 (1976) (the information specified in this section is "mandatory and not directory"). *See also* State v. Cox, *supra,* 505 P.2d 360 (Ore. App. 1973). See Appendix D, Sec. 7, for model forms.

[24]IAD, Art. III(d). *See, e.g.,* United States v. Eaddy, 595 F.2d 341, 347 (6th Cir. 1979).

[25]IAD, Art. III(e). *See, e.g.,* Cuyler v. Adams, *supra* note 9, 449 U.S. at 446 (prisoner initiating transfer procedure under Art. III waives rights, including a pre-transfer hearing, which the sending state affords persons being extradited; but prisoner's extradition rights are preserved when the receiving state seeks prisoner's involuntary transfer under Art. IV). A prisoner's waiver of rights under the IAD must be the product of an understanding and knowing decision s/he is not necessarily bound by decision or default of counsel. Enright v. United States, 434 F. Supp. 1056 (S.D.N.Y. 1977), *motion granted for reargument,* 437 F. Supp. 580 (S.D.N.Y. 1977), *rev'd and rem'd,* 537 F.2d 1289 (2d Cir. 1978). *See also* Franks v. Johnson, 401 F. Supp. 669, 672 (E.D. Mich. 1975; People v. Uplinger, *supra,* 370 N.E.2d at 1058 ("Had [prisoner] not blocked his return to the state by refusing to waive extradition, it is likely that the charges against him would have been disposed of within the time period mandated by the [IAD].").

[26]IAD, Art. III(a). *See, e.g.,* Nelson v. George, 399 U.S. 224, 90 S.Ct. 1963 (1970) (the 180-day period begins to run after there has been full compliance with IAD provisions); Isaacs v. State, *supra,* 358 A.2d at 278 (the 180-day period did

be dismissed *with prejudice* and the detainer is removed.[27] You are not required to show that you have been prejudiced or injured by the failure of the demanding jurisdiction to comply with the 180-day statutory period within which you must be brought to trial.[28] You are entitled to dismissal of the charges and the detainer itself as a matter of right when the demanding jurisdiction fails to comply with that IAD provision.[29]

not begin to run "since it was not established that the [prisoner] and prison officials did all that they were called upon to do by the provisions of the Act, the Act was not invoked no matter where the fault lay"). *Compare* Commonwealth v. Eisenhauer, 331 A.2d 786 (Pa. Super. 1974) (the 180-day period begins to run when the prisoner makes a written request to the custodian for prompt disposition); State v. Wood, 241 N.W.2d 8 (Iowa 1976) (the 180-day period begins to run when the custodian mails the written request and certificate to the prosecutor and court), *with* Graham v. Commonwealth ex rel. Costa, 368 F. Supp. 846 (W.D. Pa. 1973) (the 180-day period begins when the prosecutor and the court receive the written request and certificate). For cases with holdings similar to *Graham, supra, see* Holland v. State, 352 N.E.2d 752 (Ind. Supr. 1976); State v. Ternaku, 156 N.J. Super. 30, 383 A.2d 437 (1978). *But see* Gardner v. State, 29 Md. App. 314, 347 A.2d 881 (1975) (since no date was stamped by the court on the prisoner's request for immediate and speedy trial after the prosecutor's request for final disposition, the 120-day period commenced from the date on which the Certificate of Inmate Status was executed by the Division of Correction and the prisoner should be released). People v. Jones, 457 N.Y.S.2d 870 (N.Y.A.D. 1982) (prisoner's request for suppression hearing served as waiver of right to trial within 180 days).

[27]IAD, Art. V(c). *See, e.g.,* Commonwealth v. Fisher, 451 Pa. 102, 301 A.2d 605, 606 (1973) (the dismissal sanction is intended to produce general compliance with the IAD). *See also* Commonwealth v. Wilson, 331 A.2d 792 (Pa. Super. 1975). *But see* Watson v. Ralston, 419 F. Supp. 536 (D. Wis. 1976) (detainers enjoy full force and effect for all purposes unless and until the appropriate court in the *charging* state dismisses the underlying charges). *Compare* State ex rel. Stanley v. Davis, 569 S.W.2d 202 (Mo. App. 1978) (dismissal not applicable where federal prisoner in state is transferred to state court for limited purpose of arraignment, appearances, or hearings and is then returned to federal facility), *with* United States v. Schrum, 504 F. Supp. 23 (D. Kan. 1980), *aff'd,* 638 F.2d 214 (10th Cir. 1981) (interjurisdicational transfers subject to IAD even though no transfer across a state boundary).

[28]*See, e.g.,* Ridgeway v. United States, 558 F.2d 357, 359 (6th Cir. 1977) (the jurisdiction in which the outstanding charge is pending is required to dismiss the charge with prejudice). *Contra,* Young v. Mabry, 471 F. Supp. 553, 562 (E.D. Ark. 1978) (the prisoner must not only show a clear violation of Art. III, but also that s/he was prejudiced as a direct result of the violation). *Compare* Stroble v. Anderson, 587 F.2d 830, 840 (6th Cir. 1978), *cert. denied,* 99 S.Ct. 2032 (1979), *with* Stroble v. Egeler, 547 F.2d 339 (6th Cir. 1977), *rev'g,* 408 F. Supp. 630 (E.D. Mich. 1976); People v. Bean, 650 P.2d 565 (Colo. 1982) (no prejudice need be shown by prisoner).

[29]"The legislation adopting the agreement is obviously remedial in character

The purpose of the dismissal sanction is not to redress any injury or prejudice you will in fact suffer by the delay in being brought to trial. Its purpose is to force prosecutors of demanding jurisdictions to comply with the time limits imposed by the IAD.[30]

There are two important exceptions to the IAD dismissal sanction. The first exception is contained in IAD, Art. III(a) which provides that "for good cause shown in open court, the prisoner or his counsel being present, the court having jurisdiction of the matter may grant any necessary or reasonable continuance" of the 180-day period.[31] This provision of the IAD serves as a valuable and effective tool for a prosecutor when the 180-day time period is about to end and you cannot be brought to trial within that period. It is also the source of much litigation concerning whether a proper continuance was granted.[32] Such litigation commonly involves whether the continuance was granted in "open court,"[33] whether "good cause" was shown for granting the continuance,[34] whether it was "necessary or reasonable" to grant the continuance,[35] whether you or your counsel were present at the

---

and, thus, by familiar principle should be construed liberally in favor of the prisoner." State v. West, 79 N.J. Super. 379, 191 A.2d 758, 760 (1963). *See also* United States v. Mason, 372 F. Supp. 651 (N.D. Ohio 1973); Barnes v. State, 20 Md. App. 262, 315 A.2d 117 (1974); State v. Chirra, *supra,* 191 A.2d at 312; Commonwealth v. Fisher, *supra,* 301 A.2d at 607. *But see* United States v. Palmer, 574 F.2d 164 (3d Cir. 1978) (violation does *not* result in dismissal as of right).

[30]*See, e.g.,* Pittman v. State, 301 A.2d 509 (Del. 1973); Dennet v. State, 311 A.2d 437 (Md. App. 1973); Nelms v. State, 532 S.W.2d 923 (Tenn. 1976). *See also* United States v. Thompson, 562 F.2d 232 (3d Cir. 1977), *cert. denied,* United States v. Sorrell, 436 U.S. 949 (1978) (IAD should be enforced according to its terms).

[31]IAD, Art. III(a). *See, e.g.,* Neville v. Friedman, 67 Ill.2d 488, 367 N.E.2d 1341 (1977). If a continuance is granted, your warden will be notified and s/he should notify you.

[32]*See, e.g.,* Gardner v. State, 29 Md. App. 314, 347 A.2d 881 (1975); Davis v. State, 24 Md. App. 567, 332 A.2d 733 (1975); State v. Chirra, 79 N.J. Super. 270, 191 A.2d 308 (1963); Commonwealth v. Gregg, 368 A.2d 651 (Pa. 1977); Commonwealth v. Fisher, 451 Pa. 102, 301 A.2d 605 (1973).

[33]*See, e.g.,* Stroble v. Anderson, 587 F.2d 830, 838 (6th Cir. 1978), *cert. denied,* 99 S.Ct. 1289 (1979) ("in open court" means that there must be a judge present conducting the proceeding in a courtroom).

[34]*See, e.g.,* Stroble v. Anderson, *supra* (a rationale must be given as justification).

[35]*See, e.g.,* United States v. Ford, 550 F.2d 732 (2d Cir. 1977), *aff'd,* 436 U.S. 340 (1978) (delays caused by transfer of prisoner's case to a judge with a full calendar were not necessary, reasonable, or for good cause); State v. Chirra, *supra,* 191 A.2d 308 (delay cannot be justified by the presence of a heavy court calendar). *See also,* Commonwealth v. Gregg, 368 A.2d 651 (Pa. 1977).

proceeding,[36] and whether the continuance was sought before or after the 180-day period had elapsed.[37] In any event, because the judicial proceedings of a jurisdiction or state are presumed to be correct, the burden is on you to show any defects in the granting of the continuance.[38]

The second exception to the IAD, Art. III(a) dismissal sanction is contained in Art. VI(a).[39] That article provides that "[i]n determining the duration and expiration dates of the time periods provided in Articles III and IV of this agreement, the running of said time periods shall be tolled whenever and for as long as the prisoner is unable to stand trial, as determined by the court having jurisdiction of the matter."[40]

The critical language of Art. VI(a) is contained in the phrase "unable to stand trial." A determination must be made by the court of the demanding jurisdiction having jurisdiction over the detainer and its charges to the effect that you are unable to stand trial because you are not present in the demanding jurisdiction or are physically or mentally disabled.[41] When that determination is made, the running of the 180-day period is tolled or stopped for so long as you are unable to stand trial on the charges underlying the detainer. Thereafter, when a *determination* is made by the court having jurisdiction of the matter that you are able to stand trial on the charges, the 180-day "clock" will begin to run again. After your disability is removed, you should write a letter to the court and prosecutor telling them that you are available for trial. Attach to your letter copies of any relevant documents. The point here is that the period of time during which you are unable to stand trial is not included in the calculation of the 180-day period.[42]

---

[36]*See, e.g.,* Stroble v. Anderson, *supra,* 587 F.2d at 838; Stroble v. Egeler, *supra,* 547 F.2d 339; Davis v. State, 24 Md. App. 567, 332 A.2d 733 (1975).

[37]*See, e.g.,* Commonwealth v. Fisher, *supra,* 301 A.2d at 607-08.

[38]*See, e.g.,* Stroble v. Egeler, 408 F. Supp. 630 (E.D. Mich.), *rem'd,* 547 F.2d 339 (6th Cir. 1976), *later app. sub nom.* Stroble v. Anderson, 587 F.2d 830 (1978), *cert. denied,* 99 S.Ct. 2032.

[39]IAD, Art. VI(a). It is important to note that under Art. VI(b) the provisions of the IAD do not apply to prisoners who are insane.

[40]IAD, Art. VI(a). The court having jurisdiction is the court in which the charges will be tried.

[41]*See, e.g.,* Stroble v. Anderson, *supra,* 587 F.2d at 838; Young v. Mabry, 471 F. Supp. 553, 561 (E.D. Ark. 1978), *aff'd,* 596 F.2d 339 (8th Cir.), *cert. denied,* 100 S.Ct. 107 (1981). *See also* United States v. Mason, 372 F. Supp. 651 (N.D. Ohio 1973); Gray v. Benson, 458 F. Supp. 1209 (D. Kan. 1978), *aff'd,* 608 F.2d 825 (10th Cir. 1979) (prisoner requested return to state prison prior to completion of federal prosecution).

[42]*See, e.g.,* United States v. Mason, *supra* (period for defendant-prisoner's

If, for example, you are standing trial in one state on charges underlying a detainer lodged against you by that state, you cannot simultaneously stand trial in a second state on charges underlying a detainer lodged against you by the second state. The running of the 180-day period must therefore be tolled or stopped until such time as you are able to stand trial in the second state.[43] As one court has put it, "[o]therwise an interstate bandit, having committed crimes in numerous states, upon his arrest, could make Article III requests as to all his crimes and only a few states could try him in the 180 days allowed if the [IAD] were not tolled by the several trials."[44]

Even though the prosecuting authorities of the demanding jurisdiction can seek and obtain a continuance or temporary stay of the 180-day period under the IAD provisions we have discussed, once you have been transferred to the demanding jurisdiction you must be tried on the charges underlying the detainer before you are returned to your original place of imprisonment.[45] If you are not tried on all charges existing against you in the demanding jurisdiction before your return to the sending jurisdiction, or your original place of imprisonment, those charges must be dismissed with prejudice.[46] It is the fact of your transfer to the demanding jurisdiction[47] and the fact that the IAD was designed to avoid the shuttling of prisoners back and forth between two prisons of two jurisdictions[48] that make Art. III(e) operative and mandate dismissal of the detainer and its underlying charges with prejudice.

---

prosecution was tolled while he was standing trial in another state). *See also,* Price v. State, 237 Ga. 352, 227 S.E.2d 368 (1976); State v. Wood, 241 N.W.2d 8 (Iowa 1976).

[43]*See, e.g.,* United States v. Mason, *supra,* 372 F. Supp. at 653 (this is the only logical result).

[44]Price v. State, *supra,* 227 S.E.2d at 371.

[45]IAD, Art. III(d). *See, e.g.,* United States v. Mauro, 436 U.S. 340, 98 S.Ct. 1834 (1978); Walker v. King, 448 F. Supp. 580 (E.D.N.Y. 1978). *See also* Commonwealth v. Merlo, 364 A.2d 391 (Pa. 1976).

[46]IAD, Art. III(d). *See, e.g.,* Commonwealth v. Merlo, *supra. See* note 24, *supra.*

[47]*See, e.g.,* United States v. Sorrell, 413 F. Supp. 138 (D. Pa. 1976), *aff'd,* 562 F.2d 227 (3d Cir. 1977), *cert. denied,* 436 U.S. 949 (1978).

[48]See, e.g., United States v. Mauro, *supra*; Walker v. King, 448 F. Supp. 580 (E.D.N.Y. 1978).

(2) Prosecutor's Request for Final Disposition Under IAD, Article IV

Under IAD, Article IV, the appropriate prosecuting officer[49] of the demanding jurisdiction in which an untried indictment, information, or complaint is pending against you can request final disposition of the charges underlying the detainer in much the same way that you can under Article III.[50] There are, however, important differences between the procedural aspects of the two requests of which you should be aware.

If the prosecutor of another IAD jurisdiction decides to prosecute the charges underlying a detainer, which that jurisdiction has lodged against you, s/he must make a written request of the appropriate authorities, usually your warden, for temporary custody of you for trial on those charges.[51] The request must have been duly approved, recorded, and transmitted by the court of the demanding jurisdiction having jurisdiction over the underlying charges.[52]

Nothing in the IAD explicitly provides for a pre-transfer hearing before your transfer to the demanding jurisdiction pursuant to an Article IV prosecutor's request for temporary custody. However, the Supreme Court in *Cuyler v. Adams* interpreted IAD, Article IV(d) as having preserved the rights conferred on prisoners by extradition laws, including the right to a pre-transfer hearing at which you can contest the legality of your transfer.[53] First, as a matter of federal law, prisoners transferred

---

[49]*See, e.g.,* United States v. Woods, 465 F. Supp. 89 (E.D. Ky. 1979), *cert. denied,* 101 S.Ct. 222 ("appropriate officer" indicates prosecutor).

[50]IAD, Art. IV(a). *See supra,* notes 14 and 15 (prisoner must be notified of the filing of a detainer and its source).

[51]IAD, Art. IV(a). Your warden should notify you that the prosecutor has requested temporary custody of you for trial on the charges. See Appendix D, Sec, 7, Form V. *See* Culyer v. Adams, *supra* note 9; Dobson v. United States, 449 A.2d 1082 (D.C. App. 1982); People v. Bentley, 328 N.W.2d 389 (Mich. App. 1982) (although not in proper form, letter from prosecutor triggered IAD). *See also* People v. Lincoln, 601 P.2d 641, 644 (Colo. App. 1979) (official oversights of warden should result in dismissal of charges). See also cases compiled under note 14, *supra.*

[52]IAD, Art. IV(a); *See,* Culyer v. Adams, *supra* note 9.

[53]449 U.S. 433, 101 S.Ct. 703 (1981). *See, e.g.,* Adams v. Cuyler, 592 F.2d 720 (3d Cir. 1979). Forty-eight states have adopted the Uniform Criminal Extradition Act ("UCEA"), *reprinted in* 11 UNIFORM LAWS ANNOTATED, 51 (1974). See Appendix D, Sec. 8, for a copy of the UCEA, and Sec. 9, for a list of the states that have adopted it and their respective statutes. The UCEA has not been adopted in the District of Columbia, Mississippi, or South Carolina. The extradition statute for each of those states is as follows:

pursuant to the provisions of the IAD are not required to forfeit any pre-existing rights they may have under state or federal law to challenge their transfer to the receiving state. Second, under provisions of the IAD and applicable extradition laws, such prisoners have the right to a judicial hearing in which they can bring a limited challenge to the receiving state's custody request. Third, a prisoner sought to be transferred against his or her will under Article IV is entitled to all the safeguards of the Uniform Criminal Extradition Act, including a pre-transfer hearing, in states having adopted that act (see Appendix D, Sec. 9, for a listing of states that have adopted this Act.) Finally, such prisoners are also entitled to any other procedural protections the sending state (or jurisdiction) guarantees persons being extradited from within its borders.

You are also afforded some pre-transfer protection by Art. IV(a). The relevant portion of that article provides that "there shall be a period of thirty days after receipt by the appropriate authorities [of the holding or sending jurisdiction] before the request [is] honored, within which period the governor of the sending state may disapprove the request for temporary custody. . . , either upon his own motion or upon the motion of the prisoner."[54] If you fail to request that the governor disapprove the demanding jurisdiction's request for temporary custody, your right to contest delivery to the demanding state is deemed waived.[55]

If you are faced with the 30-day deadline of Art. IV(a) and can arguably claim injustice if transferred to the demanding jurisdiction, you

---

D.C. Code Ann., §§23-401 to 23-411 (1983).
Miss. Code Ann., §§99-21-1 to 99-21-11 (1972).
S.C. Code Ann., §§17-9-10 to 17-9-70 (1976).
The federal extradition statute is 18 U.S.C. §3182 (1976).

[54]IAD, Art. IV(a). *See* IAD, Sec. 3 (governor in a federal context means the attorney general). *See, e.g.,* Lopez v. Levi, 422 F. Supp. 846 (S.D.N.Y. 1976) (an appropriate official with proper authority). The 30-day period runs from the date the prosecutor makes a request for custody until the date the prisoner can be transferred. Cuyler v. Adams, *supra* note 9. *See* United States v. Bryant, 612 F.2d 799 (4th Cir. 1979), *cert. denied,* 446 U.S. 919 (1980) (does not apply to writs of *ad prosequendum*); United States v. Ford, 550 F.2d 732 (2d Cir. 1977), *cert. denied,* 434 U.S. 816 (1978), *aff'd,* United States v. Mauro, 436 U.S. 340, 98 S.Ct. 1834 (1978). *See also* [1970] U.S.C.C.A.N., p. 4865 ("a governor's right to refuse to make a prisoner available is preserved"); Council of State Governments, Suggested State Legislation Program for 1957, p. 78 (1956) ("a governor's right to refuse to make the prisoner available (on public policy grounds) is retained").

Although the Supreme Court has recognized that the terms of the IAD may entitle a prisoner to notification of his right to petition the governor, it has so far failed to rule on the issue. *See* Cuyler v. Adams, *supra* note 9, 436 U.S. 439.

[55]IAD, Art. IV(d). *See, e.g.,* State v. Thompson, 133 N.J. Super. 180, 336 A.2d 11, 14 (1975).

must quickly petition the governor or appropriate officer.[56] You should be realistic in assessing your particular case, the evidence in support thereof, and the advantage to be gained by petitioning the governor for disapproval of the request for temporary custody. If you decide that you should petition the governor, you should review the considerations discussed in the "Negotiation" subsection and make a written request demonstrating why the governor should disapprove the request. You should emphasize how your rights will be violated if you are transferred. Although you can successfully petition for the governor's disapproval, you should realize that this is the exception and not the rule.

When the prosecutor of the demanding jurisdiction makes a request for final disposition, your warden or prison authorities must furnish the demanding jurisdiction with a certificate of your status.[57] They must also furnish information of other detainers and similar certificates lodged against you by that state or by any other jurisdiction.[58] Once you arrive in the demanding jurisdiction, trial on the charges must be held within 120 days.[59] If trial is not held within 120 days of your arrival, the detainer and the charges are dismissed with prejudice[60] unless a continuance,[61]

---

[56]*See, e.g.,* United States v. Bryant, 612 F.2d 799 (3d Cir. 1979), *cert. denied,* 100 S.Ct. 1855 (no more than 30 days are allowed); Dobson v. United States, 449 A.2d 1082 (D.C. App. 1982).

[57]IAD, Art. IV(b). *See supra,* note 23. See also Appendix D, Sec. 7, Form III.

[58]IAD, Art. IV(b). See Appendix D, Sec. 7, Form III.

[59]IAD, Art. IV(c), requires "commencement of trial within 120 days whenever the receiving state initiates the disposition of charges underlying a detainer it has previously lodged against a state prisoner." United States v. Mauro, 436 U.S. 340, 98 S.Ct. 1834, 1849 (1978).
Compare State v. Sasoon, 242 S.E.2d 121 (Ga. 1978) (brief removal to receiving jurisdiction and prompt return to sending jurisdiction after arraignment and prior to trial consonant with IAD where prisoner returned for medical and rehabilitative treatment); Haley v. State, 421 A.2d 982 (Md. App. 1980) (state's request for temporary custody not within ambit of IAD where transfer requested by prisoner to pursue his application for post-conviction relief), *with* People v. Cella, 170 Cal. Rptr. 915 (Cal. App. 1981) (brief but repetitive visits for several pretrial proceedings, at times, can violate provisions of IAD). *See* State v. Chirra, 79 N.J. Super. 270, 191 A.2d 308 (1963) (a prisoner must be transported to the demanding state within a reasonable time after the request is made). *See also* Foran v. Metz, 463 F. Supp. 1088 (S.D.N.Y. 1979) (120-day limit and not 180-day limit is applicable where prisoner was actually produced in the demanding state).

[60]IAD, Art. V(c). *See supra,* notes 27-30. *See also* State v. Keener, 577 P.2d 1182 (1978), *cert. denied,* 439 U.S. 953 (1979). *But see* People v. Housewright, 268 N.W.2d 401 (Mich. App. 1978) ("trial" in IAD means determination of guilty; dismissal sanction does not apply where guilty plea entered).

which is necessary or reasonable,[62] is granted for good cause shown[63] in open court[64] with you or your counsel present,[65] or unless you are unable to stand trial.[66]

Even if a continuance is granted for good cause shown or because you are physically or mentally unable to stand trial, once you have been transported to the demanding jurisdiction, generally you must be tried on the charges underlying the detainer before return to the sending jurisdiction.[67] If you are not tried before that return, the charges and the detainer itself are dismissed with prejudice.[68]

Although IAD, Art. III(d) provides that your single request for final disposition of charges operates as a request on *all* untried indictments, information, or complaints on the basis of which detainers have been lodged against you by the demanding jurisdiction, there is no such provision covering prosecutors' requests under IAD, Art. IV. Consequently, it is possible for the demanding jurisdiction to request custody of you at different times for trial on the different charges underlying different detainers.[69]

---

[61]IAD, Art. IV(c). *See supra,* notes 32-40. If a continuance is granted, your warden will be notified and s/he should notify you.

[62]IAD, Art. IV(c). *See, e.g.,* Stroble v. Anderson, 587 F.2d 830 (6th Cir. 1978), *cert. denied,* 99 S.Ct. 1289 (1979); United States v. Ford, 550 F.2d 732 (2d Cir. 1977), *aff'd,* United States v. Mauro, 436 U.S. 340 (1978).

[63]IAD, Art. IV(c). *See, e.g.,* United States v. Mauro, *supra*; United States v. Ford, *supra.*

[64]IAD, Art. IV(c). *See, e.g.,* Stroble v. Anderson, *supra. See supra,* note 33.

[65]IAD, Art. IV(c). *See supra,* note 36.

[66]IAD, Art. VI(a). *See, e.g.,* Stroble v. Anderson, *supra;* Prince v. State, 638 S.W.2d 550 (Tex. App. 1982) (prisoner has burden of proof when moving for dimissal of charges). *See supra,* notes 41-44.

[67]IAD, Art. IV(e). Walker v. King, 448 F. Supp. 580 (E.D.N.Y. 1978) (once temporary custody assumed, receiving jurisdiction must resolve all matters pertaining to the indictment while prisoner is in its custody).

[68]IAD, Art. IV(e). *See, e.g.,* United States v. Mauro, *supra*; United States v. Ford, *supra* note 45; United States v. Cyphers, 556 F.2d 630 (2d Cir. 1977), *cert. denied,* 431 U.S. 972, *and cert. denied,* 436 U.S. 950 (1978). *See also* Gray v. Benson, 443 F. Supp. 1284 (D. Kan. 1978); Walker v. King, 448 F. Supp. 580 (D.N.Y. 1978); United States v. Cappucci, 342 F. Supp. 790 (E.D. Pa. 1972); People v. Squitierri, 91 Misc.2d 290, 39 N.Y.S.2d 888 (1977); *supra,* notes 41-44. *But see* United States v. Boniface, 601 F.2d 390 (9th Cir. 1979) (such error does not entitle a prisoner to vacation of new sentence if it falls short of a fundamental defect causing complete miscarriage of justice or of exceptional circumstances).

[69]*See, e.g.,* United States v. Cumberbatch, 438 F. Supp. 976 (S.D.N.Y. 1976),

Before discussing relief from violations of the IAD, we shall consider the federal writ of habeas corpus ad prosequendum. You may encounter this writ in lieu of or in conjunction with a detainer, and the provisions of the IAD are often applicable to such writs.

Writs *ad prosequendum* are issued by the prosecutor of a federal jurisdiction pursuant to a court order. They demand immediate custody of you for trial on an outstanding criminal charge. They differ from detainers in that they are immediately executed, that is, you are immediately transferred to the demanding federal jurisdiction. Detainers, on the other hand, have a tendency to dangle for an indefinite time until either you or the prosecutor initiate a request for final disposition.

The provisions of the IAD apply to situations where the federal government has filed a detainer against you and uses the writ ad prosequendum to secure temporary custody of you for trial. In that situation, the federal government is bound by the terms of the IAD and you are entitled to dismissal of the charges if you are not tried on those charges within the statutory period provided in IAD, Art. IV.[70] If, on the other hand, no detainer has been lodged against you by the federal jurisdiction, the mere use of the writ ad prosequendum does not trigger the provisions of the IAD.[71]

(3) Obtaining Relief for Violations of the IAD

Relief from government violations of provisions of the IAD is provid-

---

cert. denied, 436 U.S. 946 (Art. IV(e) does not bar later trial of a prisoner on charges arising out of the same incident absent prejudice to the prisoner); Boyd v. State, 441 A.2d 1133 (Md. App. 1982), *aff'd,* 447 A.2d 871 (1982) (Art. IV(e) does not require dismissal of every indictment remaining untried after return of prisoner, but only dismissal of those indictments contemplated in Art. IV(e), that is, (1) an indictment which forms the basis of a detainer lodged against the prisoner pursuant to Art. III(a), and (2) which is the object of either a request by the prisoner pursuant to Art. III(a) or a request by the prosecutor under Art. IV(a)).

[70]*See, e.g.,* United States v. Ford, 550 F.2d 732 (2d Cir. 1977), *aff'd,* United States v. Mauro, 436 U.S. 340, 98 S.Ct. 1834 (1978); Dobson v. United States, *supra.*

[71]United States v. Mauro, 436 U.S. 340, 98 S.Ct. 1834 (1978); United States v. Kenann, 557 F.2d 912 (1st Cir. 1977), *cert. denied,* 436 U.S. 943. *See generally* Note, "The Interrelationship Between Habeas Corpus Ad Prosequendum, the Interstate Agreement on Detainers, and the Speedy Trial Act of 1974: *United States v. Mauro,*" 40 U. Pitt. L. Rev. 285 (1979). *See also* Mars v. United States, 443 F. Supp. 774, 776 (E.D. Mich. 1978), *aff'd,* 615 F.2d 704 (6th Cir. 1980), *cert. denied,* 101 S.Ct. 138 (1981); United States v. Gravitt, 590 F.2d 123 (11th Cir. 1979) (where no detainer lodged, obtaining custody of prisoner does not invoke operation of IAD).

ed by administrative, state, and federal remedies. Before discussing each of these remedies, it is important to reiterate that a violation of the IAD does not automatically result in dismissal of the detainer and its underlying charges.[72] Consequently, it is important that you allege in your legal action not only that your IAD rights have been violated, but that those violations caused such a fundamental defect resulting in such a complete miscarriage of justice that court intervention is required to remedy the injustice.[73] It is also important to exhaust your administrative remedies.

Before alleging a violation of your IAD rights in a court proceeding, you should pursue the administrative remedies provided in the IAD.[74] If the jurisdiction that filed the detainer against you is not actively seeking custody of you, and your circumstances make it appropriate, you should request final disposition of the charges underlying the detainer.[75] If you decide not to request final disposition of the charges, at least you should write a "protest" letter to the department of corrections where you are confined and to the prosecutor and court of the jurisdiction where the charges are pending. Your protest letter should notify the authorities that you are *not* requesting final disposition, but that you will contest any transfer to the demanding jurisdiction as being a violation of your rights. At a later date, such a letter may provide support for any speedy trial claims you may have. If nothing else, a protest letter will notify the authorities that you are aware of your rights and will zealously pursue them.

If the prosecutor of the jurisdiction that lodged the detainer against you has requested temporary custody of you for trial on the charges underlying the detainer, if appropriate, you should promptly petition the governor, or other proper authority,[76] of the jurisdiction where you are imprisoned to disapprove the prosecutor's request.[77] In the event of a prosecutor's Article IV request, remember that you are entitled to a pre-transfer hearing under the provisions of the Uniform Criminal Ex-

---

[72]*See supra,* notes 27-30.

[73]*See generally* Fasano v. Hall, 615 F.2d 555 (1st Cir. 1980), *cert. denied,* 101 S.Ct. 201; United States v. Williams, 615 F.2d 585 (3d Cir. 1980); Mars v. United States, 615 F.2d 704 (6th Cir. 1980), *cert. denied,* 101 S.Ct. 138.

[74]*See, e.g.,* Lovell v. Arnold, 391 F. Supp. 1047 (E.D. Pa. 1975). *See also* Hurst v. Hogan, 435 F. Supp. 125 (D. Ga. 1977).

[75]IAD, Art. III(a). *See, e.g.,* Fells v. Kansas, 343 F. Supp. 678 (D. Kan. 1972). *See generally* Gilstrap v. Godwin, 517 F.2d 52 (8th Cir. 1976); Camp v. United States, 587 F.2d 397 (8th Cir. 1978). See discussion under Sec. B for assistance in this regard.

[76]*See supra,* note 54. If the request is not timely made, it is waived and lost.

[77]IAD, Art. IV(a). *See supra,* notes 54-56.

tradition Act, or similar law, to contest the legality of your transfer under a petition for a writ of habeas corpus. If you are not provided with a pre-transfer hearing and are about to be transferred, you may be able to obtain a temporary restraining order from a state court in the jurisdiction where you are imprisoned. Such an order would prevent your transfer until such time as you are provided with the statutorily required pre-transfer hearing. In the event that your request for a temporary restraining order is denied by the state trial and appellate courts, you should seek a similar restraining order in federal court under 42 U.S.C. §1983. (See Ch. VI, Secs. B and H, for a discussion of a §1983 action and temporary restraining order, respectively.)

You should also consult your prison rules, regulations, policy directives, and other procedures provided by the jurisdiction holding you to determine whether any other administrative remedies have been provided "to carry out more effectively the terms and provisions of [the IAD]."[78] If you are in federal custody, the federal prison system provides the following administrative remedies you must exhaust before seeking relief in the courts: (1) a Request for Administrative Remedy, (2) a Regional Appeal, and (3) a Central Office Appeal.[79] Other administrative remedies may be provided by the rules, regulations, and directives of the jurisdiction demanding your custody. These should be consulted because you may have to exhaust them before seeking relief in court for violations of the IAD.

After exhausting all your administrative remedies, you should petition the trial court of the demanding jurisdiction where the charges are pending for dismissal of those charges based on the violation of the IAD.[80]

---

[78]IAD, Art. VII.

[79]See, e.g., Schofs v. Warden, 509 F. Supp. 78, 80 (E.D. Ky. 1981) (Request for Administrative Remedy and Regional Appeal were sufficient evidence of exhaustion where government response was not timely filed under terms of policy statement of prison).

[80]You should file a motion to dismiss the indictment pursuant to IAD Art. IV(e). Braden v. 30th Judicial Circuit of Kentucky, 410 U.S. 484, 93 S.Ct. 1123 (1973) (petitioner for federal habeas corpus relief, alleging improper state action, generally must exhaust state judicial remedies); Peyton v. Rowe, 391 U.S. 54, 88 S.Ct. 1549 (1968); Wingo v. Ciccone, 507 F.2d 354 (8th Cir. 1974); Campbell v. Virginia, 453 F.2d 1230 (10th Cir. 1972). See, e.g., United States ex rel. Esola v. Groomes, 520 F.2d 830 (3d Cir. 1975), cert. denied, 436 U.S. 949; Fells v. Kansas, 343 F. Supp. 678 (D. Kan. 1972); Williams v. Maryland, 445 F. Supp. 1216 (D. Md. 1978); Williams v. Dalsheim, 480 F. Supp. 1049 (D.N.Y. 1979); Sorenson v. Bell, 441 F. Supp. 265 (D.N.Y. 1977) (prisoner must request dismissal of indictment in state trial court before seeking federal habeas corpus relief); Royals v. Day, 446 F. Supp. 887 (D. Okla. 1978) (remedy under Art. IV(c) for alleged denial of speedy trial is by application to state court where charges were pending, rather than by habeas corpus application to federal

Generally, the receiving (or demanding) jurisdiction must bear the burden of assuming that the provisions of the IAD are enforced in the sending (or holding) jurisdiction.[81] However, in an appropriate case, the court of the jurisdiction in which you are confined may relieve you from the burden of the detainer under a writ of habeas corpus. If relief is not granted at the trial level, you should appeal the denial to appellate courts of the jurisdiction.[82]

After exhaustion of your administrative and "adequate and currently available" state post-conviction remedies, you can pursue in federal court, by a petition for a federal writ of habeas corpus,[83] a challenge to your transfer to the demanding jurisdiction based on a violation of the IAD.[84] A prisoner confined in one jurisdiction may challenge an in-

---

court). *See also* Picard v. Connor, 404 U.S. 270, 275-76, 92 S.Ct. 509 (1971); United States ex rel. Scranton v. New York, 532 F.2d 292 (2d Cir. 1976); Moore v. De Young, 515 F.2d 437, 442 (3d Cir. 1975); Grant v. Hogan, 505 F.2d 1220, 1224 (3d Cir. 1974); Kane v. Virginia, 419 F.2d 1369, 1372 (4th Cir. 1970); Brown v. Estelle, 530 F.2d 1280 (5th Cir. 1976); Beck v. United States, 442 F.2d 1037 (5th Cir. 1971); Eschevarria v. Bell, 579 F.2d 1022 (7th Cir. 1978); Chauncey v. Seccond Judicial District Court, 453 F.2d 389, 390 n.1 (9th Cir. 1971); Trigg v. Mosely, 433 F.2d 364 (10th Cir. 1970); Graham v. Commonwealth ex rel. Costa, 368 F. Supp. 846, 850 (W.D. Pa. 1973); Franks v. Johnson, 401 F. Supp. 669, 671 (E.D. Mich. 1975); Palmer v. Judge and District Attorney General, 411 F. Supp. 1029 (W.D. Tenn. 1976).

[81]*See* Shakur v. Bell, 447 F. Supp. 958 (S.D.N.Y. 1978) (hearing would be provided by receiving state); Peopie v. Lincoln, 601 P.2d 641 (Colo. App. 1979) (burden on receiving state to show compliance with IAD by sending state). *But see* Schofs v. Warden, *supra* note 79, at 81 (in a proper case, federal court has jurisdiction to relieve a federal prisoner from the burden of a state detainer); Campbell v. Virginia, 453 F.2d 1230 (10th Cir. 1972); Bedwell v. Harris, 451 F.2d 122 (10th Cir. 1971); Trigg v. Moseley, 433 F.2d 364 (10th Cir. 1970).

[82]Lovell v. Arnold, 391 F. Supp. 1047 (E.D. Pa. 1975). *See also* Picard v. Connor, 404 U.S. 270, 92 S.Ct. 509 (1971); Fay v. Noia, 372 U.S. 391, 83 S.Ct. 822 (1963) (state remedies exhausted when highest state court has ruled on the merits).

You should consult local law concerning court orders before using the appellate courts. Many jurisdictions permit a challenge to the lower court's denial of your claim through a petition for a writ of mandamus.

[83]28 U.S.C. §2254. Braden v. 30th Judicial Circuit of Kentucky, *supra* note 80, 410 U.S. at 489; Nelson v. George, 399 U.S. 224, 229-230, 90 S.Ct. 1963 (1970); Fay v. Noia, *id. See also* Frazier v. Lane, 446 F. Supp. 19 (D. Tenn. 1977) (only where states withhold effective remedy do federal courts have power and duty to provide it). *See, e.g.,* United States ex rel. Esola v. Groomes, *supra* note 80; Williams v. Maryland, *supra;* Fasano v. Hall, 476 F. Supp. 291 (D. Mass. 1979), *cert. denied,* 101 S.Ct. 201. *See also* Preiser v. Rodriguez, 411 U.S. 475, 499-500, 93 S.Ct. 1827 (1973). See "Post-Conviction Remedies," Ch. IX.

[84]Cuyler v. Adams, 449 U.S. 433, 101 S.Ct. 703 (1981). *See generally* Foran v.

terstate (or interjurisdictional) detainer lodged against him or her and the legality of the charges on which it was based by means of a petition for federal habeas corpus *both* in the district in which the prisoner is confined and in the district where the detainer was issued.[85]

The federal district court in the district of the state (or jurisdiction) that lodged the detainer against you will ordinarily be the most convenient forum for a trial concerning violations of the IAD. However, the Supreme Court has carefully noted that the convenience of the forum should not "preclude the exercise of concurrent habeas corpus jurisdiction over [a prisoner's IAD] claim by a federal district court in the district of confinement."[86] In this regard, the federal court in which you have filed will have to make a venue determination on the basis of the venue (the location) which is most convenient to the parties involved. As indicated by the Supreme Court, "[w]here a prisoner brings an action in the district of confinement attacking a detainer lodged by another state [or jurisdiction], the court can, of course, transfer the suit to a more convenient forum," namely, to the district where the detainer was issued.[87]

Another possible challenge to your transfer to the demanding jurisdiction, or other state IAD actions, is based on the fact that the IAD is a congressionally sanctioned interstate compact the interpretation of which presents a question of federal law.[88] A federal court is not bound by a state court's interpretation of the provisions of the IAD because it is an interstate compact approved by Congress and is thus a federal law subject to federal rather than state construction or interpretation.[89] If a state court has misinterpreted the provisions of the IAD or the rights you possess thereunder, and thereby has violated them, you can bring an action in the federal district court for the district where you are confined

---

Metz, 463 F. Supp. 1088 (S.D.N.Y. 1979). See also cases compiled at note 80, *supra*. Only when the highest state court has ruled adversely to petitioner on the merits of his contentions can his state remedies be deemed exhausted for purposes of federal habeas corpus review. Picard v. Connor, 404 U.S. 270, 92 S.Ct. 509 (1971); Fay v. Noia, 372 U.S. 391, 83 S.Ct. 822 (1963). *See also* 28 U.S.C. §2254.

[85]Braden v. 30th Judicial Circuit of Kentucky, *supra* note 80. *See also* Brazer v. State, 367 F. Supp. 753, 757 (W.D. Mo. 1973); Norris v. State, 357 F. Supp. 1200, 1204 (W.D.N.C. 1973).

[86]Braden v. 30th Judicial Circuit of Kentucky, *supra* note 80, 410 U.S. at 499.

[87]*Id.,* 410 U.S. at 499 n.15, *citing* 28 U.S.C. §1404(a), and Hoffman v. Blaski, 363 U.S. 335, 80 S.Ct. 1084 (1960).

[88]Cuyler v. Adams, *supra* note 9. Refer to this case for the legal basis for bringing such an action.

[89]*Id.*

under 42 U.S.C. §1983 seeking declaratory, injunctive, and other appropriate relief from the state's misinterpretation and violation of your IAD rights.[90] The major restriction on the §1983 remedy is that you cannot get your conviction set aside; you can only do this through a post-conviction proceeding. However, in a §1983 action, you can obtain an injunction requiring the authorities to provide the hearing and other procedural protections to which you are entitled. The Supreme Court has ruled as a matter of federal law, in opposition to a state court's interpretation of the IAD, that the IAD preserves any preexisting rights you may have under applicable post-conviction and extradition laws.[91]

If you seek to set aside your conviction on the charges underlying the detainer, or seek to obtain release after your transfer, a similar action can be brought in federal court in a petition for a writ of habeas corpus based on the misinterpretation and violation of the IAD as a violation of the rights you possess under federal law.[92]

Any time you contest the propriety or legality of a jurisdiction's actions under the IAD, be sure to include a statement citing IAD, Article IX. Article IX provides that the IAD "shall be liberally construed so as to effectuate its purpose." As stated by the Supreme Court,

> The legislative history of the [IAD], including the comments of the Council of State Governments and the congressional reports and debates preceding the adoption of the Agreement on behalf of the District of Columbia and the federal government, emphasizes that a primary purpose of the Agreement is *to protect prisoners* against whom detainers are outstanding.[93]

(4) Relationship of the IAD and Constitutional Speedy Trial Guarantees

The central purposes of the IAD are "to encourage the expeditious and orderly disposition" of the charges underlying an interjurisdictional detainer and to remove the "uncertainties which obstruct programs of prisoner treatment and rehabilitation" that occur when the detainer is lodged against a prisoner.[94] The central purpose of the Sixth Amend-

---

[90]*See* Maine v. Thiboutot, 448 U.S. 1, 100 S.Ct. 2502 (1980) (§1983 encompasses claims based on all federal statutory violations). See also Ch. VI, Sec. B3, for a discussion of the differences between §1983 and habeas corpus. See also Ch. VI, Secs. G and H, for a discussion of injunctive and declaratory relief.

[91]Cuyler v. Adams, *supra* note 9.

[92]See Ch. IX for a discussion of habeas corpus actions. See also cases compiled at notes 80-87, *supra*.

[93]Cuyler v. Adams, *supra* note 9, 449 U.S. at 448-49 (emphasis added).

[94]IAD, Art. I. *See, e.g.,* Camp v. United States, 587 F.2d 397 (8th Cir. 1978) (IAD is nothing more than a statutory set of procedural rules which do not rise to

ment right to speedy trial is to ensure that a defendant will "enjoy" a speedy trial of criminal charges lodged against him/her.[95]

You should distinguish your rights under the IAD and your rights under the Sixth Amendment to the Constitution of the United States when considering the legal effect of a detainer lodged against you. Under the IAD, you are generally entitled to a trial of the charges underlying the detainer within set statutory periods[96] to avoid the "uncertainties" created by outstanding detainers which tend to obstruct your "treatment and rehabilitation."[97] Under the Sixth Amendment right to a speedy trial of criminal charges, on the other hand, there is no set period within which you must be tried. Instead, in determining whether you have enjoyed a speedy criminal trial, the courts analyze the facts and circumstances of your case by balancing the conduct of the prosecution against that of the defense, and the rights of society against your right to a speedy criminal trial.[98]

Although your rights protected by the IAD and those protected by the Sixth Amendment are related, they are not the same. Conduct by the prosecutor that obeys the provisions of the IAD may still violate your Sixth Amendment rights, and conduct that is permissible under the Sixth Amendment may violate your IAD rights.

For example, a prosecutor could use the IAD to obtain temporary custody of you for trial on the charges underlying a detainer to avoid an allegation that your speedy trial right has been denied. But, even though the prosecutor may have observed your right to a speedy criminal trial, the prosecutor must still observe your rights under the IAD. If your IAD rights, such as trial within 120 days of arrival in the demanding jurisdiction are not observed, you are entitled to dismissal of the charges with prejudice, even though your speedy trial rights have been observed. Likewise, even though you are tried within the IAD statutory period, if the prosecutor has delayed too long in resorting to the IAD to bring you

---

the level of constitutionally guaranteed rights and has nothing to do with a fair trial); United States v. Cogdell, 585 F.2d 1130 (D.C. Cir. 1978), *cert. denied,* 99 S.Ct. 1509 (1979), *rev'd,* United States v. Bailey, 444 U.S. 394, 100 S.Ct. 624 (1980). *But see* Rhodes v. Schoen, 574 F.2d 968 (8th Cir. 1978), *cert. denied,* 439 U.S. 868 (1978).

[95]U.S. Const., Amend. VI. Consult state constitutions for similar constitutional rights.

[96]IAD, Art. III(a) (trial within 180 days after written request for final disposition has been caused to be delivered); IAD, Art. IV(a) (trial within 120 days of prisoner's arrival in the demanding jurisdiction). *See supra,* notes 26 and 59.

[97]IAD, Art. I.

[98]*See* Barker v. Wingo, 407 U.S. 514, 92 S.Ct. 2182 (1972). *See also* Branch v. United States, 372 A.2d 998 (D.C. Ct. App. 1977).

to trial on the charges, you may successfully assert your constitutional right to a speedy criminal trial which may have been denied by prosecutorial inaction. The Supreme Court has held that a state has a continuing speedy trial obligation to a defendant, even though s/he may be imprisoned in another jurisdiction.[99]

b. Speedy Trial Guarantees

The fact that you are imprisoned does not relieve a jurisdiction where criminal charges are pending against you of its Sixth Amendment duty[100] to provide you with a speedy trial.[101] That duty must be observed whether the charges underlie an interstate or an intrastate detainer[102] and whether the provisions of the IAD are applicable[103] or have been invoked by you or by the prosecutor of the demanding jurisdiction.[104] Additional speedy trial duties may be imposed on a jurisdiction by pertinent statutory provisions promulgated by the legislature of that jurisdiction.[105]

You should employ constitutional and statutory speedy trial arguments whenever there has been excessive delay of a trial on the charges underlying the detainer. The most common situation in which they should be employed is where there has been a delay in bringing you

---

[99]Smith v. Hooey, 393 U.S. 374, 89 S.Ct. 575 (1969); Dickey v. Florida, 398 U.S. 30, 90 S.Ct. 1564 (1970). For a further discussion of this issue, *see* United States v. Mauro, 436 U.S. 340, 98 S.Ct. 1834 (1978). *See generally* Godbold, "Speedy Trial—Major Surgery for a National Ill," 24 Ala. L. Rev. 265 (1972).

[100]U.S. Const., Amend. VI. Three interests are protected by the Sixth Amendment right to speedy trial. First is your interest in avoiding prolonged imprisonment prior to trial. Second is your interest in avoiding prolonged psychological pressure and public suspicion while the charges are pending against you. Third is your interest in disposing of your case before witnesses and other evidence are lost, that is, before your defense is lost. *See* Dickey v. Florida, 398 U.S. 30, 90 S.Ct. 1564 (1970); Smith v. Hooey, 393 U.S. 374, 89 S.Ct. 575 (1969).

[101]United States v. Mauro, 436 U.S. 340, 98 S.Ct. 1834 (1978); United States v. Dowl, 394 F. Supp. 1250 (D. Minn. 1975).

[102]*See generally* Klopfer v. North Carolina, 386 U.S. 213, 87 S.Ct. 988 (1967) (guarantee of speedy trial is applicable to the states through the Due Process Clause of the Fourteenth Amendment).

[103]*See supra,* note 11 and accompanying text.

[104]*See supra,* notes 20-23 and 49-52.

[105]*See, e.g.,* The federal Speedy Trial Act, 18 U.S.C. §§3161-74. Consult Appendix D, Sec. 3, for state statutory provisions. Courts also have the inherent power to control their own calendars and can dismiss an action for lack of government prosecution. *See, e.g.,* FRCrP 48(b) and 50.

to trial and where the IAD is inapplicable either because the demanding jurisdiction is not a party to the IAD or because the detainer is an intra-state detainer.[106] You should also employ speedy trial arguments to supplement arguments under the IAD whenever the IAD is applicable.[107]

(1) When Do Constitutional Speedy Trial Rights Attach?

(a) Pre-Charge or Pre-Arrest Delay

The Sixth Amendment right to speedy trial generally does not apply prior to indictment, information, or arrest.[108] In other words, your speedy trial rights do not attach until you become an "accused."[109] If you are formally charged before the demanding jurisdiction lodges a detainer against you, your speedy trial rights attach when that formal charge is made.[110] The Supreme Court has held that the actual restraints imposed by arrest and holding to answer a criminal charge engage the particular protections of the speedy trial provision of the Sixth Amendment.[111] Thus, you "need not await indictment, information, or other formal charge" to invoke the speedy trial provisions of the Sixth Amendment.[112] The fact that you are presently imprisoned on another charge and are subject to criminal prosecution in another jurisdiction might cause the court to conclude that you are or were an "accused" entitled to the Sixth Amendment guarantees.[113] Whether you stand accused can

---

[106]The federal government is one jurisdiction under the IAD. *See supra,* note 10.

[107]*See supra,* note 11.

[108]United States v. Marion, 404 U.S. 307, 92 S.Ct. 455 (1971).

[109]*Id.* at 313.

[110]*Id.* at 320.

[111]*See* United States v. Marion, *supra* note 108, at 321; Dodge v. People, 495 P.2d 312 (Colo. 1972); Commonwealth v. Hamilton, 297 A.2d 127 (Pa. 1972). You should consult the statutes and case law of the holding and demanding jurisdiction to determine when your speedy trial right attaches. *See, e.g.,* FRCrP 48(b).

[112]United States v. Marion, *id.*

[113]Smith v. Hooey, *supra* note 99, at 387-383 (speedy trial right protects prisoners who are subject to criminal prosecutions in another jurisdiction). *Cf.* United States v. Gouveia, 704 F.2d 1116, 1120 (9th Cir. 1983) (arrest will trigger speedy trial right even if no formal indictment brought because arrest is public act seriously interfering with suspect's liberty in a way that speedy trial provision is designed to mitigate).

only be determined by the court from "the totality of the circumstances."[114]

Although the Sixth Amendment right to speedy trial generally does not attach prior to arrest, indictment, or information, the Due Process Clause of the Fifth and Fourteenth Amendments, which guarantee a fair trial, always have a limited role to play in protecting you from oppressive pre-charge delay.[115] To get your case dismissed for delay at this preliminary stage, you must show "actual prejudice" from the delay.[116] However, your showing of actual prejudice merely makes your due process claim "concrete and ripe for adjudication, not . . . automatically valid."[117] For example, where the reason for the pre-charge delay was the prosecution's further investigation of the case, the delay does not necessarily deprive you of due process, even if your defense might have been somewhat prejudiced by the lapse of time.[118] A full and thorough investigation serves the interests of justice and often your own interests, and as such often fulfills rather than violates the requirements of the Due Process Clause.[119] But if the delay is intended to gain a tactical and one-sided advantage over you, due process has been violated and the charge should be dismissed to protect you from the effects of the prejudicial delay.[120]

Where the prosecution provides an investigative or similar justification for the pre-charge delay, your due process claim will be denied. But, where no such justification for the delay is given or where it is not supported by the record, the Due Process Clause can support dismissal of the case if your defense has been prejudiced.

---

[114]*See* Escobedo v. Illinois, 378 U.S. 478, 485-86, 84 S.Ct. 1758 (1962); United States v. Gouveia, *id.* at 1120.

[115]United States v. Marion, *supra,* 404 U.S. at 326.

[116]United States v. Marion, *supra*; United States v. Lavasco, 431 U.S. 783, 789, 97 S.Ct. 2044 (1977).

[117]United States v. Lavasco, *supra.* If prolonged delay adversely affects your ability to prepare, preserve, and present evidence in your defense, your due process right to a fair trial may be violated. United States v. Lamasco, 431 U.S. at 789, 795-97 and n.17; United States v. Marion, 404 U.S. at 324-26; Fontaine v. California, 390 U.S. 593, 595-96, 88 S.Ct. 1229 (1968); Taylor v. United States, 238 F.2d 259 (D.C. Cir. 1956); United States v. Chase, 135 F. Supp. 230 (N.D. Ill. 1955).

[118]*Id.* at 796.

[119]*See generally* United States v. Lavasco, *supra,* 431 U.S. at 795-96. *See also* Tolliver v. United States, 378 A.2d 679 (D.C. Ct. App. 1977).

[120]United States v. Marion, *supra,* 404 U.S. at 324.

(b) Post-Charge or Post-Arrest Delay

The right to a speedy criminal trial is specifically guaranteed by the Sixth Amendment to the Constitution of the United States.[121] It is applicable to the states through the Fourteenth Amendment.[122] Generally, the right attaches and computation of the delay begins when you are arrested or when you are arraigned on an information or indictment, whichever occurs first.[123] If you are accused of a crime, even if you are confined in prison at the time of the accusation, the charging jurisdiction has a constitutional duty to make a diligent, good-faith effort to bring you to trial after you demand a speedy trial.[124] When a court determines that you have been deprived of your right to a speedy trial, you are entitled to dismissal with prejudice of the charges against you.[125]

Generally, you are entitled to dismissal with prejudice of the charges against you only if you can prove that there are aggravated circumstances which entitle you to such relief.[126] The Supreme Court has identified four factors which a court should consider on a case-by-case basis to determine whether you are entitled to such relief because you have been denied a speedy trial.[127] Those factors are (1) the length of the delay, (2) the reason for the delay, (3) your assertion of or failure to assert your right to a speedy trial, and (4) the presence or absence of prejudice to you resulting from the delay.[128] Although none of these factors has any "talismanic qualities," they are interrelated and "must be considered

---

[121]Consult state constitutions for a similar provision.

[122]Klopfer v. North Carolina, 386 U.S. 213, 87 S.Ct. 988 (1967).

[123]Dillingham v. United States, 423 U.S. 64, 96 S.Ct. 303 (1975); United States v. Marion, 404 U.S. 307, 320-21, 92 S.Ct. 455 (1971). See discussion under subsection (a), pre-charge or pre-arrest delay, *supra.*

[124]Smith v. Hooey, 393 U.S. 374, 382-83, 89 S.Ct. 575 (1969); United States v. Elwell, 383 U.S. 116, 120, 86 S. Ct. 773 (1966).

[125]Strunk v. United States, 412 U.S. 434, 439-40, 93 S.Ct. 2260 (1973); Dickey v. Florida, 398 U.S. 30, 90 S.Ct. 1564 (1970).

[126]*See, e.g.,* United States v. Ellis, 408 A.2d 971 (D.C. Ct. App. 1979) (extraordinarily long period of delay in prosecuting a simple misdemeanor); Branch v. United States, 372 A.2d 998 (D.C. Ct. App. 1977) (government failed to give an adequate justification for the delay while defendant asserted his right while imprisoned). *But see* Day v. United States, 390 A.2d 957 (D.C. Ct. App. 1978) (nearly three-year delay did not violate defendant's right to speedy trial where defendant failed to assert his right and where there was an absence of cognizable prejudice).

[127]Barker v. Wingo, 407 U.S. 514, 92 S.Ct. 2182 (1972).

[128]Barker v. Wingo, *id.,* 407 U.S. at 530. *See also* United States v. Dowl, 394 F. Supp. 1250 (D. Minn. 1975).

together with such other circumstances as may be relevant"[129] in the "difficult and sensitive balancing process" by which a court determines whether your speedy trial right has been denied.[130]

(2) Assessing Adherence to the Speedy Trial Right

(a) Length of Delay

There is no constitutional basis for holding that the speedy trial right can be quantified into a specified number of days or months.[131] But

> [t]he length of delay is to some extent a triggering mechanism. Until there is some delay which is presumptively prejudicial, there is no necessity for inquiry into the other factors that go into the balance. Nevertheless, because of the imprecision of the right to speedy trial, the length of delay that will provoke such an inquiry is necessarily dependent upon the peculiar circumstances of the case. To take but one example, the delay that can be tolerated for an ordinary street crime is considerably less than for a serious, complex conspiracy charge.[132]

To determine whether the length of delay in bringing you to trial has been excessive, you should consult the court rules and case law of the jurisdiction in which the charges are pending against you. That jurisdiction may have certain specific criteria for evaluating the significance of the delay in any given case.[133]

---

[129]*See, e.g.,* Moore v. Arizona, 414 U.S. 25, 94 S.Ct. 188 (1973) (a court should examine the effect of an additional charge on a prisoner's prospects for parole and rehabilitation).

[130]Barker v. Wingo, *supra,* 407 U.S. at 533.

[131]Barker v. Wingo, *supra,* 407 U.S. at 523.

[132]Barker v. Wingo, *supra,* 407 U.S. at 530.

[133]*See, e.g.,* Branch v. United States, *supra,* 372 A.2d at 1000 n.3 (delay in excess of six months warrants inquiry and justification); Glass v. United States, 395 A.2d 796, 801 (D.C. Ct. App. 1978) (delay in excess of one year gives claim of denial prima facie merit); Reed v. United States, 383 A.2d 316, 319 (D.C. Ct. App. 1978) (one-year delay period is a simple rule of thumb which triggers review, but which does not attach any evidentiary presumption to the delay); Day v. United States, *supra,* 390 A.2d at 970 (the longer the delay, the heavier the burden on the government to justify it); Branch v. United States, *supra,* 372 A.2d at 1000 (the more serious and complicated the offense, the greater pretrial delay allowed). *See also* United States v. Lara, 520 F.2d 460, 464 (D.C. Cir. 1975); United States v. Ransom, 465 F.2d 672, 673 (D.C. Cir. 1972); United States v. Jones, 524 F.2d 834, 849 (D.C. Cir. 1975); Coleman v. United States, 442 F.2d 150, 153 (D.C. Cir. 1971).

(b) Reason for Delay

The reason the government assigns to justify the delay is closely related to the length of delay.[134]

> Here, too, different weights should be assigned to different reasons. A deliberate attempt to delay the trial in order to hamper the defense should be weighted heavily against the government. A more neutral reason such as negligence or overcrowded courts should be weighted less heavily but nevertheless should be considered since the ultimate responsibility for such circumstances must rest with the government rather than with the defendant. Finally, a valid reason, such as a missing witness, should serve to justify appropriate delay.[135]

If the prosecution purposefully delays trial to hamper your defense, to gain some tactical advantage over you, or to harass you, these factors should weigh heavily against the government.[136] "Whenever the government's action at any stage of the proceedings indicates bad faith, neglect, or a purpose to secure delay itself or some other procedural advantage, the resulting delay is not justified."[137] Similarly, because the government has a duty to bring you to trial, delay caused by crowded court calendars and other "neutral" reasons should weigh against the government.[138] But these neutral reasons will weigh less heavily against the government.[139]

When *you* cause the delay, you may forfeit the right to have that delay counted in the speedy trial equation.[140] If, for example, you request a trial continuance, the period of the continuance may be excluded from the calculation of the delay.[141] Similarly, if you mutually agree with the prosecution to a trial continuance, the period of that continuance may be disregarded by a court when it calculates the delay caused by the govern-

---

[134]Barker v. Wingo, *supra,* 407 U.S. at 531.

[135]Barker v. Wingo, *supra.*

[136]Barker v. Wingo, *supra,* 407 U.S. at 531 and n.32.

[137]United States v. Lara, *supra,* 520 F.2d at 464.

[138]Barker v. Wingo, *supra,* 407 U.S. at 531.

[139]Barker v. Wingo, *supra. See* Bethea v. United States, 395 A.2d 787, 791 (D.C. Ct. App. 1978) (institutional delays, like court congestion, may easily be outweighed by an inadequate assertion of the speedy trial right or a low threshold of prejudice).

[140]*See, e.g.,* Forbes v. United States, 390 A.2d 453, 456 (D.C. Ct. App. 1978) (delay caused by your other trials cannot be held against the government). *See also* Cates v. United States, 379 A.2d 968, 972 (D.C. Ct. App. 1977).

[141]*See, e.g.,* Chatman v. United States, 377 A.2d 1155, 1157 n.3 (D.C. Ct. App. 1977).

ment.[142] Finally, if you fail to object to the continuance, or if you fail to demand a speedy trial at that time, a court calculating the delay against the government may assign minimal weight to the period of the continuance.[143]

(c) Assertion of the Speedy Trial Right

Whether and how you assert your speedy trial right is closely related to the other factors we have mentioned.[144] As with them, the facts and circumstances of your case must be weighed and measured by a court to determine when you must assert or have waived your right to a speedy trial.[145] The Supreme Court expressed this sentiment in the following passage:

> The strength of his efforts [at asserting the right] will be affected by the length of the delay, to some extent by the reason for the delay, and most particularly by the personal prejudice, which is not always readily identifiable, that he experiences. *The more serious the deprivation, the more likely a defendant is to complain.* The defendant's assertion of his speedy trial right, then, is entitled to strong evidentiary weight in determining whether the defendant is being deprived of the right. We emphasize that failure to assert the right will make it difficult for a defendant to prove that he was denied a speedy trial.[146]

Although you do not forever waive your right to a speedy trial if you fail to assert it, you do have a responsibility to assert or demand it.[147] In fact, if you do assert your right to a speedy trial, the government bears a heavier burden of meeting your demand and the reasons for delay take on greater significance. As a rule of thumb, any delay prior to your demand for speedy trial is accorded less significance than delay occurring after you assert your right.[148]

---

[142]*See, e.g.,* United States v. Calhoun, 363 A.2d 277, 280 n.3 (D.C. Ct. App. 1976).

[143]*See, e.g.,* Reed v. United States, *supra,* 383 A.2d at 319. *See also* Bowman v. United States, 385 A.2d 28, 31 (D.C. Ct. App. 1978).

[144]Barker v. Wingo, *supra,* 407 U.S. at 531.

[145]Barker v. Wingo, *supra* at 528 (it is impossible to pinpoint a precise time when you must assert or waive the right).

[146]Barker v. Wingo, *supra* at 531-32 (emphasis added).

[147]Barker v. Wingo, *supra* at 531.

[148]*Compare* Glass v. United States, *supra,* 395 A.2d at 802 (delay prior to assertion of right), *with* Bethea v. United States, 395 A.2d 787, 792 (D.C. Ct. App. 1978) (delay after assertion of right). *See* Reed v. United States, *supra,* 383 A.2d at 319.

(d) Prejudice

If the length of delay is unjustified and excessive, or presumptively prejudicial, theoretically, you do not have to show actual prejudice to establish that you were denied your right to a speedy trial by the delay.[149] Practically, however, you must show prejudice to prevail on your claim. Even if you believe that the other factors in the speedy trial equation will convince the court that your right to a speedy trial has been denied, you should still allege and establish that you have been prejudiced by the delay.

Prejudice should be assessed in light of your interests which the speedy trial right was designed to protect.[150] Three such interests have been identified by the Supreme Court: (1) to prevent your oppressive pretrial imprisonment,[151] (2) to minimize your anxiety and concern,[152] and (3) to limit the possibility that your defense will be impaired.[153] As the Court pointed out,

> Of these, the most serious is the last, because the inability of a defendant adequately to prepare his case skews the fairness of the entire system. If witnesses die or disappear during a delay, the prejudice is obvious. There is also prejudice if defense witnesses are unable to recall accurately events of the distant past. Loss of memory, however, is not always reflected in the record because what has been forgotten can rarely be shown.[154]

When claiming prejudice from the delay, you must *substantiate* your claim. You cannot merely speculate that you have been prejudiced. Although it may be relatively easy for you to substantiate a violation of

---

[149]Moore v. Arizona, 414 U.S. 25, 94 S.Ct. 188 (1973) (showing of prejudice is not required by Barker v. Wingo, *supra*).

[150]Barker v. Wingo, *supra,* 407 U.S. at 532.

[151]*See, e.g.,* Smith v. Hooey, *supra,* 393 U.S. at 378-79; Day v. United States, *supra,* 390 A.2d at 972.

[152]*See, e.g.,* Reed v. United States, *supra,* 383 A.2d at 320 (mere assertion that you have been upset or concerned about a pending criminal prosecution is not sufficient); United States v. Bolden, 381 A.2d 624 (D.C. Ct. App. 1977) (little additional apprehension or anxiety from pending misdemeanor charge where defendant is also pending trial on a felony charge); United States v. Clark, 376 A.2d 434, 436 (D.C. Ct. App. 1977) (strain by itself does not establish prejudice where defendant neither asserts nor shows that the delay weighed particularly heavily on him in specific instances).

[153]Barker v. Wingo, *supra,* 407 U.S. at 532. *See* Crowder v. United States, 383 A.2d 336, 339-40 (D.C. Ct. App. 1978) (delay which strengthens the government's case should be distinguished from delay which weakens the defendant's case).

[154]Barker v. Wingo, *supra* at 532.

the first two interests protected by the speedy trial right, substantiating a violation of the third interest may be more difficult because you are imprisoned and cannot adequately investigate your defense to show that it has been impaired by the delay. Since you are unable to investigate your defense, you should compile a list of your evidence and witnesses and how you expected them to testify. This record will form the basis of your claim that your defense has been impaired by the delay.

It is important to mention that the extent to which your defense has been impaired can often only be accurately determined after your trial.[155] Consequently, if the evidence presented at your trial establishes more clearly the prejudice to your defense from the delay, you may want to renew *after* your trial a motion to dismiss the indictment for lack of speedy trial.[156]

(3) Making a Speedy Trial Demand and Obtaining Relief for Constitutional Speedy Trial Violations

You should put the prosecutor on notice that you are demanding a speedy trial of the charges pending against you. When the prosecutor is aware of your request or demand for speedy trial, s/he bears a heavier burden of meeting your right.[157] The time that passes after your demand for speedy trial and the reasons for its passage take on greater significance for a court calculating through the speedy trial equation whether you have been denied a speedy trial.[158]

The simplest way for you to make the prosecutor and court aware of your demand for speedy trial is to write them a letter in which you explicitly ask for a speedy trial of the charges pending against you.[159] Your letter should ask the prosecutor and court to schedule your case for trial.

Oftentimes, the prosecutor will ignore your letter and request for speedy trial. If that happens and a reasonable period has passed without a reply, you should write the prosecutor and court another letter

---

[155]United States v. McDonald, 435 U.S. 850, 98 S.Ct. 1816 (1978). *See* Day v. United States, *supra*, 390 A.2d at 971-72; Bethea v. United States, *supra*, 395 A.2d at 793.

[156]*Id.*

[157]See discussion and notes under subsection "Assertion of Speedy Trial Right," *supra.*

[158]*See supra,* note 148.

[159]Your letter should contain information similar to that contained in an IAD request for final disposition. *See, e.g.,* Appendix D, Sec. 7, Form I. See discussion under subsection "Prisoner's Request for Final Disposition Under IAD Article III," *supra.*

demanding a speedy trial and making reference to your previous speedy trial demand.[160] If the prosecutor ignores your second letter, you have two options. If you want a speedy trial, you can file a formal *pro se* motion for speedy trial in the court where the charges are pending against you. If instead you only want to make a demand for speedy trial to make a record so you can later move for a dismissal, it may make sense to stop after you have written the prosecutor twice.

If you decide to make a motion for speedy trial and it is denied by the trial court, you should first consult local law for further remedy since the trial court's denial can often be challenged by writ of mandamus.[161] This writ, if available, can be used to compel the trial court to grant your request for speedy trial.

If your motion for speedy trial is denied and mandamus is unavailable or also denied, you should appeal the denial to the appellate courts of the jurisdiction in which the charges are pending against you.[162] After you exhaust your state remedies, you should petition by writ of habeas corpus[163] the federal court of the district in which the charges are pending against you for relief from the denial of your right to speedy trial.

If you believe that you have been denied a speedy trial in violation of your constitutional right, you should file a *pro se* motion to dismiss the charges against you in the court of the jurisdiction where those charges are pending.[164] Your motion should allege in general and establish in particular the factors of the speedy trial equation we have previously discussed in this section: length of delay, reason for delay, assertion of your right to speedy trial, and prejudice to you. If the trial court of that jurisdiction denies your motion to dismiss the charges, you must appeal the denial to the appellate courts of that jurisdiction. If the appellate courts deny your motion, and you are facing state charges, you can petition by writ of habeas corpus the federal court of the jurisdiction in which the charges are pending for relief from the violation of your constitutional right to a speedy trial.[165]

---

[160]You should make and keep copies of all correspondence you have with the prosecutor.

[161]*See, e.g.,* The federal Mandamus Act, 28 U.S.C. §1361 (1970) (claim to compel federal official brought in federal court). *See* Thompson v. State, 482 P.2d 627 (Okla. Crim. 1971); Rudisill v. District Court, 453 P.2d 598 (Colo. 1969), *cert. denied,* 395 U.S. 925 (1969).

[162]See discussion under Sec. B3a(3) "Obtaining Relief for Violations of the IAD," *supra.*

[163]See Ch. IX, "Post-Conviction Relief." *See also supra,* notes 79-82.

[164]See Ch. III, Sec. B, concerning drafting of a motion. You must include detailed allegations concerning the denial of your speedy trial, including dates of letters and the factors discussed *supra* concerning the speedy trial equation.

[165]*See, e.g.,* Strunk v. United States, 412 U.S. 434, 93 S.Ct. 2260 (1973);

(4) Statutory Speedy Trial Rights: Intrastate (Intrajurisdictional) Detainers and Interstate Detainers *Not* Covered by the Interstate Agreement on Detainers (IAD)

Most states and the federal government have enacted statutes to implement and define your constitutional right to a speedy trial.[166] Unlike the IAD, which was primarily enacted for administrative efficiency and to alleviate the uncertainties connected with detainers, your imprisonment, and rehabilitation, these statutes were enacted to clearly define your right to speedy trial.[167] They were not designed to limit the scope of your constitutional rights. They are very important and may provide your only statutory remedy in three situations:

1. When a federal detainer is lodged against you by a federal jurisdiction while you are imprisoned on a federal conviction in another federal jurisdiction;[168]

2. When an intrastate detainer is lodged against you by a state which has not adopted intrastate detainer legislation;[169] and

3. When an interstate detainer is lodged against you by a non-signatory of the IAD.[170]

In each of these situations, in addition to relying on constitutional speedy trial guarantees, you should rely on the statutory speedy trial provisions of the demanding jurisdiction. Often, the speedy trial statute will have provisions which specifically concern prisoners and detainers.[171]

Generally, it will be easier for you to make a speedy trial argument based on these statutes than it will be for you to make similar arguments

---

Braden v. 30th Judicial Circuit Court, 410 U.S. 484, 93 S.Ct. 1123 (1973). See previous discussion and "Post-Conviction Relief," Chapter X. In response to your petition for habeas corpus, a federal court may direct the following relief: (1) the detainer will have no effect on you, (2) the detainer will be withdrawn from your prison file, (3) the charges underlying the detainer will be dismissed, or (4) the charges underlying the detainer will be resolved by an immediate trial.

[166]See Appendix D, Sec. 3, for a list of speedy trial statutes.

[167]*See supra,* notes 84-89 and accompanying text.

[168]The IAD does not apply in this situation. The federal government is one jurisdiction for purposes of the IAD. *See supra,* note 10.

[169]An example of intrastate detainer legislation is the Uniform Mandatory Disposition of Detainers Act (UMDDA). See Appendix D, Secs. 4 and 5, for the text of the UMDDA and states which have enacted it or similar legislation.

[170]See Appendix D, Sec. 2, for a list of signatory states and statutes.

[171]*See, e.g.,* the federal Speedy Trial Act, 18 U.S.C. §§3161-74, discussed *infra. See also* State v. Barnes, 328 A.2d 737 (Md. 1974); Hoss v. State, 242 A.2d 48 (Md. 1972) (indictment dismissed with prejudice; state failed to comply with 180-day rule of Md. Code, Art. 27, §616).

based on your constitutional right to a speedy trial since your right to a speedy trial can be easily measured by the statutory provisions. But, you should always supplement your statutory speedy trial arguments with arguments based on the constitutional guarantee of a speedy trial. There is always the possibility that a court will dismiss the prosecution's case against you, even though the prosecution has complied with the time limits of the speedy trial statute. This possibility exists because your constitutional right to a speedy trial may be denied nonetheless when there has been compliance with the statutory time limits.[172] However, when there has been compliance with the speedy trial statute, you will have to show extremely aggravated or unusual circumstances to justify a dismissal of the charges on constitutional grounds.[173]

As just indicated, when the facts of your case fit the terms of the speedy trial statute of the demanding jurisdiction, your right to a speedy trial will be determined in the first instance by the provisions of that statute. (Remember, these statutes do not limit your constitutional rights, they augment them.) You should carefully review the provisions of the statute to determine the time limits and specific exclusions from those time limits.[174] Speedy trial statutes commonly provide that you must be brought to trial within a certain number of days, or within a prescribed number of terms of the court where the charge against you is pending, after one of the following has occurred: 1) an indictment, information, or complaint is filed; or 2) an arrest occurs; or 3) you demand a speedy trial. If the time limits of the statute are violated, and no exclusion is applicable, the charge against you must be dismissed, often with prejudice.[175] A dismissal of the charge causes the detainer to be removed from your prison file.

(a) Federal Speedy Trial Act

A good example of statutory implementation of the constitutional

---

[172]*See* 18 U.S.C. §3173; Fed. R. Crim. P. 48(b). *See, e.g.,* United States v. Peters, 587 F.2d 1267, 1270 n.6 (D.C. Cir. 1978).

[173]Your burden is heavy in this regard because such statutes evidence a legislative sanction of the permissible time limits for the disposition of criminal charges and some specific exclusions from those time limits. For an analysis of constitutional speedy trial considerations, consult the subsection on constitutional speedy trial rights, *supra.*

[174]Consult appropriate local court rules, including the rules of criminal procedure, for additional provisions.

[175]Frequently, however, there is not a mandatory dismissal of the charges. The court usually considers the circumstances of the case in reaching its decision. *See, e.g.,* 18 U.S.C. §3162. You should always ask for a dismissal with prejudice in your prayer for relief.

right to speedy trial is the federal Speedy Trial Act.[176] We will consider the provisions of the Act which specifically concern prisoners and detainers. A federal court will determine whether your statutory speedy trial right has been observed by determining whether the prosecution has complied with these provisions of the Act.

The provisions of the Act which specifically concern prisoners and detainers provide the following:

(j)(1) If the attorney for the government knows that a person charged with an offense is serving a term of imprisonment in any penal institution, he shall promptly—
  (A) undertake to obtain the presence of the prisoner for trial; or
  (B) cause a detainer to be filed with the person having custody of the prisoner and request him to so advise the prisoner and to advise the prisoner of his right to demand trial.
(2) If the person having custody of such prisoner receives a detainer, he shall promptly advise the prisoner of the charge and of the prisoner's right to demand trial. If at any time thereafter the prisoner informs the person having custody that *he does demand trial,* such person shall cause notice to that effect to be sent promptly to the attorney for the government who caused the detainer to be filed.
(3) Upon receipt of such notice, the attorney for the government shall *promptly* seek to obtain the presence of the prisoner for trial.
(4) When the person having custody of the prisoner receives from the attorney for the government a properly supported request for temporary custody of such prisoner for trial, the prisoner shall be made available to that attorney for the government (subject, in cases of interjurisdictional transfer, to any right of the prisoner to contest the legality of his delivery).[177]

If you are imprisoned and are charged with a federal offense, the prosecutor of the demanding federal district must either request your presence for trial[178] or file a detainer against you. When s/he files a detainer with your warden, your warden must advise you of the detainer and of your right to demand trial of the charges underlying it.[179]

If you demand trial, the prosecutor must *promptly* seek to obtain your presence or trial. Similarly, if the prosecutor does not file a detainer

---

[176]18 U.S.C. §§3161-74.

[177]18 U.S.C. §3161(j) (emphasis added). *See* United States v. Bryant, 612 F.2d 806 (4th Cir. 1979), *cert. denied,* 446 U.S. 920 (1980) (demand is prerequisite to speedy trial).

[178]This is usually accomplished by a writ ad prosequendum. *See supra,* notes 70-71.

[179]Note that when both the Speedy Trial Act and the IAD apply, the government should make every effort to comply with the provisions of both. United States v. Mauro, 436 U.S. 340, 356-57 n.24, 98 S.Ct. 1834 (1978).

against you and instead directly seeks your presence for trial, s/he must do so *promptly*. The standard for promptly obtaining your presence for trial is established by the Plans for Achieving Prompt Disposition of Criminal Cases adopted by individual federal district courts pursuant to the Speedy Trial Act.[180] To determine this standard, you should consult the local court rules of the federal district seeking your presence for trial.

Many states have similar provisions concerning prisoners and detainers. You should consult them to determine the time limits for trial and any exclusions that may apply to prisoners. You should also consult the court rules, including the rules of criminal procedure, of the demanding jurisdiction to determine other applicable rules and regulations. If there are no provisions specifically concerning prisoners, you should rely on the general speedy trial provisions of the demanding jurisdiction.

C. Parole/Probation Detainers

A prisoner who has in his/her file a detainer based on a parole/probation violation may encounter adverse consequences similar to those encountered by prisoners with other detainers in their files.[181] A prisoner in this situation should seek to have the parole/probation detainer resolved so that s/he can either have the detainer dismissed or be sentenced on the charged violation in time to serve his/her sentences concurrently.[182]

When you are first arrested, your parole/probation officer will usually lodge a parole/probation violator warrant against you. This does not revoke your parole/probation, but it does inform the people holding you that revocation of your parole/probation is being considered. If you have been convicted and sentenced on a new charge, the parole/probation authority instead of holding a revocation hearing immediately[183] may decide to file with prison officials a parole/probation warrant that will act as a detainer.[184] This detainer

---

[180]18 U.S.C. §3166. *See* United States v. Bryant, 612 F.2d 806, 811 (4th Cir. 1979). Note that a federal charge must be filed before the Federal Speedy Trial Act applies. United States v. Burkhalter, 583 F.2d 389 (8th Cir. 1978).

[181]See Sec. A1, *supra,* for a discussion of the adverse impact of a detainer.

[182]You do not have an automatic right to concurrent sentences. However, depending on your local statute, the parole/probation authority seeking revocation may have the power to grant retroactively the equivalent of concurrent sentences and to provide for unconditional or conditional release upon completion of the subsequent sentence. *See, e.g.,* 18 U.S.C. §§4211, 4214(d); 28 CFR §§2.21, 2.52(c)(2).

[183]See Ch. VIII, Sec. B, for a discussion of parole revocation.

[184]Moody v. Daggett, 429 U.S. 78, 87, 97 S.Ct. 274 (1976).

informs prison officials that prior to releasing you, the parole/probation authority should be contacted and given an opportunity to hold a revocation hearing.[185] The parole/probation authority is not required to wait until you have completed your present sentence to hold the revocation hearing; it may be held immediately after your conviction if that is the basis of the parole/probation violation warrant, or at some later date.[186]

After a detainer has been lodged against you, prison officials will usually inform you of its presence in your file. They will not take action to eliminate the warrant. Instead they will either wait until completion of your sentence and then notify the proper parole/probation authority or wait until that authority executes the parole/probation violator warrant.[187] If the parole/probation warrant has been lodged against you by another state or the federal government, you should check the statutes and case law where you are confined to determine if you are entitled to any procedural protections, such as a hearing, before being transferred to the demanding jurisdiction.

1. Strategies

There are at least three alternatives to pursue when trying to remove from your prison file a detainer based on a parole/probation violator warrant. First, you can seek to negotiate with the parole/probation authority. (See Sec. B2, *supra,* for a general discussion of negotiation.) It is unlikely that the authority will dismiss the parole/probation violator warrant, but you may convince them to hold the revocation hearing immediately and allow you to serve concurrently any violation sentence and your present sentence. Second, you can examine the procedures found in the parole/probation authority's statutes and regulations. These may provide a method to have either an immediate revocation hearing so you may serve concurrent sentences, or to have the detainer dismissed. Third, you may be able to obtain relief from the court if the parole/probation authority has violated its regulations or statutes.

---

[185]*Id.* at 82 n.2.

[186]*Id.* at 82-84 (after a parolee is convicted of a new offense, parole board has discretion to review parole immediately or to defer review until the intervening sentence has been served). *See* Carlton v. Keohane, 601 F.2d 992, 993 (11th Cir. 1982); Goodman v. Keohane, 663 F.2d 1044, 1046-47 (11th Cir. 1981). *See also* FRCrP, 32.1(a)(2) (probation revocation hearing, unless waived by probationer, shall be held within reasonable time); United States v. Blunt, 680 F.2d 1216 (8th Cir. 1982).

[187]Moody v. Daggett, *supra* note 184, at 87.

2. Federal Parolees' Strategies

If you are a federal parolee and are convicted and imprisoned on a state charge, the U.S. Parole Commission may lodge with state prison officials a detainer against you based on the state conviction. The U.S. Parole Commission must review the detainer within 180 days after it is lodged.[188] The Parole Commission must also give you prior notice of the review and appoint counsel, if you cannot afford it, to assist with preparation of your written response.[189] If the Parole Commission fails to provide a timely review of the detainer lodged against you, or violates some other procedure, you can file an action under 28 U.S.C. §1331 to compel them to comply with their rules. You can also file for a writ of habeas corpus seeking dismissal of the detainer and/or release from custody if you can show prejudice and are serving the sentence on the charge underlying the detainer when the court rules.[190] In either action, the court will generally provide the Parole Commission with an opportunity to hold a hearing in accordance with its rules before issuance of a writ of habeas corpus releasing you.[191] The court, in considering whether to issue the writ ordering dismissal of the detainer or your release from custody, will examine any delay to determine whether it was unreasonable and whether your interests were prejudiced.[192]

---

[188]18 U.S.C. §4214(b)(1); 28 CFR §§2.47(a), 2.47(a)(2). Abbreviated revocation proceedings are provided in cases in which the parolee has a new criminal conviction since the new criminal conviction satisfies the probable cause requirement in parole revocation. *See* United States v. Tucker, 524 F.2d 77 (5th Cir. 1975).

[189]18 U.S.C. §4214(a)(2)(B).

[190]Carlton v. Keohane, 691 F.2d 992, 993 (11th Cir. 1982); Lambert v. Warden, 591 F.2d 4, 7 (5th Cir. 1977). *See* Veneri v. Circuit Court of Gasconade County, 528 F. Supp. 496 (E.D. Mo. 1981). See Ch. VI, Sec. C1, for a discussion of bringing an action under 28 U.S.C. §1331; see also Ch. IX for a discussion of bringing a habeas corpus action.

[191]Carlton v. Keohane, *id.* at 993; Wright v. Young, 443 F. Supp. 617, 618-19 (D. Conn. 1977) (subsequent parole revocation hearing remedied any error in failure to provide an earlier dispositional hearing).

[192]Hooper v. U.S. Parole Commission, 702 F.2d 842, 847 (9th Cir. 1982); Goodman v. Keohane, *supra* note 186, at 1046; Maslauskas v. United States Board of Parole, 639 F.2d 935, 938 (3d Cir. 1980); Lambert v. Warden, *supra* note 190. *See* Smith v. United States, 577 F.2d 1025 (5th Cir. 1978); Bryant v. Grinner, 563 F.2d 871 (7th Cir. 1977); Reese v. United States Board of Parole, 530 F.2d 231, 235 (9th Cir. 1976), *cert. denied,* 429 U.S. 999 (1976); United States ex rel. Fitzpatrick v. U.S. Parole Commission, 444 F. Supp. 1302 (M.D. Pa. 1978).

D. Right to Appointed Counsel in Detainer Proceedings

The Sixth Amendment guarantees that "In all criminal prosecutions, the accused shall enjoy the right . . . to have the Assistance of Counsel for his defence."[193] This guarantee is meant to assure fairness in the adversary criminal process.[194] The right to counsel is primarily a trial right.[195] It attaches at any point in the prosecution of a criminal offense where an attorney is necessary to preserve the accused's right to a fair trial or to ensure that the accused will receive the effective assistance of counsel at the trial itself.[196]

The right to counsel is applicable to convicted prisoners being tried on additional charges.[197] Whether you have the right to appointed counsel in proceedings concerning a detainer will depend upon the nature of the detainer and the particular stage of the proceedings. It will also depend upon the statutes, regulations, court rules, and case law of the holding and demanding jurisdictions concerning prisoners, detainer proceedings, and criminal prosecutions. To determine when you have the right to appointed counsel, you should consult those sources.

Generally, you are not entitled to appointed counsel in the administrative proceedings concerning a detainer. For example, you will probably not be entitled to appointed counsel in the holding jurisdiction to assist you in making a request for final disposition of a detainer under IAD, Article III. Similarly, you will probably not be entitled to appointed counsel when you request the governor of the holding jurisdiction to deny the demanding jurisdiction's request for custody of you for trial under IAD, Article IV. You also will probably not be entitled to counsel in any proceedings before prison authorities of the holding jurisdiction in which you seek to review a detainer lodged against you.

You may be entitled to appointed counsel when the prosecutor of the demanding jurisdiction makes an IAD, Article IV, request for temporary custody of you for trial if the holding jurisdiction has adopted the

---

[193]U.S. Const., Amend. VI.

[194]United States v. Morrisson, 449 U.S. 361, 364, 101 S.Ct. 665, 667 (1981). *See* United States v. Gouveia, 704 F.2d 1116, 1119 (9th Cir. 1983).

[195]Brewer v. Williams, 430 U.S. 387, 97 S.Ct. 1232 (1977) (right to counsel at or after judicial proceedings initiated by formal charge, preliminary hearing, indictment, information, or arraignment).

[196]United States v. Morrisson, *supra* note 194, at 364; United States v. Wade, 388 U.S. 218, 225-27, 87 S.Ct. 1926, 1931-32 (1967).

[197]Taylor v. Sterrett, 532 F.2d 462, 472 (5th Cir. 1976); Lock v. Jenkins, 464 F. Supp. 541 (D. Ind. 1978).

Uniform Criminal Extradition Act (UCEA).[198] Under provisions of the UCEA, you have the right to counsel in the holding state.[199] The right to appointed counsel in the extradition proceedings may extend to proceedings concerning any habeas corpus review you pursue in the holding state.[200]

Federal prisoners have the right to appointed counsel to assist them when responding to a detainer lodged against them based on a parole or probation violation.[201] State prisoners do not have a federal constitutional right to appointed counsel to assist them when responding to a parole/probation detainer. But they may have a state law right and should check the state statutes and case law.

You definitely have a right to appointed counsel after your custody is first transferred to the demanding jurisdiction for trial on charges against you[202] or, in some cases, for a hearing on your alleged parole/probation violation.[203]

In most cases, the demanding jurisdiction will not appoint counsel for you until you actually arrive in that jurisdiction. If there is substantial delay between the filing of the detainer and your removal to the demanding jurisdiction, the absence of counsel during this period may be prejudicial to you because no one was responsible for helping you prepare a defense. In this situation, you may wish to argue that your Sixth Amendment right to counsel was violated because you were "accused" at the time the detainer was lodged.[204]

---

[198]See Appendix D, Sec. 8, for a copy of the Uniform Criminal Extradition Act (UCEA).

[199]UCEA, §§10, 25-A. Consult the extradition laws of the confining (holding) jurisdiction to determine whether you have the right to appointed counsel. See Appendix D, Sec. 9, for a list of the different state extradition statutes.

[200]Id.

[201]See 18 U.S.C. §4214(a)(2)(B) and 18 U.S.C. §3006A(a) concerning the right to appointed counsel in parole and probation revocation proceedings.

[202]United States v. Thompson, 562 F.2d 233, 234 (3d Cir. 1977).

[203]Gagnon v. Scarpelli, 411 U.S. 778, 93 S.Ct. 1756 (1973).

[204]This issue has not been explored by the courts. You will have to argue that in the special circumstances of an incarcerated person with a detainer, the period before you are brought to the demanding jurisdiction is part of the accusatory stage of the prosecution. The argument will be similar to that in United States v. Gouveia, 704 F.2d 1116 (9th Cir. 1983), where the court held that placement in administrative segregation triggered the right to counsel where the prisoner was later indicted and arraigned.

E. Extradition

Interstate extradition is a legal process by which the states or the federal government can obtain prisoners from other jurisdictions for trial on outstanding criminal charges.[205] It is derived from the Extradition Clause of the United States Constitution[206] and is intended to preclude any state from becoming "a sanctuary for fugitives from the justice of another state and thus 'balkanize' the administration of justice among the several states."[207]

The Extradition Clause sets forth in mandatory language the concepts of comity and full faith and credit between the states.[208] It creates a constitutional duty in the asylum state to deliver a fugitive to the demanding state. It is clear from the language of the Extradition Clause that "interstate extradition was intended to be a summary and mandatory executive proceeding."[209]

The provisions for extradition found in the Constitution have been codified by the federal government[210] and by the states.[211] Their re-

---

[205]United States v. Mauro, 436 U.S. 340, 98 S.Ct. 1834 (1978). An excellent review of extradition procedures is contained in Abramson, "Extradition in America: Of Uniform Acts and Governmental Discretion," 33 BAYLOR L. REV. 793 (1981).

[206]U.S. Const., Art. IV, sec. 2, cl. 2.

[207]Michigan v. Doran, 439 U.S. 282, 288, 99 S.Ct. 530 (1978). See Biddinger v. Commissioner of Police, 245 U.S. 138, 38 S.Ct. 41 (1917); Appleyard v. Massachusetts, 203 U.S. 22, 27 S.Ct. 122 (1906).

[208]Michigan v. Doran, id. at 288; Kentucky v. Dennison, 65 U.S. (24 How.) 66, 107 (1860) (no obligation of governor to deliver, only a moral duty).

[209]Pacileo v. Walker, 449 U.S. 86, 101 S. Ct. 308 (1980), quoting Michigan v. Doran, id. at 288.

[210]18 U.S.C. §3182 (1976). The original federal extradition act is found at Act of Feb. 12, 1793, ch. 7, 1 Stat. 302.

[211]Forty-eight states have adopted the Uniform Criminal Extradition Act ("UCEA"), 11 Uniform Laws Annotated 51 (1974). See Appendix D, Sec. 8, for a copy of the UCEA. See also Appendix D, Sec. 9, for a list of the states that have adopted the UCEA.
It is important for you to refer to the extradition statute of the jurisdiction in which you are imprisoned to determine your extradition rights since some states have modified the provisions of the UCEA.
Jurisdictions that have not adopted the UCEA and their respective extradition statutes are as follows:
D.C. Code Ann. §§23-401 to 411 (1983);
Miss. Code Ann. §§99-21-1 to 11 (1972);
S.C. Code §§17-9-10 to -70 (1976);
U.S. 18 U.S.C. §3182 (1976).

spective statutes provide detailed extradition procedures and time limits within which extradition should be accomplished.[212] You should consult the appropriate statutes and case law of the jurisdiction where you are confined to determine your extradition rights.

In general terms, the extradition process operates as follows. First, a written request seeking custody of you for trial in the demanding jurisdiction must be sent in proper form by the governor of the demanding (or receiving) jurisdiction to the governor of the asylum (or holding) jurisdiction.[213] Next, the govenor of the asylum jurisdiction, with the help of prosecuting authorities, may investigate the circumstances surrounding the request to determine whether you should be surrendered.[214] Thereafter, if the governor of the asylum jurisdiction agrees to the extradition request s/he must execute in proper form a fugitive warrant of arrest.[215] You are thereupon arrested on the fugitive warrant and have the right to a pre-transfer hearing before a state court magistrate who will advise you of your extradition rights.[216] At the hearing, the magistrate must advise you of the following: (1) a request for your extradition has been lodged by the demanding jurisdiction; (2) the request for extradition and accompanying arrest warrant are based on certain enumerated charges against you; (3) you have the right to counsel; (4) you have the right to have the governor of the demanding jurisdiction issue an extradition warrant; and (5) you have the right to habeas corpus review in the asylum state.[217] At that point, you have two options. You can waive extradition or test the legality of the fugitive warrant of arrest by petitioning the appropriate court of the asylum jurisdiction for a writ of habeas corpus. If you waive extradition, you must execute a written waiver in open court wherein you acknowledge that you have been informed of your extradition rights.[218] After the waiver of extradition, the demanding jurisdiction is notified and you will be transferred to the demanding jurisdiction when it requests custody

---

[212]UCEA §3. See note 53 and accompanying text, *supra,* for discussion of your rights when the UCEA and IAD are both involved in your transfer.

[213]UCEA §4.

[214]UCEA §7.

[215]UCEA §10. *See* UCEA §25-A and §23.

[216]UCEA §§8, 9, 10. *See* Cuyler v. Adams, 449 U.S. 433, 101 S.Ct. 703 (1981).

[217]UCEA §§10, 25-A. You have no right to challenge the facts surrounding the underlying crime or the lodging of the custody request. You are only permitted to question matters related directly to the extradition documents and your identification as the accused. Cuyler v. Adams, *id*. at 443 n.11.

[218]UCEA §25-A. The waiver must be a voluntary and intelligent waiver of rights as evidenced by the record of the waiver proceeding. Boykin v. Alabama, 395 U.S. 238, 89 S.Ct. 1709 (1969).

under an application for requisition.[219] If you decide to contest the legality of the arrest or the extradition process, you have the right, within a reasonable time, to petition the appropriate court of the asylum jurisdiction for a writ of habeas corpus.[220] The demanding jurisdiction will then be notified that you intend to contest the transfer.[221]

Prior to removal to the demanding jurisdiction, the only remedy available to you is habeas corpus.[222] Depending upon the jurisdiction in which you are imprisoned, the remedy will be either federal or state habeas corpus relief. If you are a state prisoner, you must exhaust your state remedies before seeking federal habeas corpus relief.[223] At the habeas corpus hearing, the court cannot inquire into your guilt or innocence of the charges upon which your extradition is sought, except so far as it may be involved in identifying you as the person charged with the crime.[224]

If you have been extradited, once you are returned to the asylum (or sending) jurisdiction, you cannot bring a habeas action to challenge your earlier transfer. You are limited to obtaining relief for violation of your rights under 42 U.S.C. §1983.[225] You would allege that your extradition was a violation of your rights protected by the Constitution and laws of

---

[219]UCEA §23.

[220]UCEA §10. *See* McBride v. Soos, 594 F.2d 610 (7th Cir. 1979), *on remand* 512 F. Supp. 1207 (N.D. Ind. 1981), *aff'd,* 679 F.2d 1223 (7th Cir. 1982).

[221]UCEA §10.

[222]Pacileo v. Walker, *supra* note 209; Michigan v. Doran, *supra* note 208.

[223]Preiser v. Rodriguez, 411 U.S. 475, 93 S.Ct. 1827 (1973); Peyton v. Rowe, 391 U.S. 54, 58, 88 S.Ct. 1549 (1968); Fay v. Noia, 372 U.S. 391, 83 S.Ct. 822 (1963). See note 82 and accompanying text, *supra.* See also Ch. IX, Sec. B2, for a discussion of exhausting state remedies.

[224]UCEA §20. The prisoner is permitted to question only "(a) whether the extradition documents on their face are in order; (b) whether [he] has been charged with a crime in the demanding state; (c) whether [he] is the person named in the request for extradition; and (d) whether [he] is a fugitive." Michigan v. Doran, *supra* note 207, at 289. *See* Cuyler v. Adams, *supra* note 216, at 443, where the Supreme Court indicated that a habeas corpus hearing may not be mandatory.

[225]Brown v. Nutsch, 619 F.2d 758 (8th Cir. 1980); Ricks v. Summers, 647 F.2d 76 (9th Cir. 1981) (prisoner may maintain damage action under §1983 based on denial of procedural safeguards of UCEA). *See* Cuyler v. Adams, *supra* note 216; Maine v. Thiboutot, 448 U.S. 1, 100 S.Ct. 2502 (1980). See also note 90, *supra,* and Ch. VI, Sec. B, for a discussion of §1983 action. *See generally* Manheimer, "Interstate Rendition Violations and Section 1983: Locating the Federal Rights of Fugitives," 50 FORDHAM L. REV. 1268 (1982).

the United States and that it was done under color of state law.[226] A federal court hearing a §1983 action cannot reverse your conviction regardless of any illegality or improprieties in the extradition process.[227] But you can receive damages for a violation of your extradition rights in certain cases.[228]

---

[226]See Ch. VI, Sec. B, for a discussion of actions under color of state law.

[227]Brown v. Nutsch, 619 F.2d 758 (8th Cir. 1980) (force, improprieties, or irregularities in the extradition process do not invalidate a subsequent conviction).

[228]See Ch. VI, Sec. F, for a discussion of damages.

XI
Prison Officials and You – Protecting Yourself

A. Know Your Rights

[E]very prisoner has a constitutional right of access to the courts to present any complaints he might have concerning his confinement. He cannot be disciplined in any manner for making a reasonable attempt to exercise that right. Access to the courts is a fundamental precept of our legal system of government. No citizen, regardless of his transgressions, is ever to be legally consigned to the total and unreviewed power of any branch of government. To make the system work, to maintain the proper checks and the proper balance, no person subject to the power of government can be denied communication with or access to each of the three spheres of governmental authority. This principle serves the highest interest of government as much as it serves the needs of the individual.[1]

Even though prisoners have a constitutional right to meaningful access to the courts[2] which prison officials may not abridge, impair, nor impermissibly burden its exercise,[3] this rule of law has frequently ·been ignored by prison officials.[4]

A right of access to the courts is based upon the First and Fourteenth Amendment rights to petition all branches of the government for redress

---

[1]Andrade v. Hauck, 452 F.2d 1071, 1072 (5th Cir. 1971). See Ch. V, *Overview of Prisoners' Rights,* for a more in-depth discussion of your procedural and substantive rights.

[2]See Ch. V, Sec. C4, "Access to the Courts."

[3]*See* Bounds v. Smith, 430 U.S. 817, 823-24, 97 S.Ct. 1491 (1977). *See also* Laaman v. Perrin, 435 F.2d 319, 326 (D.N.H. 1977).

[4]*See* Ruiz v. Estelle, 503 F. Supp. 1265, 1371-73 (S.D. Texas 1980) (court had issued five protective orders during pendency of case), *aff'd in pertinent part, rev'd on other grounds,* 679 F.2d 1115 (5th Cir. 1982); Vaughn v. Trotter, 516 F. Supp. 86 (M.D. Tenn. 1980) (jailhouse lawyer transferred because of his activities).

of grievances; the Fifth and Fourteenth Amendment guarantees of due process; and the Sixth and Fourteenth Amendment rights to counsel. The right of access to the courts includes the right to give as well as to receive legal assistance.[5] The right of mutual assistance is ultimately to protect and guarantee meaningful access to the courts for the blind, illiterate, mentally handicapped, or simply the legally unsophisticated. The district court, in *Nickl v. Schmidt*,[6] held that

> [I]t is clear that the right to receive legal aid would be empty if correctional authorities were free to punish its donation. Thus, in order to protect the right of the donee to legal help, the donor threatened with punishment for providing legal assistance must be permitted to assert the donee's right.[7]

Some of the other First Amendment rights you retain as a prisoner that prison officials may seek to curtail are: the right to receive political publications;[8] the right to engage in political writing;[9] the right to correspond with legitimate representatives of the press;[10] the right to correspond with attorneys and other officers of the court;[11] and the right to engage in political discussion with other prisoners.[12]

B. Organizing Together To Defend Your Rights

If your legal work consists only of challenges to criminal convictions, prison officials probably will not harass you since you are not bothering them. But, if your legal work consists also of challenging prison conditions and bringing damage claims against prison officials, you will be harassed. This harassment, or more commonly called retaliation, can come in many different forms. You may receive disciplinary actions one

---

[5]*See* Johnson v. Avery, 393 U.S. 483, 89 S.Ct. 747 (1969) (prisoner not only has a right to receive legal assistance, but s/he has a right to give legal assistance); Wolff v. McDonnell, 418 U.S. 539 94 S.Ct. 2963 (1974) (rule prohibiting prisoners giving assistance to or receiving assistance from other prisoners on civil matters unconstitutional unless provided with reasonable alternative).

[6]351 F. Supp. 385 (W.D. Wisc. 1972) (on the issue of standing).

[7]*Id.* at 389. *See also* Vaughn v. Trotter, 516 F. Supp. 886 (M.D. Tenn. 1980) ("To persecute the jailhouse lawyer ultimately threatens, both directly and indirectly, those for whom the rule of mutual assistance was primarily intended, *i.e.,* the blind, the illiterate, the mentally handicapped, etc.").

[8]Walker v. Blackwell, 411 F.2d 23 (5th Cir. 1969).

[9]Sostre v. McGinnis, 442 F.2d 178 (2d Cir. 1971).

[10]Guarjardo v. Estelle, 580 F.2d 748 (5th Cir. 1978).

[11]Taylor v. Sterrett, 532 F.2d 462 (5th Cir. 1976).

[12]Diamond v. Thompson, 364 F. Supp. 659 (M.D. Ala. 1973).

after another, each of which you are found guilty of and then the maximum punishment as to time in segregation and loss of good time imposed. Other types of retaliation are either being transferred far from family and friends[13] or denied a transfer to a lesser security level prison. Your furlough, work release, or parole may not be granted when you first become eligible. There are many more overt and covert methods prison officials use to get "even" with a prisoner for exercising his/her constitutional rights.

> Disciplining inmates for pursuing legal remedies to redress alleged abuses of their rights, either by direct deprivation of privileges or by denial of potentially available privileges, can similarly severely discourage them from effectively and appropriately utilizing the courts. . . . Classification decisions, be it for parole or for work release in correctional system, should not be affected by an individual's effort to petition the courts for a redress of grievances.[14]

If you are still serious about being a "jailhouse lawyer" and helping other prisoners with their legal problems, you must consider ways you can protect yourself from retaliation from prison officials. This protection does not guarantee prison officials will not take retaliatory actions against you. It, hopefully, provides a means for restricting the type and duration of any retaliation taken against you. Due to your confinement, and your being under the almost absolute control of prison officials, they can always place you in segregation or administrative detention without your having a chance to contact outside people. Often, it is only after the retaliatory action by prison officials that people can come to your aid. Most of the time, this aid will be in the form of letters and phone calls to the warden where you are incarcerated, the director of the Department of Corrections, legislators, and, hopefully, the press.

But, things do not have to be this way. Retaliation by officials is best handled by preventive organizing: if they realize you are strong and too well connected with the outside, they may decide it is a bad idea to harass you. Also, if you have established an organization which represents the prisoners at the institution, and if you have outside contacts, you will be able to respond faster to incidents of harassment.

The following are some suggestions of ways to protect yourself:

(1) a. You should organize with other prisoners into some type of club/organization, such as the Jaycees, Prisoners' Progress Association, The Committee To Safeguard Prisoners' Rights, the National Lawyers Guild, etc. You should seek help from outside organizations in establishing yourself, such as churches, colleges, law schools, political groups,

---

[13]*See* Vaughn v. Trotter, 516 F. Supp. 886, 899 (M.D. Tenn. 1980), for a listing of the punitive characteristics of a transfer.

[14]Moore v. Howard, 410 F. Supp. 1079, 1080 (E.D. Va. 1976).

etc. If necessary, affiliate with one of these outside organizations. This organization can assist you in getting recognized by prison officials. See the list of organizations, *infra,* Secs. C and D.

b. If there is no outside group nearby that you can affiliate with, the members of your group should organize your family and friends into an outside group. This outside group should become incorporated as a nonprofit corporation pursuant to the law of the state in which you are confined. They are then a legitimate organization in the eyes of the state. This may carry a little more weight in helping your inside group receive recognition.

c. Once you have established an outside group and have received recognition by prison officials, you can then consider expanding your group into other prisons. Most likely your communication with these other prison groups will need to be through your outside affiliate. The court, in *McKinney v. De Bord,*[15] found that "[t]here is no constitutional right for inmates at different institutions to correspond, whether on legal matters or otherwise."[16]

d. Keep all your organizational activities within the bounds of prison rules. Prison officials will be watching closely and will take advantage of any excuse to shut you down.

(2) Your organization should also communicate with legal and other organizations involved in the area of prison rights (*e.g.,* National Lawyers Guild). Keep these different organizations aware of what your members are doing. Prison administrators who know that you are in close contact with legal or national organizations are aware that placing your members in segregation or administrative detention may cause close scrutiny of their actions. These organizations may be able to provide legal advice or access to materials that you cannot readily obtain. Some outside organizations are happy to assist groups of prisoners who are actively helping themselves.

(3) You must learn to document all of your involvements with prison officials. Every time you correspond with them, you must keep a copy, and, if necessary, send a copy to your outside affiliate. If you have a meeting scheduled with a prison official, try not to meet alone. If you have just had a run-in with a prison guard and did not then receive a disciplinary ticket, prepare a memorandum as to the events and the conversation. Always make sure at least one copy of any of the above written records is sent to an outside person.

(4) If you can, keep in close contact with the news media. There is usually someone in every state who occasionally will write an article

---

[15]324 F. Supp. 928 (E.D. Cal. 1970), *aff'd in part, rev'd in part,* 507 F.2d 501 (9th Cir. 1974).

[16]*Id.* 324 F. Supp. at 932.

concerning the prison situation. Make contact with this person. Keep him/her informed about your organization and what you are doing.

(5) a. Members of Congress and your state legislature are also good people to write. They usually will not do more than write a letter to prison officials asking for a response concerning your complaint. But, even this level of scrutiny may help keep prison officials in line, and some legislators will take a more personal interest in prison matters. If you are allowed to have outside speakers attend your meetings, invite them.

b. Your organization should also request to be placed on the mailing list of certain congressional and state legislative committees. You can receive copies of all proposed laws being considered by that committee and prepare a response to any of these proposed bills. Even though you will not be there to testify in person (someone from your outside affiliate could testify for you), you could have an impact on the laws being passed by your state that will affect you. You may also be able to persuade outside organizations to take helpful positions.

(6) Once your organization is established solidly within your state, you can consider expanding to other states.

The following is a list of national and state organizations you should consider contacting. You should ask these organizations for referral to other groups you can contact. Every state also has many different educational institutions. Most of these educational institutions have psychology, sociology, criminal justice, political science, etc., departments which may have at least one faculty member who would be interested in communicating with your organization. Do not leave any stone unturned. Prisons will only change from the hell holes that they are when those that are incarcerated within the walls unite their political voices with their many friends on the outside.

I weep not that you are incarcerated and suffer such. I weep that you remain divided by petty jealousies. The future and the power to change the prison system lies in each of our hands. As Justice Rehnquist said when referring to those incarcerated, and I now say to you in your struggles for decency and humanity:[17] "[N]obody promised [us] a rose garden. . . ."[18]

C. National Organizations

Legal
Center for Constitutional Rights
853 Broadway
New York, NY 10003

NAACP Legal Defense and
Educational Fund, Inc.
10 Columbus Circle, Ste. 2030
New York, NY 10019

---

[17]Atiyeh v. Capps, 449 U.S. 1312, 101 S.Ct. 829 (1981).

[18]*Id.* at 831.

NAACP Prison Program
1790 Broadway
New York, NY 10019

National Gay Task Force
80 Fifth Ave., Ste. 1601
New York, NY 10011

National Lawyers Guild
853 Broadway
New York, NY 10003

National Legal Aid and
 Defender Association
1625 K St., NW, 8th Fl.
Washington, DC 20006

National Prison Project
 of the ACLU
1346 Conn. Ave., NW, Ste. 1031
Washington, DC 20036

Pretrial Services Resources Ctr.
918 F St., NW, Ste. 500
Washington, DC 20004

Prisoner Visitation and Support(PVS)
1501 Cherry St.
Philadelphia, PA 19102

U.S. Dept. of Justice,
 Civil Rights Division
Civil Rights Division
U.S. Dept. of Justice
Washington, DC 20530

Juveniles
National Ctr. for Youth Law
1663 Mission St., 5th Fl.
San Francisco, CA 94103

National Youth Work Alliance
1346 Conn. Ave., NW
Washington, DC 20036

Juvenile Rights Project
 of the ACLU
132 W. 43rd St.
New York, NY 10036

Medical
American Medical Association—Dept.
 of Correctional Activities
535 N. Dearborn
Chicago, IL 60657

American Public Health Assn.
1015 15th St., NW
Washington, DC 20005

Veterans
National Vets Law Center
4900 Mass. Ave., NW
Washington, DC 20016

Veterans Education Project
P.O. Box 42130
Washington, DC 20015

D.   State and Local Organizations

Alabama
Southern Poverty Law Ctr.
1001 S. Hull St.
Montgomery, AL 36104

Alaska
Alaska CLU
425 G St., #930
Anchorage, AK 99501

Arizona
American Civil Lib. Union
745 E. Fifth St.
Tucson, AZ 85719

Cummins and Texarkana Prison
 Projects
Waterman Hall, Rm. 102B
U. of Arkansas Sch. of Law
Fayetteville, AR 72701

California
ACLU of Northern California
814 Mission St.
San Francisco, CA 94103

ACLU Found. of Southern Calif.
633 S. Shatto Place
Los Angeles, CA 90005

Calif. Western Sch. of Law
350 Cedar St.
San Diego, CA 92101

Legal Serv. for Prisoners
 With Children
693 Mission St., 7th Fl.
San Francisco, CA 94105

Prisoners Union
1317 18th St.
San Francisco, CA 94107

Colorado
National Lawyers Guild
1760 Lafayette St.
Denver, CO 80218

Connecticut
J.N. Frank Leg. Serv. Organ.
Yale Law School
Box 401-A Yale Station
New Haven, CT 06520

Legal Assist. to Prisoners
340 Capitol Ave.
Hartford, CT 06106

Delaware
ACLU of Delaware
1707 Farmers Bank Bldg.
Wilmington, DE 19801

District of Columbia
Legal Assist. Branch, D.C.
 Superior Court
451 Indiana Ave, NW, #237
Washington, DC 20001

Florida
Fla. Clearinghouse on Crim. Just.
222 W. Pensacola St.
Tallahassee, FL 32301

Fla. Inst. Leg. Serv., Inc.
2614 S.W. 34th St.
Gainesville, FL 32608

Georgia
Clearinghouse on Georgia Prisons
 and Jails
88 Walton St.
Atlanta, GA 30303

E.O.A.—Disch. Upgrade Project
75 Marietta St., NW, #506
Atlanta, GA 30303

Prisoner Leg. Coun. Project
475 N. Lumpkin St.
Athens, GA 30601

Hawaii
American Civil Lib. of Hawaii
217 S. King, Ste. 307
Honolulu, HI 96813

Idaho
ACLU of Idaho—Boise Valley
 Chapter
P.O. Box 968
Boise, ID 83701

Illinois
Chicago Connections
P.O. Box 469
Chicago, IL 60690

John Howard Assoc.
67 E. Madison St., #1216
Chicago, IL 60603

People's Law Office
343 S. Deaborn, #1607
Chicago, IL 60604

Prisoner's Research Project
U. of Ill. College of Law
504 E. Pennsylvania
Champaign, IL 61820

Indiana
Notre Dame Leg. Aid and
 Defender Assn.—Post-Conviction
 Remedies Division
Notre Dame Law School
Notre Dame, IN 46556

Iowa
Prisoner Assist. Clinic
U. of Iowa Coll. of Law
Iowa City, IA 52242

Kansas
Leg. Serv. for Prisoners, Inc.
P.O. Box 829
5600 W. 6th
Topeka, KS 66601

Leg. Serv. for Prisoners, Inc.
Box 1568
Hutchinson, KS 67501

Leg. Serv. for Prisoners, Inc.
P.O. Box 2
Lansing, KS 66043

Kentucky
Female Offender Res. Ctr.
208 S. 5th St., #304
Lexington, KY 40202

Ky. Prisoners' Supp. Council
P.O. Box 3743
Louisville, KY 40201

Louisiana
ACLU of Louisiana
606 Common
New Orleans, LA 70130

La. Coal. on Jails and Prisons
2010 Magazine St.
New Orleans, LA 70130

So. Prisoners' Def. Comm., Inc.
344 Camp St., #708
New Orleans, LA 70130

Maine
Maine Civ. Lib. Union
97A Exchange St.
Portland, ME 04101

Maryland
Prisoners Aid Assn. of Md., Inc.
109 Old Town Bank Bldg.
Baltimore, MD 21202

Massachusetts
Mass. Corr. Leg. Serv., Inc.
294 Wash. St., #744
Boston, MA 02108

Michigan
Amer. Civ. Lib. Union of Mich.
1110 Woodward Tower
10 Witherell
Detroit, MI 48226

Center for Urban Law
3550 Cadillac Tower
Detroit, MI 48226

Minnesota
Leg. Assist. to Minn. Prisoners
95 Law Bldg.
Univ. of Minnesota
Minneapolis, MN 55455

Mississippi
Miss. Prisoners' Def. Comm.
210 S. Lamar St., #750
Jackson, MS 39201

N. Miss. Rural Leg. Serv.
P.O. Box 928
Oxford, MS 38655

Missouri
ACLU of Eastern Missouri
5756 W. Park Ave.
St. Louis, MO 63110

Toby Hollander
3109 S. Grand, #24
St. Louis, MO 63118

Montana
Missoula Women's Res. Ctr.
Univ. of Montana
Missoula, MT 59812

Nebraska
Neb. Civ. Lib. Union
P.O. Box 81455
Lincoln, NE 68501

Nevada
ACLU of Nevada
2105C Capurro Way
Sparks, NV 89431

Washoe Leg. Services
2105 Capurro Way, Ste. C
Sparks, NV 89431

New Hampshire
New Hamp. Civ. Lib. Union
11 S. Main St.
Concord, NH 03301

New Jersey
Amer. Civ. Lib. Union of NJ
38 Walnut St.
Newark, NJ 07102

Inmate Leg. Assn.
3rd & Federal Sts.
Trenton, NJ 08625

New Mexico
ACLU of New Mexico
1330 San Pedro, NE, #110
Albuquerque, NM 87110

Concerned Citizens for Comm.
  and Prison Reform (CCCPR)
P.O. Box 25951
Albuquerque, NM 87101

New York
Prisoners' Rights Proj. of
  the Legal Aid Society
15 Park Row, 19th Fl.
New York, NY 10038

Prisoners' Leg. Serv. of N.Y.
Offices:
20 Vesey St.
New York, NY 10007

84 Holland Ave.
Albany, NY 12208

55-59 Clinton St.
Plattsburgh, NY 12901

2 Catharine St.
Poughkeepsie, NY 12601

111 S. Cayuga St.
Ithaca, NY 14850

487 Niagara St.
Buffalo, NY 14201

Women Free Women in Prison
P.O. Box 90
Brooklyn, NY 11215

North Carolina
N.C. CLU—ACLU Prisoners' Rts.
P.O. Box 3094
Greensboro, NC 27402

Prisoners' Rights Project
UNC, School of Law
Durham, NC 27701

Ohio
ACLU of Ohio Found.
360 S. 3rd St., #150
Columbus, OH 43215

Cleve.-Marshall Leg. Clinic
Cleve.-Marshall Coll. of Law
Cleve. State Univ.
Cleveland, OH 44115

Oklahoma
Leg. Aid of West. Okla., Inc.
980 Court Plaza
228 R.S. Kerr Ave.
Oklahoma City, OK 73102

Women Offenders' Res. Ctr.
1808 N.W. 23rd
Oklahoma City, OK 73106

Oregon
ACLU of Oregon
601 Willamette Bldg.
534 SW 3rd Ave.
Portland, OR 97204

Prisoners' Leg. Serv. of Ore.
875 Idylwood Dr., SE
Salem, OR 97302

Pennsylvania
Legal Services, Inc.
7 N. Harbour St.
Carlisle, PA 17013

Penn. Prison Society
311 S. Juniper St.
Philadelphia, PA 19107

Susquehanna Leg. Serv.
416 Pine St.
Williamsport, PA 17701

Rhode Island
ACLU of R.I.
235 Promenade St., #203
Providence, RI 02908

South Carolina
ACLU of South Carolina
533-B Harden St.
Columbia, SC 29205

S.C. Crim. Just. Project
2112 Hampton St.
Columbia, SC 29204

South Dakota
South Dakota ACLU
USD, School of Law
Vermillion, SD 57069

Tennessee
The Lifer's Club of Davidson
 Co. Tenn., Inc.
c/o Exec. Sec.
3865 Georgia Ct.
Nashville, TN 37209

So. Prisoners' Def. Comm., Inc.
P.O. Box 120636
Acklen Station
Nashville, TN 37212

Texas
Tex. Civ. Lib. Union
600 W. 7th St.
Austin, TX 78701

Tex. Ctr. for Corr. Serv.
P.O. Box 12487
Austin, TX 78711

Utah
ACLU of Utah
632 Judge Bldg.
#8 East Broadway
Salt Lake City, UT 84111

Vermont
Amer. Civ. Lib. Union of Vt.
43 State St.
Montpelier, VT 05602

Corr. Fac. Defender
State Office Bldg.
Montpelier, VT 05602

Virginia
ACLU of Virginia
112A N. 7th St.
Richmond, VA 23219

Post-Conviction Assist. Proj.
U. of Va. Law School
Charlottesville, VA 22903

Washington
ACLU of Washington
2101 Smith Tower
506 2nd Ave.
Seattle, WA 98104

Inst. Legal Services
1702 Smith Tower
506 2nd Ave.
Seattle, WA 98104

West Virginia
West Va. CLU
800 Monongahela Bldg.
235 High St.
Morgantown, WV 26505

Wisconsin
Leg. Assist. to Inst.
 Persons Program
U. of Wisc.—Extension
913 Univ. Ave.
Madison, WI 53706

Wyoming
ACLU of Laramie Cty.
418 S. 12th St.
Laramie, WY 82070

Appendices

Appendix A
United States Federal Courts Directory

District Courts

Alabama
Northern Alabama
104 Fed. Courthouse
Birmingham, AL 35104

Middle Alabama
P.O. Box 711
Montgomery, AL 36101

Southern Alabama
P.O. Box 2625
Mobile, AL 36601

Alaska
Alaska
701 C St., Box 4
Anchorage, AK 99513

Arizona
A
Rm. 6218, Fed. Bldg.
Phoenix, AZ 85025

Arkansas
Eastern Arkansas
P.O. Box 869
Little Rock, AR 72203

Western Arkansas
P.O. Box 1523
Ft. Smith, AR 72902

California
Northern California
P.O. Box 36060
San Francisco, CA 94102

Central California
U.S. Courthouse
312 N. Spring St.
Los Angeles, CA 90012

Southern California
U.S. Courthouse
940 Front St.
San Diego, CA 92189

Eastern California
2546 U.S. Courthouse
650 Capitol Mall
Sacramento, CA 95814

Colorado
Colorado
C-145, U.S. Cthse.
1929 Stout St.
Denver, CO 80294

Connecticut
Connecticut
Federal Bldg.
141 Church St.
New Haven, CT 06505

Delaware
Lockbox 18, Fed. Bldg.
844 King St.
Wilmington, DE 19801

District of Columbia
District of Columbia
U.S. Courthouse
3rd & Constitution, NW
Washington, DC 20001

Florida
Northern Florida
P.O. Box 958
Tallahassee, FL 32302

Middle Florida
P.O. Box 53558
Jacksonville, FL 32201

Southern Florida
P.O. Box 010669
Flagler Station
Miami, FL 33101

Georgia
Northern Georgia
100 U.S. Cthse.
56 Forsyth St., NW
Atlanta, GA 30303

Middle Georgia
P.O. Box 128
Macon, GA 31202

Southern Georgia
P.O. Box 8286
Savannah, GA 31402

Guam
Guam
P.O. Box DC
Agana, Guam 96910

Hawaii
P.O. Box 50129
Honolulu, HI 96850

Idaho
Idaho
U.S. Cthse., Box 039
550 W. Fort St.
Boise, ID 83724

Illinois
Northern Illinois
U.S. Courthouse
219 S. Dearborn St.
Chicago, IL 60604

Central Illinois
P.O. Box 238
Peoria, IL 61601

Southern Illinois
P.O. Box 249
East St. Louis, IL 62202

Indiana
Northern Indiana
305 Fed. Bldg.
204 S. Main St.
South Bend, IN 46601

Southern Indiana
105 U.S. Cthse.
46 E. Ohio St.
Indianapolis, IN 46204

Iowa
Northern Iowa
Fed. Bldg.
P.O. Box 4411
Cedar Rapids, IA 52407

Southern Iowa
200 U.S. Cthse.
E. 1st & Walnut Sts.
Des Moines, IA 50309

Kansas
Kansas
P.O. Box 2201
Witchita, KS 67201

Kentucky
Eastern Kentucky
P.O. Box 741
Lexington, KY 40586

Western Kentucky
230 U.S. Cthse. Bldg.
Louisville, KY 40202

Louisiana
Eastern Louisiana
C-151 U.S. Cthse.
500 Camp St.
New Orleans, LA 70130

Middle Louisiana
139 Fed. Bldg.
707 Florida St.
Baton Rouge, LA 70801

Western Louisiana
P.O. Box 106
Shreveport, LA 71161

Maine
Maine
156 Federal St.
Portland, ME 04101

Maryland
Maryland
U.S. Courthouse
101 W. Lombard St.
Baltimore, MD 21201

Massachusetts
Massachusetts
McCormack PO&CH
Boston, MA 02109

Michigan
Eastern Michagan
133 Fed. Bldg.
Detroit, MI 48226

Western Michigan
458 Fed. Bldg.
110 Michigan St., NW
Grand Rapids, MI 49503

Minnesota
Minnesota
708 Fed. Bldg.
316 N. Robert St.
St. Paul, MN 55101

Mississippi
Northern Mississippi
P.O. Box 727
Oxford, MS 38655

Southern Mississippi
P.O. Box 769
Jackson, MS 39205

Missouri
Eastern Missouri
U.S. Ct. and Custom House
1114 Market St.
St. Louis, MO 63101

Western Missouri
201 U.S. Cthse.
811 Grand Ave.
Kansas City, MO 64106

Montana
Montana
5405 Fed. Bldg.
316 N. 26th St.
Billings, MT 59101

Nebraska
Nebraska
9000 U.S. Cthse.
Box 129, Downtown Sta.
Omaha, NE 68101

Nevada
Nevada
300 Las Vegas Blvd., #3-632
Las Vegas, NV 89101

New Hampshire
New Hampshire
P.O. Box 1498
Concord, NH 03301

New Jersey
New Jersey
U.S. Courthouse
Trenton, NJ 08605

New Mexico
New Mexico
P.O. Box 689
Albuquerque, NM 87103

New York
Northern New York
Box 950, Cthse. Bldg.
Albany, NY 12201

Southern New York
U.S. Cthse., Foley Sq.
New York, NY 10007

Eastern New York
U.S. Courthouse
225 Cadman Plaza East
Brooklyn, NY 11201

Western New York
604 U.S. Cthse.
Buffalo, NY 14202

North Carolina
Eastern North Carolina
P.O. Box 25670
Raleigh, NC 27611

Middle North Carolina
P.O. Box V-1
Greensboro, NC 27402

Western North Carolina
P.O. Box 92
Asheville, NC 28802

North Dakota
North Dakota
P.O. Box 1193
Bismarck, ND 58501

Ohio
Northern Ohio
328 U.S. Cthse.
Cleveland, OH 44114

Southern Ohio
328 U.S. Cthse.
85 Marconi Blvd.
Columbus, OH 43215

Oklahoma
Northern Oklahoma
411 U.S. Cthse.
Tulsa, OK 74103

Eastern Oklahoma
Box 607, U.S. Cthse.
Muskogee, OK 74401

Western Oklahoma
3210 U.S. Cthse.
Oklahoma City, OK 73102

Oregon
Oregon
P.O. Box 1150
Portland, OR 97207

Pennsylvania
Eastern Pennsylvania
2609 U.S. Cthse.
Independence Mall West
601 Market St.
Philadelphia, PA 19106

Middle Pennsylvania
P.O. Box 1148
Scranton, PA 18501

Western Pennsylvania
P.O. Box 1805
Pittsburgh, PA 15219

Puerto Rico
Puerto Rico
P.O. Box 3671
San Juan, PR 00904

Rhode Island
Rhode Island
Providence, RI 02903

South Carolina
South Carolina
P.O. Box 867
Columbia, SC 29202

South Dakota
South Dakota
207 U.S. Cthse.
400 S. Phillips Ave.
Sioux Falls, SD 57102

Tennessee
Eastern Tennessee
P.O. Box 2348
Knoxville, TN 37901

Middle Tennessee
800 U.S. Cthse.
Nashville, TN 37203

Western Tennessee
950 Fed. Bldg.
167 N. Main St.
Memphis, TN 38103

Texas
Northern Texas
15C22 U.S. Cthse.
1100 Commerce St.
Dallas, TX 75242

Southern Texas
P.O. Box 61010
Houston, TX 77208

Eastern Texas
P.O. Box 231
Beaumont, TX 77704

Western Texas
Hemisfair Plaza
655 E. Durango Blvd.
San Antonio, TX 78206

Utah
Utah
U.S. Courthouse
Salt Lake City, UT 84101

Vermont
Vermont
Box 945, Fed. Bldg.
Burlington, VT 05402

Virgin Islands
Virgin Islands
P.O. Box 720
Charlotte Amalie,
St. Thomas 00801

Virginia
Eastern Virginia
P.O. Box 1318
Norfolk, VA 23501

Western Virginia
P.O. Box 1234
Roanoke, VA 24006

Washington
Eastern Washington
P.O. Box 1493
Spokane, WA 99210

Western Washington
308 U.S. Cthse.
Seattle, WA 98104

West Virginia
Northern West Virginia
P.O. Box 1518
Elkins, WV 26241

Southern West Virginia
P.O. Box 2546
Charleston, WV 25329

Wisconsin
Eastern Wisconsin
362 U.S. Cthse.
517 E. Wisconsin Ave.
Milwaukee, WI 53202

Western Wisconsin
P.O. Box 432
Madison, WI 53701

Wyoming
Wyoming
P.O. Box 727
Cheyenne, WY 82001

United States Courts of Appeals

District of Columbia Circuit
Washington, DC 20001

First Circuit
1634 McCormack PO&CH
Boston, MA 02109

Second Circuit
New York, NY 10007

Third Circuit
21400 U.S. Cthse.
Indpendence Mall West
601 Market St.
Philadelphia, PA 19106

Fourth Circuit
10th & Main Sts.
Richmond, VA 23219

Fifth Circuit
600 Camp St., #102
New Orleans, LA 70130

Sixth Circuit
502 U.S. PO&CH
Cincinnati, OH 45202

Seventh Circuit
502 U.S. Cthse.
Chicago, IL 60604

Eighth Circuit
  1114 Market St., #542
  St. Louis, MO 63101

Ninth Circuit
  P.O. Box 547
  San Francisco, CA 94101

Tenth Circuit
  C404 U.S. Cthse.
  Denver, CO 80294

Eleventh Circuit
  56 Forsyth St., NW
  Atlanta, GA 30303

United States Supreme Court

United States Supreme Court
  U.S. Supreme Ct. Bldg.
  Washington, DC 20005

Appendix B
Civil Rights Forms

The forms in this appendix will be useful when you are bringing an action in federal court seeking damages, injunctive relief, or a declaratory judgment. The facts contained in the complaint (Form 1a) are the basis for the other pleadings you will use when litigating in the trial court.

All papers you file in court should be headed by a caption which consists of the name of the court where you filed the case and the names of the plaintiff(s) and defendant(s). (The caption on the enclosed forms is only placed on Form 1a and 1b.) Once you have filed your complaint, you will receive a case or docket number that must be placed on all your future papers filed with the court. Any time you write the court concerning your case, you will want to list the case or docket number.

These sample pleadings are single spaced. The legal pleadings you filed with the federal courts should be on 8½ by 11 inch paper and double spaced.

Note of Motion Practice

The form of motion papers is not uniform in all federal courts. For example, in Michigan, for most motions, a litigant will file a document called a "Motion," stating what the motion is for and what the factual basis of the motion is; along with this, the litigant will file a brief. An affidavit is only required in connection with certain motions, such as motions for summary judgment and for a default judgment. In New York, on the other hand, there is no document called "Motion"; instead, a litigant files a "Notice of Motion" with a return date, an affidavit or declaration stating any facts relevant to the motion, and a brief (or "memorandum of law"). There may be other local variations in the form of papers in the federal jurisdiction where you are incarcerated.

The forms in this Appendix mostly conform to the Michigan style. We have included a "Notice of Motion" form (see Form 1f). In most cases, if an affidavit or declaration is required, the "Motion" form we present can be easily converted. If there are other variations in local practice in your jurisdiction, you should follow the local style. The forms in this Appendix will still be useful as a general guide to writing legal documents.

1. Complaint

The forms in this Appendix are based on a § 1983 action filed by a state prisoner against state prison officials. These forms also can be used by federal prisoners and the different requirements for the filing of a federal question action are contained in the footnotes.

1a. Complaint

IN THE UNITED STATES DISTRICT COURT[1]
FOR THE EASTERN DISTRICT OF MICHIGAN

DANIEL E. MANVILLE,
    Plaintiff,

-v-   C.A. No.

BARRY POGATS, Warden, State
Prison of Southern Michigan;
DON SMITH, Lieutenant at the
State Prison of Southern Mich-
igan; AND JOHN DOE, Correctional
Officer at the State Prison of
Southern Michigan, in their indi-
vidual and official capacities,

    Defendants.[2] _____/

CIVIL RIGHTS COMPLAINT
WITH A JURY DEMAND

This is a § 1983 action filed by Daniel E. Manville, a state prisoner,[3] alleging violation of his constitutional rights[4] and seeking money damages, declaratory judgment, and injunctive relief.[5] The plantiff requests a trial by jury.[6]

Jurisdiction

1. This is a civil rights action under 42 U.S.C. § 1983.[7] This Court has jurisdiction under 28 U.S.C. § 1343.[8] Plaintiff also invokes the pendent jurisdiction of this Court.[9]

Parties

2. Plaintiff Daniel E. Manville is presently incarcerated at the State Prison of Southern Michigan, Jackson (SPSM).

3. Defendant Barry Pogats is the Warden of the State Prison of Southern Michigan, Jackson (SPSM), and is responsible for the operation and management of SPSM. See M.S.A. §§ 28.1431-.1443; Policy Directive 28.02. He is ultimately responsible for the training and supervision

---

[1] You will need to change "Eastern" and "Michigan" to reflect the federal district and state where you are filing your lawsuit.

[2] If you are suing more than one defendant, once you have filed your complaint you need only list on future legal papers the name of the first defendant and place "et al." after his/her name (e.g., "Barry Pogats, et al."). See Form 1b, vor an example.

[3] A non-state prisoner (e.g., federal prisoner or pretrial detainee) would list his/her status.

[4] For a discussion of your constitutional rights, see Ch. V.

[5] For a discussion of damages, injunctive relief, and declaratory judgment, see Ch. VI, Secs. F, G, and H, respectively.

[6] For a discussion of the right to a jury trial, see Rule 38, FRCP.

[7] For a discussion of 42 U.S.C. §1983, See Ch. VI, Sec. B. Federal prisoners would bring a "federal question action under the U.S. Constitution." See Ch. VI, Sec. C.

[8] For a discussion of jurisdiction over civil rights action, see Ch. VI, Sec. Bla. Federal prisoners would invoke jurisdiction uder 28 U.S.C. § 1331(a). For a discussion of federal question jurisdiction, see Ch. VI, Sec. Cla.

[9] For a discussion of pendent claims, see Ch. VI, Sec. B3. Federal prisoners would not bring a pendent claim.

of the correctional personnel employed at SPSM. See Policy Directive 28.146. He is sued in his individual and official capacities.

   4. Defendant Don Smith, an agent of defendant Pogats, is a Lieutenant at SPSM and is the officer-in-charge of the 8am to 4pm shift of correctional personnel. He is sued in his individual and official capacities.

   5. Defendant John Doe, an agent of defendant Pogats, is a correctional officer at SPSM, whose name is presently unknown to plaintiff.

   6. All defendants have acted under "color of state law" during all times relevant to this complaint.

Facts

   7. At approximately 11:30 am on February 19, 1983, defendants Smith and John Doe approached plaintiff's cell located at 32-B-2.

   8. Defendant Smith ordered plaintiff to place his hands between one set of bars so that he could be handcuffed and his cell searched.

   9. Plaintiff asked defendant Smith why his cell was to be searched.

   10. Defendant Smith ordered defendant John Doe to mace plaintiff if he did not immediately place his hands between a set of bars.

   11. Once the handcuffs were placed on plaintiff, defendant Smith ordered defendant John Doe to give plaintiff a short burst of mace to teach him a lesson.

   12. Defendant John Doe sprayed mace into plaintiff's face while he was locked in his cell handcuffed.

   13. Approximately five minutes later plaintiff's cell was searched by defendant John Doe.

   14. Defendant John Doe took from plaintiff's cell and gave to defendant Smith the legal pleadings concerning plaintiff's pro se challenge to his criminal conviction and a criminal appeal law book.

   15. These legal pleadings and law book have not been returned to the plaintiff.

   16. Defendant Smith told plaintiff he was being taken to the "hole," formally known as administrative segregation.

   17. As plaintiff was being escorted to the "hole" in handcuffs by defendants Smith and John Doe, he was repeatedly struck with ax handles about the head and shoulders by these defendants.

   18. During the events described in paragraphs 7 through 17, supra, plaintiff did not resist defendants Smith and John Doe or disobey their orders in anyway.

   19. Previously the plaintiff and other prisoners had filed grievances, or otherwise provided notification, to defendant Pogats concerning defendant Smith's use of mace against handcuffed prisoners and the use of ax handles to beat prisoners.[10]

   20. Defendant Pogats failed to take corrective actions concerning the allegations contained in paragraph 19.

Claims

First Cause of Action

   21. The actions of the defendants stated in paragraphs 7 through 20 denied plaintiff due process of law in violation of the Fourteenth Amendment.[11]

   22. Plaintiff's Fourteenth Amendment right to be free of unjustified and excessive use of force was violated when
        a) he was sprayed with mace and
        b) he was beaten with ax handles.[12]

Second Cause of Action

   23. The actions of the defendants stated in paragraphs 7 through 20 denied plaintiff his First and Fourteenth Amendment rights.

   24. Plaintiff's First and Fourteenth Amendment right of access to the courts was violated when his legal pleadings concerning his pro se criminal appeal and his law book were taken and not returned.[13]

Third Cause of Action

   25. The actions of the defendants stated in paragraphs 7 through 20 violated state law.

---

[10]For a discussion of establishing personal involvement of prison officials not directly involved with your injuries, see Ch. VI, Sec. E2a.

[11]Federal prisoners should allege a violation of the Fifth Amendment due process clause.

[12]For a discussion of use of force and mace by prison officials, see Ch. V, Sec. C2b.

[13]For a discussion of your right of access to the courts, See Ch. V, Sec. C4.

26. Plaintiff alleges that defendants violated state law of assault and battery and the regulations of Michigan Department of Corrections with respect to the lawful use of force when
>   a) he was sprayed with mace while confined handcuffed in his cell, and
>   b) he was beaten with ax handles while handcuffed.

Fourth Cause of Action

27. The actions of the defendants stated in paragraphs 7 through 20 violated state law.

28. Plaintiff alleges that defendants Smith and John Doe violated the state law of conversion and the regulations of Michigan Department of Corrections with respect to the handling of prisoners' property and prisoners' right to possession of legal materials when his legal pleadings concerning his pro se criminal appeal and his law book were taken and not returned.[14]

Relief

WHEREFORE, plaintiff requests this Honorable Court grant the following relief:

A. Issue a declaratory judgment that defendants violated the United States Constitution and state law when they:
>   1) used mace on the plaintiff without justification;
>   2) struck plaintiff with ax handles without justification;
>   3) confiscated plaintiff's personal legal pleadings and law book.

B. Issue an injunction ordering that defendants or their agents
>   1) refrain from using mace against plaintiff, except when immediately necessary to prevent injury, death, or the destrution of valuable property;
>   2) refrain from using ax handles to strike plaintiff, except when immediately necessary to prevent injury, death, or the destruction of valuable property;
>   3) refrain from using other physical force against plaintiff except when necessary to maintain order or immediately necessary to prevent injury, death, or the destruction of valuable property; and
>   4) refrain from confiscating the personal legal pleadings or law books of the plaintiff.

C. Grant compensatory damages in the following amount:
>   1) $5,000 against defendant Pogats;
>   2) $10,000 against defendant Smith; and
>   3) $10,000 against defendant John Doe.

D. Grant punitive damages of $10,000 against each of the defendants.

E. Grant such other relief as it may appear plaintiff is entitled.

> Respectfully submitted,
>
> Name
> Address

---

[14] For a discussion of pendent claims, see Ch. VI, Sec. B3.

1b. Amended Complaint

For a discussion of amending a complaint, see Ch. VII, Sec. C and Rule 15(a), FRCP. If you are going to file an amended complaint, you should completely retype your original complaint and place in CAPITAL LETTERS you changed protions. Below we will show only the paragraphs of the original complaint that are being amended.

Assume you have served your interrogatories upon the named defendants and in their reply you have obtained the name of the John Doe defendant. You now want to amend your complaint to show his name.

1b1. Motion for Leave to File an Amended Complaint

IN THE UNITED STATES DISTRICT COURT

FOR THE EASTERN DISTRICT OF MICHIGAN

DANIEL E. MANVILLE,

    Plaintiff,

-v-   Case No. 83-0001-B

BARRY POGATS, et al.,   [16]

    Defendants.

_____/

MOTION FOR LEAVE TO FILE AN AMENDED COMPLAINT[17]

    Plaintiff Daniel E. Manville, pursuant to Rules 15(a) and 19(a), Fed. R. Civ. Proc., requests leave to file an amended complaint adding a party.

    1. Plaintiff in his original complaint named a John Doe defendant.

    2. Since the filing of the complaint the plaintiff has determined the name of the John Doe defendant.

    3. This Court should grant leave freely to amend a complaint. See Foman v. Davis, 371 U.S. 178, 83 S.Ct. 227 (1962); Martens v. Hunnell, 587 F.2d 962 (7th Cir. 1978)(trial court may not deny leave to amend without any justifying reason).

                       Respectfully submitted,

                       Daniel E. Manville
                       P.O. Box E - 135706
                       Jackson, MI   49204

Dated: _____.

_____

[16] See supra note 2.

[17] If the court has dismissed your first complaint and has given you a specific time period in which to file an amended complaint, you will not need to file this motion.

1b2. Amended Complaint

[CAPTION][18]

AMENDED COMPLAINT

   * * *

    6. Defendant DAN JONES, an agent of Defendant Pogats, is a correctional officer at SPSM.

    7. At approximately 11:30 am on February 19, 1983, defendants Smith and JONES approached plaintiff's cell located at 32-B-2.

   * * *

    10. Defendant Smith ordered defendant JONES to mace plaintiff if he did not immediately place his hands between a set of bars.

    11. Once the handcuffs were placed on plaintiff, defendant Smith ordered defendant JONES to give plaintiff a short burst of mace to teach him a lesson.

_____

[18] This caption would be identical to the one on your 'Motion for Leave to File an Amended Complaint."

12. Defendant JONES sprayed mace into plaintiff's face while he was locked in his cell handcuffed.

13. Approximately five minutes later plaintiff's cell was searched by defendant JONES.

14. Defendant JONES took from plaintiff's cell and gave to defendant Smith the legal pleadings concerning plaintiff's pro se challenge to his criminal conviction and a criminal appeal law book.

  * * *

16. As plaintiff was being escorted to the hole by defendants, he was repeatedly struck with ax handles about the head and shoulders by these defendants Smith and JONES.

  * * *

       Relief

  * * *

C. * * *

  * * *

3) $10,000 against defendant JONES.

  * * *

       Name
       Address

1c. Supplemental Complaint

For a discussion of what is a supplemental complaint, see Ch. VII, Sec. C and Rule 15(d), FRCP. A motion must be filed with the supplemental complaint requesting the court's permission to file it. If permission is granted you will need to serve the supplemental complaint on the defendants and the court may order them to file an answer within a reasonable time. If the court denys your motion but you still want to pursue the claims raised in your supplemental complaint, you can retype the first page of the supplemental complaint eliminating "Supplemental" and file it as a new lawsuit.

1c1. Motion for Leave to File a Supplemental Complaint

[CAPTION]

MOTION FOR LEAVE TO FILE
SUPPLEMENTAL COMPLAINT

Plaintiff Daniel E. Manville, pursuant to Rule 15(d), Fed. R. Civ. Proc., requests leave to file a supplemental complaint.

1. Events have occurred since plaintiff filed his complaint which are similar in nature to the violations alleged in the complaint filed on ___(date filed)___.

2. Defendants will not be prejudiced by the filing of this supplemental complaint.

3. The interests of justice will be served by this Court hearing at one trial all the allegations contained in the complaint and supplemental complaint.

       Respectfully submitted,

       Name
       Address

Dated: _____.

1c2. Supplemental Complaint

The supplemental complaint is exactly like a regular complaint, See Form 1a. You would place the case No. of the original complaint on the supplemental complaint. A copy of the motion and supplemental complaint must be sent to defendants' counsel.

1d. Order Granting the Above Motions

Most judges will write on the "Motion for Leave to File an Amended Complaint" or the "Motion for Leave to File a Supplemental Complaint" whether it has been granted or denied. If you wish to submit your own order, the following is an example:

[CAPTION]

This matter having been considered by the Court on the motion of the plaintiff for leave to file an amended [supplemental] complaint and it appearing to the Court that plaintiff is entitled to the relief he seeks by his motion, it is hereby

ORDERED that plaintiff's motion to amend [supplement] the complaint is granted.

_____
Judge

Dated: _____ .

1e. Standardized §1983 Forms for Use in Federal District Court[19]
1e1. – Complaint

Instructions for Filing a Complaint by a Prisoner
Under the Civil Rights Act, 42 U.S.C. §1983

This packet includes four copies of a complaint form and two copies of a forma pauperis petition. To start an action you must file an original and one copy of your complaint for each defendant you name and one copy for the court. For example, if you name two defendants you must file the original and three copies of the complaint. You should also keep an additional copy of the complaint for your own records. All copies of the complaint must be identical to the original.

The clerk will not file your complaint unless it conforms to these instructions and to these forms.

Your complaint must be legibly handwritten or typewritten. You, the plaintiff, must sign and declare under penalty of perjury that the facts are correct. If you need additional space to answer a question, you may use the reverse side of the form or an additional blank page.

Your complaint can be brought in this court only if one or more of the named defendants is located within this district. Further, you must file a separate complaint for each claim that you have unless they are all related to the same incident or issue.

You are required to furnish, so that the United States marshal can complete service, the correct name and address of each person you have named as defendant. A PLAINTIFF IS REQUIRED TO GIVE INFORMATION TO THE UNITED STATES MARSHAL TO ENABLE THE MARSHAL TO COMPLETE SERVICE OF THE COMPLAINT UPON ALL PERSONS NAMED AS DEFENDANTS.

[19] These forms are taken from the Federal Judicial Center, Recommended Procedures for Handling Prisoner Civil Rights Cases in the Federal Courts at 93 (1980).

In order for this complaint to be filed, it must be accompanied by the filing fee of $15. In addition, the United States marshal will require you to pay the cost of serving the complaint on each of the defendants.

If you are unable to pay the filing fee and service costs for this action, you may petition the court to proceed in forma pauperis. Two blank petitions for this purpose are included in this packet. One copy should be filed with your complaint; the other copy is for your records.

You will note that you are required to give facts. THIS COMPLAINT SHOULD NOT CONTAIN LEGAL ARGUMENTS OR CITATIONS.

When these forms are completed, mail the original and the copies to the Clerk of the United States District Court for the _____ .
                                        [local court should insert address]

FORM TO BE USED BY A PRISONER IN FILING A COMPLAINT
UNDER THE CIVIL RIGHTS ACT, 42 U.S.C. §1983

                    In the United States District Court
                    For_____

_____
[Enter above the full name of
the plaintiff in this action.]

        v.

_____
_____
[Enter above the full name of the
defendant or defendants in this
action.]

I. Previous Lawsuits

    A. Have you begun other lawsuits in state or federal court dealing
        with the same facts involved in this action or otherwise relat-
        ing to your imprisonment?   Yes [ ]   No [ ]

    B. If your answer to A is yes, describe the lawsuit in the space
        below. [If there is more than one lawsuit, describe the addi-
        tional lawsuits on another piece of paper, using the same
        outline.]

        1. Parties to this previous lawsuit

            Plaintiffs_____
            _____

            Defendants_____
            _____

        2. Court [if federal court, name the district;
                   if state court, name the county]
            _____

        3. Docket number_____

        4. Name of judge to whom case was assigned_____

        5. Disposition [for example: Was the case dismissed? Was
                          it appealed? Is it still pending?]
            _____

6. Approximate date of filing lawsuit_____

7. Approximate date of disposition_____

II. Place of Present Confinement_____

A. Is there a prisoner grievance procedure in this institution?
    Yes [ ]   No [ ]

B. Did you present the facts relating to your complaint in the
    state prisoner grievance procedure?   Yes [ ]   No [ ]

C. If your answer is YES,

    1. What steps did you take?_____
        _____

    2. What was the result?_____
        _____

D. If your answer is NO, explain why not_____
    _____

E. If there is no prison grievance procedure in the institution,
    did you complain to prison authorities?   Yes [ ]   No [ ]

F. If your answer is YES,

    1. What steps did you take?_____
        _____

    2. What was the result?_____
        _____

III. Parties

[In item A below, place your name in the first blank and place
your present address in the second blank. Do the same for
additional plaintiffs, if any.]

A. Name of Plaintiff_____

    Address_____ _____

[In item B below, place the full name of the defendant in the first
blank, his official position in the second blank, and his place of
employment in the third blank. Use item C for the names, positions
and places of employment of any additional defendants.]

B. Defendant _____ is employed as _____

    _____ at _____

C. Additional Defendants_____
    _____
    _____

IV. Statement of Claim

[State here as briefly as possible the facts of your case.
Describe how each defendant is involved. Include also the names
of other persons involved, dates, and places. Do not give any

legal arguments or cite any cases or statutes. If you intend
to allege a number of related claims, number and set forth each
claim in a separate paragraph. Use as much space as you need.
Attach extra sheet if necessary.]

_____

_____

_____

_____

_____

V. Relief

[State briefly exactly what you want the court to do for you.
Make no legal arguments. Cite no cases or statutes.]

_____

_____

_____

Signed this _____ day of _____, 19___ .

_____
                                  [Signature of Plaintiff]

I declare under penalty of perjury that the foregoing is true and
correct.

_____   _____
     [Date]   [Signature of Plaintiff]

1e2. – Declaration in Support of Request to Proceed In Forma Pauperis

Instructions to court:

This form is to be sent to the prisoner-plaintiff.

If there is reason to believe that the information received is not accurate or
complete, the court may want to use form 3 in addition. Form 3 is an order
asking the records officer at the institution to submit a certificate stating
the current balance in the plaintiff's institutional account.

Form 2

_____
       [insert appropriate court]

[petitioner]
_____
                                    DECLARATION IN SUPPORT OF
          v.   REQUEST TO PROCEED
                                    IN FORMA PAUPERIS
_____
[respondent]

I, _____, am the petitioner in the above
entitled case. In support of my motion to proceed without being
required to prepay fees or costs or give security therefor, I
state that because of my poverty I am unable to pay the costs of
said proceeding or to give security therefor; that I believe I
am entitled to redress.

I declare that the responses which I have made below are true.

1. Are you presently employed? Yes___ No___

   a. If the answer is yes, state the amount of your salary
      per month and give the name and address of your employer.
      _____

   b. If the answer is no, state the date of last employment and
      the amount of the salary per month which you received.
      _____

2. Have you received within the past twelve months any money
   from any of the following sources?

   a. Business, profession, or form of self-employment? Yes__ No__
   b. Rent payments, interest, or dividends? Yes___ No___
   c. Pensions, annuities, or life insurance payments? Yes__ No__
   d. Gifts or inheritances? Yes___ No___
   e. Any other sources? Yes___ No___

   If the answer to any of the above is yes, describe each source
   of money and state the amount received from each during the
   past twelve months._____

3. Do you own any cash or do you have money in a checking or
   savings account? Yes___ No___ (Include any funds in
   prison accounts)

   If the answer is yes, state the total value owned.
   _____

4. Do you own any real estate, stocks, bonds, notes, automobiles,
   or other valuable property (excluding ordinary household
   furnishings and clothing)? Yes___ No___

   If the answer is yes, describe the property and state its
   approximate value._____

5. List the persons who are dependent upon you for support;
   state your relationship to those persons; and indicate how
   much you contribute toward their support._____
   _____   _____

I understand that a false statement or answer to any questions
in this declaration will subject me to penalties for perjury.

                              _____
                              [Petitioner's Signature]

I declare under penalty of perjury that the foregoing is true
and correct.

Signed this _____ day of _____, 19___.

                              _____
                              [Signature]

1f. Notice of Motion

For a discussion of notice of motion, see "Note on Motion Practice" at the beginning of this Appendix.

[CAPTION]

PLEASE TAKE NOTICE that on the attached affidavit of Daniel E. Manville and exhibit attached thereto the undersigned will move the court on the____day of_____, 198__[20] or as soon thereafter as the parties may be heard at the U.S. Courthouse, 156 Bagley St., Detroit, Michigan, for an order [insert nature of relief sought], pursuant to [insert Federal Rule   of Civil Procedure or other statute relied upon].

                    Name
                    Address

---

[20] The length of time you have to give the defendant to respond to a motion is set forth in Rule 6(d), FRCP; the local court rules may make some modification of these time limits. In addition, the local rules may specify particular days or times when motions may be heard, or the judge may have established a particular "motion day" in each week or month.

2. In Forma Pauperis

For a discussion of in forma pauperis motions, see Ch. VII, Sec. A3a.

2a. Motion for Leave to Proceed In Forma Pauperis

[CAPTION]

MOTION FOR LEAVE TO PROCEED IN FORMA PAUPERIS

Plaintiff Daniel E. Manville, pursuant to 28 U.S.C. §1915, move this Court for an order permitting him to proceed without prepayment of fees and costs or security. Plaintiff has attached a declaration in support of this motion.

                    Respectfully submitted,

                    Name
                    Address

Dated:

2b. Declaration in Support of Request to Proceed In Forma Pauperis

[CAPTION]

DECLARATION IN SUPPORT OF REQUEST
TO PROCEED IN FORMA PAUPERIS

I, Daniel E. Manville, am the plaintiff in the above entitled case. In support of my motion to proceed without being required to prepay fees or costs or give security therefor, I state that because of my poverty I am unable to pay the costs of said proceedings or to give security therefor and that I believe I am entitled to redress.

I declare that the responses which I have made below are true.

1. Are you presently employed? Yes_____ No_____

     a. If the answer is yes, state the amount of your salary
        per month and give the name and address of your employer.

_____

b. If the answer is no, state the date of last employment and the amount of salary per month which you received.

_____

2. Have you received within the past twelve months any money from any of the following sources?

    a. Business, profession, or form of self-employment? Yes__No__
    b. rent payments, interest, or dividends? Yes__No__
    c. Pensions, annuities, or life insurance payments? Yes__No__
    d. Gifts or inheritance? Yes___ No___
    e. Any other sources? Yes___ No___

If the answer to any of the above is yes, describe each source of money and state the amount received from each during the past twelve months._____

3. Do you own any cash or do you have money in a checking or savings account: Yes ___No___(Include any funds in prison accounts.)

If the answer is yes, state the total value owned.

_____

4. Do you own any real estate, stocks, bonds, notes, automoviles, or other valuable property (excluding ordinary household furnishings and clothing)? Yes___ No___

If the answer is yes, describe the property and state its approximate value._____

5. List the persons who are dependent upon you for support; state your relationship to those persons; and indicate how much you contribute toward their support._____

I understand that a false statement or answer to any questions in this declaration will subject me to penalties for perjury.

_____
(Your signature)

I declare under penalty of perjury that the foregoing is true and correct.

Signed this_____day of_____, 19___.

_____
(Your signature)

2c. Order Granting Leave to Proceed In Forma Pauperis

For a discussion of drafting of orders, see Ch. IV, Sec. C. If a judge does not grant your motion, s/he will either have a clerk type the order denying you relief or will write on your proposed order denying you the relief requested.

ORDER

Plaintiff Daniel E. Manville, a prisoner at the State Prison of Southern Michigan, Jackson, has submitted a complaint for filing in this district, together with a request for leave to proceed in forma pauperis. Since it appears that he is unable to pay the costs for commencement of suit, the following order is entered this_____ day of_____, 19___:

IT IS HEREBY ORDERED that plaintiff's motion for leave to proceed in forma pauperis is granted and the clerk is directed to file the complaint.

_____

3. Cover Letter to the Clerk of the Court

A cover letter should be submitted with every legal pleading submitted to the clerk of the court for filing informing him/her what you wish done.

Date:

Clerk of the Court[1]
United States District Court
Federal Courthouse
Detroit, MI 48226

Dear Clerk:

Find enclosed for filing an original of a complaint, motion for leave to proceed in forma pauperis, declaration in support, and an order. I have also submitted three copies[2] of the summons and the complaint that will need to be stamped as filed and returned to me so that I can seek service of these documents by "Notice and Acknowledgement of Receipt."[3] Also enclosed is an extra copy of the motion for leave to proceed in forma pauperis that I wish stamped and returned to me for my files.

Thank you.

Sincerely,

Name
Address

---

[1] See Appendix A for the addresses of the federal courts.

[2] The original of all legal pleadings must be filed with the court. You need to send to the clerk a copy of the summons and complaint for each defendant so that these documents can be stamped and returned to you for service.

[3] For a discussion of service of a summons and complaint, see Ch. VII, Sec. A2. State prisoners should also see Ch. VI, Sec. B1c, and federal prisoners should see Sec. C1c.

4. Summons

You can either prepare your own summons to submit to the Court or you can write to the clerk of the court before filing your complaint and ask him/her to send you the standard form summons. For a discussion of filing and service of the complaint, see Ch. VII, Sec. A2.

[CAPTION]

SUMMONS

To the above-named Defendant:[1] _____

You are hereby summoned and required to serve upon plaintiff Daniel E. Manville, whose address is P.O. Box E - 135760, Jackson, Michigan, 49204, an answer to the complaint which is herewith served upon you, within 20[2] days after service of this summons upon you, exclusive of the day of service. If you fail to do so, judgment by default will be taken against you for the relief demanded in the complaint.

---

[1] You must draft a summons for each named defendant listed in your complaint. The John Does cannot be served since you do not have their names. When you discover their names later and have amended your complaint (see Form 1b, supra) you will need to draft a summons for each. You should make an extra copy of each summons for your file.

[2] If federal prisoners are suing the United States or an officer or agency thereof is a defendant, the time to be inserted is 60 days.

Clerk of the Court

[Seal of the U.S. District Court]

Dated_____

4a. Notice and Acknowledgement of Receipt of Summons and Complaint

If you do not have anyone on the outside to serve your summons and complaint, you will need first to try and have them served by mail using the form below before the court will issue an order requiring the U.S. Marshal to serve your papers. You will send two copies of this form to the named defendant. You should mail this Notice and Acknowledgement by certified or registered mail with return receipt requested so that you have proof of the date it was received by the named defendant.

[CAPTION]

NOTICE AND ACKNOWLEDGEMENT OF RECEIPT OF
SUMMONS AND COMPLAINT

TO: (insert the name and address of the person to be served)

The enclosed summons and complaint are served pursuant to Rule 4(c)(2)(C)(ii) of the Federal Rules of Civil Procedure.

You must complete the acknowledgement part of this form and return one copy of the completed form to the sender within 20 days.

You must sign and date the acknowledgement. If you are served on behalf of a corporation, unincorporated association (including a partnership), or other entity, you must indicate under your signature your relationship to that entity. If you are served on behalf of another person and you are authorized to receive process, you must indicate under your signature your authority.

If you do not complete and return the form to the sender within 20 days, you (or the party on whose behalf you are being served) may be required to pay any expense incurred in serving a summons and complaint in any other manner permitted by law.

If you do not complete and return this form, you (or the party on whose behalf you are being served) must answer the complaint within 20 days. If you fail to do so, judgment by default will be taken against you for the relief demanded in the complaint.

I declare, under penalty of perjury, that this Notice and Acknowledgement of Receipt of Summons and Complaint was mailed on __(insert date)__ .

_____
Name
Address

_____
Date of Signature

ACKNOWLEDGEMENT OF RECEIPT OF SUMMONS[1]
AND COMPLAINT

I declare under penalty of perjury, that I received a copy of

_____

[1] If the defendant signs the acknowledgement of receipt of summons and complaint, s/he should return at least one copy to you and you should make a copy for your files before sending the original to the court for filing.

the summons and of the complaint in the above-captioned manner at
_____(Leave blank for defendant to complete.)_____

_____
(Defendant's Name)

_____
(Relationship to Entity/Authority
to Receive Service of Process.)

_____
Date of Signature

5. Interrogatories

You can submit either a set of interrogatories to each named defendant or one set of interrogatories to all the defendants which contain questions addressed to each defendant. The below interrogatories are based on the complaint (Form 1a) and not the supplemental complaint (Form 1c). The sample interrogatories below are addressed to all the defendants.

For a discussion of interrogatories, see Ch. VII, Sec. E2d. If you submit another set of interrogatories, you would entitle it "Second Set of Interrogatories." The same goes for a third or fourth set of interrogatories.

[CAPTION]

FIRST SET OF INTERROGATORIES[1]

Plaintiff submits the following interrogatories to the defendants pursuant to Rule 33, FRCP. You are directed to answer them in writing under oath and within 30 days of service.

1. Define what the duties and responsibilities or each defendant are.

2. On February 19, 1983, did defendant Smith go to plaintiff Manville's cell (32-B-2)? If yes, state the reasons.

3. Were there any other correctional officers with defendant Smith at the time he arrived at plaintiff Manville's cell? If yes, provide the names and titles.

4. What occurred while defendant Smith and any other officers were at plaintiff Manville's cell on February 19, 1983?

5. While defendant Smith and any other officers were at plaintiff Manville's cell on February 19, 1983, did defendant Smith order that plaintiff be sprayed with mace? If yes, state the reasons and the name and title of the person spraying the mace.

6. Assuming that mace was sprayed into plaintiff Manville's cell on February 19, 1983, did defendant Smith or any other person report this use of mace to the medical staff? If yes, state when and how.

7. Assuming that mace was sprayed into plaintiff Manville's cell on February 19, 1983, did he ever receive medical treatment in regard to the mace? If yes, state when, where, and by whom; if no, state why not.

8. On February 19, 1983, did defendant Smith order that plaintiff's hands be placed in handcuffs? If yes, state why.

9. On February 19, 1983, did defendant Smith order that plaintiff's cell be searched? If yes, what was defendant Smith searching for?

10. What is the name of the correctional officer that defendant Smith ordered to search plaintiff's cell?

_____

[1] You would mail the original to the Clerk of the Court for filing and a copy to defendant's counsel. You would also need to file with the Clerk a Proof of Service. See Form 17, acknowledging that you sent a copy to defendant's counsel.

11. During the search of plaintiff's cell were any items removed from it? If so, identify the items and who removed the items.

12. If items were removed form plaintiff's cell on February 19, 1983, whom were they given to and what was done with these items?

13. Did defendants Pogats or Smith order that the items removed from plaintiff's cell on February 19, 1983, be confiscated? If yes, state the reasons and the authority for the confiscation.

14. Was plaintiff given a receipt for the items confiscated? If not, why not?

15. Does the Department of Corrections policy provide that a receipt will be given to a prisoner when items are confiscated? If not, state why not.

_____
Name
Address

6. Compelling Discovery

Once the time period for defendants to respond to either a set of interrogatories or a request for production of documents has passed you should write defendants' counsel a letter concerning the delay in producing your discovery request. If an agreement can't be worked out between you and defendants' counsel, you might consider filing a motion to compel. You will not want to file a motion to compel concerning a set of admissions since the rule provides that if a defendant does not deny the admissions within the time period provided, the admissions will be taken as admitted.

6a. Motion to Compel

This motion and brief relate to the denial of a request for production of documents. You can use it with modifications for challenging other denials of discovery.

[CAPTION]

MOTION TO COMPEL PRODUCTION OF DOCUMENTS

Plaintiff Daniel E. Manville, pursuant to Rule 34(b) and 37(a), FRCP, moves this Court for an Order compelling the defendants to produce for inspection and copying the documents requested on _____.

_____
Daniel E. Manville
P.O. Box E - 135706
Jackson, MI 49204

Dated:_____

6b. Brief in Support

[CAPTION]

BRIEF IN SUPPORT OF MOTION TO COMPEL

Statement of the Case

This is a §1983 action filed by a prisoner at the State Prison of Southern Michigan, Jackson, seeking damages, a declaratory judgment, and injunctive relief based on prison officials' use of excessive and

unjustified force against him, the use of mace against him without
justification, and the confiscation of his personal legal materials.
     This motion seeks to compel answers to plaintiff's request for
production of documents pursuant to Rule 37, FRCP.

Statement of Facts[2]

     On June 20, 1983, plaintiff filed a request for production of
documents pursuant to Rule 34, FRCP. See Exhibit A (Request for
Production of Documents) attached to this Motion. On August 29,
1983, defendants responded by filing objections. See Exhibit B
(Objections). Defendants claim in their objections that plaintiff's request is burdensome and irrelevant. Plaintiff has
attempted without success to persuade the defendants to turn over
the requested materials without resorting to a motion to compel.
See Exhibits C and D (Plaintiff's letter to defendants' counsel
and defendants' counsel's response).

Argument

     I. THE REQUESTED DISCOVERY IS RELEVANT TO THE SUBJECT
          MATTER OF THE LAWSUIT.

     Rule 26(b)(1), FRCP, provides that a party "may obtain discovery
regarding any matter, not privileged, which is relevant ot the subject matter involved in the pending action...." Each item in plaintiff's request is relevant to the subject matter of the lawsuit.
     Request 1, for grievances received by defendants or their agents
concerning the use of mace against prisoners, is relevant to the
allegation in the complaint, at paragraph 19, that defendant Pogats
was on notice of the abuse of mace by his subordinates but failed
to take any action to control it. Proof of Pogats' knowledge and
failure to act is necessary to establish Pogats' personal liability
under §1983. *Holland v. Connors, 491 F.2d 539 (5th Cir. 1974);
Wright v. McMann, 460 F.2d 126, 134-35 (2d Cir. 1972).

     [Relevance of other requests should be explained.]

     II. DEFENDANTS' OBJECTIONS ON THE GROUNDS OF BURDEN
          HAS NO MERIT.

     Defendants claim that plaintiff's request is burdensome. However,
they have not provided any factual support for this claim. An objection that discovery is burdensome does not even present an issue
unless specific reasons are shown. Leumi Financial Corp. v. Hartford
Accident and Indemnity Co., 295 F.Supp. 539, 544 (S.D.N.Y. 1969).
The discovery sought is obviously not burdensome in any case. It
consists only of documents concerning the plaintiff, policies used
in the daily operation of the prison, and complaints defendants
have received about certain specified practices. Even if the
requested discovery were burdensome, it would be required if relevant
to the case. King v. Georgia Power Co., 50 F.R.D. 134 (N.D.Ga. 1970).
The relevance of the items sought is demonstrated in point 1, supra.

Conclusion

     WHEREFORE, the Court should grant plaintiff's motion to compel
discovery.

                    Respectfully submitted,

                    Name
                    Address

----

[1] This brief present examples of legal arguments that might arise based on the complaint,
see Form 1a, supra, and the request for production of documents, see Form 7, infra.
[2] All facts asserted in the motion and stated in the brief would be presented to the
court in an affidavit. See Form 11c, infra, for a sample affidavit.

7. Request for Production of Documents

For a discussion of requests for production of documents, see Ch. VII, Sec. E2e. If you submitted another request for production of documents, you would entitle it "Second Request for Production of Documents." The same goes for a third or fourth request.

[CAPTION]

REQUEST FOR PRODUCTION OF DOCUMENTS

Plaintiff, pursuant to Rule 34, FRCP, requests that the defendants respond within 30 days by either allowing plaintiff to inspect and copy or by providing plaintiff with a copy of the following documents.

1. Any and all letters or grievances received by the defendants or their agents within the past two years concerning the use of mace against a prisoner at the State Prison of Southern Michigan (SPSM).

2. Any and all policies concerning the use of mace by correctional officials at SPSM.

3. Any and all court decisions or consent decree entered against defendants or their agents concerning the use of mace.

4. Any and all letters or grievances received by the defendants or their agents within the past two years concerning the use of strip cells within the segregation unit at SPSM.

5. A copy of any records of plaintiff's medical treatment relating to his being sprayed with mace or any record of any medical treatment of plaintiff from February 19, 1983 to present.

6. Any and all disciplinary reports written concerning the plaintiff from January 1983 to the present.

7. Any and all policies concerning access to or possession of legal materials.

8. Any and all policies, relating to confiscation of property from a prisoner.

9. Any and all policies that establish the duties and responsibilities of defendant Smith.

Name
Address

8. Admissions

For a discussion of admissions, see Ch. VII, Sec. E2f. If you submit another set of admissions, you would entitle it "Second Request for Admissions." The same goes for a third of fourth request.

[CAPTION]

REQUEST FOR ADMISSIONS

Plaintiff requests the defendants to make the following admissions within 30 days after service of this request

1. The State Prison of Southern Michigan institutional policy about the use of mace is contained in Policy Directive 39.01.

2. The document attached as Exhibit A is an authentic copy of Policy Directive 39.01 mentioned in Admission No. 1.

3. Defendant Pogats has received in the past two years letters and grievances concerning defendant Smith's use of mace in violation of Policy Directive 39.01.

4. Defendant Pogats has not taken corrective action against defendant Smith for use of mace in violation of Policy Directive 39.01.

5. On February 19, 1983, defendants Smith and Jones went to plaintiff's cell.

6. On February 19, 1983, at approximately 11:30 am, defendant Smith told plaintiff to place his hands between the bars so that they could be handcuffed.

7. On February 19, 1983, defendant Smith told plaintiff his cell was to be searched.

8. On February 19, 1983, defendant Jones placed handcuffs on the plaintiff while he was confined in his cell.

9. On February 19, 1983, defendant Smith ordered defendant Jones to spray mace into plaintiff's cell.

10. On February 19, 1983, defendant Jones pursuant to an order of defendant Smith sprayed mace into plaintiff's face while he was confined handcuffed in his cell.

11. Plaintiff while confined in his cell did not present an immediate risk of death or injury to any person, escape, or destruction of property.

12. On February 19, 1983, defendant Smith ordered confiscated from plaintiff's cell the following items:

    a. legal papers and

    b. a law book.

       Name
       Address

9. Subpoena
9a. For Non-Prisoner Witnesses

-If you wish to have a prison official who is not a named defendant or some other free-world person testify at your trial, you will need to write the clerk of the court requesting that you be sent some witness subpoena forms you can complete. For a discussion of subpoenaing witnesses, see Ch. VII, Sec. F.

Dated

Clerk of the Court
(For the addresses of
the federal courts, see
Appendix A, supra.)

Re: Manville v. Pogats, et al., No. 83-17

Dear Clerk:

Please send me five witness subpoenas so that I can obtain the attendance of non-parties at the trial scheduled for October 28, 1983.

Sincerely,

Name
Address

9b. For Prisoners
9b1. Habeas Corpus Ad Testificandum

You will need to file with the trial judge separate "Petition for Writ of Habeas Corpus Ad Testificandum" concerning you and each prisoner/witness you want brought to the courthouse to testify. For a discussion of court appearance of a plaintiff and his/her prisoner witnesses, see Ch. VII, Sec. M.

[CAPTION]

PETITION FOR WRIT OF HABEAS CORPUS AD TESTIFICANDUM[1]

Plaintiff Daniel E. Manville, pursuant to 28 U.S.C. §2241(c)(5), requests that this Court issue a writ of habeas corpus ad testificandum requiring Warden Pogats[2] to bring the plaintiff[3] before the Court for the trial to start on August 5, 1983, and states in support:[4]

1. The plaintiff is proceeding pro se in this matter.
2. The credibility of witnesses will be an issue in this matter and the jury should be allowed to observe the plaintiff.
3. Plaintiff should also be allowed to personally cross-examine the defendants who testify and their witnesses.

Plaintiff requests that defendants bear the costs of the implementation of the terms of the writs.

Name
Address

---

[1] In some jurisdictions the material in this petition should be in the form of an affidavit. If you aren't sure of how to proceed, the safe course is to notarize or sign under the penalty of perjury to what you state in your petition. See Form 10a2, infra, for an example of signing under the penalty of perjury.

[2] If your witnesses are incarcerated in a different prison than you are, you will need to name the warden of the prison that has custody of them.

[3] A separate petition must be submitted to the trial court for each prisoner/witness you want brought to the courtroom regardless of whether that prisoner is confined at the same prison as you are. You will use the caption in your case when requesting that other prisoners be brought to your trial, and place the name and other information in the body of the petition concerning the prisoner you are seeking a writ for.

[4] You are required to list what the prisoner witness would testify concerning. See Ch. VII, Sec. M; Cook v. Bounds, 518 F.2d 779 (4th Cir. 1975).

9b2. Order Granting Writ

You should draft an order for each petition you submit to the court.

[CAPTION]

WRIT OF HABEAS CORPUS AD TESTIFICANDUM

THE PRESIDENT OF THE UNITED STATES OF AMERICA

TO: Warden Pogats, State Prison of Southern Michigan, Jackson.

—Greeting!

We command that you have the body of Daniel E. Manville, 135706, detained in the State Prison of Southern Michigan, Jackson, under your custody as it is said, under safe and secure conduct before the judges of our District Court within and for the Eastern District of Michigan, at Detroit, Michigan, on August 4, 1983, there to testify to the truth according to his knowledge in a certain cause now pending in said court, and there to be tried, entitled Manville v. Pogats, et al., No. 83-17, before the said court, and immediately after the said Manville has completed presenting his case and[5] shall

---

[5] Your order concerning your prisoner witness would not contain the words "Manville has completed his case" but would contain "[witness name] shall have given ...."

have given his testimony in the above-entitled matter that you
return him to the said State Prison of Southern Michigan, Jackson,
under safe and secure conduct, and have you then and there this writ.

Witness the Honorable George Brezna, Judge of the United States
District Court for the Eastern District of Michigan, this 15th day
of July, 1983.

$$\overline{\text{Clerk} \hspace{4cm}}$$

[Seal]

9c. For Documents

If the defendants have certain documents you will need for trial
and you were not able to obtain the documents in discovery or obtain
admissions concerning the authenticity of your copies of them, you
will probably want to subpoena these documents. You will first write
the clerk of the court and obtain copies of a subpoena duces tecum
form. Once you have these forms you will complete them and have
them served on the party or person having possession of the documents.
For a discussion of supoenas, see Ch. VII, Sec. F.

10. Default

When seeking a default judgment you will need first to submit
a request to the clerk for entry of a default with an affidavit
attached. Second, you will need to request either the clerk (if the
relief sought is a definite dollar amount) or the judge (if the relief
sought is an injunction or not a definite amount) for a default judgment. Third, if the relief is a definite dollar amount and your request
is to the clerk, you will need to attach an affidavit to your request;
if your request is to the judge, you will need to send a notice of
application for default judgment to the defendant and submit an
affiavit that the defendant is not in military service. Fourth, a
proposed judgment should be submitted for signing by either the
clerk or the judge. For a further discussion of default, see Ch.
VII, Sec. H.

10a. Entry of Default
10a1. Request for Entry of Default

[CAPTION]

REQUEST TO ENTER DEFAULT

TO: Clerk of the Court for the Eastern District of Michigan

You will please enter the default of defendant Don Smith for
failure to plead or otherwise defend as provided by the Federal
Rules of Civil Procedures, as appears from the attached affidavit
of Daniel E. Manville.

$$\overline{\hspace{6cm}}$$
Name
Address

10a2. Affidavit for Entry of Default

[CAPTION]

AFFIDAVIT FOR ENTRY OF DEFAULT

State of Michigan   )
) -ss-
County of Jackson   )

Plaintiff Daniel E. Manville, being duly sworn, deposes and
says:

1. That he is the pro se counsel in the above-entitled matter.
2. That defendant Don Smith was served with a copy of the summons and complaint as appears from the proof of service on file.
3. That defendant Don Smith has not filed or served an answer or taken other actions as may be permitted by law although more than 55 days have elapsed since the date of service.

_____
Name
Address

I declare under the penalty of perjury that the foregoing is true and correct.
Signed this____day of_____, 198__.

_____
Name and Signature

10b. Request for Default Judgment by the Clerk

If the damage claims of the plaintiff are not for a sum certain, the clerk will not be able to enter judgment for the plaintiff and the plaintiff will have to seek judgment from the Court. See Form 10c, infra.

10b1. Request for Default Judgment

[CAPTION]

REQUEST FOR DEFAULT JUDGMENT

TO: Clerk of the Court

Plaintiff Daniel E. Manville requests that you enter judgment by default based upon the attached affidavit against defendant Don Smith in the above-entitled matter for $_____, plus interest[1] at the rate of_____% and costs.

Name
Address

10b2. Affidavit in Support

[CAPTION]

AFFIDAVIT FOR DEFAULT JUDGMENT

State of Michigan   )
) -ss-
County of Jackson   )

Daniel E. Manville being duly sworn, deposes and says:
1. That he is the pro se counsel in the above-entitled matter.
2. That the amount due plaintiff from defendant Smith is $84.34:
    a. Value of law book destroyed-------$45.00
    b. Value of legal papers--------------15.00
                                     $60.00
    c. Interest for one year at 6%----------------3.60
    d. Costs:
      -Service of summons and complaint-$20.00
      -Postage, paper, and xeroxing-------7.00
                                     $27.40
    TOTAL---------------------------------------$91.00
3. That the default of the defendant has been entered for failure to appear in this action.

---
[1]Since the interest rate that can be obtained from a court judgment is usually established by state statutes, you will need to examine your state statutes.

4. That the amount listed above is due and owing and that no part has been paid.
5. That the costs sought to be recover have occurred in this action.
6. That the defendant is not in the military service as shown by the attached affidavit.

                              Name
                              Address

10b3. Affidavit that Defendant is not in Military Service

    This affidavit is required to be submitted in every case which a default judgment is sought. See 28 U.S.C. §520(1).

                         [CAPTION]

                  AFFIDAVIT AS TO MILITARY SERVICE

State of Michigan)
)   -ss-
County of Jackson)

    Daniel E. Manville, being duly sworn, deposes and says:
    1. That he is the pro se counsel in the above-entitled matter. and makes this affidavit pursuant to the provision of the Soldiers' and Sailors Civil Relief Act.
    2. That defendant Don Smith has worked at the State Prison of Southern Michigan, Jackson, since plaintiff was first incarcerated there in June 1973.
    3. That from the above fact, plaintiff is convinced that defendant Smith is not in the military service of the United States.

                         Name
                         Address

10b4. Default Judgment by the Clerk

                         [CAPTION]

                         JUDGMENT

    Defendant Don Smith having failed to plead or otherwise defend in this action and his default having been obtained,
    Now upon application of the plaintiff and upon affidavit that defendant is indebted to plaintiff in the sum of $60.00, that defendant has been defaulted for failure to appear and that the defendant is not an infant or incompetent person, and is not in the military service of the United States, it is hereby
    ORDERED, ADJUDGED AND DECREED that plaintiff recover the sum of $60.00, with interest of $3.60, at the rate of 6% per year from the date of February 19, 1983, and costs in the sum of $27.40.

                         _____Clerk_____

Dated: _____

_____
³This judgment is used only when the sum is certain.

10c. Default Judgment from the Court

    Before you file for a default judgment from the court you must have submitted to the clerk a "Request for Entry of Default" and affidavit in support. See Form 10a, supra.

10c1. Motion for Default Judgment

[CAPTION]

MOTION FOR DEFAULT JUDGMENT

Plaintiff Daniel E. Manville moves the Court to enter a default judgment against defendant Don Smith for $20,000. and states:
1. That a default has been entered against defendant Don Smith for failure to answer or otherwise defend in the above-entitled matter.
2. That defendant Don Smith is not in the military service as shown by the attached affidavit.

Name
Address

10c2. Notice of Motion to the Court for Default Judgment

You will need to contact the clerk of the court and schedule a day for a hearing so you can present evidence concerning the value of the substantive and procedural violations of your constitutional rights. The defendant must receive a copy of this notice so that s/he has the opportunity to attend the hearing to present contrary evidence as to the value of the harm you suffered.

[CAPTION]

NOTICE OF MOTION FOR JUDGMENT

TO: Don Smith

Please Take Notice that plaintiff will make application to the Court, at Room ___, United States Courthouse, 156 Bagley St., Detroit, Michigan, on the 29th day of September, 1983, at 10:00 am or as soon thereafter as pro se counsel can be heard, for entry of a default judgment in favor of the plaintiff and against you for $20,000. [2]

Name
Address

---

[2] This is the amount of compensatory and punitive damages the plaintiff had requested in the relief section of his complaint. See Form 1a, supra.

10c3. Proof of Service

See Form 17, infra.

10c4. Affidavit that Defendant Is Not in Military Service

See Form 10b3, supra.

10c5. Default Judgment

If you had requested a jury trial in your complaint, a jury would hear your evidence concerning the value of the your injuries.

[CAPTION]

JUDGMENT

The Court having ordered that the plaintiff herein recover of the defendant the damages sustained by him and that an inquest be taken before a jury to assess plaintiff's damages and that, upon rendering of a verdict by the jury, judgment be entered in accordance therewith; and this cause having been regularly brought on for hearing on the 29th day of September, 1983, before the Court and a jury, after due notice thereof to said defendant, and the jury having rendered a verdict for the plaintiff and against defendant Don Smith in the sum of $4,500 compensatory and $5,000 punitive damages, it is hereby

ORDERED, ADJUDGED, AND DECREED, that the plaintiff recover of the defendant Don Smith the sum of $9,500, together with costs.

_____
Judge

Dated: _____

11. Summary Judgment

You can't file a motion for summary judgment until the time period allowed for the defendant(s) to file an answer has passed. You very seldom will file a motion for summary judgment until you have completed your discovery. If the defendant has filed a motion for summary judgment, when you file your opposition you may wish to file your request for summary judgment. In the sample summary judgment motion below, plaintiff has requested summary judgment only as to the issue of liability as to the use of mace. You can move for summary judgment for all or part of the case depending on whether there is a factual dispute as to any part of the case. For a discussion of summary judgment, see Ch. VII, Sec. G.

11a. Motion for Summary Judgment

MOTION FOR PARTIAL SUMMARY JUDGMENT

Plaintiff Daniel E. Manville, pursuant to Rule 56, FRCP, requests this court to grant him summary judgment as to defendants' liability for damages alleging illegal and unlawful use of mace. See plaintiff's brief and affidavit in support.

                               _____
                               Daniel E. Manville, Pro se
                               P.O. Box E - 135706
                               Jackson, MI   49204

Dated:_____

11b. Brief in Support

[CAPTION]

BRIEF IN SUPPORT OF MOTION FOR SUMMARY JUDGMENT

Statement of Claim

[See first paragraph of the Statement of the Case in Form 6b, supra, Brief in Support of Motion to Compel.]

This motion seeks partial summary judgment against defendants Smith and Jones as to their liability[1] for use of mace against the plaintiff.

Statement of Facts

Defendants have admitted that on February 19, 1983, defendant Smith ordered Defendant Jones to spray mace into plaintiff's face while plaintiff was handcuffed and locked in his cell. Defendants further admit that plaintiff did not present an immediate risk of death or injury to any person, escape, or destruction of property. See Admissions No. 11, attached to this Motion as Exhibit A.

Argument

THERE ARE NO MATERIAL FACTS IN DISPUTE AS TO THE UNLAWFULNESS OF DEFENDANTS USE OF MACE AGAINST THE PLAINTIFF.

Summary judgment should be granted where a party shows that

_____

[1] In this example, the facts pertaining to liability (i.e., whether defendants violated plaintiff's rights) are undisputed but there might be a dispute about the amount of damages plaintiff is entitled to which would have to be settled at a trial on the issue of damages. See Rule 56(c), FRCP.

"there is no genuine issue as to any material fact and...the moving party is entitled to judgment as a matter of law." Rule 56, FRCP. The undisputed facts of this case show that the plaintiff was subjected to the unlawful use of mace. Thus, there is no factual dispute preventing the entry of summary judgment for the plaintiff on this issue.

Courts have "condemned the unnecessary use of tear gas and chemical agents as violative of the eighth amendment." Ruiz v. Estelle, 503 F.Supp. 1265, 1305 (S.D.Tex. 1980), aff'd in part and rev'd in part on other grounds, 679 F.2d 1115 (5th Cir. 1982), and cases cited. Use of chemical agents has been limited to situations involving an imminent threat of death or bodily harm, the destruction of substantial amounts of valuable property, or escape. Spain v. Procunier, 600 F.2d 189, 196, (9th Cir. 1979); Battle v. Anderson, 376 F.Supp. 402, 433 (E.D.Okla, 1974), aff'd, 564 F.2d 388 (10th Cir. 1977). Their use against individual prisoners and prisoners locked in their cells is prohibited except in extreme circumstances. Lock v. Jenkins, 641 F.2d 488 (7th Cir. 1981); Stringer v. Rowe, 616 F.2d 993 (7th Cir. 1980).

In this case, plaintiff was sprayed with mace while locked alone in his cell in handcuffs. He posed no threat of death, injury, escape, or destruction of property. The use of mace against him was therefore illegal under the above stated constitutional standards.

Conclusion

WHEREFORE, the Court should grant summary judgment to plaintiff as to the liability of defendants Smith and Jones for the use of mace against plaintiff.

Respectfully submitted,

Name
Address

11c. Affidavit in Support

[CAPTION]

AFFIDAVIT IN SUPPORT OF PLAINTIFF'S
MOTION FOR SUMMARY JUDGMENT

Daniel E. Manville, under the penalty of perjury, states:
1. I am the plaintiff in the above-entitled case. I make this affidavit in support of my motion for partial summary judgment as to the liability of defendants Smith and Jones for the unjustified use of mace against me.
2. On February 19, 1983, defendants Smith and Jones came to my cell in the State Prison of Southern Michigan, Jackson. Defendant Smith ordered me to place my hands through the bars so I could be handcuffed and my cell searched.
3. I asked defendant Smith the reason for the search. Defendant Smith ordered defendant Jones to mace me if I did not immediately place my hands through the bars.
4. I placed my hands through the bars and defendant Jones handcuffed me. Defendant Smith then ordered defendant Jones to mace me "to teach me a lesson." Defendant Jones then sprayed mace into my face.
5. During the time these events were taking place, I did not resist defendants Smith or Jones or disobey their orders.
6. Defendants have admitted that they came to my cell on February 19, 1983, that I was handcuffed by defendant Jones, that defendant Jones sprayed me with mace while I was handcuffed and locked in my cell at the order of defendant Smith, and that I did not present an immediate risk of death or injury to any person, escape, or the destruction of property. See Admissions No. 11, attached to this Motion as Exhibit A.
7. Thus, no material facts are in dispute as to the illegality of the defendants' use of mace against me.

WHEREFORE, the court should grant partial summary judgment against defendants Smith and Jones as to their use of mace against plaintiff.

_____
Name

12. Plaintiff's Opposition to Defendants' Motion for Summary Judgment

This affidavit is based on the complaint Form 1a, supra, but we have assumed in drafting it that defendants have denied rather than admitted the facts discussed in Forms 11a - 11c and have moved for summary judgment claiming that they used mace on the plaintiff because he refused to be handcuffed or to leave his cell for a search and threatened to assault defendants Smith and Jones if they entered his cell.

We have not presented a brief in opposition to summary judgment for reasons of space. You shuld be able to draft an acceptable brief by consulting Ch. VII, Sec. G, and by looking at the various other model briefs in this Appendix.

[CAPTION]

PLAINTIFF'S AFFIDAVIT IN OPPOSITION TO
DEFENDANTS' MOTION FOR SUMMARY JUDGMENT

Daniel E. Manville delcares under penalty of perjury:

1. I am the plaintiff in the above-entitled case. I make this declaration in opposition to defendants' motion for summary judgment as to their use of mace on me.

2. Defendants claim in their motion that there were no material facts in dispute. In reality, there are many facts in dispute.

3. The defendants claim in their motion that when they came to my cell I refused to be handcuffed until they sprayed me with mace. In fact, I submitted to handcuffing and was handcuffed before they sprayed mace on me.

4. The defendants claim in their motion that I refused to leave my cell to permit it to be searched. In fact, I did not refuse to leave my cell or refuse to permit it to be searched.

5. Defendants claim in their motion that I threatened to assault them if they entered my cell. In fact, I did not threaten to assault them.

6. Defendants claim that they used mace on me because of my alleged refusal to be handcuffed or to leave my cell and because of my alleged threats of assault. In fact, defendant Smith ordered defendant Jones, in my presence, to spray me with mace "to teach me a lesson."

7. These factual disputes cannot be resolved without a trial.

WHEREFORE, defendants' motion for summary judgment should be denied.

_____
Name

I declare under the penalty of perjury that the foregoing is true and correct.
Signed this ____ day of _____, 198__.

_____
Name and Signature

13. Appellate Brief

IN THE UNITED STATES COURT OF APPEALS
FOR THE ELEVENTH CIRCUIT

No. 81-8003

CHARLES A. GRADDICK, Attorney General,
State of Alabama,

        Appellant-Defendant,

    v.

N.H. NEWMAN: et al.; JERRY LEE PUGH,
etc.; WORLEY JAMES; et al.;

        Appellee-Plaintiffs,

UNITED STATES OF AMERICA;
BARRY E. TEAGUE, etc.;
THE NATIONAL PRISON PROJECT, etc.;
et al.,

        Amici Curiae.

CERTIFICATE OF INTERESTED PARTIES

The parties are the plaintiff class consisting of Alabama prison inmates; governmental parties defendant below; and the Governor of Alabama as temporary receiver for the Alabama Prison System.

                         John L. Carroll

                         Attorney for Pugh Plaintiffs

- i -

TABLE OF CONTENTS

TABLE OF AUTHORITIES

STATEMENT OF THE CASE[1]

A.   COURSE OF PROCEEDINGS AND DISPOSITION BELOW[2]

These consolidated cases began on October 28, 1971, when a class action suit was initiated by inmate N. H. Newman which claimed that inmates in the Alabama Prison System were being subjected to cruel and unusual punishment because of a lack of adequate medical care (physical and mental) provided. A trial was held and on October 4, 1981, the court upheld the claims of the inmates and issued broad injunctive relief tailored to cure the violations. Newman v. Alabama, 349 F. Supp. 278 (M.D. Ala. 1972), aff'd. 522 F.2d 71 (5th Cir. 1975), cert. denied sub nom. Alabama v. Newman, 421 U.S. 948 (1975).

In 1974, separate cases were filed by inmates Worley James and Jerry Lee Pugh alleging that the totality of conditions in the Alabama Prison System subjected a class of all prisoners within said system to cruel and unusual punishment. The cases were consolidated for trial. On August 29, 1975, the court, after trial, joined with the United States District Court for the Southern District of

_____   [Pages 2-8 are not included.]

[1]Because of the expedited nature of this appeal, the Record concerning the December 14, 1981 order is not yet prepared. References to that record have thus been omitted.

[2]A "brief summary" of "this protracted litigation" is provided by Justice Powell in Graddick v. Newman, ___ U.S. ___ 102 S.Ct. 4 (1981).

- 1 -

B. STATEMENT OF THE FACTS

> On October 4, 1972, this Court held that
> the failure of the Board of Corrections to
> afford the basic elements of adequate medical
> care to inmates in the Alabama Prison System
> constituted "a willful and intentional viola-
> tion" of their rights under the Eighth and
> Fourteenth Amendments. Newman v. Alabama,
> D. C., 349 F.Supp. 278, 287. Four years
> later, when the Court issued its order in
> Pugh v. Locke, D. C., 406 F.Supp. 318 (1976),
> those same serious shortcomings persisted.
> What Pugh revealed, however, was that such
> shortcomings were endemic to every phase of
> the prison system's operation. The conditions
> of confinement then violated any judicial
> definition of cruel and unusual punishment.

Newman v. Alabama, 466 F. Supp. 628, 629 (M. D. Ala., 1979).

Further orders since 1976 have recognized and confirmed

continuing violation of the constitutional rights of prisoners

in the Alabama Prison System and continuing non-compliance with

the comprehensive remedial order issued to cure the violation.

See, e.g., Newman v. Alabama, 466 F. Supp. 628 (M. D. Ala.

1979); Newman, slip op. (M. D. Ala., Oct. 9, 1980); Newman,

slip op. (M. D. Ala., July 15, 1981); Graddick v. Newman,

___ U.S. ___, 102 S.Ct. 4 (1981); Newman, slip op. (M. D.

Ala., December 14, 1981). See, also, Rhodes v. Chapman,

___ U.S. ___, 101 S.Ct. 2392, 2401 (ftnte. 17)(1981).

In 1975, the Alabama Prison System was "horrendously

overcrowded" and that condition exacerbated all the other

ills of the Alabama prison system. The court, therefore,

entered an order enjoining the defendants from accepting any

[Pages 10-27 are not included.]

SUMMARY OF ARGUMENT

The orders of the district court in this case ordering
the release of state prisoners came after the defendants had
been in non-compliance with various orders of the court for
six years. In 1978, then District Judge Frank M. Johnson
issued orders forbidding the defendants from housing state
prisoners in county jails. In a later order he specifically
found that conditions in the county jails were such that "in
almost, if not every instance they fall below the minimum
constitutional standards set forth in the Pugh order. . . Overcrowding in the prisons has been relieved only at the price
of aggravated violations of the rights of the state prisoners
in county jails. Newman v. Alabama, 466 F.Supp. 628, 630
(M.D.Ala. 1978). On October 9, 1980 the defendants agreed to
remove all state prisoners from the county jails by September
1, 1981. The agreement was then entered as an order by the
Court.

The defendants failed to comply with the terms of the
October 9, 1980 order as they had previously failed to comply
with Judge Johnson's 1978 orders. In July of 1981, there were
still 2,100 state prisoners in the county jails. At that point,
the district court ordered a release of state prisoners. Despite
the efforts of the state to forestall another release by creating bedspaces, there were 1,528 state prisoners in the county
jails in November 1981. Again faced with the continued violation
of his orders, the Judge ordered another release. That release
was well within his equitable powers. Swann v. Charlotte-
Mecklenburg Board of Education, 402 U.S. 1 (1971).

[Pages 29 and 30 are not included.]

I. THE REMEDY ORDERED BY THE TRIAL COURT
    WAS WELL WITHIN THE SCOPE OF HIS REMEDIAL
    AUTHORITY.

A. THE TRIAL COURT IS EMPOWERED TO ENFORCE ITS LONG-
    IGNORED ORDERS BY APPROPRIATE REMEDIES.

There can be no argument with the general principle that

the power of a federal equity court is equal to any obstacles

placed in the way of vindication of the rights protected by

the Constitution. As the Supreme Court has noted,

> Once a right and a violation have been shown,
> the scope of the District Court's equitable
> powers to remedy past wrongs is broad.

Swann v. Charlotte-Mecklenburg Board of Education, 402 U.S.

1, 15 (1971). Further, when as here, injunctive type orders

have been issued to remedy constitutional violations, "federal

cou:ts are not reduced to issuing injunctions against state

officers and hoping for compliance. Once issued, an injunction

may be enforced." Hutto v. Finney, 437 U.S. 678, 690 (1978).

Indeed, as this court noted in Gates v. Collier, 616 F.2d 1268

(5th Cir. 1980), a district court may use "any of the weapons

generally at its disposal to ensure compliance."

This Circuit has repeatedly endorsed a broad range of

equitable relief, particularly in cases involving prisons.

See, e.g., Ruiz v. Estelle, 650 F.2d 555 (5th Cir. 1981, noting

its acceptance of the principle that "... a district court in

exercising its remedial powers may order a prison's population

reduced in order to allieviate unconstitutional conditions,"

650 F.2d at 570; Miller v. Carson, 563 F.2d 741 at 751, n.14

(5th Cir. 1977)(affirming an order placing a daily population

[pages 32 - 48 are not included.]

- 31 -

CONCLUSION

For the foregoing reasons, the order and judgment of the district court of December 14, 1981 and December 22, 1981 should be affirmed and this court's stay of those orders vacated.

Respectfully submitted,

JOHN L. CARROLL
    1001 South Hull Street
    Montgomery, AL 36104
    (205) 264-0286

RALPH I. KNOWLES
    Post Office Box DK
    University, AL 35486
    (205) 759-1234

ATTORNEYS FOR APPELLEE-PLAINTIFFS

ALVIN J. BRONSTEIN
ELIZABETH ALEXANDER
THE NATIONAL PRISON PROJECT
 of the American Civil Liberties
Union Foundation
    1346 Connecticut Avenue, N.W.
    Washington, D. C. 20036
    (202) 331-0500

ATTORNEYS FOR AMICI CURIAE

14. Temporary Restraining Order and/or Preliminary Injunction

Because a temporary restraining order (TRO) is granted without the usual notice and opportunity for the adverse party to prepare, it is considered an extraordinary form of relief and is rarely granted. A court is more likely to grant a preliminary injunction after notice to the other side. Also, when a TRO is granted, it is intended only to protect the plaintiff's rights until such time as a hearing on notice can be held. Therefore, it is common practice to move for a TRO and, in the alternative, for a preliminary injunction in the same set of papers. The following forms have been drafted in this style. If you are only asking for one of these types of relief you can easily modify the forms.

14a. Motion for TRO and/or PI

[CAPTION]

Plaintiff Daniel E. Manville, pursuant to Rule 65, FRCP, requests this court to grant him a temporary restraining and/or preliminary injunction directing defendants Smith and Jones to return plaintiff's personal legal materials which they confiscated.

Name
Address

14b. Brief in Support

[CAPTION]

BRIEF IN SUPPORT OF PLAINTIFF's MOTION FOR
TEMPORARY RESTRAINING ORDER AND/OR PRELIMINARY INJUNCTION

Statement of the Case

[See Statement of Case in Brief in Support of Motion to Compel, Form 6b, supra.]
This motion seeks a temporary restraining order and/or preliminary injunction to return plaintiff's legal pleadings and a personal law book which were confiscated by the defendants.

Statement of Facts

As set forth in detail in the affidavit of Daniel E. Manville attached, defendants Smith and Jones came to plaintiff's cell, handcuffed him, sprayed him with mace, and took him to the "hole." They also confiscated legal pleadings he had prepared for a challenge to his criminal conviction, plus a law book belonging to him. These items have not been returned. Defendants' retention of these items is delaying plaintiff in filing his case. If the defendants lose or destroy them, plaintiff will be subjected to months of further delay and enormous amounts of work while he reconstruct them.

Argument

I.   PLAINTIFF IS ENTITLED TO A TEMPORARY RESTRAINING ORDER DIRECTING DEFENDANTS TO RETURN HIS PERSONAL LEGAL MATERIALS.

A litigant may be granted a temporary restraining order (TRO) by a federal court upon a showing that the plaintiff is in danger of immediate and irreparable injury, that the adverse party will not be substantially harmed if a TRO is granted, that the TRO is consistent with the public interest, and that the plaintiff has a strong likelihood of success in the lawsuit.[1] Murphy v. Society of Real Estate Appraisers, 388 F.Supp. 1046, 1049 (E.D.Wisc. 1975).

Plaintiff is entitled to a TRO under these standards.

A.   <u>Irreparable Injury</u>.

The loss of constitutional rights, even for short periods of time, constitutes irreparable injury. <u>Elrod v. Burns</u>, 427 U.S. 347, 373 (1976); <u>Deerfield Medical Center v. City of Deerfield Beach</u>, 661 F.2d 328, 338 (5th Cir. 1981). The deprivation of plaintiff's legal materials clearly violates the constitution. See Sec. D, infra. Every day the defendants retain the materials, plaintiff is delayed in filing his challenge to his criminal conviction, and every day increases the risk that the defendants will lose or destroy the materials.

B.   <u>Absence of Harm to the Adverse Party</u>.

The defendants have no legitimate interest in keeping plaintiff's legal materials or in delaying the filing of his criminal case. Thus, there will not be harm to the defendants from a TRO.

C.   <u>Public Interest</u>.

The public interest is best served when all persons, including prisoners, enjoy unimpaired access to the courts. See <u>Bound v. Smith</u>, 430 U.S. 17 (1977).

D.   <u>Likelihood of Ultimate Success on the Merits</u>.

Plaintiff's likelihood of winning a final judgment on the issue of his legal papers is overwhelming. Prisoners' right to petition the courts, to prepare legal papers for this purpose, and to be free of confiscation of these papers is so well established as to be unquestionable. <u>Bound v. Smith</u>, supra; <u>Franklin v. State of Oregon</u>, 662 F.2d 1337 (9th Cir. 1981).

Rule 65, FRCP, requires an applicant for TRO to certify to the court the efforts that have been made to given notice to the adverse party and/or the reasons why notice or further efforts to give notice should not be required. Plaintiff's efforts are described in paragraph 6 of his affidavit attached. The TRO should be granted without further delay for notice purpose because of the irreparable injury the plaintiff is suffering and because of the risk of loss or destruction of his legal materials if the matter is further delayed.

Even if the court finds that plaintiff is not entitled to a temporary restraining order, it should grant plaintiff a preliminary injunction after notice to the defendants.

A preliminary injunction may be granted upon notice based on consideration of the same four factors discussed in Point I, supra. <u>Florida Medical Association, Inc. v. Unites States Department of Health, Education, and Welfare</u>, 601 F.2d 199 (5th Cir. 1979). Plaintiff incorporates that discussion by reference in this point.

Wherefore, the court should grant a temporary restraining order or, in the alternative a preliminary injunction, directing defendants to return his legal materials forthwith.

Name
Address

---

[1] Some courts use a slightly different outline of the factors governing temporary restraining orders and preliminary injunctions. See, e.g., Doe v. New York University, 666 F.2d 761, 773 (2d Cir. 1981). Your brief and motion should follow the law as stated by your circuit.

14c. Affidavit in Support

[CAPTION]

Daniel E. Manville states under penalty of pejury:

1. I am the plaintiff in the above-entitled case. I make

this affidavit is support of my motion for a temporary restraining order or, in the alternative, for a preliminary injunction.

2. On February 19, 1983, defendants Smith and Jones came to my cell and ordered me to submit to being handcuffed so my cell could be searched. I asked why my cell was to be searched. Defendant Smith told defendant Jones to spray me with mace unless I submitted immediately to being handcuffed. I did so, but defendant Smith directed defendant Jones to spray me with mace anyway "to teach me a lesson." After these events, my cell was searched and defendants removed the legal pleadings in my pro se challenge to my criminal conviction and a law book about criminal appeals. I was then taken to the "hole" (segregation).

3. These materials have not been returned to me despite my requests.

4. The above-described legal pleadings are almost ready to be filed. They represent approximately six months of legal research, review of my trial transcript, and writing. The confiscated law book is essential to help me finish my pleadings.

5. Every day my pleadings and my book are out of my possession represents a day's delay in filing my case. If the pleadings are lost, it will be many months before I am able to reconstruct them. Thus, I am suffering irreparable harm while I am deprived of these materials.

6.[2] I have placed a copy of these papers and a complaint in the institutional mail to defendants Smith and Jones. I have not served their attorney because no attorney has yet appeared in the case,[3] since formal service of process has not been completed. Because of the urgency of the situation, set forth in paragraph 5, supra, no further efforts at notice should be required.

7. No prior application for relief sought in this motion has been made.

Wherefore, the court should grant a temporary restraining order or, in the alternative, a preliminary injunction requiring defendants to return plaintiff's legal pleadings and law book.

Name

I declare under the penalty of perjury that the foregoing is true and correct.
    Signed this ____ day of _____, 198___.

_____
Name and Signature

---

[2] This paragraph is designed to meet the requirements of Rule 65(b), FRCP, that the party seeking a TRO certify any efforts made to give notice of the motion and the reasons why further notice should not be required.

[3] If you know that prison officials are always represented by the same office, such as the State Attorney General, you can give notice to that office.

14d. Order Granting the Motion for TRO

[CAPTION]

ORDER GRANTING MOTION FOR TEMPORARY RESTRAINING ORDER[¶]

Plaintiff has moved for a TRO pursuant to Rule 65, FRCP, seeking the return of certain personal legal papers confiscated from his cell by defendants correctional officers. Defendants' retention of these legal materials delays the filing of plaintiff's pro se challenge to his criminal conviction and subjecting plaintiff to the risk of immediate and irreparable harm consisting of loss or destr-

---

This order can be converted to an order granting a preliminary injunction by omitting the material in brackets.

uction of pleadings that would require months of work to reconstruct. [Because of this risk it is inappropriate to withhold relief until formal notice can be given to defendants.]

It is therefore ORDERED that defendants' Smith and Jones forthwith return to plaintiff any legal pleadings and/or law books seized from plaintiff's cell on February 13, 1983.

[It is further ORDERED that this TRO shall continue until _____ .]

[It is further ORDERED that a hearing on plaintiff's motion for a Preliminary Injunction should be held on _____, and that plaintiff shall be prepared to proceed with his motion at that time.]

It is further ORDERED that no security shall be required of plaintiff because it appears that he is an indigent prisoner and because this order does not appear to threaten defendants with any pecuniary loss.

_____
United States District Judge

Date: _____ .

15. Motion to Dispense with the Requirement of Security

This motion will be used when filing a request for issuance of a temporary restraining order, preliminary injunction, or stay of the enforcement of a judgment. See Ch. VI, Sec. G3, for a discussion of posting security. See also Rules 62(d), 65(c), FRCP.

[CAPTION]

Plaintiff Daniel E. Manville, pursuant to Rule 65(c), Fed. R. Civ. Proc., requests this Court not to require the plaintiff to post a security in this matter and states the following:
1. Plaintiff has been granted leave to proceed in forma pauperis in the above-entitled matter.
2. If a temporary restraining order is granted, defendants will not be required to expend money to comply with it.
3. The ends of justice are served if plaintiff is not required to post security.

Name
Address

16. Motion for Service of Process by United States Marshal

You must attempt to have your summons and complaint served using Form 4a, supra, before you can request the U.S. Marshal to serve them. If the defendants have not returned to you signed the acknowledgement of receipt of summons and complaint within the time period allowed, you will then need to either have a friend serve the defendant or submit a motion to the court asking that the U.S. Marshal be ordered to serve the summons and complaint.

[CAPTION]

MOTION FOR SERVICE OF PROCESS BY UNITED STATES MARSHAL

Plaintiff Daniel E. Manville, pursuant to Rule 4(c)(2(C)(ii), as amended February 26, 1983, moves this Court for an order requiring the U.S. Marshal to serve a copy of the summons and complaint upon defendant Don Smith, and states the following:
1. On May 20, 1983, the plaintiff mailed a copy of the summons and complaint along with two copies of the "Notice and Acknowledgement of Receipt of Summons and Complaint" to defendant Smith. See Exhibit A.
2. On May 24, 1983, defendant Smith received the documents listed in paragraph 1, supra. See Exhibit B, Return Receipt Requested containing the signature of Don Smith.
3. As of June 27, 1983, plaintiff has not received a signed copy of the "Acknowledgement of Receipt of Summons and Complaint" from defendant Smith.

4. Plaintiff requests that the U.S. Marshal be ordered to serve a copy of the summons and complaint upon defendant Smith.
5. Plaintiff requests that defendant Smith be required to pay the costs of the U.S. Marshal for service of the summons and complaint upon him.

Name
Address

17. Proof of Service (Certificate of Service)

One the summons and complaint have been served by someone other than the named plaintiff, all future legal documents can be mailed directly to counsel for the defendants. You must send the court notice that defendants' counsel has been mailed a copy of these legal documents that are being filed with the court.

[CAPTION]

PROOF OF SERVICE

Daniel E. Manville states under the penalty of perjury that he mailed a copy of the motion for summary judgment, affidavit in support, and brief in support to defendants' counsel John Roberts, Assistant Attorney General, State of Michigan, 500 Madison St., Lansing, MI., by placing them in an envelope and placed them in the Main Hall Legal Mailbox at the State Prison of Southern Michigan, Jackson, on July 17, 1983.

Name
Address

18. Appointment of Counsel

For a discussion of appointment of counsel, see Ch. VII, Sec. A3b. See also Ch. I, Sec. D, for a discussion of how to seek an attorney on your own.

18a. Motion for Appointment of Counsel

[CAPTION]

MOTION FOR APPOINTMENT OF COUNSEL

Plaintiff Daniel E. Manville, pursuant to 42 U.S.C. §1915, requests this Court to appoint counsel to represent him in this case for the following reasons:

1. Plaintiff is not able to afford counsel.
2. The issues involved in this case are complex.
3. The prison limits the hours that plaintiff may have access to the prison library and the law materials contained there are very limited.
4. Plaintiff has a limited knowledge of the law.
5. The ends of justice would best be served in this case if an attorney was appointed to represent the plaintiff.

Name
Address

18b. Brief in Support

You have no constitutional right to appointed counsel in a civil matter. See Ch. VII, Sec. Ab3, for a discussion of the factors a court will consider in its determination whether to request counsel to represent you. Your brief should list these factors and how you fit each of them.

19. Notice of Appeal

For a discussion of filing an appeal, see Ch. VII, Sec. P.

[CAPTION]

NOTICE OF APPEAL

Notice is hereby given that DANIEL E. MANVILLE, plaintiff in the above-entitled matter, appeals to the United States Court of Appeals for the Sixth[1] Circuit from the final judgment entered in this action on_____, 198__.

_____
Name
Address

_____

[1]You would place in here the name of the Circuit Court of Appeals where you are incarcerated.

20. Standard Form 95 for Use by Federal Prisoners

This form should be used by federal prisoners when filing a claim under the Federal Tort Claims Act. For a discussion of the Federal Tort Claims Act, see Ch. VI, Sec. C2.

CLAIM FOR DAMAGE, INJURY, OR DEATH	INSTRUCTIONS: Prepare in ink or typewriter. Please read carefully the instructions on the reverse side and supply information requested on both sides of this form. Use additional sheets if necessary.	OMI and B Approval No. 80-R133

1. SUBMIT TO:	2. NAME AND ADDRESS OF CLAIMANT (Number, street, city, State, and Zip Code)

3. TYPE OF EMPLOYMENT ☐ MILITARY ☐ CIVILIAN	4. AGE	5. MARITAL STATUS	6. NAME AND ADDRESS OF SPOUSE, IF ANY (Number, street, city, State, and Zip Code)

7. PLACE OF ACCIDENT (Give city or town and State; if outside city limits, indicate mileage or distance to nearest city or town)	8. DATE AND DAY OF ACCIDENT	9. TIME (A.M OR P.M)

10.   AMOUNT OF CLAIM (in dollars)

A. PROPERTY DAMAGE	B. PERSONAL INJURY	C. WRONGFUL DEATH	D. TOTAL

11. DESCRIPTION OF ACCIDENT (State below, in detail, all known facts and circumstances attending the damage, injury, or death, identifying persons and property involved and the cause thereof)

12.   PROPERTY DAMAGE

NAME AND ADDRESS OF OWNER, IF OTHER THAN CLAIMANT (Number, street, city, State, and Zip Code)

BRIEFLY DESCRIBE KIND AND LOCATION OF PROPERTY AND NATURE AND EXTENT OF DAMAGE (See instructions on reverse side for method of substantiating claim)

13.   PERSONAL INJURY

STATE NATURE AND EXTENT OF INJURY WHICH FORMS THE BASIS OF THIS CLAIM

14.   WITNESSES

NAME	ADDRESS (Number, street, city, State, and Zip Code)

I CERTIFY THAT THE AMOUNT OF CLAIM COVERS ONLY DAMAGES AND INJURIES CAUSED BY THE ACCIDENT ABOVE AND AGREE TO ACCEPT SAID AMOUNT IN FULL SATISFACTION AND FINAL SETTLEMENT OF THIS CLAIM

15. SIGNATURE OF CLAIMANT (This signature should be used in all future correspondence)	16. DATE OF CLAIM

CIVIL PENALTY FOR PRESENTING FRAUDULENT CLAIM	CRIMINAL PENALTY FOR PRESENTING FRAUDULENT CLAIM OR MAKING FALSE STATEMENTS
The claimant shall forfeit and pay to the United States the sum of $2,000, plus double the amount of damages sustained by the United States. (See R.S. §3490, 5438; 31 U.S.C. 231.)	Fine of not more than $10,000 or imprisonment for not more than 5 years or both. (See 62 Stat. 698, 749; 18 U.S.C. 287, 1001.)

GENERAL SERVICES ADMINISTRATION—FPMR 101-11.8
95-105

STANDARD FORM 95
REVISED FEBRUARY 1971
GSA FPMR 101-11.8

INSTRUCTIONS

Complete all items — Insert the word NONE where applicable

Claims for damage to or for loss or destruction of property, or for personal injury, must be signed by the owner of the property damaged or lost or the injured person. If, by reason of death, other disability or for reasons deemed satisfactory by the Government, the foregoing requirement cannot be fulfilled, the claim may be filed by a duly authorized agent or other legal representative, provided evidence satisfactory to the Government is submitted with said claim establishing authority to act.

If claimant intends to file claim for both personal injury and property damage, claim for both must be shown in item 10 of this form. Separate claims for personal injury and property damage are not acceptable.

The amount claimed should be substantiated by competent evidence as follows:

(a) In support of claim for personal injury or death, the claimant should submit a written report by the attending physician, showing the nature and extent of injury, the nature and extent of treatment, the degree of permanent disability, if any, the prognosis, and the period of hospitalization, or incapacitation, attaching itemized bills for medical, hospital, or burial expenses actually incurred.

(b) In support of claims for damage to property which has been or can be economically repaired, the claimant should submit at least two itemized signed statements or estimates by reliable, disinterested concerns, or, if payment has been made, the itemized signed receipts evidencing payment.

(c) In support of claims for damage to property which is not economically reparable, or if the property is lost or destroyed, the claimant should submit statements as to the original cost of the property, the date of purchase, and the value of the property, both before and after the accident. Such statements should be by disinterested competent persons, preferably reputable dealers or officials familiar with the type of property damaged, or by two or more competitive bidders, and should be certified as being just and correct.

Any further instructions or information necessary in the preparation of your claim will be furnished, upon request, by the office indicated in item # 1 on the reverse side.

INSURANCE COVERAGE

In order that subrogation claims may be adjudicated, it is essential that the claimant provide the following information regarding the insurance coverage of his vehicle or property.

17. DO YOU CARRY ACCIDENT INSURANCE? ☐ YES, IF YES, GIVE NAME AND ADDRESS OF INS. 'ANCE COMPANY (Number, street, city, State, and Zip Code) AND POLICY NUMBER. ☐ NO

18. HAVE YOU FILED CLAIM ON YOUR INSURANCE CARRIER IN THIS INSTANCE, AND IF SO, IS IT FULL COVERAGE OR DEDUCTIBLE?

19. IF DEDUCTIBLE, STATE AMOUNT

20. IF CLAIM HAS BEEN FILED WITH YOUR CARRIER, WHAT ACTION HAS YOUR INSURER TAKEN OR PROPOSES TO TAKE WITH REFERENCE TO YOUR CLAIM? (It is necessary that you ascertain these facts)

21. DO YOU CARRY PUBLIC LIABILITY AND PROPERTY DAMAGE INSURANCE? ☐ YES, IF YES, GIVE NAME AND ADDRESS OF INSURANCE CARRIER (Number, street, city, State, and Zip Code) ☐ NO

GPO 1971OA – 430-460 66-A

21. Petition for Writ of Certiorari

IN THE
Supreme Court of the United States
OCTOBER TERM 1982
No. _____

N.H. NEWMAN, et al.,   )
        Petitioners,   )
UNITED STATES OF AMERICA, et al.,   )
        Amicus Curiae,   )
     v.   )
STATE OF ALABAMA, et al.,   )
        Respondents.   )

PETITION FOR A WRIT OF CERTIORARI
TO THE UNITED STATES COURT OF APPEALS
FOR THE ELEVENTH CIRCUIT

ALVIN J. BRONSTEIN,
Counsel of Record
ELIZABETH ALEXANDER
National Prison Project of the
American Civil Liberties Union
Foundation, Inc.
1346 Connecticut Ave., N.W.
Washington, D.C. 20036
202/331-0500

RALPH I. KNOWLES, JR.
Drake, Knowles & Pierce
1509 University Blvd.
Tuscaloosa, AL 35401

JOHN L. CARROLL
Southern Poverty Law Center
1001 S. Hull St.
Montgomery, AL 36104

Attorneys for Petitioners

QUESTION PRESENTED

WHETHER THE COURT OF APPEALS RENDERED A DECISION IN CONFLICT WITH DECISIONS OF THIS COURT AND OF OTHER COURTS OF APPEALS, WHEN IT RULED THAT A FEDERAL DISTRICT COURT, WHICH HAS ISSUED A REMEDIAL INJUNCTIVE ORDER TO STATE OFFICIALS TO CURE LONGSTANDING CONSTITUTIONAL VIOLATIONS, IS LIMITED TO THE USE OF CONTEMPT SANCTIONS TO ENFORCE THAT ORDER AND MAY NOT ISSUE ANY FURTHER INJUNCTIVE ORDERS TO EFFECTUATE THE ORIGINAL ORDER AND CURE THE CONSTITUTIONAL VIOLATIONS?

PARTIES

The petitioners are N.H. Newman, Jerry Lee Pugh and Worley James, the named plaintiffs in the courts below for themselves and a class of all those persons who are now or may in the future be confined as prisoners by the Alabama prison system.

The respondents are George C. Wallace, Governor of Alabama; Charles Graddick, Attorney General of Alabama; and Fred Smith, Commissioner of Corrections. Governor Wallace and Commissioner Smith were automatically substituted as parties when they assumed their respective offices on January 17, 1983. Rule 25(d), Federal Rules of Civil Procedure.

(iii)

TABLE OF CONTENTS

(iv)

TABLE OF AUTHORITIES

[Page (v) is not included.]

(vi)

Page

Constitutional Provisions:

IN THE

Supreme Court of the United States
OCTOBER TERM 1982
No. _____

N.H. NEWMAN, et al.,   )
         Petitioners,   )
UNITED STATES OF AMERICA, et al.,   )
         Amicus Curiae,   )
               v.   )
STATE OF ALABAMA, et al.,   )
         Respondents.   )

PETITION FOR A WRIT OF CERTIORARI
TO THE UNITED STATES COURT OF APPEALS
FOR THE ELEVENTH CIRCUIT

DECISIONS BELOW

The decision of the United States Court of Appeals for the Eleventh Circuit is reported at 683 F.2d 1312 (11th Cir. 1982) and a copy is attached hereto as Appendix A. (A.1). The order of the United States District Court for the Middle District of Alabama is not reported and a copy is attached hereto as Appendix C. (A.19).

JURISDICTION

The judgment of the United States Court of Appeals for the Eleventh Circuit was entered on August 9, 1982. An order denying a petition for rehearing was entered on October 19, 1982 and a copy of that order is attached hereto as Appendix B. (A.17). On December 29, 1982, Justice Powell extended the time for filing this petition to and in-

2

cluding February 14, 1983.[1] Jurisdiction is conferred by 28 U.S.C. 1254(1).

CONSTITUTIONAL AND STATUTORY PROVISIONS INVOLVED

This case involves Amendment VIII to the Constitution of the United States prohibiting cruel and unusual punishment:

> Excessive bail shall not be required, nor excessive fines imposed, nor cruel and unusual punishments inflicted.

made applicable to the states by Sections 1 and 5 of Amendment XIV to the Constitution of the United States:

> SECTION 1.   All persons born or naturalized in the United States, and subject to the jurisdiction thereof, are citizens of the United States and of the State wherein they reside. No State shall make or enforce any law which shall abridge the privileges or immunities of citizens of the United States; nor shall any State deprive any person of life, liberty, or property, without due process of law; nor deny to any person within its jurisdiction the equal protection of the laws.

> SECTION 5.   The Congress shall have power to enforce, by appropriate legislation, the provisions of this article.

and enforced by Title 42, Section 1983, United States Code:

---

[1]That order was entered in Miscellaneous No. A-570.

3

Every person who, under color of any statute, ordinance, regulation, custom, or usage, of any State or Territory or the District of Columbia, subjects, or causes to be subjected, any citizen of the United States or other person within the jurisdiction thereof to the deprivation of any rights, privileges, or immunities secured by the Constitution and laws, shall be liable to the party injured in an action at law, suit in equity, or other proper proceeding for redress.

STATEMENT OF THE CASE

We recite only so much of the eleven year history of this litigation as is necessary for a determination of the issue presently before the Court. Beginning in 1971, the petitioners, all of whom are Alabama prison inmates, brought three separate lawsuits under 42 U.S.C. § 1983 and 28 U.S.C. § 1343(3) to redress alleged constitutional violations in the Alabama prisons. *See Newman v. Alabama,* 349 F.Supp. 278 (M.D. Ala. 1972), *aff'd,* 503 F.2d 1320 (5th Cir. 1974), *cert. den.* 421 U.S. 948 (1975); *Pugh v. Locke* and *James v. Wallace,* 406 F.Supp. 318 (M.D. Ala. 1976), *aff'd with modifications sub nom. Newman v. Alabama,* 559 F.2d 283 (5th Cir. 1977), *cert. den. in relevant part,* 438 U.S. 781 and 438 U.S. 915 (1978). On more than one occasion the district court held that conditions in the Alabama prison system, including overcrowding, violated the rights of inmates under the eighth and fourteenth amendments and ordered injunctive relief. (A.3).[2] At his request, the district court appointed former Alabama Governor Fob James receiver of the Alabama

[Pages 4-6 are not included.]

---

[2]Hereafter, all references to the opinions of the courts below will be cited to the Appendix to this Petition and designated A.

7

were not entitled to a mandatory injunction. The "adequate" legal remedy, according to the Court of Appeals, was again a civil contempt proceeding and coercive sanctions. (A.11, 12).

The Court of Appeals denied a petition for rehearing on October 19, 1982. On December 29, 1982, Justice Powell extended the time for filing this petition to and including February 14, 1983.

ARGUMENT IN SUPPORT OF GRANTING CERTIORARI

A. Conflicts with decisions of this court

This case is important for the issues it raises as to the proper allocation of functions between the federal district courts and federal courts of appeals. This Court has consistently recognized that "[t]he proper observance of the division of functions between federal trial courts and the federal appellate courts is important in every case," especially in cases where the district court has been asked to issue an effective remedy to cure unconstitutional conditions in public institutions. *Dayton Board of Education v. Brinkman,* 433 U.S. 406, 410 (1977), *Milliken v. Bradley,* 433 U.S. 267 (1977) (Milliken II) (public schools); *Hutto v. Finney,* 437 U.S. 678 (1978) (state prisons).

The opinion and order of the Court of Appeals vacating the remedial order of the district court are contrary to the general principles which this Court has enunciated governing the equitable powers of district courts to fashion remedies for constitutional violations and raise important questions about the proper function of appellate courts in reviewing remedial orders. In this case, the appellate court held that federal judges in complicated civil rights cases

[Pages 8-17 are not included.]

18

B. Conclusion

Certiorari should be granted because the Court of Appeals' approach to remedial orders is contrary to the decisions of this Court in *Hutto* and *Milliken* and does not respect the role of the district court in fashioning remedial orders. This case provides the proper vehicle for determining the respective roles of trial and appellate courts in determining appropriate remedial guidelines in prison conditions, as well as other, cases. The issue is presented clearly in this case since the appellate court and the district court agreed that there were serious existing constitutional violations which were not being addressed by responsible state officials.

Respectfully submitted,

ALVIN J. BRONSTEIN
ELIZABETH ALEXANDER
National Prison Project of the
American Civil Liberties Union
Foundation, Inc.
1346 Connecticut Ave., N.W.
Washington, D.C. 20036
202/331-0500

RALPH I. KNOWLESS, JR.
Drake, Knowles & Pierce
1509 University Blvd.
Tuscaloosa, AL 35401

JOHN L. CARROLL
Southern Poverty Law Center
1001 S. Hull St.
Montgomery, AL 36104

Attorneys for Petitioners

[Appendices are not included.]

22. Certification of Record to the Supreme Court

You would file this with the clerk of the court from who order you are appealing to the Supreme Court. You must send a copy of this certification to the Clerk of the Supreme Court and the attorney for the other side, with a proof of service filed with the Supreme Court.

[CAPTION][1]

REQUEST TO CLERK TO CERTIFY AND TRANSMIT RECORD

TO: Clerk of the Court
     Court of Appeals for the Sixth Circuit
     [Address]

Pursuant to Rule 19.1 of the Rules of the Supreme Court of the United States, you are requested to certify and transmit to the Supreme Court of the United States the record in the above-entitled matter.

Respectfully submitted,

_____
Name
Address

---

[1]You would use the caption previously used when before the lower court.

23. Voir Dire Questions

For a discussion of selecting a jury, see Ch. VII, Sec. K3. The following are some possible vior dire questions to be used when choosing a jury.

[CAPTION]

PLAINTIFF'S PROPOSED VOIR DIRE

Plaintiff submitts the following list of proposed voir dire questions.

Background

1.   How long have you lived in the area?
2.   Do you own your own home?
3.   Do you have children? How many? How old?
4.   Where are you employed? What is your job title?
5.   Where are the other members of your immediate family employed?
6.   To what clubs and social organizations to you belong?
7.   What are your hobbies?
8.   What magazines do you regularly read?
9.   How many years of formal education do you have?
10. Were you ever in the military?
     --What position did you hold?
     --Did you ever serve in the military police?
11. The following persons may be called as witnesses in this case. Please state whether you know or have ever heard of any of these persons? [List the name of the witnesses defendants and you may call.]
12. Do you know any of the defendants in this case?
13. Do you have any opinions concerning the [name of prison where you are confined]? What are they?
14. Have you or any member of your family or a close friend ever have been the victim of a crime? What was the nature of the crime? Was the perpetrator punished? What was the result? Were you satisfied with the results?
15. Have you or has any member of your family ever held any job in (a) a law enforcement agency, (b) any government agency, (d) the state or local police, (d) the FBI, (e) any prosecutor's office, or (f) a private detective or security guard agency?

16. Do you know anyone who was or is employed by or in any way connected with the [name of prison where your incident occurred]?

17. Do you know any one who was or is employed by or in any way connected with the [Bureau of Prisons/Michigan Department of Corrections]?

18. Do you know any, including your neighbors, friends, co-workers or relatives, who works or has worked in a jail or prison or as a parole or probation officer?

19. Does your job cause you to work with any law enforcement officer or agency?

20. In this case the defendants are represented by attorneys for the Michigan Attorney General's Office. Do you understand that this title has no particular significance, and that these attorneys are merely lawyers employed by the government?

21. In this case you may hear testimony from medical doctors and psychiatrists. Have you ever had any experience with either doctors or psychiatrists which affected you in some way so that you could not be an impartial juror on a case involving such testimony?

Attitudes toward punishment, use of force

22. Have you ever been inside a jail or prison?
   --In what circumstances?

23. Do you think prisoners are treated too lightly?

24. Do you think prisoners are afforded too many privileges?

25. Do you think a person loose: any rights when s/he goes to prison?
   --What are they?

26. What is the purpose of prison?

27. If a prisoner disobeys an order, should s/he be punished, and if so, how?

28. Under what circumstances do you think corporal punishment of a prisoner is appropriate?

29. Under what circumstances do you think it would be appropriate for a prison official to hit a prisoner or use physical force against a prisoner when the prisoner is in restrains and unable to resist?

Race[1]

30. Do you know anyone who is black, such as a co-worker, friend, neighbor?
   --How frequently do you see these persons?
   --In what settings?

31. How would you feel if a black family moved onto your street?

32. Do you belong to social clubs or organizations that bar membership to certain individuals based on their race or ethnic origin?

Credibility

33. Do you know anyone who has been in prison?
   --What is your relationship with that person?
   --What was the person imprisoned for?
   --How long was the sentence?

34. If a prisoner and a prison official give conflicting testimony about the same incident, which one would you be inclined to believe and why?

35. If you knew someone was convicted of a crime, would that make you less likely to believe s/he was telling the truth?

36. Under what circumstances, if any, would a prison official be likely to give false testimony?

37. Do you think that a prison guard is more likely to tell the truth than a prisoner?

38. Under what circumstances do you think people who work together on the same jobs are likely to protect a co-worker they suspect of wrongdoing?

39. If you were in a position to hire someone, under what circumstances would you hire a person with a criminal record?

Right to sue

40. Does your religious or ethical training teach that all human beings are entitled to fair and equitable treatment?

41. Do you believe that?

42. Do you believe that prisoners are entitled to the same humane and fair treatment other human beings receive?

---

[1]You would substitute for black whatever ethnic group you are a member of.

43. Under what circumstances does a prisoner forfeit his right to humane and equitable treatment?

44. If someone is harmed by the actions of another person, under what circumstances should he bring a lawsuit and be compensated by the person who did the harm for the injury inflicted?

45. If a prisoner is harmed by the actions of a prison official, under what circumstances do you think the prisoner should bring a lawsuit and be compensated for the harm inflicted by the prison official?

46. What do you think should be done to a prison official if it is shown that he beat a prisoner without provocation or saw others doing so and did not intervene?

Name
Address

CERTIFICATE OF SERVICE

[See Form 17, supra.]

Appendix C
Post Conviction, Habeas Corpus

1. 28 U.S.C. §§2241-2255

§ 2241. Power to grant writ

(a) Writs of habeas corpus may be granted by the Supreme Court, any justice thereof, the district courts and any circuit judge within their respective jurisdictions. The order of a circuit judge shall be entered in the records of the district court of the district wherein the restraint complained of is had.

(b) The Supreme Court, any justice thereof, and any circuit judge may decline to entertain an application for a writ of habeas corpus and may transfer the application for hearing and determination to the district court having jurisdiction to entertain it.

(c) The writ of habeas corpus shall not extend to a prisoner unless—

(1) He is in custody under or by color of the authority of the United States or is committed for trial before some court thereof; or

(2) He is in custody for an act done or omitted in pursuance of an Act of Congress, or an order, process, judgment or decree of a court or judge of the United States; or

(3) He is in custody in violation of the Constitution or laws or treaties of the United States; or

(4) He, being a citizen of a foreign state and domiciled therein is in custody for an act done or omitted under any alleged right, title, authority, privilege, protection, or exemption claimed under the commission, order or sanction of any foreign state, or under color thereof, the validity and effect of which depend upon the law of nations; or

(5) It is necessary to bring him into court to testify or for trial.

(d) Where an application for a writ of habeas corpus is made by a person in custody under the judgment and sentence of a State court of a State which contains two or more Federal judicial districts, the application may be filed in the district court for the district wherein such person is in custody or in the district court for the district within which the State court was held which convicted and sentenced him and each of such district courts shall have concurrent jurisdiction to entertain the application. The district court for the district wherein such an application is filed in the exercise of its discretion and in furtherance of justice may transfer the application to the other district court for hearing and determination.

As amended May 24, 1949, c. 139, § 112, 63 Stat. 105; Sept. 19, 1966, Pub.L. 89–590, 80 Stat. 811.

§ 2242. Application

Application for a writ of habeas corpus shall be in writing signed and verified by the person for whose relief it is intended or by someone acting in his behalf.

It shall allege the facts concerning the applicant's commitment or detention, the name of the person who has custody over him and by virtue of what claim or authority, if known.

It may be amended or supplemented as provided in the rules of procedure applicable to civil actions.

If addressed to the Supreme Court, a justice thereof or a circuit judge it shall state the reasons for not making application to the district court of the district in which the applicant is held.

§ 2243. Issuance of writ; return; hearing; decision

A court, justice or judge entertaining an application for a writ of habeas corpus shall forthwith award the writ or issue an order directing the respondent to show cause why the writ should not be granted, unless it appears from the application that the applicant or person detained is not entitled thereto.

The writ, or order to show cause shall be directed to the person having custody of the person detained. It shall be returned within three days unless for good cause additional time, not exceeding twenty days, is allowed.

The person to whom the writ or order is directed shall make a return certifying the true cause of the detention.

When the writ or order is returned a day shall be set for hearing, not more than five days after the return unless for good cause additional time is allowed.

Unless the application for the writ and the return present only issues of law the person to whom the writ is directed shall be required to produce at the hearing the body of the person detained.

The applicant or the person detained may, under oath, deny any of the facts set forth in the return or allege any other material facts.

The return and all suggestions made against it may be amended, by leave of court, before or after being filed.

The court shall summarily hear and determine the facts, and dispose of the matter as law and justice require.

§ 2244. Finality of determination

(a) No circuit or district judge shall be required to entertain an application for a writ of habeas corpus to inquire into the detention of a person pursuant to a judgment of a court of the United States if it appears that the legality of such detention has been determined by a judge or court of the United States on a prior application for a writ of habeas corpus and the petition presents no new ground not theretofore presented and determined, and the judge of court is satisfied that the ends of justice will not be served by such inquiry.

(b) When after an evidentiary hearing on the merits of a material factual issue, or after a hearing on the merits of an issue of law, a person in custody pursuant to the judgment of a State court has been denied by a court of the United States or a justice or judge of the United States release from custody or other remedy on an application for a writ of habeas corpus, a subsequent application for a writ of habeas corpus in behalf of such person need not be entertained by a court of the United States or a justice or judge of the United States unless the application alleges and is predicated on a factual or other ground not adjudicated on the hearing of the earlier application for the writ, and unless the court, justice, or judge is satisfied that the applicant has not on the earlier application deliberately withheld the newly asserted ground or otherwise abused the writ.

(c) In a habeas corpus proceeding brought in behalf of a person in custody pursuant to the judgment of a State court, a prior judgment of the Supreme Court of the United States on an appeal or review by a writ of certiorari at the instance of the prisoner of the decision of such State court, shall be conclusive as to all issues of fact or law with respect to an asserted denial of a Federal right which constitutes ground for discharge in a habeas corpus proceeding, actually adjudicated by the Supreme Court therein, unless the applicant for the writ of habeas corpus shall plead and the court shall find the existence of a material and controlling fact which did not appear in the record of the proceeding in the Supreme Court and the court shall further find that the applicant for the writ of habeas corpus could not have caused such fact to appear in such record by the exercise of reasonable diligence.

As amended Nov. 2, 1966, Pub.L. 89–711, § 1, 80 Stat. 1104.

§ 2245. Certificate of trial judge admissible in evidence

On the hearing of an application for a writ of habeas corpus to inquire into the legality of the detention of a person pursuant to a judgment the certificate of the judge who presided at the trial resulting in the judgment, setting forth the facts occurring at the trial, shall be admissible in evidence. Copies of the certificate shall be filed with the court in which the application is pending and in the court in which the trial took place.

§ 2246. Evidence; depositions; affidavits

On application for a writ of habeas corpus, evidence may be taken orally or by deposition, or, in the discretion of the judge, by affidavit. If affidavits are admitted any party shall have the right to propound written interrogatories to the affiants, or to file answering affidavits.

§ 2247. Documentary evidence

On application for a writ of habeas corpus documentary evidence, transcripts of proceedings upon arraignment, plea and sentence and a transcript of the oral testimony introduced on any previous similar application by or in behalf of the same petitioner, shall be admissible in evidence.

§ 2248. Return or answer; conclusiveness

The allegations of a return to the writ of habeas corpus or of an answer to an order to show cause in a habeas corpus proceeding, if not traversed, shall be accepted as true except to the extent that the judge finds from the evidence that they are not true.

§ 2249. Certified copies of indictment, plea and judgment; duty of respondent

On application for a writ of habeas corpus to inquire into the detention of any person pursuant to a judgment of a court of the United States, the respondent shall promptly file with the court certified copies of the indictment, plea of petitioner and the judgment, or such of them as may be material to the questions raised, if the petitioner fails to attach them to his petition, and same shall be attached to the return to the writ, or to the answer to the order to show cause.

§ 2250. Indigent petitioner entitled to documents without cost

If on any application for a writ of habeas corpus an order has been made permitting the petitioner to prosecute the application in forma pauperis, the clerk of any court of the United States shall furnish to the petitioner without cost certified copies of such documents or parts of the record on file in his office as may be required by order of the judge before whom the application is pending.

§ 2251. Stay of State court proceedings

A justice or judge of the United States before whom a habeas corpus proceeding is pending, may, before final judgment or after final judgment of discharge, or pending appeal, stay any proceeding against the person detained in any State court or by or under the authority of any State for any matter involved in the habeas corpus proceeding.

After the granting of such a stay, any such proceeding in any State court or by or under the authority of any State shall be void. If no stay is granted, any such proceeding shall be as valid as if no habeas corpus proceedings or appeal were pending.

§ 2252. Notice

Prior to the hearing of a habeas corpus proceeding in behalf of a person in custody of State officers or by virtue of State laws notice shall be served on the attorney general or other appropriate officer of such State as the justice or judge at the time of issuing the writ shall direct.

§ 2253. Appeal

In a habeas corpus proceeding before a circuit or district judge, the final order shall be subject to review, on appeal, by the court of appeals for the circuit where the proceeding is had.

There shall be no right of appeal from such an order in a proceeding to test the validity of a warrant to remove, to another district or place for commitment or trial, a person charged with a criminal offense against the United States, or to test the validity of his detention pending removal proceedings.

An appeal may not be taken to the court of appeals from the final order in a habeas corpus proceeding where the detention complained of arises out of process issued by a State court, unless the justice or judge who rendered the order or a circuit justice or judge issues a certificate of probable cause. As amended May 24, 1949, c. 139, § 113, 63 Stat. 105; Oct. 31, 1951, c. 655, § 52, 65 Stat. 727.

§ 2254. State custody; remedies in Federal courts

(a) The Supreme Court, a Justice thereof, a circuit judge, or a district court shall entertain an application for a writ of habeas corpus in behalf of a person in custody pursuant to the judgment of a State court only on the ground that he is in custody in violation of the Constitution or laws or treaties of the United States.

(b) An application for a writ of habeas corpus in behalf of a person in custody pursuant to the judgment of a State court shall not be granted unless it appears that the applicant has exhausted the remedies available in the courts of the State, or that there is either an absence of available State corrective process or the existence of circumstances rendering such process ineffective to protect the rights of the prisoner.

(c) An applicant shall not be deemed to have exhausted the remedies available in the courts of the State, within the meaning of this section, if he has the right under the law of the State to raise, by any available procedure, the question presented.

(d) In any proceeding instituted in a Federal court by an application for a writ of habeas corpus by a person in custody pursuant to the judgment of a State court, a determination after a hearing on the merits of a factual issue, made by a State court of competent jurisdiction in a proceeding to which the applicant for the writ and the State or an officer or agent thereof were parties, evidenced by a written finding, written opinion, or other reliable and adequate written indicia, shall be presumed to be correct, unless the applicant shall establish or it shall otherwise appear, or the respondent shall admit—

(1) that the merits of the factual dispute were not resolved in the State court hearing;

(2) that the factfinding procedure employed by the State court was not adequate to afford a full and fair hearing;

(3) that the material facts were not adequately developed at the State court hearing;

(4) that the State court lacked jurisdiction of the subject matter or over the person of the applicant in the State court proceeding;

(5) that the applicant was an indigent and the State court, in deprivation of his constitutional right, failed to appoint counsel to represent him in the State court proceeding;

(6) that the applicant did not receive a full, fair, and adequate hearing in the State court proceeding; or

(7) that the applicant was otherwise denied due process of law in the State court proceeding;

(8) or unless that part of the record of the State court proceeding in which the determination of such factual issue was made, pertinent to a determination of the sufficiency of the evidence to support such factual determination, is produced as provided for hereinafter, and the Federal court on a consideration of such part of the record as a whole concludes that such factual determination is not fairly supported by the record:

And in an evidentiary hearing in the proceeding in the Federal court, when due proof of such factual determination has been made, unless the existence of one or more of the circumstances respectively set forth in paragraphs numbered (1) to (7), inclusive, is shown by the applicant, otherwise appears, or is admitted by the respondent, or unless the court concludes pursuant to the provisions of paragraph numbered (8) that the record in the State court proceeding, considered as a whole, does not fairly support such factual determination, the burden shall rest upon the applicant to establish by convincing evidence that the factual determination by the State court was erroneous.

(e) If the applicant challenges the sufficiency of the evidence adduced in such State court proceeding to support the State court's determination of a factual issue made therein, the applicant, if able, shall produce that part of the record pertinent to a determination of the sufficiency of the evidence to support such determination. If the applicant, because of indigency or other reason is unable to produce such part of the record, then the State shall produce such part of the record and the Federal court shall direct the State to do so by order directed to an appropriate State official. If the State cannot provide such pertinent part of the record, then the court shall determine under the existing facts and circumstances what weight shall be given to the State court's factual determination.

(f) A copy of the official records of the State court, duly certified by the clerk of such court to be a true and correct copy of a finding, judicial opinion, or other reliable written indicia showing such a factual determination by the State court shall be admissible in the Federal court proceeding.

As amended Nov. 2, 1966. Pub.L. 89–711, § 2, 80 Stat. 1105.

§ 2255. Federal custody; remedies on motion attacking sentence

A prisoner in custody under sentence of a court established by Act of Congress claiming the right to be released upon the ground that the sentence was imposed in violation of the Constitution or laws of the United States, or that the court was without jurisdiction to impose such sentence, or that the sentence was in excess of the maximum authorized by law, or is otherwise subject to collateral attack, may move the court which imposed the sentence to vacate, set aside or correct the sentence.

A motion for such relief may be made at any time.

Unless the motion and the files and records of the case conclusively show that the prisoner is entitled to no relief, the court shall cause notice thereof to be served upon the United States attorney, grant a prompt hearing thereon, determine the issues and make findings of fact and conclusions of law with respect thereto. If the court finds that the judgment was rendered without jurisdiction, or that the sentence imposed was not authorized by law or otherwise open to collateral attack, or that there has been such a denial or infringement of the constitutional rights of the prisoner as to render the judgment vulnerable to collateral attack, the court shall vacate and set the judgment aside and shall discharge the prisoner or resentence him or grant a new trial or correct the sentence as may appear appropriate.

A court may entertain and determine such motion without requiring the production of the prisoner at the hearing.

The sentencing court shall not be required to entertain a second or successive motion for similar relief on behalf of the same prisoner.

An appeal may be taken to the court of appeals from the order entered on the motion as from a final judgment on application for a writ of habeas corpus.

An application for a writ of habeas corpus in behalf of a prisoner who is authorized to apply for relief by motion pursuant to this section, shall not be entertained if it appears that the applicant has failed to apply for relief, by motion, to the court which sentenced him, or that such court has denied him relief, unless it also appears that the remedy by motion is inadequate or ineffective to test the legality of his detention. As amended May 24, 1949, c. 139, § 114, 63 Stat. 105.

2. Rules Governing Proceedings Under §2254

Rule
1. Scope of Rules.
2. Petition.
3. Filing Petition.
4. Preliminary Consideration by Judge.
5. Answer; Contents.
6. Discovery.
7. Expansion of Record.
8. Evidentiary Hearing.
9. Delayed or Successive Petitions.
10. Powers of Magistrates.
11. Federal Rules of Civil Procedure; Extent of Applicability.

Rule 1. Scope of Rules

(a) **Applicable to cases involving custody pursuant to a judgment of a state court.** These rules govern the procedure in the United States district courts on applications under 28 U.S.C. § 2254:

(1) by a person in custody pursuant to a judgment of a state court, for a determination that such custody is in violation of the Constitution, laws, or treaties of the United States; and

(2) by a person in custody pursuant to a judgment of either a state or a federal court, who makes application for a determination that custody to which he may be subject in the future under a judgment of a state court will be in violation of the Constitution, laws, or treaties of the United States.

(b) **Other situations.** In applications for habeas corpus in cases not covered by subdivision (a), these rules may be applied at the discretion of the United States district court.

Rule 2. Petition

(a) **Applicants in present custody.** If the applicant is presently in custody pursuant to the state judgment in question, the application shall be in the form of a petition for a writ of habeas corpus in which the state officer having custody of the applicant shall be named as respondent.

(b) **Applicants subject to future custody.** If the applicant is not presently in custody pursuant to the state judgment against which he seeks relief but may be subject to such custody in the future, the application shall be in the form of a petition for a writ of habeas corpus with an added prayer for appropriate relief against the judgment which he seeks to attack. In such a case the officer having present custody of the applicant and the attorney general of the state in which the judgment which he seeks to attack was entered shall each be named as respondents.

(c) **Form of Petition.** The petition shall be in substantially the form annexed to these rules, except that any district court may by local rule require that petitions filed with it shall be in a form prescribed by the local rule. Blank petitions in the prescribed form shall be made available without charge by the clerk of the district court to applicants upon their request. It shall specify all the grounds for relief which are available to the petitioner and of which he has or by the exercise of reasonable diligence should have knowledge and shall set forth in summary form the facts supporting each of the grounds thus specified. It shall also state the relief requested. The petition shall be typewritten or legibly handwritten and shall be signed under penalty of perjury by the petitioner.

(d) **Petition to be directed to judgments of one court only.** A petition shall be limited to the assertion of a claim for relief against the judgment or judgments of a single state court (sitting in a county or other appropriate political subdivision). If a petitioner desires to attack the validity of the judgments of two or more state courts under which he is in custody or may be subject to future custody, as the case may be, he shall do so by separate petitions.

(e) **Return of insufficient petition.** If a petition received by the clerk of the district court does not substantially comply with the requirements of rule 2 or rule 3, it may be returned to the petitioner, if a judge of the court so directs, together with a statement of the reason for its return. The clerk shall retain a copy of the petition. As amended Pub.L. 94–426, § 2(1), (2), Sept. 28, 1976, 90 Stat. 1334.

Rule 3. Filing Petition

(a) **Place of filing; copies; filing fee.** A petition shall be filed in the office of the clerk of the district court. It shall be accompanied by two conformed copies thereof. It shall also be accompanied by the filing fee prescribed by law unless the petitioner applies for and is given leave to prosecute the petition in forma pauperis. If the petitioner desires to prosecute the petition in forma pauperis, he shall file the affidavit required by 28 U.S.C. § 1915. In all such cases the petition shall also be accompanied by a certificate of the warden or other appropriate officer of the institution in which the petitioner is confined as to the amount of money or securities on deposit to the petitioner's credit in any account in the institution, which certificate may be considered by the court in acting upon his application for leave to proceed in forma pauperis.

(b) **Filing and service.** Upon receipt of the petition and the filing fee, or an order granting leave to the petitioner to proceed in forma pauperis, and having ascertained that the petition appears on its face to comply with rules 2 and 3, the clerk of the district court shall file the petition and enter it on the docket in his office. The filing of the petition shall not require the respondent to answer the petition or otherwise move with respect to it unless so ordered by the court.

Rule 4. Preliminary Consideration by Judge

The original petition shall be presented promptly to a judge of the district court in accordance with the procedure of the court for the assignment of its business. The petition shall be examined promptly by the judge to whom it is assigned. If it plainly appears from the face of the petition and any exhibits annexed to it that the petitioner is not entitled to relief in the district court, the judge shall make an order for its summary dismissal and cause the petitioner to be notified. Otherwise the judge shall order the respondent to file an answer or other pleading within the period of time fixed by the court or to take such other action as the judge deems appropriate. In every case a copy of the petition and any order shall be served by certified mail on the respondent and the attorney general of the state involved.

Rule 5. Answer; Contents

The answer shall respond to the allegations of the petition. In addition it shall state whether the petitioner has exhausted his state remedies including any post-conviction remedies available to him under the statutes or procedural rules of the state and including also his right of appeal both from the judgment of conviction and from any adverse judgment or order in the post-conviction proceeding. The answer shall indicate what transcripts (of pretrial, trial, sentencing, and post-conviction proceedings) are available, when they can be furnished, and also what proceedings have been recorded and not transcribed. There shall be attached to the answer such portions of the transcripts as the answering party deems relevant. The court on its own motion or upon request of the petitioner may order that further portions of the existing transcripts be furnished or that certain portions of the non-transcribed proceedings be transcribed and furnished. If a transcript is neither available nor procurable, a narrative summary of the evidence may be submitted. If the petitioner appealed from the judgment of conviction or from an adverse judgment or order in a post-conviction proceeding, a copy of the petitioner's brief on appeal and of the opinion of the appellate court, if any, shall also be filed by the respondent with the answer.

Rule 6. Discovery

(a) **Leave of court required.** A party shall be entitled to invoke the processes of discovery available under the Federal Rules of Civil Procedure if, and to the extent that, the judge in the exercise of his discretion and for good cause shown grants leave to do so, but not otherwise. If necessary for effective utilization of discovery procedures, counsel shall be appointed by the judge for a petitioner who qualifies for the appointment of counsel under 18 U.S.C. § 3006A(g).

(b) **Requests for discovery.** Requests for discovery shall be accompanied by a statement of the interrogatories or requests for admission and a list of the documents, if any, sought to be produced.

(c) **Expenses.** If the respondent is granted leave to take the deposition of the petitioner or any other person the judge may as a condition of taking it direct that the respondent pay the expenses of travel and subsistence and fees of counsel for the petitioner to attend the taking of the deposition.

Rule 7. Expansion of Record

(a) **Direction for expansion.** If the petition is not dismissed summarily the judge may direct that the record be expanded by the parties by the inclusion of additional materials relevant to the determination of the merits of the petition.

(b) **Materials to be added.** The expanded record may include, without limitation, letters predating the filing of the petition in the district court, documents, exhibits, and answers under oath, if so directed, to written interrogatories propounded by the judge. Affidavits may be submitted and considered as a part of the record.

(c) **Submission to opposing party.** In any case in which an expanded record is directed, copies of the letters, documents, exhibits, and affidavits proposed to be included shall be submitted to the party against whom they are to be offered, and he shall be afforded an opportunity to admit or deny their correctness.

(d) **Authentication.** The court may require the authentication of any material under subdivision (b) or (c).

Rule 8. Evidentiary Hearing

(a) **Determination by court.** If the petition is not dismissed at a previous stage in the proceeding, the judge, after the answer and the transcript and record of state court proceedings are filed, shall, upon a review of those proceedings and of the expanded record, if any, determine whether an evidentiary hearing is required. If it appears that an evidentiary hearing is not required, the judge shall make such disposition of the petition as justice shall require.

(b) **Function of the magistrate.**

(1) When designated to do so in accordance with 28 U.S.C. § 636(b), a magistrate may conduct hearings, including evidentiary hearings, on the petition, and submit to a judge of the court proposed findings of fact and recommendations for disposition.

(2) The magistrate shall file proposed findings and recommendations with the court and a copy shall forthwith be mailed to all parties.

(3) Within ten days after being served with a copy, any party may serve and file written objections to such proposed findings and recommendations as provided by rules of court.

(4) A judge of the court shall make a de novo determination of those portions of the report or specified proposed findings or recommendations to which objection is made. A judge of the court may accept, reject, or modify in whole or in part any findings or recommendations made by the magistrate.

(c) **Appointment of counsel; time for hearing.** If an evidentiary hearing is required the judge shall appoint counsel for a petitioner who qualifies for the appointment of counsel under 18 U.S.C. § 3006A (g) and the hearing shall be conducted as promptly as practicable, having regard for the need of counsel for both parties for adequate time for investigation and preparation. These rules do not limit the appointment of counsel under 18 U.S.C. § 3006A at any stage of the case if the interest of justice so requires.

As amended Pub.L. 94–426, § 2(5), Sept. 28, 1976, 90 Stat. 1334; Pub. L. 94–577, § 2(a)(1), (b)(1), Oct. 21, 1976, 90 Stat. 2730, 2731.

Rule 9.   Delayed or Successive Petitions

(a) **Delayed petitions.** A petition may be dismissed if it appears that the state of which the respondent is an officer has been prejudiced in its ability to respond to the petition by delay in its filing unless the petitioner shows that it is based on grounds of which he could not have had knowledge by the exercise of reasonable diligence before the circumstances prejudicial to the state occurred.

(b) **Successive petitions.** A second or successive petition may be dismissed if the judge finds that it fails to allege new or different grounds for relief and the prior determination was on the merits or, if new and different grounds are alleged, the judge finds that the failure of the petitioner to assert those grounds in a prior petition constituted an abuse of the writ.

As amended Pub.L. 94–426, § 2(7), (8), Sept. 28, 1976, 90 Stat. 1335.

Rule 10.   Powers of Magistrates

The duties imposed upon the judge of the district court by rules 2, 3, 4, 6, and 7 may be performed by a United States magistrate if and to the extent that he is so empowered by rule of the district court, and to the extent the district court has established standards and criteria for the performance of such duties, except that when such duties involve the making of an order, under rule 4, dismissing the petition the magistrate shall submit to the court his report as to the facts and his recommendation with respect to the order to be made by the court.

As amended Pub.L. 94–426, § 2(11), Sept. 28, 1976, 90 Stat. 1335.

Rule 11. Federal Rules of Civil Procedure; extent of applicability

The Federal Rules of Civil Procedure, to the extent that they are not inconsistent with these rules, may be applied, when appropriate, to petitions filed under these rules.

3. Rules Governing Proceedings Under §2255

Rule
1. Scope of Rules.
2. Motion.
3. Filing Motion.
4. Preliminary Consideration by Judge.
5. Answer; Contents.
6. Discovery.
7. Expansion of Record.
8. Evidentiary Hearing.
9. Delayed or Successive Motions.
10. Powers of Magistrates.
11. Time for Appeal.
12. Federal Rules of Criminal and Civil Procedure; Extent of Applicability.

Rule 1. Scope of Rules

These rules govern the procedure in the district court on a motion under 28 U.S.C. § 2255:

(1) by a person in custody pursuant to a judgment of that court for a determination that the judgment was imposed in violation of the Constitution or laws of the United States, or that the court was without jurisdiction to impose such judgment, or that the sentence was in excess of the maximum authorized by law, or is otherwise subject to collateral attack; and

(2) by a person in custody pursuant to a judgment of a state or other federal court and subject to future custody under a judgment of the district court for a determination that such future custody will be in violation of the Constitution or laws of the United States, or that the district court was without jurisdiction to impose such judgment, or that the sentence was in excess of the maximum authorized by law, or is otherwise subject to collateral attack.

Rule 2. Motion

(a) **Nature of application for relief.** If the person is presently in custody pursuant to the federal judgment in question, or if not presently in custody may be subject to such custody in the future pursuant to such judgment, the application for relief shall be in the form of a motion to vacate, set aside, or correct the sentence.

(b) Form of motion. The motion shall be in substantially the form annexed to these rules, except that any district court may by local rule require that motions filed with it shall be in a form prescribed by the local rule. Blank motions in the prescribed form shall be made available without charge by the clerk of the district court to applicants upon their request. It shall specify all the grounds for relief which are available to the movant and of which he has or, by the exercise of reasonable diligence, should have knowledge and shall set forth in summary form the facts supporting each of the grounds thus specified. It shall also state the relief requested. The motion shall be typewritten or legibly handwritten and shall be signed under penalty of perjury by the petitioner

(c) Motion to be directed to one judgment only. A motion shall be limited to the assertion of a claim for relief against one judgment only of the district court. If a movant desires to attack the validity of other judgments of that or any other district court under which he is in custody or may be subject to future custody, as the case may be, he shall do so by separate motions.

(d) Return of insufficient motion. If a motion received by the clerk of a district court does not substantially comply with the requirements of rule 2 or 3, it may be returned to the movant, if a judge of the court so directs, together with a statement of the reason for its return. The clerk shall retain a copy of the motion.
As amended Pub.L. 94–426, § 2(3), (4), Sept. 28, 1976, 90 Stat. 1334.

Rule 3.   Filing Motion

(a) Place of filing; copies. A motion under these rules shall be filed in the office of the clerk of the district court. It shall be accompanied by two conformed copies thereof.

(b) Filing and service. Upon receipt of the motion and having ascertained that it appears on its face to comply with rules 2 and 3, the clerk of the district court shall file the motion and enter it on the docket in his office in the criminal action in which was entered the judgment to which it is directed. He shall thereupon deliver or serve a copy of the motion together with a notice of its filing on the United States Attorney of the district in which the judgment under attack was entered. The filing of the motion shall not require said United States Attorney to answer the motion or otherwise move with respect to it unless so ordered by the court.

Rule 4. Preliminary Consideration by Judge

(a) **Reference to judge; dismissal or order to answer.** The original motion shall be presented promptly to the judge of the district court who presided at the movant's trial and sentenced him, or, if the judge who imposed sentence was not the trial judge, then it shall go to the judge who was in charge of that part of the proceedings being attacked by the movant. If the appropriate judge is unavailable to consider the motion, it shall be presented to another judge of the district in accordance with the procedure of the court for the assignment of its business.

(b) **Initial consideration by judge.** The motion, together with all the files, records, transcripts, and correspondence relating to the judgment under attack, shall be examined promptly by the judge to whom it is assigned. If it plainly appears from the face of the motion and any annexed exhibits and the prior proceedings in the case that the movant is not entitled to relief in the district court, the judge shall make an order for its summary dismissal and cause the movant to be notified. Otherwise, the judge shall order the United States Attorney to file an answer or other pleading within the period of time fixed by the court or to take such other action as the judge deems appropriate.

Rule 5. Answer; Contents

(a) **Contents of answer.** The answer shall respond to the allegations of the motion. In addition it shall state whether the movant has used any other available federal remedies including any prior post-conviction motions under these rules or those existing previous to the adoption of the present rules. The answer shall also state whether an evidentiary hearing was accorded the movant in a federal court.

(b) **Supplementing the answer.** The court shall examine its files and records to determine whether it has available copies of transcripts and briefs whose existence the answer has indicated. If any of these items should be absent, the government shall be ordered to supplement its answer by filing the needed records. The court shall allow the government an appropriate period of time in which to do so, without unduly delaying the consideration of the motion.

Rule 6. Discovery

(a) **Leave of court required.** A party may invoke the processes of discovery available under the Federal Rules of Criminal Procedure or the Federal Rules of Civil Procedure or elsewhere in the usages and principles of law if, and to the extent that, the judge in the exercise of his discretion and for good cause shown grants leave to do so, but not otherwise. If necessary for effective utilization of discovery procedures, counsel shall be appointed by the judge for a movant who qualifies for appointment of counsel under 18 U.S.C. § 3006A(g).

(b) Requests for discovery. Requests for discovery shall be accompanied by a statement of the interrogatories or requests for admission and a list of the documents, if any, sought to be produced.

(c) Expenses. If the government is granted leave to take the deposition of the movant or any other person, the judge may as a condition of taking it direct that the government pay the expenses of travel and subsistence and fees of counsel for the movant to attend the taking of the disposition.

Rule 7. Expansion of Record

(a) Direction for expansion. If the motion is not dismissed summarily, the judge may direct that the record be expanded by the parties by the inclusion of additional materials relevant to the determination of the merits of the motion.

(b) Materials to be added. The expanded record may include, without limitation, letters predating the filing of the motion in the district court, documents, exhibits, and answers under oath, if so directed, to written interrogatories propounded by the judge. Affidavits may be submitted and considered as a part of the record.

(c) Submission to opposing party. In any case in which an expanded record is directed, copies of the letters, documents, exhibits, and affidavits proposed to be included shall be submitted to the party against whom they are to be offered, and he shall be afforded an opportunity to admit or deny their correctness.

(d) Authentication. The court may require the authentication of any material under subdivision (b) or (c).

Rule 8. Evidentiary Hearing

(a) Determination by court. If the motion has not been dismissed at a previous stage in the proceeding, the judge, after the answer is filed and any transcripts or records of prior court actions in the matter are in his possession, shall, upon a review of those proceedings and of the expanded record, if any, determine whether an evidentiary hearing is required. If it appears that an evidentiary hearing is not required, the judge shall make such disposition of the motion as justice dictates.

(b) Function of the magistrate.

(1) When designated to do so in accordance with 28 U.S.C. § 636 (b), a magistrate may conduct hearings, including evidentiary hearings, on the motion, and submit to a judge of the court proposed findings and recommendations for disposition.

(2) The magistrate shall file proposed findings and recommendations with the court and a copy shall forthwith be mailed to all parties.

(3) Within ten days after being served with a copy, any party may serve and file written objections to such proposed findings and recommendations as provided by rules of court.

(4) A judge of the court shall make a de novo determination of those portions of the report or specified proposed findings or recommendations to which objection is made. A judge of the court may accept, reject, or modify in whole or in part any findings or recommendations made by the magistrate.

(c) Appointment of counsel; time for hearing. If an evidentiary hearing is required, the judge shall appoint counsel for a movant who qualifies for the appointment of counsel under 18 U.S.C: § 3006A (g) and the hearing shall be conducted as promptly as practicable, having regard for the need of counsel for both parties for adequate time for investigation and preparation. These rules do not limit the appointment of counsel under 18 U.S.C. § 3006A at any stage of the proceeding if the interest of justice so requires.
As amended Pub.L. 94–426, § 2(6), Sept. 28, 1976, 90 Stat. 1335; Pub. L. 94–577, § 2(a)(2), (b)(2), Oct. 21, 1976, 90 Stat. 2730, 2731.

Rule 9. Delayed or Successive Motions

(a) Delayed motions. A motion for relief made pursuant to these rules may be dismissed if it appears that the government has been prejudiced in its ability to respond to the motion by delay in its filing unless the movant shows that it is based on grounds of which he could not have had knowledge by the exercise of reasonable diligence before the circumstances prejudicial to the government occurred.

(b) Successive motions. A second or successive motion may be dismissed if the judge finds that it fails to allege new or different grounds for relief and the prior determination was on the merits or, if new and different grounds are alleged, the judge finds that the failure of the movant to assert those grounds in a prior motion constituted an abuse of the procedure governed by these rules.
As amended Pub.L. 94–426, § 2(9), (10), Sept. 28, 1976, 90 Stat. 1335.

Rule 10. Powers of Magistrates

The duties imposed upon the judge of the district court by rules 2, 3, 4, 6, and 7 may be performed by a United States magistrate if and to the extent that he is so empowered by rule of the district court, and to the extent the district court has established standards and criteria for the performance of such duties, except that, when such duties involve the making of an order under rule 4 dismissing the motion, the magistrate shall submit to the court his report as to the facts and his recommendation with respect to the order to be made by the court.

As amended Pub.L. 94–426, § 2(12), Sept. 28, 1976, 90 Stat. 1335.

Rule 11. Time for Appeal

Nothing in these rules shall be construed as extending the time to appeal from the original judgment of conviction in the district court.

Rule 12. Federal Rules of Criminal and Civil Procedure; Extent of Applicability

If no procedure is specifically prescribed by these rules, the district court may proceed in any lawful manner not inconsistent with these rules, or any applicable statute, and may apply the Federal Rules of Criminal Procedure or the Federal Rules of Civil Procedure, whichever it deems most appropriate, to motions filed under these rules.

4. State Prisoners' Model Federal Court Habeas Forms

4a. Application for Habeas Corpus Under 28 U.S.C. §2254

Name _____ _____

Prison number _____ ._____

Place of confinement _____

_____

United States District Court _____ District of _____

Case No. _____. _____

(To be supplied by Clerk of U. S. District Court)

_____, **PETITIONER**

(Full name)

v.

_____, **RESPONDENT**

(Name of Warden, Superintendent, Jailor, or authorized person having custody of petitioner)

and

THE ATTORNEY GENERAL OF THE STATE OF _____

_____, **ADDITIONAL RESPONDENT.**

   (If petitioner is attacking a judgment which imposed a sentence to be served in the future, petitioner must fill in the name of the state where the judgment was entered. If petitioner has a sentence to be served in the future under a federal judgment which he wishes to attack, he should file a motion under 28 U.S.C. § 2255, in the federal court which entered the judgment.)

PETITION FOR WRIT OF HABEAS CORPUS BY A
PERSON IN STATE CUSTODY

Instructions.—Read Carefully

(1) This petition must be legibly handwritten or typewritten, and signed

by the petitioner under penalty of perjury. Any false statement of a material fact may serve as the basis for prosecution and conviction for perjury. All questions must be answered concisely in the proper space on the form.

(2) Additional pages are not permitted except with respect to the facts which you rely upon to support your grounds for relief. No citation of authorities need be furnished. If briefs or arguments are submitted, they should be submitted in the form of a separate memorandum.

(3) Upon receipt of a fee of $5 your petition will be filed if it is in proper order.

(4) If you do not have the necessary filing fee, you may request permission to proceed in forma pauperis, in which event you must execute the declaration on the last page, setting forth information establishing your inability to prepay the fees and costs or give security therefor. If you wish to proceed in forma pauperis, you must have an authorized officer at the penal institution complete the certificate as to the amount of money and securities on deposit to your credit in any account in the institution. If your prison account exceeds $_____, you must pay the filing fee as required by the rule of the district court.

(5) Only judgments entered by one court may be challenged in a single petition. If you seek to challenge judgments entered by different courts either in the same state or in different states, you must file separate petitions as to each court.

(6) Your attention is directed to the fact that you must include all grounds for relief and all facts supporting such grounds for relief in the petition you file seeking relief from any judgment of conviction.

(7) When the petition is fully completed, the original and two copies must be mailed to the Clerk of the United States District Court whose address is _____

_____

(8) Petitions which do not conform to these instructions will be returned with a notation as to the deficiency.

PETITION

1. Name and location of court which entered the judgment of conviction under attack _____

2. Date of judgment of conviction _____

3. Length of sentence _____

4. Nature of offense involved (all counts) _____

_____

_____

_____

5. What was your plea? (Check one)
    (a) Not guilty ☐
    (b) Guilty ☐
    (c) Nolo contendere ☐

If you entered a guilty plea to one count or indictment, and a not guilty plea to another count or indictment, give details:

_____

_____

6. Kind of trial: (Check one)
    (a) Jury ☐
    (b) Judge only ☐

7. Did you testify at the trial?
Yes ☐ No ☐

8. Did you appeal from the judgment of conviction?
Yes ☐ No ☐

9. If you did appeal, answer the following:
    (a) Name of court _____
    (b) Result _____
    (c) Date of result _____

10. Other than a direct appeal from the judgment of conviction and sentence, have you previously filed any petitions, applications, or motions with respect to this judgment in any court, state or federal?
Yes ☐ No ☐

11. If your answer to 10 was "yes," give the following information:
    (a)(1) Name of court _____
    (2) Nature of proceeding _____
    _____

    (3) Grounds raised _____
    _____
    _____
    _____

    (4) Did you receive an evidentiary hearing on your petition, application or motion?
Yes ☐ No ☐
    (5) Result _____
    (6) Date of result _____

    (b) As to any second petition, application or motion give the same information:
    (1) Name of court _____
    (2) Nature of proceeding _____
    _____

    (3) Grounds raised _____
    _____
    _____
    _____

    (4) Did you receive an evidentiary hearing on your petition, application or motion?
Yes ☐ No ☐
    (5) Result _____
    (6) Date of result _____

    (c) As to any third petition, application or motion, give the same information:

(1) Name of court _____

(2) Nature of proceeding _____

_____

(3) Grounds raised _____

_____

_____

_____

_____

(4) Did you receive an evidentiary hearing on your petition, application or motion?

Yes ☐ No ☐

(5) Result _____

(6) Date of result _____

(d) Did you appeal to the highest state court having jurisdiction the result of action taken on any petition, application or motion?

(1) First petition, etc.   Yes ☐   No ☐

(2) Second petition, etc.   Yes ☐   No ☐

(3) Third petition, etc.   Yes ☐   No ☐

(e) If you did not appeal from the adverse action on any petition, application or motion, explain briefly why you did not:

_____

_____

_____

12. State concisely every ground on which you claim that you are being held unlawfully. Summarize briefly the facts supporting each ground. If necessary, you may attach pages stating additional grounds and facts supporting same.

Caution: In order to proceed in the federal court, you must ordinarily first exhaust your state court remedies as to each ground on which you request action by the federal court. If you fail to set forth all grounds in this petition, you may be barred from presenting additional grounds at a later date.

For your information, the following is a list of the most frequently raised grounds for relief in habeas corpus proceedings. Each statement preceded by a letter constitutes a separate ground for possible relief. You may raise any grounds which you may have other than those listed if you have exhausted your state court remedies with respect to them. However, you should raise in this petition all available grounds (relating to this conviction) on which you base your allegations that you are being held in custody unlawfully.

Do not check any of these listed grounds. If you select one or more of these grounds for relief, you must allege facts. The petition will be returned to you if you merely check (a) through (j) or any one of these grounds.

(a) Conviction obtained by plea of guilty which was unlawfully induced or not made voluntarily with understanding of the nature of the charge and the consequences of the plea.

(b) Conviction obtained by use of coerced confession.

(c) Conviction obtained by use of evidence gained pursuant to an unconstitutional search and seizure.

(d) Conviction obtained by use of evidence obtained pursuant an unlawful arrest.

(e) Conviction obtained by a violation of the privilege against self-incrimination.

(f) Conviction obtained by the unconstitutional failure of the prosecution to disclose to the defendant evidence favorable to the defendant.

(g) Conviction obtained by a violation of the protection against double jeopardy.

(h) Conviction obtained by action of a grand or petit jury which was unconstitutionally selected and impaneled.

(i) Denial of effective assistance of counsel.

(j) Denial of right of appeal.

A. Ground one: _____

Supporting FACTS (tell your story *briefly* without citing cases or law): _____

_____
_____
_____
_____
_____
_____

B. Ground two: _____

Supporting FACTS (tell your story *briefly* without citing cases or law): _____

_____
_____
_____
_____
_____

C. Ground three: _____

Supporting FACTS (tell your story *briefly* without citing cases or law): _____

_____
_____
_____
_____
_____
_____

D. Ground four: _____

Supporting FACTS (tell your story *briefly* without citing cases or law): _____

_____
_____
_____
_____
_____

13. If any of the grounds listed in 12A, B, C, and D were not previously presented in any other court, state or federal, state *briefly* what grounds were not so presented and give your reasons for not presenting them:

_____
_____
_____
_____

14. Do you have any petition or appeal now pending in any court, either state or federal, as to the judgment under attack?
Yes ☐ No ☐

15. Give the name and address, if known, of each attorney who represented you in the following stages of the judgment attacked herein:

    (a) At preliminary hearing _____
_____

    (b) At arraignment and plea _____
_____

    (c) At trial _____
_____

    (d) At sentencing _____
_____

    (e) On appeal _____
_____

    (f) In any post-conviction proceeding _____
_____

    (g) On appeal from any adverse ruling in a post-conviction proceeding _____
_____
_____

16. Were you sentenced on more than one count of an indictment, or on more than one indictment, in the same court and at the same time?
Yes ☐ No ☐

17. Do you have any future sentence to serve after you complete the sentence imposed by the judgment under attack?
Yes ☐ No ☐

    (a) If so, give name and location of court which imposed sentence to be served in the future: _____
_____

    (b) And give date and length of sentence to be served in the future: _____
_____

    (c) Have you filed, or do you contemplate filing, any petition attacking the judgment which imposed the sentence to be served in the future?
Yes ☐ No ☐

Wherefore, petitioner prays that the Court grant petitioner relief to which he may be entitled in this proceeding.

Signature of Attorney (if any)

I declare (or certify, verify, or state) under penalty of perjury that the foregoing is true and correct.   Executed on _____.

(date)

Signature of Petitioner

4b. In Forma Pauperis Declaration

[Insert appropriate court]

DECLARATION IN SUPPORT
OF REQUEST
TO PROCEED
IN FORMA PAUPERIS

(Petitioner)
v.

(Respondent(s))

I, _____, declare that I am the petitioner in the above entitled case; that in support of my motion to proceed without being required to prepay fees, costs or give security therefor, I state that because of my poverty I am unable to pay the costs of said proceeding or to give security therefor; that I believe I am entitled to relief.

1. Are you presently employed? Yes ☐ No ☐
    a. If the answer is "yes," state the amount of your salary or wages per month, and give the name and address of your employer.

    _____   _____

    b. If the answer is "no," state the date of last employment and the amount of the salary and wages per month which you received.

    _____   _____

2. Have you received within the past twelve months any money from any of the following sources?
    a. Business, profession or form of self-employ-
        ment?   Yes ☐ No ☐
    b. Rent payments, interest or dividends?   Yes ☐ No ☐
    c. Pensions, annuities or life insurance pay-
        ments?   Yes ☐ No ☐
    d. Gifts or inheritances?   Yes ☐ No ☐
    e. Any other sources?   Yes ☐ No ☐

    If the answer to any of the above is "yes," describe each source of money and state the amount received from each during the past twelve months. _____

_____
_____
_____
_____

3. Do you own cash, or do you have money in checking or savings account?
   Yes ☐ No ☐ (include any funds in prison accounts.)
   If the answer is "yes," state the total value of the items owned.

_____
_____

4. Do you own any real estate, stocks, bonds, notes, automobiles, or other valuable property (excluding ordinary household furnishings and clothing)?
   Yes ☐ No ☐
   If the answer is "yes," describe the property and state its approximate value. _____

_____
_____

5. List the persons who are dependent upon you for support, state your relationship to those persons, and indicate how much you contribute toward their support. _____

_____

I declare (or certify, verify, or state) under penalty of perjury that the foregoing is true and correct. Executed on _____.

(date)

_____
Signature of Petitioner

Certificate

I hereby certify that the petitioner herein has the sum of $_____ on account to his credit at the _____ institution where he is confined. I further certify that petitioner likewise has the following securities to his credit according to the records of said _____ institution: _____

_____
_____
_____

_____
Authorized Officer of
. Institution

4c. Rule 9 Response in 28 U.S.C. §2254 Cases

Form No. 9

United States District Court,
_____ District of _____

Case No. _____
_____, PETITIONER

v.

_____, RESPONDENT

and

————————————, ADDITIONAL RESPONDENT
Petitioner's Response as to Why His Petition Should
Not Be Barred Under Rule 9

Explanation and Instructions—Read Carefully

(I) Rule 9. Delayed or successive petitions.

(a) Delayed petitions. A petition may be dismissed if it appears that the state of which the respondent is an officer has been prejudiced in its ability to respond to the petition by delay in its filing unless the petitioner shows that it is based on grounds of which he could not have had knowledge by the exercise of reasonable diligence before the circumstances prejudicial to the state occurred.

(b) Successive petitions. A second or successive petition may be dismissed if the judge finds that it fails to allege new or different grounds for relief and the prior determination was on the merits or, if new and different grounds are alleged, the judge finds that the failure of the petitioner to assert those grounds in a prior petition constituted an abuse of the writ.

(II) Your petition for habeas corpus has been found to be subject to dismissal under rule 9 (   ) for the following reasons(s):

————————————————————————————————
————————————————————————————————
————————————————————————————————
————————————————————————————————

(III) This form has been sent so that you may explain why your petition contains the defect(s) noted in (II) above. It is required that you fill out this form and send it back to the court within ———— days. Failure to do so will result in the automatic dismissal of your petition.

(IV) When you have fully completed this form, the original and two copies must be mailed to the Clerk of the United States District Court whose address is ——————————————————
————————————————————————————————

(V) This response must be legibly handwritten or typewritten, and signed by the petitioner under penalty of perjury. Any false statement of a material fact may serve as the basis for prosecution and conviction for perjury. All questions must be answered concisely in the proper space on the form.

(VI) Additional pages are not permitted except with respect to the *facts* which you rely upon in item 4 or 5 in the response. Any citation of authorities should be kept to an absolute minimum and is only appropriate if there has been a change in the law since the judgment you are attacking was rendered.

(VII) Respond to 4 *or* 5 below, not to both, unless (II) above indicates that you must answer both sections.

RESPONSE

1. Have you had the assistance of an attorney, other law-trained personnel, or writ writers since the conviction your petition is attacking was entered?
   Yes ☐   No ☐

2. If you checked "yes" above, specify as precisely as you can the period(s) of time during which you received such assistance, up to and including the present. _____

_____

3. Describe the nature of the assistance, including the names of those who rendered it to you. _____

_____

_____

_____

4. If your petition is in jeopardy because of delay prejudicial to the state under rule 9(a), explain why you feel the delay has not been prejudicial and/or why the delay is excusable under the terms of 9(a). This should be done by relying upon FACTS, not your opinions or conclusions. _____

_____

_____

_____

_____

5. If your petition is in jeopardy under rule 9(b) because it asserts the same grounds as a previous petition, explain why you feel it deserves a reconsideration. If its fault under rule 9(b) is that it asserts new grounds which should have been included in a prior petition, explain why you are raising these grounds now rather than previously. Your explanation should rely on FACTS, not your opinions or conclusions. _____

_____

_____

_____

_____

_____

_____

I declare (or certify, verify, or state) under penalty of perjury that the foregoing is true and correct. Executed on _____.

(date)

_____

Signature of Petitioner

5. Federal Prisoners' Model Post-Conviction Forms

5a. Motion Under 28 U.S.C. §2255

Name _____

Prison Number _____

Place of Confinement _____

United States District Court _____ District of _____

Case No. _____ (to be supplied by Clerk of U. S. District Court)

United States,

v.

_____

(full name of movant)

(If movant has a sentence to be served in the future under a federal judgment which he wishes to attack, he should file a motion in the federal court which entered the judgment.)

MOTION TO VACATE, SET ASIDE, OR CORRECT SENTENCE BY A PERSON IN FEDERAL CUSTODY

(1) This motion must be legibly handwritten or typewritten, and signed by the movant under penalty of perjury. Any false statement of a material fact may serve as the basis for prosecution and conviction for perjury. All questions must be answered concisely in the proper space on the form.

(2) Additional pages are not permitted except with respect to the facts which you rely upon to support your grounds for relief. No citation of authorities need be furnished. If briefs or arguments are submitted, they should be submitted in the form of a separate memorandum.

(3) Upon receipt, your motion will be filed if it is in proper order. No fee is required with this motion.

(4) If you do not have the necessary funds for transcripts, counsel, appeal, and other costs connected with a motion of this type, you may request permission to proceed in forma pauperis, in which event you must execute the declaration on the last page, setting forth information establishing your inability to pay the costs. If you wish to proceed in forma pauperis, you must have an authorized officer at the penal institution complete the certificate as to the amount of money and securities on deposit to your credit in any account in the institution.

(5) Only judgments entered by one court may be challenged in a single motion. If you seek to challenge judgments entered by different judges or divisions either in the same district or in different districts, you must file separate motions as to each such judgment.

(6) Your attention is directed to the fact that you must include all grounds for relief and all facts supporting such grounds for relief in the motion you file seeking relief from any judgment of conviction.

(7) When the motion is fully completed, the original and two copies must be mailed to the Clerk of the United States District Court whose address is _____

(8) Motions which do not conform to these instructions will be returned with a notation as to the deficiency.

MOTION

1. Name and location of court which entered the judgment of conviction under attack _____

2. Date of judgment of conviction _____

3. Length of sentence _____

4. Nature of offense involved (all counts) _____

5.   What was your plea?   (Check one)
     (a) Not guilty   ☐
     (b) Guilty   ☐
     (c) Nolo contendere   ☐
     If you entered a guilty plea to one count or indictment, and a not guilty plea to another count or indictment, give details:

_____

_____

_____

6.   Kind of trial: (Check one)
     (a) Jury   ☐
     (b) Judge only   ☐

7.   Did you testify at the trial?
     Yes ☐   No ☐

8.   Did you appeal from the judgment of conviction?
     Yes ☐   No ☐

9.   If you did appeal, answer the following:
     (a) Name of court _____
     (b) Result _____
     (c) Date of result _____

10.   Other than a direct appeal from the judgment of conviction and sentence, have you previously filed any petitions, applications or motions with respect to this judgment in any federal court?
     Yes ☐   No ☐

11.   If your answer to 10 was "yes," give the following information:
     (a) (1) Name of court _____
         (2) Nature of proceeding _____

         (3) Grounds raised _____

_____

_____

_____

         (4) Did you receive an evidentiary hearing on your petition, application or motion?
            Yes ☐   No ☐
         (5) Result _____
         (6) Date of result _____
     (b) As to any second petition, application or motion give the same information:
         (1) Name of court _____
         (2) Nature of proceeding _____

         (3) Grounds raised _____

_____

_____

_____

         (4) Did you receive an evidentiary hearing on your petition, application or motion?
            Yes ☐   No ☐
         (5) Result _____

(6) Date of result _____

(c) As to any third petition, application or motion, give the same information:
    (1) Name of court _____
    (2) Nature of proceeding _____
    _____

    (3) Grounds raised _____
    _____
    _____
    _____
    _____

    (4) Did you receive an evidentiary hearing on your petition, application or motion?
    Yes ☐ No ☐

(d) Did you appeal, to an appellate federal court having jurisdiction, the result of action taken on any petition, application or motion?
    (1) First petition, etc.   Yes ☐ No ☐
    (2) Second petition, etc. Yes ☐ No ☐
    (3) Third petition, etc.   Yes ☐ No ☐

(e) If you did not appeal from the adverse action on any petition, application or motion, explain briefly why you did not·
_____
_____
_____

12. State concisely every ground on which you claim that you are being held unlawfully. Summarize briefly the fact supporting each ground. If necessary, you may attach pages stating additional grounds and facts supporting same.

    Caution: If you fail to set forth all grounds in this motion, you may be barred from presenting additional grounds at a later date.

    For your information, the following is a list of the most frequently raised grounds for relief in these proceedings. Each statement preceded by a letter constitutes a separate ground for possible relief. You may raise any grounds which you have other than those listed. However, you should raise in this motion all available grounds (relating to this conviction) on which you based your allegations that you are being held in custody unlawfully.

Do not check any of these listed grounds. If you select one or more of these grounds for relief, you must allege facts. The motion will be returned to you if you merely check (a) through (j) or any one of the grounds.

    (a) Conviction obtained by plea of guilty which was unlawfully induced or not made voluntarily or with understanding of the nature of the charge and the consequences of the plea.
    (b) Conviction obtained by use of coerced confession.
    (c) Conviction obtained by use of evidence gained pursuant to an unconstitutional search and seizure.
    (d) Conviction obtained by use of evidence obtained pursuant to an unlawful arrest.

(e) Conviction obtained by a violation of the privilege against self-incrimination.

(f) Conviction obtained by the unconstitutional failure of the prosecution to disclose to the defendant evidence favorable to the defendant.

(g) Conviction obtained by a violation of the protection against double jeopardy.

(h) Conviction obtained by action of a grand or petit jury which was unconstitutionally selected and impanelled.

(i) Denial of effective assistance of counsel.

(j) Denial of right of appeal.

A. Ground one: _____

Supporting FACTS (tell your story briefly without citing cases or law): _____
_____
_____
_____
_____
_____

B. Ground two: _____

Supporting FACTS (tell your story briefly without citing cases or law): _____
_____
_____
_____
_____

C. Ground three: _____

Supporting FACTS (tell your story briefly without citing cases or law): _____
_____
_____
_____
_____

D. Ground four: _____

Supporting FACTS (tell your story briefly without citing cases or law): _____
_____
_____
_____
_____

13. If any of the grounds listed in 12A, B, C, and D were not previously presented, state briefly what grounds were not so presented, and give your reasons for not presenting them: _____

_____

_____

_____

14. Do you have any petition or appeal now pending in any court as to the judgment under attack?
    Yes ☐ No ☐

15. Give the name and address, if known, of each attorney who represented you in the following stages of the judgment attacked herein:

    (a) At preliminary hearing _____

    _____

    (b) At arraignment and plea _____

    _____

    (c) At trial _____

    _____

    (d) At sentencing _____

    _____

    (e) On appeal _____

    _____

    (f) In any post-conviction proceeding _____

    _____

    (g) On appeal from any adverse ruling in a post-conviction proceeding _____

    _____

16. Were you sentenced on more than one count of an indictment, or on more than one indictment, in the same court and at approximately the same time?
    Yes ☐ No ☐

17. Do you have any future sentence to serve after you complete the sentence imposed by the judgment under attack?
    Yes ☐ No ☐

    (a) If so, give name and location of court which imposed sentence to be served in the future: _____

    _____

    (b) And give date and length of sentence to be served in the future: _____

    _____

    (c) Have you filed, or do you contemplate filing, any petition attacking the judgment which imposed the sentence to be served in the future?
        Yes ☐ No ☐

Wherefore, movant prays that the Court grant him all relief to which he may be entitled in this proceeding.

_____

Signature of Attorney (if any)

I declare (or certify, verify, or state) under penalty of perjury that the foregoing is true and correct. Executed on _____.

(date)

_____

Signature of Movant

5b. In Forma Pauperis Declaration

_____

[Insert appropriate court]

United States
v.
_____
(Movant)

DECLARATION IN SUPPORT
OF REQUEST
TO PROCEED
IN FORMA PAUPERIS

I, _____, declare that I am the movant in the above entitled case; that in support of my motion to proceed without being required to prepay fees, costs or give security therefor, I state that because of my poverty, I am unable to pay the costs of said proceeding or to give security therefor; that I believe I am entitled to relief.

1. Are you presently employed? Yes ☐ No ☐
    a. If the answer is "yes," state the amount of your salary or wages per month, and give the name and address of your employer.

    _____
    _____

    b. If the answer is "no," state the date of last employment and the amount of the salary and wages per month which you received.

    _____
    _____

2. Have you received within the past twelve months any money from any of the following sources?
    a. Business, profession or form of self-employment? Yes ☐ No ☐
    b. Rent payments, interest or dividends? Yes ☐ No ☐
    c. Pensions, annuities or life insurance payments? Yes ☐ No ☐
    d. Gifts or inheritances? Yes ☐ No ☐
    e. Any other sources? Yes ☐ No ☐

    If the answer to any of the above is "yes," describe each source of money and state the amount received from each during the past twelve months. _____
    _____
    _____
    _____

3. Do you own any cash, or do you have money in a checking or savings account?
    Yes ☐ No ☐ (Include any funds in prison accounts)
    If the answer is "yes," state the total value of the items owned.

    _____
    _____

4. Do you own real estate, stocks, bonds, notes, automobiles, or other

valuable property (excluding ordinary household furnishings and clothing)?
Yes ☐ No ☐
If the answer is "yes," describe the property and state its approximate value. _____

_____
_____

5. List the persons who are dependent upon you for support, state your relationship to those persons, and indicate how much you contribute toward their support. _____

_____
_____

I declare (or certify, verify, or state) under penalty of perjury that the foregoing is true and correct. Executed on _____.

(date)

_____
Signature of Movant

CERTIFICATE

I hereby certify that the movant herein has the sum of $_____ on account to his credit at the _____ institution where he is confined.

I further certify that movant likewise has the following securities to his credit according to the records of said _____ institution: _____

_____
_____
_____
_____

_____
Authorized Officer of
Institution

5c. Rule 9 Response in 28 U.S.C. §2255 Cases

Form No. 9
United States District Court
_____ District of _____
Case No. _____
United States
v.

_____
(Name of Movant)

*Movant's Response as to Why His Motion Should
Not be Barred Under Rule 9*

Explanation and Instructions—Read Carefully

(I) Rule 9. Delayed or Successive Motions.

(a) Delayed motions. A motion for relief made pursuant to these rules may be dismissed if it appears that the government has been prejudiced in its ability to respond to the motion by delay in its filing unless the movant shows that it is based on grounds of which he could not have had knowledge by the exercise of reasonable diligence before the circumstances prejudicial to the government occurred.

   (b) Successive Motions. A second or successive motion may be dismissed if the judge finds that it fails to allege new or different grounds for relief and the prior determination was on the merits or, if new and different grounds are alleged, the judge finds that the failure of the movant to assert those grounds in a prior motion constituted an abuse of the procedure governed by these rules.

(II) Your motion to vacate, set aside, or correct sentence has been found to be subject to dismissal under rule 9 (   ) for the following reason(s): _____

_____

_____

_____

(III) This form has been sent so that you may explain why your motion contains the defect(s) noted in (II) above. It is required that you fill out this form and send it back to the court within _____ days. Failure to do so will result in the automatic dismissal of your motion.

(IV) When you have fully completed this form, the original and two copies must be mailed to the Clerk of the United States District Court whose address is _____

_____

(V) This response must be legibly handwritten or typewritten, and signed by the movant under penalty of perjury. Any false statement of a material fact may serve as the basis for prosecution and conviction for perjury. All questions must be answered concisely in the proper space on the form.

(VI) Additional pages are not permitted except with respect to the facts which you rely upon in item 4 or 5 in the response. Any citation of authorities should be kept to an absolute minimum and is only appropriate if there has been a change in the law since the judgment you are attacking was rendered.

(VII) Respond to 4 or 5, not to both, unless (II) above indicates that you must answer both sections.

RESPONSE

1. Have you had the assistance of an attorney, other law-trained personnel, or writ writers since the conviction your motion is attacking was entered?
    Yes ☐   No ☐

2. If you checked "yes" above, specify as precisely as you can the period(s) of time during which you received such assistance, up to and including the present. _____

_____

3. Describe the nature of the assistance, including the names of those who rendered it to you. _____

_____

_____

4. If your motion is in jeopardy because of delay prejudicial to the government under rule 9(a), explain why you feel the delay has not been prejudicial and/or why the delay is excusable under the terms of 9(a). This should be done by relying upon FACTS, not your opinions or conclusions. _____

_____
_____
_____
_____

5. If your motion is in jeopardy under rule 9(b) because it asserts the same grounds as a previous motion, explain why you feel it deserves a reconsideration. If its fault under rule 9(b) is that it asserts new grounds which should have been included in a prior motion, explain why you are raising these grounds now rather than previously. Your explanation should rely on FACTS, not your opinions or conclusions. _____

_____
_____
_____
_____
_____
_____
_____

   I declare (or certify, verify, or state) under penalty of perjury that the foregoing is true and correct. Executed on _____.

                                                  (date)

                                        _____
                                        Signature of Movant

As amended Apr. 28, 1982, eff. Aug. 1, 1982.

   (I) Rule 9. Delayed or Successive Motions.

   (a) Delayed motions. A motion for relief made pursuant to these rules may be dismissed if it appears that the government has been prejudiced in its ability to respond to the motion by delay in its filing unless the movant shows that it is based on grounds of which he could not have had knowledge by the exercise of reasonable diligence before the circumstances prejudicial to the government occurred. If the motion is filed more than five years after the judgment of conviction, there shall be a presumption, rebuttable by the movant, that there is prejudice to the government.

   (b) Successive motions. A second or successive motion may be dismissed if the judge finds that it fails to allege new or different grounds for relief and the prior determination was on the merits or, if new and different grounds are alleged, the judge finds that the failure of the movant to assert those grounds in a prior motion is not excusable.

   (II) Your motion to vacate, set aside, or correct sentence has been found to be subject to dismissal under rule 9( ) for the following reason(s): _____

_____

(III) This form has been sent so that you may explain why your motion contains the defect(s) noted in (II) above. It is required that you fill out this form and send it back to the court within _____ days. Failure to do so will result in the automatic dismissal of your motion.

(IV) When you have fully completed this form, the original and two copies must be mailed to the Clerk of the United States District Court whose address is _____

(V) This response must be legibly handwritten or typewritten, signed by the movant, and sworn to before a notary public or institutional officer authorized to administer an oath. Any false statement of a material fact may serve as the basis for prosecution and conviction for perjury. All questions must be answered concisely in the proper space on the form.

(VI) Additional pages are not permitted except with respect to the *facts* which you rely upon in item 4 or 5 in the response. Any citation of authorities should be kept to an absolute minimum and is only appropriate if there has been a change in the law since the judgment you are attacking was rendered.   -

(VII) Respond to 4 *or* 5, not to both, unless (II) above indicates that you must answer both sections.

RESPONSE

1. Have you had the assistance of an attorney, other law-trained personnel, or writ writers since the conviction your motion is attacking was entered?
   Yes ☐ No ☐

2. If you checked "yes" above, specify as precisely as you can the period(s) of time during which you received such assistance, up to and including the present. _____

3. Describe the nature of the assistance, including the names of those who rendered it to you. _____

4. If your motion is in jeopardy because of delay prejudicial to the government under rule 9(a), explain why you feel the delay has not been prejudicial and/or why the delay is excusable under the terms of 9(a). This should be done by relying upon FACTS, not your opinions or conclusions. _____

5. If your motion is in jeopardy under rule 9(b) because it asserts the same grounds as a previous motion, explain why you feel it deserves a reconsideration. If its fault under rule 9(b) is that it asserts new grounds which should have been included in a prior motion, explain why you are raising these grounds now rather than previously. Your explanation should rely on FACTS, not your opinions or conclusions. _____

_____
_____
_____
_____
_____
_____
_____
_____

State of _____
County (City) of _____ ___
_____, being first duly sworn under oath, presents
(Name of Movant)
that he has read and subscribed to the above and states that the information therein is true and correct.

_____
Signature of Movant
(Required as to each
movant)

Subscribed and sworn to before me this _____ day of
_____, 19___.

_____
Notary Public or other
person authorized to
administer an oath

6. Notice of Appeal From a Judgment/Order of a District Court in a Post-Conviction Proceeding

(CAPTION)

NOTICE OF APPEAL

PLEASE TAKE NOTICE that the above petitioner appeals to the United States Court of Appeals for the Sixth[1] Circuit from the order entered March 31, 1983, dismissing petitioner's petition for writ of habeas corpus brought pursuant to 28 U.S.C. § 2254.[2]

_____
Name
Address

_____
[1] You would place the number of the circuit in which your prison is located.
[2] A federal prisoner would list § 2255.

7. Habeas Corpus Petition
7a. Petition for Writ of Habeas Corpus

The following petition and brief are sample documents. The statement of the procedures used in the case is not the procedures used in evey state.

a.   Petition for Writ of Habeas Corpus

IN THE UNITED STATE DISTRICT COURT
FOR THE EASTERN DISTRICT OF MICHIGAN

DANIEL E. MANVILLE,
P.O. Box E - 135706
Attica, N.Y. 14011

Petitioner,

-v-   C.A. No.

BARRY POGATS, Warden,
State Prison of South-
ern Michigan, Jackson,
Michigan 49204,

Respondent.
_____/

PETITION FOR WRIT OF HABEAS CORPUS

Petitioner Daniel E. Manville, pursuant to 28 U.S.C. §2254, seeks a writ of habeas corpus and states:

1.   Petitioner is presently in the custody of the Michigan Department of Corrections and is confined at the State Prison of Southern Michigan, Jackson.(SPSM).

2.   Petitioner is presently unconstitutionally detained and imprisoned at Michigan State Prison by Barry Pogats, Warden, by virtue of a judgment and sentence of four years, pronounced by the Honorable Judge Edward, Circuit Court Judge of Isabella County, Mt. Pleasant, Michigan, on June 17, 1980, for the conviction by guilty plea of manslaughter, M.C.L.A. §790.123.

3.   Petitioner has exhausted all adequate and currently available state remedies in the following manner:

   a)   Petitioner filed an appeal as of right which was denied by the Court of Appeals of Michigan on September 28, 1982, for lack of merit on the grounds presented.

   b)   Petitioner filed an application for leave to appeal his conviction in the Michigan Supreme Court which leave to appeal was denied on November 28, 1982.

4.   Petitioner is imprisoned pursuant to an illegal and void sentence because his guilty plea was constitutionally defective for the following reasons:

   a)   The trial court committed reversible error when it decided not to carry out the plea bargain agreement reached between the prosecutor and defense counsel and refused petitioner's timely request to withdraw his guilty plea. See Affidavit of Petitioner and Exhibit A attached.

   b)   The guilty plea was the result of beatings and threats petitioner received from police officers and inmates at the county jail. See Petitioner's Affidavit and Exhibit B attached.

   c)   The trial court committed reversible error when it failed to advise petitioner of the consequences of his pleas as required by law.

   d)   The trial court committed reversible error when it failed to advise petitioner of the constitutional rights he would waive by pleading guilty.

   e)   The trial court committed reversible error when it failed to advise petitioner of the minimum and maximum sentence he could receive by pleading guilty.

5.   Petitioner is innocent of the crime for which he was charged, and to which he pled guilty.

6.   Petitioner is imprisoned prusuant to a sentence that is illegal and void for the reasons presented above and those set forth in the Brief in Support of the Petition for Habeas Corpus, in

Petitioner's Affidavit, and in the Exhibits attached hereto, all of which are incorporated by reference herein.

WHEREFORE, Petitioner respectfully requests:

A.   That Respondent be required to appear and answer the allegations of this petition.

B.   That after full consideration this court relieve Petitioner of the unconstitutional restraint on his liberty by issuing a writ of habeas corpus. .

C.   That this court declare Petitioner's guilty plea and conviction void.

D.   That this Court grant reasonable bond so that Petitioner does not have to remain confined under an illegal sentence.

E.   That the Court, if necessary, grant an evidentiary hearing.

F.   That this Court grant such other, further and different relief as it may deem just and proper.

> Respectfully submitted,
> Name
> Address

* I declare (or certify, verify, or state) under penalty of perjury that the foregoing is true and correct. Executed on ____ ___date___ .

_____
Signature

7b. Brief in Support of Petition for Writ of Habeas Corpus

[CAPTION]

BRIEF IN SUPPORT OF
PETITION FOR WRIT OF HABEAS CORPUS

[You should prepare a cover page with just the caption, the title of what you are filing, and your name and address down in the right hand corner. The next page would contain the "Table of Contents," see example below.

TABLE OF CONTENTS

[For examples of a Table of Contents, see Appenidx B, Forms 13 and 21, supra.]

Statement of Issues Presented

I.   IS THE WRIT OF HABEAS CORPUS UNDER 28 U.S.C. §THE PROPER REMEDY FOR SETTING ASIDE PETITIONER'S GUILTY PLEA?

Petitioner answers YES.

II. IS A GUILTY PLEA VOLUNTARILY AND INTELLIGENTLY ENTERED WHEN THE TRIAL COURT DOES NOT ADVISE THE DEFENDANT OF SPECIFIC CONSTITUTIONAL RIGHTS HE WAIVES BY PLEADING GUILTY?

Petitioner answers NO.

[You would list all of the issues you will present in the brief here in question form.]

Statement of the Case

[For examples of Statement of The Case, see Appendix B, Forms 13 and 21, infra. In a Statement of the Case you will first list the procedural history of the case to date and then the facts upon which the issues are based.]

Summary of the Arguments

Petitioner alleges that his guilty plea was the result of a plea agreement with the prosecutor that was not followed by the sentencing judge. When petitioner sought to withdraw his guilty plea before sentence was imposed, the sentencing judge denied his request. Petitioner also alleges that his guilty plea was not voluntarily and

intelligently made insofar as the trial court did not advise him of
the constitutional rights he would waive by pleading guilty. Finally,
petitioner alleges that his guilty plea resulted from beatings, coercion,
intimidation, and threats, and consequently, was not entered voluntarily
and intelligently.

Arguments

I. A GUILTY PLEA IS NOT VOLUNTARILY AND INTELLIGENTLY
    ENTERED WHEN THE TRIAL COURT DOES NOT ADVISE THE DE-
    FENDANT OF THE SPECIFIC CONSTITUTIONAL RIGHTS HE
    WAIVES BY PLEADING GUILTY.

It is well-settled law that a defendant's guilty plea is only
properly accepted upon satisfaction of the requisites of Boykin v.
Alabama, 395 U.S. 238 (1969). Boykin established that a guilty plea
must be intelligently and voluntarily entered and that the record
must affirmately disclose that the accused entered his/her plea
understandingly and voluntarily. Brady v. United States, 387 U.S.
742 (1970).

Boykin requires that in order for a guilty plea to be made
intelligently and voluntarily, the record must affirmately reveal
that the accused voluntarily waived his privileged against compulsory
self-incrimination, the right to trial by jury, and the right to confront one's accusers. Boykin v. Alabama, at 243. "Presuming waiver
from a silent record is impermissible." Id. at 242.

Before accepting a defendant's plea of guilty the trial judge
must "canvass[ ]the matter with the accused to make sure he has a
full understanding of what the plea connotes and of its consequences.
When the judge discharges that function, he leaves a record adequate
for any review that may be later sought...." Id. at 244 (citations
omitted.) The trial judge must undertake a factual inquiry to
determine if the plea is voluntarily made with an understanding of
the nature of the charge and consequences of the plea.

Failure of a judge to engage in such colloquy with an accused
is fatal error and must result in reversal of conviction. Id. at 245.

Acceptance of petitioner's guilty plea as to the manslaughter
charge lodged against him violated his constitutional rights and was
imporper because the requirements of Boykin v. Alabama, and the case
law of the federal courts of Michigan were not satisified by the trial
court when he accepted petitioner's plea of guilty. Consequently,
petitioner's conviction on the manslaughter charge must be reversed
by this Honorable Court for the following reasons.

The record of the proceedings against the petitioner in each
of the cases against him is completely devoid of any colloquy between the judge and the petitioner which is necessary to show compliance
with Boykin and numerous other cases concerning this issue.

The only record of petitioner's entry of a guilty plea to the
charge against him is found in the minute entries of the "Case Action
Summary-----Criminal" for his case. See Petitioner's Exhibit G attached.
The revelant entry reads as follows:

[You would place the relevant portions here.]

The minute entry described above does not disclose the judge
"canvassing the matter with the accused to make sure he has a full
understanding of what the plea connotes and of its consequences."
Boykin v. Alabama, Id. at 244.

Because of the case against petitioner does not
"affirmative reveal" that he voluntarily waived his constitutional
privilege against compulsory self-incrimination, right to trial by
jury, and right to confront his accusers, his criminal conviction
must be reversed based on the authority of Boykin v. Alabama.

[Your other arguments would be presented in a similar
manner.

Relief Requested

[For examples of how to frame your relief, see Appendix B,
Forms 13 and 21, supra.]

                        Respectfully submitted,

                        Name
                        Address

8. Habeas Corpus Cover Letter to the Clerk

February 1, 1983

Daniel E. Manville
P.O. Box E - 135706
Jackson, MI. 49204

Dear Clerk:

Please find enclosed an original and three copies of the following: Petition for Writ of Habeas Corpus, Motion for Leave to Proceed In Forma Pauperis and Declaration in Support, Motion for Appointment of Counsel, and Proof of Service, for filing.

Once the Petition has been filed please return the copy of each of the above pleadings marked "Petitioner's File Copy."

Thank you.

Sincerely,

Name
Address

9. Motion for Leave to Proceed In Forma Pauperis

[CAPTION]

MOTION FOR LEAVE TO PROCEED IN FORMA PAUPERIS

Petitioner Daniel E. Manville requests this Court to grant him leave to file the attached Petition for Writ of Habeas Corpus without prepayment of costs and to proceed in forma pauperis. A declaration in support is attached.

Name
Address

10. In Forma Pauperis Declaration

See Appenidx C, Form 4a, supra, for a sample of an in forma pauperis declaration; see also Appendix B, Form 2b, supra.

11. Proof of Service/Certification of Service

See Appenidx B, Form 17, for a sample proof of service.

12. Request for Counsel

For a discussion of appointment of counsel in a habeas matter, see Ch. IX, Sec. E5.

12a. Motion for Appointment of Counsel

[CAPTION]

Petitioner Daniel E. Manville, pursuant to 18 U.S.C. & 3006A(g), requests this Court to appoint counsel to represent him in this habeas petition for the following reasons:

1. Plaintiff is not able to afford counsel, see the motion
to proceed in forma pauperis and affidavit in support filed with
this court.
2. The issues involved in this case are complex.
3. The issues involved in this case will require investigation
which the petitioner cannot do while confied in prison.
4. The prison limits the hours that the petitioner may have
access to the law library and the law materials contained there are
very limited.
5. Petitioner has a very limited knowledge of the law.
6. The end of justice would best be served in this case if an
attorney was appointed to represent the petitioner.

_____
Name
Address

12b. Brief in Support of Appointment of Counsel

[CAPTION]

Petitioner has requested this Court to appoint counsel to
represent him concerning the attached Petition for Writ of Habeas
Corpus. The Court has discretion pursuant to 18 U.S.C. § 3006A(g)
to appoint counsel concering matters brought pursuant to 28 U.S.C.
§§ 2241, 2254, 2255. For the reasons stated in petitioner's motin
for appointment of counsel and based on the allegations contained in
his petition this Court should appoint counsel.

Name
Address

13. Motion for Certification of Probable Cause of Appeal for Use in 28 U.S.C. §2254 Cases

[CAPTION]

MOTION FOR CERTIFICATE OF PROBABLE CAUSE AND
APPOINTMENT OF COUNSEL
_____

Daniel E. Manville requests this Court to issue a certificate
of probable cause in the above-entitled matter so that he may appeal
his denial of his writ of habeas corpus, dated March 31, 1983. In
support of his motion, he states

1. Petitioner has raised a substantial issue concerning
whether his guilty plea was voluntary or coerced. See discussion
in the district court's opinion, pp. 7-10.
2. Petitioner should be allowed to have the denial of the
Writ of Habeas Corpus reviewed by the Sixth Circuit Court of Appeals.

_____
Name
Address

14. Writ of Habeas Corpus Ad Testificandum and Order

See Appendix B, Form 9b, for a sample of a petition for writ
of habeas corpus ad testificandum and order.

Appendix D
Detainers

1. Interstate Agreement on Detainers (IAD)

The contracting states solemnly agree that:

Article I

The party states find that charges outstanding against a prisoner, detainers based on untried indictments, informations or complaints, and difficulties in securing speedy trial of persons already incarcerated in other jurisdictions, produce uncertainties which obstruct programs of prisoner treatment and rehabilitation. Accordingly, it is the policy of the party states and the purpose of this agreement to encourage the expeditious and orderly disposition of such charges and determination of the proper status of any and all detainers based on untried indictments, informations or complaints. The party states also find that proceedings with reference to such charges and detainers, when emanating from another jurisdiction, cannot properly be had in the absence of cooperative procedures. It is the further purpose of this agreement to provide such cooperative procedures.

Article II

As used in this agreement:

(a) "State" shall mean a state of the United States; the United States of America; a territory or possession of the United States; the District of Columbia; the Commonwealth of Puerto Rico.

(b) "Sending state" shall mean a state in which a prisoner is incarcerated at the time that he initiates a request for final disposition pursuant to Article III hereof or at the time that a request for custody or availability is initiated pursuant to Article IV hereof.

(c) "Receiving state" shall mean the state in which trial is to be had on an indictment, information or complaint pursuant to Article III or Article IV hereof.

Article III

(a) Whenever a person has entered upon a term of imprisonment in a penal or correctional institution of a party state, and whenever during the continuance of the term of imprisonment there is pending in any other party state any untried indictment, information or complaint on the basis of which a detainer has been lodged against the prisoner, he shall be brought to trial within one hundred eighty days after he shall have caused to be delivered to the prosecuting officer and the appropriate court of the prosecuting officer's jurisdiction written notice of the place of his imprisonment and his request for a final disposition to be made of the indictment, information or complaint: provided that for good cause shown in open court, the prisoner or his counsel being present, the court having jurisdiction of the matter may grant any necessary or reasonable continuance. The request of the prisoner shall be accompanied by a certificate of the appropriate official having custody of the prisoner, stating the term of commitment under which the prisoner is being held, the time already served, the time remaining to be served on the sentence, the amount of good time earned, the time of parole eligibility of the prisoner, and any decisions of the state parole agency relating to the prisoner.

(b) The written notice and request for final disposition referred to in paragraph (a) hereof shall be given or sent by the prisoner to the warden, commissioner of corrections or other official having custody of him, who shall promptly forward it together with the certificate to the appropriate prosecuting official and court by registered or certified mail, return receipt requested.

(c) The warden, commissioner of corrections or other official having custody of the prisoner shall promptly inform him of the source and contents of any detainer lodged against him and shall also inform him of his right to make a request for final disposition of the indictment, information or complaint on which the detainer is based.

(d) Any request for final disposition made by a prisoner pursuant to paragraph (a) hereof shall operate as a request for final disposition of all untried indictments, informations or complaints on the basis of which detainers have been lodged against the prisoner from the state to whose prosecuting official the request for final disposition is specifically directed. The warden, commissioner of corrections or other official having custody of the prisoner shall forthwith notify all appropriate prosecuting officers and courts in the several jurisdictions within the state to which the prisoner's request for final disposition is being sent of the proceeding being initiated by the prisoner. Any notification sent pursuant to this paragraph shall be accompanied by copies of the prisoner's written notice, request, and the certificate. If trial is not had on any indictment, information or complaint contemplated hereby prior to the return of the prisoner to the original place of imprisonment, such indictment, information or complaint shall not be of any further force or effect, and the court shall enter an order dismissing the same with prejudice.

(e) Any request for final disposition made by a prisoner pursuant to paragraph (a) hereof shall also be deemed to be a waiver of extradition with respect to any charge or proceeding contemplated thereby or included therein by reason of paragraph (d) hereof, and a waiver of extradition to the receiving state to serve any sentence there imposed upon him after completion of his term of imprisonment in the sending state. The request for final disposition shall also constitute a consent by the prisoner to the production of his body in any court where his presence may be required in order to effectuate the purposes of this agreement and a further consent voluntarily to be returned to the original place of imprisonment in accordance with the provisions of this agreement. Nothing in this paragraph shall prevent the imposition of a concurrent sentence if otherwise permitted by law.

(f) Escape from custody by the prisoner subsequent to his execution of the request for final disposition referred to in paragraph (a) hereof shall void the request.

Article IV

(a) The appropriate officer of the jurisdiction in which an untried indictment, information or complaint is pending shall be entitled to have a prisoner against whom he has lodged a detainer and who is serving a term of imprisonment in any party state made available in accordance with Article V(a) hereof upon presentation of a written request for temporary custody or availability to the appropriate authorities of the state in which the prisoner is incarcerated: provided that the court having jurisdiction of such indictment, information or complaint shall have duly approved, recorded and transmitted the request: and provided further that there shall be a period of thirty days after receipt by the appropriate authorities before the request be honored, within which period the governor of the sending state may disapprove the request for temporary custody or availability, either upon his own motion or upon motion of the prisoner.

(b) Upon receipt of the officer's written request as provided in paragraph (a) hereof, the appropriate authorities having the prisoner in custody shall furnish the officer with a certificate stating the term of commitment under which the prisoner is being held, the time already served, the time remaining to be served on the sentence, the amount of good time earned, the time of parole eligibility of the prisoner, and any decisions of the state parole agency relating to the prisoner. Said authorities simultaneously shall furnish all other officers and appropriate courts in the receiving state who lodged detainers against the prisoner with similar certificates and with notices informing them of the request for custody or availability and of the reasons therefor.

(c) In respect to any proceeding made possible by this Article, trial shall be commenced within one hundred twenty days of the arrival of the prisoner in the receiving state, but for good cause shown in open court, the prisoner or his counsel being present, the court having jurisdiction of the matter may grant any necessary or reasonable continuance.

(d) Nothing contained in this Article shall be construed to deprive any prisoner of any right which he may have to contest the legality of his delivery as provided in paragraph (a) hereof, but such delivery may not be opposed or denied on the ground that the executive authority of the sending state has not affirmatively consented to or ordered such delivery.

(e) If trial is not had on any indictment, information or complaint contemplated hereby prior to the prisoner's being returned to the original place of imprisonment pursuant to Article V(e) hereof, such indictment, information or complaint shall not be of any further force or effect, and the court shall enter an order dismissing the same with prejudice.

Article V

(a) In response to a request made under Article III or Article IV hereof, the appropriate authority in a sending state shall offer to deliver temporary custody of such prisoner to the appropriate authority in the state where such indictment, information or complaint is pending against such person in order that speedy and efficient prosecution may be had. If the request for final authority is made by the prisoner, the offer of temporary custody shall accompany the written notice provided for in Article III of this agreement. In the case of a federal prisoner, the appropriate authority in the receiving state shall be entitled to temporary custody as provided by this agreement or to the prisoner's presence in federal custody at the place for trial whichever custodial arrangement may be approved by the custodian.

(b) The officer or other representative of a state accepting an offer of temporary custody shall present the following upon demand:

(1) Proper identification and evidence of his authority to act for the state into whose temporary custody the prisoner is to be given.

(2) A duly certified copy of the indictment, information or complaint on the basis of which the detainer has been lodged and on the basis of which the request for temporary custody of the prisoner has been made.

(c) If the appropriate authority shall refuse or fail to accept temporary custody of said person, or in the event that an action on the indictment, information or complaint on the basis of which the detainer has been lodged is not brought to trial within the period provided in Article III or Article IV hereof, the appropriate court of the jurisdiction where the indictment, information of complaint has been pending shall enter an order dismissing the same with prejudice, and any detainer based thereon shall cease to be of any force or effect.

(d) The temporary custody referred to in this agreement shall be only for the purpose of permitting prosecution on the charge or charges contained in one or more untried indictments, informations or complaints which form the basis of the detainer or detainers or for prosecution on any charge or charges arising out of the same transactions. Except for his attendance at court and while being transported to or from any place at which his presence may be required, the prisoner shall be held in a suitable jail or other facility regularly used for persons awaiting prosecution.

(e) At the earliest practicable time consonant with the purposes of this agreement, the prisoner shall be returned to the sending state.

(f) During the continuance of temporary custody or while the prisoner is otherwise being made available for trial as required by this agreement, time being served on the sentence shall continue to run but good time shall be earned by the prisoner only if, and to the extent that, the law and practice of the jurisdiction which imposed the sentence may allow.

(g) For all purposes other than that for which temporary custody as provided in this agreement is exercised, the prisoner shall be deemed to remain in the custody of and subject to the jurisdiction of the sending state and any escape from temporary custody may be dealt with in the same manner as an escape from the original place of imprisonment or in any other manner permitted by law.

(h) From the time that a party state receives custody of a prisoner pursuant to this agreement until such prisoner is returned to the territory and custody of the sending state, the state in which the one or more untried indictments, informations or complaints are pending or in which trial is being had shall be responsible for the prisoner and shall also pay all costs of transporting, caring for, keeping and returning the prisoner. The provisions of this paragraph shall govern unless the states concerned shall have entered into a supplementary agreement providing for a different allocation of costs and responsibilities as between or among themselves. Nothing herein contained shall be construed to alter or affect any internal relationship among the departments, agencies and officers of and in the government of a party state, or between a party state and its subidivisions, as to the payment of costs, or responsibilities therefor.

Article VI

(a) In determining the duration and expiration dates of the time periods provided in Articles III and IV of this agreement, the running of said time periods shall be tolled whenever and for as long as the prisoner is unable to stand trial, as determined by the court having jurisdiction of the matter.

(b) No provision of this agreement, and no remedy made available by this agreement, shall apply to any person who is adjudged to be mentally ill.

Article VII

Each state party to this agreement shall designate an officer who, acting jointly with like officers of other party states, shall promulgate rules and regulations to carry out more effectively the terms and provisions of this agreement, and who shall provide, within and without the state, information necessary to the effective operation of this agreement.

Article VIII

This agreement shall enter into full force and effect as to a party state when such state has enacted the same into law. A state party to this agreement may withdraw herefrom by enacting a statute repealing the same. However, the withdrawal of any state shall not affect the status of any proceedings already initiated by inmates or by state officers at the time such withdrawal takes effect, nor shall it affect their rights in respect thereof.

Article IX

This agreement shall be liberally construed so as to effectuate its purposes. The provisions of this agreement shall be severable and if any phrase, clause, sentence or provision of this agreement is declared to be contrary to the constitution of any party state or of the United States or the applicability thereof to any government, agency, person or circumstance is held invalid, the validity of the remainder of this agreement and the applicability thereof to any government, agency, person or circumstance shall not be affected thereby. If this agreement shall be held contrary to the constitution of any state party thereto, the agreement shall remain in full force and effect as to the remaining states and in full force and effect as to the state affected as to all severable matters.

2. Signatories of the Interstate Agreement on Detainers (IAD) and Statutory Provisions of Each State

Ak.   Stat.   §§ 33.35.010 to 33.35.040

Ariz. Rev. Stat. §§ 31-481, 31-482

Ark. Stat. Ann. §§ 43-3201 to 43-4308

Cal. Penal Code §§ 1389 to 1389.8

Colo. Rev. Stat. §§ 24-60-501 to 24-60-507

Conn. Gen. Stat. §§ 54-186 to 54-192

Del. Code tit. 11, §§ 2540 to 2550

D.C. Doce §§ 24-701 to 24-705

Fla. Stat. §§ 941.45 to 941.50

Ga. Code §§42-6-20 to 42-6-25

Haw. Rev. Stat. §§ 834-1 to 834-6

Idaho Code §§ 19-5001 to 19-5008

Ill. Rev. State. ch. 38, § 1003-8-9

Ind. Code § 35-33-10-4

Iowa Code §§ 821.1 to 821.8

Kan. Stat. §§ 22-4401 to -4408

Ky. Rev. Stat. §§ 440.450 to 440.510

Me. Rev. Stat. tit. 34, §§ 1411 to 1419

Md. Ann. Code art. 27, §§ 616A to 616S

Mass. Gen. Laws Ann. ch. 276, §§ 1-1 to 1-8

Mich. Comp. Laws Ann. §§ 780.601 to 780.608

Minn. Stat. § 629.294

Mo. Rev. Stat. §§ 217.490 to 217.520

Mont. Rev. Codes. Ann. §§ 46-31-101 to 46-31-204

Neb. Rev. Stat. §§ 29-759 to 29-765

N.H. Rev. Stat. Ann. §§ 606-A:1 to 606-A:6

N.J. Rev. Stat. §§ 2A:159A-1 to 2A:159A-15

N.M. Stat. Ann. § 31-5-12

N.Y. Crim Proc. Law § 580.20

N.C. Gen. Stat. §§ 15A-761 to 1A-767

N.D. Cent. Code §§29-34-01 to 29-34-08

Ohio Rev. Code Ann. §§ 2963.30 to 2963.35

Okla. Stat. tit. 22, §§ 1345 to 1349

Or. Rev. Stat. §§ 135.775 to 135.793

42 Pa. Cons. Stat. §§ 9101 to 9108

R.I. Gen. Laws §§ 13-13-1 to 13-13-8

S.C. Code §§ 17-11-10 to 17-11-80

S.D. Compiled Laws Ann. §§ 23-24A-1 to 23-24A-34

Tenn. Code Ann. §§ 40-3901 to 40-3908

Tex. Code. Crim. Proc. Ann. art. 51.14

Utah Code Ann. §§ 77-29-5 to 77-29-11

Vt. Stat. Ann. tit. 28, §§ 1501, 1509, 1531 to 1537

Va. Code §§ 53.1-210 to 53.1-215

Wash. Rev. Code Ann. §§ 9.100.010 to 9.100.080

W.Va. Code §§ 62-14-1 to 62-14-7

Wis. Stat. §§ 976.05, 976.06

Wyo. Stat. §§ 7-15-101 to 7-15-107

3. State Constitutional and Statutory Speedy Trial Provisions

	Constitution	Statute
Alabama	art. I, §6	
Alaska	art. I, §11	Alas. R. Crim. P. 43(b) (1968)
Arizona	art. 2, §§11, 24	Ariz. Rev. Stat. Rules of Crim. Proc. rule 8.2 (Supp. 1978)
Arkansas	art. 2, §10	Ark. Stat. Ann. §43-1708 (1977)
California	art. 1, §13	Cal. Penal Code §§1381, 1382 (West Supp. 1978)
Colorado	art. 2, §16	Colo. Rev. Stat. §18-1-405 (1974)
Connecticut	·art. 1, §8	
Delaware	art. 1, §7	Del. Code tit. 10,· §6910 (1975)
Florida	art. 1, §16	Fla. Stat. R. Crim. Proc. 3.191(1)(1) (1975)
		Fla. Stat. R. Crim. Proc. 3.191(a)(2) (1975)
Georgia	art. 1, §2-105	Ga. Code §27-1901 (1978)
Hawaii	art. 1, §11	
Idaho	art. 1, §13	Idaho Code §19-106, §19-3501 (1948)
Illinois	art. 1, §8	Ill. Rev. Stat. ch. 38, §103-5 (Supp. 1978)
Indiana	art. 1, §13	Ind. Code R. Crim. Proc. 4(A)-(D) (1973)
Iowa	art. 1, §10	Iowa Code §795.2 (Supp. 1978)
Kansas	art. 1, §10	Kan. Stat. §22-3402 (Supp. 1977)

	Constitution	Statute
Kentucky	§11	Ky. Rev. Stat. R. Crim. Proc. 9.02 (1975)
Louisiana	art. 1, §9	La. Code Crim. Pro. Ann. art. 701 (West) (1967)
Maine	art. 1, §6	
Maryland	art. 21	
Massachusetts		Mass. Gen. Laws Ann. ch. 277, §72 (1968)
Michigan	art. 1, §20	Mich. Comp. Laws Ann. §768.1 (1968)
Minnesota	art. 1, §6	Minn. R. Crim. Proc. 30.02 (1978)
Mississippi	art. 3, §26	
Missouri	art. 1, §18(a)	Mo. R. Crim. Proc. 25.01 (1979)
Montana	art. III, §16	
Nebraska	art. 1, §11	Neb. Rev. Stat. 29-1207(2) (1975)
Nevada		Nev. Rev. Stat. §178.556 (1973)
New Hampshire	pt. 1, art. 14	
New Jersey	art. 1, §10	
New Mexico	art. II, §14	
New York		N.Y. Crim. Proc. Law §30.30 (McKinney) (Supp. 1978)
North Carolina	art. 1, §18	N.C. Gen. Stat. §15-10 (1978)
North Dakota	art.1, §13	N.D. Cent. Code R. Crim. Proc. 48(b) (1974)
Ohio	art. 1, §10	Ohio Rev. Code Ann. §2945.7 (Supp. 1978)
Oklahoma	art.2 §20	Okla. Stat. tit. 22, §812 (1969)
Oregon	art. I, §10	Or. Rev. Stat. §135.747 (1978)
Pennsylvania	art. 1, §9	Pa. Cons. Stat. R. Crim. Proc. §1100 (1978)
Rhode Island	art.1, §10	R.I. Gen. Laws §12-13-7 (Supp. 1979)
South Carolina	art. 1, §18	S.C. Code §17-23-90 (1977)
South Dakota	art. VI, §7	
Tennessee	art. 1, §9	Tenn. Code Ann. §40-2102 (1975)
Texas	art. 1, §10	
Utah		Utah Code Ann. §77-51-1 (1978)
Vermont	ch. 1, art. 10	Vt. R. Crim. Proc. 48(b) (1974)
Virginia	art. 1, §8'	Va. Code §19.2-243 (1975)
Washington	art. 1, §10	Wash. Rev. Code Ann. §10.46.010 (1961)
West Virginia	art. 3, §14	W.Va. Code §62-3-21 (1966)
Wisconsin	art. 1, §7	Wis. Stat. §971.10 (Supp. 1978)
Wyoming	art. 1, §10	Wyo. Stat. R. Crim. Proc. 45(b) (1977)

4. Uniform Mandatory Disposition of Detainers Act (UMDDA)

§1. Request for Disposition of Untried Charges; Notification to Prisoner of Charges; Effect of Failure to Notify

(a) Any person who is imprisoned in a penal or correctional institution of this state may request final disposition of any untried [indictment, information or complaint] pending against him in this state. The request shall be in writing addressed to the court in which the [indictment, information or complaint] is pending and to the [prosecuting official] charged with the duty of prosecuting it, and shall set forth the place of imprisonment.

(b) The [warden, commissioner of corrections or other official] having custody of prisoners shall promptly inform each prisoner in writing of the source and nature of any untried [indictment, information or complaint] against him of which the [warden, commission of corrections or other official] had knowledge [or notice] and of his right to make a request for final disposition thereof.

(c) Failure of the [warden, commissioner of corrections or other official] to inform a prisoner, as required by this section, within one year after a detainer has been filed at the institution shall entitle him to a final dismissal of the [indictment, information or complaint] with prejudice.

§2. Procedure on Receipt of Request

The request shall be delivered to the [warden, commissioner of corrections or other officials] having custody of the prisoner, who shall forthwith

(1) certify the term of commitment under which the prisoner is being held, the time already served on the sentence, the time remaining to be served, the good time earned, the time of parole eligibility of the prisoner, and any decisions of the [state parole agency] relating to the prisoner; and

(2) send by registered or certified mail, return receipt requested, one copy of the request [and certificate] to the court and one copy to the [prosecuting official] to whom it is addressed.

§3. Period Within Which Trial Must Be Brought

Within [ninety days] after the receipt of the request and certificate by the court and [prosecuting official] or within such additional time as the court for good cause shown in open court may grant, the prisoner or his counsel being present, the [indictment, information or complaint] shall be brought to trial; but the parties may stipulate for a continuance or a continuance may be granted on notice to the attorney of record and opportunity for him to be heard. If, after such a request, the [indictment, information or complaint] is not brought to trial within that period, no court of this state shall any longer have jurisdiction thereof, nor shall the untried [indictment, information or complaint] be of any further force or effect, and the court shall dismiss it with prejudice.

§4. Avoidance of Request on Escape of Prisoner

Escape from custody by any prisoner subsequent to his execution of a request for final disposition of an untried [indictment, information or complaint] voids the request.

§5. Mentally Ill Persons

This Act does not apply to any person adjudged to be mentally ill [or a defective delinquent].

§6. Informing Prisoners of Available Procedure

The [warden, commissioner of corrections or other official] having custody of prisoners shall arrange for all prisoners to be informed in writing of the provisions of this Act, and for a record thereof to be placed in the prisoner's file.

§7. Uniformity of Interpretation

This Act shall be so construed as to effectuate its general purpose make uniform the law of those states which enact it.

§8. Short Title

This Act may be cited as the Uniform Mandatory Disposition of Detainers Act.

5. Signatories of the Uniform Mandatory Disposition of Detainers Act (UMDDA)

Arizona--17 Ariz. Rev. Stat., Rules of Crim. Proc., Rule 8.3(b)

Colorado--Colo. Rev. Stats.§§16-14-101 to 16-14-108 (1974)

Kansas--Kan. Stat. §§22-4301 to 22-4308 (1974)

Minnesota--Minn. Stat. §629.292 (Supp. 1978)

Missouri--Mo. Rev. Stat. §§222.080 to 222.150

North Dakota--N.D. Cent. Code §§29-33-01 to 29-33-08 (1974)

Utah--Utah Code Ann. §§77-65-1 to 77-65-3 (1978)

6. Comparable Legislation Covering Intrastate Detainers

California--Cal. Penal Code § 1381 (West)(Supp. 1978)
Connecticut--Conn. Gen. Stat. §54-139 (Supp. 1978)
Florida--Fla. Rules of Crim. Proc. 3.191(b)(1),
          (2) (1975)
Illinois--Ill. Rev. Stat. ch. 38 §103-5(e)(Supp. 1978)
Oregon--Oreg. Rev. Stat. § 135.760 (1977)
Pennsylvania--19 Pa. Cons. Stat. §881 (1964)
Washington--Wash. Rev. Code Ann. §9.98.010 (1977)
Wisconsin--Wis. Stat. Ann. §971.11 (1971)

7. FORMS*

I. Notice of Untried Indictment, Information, or Complaint and of Right to Request Disposition

In duplicate. One copy of this form, signed by the prisoner and the warden should be retained by the warden. One copy, signed by the warden should be retained by the prisoner.

NOTICE OF UNTRIED INDICTMENT, INFORMATION OR COMPLAINT AND OF RIGHT TO REQUEST DISPOSITION

Inmate_____ No._____ Inst._____

Pursuant to the Agreement on Detainers, you are hereby informed that the following are the untried indictments, informations, or complaints against you concerning which the undersigned has knowledge, and the source and contexts of each.

You are hereby further advised that by the provisions of said Agreement you have the right to request the appropriate prosecuting officer of the jurisdiction in which any such indictment, information, or complaint is pending and the appropriate court that a final disposition be made thereof. You shall then be brought to trial within 180 days, unless extended pursuant to provisions of the Agreement, after you have caused to be

---

* Reprinted with permission from Leslie W. Abramson's Criminal Detainers, Copyright 1977, Ballinger Publishing Company.

delivered to said prosecuting officer and said court written notice of the place of your imprisonment and your said request, together with a certificate of the custodial authority as more fully set forth in said Agreement. However, the court having jurisdiction of the matter may grant any necessary or reasonable continuance.

Your request for final disposition will operate as a request for final disposition of all untried indictments, informations, or complaints on the basis of which detainers have been lodged against you from the state to whose prosecuting official your request for final disposition is specifically directed. Your request will also be deemed to be a waiver of extradition with respect to any charge or proceeding contemplated thereby or included therein and a waiver of extradition to the state of trial to serve any sentence there imposed upon you, after completion of your term of imprisonment in this state. Your request will also constitute a consent by you to the production of your body in any court where your presence may be required in order to effectuate the purposes of the Agreement on Detainers and a further consent voluntarily to be returned to the institution in which you are now confined.

Should you desire such a request for final disposition of any untried indictment, information or complaint, you are to notify_____
_____of the institution in which you are confined.

You are also advised that under provisions of said Agreement the prosecuting officer of a jurisdiction in which any such indictment, information, or complaint is pending may institute proceedings to obtain a final disposition thereof. In such event, you may oppose the request that you be delivered to such prosecuting officer or court. You may request the Governor of this state to disapprove any such request for your temporary custody but you cannot oppose delivery on the grounds that the Governor has not affirmatively consented to or ordered such delivery.

DATED:_____   _____
                                  (insert name and title of custodial authority)

                       BY: _____
                            Warden—Superintendent—Director

            RECEIVED

DATE_____

INMATE _____ NO. _____

II. Inmate's Notice of Place of Imprisonment and Request for Disposition of Indictments, Information, or Complaints

Five copies, if only one jurisdiction within the state involved has an indictment, information or complaint pending. Additional copies will be necessary for prosecuting officials and clerks of court if detainers have been lodged by other jurisdictions within the state involved. One copy should be retained by the prisoner. One signed copy should be retained by the warden. Signed copies must be sent to the Agreement Administrator of the state which has the prisoner incarcerated, the prosecuting official of the jurisdiction which placed the detainer, and the clerk of the court which has jurisdiction over the matter. The copies for the prosecuting officials and the court must be transmitted by certified or registered mail, return receipt requested.

INMATE'S NOTICE OF PLACE OF IMPRISONMENT AND REQUEST FOR DISPOSITION OF INDICTMENTS, INFORMATIONS OR COMPLAINTS

TO: _____ _____,   Prosecuting Officer _____ _____

(jurisdiction)

_____,   Court _____

(jurisdiction)

And to all other prosecuting officers and courts of jurisdictions listed below from which indictments, informations or complaints are pending.

You are hereby notified that the undersigned is now imprisoned in

_____ at _____

(institution)   (town and state)

and I hereby request that a final disposition be made of the following indictments, informations or complaints now pending against me:

Failure to take action in accordance with the Agreement on Detainers, to which your state is committed by law, will result in the invalidation of the indictments, informations or complaints.

I hereby agree that this request will operate as a request for final disposition of all untried indictments, informations or complaints on the basis of which detainers have been lodged against me from your state. I also agree that this request shall be deemed to be my waiver of extradition with respect to any charge or proceeding contemplated hereby or included herein, and a waiver of extradition to your state to serve any sentence there imposed upon me, after completion of my term of imprisonment in this state. I also agree that this request shall constitute a consent by me to the production of my body in any court where my presence may be required in order to effectuate the purposes of the Agreement on Detainers and a further consent voluntarily to be returned to the institution in which I now am confined.

If jurisdiction over this matter is properly in another agency, court or officer, please designate the proper agency, court or officer and return this form to the sender.

The required Certificate of Inmate Status and Offer of Temporary Custody are attached.

DATED: _____

_____
(Inmate's name and number)

The inmate must indicate below whether he has counsel or wishes the court in the receiving state to appoint counsel for purposes of any proceedings preliminary to trial in the receiving state which may take place before his delivery to the jurisdiction in which the indictment, information or complaint is pending. Failure to list the name and address of counsel will be construed to indicate the inmate's consent to the appointment of counsel by the appropriate court in the receiving state.

A. My counsel is _____,
                              (name of counsel)

  whose address is _____.
                              (street, city and state)

B. I request the court to appoint counsel.

                              _____
                              (inmate's signature)

III. Certification of Inmate Status

In the case of an inmate's request for disposition under Article III, copies of this Form should be attached to all copies of Form II. In the case of a request initiated by a prosecutor under Article IV, copy of this Form should be sent to the prosecutor upon receipt by the warden of Form V. Copies also should be sent to all other prosecutors in the same state who have lodged detainers against the inmate. A copy may be given to the inmate.

CERTIFICATE OF INMATE STATUS

RE: _____   _____
          (inmate)   (number)

  _____   _____
          (institution)   (location)

The [custodial authority] hereby certifies:

1. The term of commitment under which the prisoner above named is being held:
    _____

2. The time already served: _____

3. Time remaining to be served on the sentence: _____

4. The amount of good time earned:_____

5. The date of parole eligibility of the prisoner:_____

6. The decisions of the Board of Parole relating to the prisoner: (if additional space is needed use reverse side) _____

7. Maximum expiration date under present sentence: _____

8. Detainers currently on file against this inmate from your state are as follows: ____
    _____
    _____
    _____

DATED: _____   _____
                                           Custodial Authority

                    BY: _____
                              Warden—Superintendent—Director

IV. Offer to Deliver Temporary Custody

In the case of an inmate's request for disposition under Article III, copies of this Form should be attached to all copies of Form II. In the case of a request initiated by a prosecutor, this Form should be completed after the Governor has indicated his approval of the request for temporary custody or after the expiration of the 30 day period. Copies of this Form should then be sent to all officials who previously received copies of Form III. One copy also should be given to the prisoner and one copy should be retained by the warden. Copies mailed to the prosecutor should be sent by certified or registered mail, return receipt requested.

OFFER TO DELIVER TEMPORARY CUSTODY

Date _____

TO: _____ Prosecuting Officer
    (insert name and title if known)

_____
    (jurisdiction)

and to all other prosecuting officers and courts of jurisdictions listed below from which indictments, informations or complaints are pending.

RE: _____   Number _____
    (inmate)

Dear Sir:

Pursuant to the provisions of Article V of the Agreement on Detainers between this state and your state, the undersigned hereby offers to deliver temporary custody of the above-named prisoner to the appropriate authority in your state in order that speedy and efficient prosecution may be had of the indictment, information or complaint which is [described in the attached inmate's request] [described in your request for custody of _____].
    (date)

[The required Certificate of Inmate Status is enclosed.] [The required Certificate of Inmate Status was sent to you with our letter of _____.]
                                  (date)

If proceedings under Article IV(d) of the Agreement are indicated, an explanation is attached.

Indictments, informations or complaints charging the following offenses also are pending against the inmate in your state and you are hereby authorized to transfer the inmate to custody of appropriate authorities in these jurisdictions for the purposes of disposing of these indictments, informations or complaints.

Offense	County or Other Jurisdiction
_____	_____
_____	_____
_____	_____
_____	_____

If you do not intend to bring the inmate to trial, will you please inform us as soon as possible?

Kindly acknowledge.

_____
(name and title of custodial authority)

BY: _____
(Warden—Superintendent—Director)

_____
(Institution and address)

. . . .

A.   My counsel is _____
(name of counsel)

whose address is _____
(street, city and state)

_____

B.   I request the court to appoint counsel.

_____
(inmate's signature)

V. Request for Temporary Custody

Five copies. Signed copies must be sent to the prisoner and to the official who has the prisoner in custody. A copy should be sent to the Agreement Administrator of the state which has the prisoner incarcerated. Copies should be retained by the person filing the request and the judge who signs the request.

REQUEST FOR TEMPORARY CUSTODY

TO: _____   _____
(Warden—Superintendent—Director)   (Institution)

_____   _____
(address)

Please be advised that _____, who is presently an inmate of your institution, is under [indictment] [information] [complaint] in the _____ of which I am the _____.
(jurisdiction)   (title of prosecuting officer)

Said inmate is therein charged with the [offense] [offenses] enumerated below:

Offense

_____

_____

_____

I propose to bring this person to trial on this [indictment] [information] [complaint] within the time specified in Article IV(c) of the Agreement.

In order that proceedings in this matter may be properly had, I hereby request temporary custody of such person pursuant to Article IV(a) of the Agreement on Detainers.

I hereby agree that immediately after trial is completed in this jurisdiction I will return the prisoner directly to you or allow any jurisdiction you have designated to take temporary custody. I agree also to complete Form IX, the Notice of Disposition of a Detainer, immediately after trial.

Signed _____

Title _____

I hereby certify that the person whose signature appears above is an appropriate officer within the meaning of Article IV(a) and that the facts recited in this request for temporary custody are correct and that having duly recorded said request I hereby transmit it for action in accordance with its terms and the provisions of the Agreement on Detainers.

DATED: _____   Signed _____
(Judge)

_____

VI. Evidence of Agent's Authority To Act for Receiving State

In quadruplicate. All copies, signed by the prosecutor and the agent should be sent to the Administrator of their own state. After signing all copies, the Administrator should retain one for his files, send one to the warden of the institution in which the prisoner is located and return two copies to the prosecutor who will give one to the agent for use in establishing his authority and place one in his files.

EVIDENCE OF AGENT'S AUTHORITY TO ACT FOR
RECEIVING STATE

TO: _____
Administrator of the Agreement on Detainers
_____ is confined in _____
(inmate)   (institution)

_____
(address)
and will be taken into custody at the institution on _____
for return to this jurisdiction for trial on or about _____.

In accordance with Article V(b), I have designated _____
whose signature appears below as agent to return the prisoner.

_____
(prosecuting official)

_____
(agent's signature)

TO: Warden

    In accordance with the above representation and the provisions of the Agreement
on Detainers, _____ is hereby designated as agent for this
                      (agent)
state to return _____ for trial.
                     (inmate)

_____
Administrator

VII. Prosecutor's Acceptance of Temporary Custody Offered in Connection With a Prisoner's Request for Disposition of a Detainer

IMPORTANT: This form should only be used when an offer of temporary
custody has been received as the result of a *prisoner's* request for disposition of a
detainer. If the offer has been received because another prosecutor in your state
has initiated the request, use Form VIII. Copies of Form VII should be sent to
the warden, the prisoner, the other jurisdictions in your state listed in the offer of
temporary custody, and the Agreement Administrator of the state which has the
prisoner incarcerated. Copies should be retained by the person filing the acceptance and the judge who signs it.

PROSECUTOR'S ACCEPTANCE OF TEMPORARY CUSTODY
OFFERED IN CONNECTION WITH A PRISONER'S
REQUEST FOR DISPOSITION OF A DETAINER

TO: _____   _____
    (Warden, Superintendent, Director)   (Institution)

_____
(address)

    In response to your letter of _____ and offer of temporary custody
  "   (date)
regarding _____ who is presently under indictment, in-
         (name of prisoner)
formation, complaint in the _____ of which I am
                 (jurisdiction)
_____, please be advised that I accept temporary
    (title of prosecuting officer)
custody and that I propose to bring this person to trial on the indictment, information
or complaint named in the offer within the time specified in Article III(a) of the Agreement on Detainers.

I hereby agree that immediately after trial is completed in this jurisdiction, I will return the prisoner directly to you or allow any jurisdiction you have designated to take temporary custody. I agree also to complete Form IX, the Notice of Disposition of a Detainer, immediately after trial.

COMMENTS: [If your jurisdiction is the only one named in the offer of temporary custody use the space below to indicate when you would like to send your agents to conduct the prisoner to your jurisdiction. If the offer of temporary custody has been sent to other jurisdictions in your state, use the space below to make inquiry as to the order in which you will receive custody, or to indicate any arrangements you have already made with other jurisdictions in your state in this regard.]

Signed: _____

Title: _____

I hereby certify that the person whose signature appears above is an appropriate officer within the meaning of Article IV(a) and that the facts recited in this request for temporary custody are correct and that having duly recorded said request I hereby transmit it for action in accordance with its terms and the provisions of the Agreement on Detainers.

DATED: _____   Signed: _____

                                         (Judge)

                                   _____

                                         (Court)

VIII. Prosecutor's Acceptance of Temporary Custody Offered in Connection With Another Prosecutor's Request for Disposition of a Detainer

IMPORTANT: This form should only be used when an offer of temporary custody has been received as the result of another prosecutor's request for disposition of a detainer. If the offer has been received because a prisoner has initiated the request, use Form VII to accept such an offer. Copies of Form VIII should be sent to the warden, the prisoner, the other jurisdictions in your state listed in the offer of temporary custody, and the Agreement Administrator of the state which has the prisoner incarcerated. Copy should be retained by the person filing the acceptance and the judge who signs it.

PROSECUTOR'S ACCEPTANCE OF TEMPORARY CUSTODY OFFERED IN CONNECTION WITH ANOTHER PROSECUTOR'S REQUEST FOR DISPOSITION OF A DETAINER

TO: _____   _____
     (Warden, Superintendent, Director)   (Institution)

                           (Address)

According to your letter of _____, _____
                         (Date)   (Name of Prisoner)

_____ is being returned to this state at the

request of _____ of _____

(Title of Prosecuting Officer)   (Jurisdiction)

I hereby accept your offer of temporary custody of _____

(Name of Prisoner)

who also is under indictment, information or complaint in the _____

(Jurisdiction)

_____of which I am the _____

(Title of Prosecuting Officer)

I plan to bring this person to trial on said indictment, information or complaint within the time specified in Article IV(c) of the Agreement on Detainers.

I hereby agree that immediately after trial is completed in this jurisdiction, I will return the prisoner directly to you or allow any jurisdiction you have designated to take temporary custody. I agree also to complete Form IX, the Notice of Disposition of a Detainer, immediately after trial.

COMMENTS: [Use the space below to make inquiry as to order in which your jurisdiction will receive custody or to inform the warden of arrangements you have already made with other jurisdictions in your state in this regard.]

Signed: _____

Title: _____

I hereby certify that the person whose signature appears above is an appropriate officer within the meaning of Article IV(a) and that the facts recited in this request for temporary custody are correct and that having duly recorded said request I hereby transmit it for action in accordance with its terms and the provisions of the Agreement on Detainers.

DATED: _____ Signed: _____

(Judge)

IX. Prosecutor's Report on Disposition of Charges

In quadruplicate—one copy to be retained by the prosecutor; one copy to be sent to the warden of the state of original imprisonment, one copy to be sent to the compact administrator of the state of original imprisonment, one copy to be sent to the warden or agency who will have jurisdiction over the prisoner when he returns to the state which placed the detainer to serve his new sentence.

PROSECUTOR'S REPORT ON DISPOSITION OF CHARGES

TO: _____   _____

(Superintendent)   (Date)

_____

(Name of Institution in which the Prisoner
was originally imprisoned)

_____

(Street Address)

_____ _____ _____
    (City)   (State)   (Zip Code)

_____, _____ was transferred to the State of
    (Name of Inmate)   (Number)
_____ pursuant to the Interstate Agreement on Detainers for
   (Name of State)
trial based on the pending charge or charges contained in the Agreement on Detainers,
Form II (if transfer was at the request of inmate) or in Forms IV and V (if transfer was
at request of the prosecutor).

The disposition of the pending charge or charges in *this* jurisdiction was as follows:
Disposition: _____
_____
_____

_____
                            Prosecuting Officer

_____
                            Jurisdiction

8. Uniform Criminal Extradition Act (UCEA)

An Act relating to the extradition of persons charged with crime, and to make uniform the law with reference thereto.

1936 ACT

Sec.
1. Definitions.
2. Fugitives from Justice; Duty of Governor.
3. Form of Demand.
4. Governor May Investigate Case.
5. Extradition of Persons Imprisoned or Awaiting Trial in Another State or Who Have Left the Demanding State Under Compulsion.
6. Extradition of Persons Not Present in Demanding State at Time of Commission of Crime.
7. Issue of Governor's Warrant of Arrest: Its Recitals.
8. Manner and Place of Execution.
9. Authority of Arresting Officer.
10. Rights of Accused Person; Application for Writ of Habeas Corpus.
11. Penalty for Non-Compliance with Preceding Section.
12. Confinement in Jail When Necessary.

Be it enacted . . . .

§ 1.   Definitions

Where appearing in this act, the term "Governor" includes any person performing the functions of Governor by authority of the law of this state. The term "Executive Authority" includes the Governor, and any person performing the functions of Governor in a state other than this state, and the term "State," referring to a state other than this state, includes any other state or territory, organized or unorganized, of the United States of America.

§ 2.   Fugitives from Justice; Duty of Governor

Subject to the provisions of this act, the provisions of the Constitution of the United States controlling, and any and all acts of Congress enacted in pursuance thereof, it is the duty of the Governor of this state to have arrested and delivered up to the Executive Authority of any other state of the United States any person charged in that state with treason, felony, or other crime, who has fled from justice and is found in this state.

§ 3.   Form of Demand

No demand for the extradition of a person charged with crime in another state shall be recognized by the Governor unless in writing alleging, except in cases arising under Section 6, that the accused was present in the demanding state at the time of the commission of the alleged crime, and that thereafter he fled from the state, and accompanied by a copy of an indictment found or by information supported by affidavit in the state having jurisdiction of the crime, or by a copy of an affidavit made before a magistrate there, together with a copy of any warrant which was issued thereupon; or by a copy of a judgment of conviction or of a sentence imposed in execution thereof, together with a statement by the Executive Authority of the demanding state that the person claimed has escaped from confinement or has broken the terms of his bail, probation or parole. The indictment, information, or affidavit made before the magistrate must substantially charge the person demanded with having committed a crime under the law of that state; and the copy of indictment, information, affidavit, judgment of conviction or sentence must be authenticated by the Executive Authority making the demand.

§ 4.   Governor May Investigate Case

When a demand shall be made upon the Governor of this state by the Executive Authority of another state for the surrender of a person so charged with crime, the Governor may call upon the Attorney-General or any prosecuting officer in this state to investigate or assist in investigating the demand, and to report to him the situation and circumstances of the person so demanded, and whether he ought to be surrendered.

§ 5.   Extradition of Persons Imprisoned or Awaiting Trial in Another State or Who Have Left the Demanding State Under Compulsion

When it is desired to have returned to this state a person

charged in this state with a crime, and such person is imprisoned or is held under criminal proceedings then pending against him in another state, the Governor of this state may agree with the Executive Authority of such other state for the extradition of such person before the conclusion of such proceedings or his term of sentence in such other state, upon condition that such person be returned to such other state at the expense of this state as soon as the prosecution in this state is terminated.

The Governor of this state may also surrender on demand of the Executive Authority of any other state any person in this state who is charged in the manner provided in Section 23 of this act with having violated the laws of the state whose Executive Authority is making the demand, even though such person left the demanding state involuntarily.

§ 6.   Extradition of Persons not Present in Demanding State at Time of Commission of Crime

The Governor of this state may also surrender, on demand of the Executive Authority of any other state, any person in this state charged in such other state in the manner provided in Section 3 with committing an act in this state, or in a third state, intentionally resulting in a crime in the state whose Executive Authority is making the demand, and the provisions of this act not otherwise inconsistent, shall apply to such cases, even though the accused was not in that state at the time of the commission of the crime, and has not fled therefrom.

§ 7.   Issue of Governor's Warrant of Arrest; Its Recitals

If the Governor decides that the demand should be complied with, he shall sign a warrant of arrest, which shall be sealed with the state seal, and be directed to any peace officer or other person whom he may think fit to entrust with the execution thereof. The warrant must substantially recite the facts necessary to the validity of its issuance.

§ 8.   Manner and Place of Execution

Such warrant shall authorize the peace officer or other person to whom directed to arrest the accused at any time and any place where he may be found within the state and to command the aid of all peace officers or other persons in the éxecution of the warrant, and to deliver the accused, subject to the provisions of this act to the duly authorized agent of the demanding state.

§ 9.   Authority of Arresting Officer

Every such peace officer or other person empowered to make the arrest, shall have the same authority, in arresting the accused, to command assistance therein, as peace officers have by law in the execution of any criminal process directed to them, with like penalties against those who refuse their assistance.

§ 10.   Rights of Accused Person; Application for Writ of Habeas Corpus

No person arrested upon such warrant shall be delivered over to the agent whom the Executive Authority demanding him shall have appointed to receive him unless he shall first be taken forthwith before a judge of a court of record in this state, who shall inform him of the demand made for his surrender and of the crime with which he is charged, and that he has the right to demand and procure legal counsel; and if the prisoner or his counsel shall state that he or they desire to test the legality of his arrest, the judge of such court of record shall fix a reasonable time to be allowed him within which to apply for a writ of habeas corpus. When such writ is applied for, notice thereof, and of the time and place of hearing thereon, shall be given to the prosecuting officer of the county in which the arrest is made and in which the accused is in custody, and to the said agent of the demanding state.

§ 11.   Penalty for Non-Compliance with Preceding Section

Any officer who shall deliver to the agent for extradition of the demanding state a person in his custody under the Governor's warrant, in wilful disobedience to the last section, shall be guilty of a misdemeanor and, on conviction, shall be fined [not more than $1,000.00 or be imprisoned not more than six months, or both].

§ 12.   Confinement in Jail When Necessary

The officer or persons executing the governor's warrant of arrest, or the agent of the demanding state to whom the prisoner may have been delivered may, when necessary, confine the prisoner in the jail of any county or city through which he may pass; and the keeper of such jail must receive and safely keep the prisoner until the officer or person having charge of him is ready to proceed on his route, such officer or person being chargeable with the expense of keeping.

The officer or agent of a demanding state to whom a prisoner may have been delivered following extradition proceedings in another state, or to whom a prisoner may have been delivered after waiving extradition in such other state, and who is passing through this state with such a prisoner for the purpose of immediately returning such prisoner to the demanding state may, when necessary, confine the prisoner in the jail of any county or city through which he may pass; and the keeper of such jail must receive and safely keep the prisoner until the officer or agent having charge of him is ready to proceed on his route, such officer or agent, however, being chargeable with the expense of keeping; provided, however, that such officer or agent shall produce and show to the keeper of such jail satisfactory written evidence of the fact that he is actually transporting such prisoner to the demanding state after a requisition by the Executive Authority of such demanding state. Such prisoner shall not be entitled to demand a new requisition while in this state.

§ 13.   Arrest Prior to Requisition

Whenever any person within this state shall be charged on the oath of any credible person before any judge or magistrate of this state with the commission of any crime in any other state and, except in cases arising under Section 6, with having fled from justice, or with having been convicted of a crime in that state and having escaped from confinement, or having broken the terms of his bail, probation or parole, or whenever complaint shall have been made before any judge or magistrate in this state setting forth on the affidavit of any credible person in another state that a crime has been committed in such other state and that the accused has been charged in such state with the commission of the crime, and, except in cases arising under Section 6, has fled from justice, or with having been convicted of a crime in that state and having escaped from confinement, or having broken the terms of his bail, probation or parole and is believed to be in this state, the judge or magistrate shall issue a warrant directed to any peace officer commanding him to apprehend the person named therein, wherever he may be found in this state, and to bring him before the same or any other judge, magistrate or court who or which may be available in or convenient of access to the place where the arrest may be made, to answer the charge or complaint and affidavit, and a certified copy of the sworn charge or complaint and affidavit upon which the warrant is issued shall be attached to the warrant.

§ 14.   Arrest Without a Warrant

The arrest of a person may be lawfully made also by any peace officer or a private person, without a warrant upon reasonable information that the accused stands charged in the courts of a state with a crime punishable by death or imprisonment for a term exceeding one year, but when so arrested the accused must be taken before a judge or magistrate with all practicable speed and complaint must be made against him under oath setting forth the ground for the arrest as in the preceding section; and thereafter his answer shall be heard as if he had been arrested on a warrant.

§ 15.   Commitment to Await Requisition; Bail

If from the examination before the judge or magistrate it appears that the person held is the person charged with having committed the crime alleged and, except in cases arising under Section 6, that he has fled from justice, the judge or magistrate must, by a warrant reciting the accusation, commit him to the county jail for such a time not exceeding thirty days and specified in the warrant, as will enable the arrest of the accused to be made under a warrant of the Governor on a requisition of the Executive Authority of the state having jurisdiction of the offense, unless the accused give bail as provided in the next section, or until he shall be legally discharged.

§ 16.   Bail; in What Cases; Conditions of Bond

Unless the offense with which the prisoner is charged is shown to be an offense punishable by death or life imprisonment under the laws of the state in which it was committed, a judge or magistrate in this state may admit the person arrested to bail by bond, with sufficient sureties, and in such sum as he deems proper, conditioned for his appearance before him at a time specified in such bond, and for his surrender, to be arrested upon the warrant of the Governor of this state.

§ 17.   Extension of Time of Commitment; Adjournment

If the accused is not arrested under warrant of the Governor by the expiration of the time specified in the warrant or bond, a judge or magistrate may discharge him or may recommit him for a further period not to exceed sixty days, or a judge or magistrate judge may again take bail for his appearance and surrender, as provided in Section 16, but within a period not to exceed sixty days after the date of such new bond.

§ 18.   Forfeiture of Bail

If the prisoner is admitted to bail, and fails to appear and surrender himself according to the conditions of his bond. the judge, or magistrate by proper order, shall declare the bond forfeited and order his immediate arrest without warrant if he be within this state. Recovery may be had on such bond in the name of the state as in the case of other bonds given by the accused in criminal proceedings within this state.

§ 19.   Persons under Criminal Prosecution in This State at Time of Requisition

If a criminal prosecution has been instituted against such person under the laws of this state and is still pending the Governor. in his discretion, either may surrender him on demand of the Executive Authority of another state or hold him until he has been tried and discharged or convicted and punished in this state.

§ 20.   Guilt or Innocence of Accused, when Inquired into

The guilt or innocence of the accused as to the crime of which he is charged may not be inquired into by the Governor or in any proceeding after the demand for extradition accompanied by a charge of crime in legal form as above provided shall have been presented to the Governor, except as it may be involved in identifying the person held as the person charged with the crime.

§ 21.　Governor May Recall Warrant or Issue Alias

The Governor may recall his warrant of arrest or may issue another warrant whenever he deems proper.

§ 22.　Fugitives from This State; Duty of Governors

Whenever the Governor of this State shall demand a person charged with crime or with escaping from confinement or breaking the terms of his bail, probation or parole in this state, from the Executive Authority of any other state, or from the chief justice or an associate justice of the Supreme Court of the District of Columbia authorized to receive such demand under the laws of the United States, he shall issue a warrant under the seal of this state, to some agent, commanding him to receive the person so charged if delivered to him and convey him to the proper officer of the county in this state in which the offense was committed.

§ 23.　Application for Issuance of Requisition; by Whom Made; Contents

I. When the return to this state of a person charged with crime in this state is required, the prosecuting attorney shall present to the Governor his written application for a requisition for the return of the person charged in which application shall be stated the name of the person so charged, the crime charged against him, the approximate time, place and circumstances of its commission, the state in which he is believed to be, including the location of the accused therein at the time the application is made and certifying that, in the opinion of the said prosecuting attorney the ends of justice require the arrest and return of the accused to this state for trial and that the proceeding is not instituted to enforce a private claim.

II. When the return to this state is required of a person who has been convicted of a crime in this state and has escaped from confinement or broken the terms of his bail, probation or parole, the prosecuting attorney of the county in which the offense was committed, the parole board, or the warden of the institution or sheriff of the county, from which escape was made, shall present to the Governor a written application for a requisition for the return of such person, in which application shall be stated the name of the person, the crime of which he was convicted, the circumstances of his escape from confinement or of the breach of the terms of his bail, probation or parole, the state in which he is believed to be, including the location of the person therein at the time application is made.

III.   The application shall be verified by affidavit, shall be executed in duplicate and shall be accompanied by two certified copies of the indictment returned, or information and affidavit filed, or of the complaint made to the judge or magistrate, stating the offense with which the accused is charged, or of the judgment of conviction or of the sentence.   The prosecuting officer, parole board, warden or sheriff may also attach such further affidavits and other documents in duplicate as he shall deem proper to be submitted with such application.   One copy of the application, with the action of the Governor indicated by endorsement thereon, and one of the certified copies of the indictment, complaint, information, and affidavits, or of the judgment of conviction or of the sentence shall be filed in the office of [the secretary of state] to remain of record in that office.   The other copies of all papers shall be forwarded with the Governor's requisition.

§ 24.   Costs and Expenses

[When the punishment of the crime shall be the confinement of the criminal in the penitentiary, the expenses shall be paid out of the state treasury, on the certificate of the Governor and warrant of the Auditor; and in all other cases they shall be paid out of the county treasury in the county wherein the crime is alleged to have been committed.   The expenses shall be the fees paid to the officers of the state on whose Governor the requisition is made, and not exceeding .   .   .   .   cents a mile for all necessary travel in returning such prisoner.]

§ 25.   Immunity from Service of Process in Certain Civil Actions

A person brought into this state by, or after waiver of, extradition based on a criminal charge shall not be subject to service of personal process in civil actions arising out of the same facts as the criminal proceeding to answer which he is being or has been returned, until he has been convicted in the criminal proceeding, or, if acquitted, until he has had reasonable opportunity to return to the state from which he was extradited.

§ 25-A. Written Waiver of Extradition Proceedings

Any person arrested in this state charged with having committed any crime in another state or alleged to have escaped from confinement, or broken the terms of his bail, probation or parole may waive the issuance and service of the warrant provided for in sections 7 and 8 and all other procedure incidental to extradition proceedings, by executing or subscribing in the presence of a judge of any court of record within this state a writing which states that he consents to return to the demanding state; provided, however, that before such waiver shall be executed or subscribed by such person it shall be the duty of such judge to inform such person of his rights to the issuance and service of a warrant of extradition and to obtain a writ of habeas corpus as provided for in Section 10.

If and when such consent has been duly executed it shall forthwith be forwarded to the office of the Governor of this state and filed therein. The judge shall direct the officer having such person in custody to deliver forthwith such person to the duly accredited agent or agents of the demanding state, and shall deliver or cause to be delivered to such agent or agents a copy of such consent; provided, however, that nothing in this Section shall be deemed to limit the rights of the accused person to return voluntarily and without formality to the demanding state, nor shall this waiver procedure be deemed to be an exclusive procedure or to limit the powers, rights or duties of the officers of the demanding state or of this state.

§ 25-B. Non-Waiver by This State

Nothing in this act contained shall be deemed to constitute a waiver by this state of its right, power or privilege to try such demanded person for crime committed within this state, or of its right, power or privilege to regain custody of such person by extradition proceedings or otherwise for the purpose of trial, sentence or punishment for any crime committed within this state, nor shall any proceedings had under this act which result in, or fail to result in, extradition be deemed a waiver by this state of any of its rights, privileges or jurisdiction in any way whatsoever.

§ 26. No Right of Asylum. No Immunity from Other Criminal Prosecutions while in This State

After a person has been brought back to this state by, or after waiver of extradition proceedings, he may be tried in this state for other crimes which he may be charged with having committed here as well as that specified in the requisition for his extradition.

§ 27. Interpretation

The provisions of this act shall be so interpreted and construed as to effectuate its general purposes to make uniform the law of those states which enact it.

§ 28. Constitutionality

If any provision of this act or the application thereof to any person or circumstances is held invalid, such invalidity shall not affect other provisions or applications of the act which can be given effect without the invalid provision or application, and to this end the provisions of this act are declared to be severable.

§ 29. Repeal

All acts and parts of acts inconsistent with the provisions of this act and not expressly repealed herein are hereby repealed.

§ 30. Short Title

This act may be cited as the Uniform Criminal Extradition Act.

§ 31. Time of Taking Effect

This act shall take effect on the _____ day of _____, 19__.

9. The Uniform Criminal Extradition Act (UCEA) Has Been Adopted by the Following States*:

Ala. Code §§15-9-20 to 15-9-65

Alas. Stat. 12.70.010 to 12.70.290

Ariz. Rev. Stat. §§13-3841 to 13-3868

Ark. Stat. §§43-3001 to 43-3030

Cal. Penal Code §§1547 to 1556.2

Colo. Rev. Stat. 16-19-101 to 16-19-133

Conn. Ren. Stat. §§54-157 to 54-185

Del. Code tit. 11, §§2501 to 2530

Fla. Stat. §§941.01 to 941.30

Ga. Code §§17-13-20 to 17-13-49

Haw. Rev. Stat. §§832-1 to 832-27

Idaho Code §§19-4501 to 4527

Ill. Rev. Stat. ch. 60, §§18 to 49

Ind. Code 35-33-10-3

Iowa Code §§820.1 to 820.29

Kan. Stat. §§22-2701 to 22-2730

Ky. Rev. Stat. §§440.150 to 440.420

La. Stat. Cts. Cr. P. arts 261 to 280

Me. Rev. Stat. tit. 15, §§201 to 229

Md. Code art. 41, §§16-43

Mass. Gen. Laws Ann. ch. 276, §§11 to 20R

Mich. Comp. Laws Ann. §§780.1 to 780.31

Minn. Stat. §§629.01 to 629.29

-----

* You must check your local statutes to determine whether there has been any change in the language of the original Act.

Mo. Rev. Stat. §§548.011 to 548.300

Mont. Rev. Code Ann. 46-30-101 to 46-30-413

Neb. Rev. Stat. §§29-729 to 29-758

Nev. Rev. Stat. 179.177 to 179.235

N.H. Rev. Stat. §§612:1 to 612:30

N.J. Rev. Stat. §§2A:160-6 to 2A:160-35

N.M. Stat. Ann. §§31-4-1 to 31-4-30

N.Y. Crim. Proc. Law §§570.02 to 570.66

N.C. Gen. Stat. §§15A-721 to 15A-750

N.D. Cent. Code §§29-30.2-01 to 29-30.2-29

Ohio Rev. Code §§2963.01 to 2963.29

Okla. Stat. tit. 22, §§1141.1 to 1141.30

Or. Rev. Stat. §§133.743 to 133.857

42 Pa. Cons. Stat. §§9121 to 9148

P.R. Laws tit. 34, §§1881 to 1881bb

R.I. Gen. Laws §§12-9-1 to 12-9-35

S.D. Compiled Laws Ann. §§23-24-1 to 23-24-39

Tenn. Code Ann. §§40-1001 to 40-1035

Tex. Code Crim. Proc. Ann. art. 51.13

Utah Code Ann. §§77-30-1 to 77-30-28

Vt. Stat. Ann. tit. 13, §§4941 to 4969

V.I. Code tit. 5, §§3801 to 3829

Va. Code §§19.2-85 to 19.2-118

Wash. Rev. Code Ann. §§10.88.200 to 10.88.930

W.Va. Code §§5-1-7 to 5-1-13

Wis. Stat. §976.03

Wyo. Stat. §§7-3-201 to 7-3-227

Comparable legislation covering extradition:

D.C. Code Ann. §§23-401 to 23-411

Miss. Code Ann. §§99-21-1 to 99-21-11

S.C. Code §§17-9-10 to 17-9-70

18 U.S.C. §3182

Appendix E
Law Library Requirements

American Association of Law Libraries
Special Committee on
Law Library Services to Prisoners

CHECKLIST ONE:
MINIMUM COLLECTION FOR PRISON LAW LIBRARIES

I. Federal and State Prisons
   A. Federal Materials
      1. *United States Code Annotated.* Constitution; Titles 18, 28 (Sec. 2241–2255, Federal Rules of Appellate Procedure, Rules of Supreme Court) ; 42 (Sec. 1981–1985). St. Paul: West. 26 vols. and two pamphlets. $195.00 ($58.50 annual upkeep)

         or

         Federal Code Annotated. Constitution; Court Rules–Criminal Proceedings; Titles 18; 28 (Sec. 2241–2255) ; 42 (Sec. 1981–1985). Rochester: Lawyers Cooperative. 7 vols. and pamphlet. $129.00 ($31? annual upkeep)

      2. *United States Reports.* Washington, D.C.: U.S. Government Printing Office. Vol. 361–, 1960–. 36 vols. $204.00? ($35 annual upkeep)

         or

         Supreme Court Reporter. St. Paul: West. Vol. 80–, 1960–. 12 vols. $255.00 ($42.50 annual upkeep)

         or

         United States Supreme Court Reports. (Lawyers Edition 2d Series). Rochester: Lawyers Cooperative. Vol. 4–, 1960–. 23 vols. $402.50 ($82.50 annual upkeep)

      3. *Federal Reporter.* (2d Series). St. Paul: West. Vol. 273–, 1960–. 177 vols. $1,564.00 ($180 annual upkeep)

---

*Title changed, See Expanded Collection I.A.I.

597

4. *Federal Supplement.* St. Paul: West. Vol. 180–, 1960–. 155 vols. $1,114.00 ($180 annual upkeep)

5. *Shepard's United States Citations.* Colorado Springs: Shepard, 1968. 5 vols. $145.00 ($48 annual upkeep)

6. *Shepard's Federal Citations.* Colorado Springs: Shepard. Federal Supplement; Federal Reporter, 2d Series. 201–390 vol. (6th ed.) 1969 Series. $90.00 ($48 annual upkeep)

7. Rules of local federal district courts. Free from court clerks.

B. General Materials

1. Bailey, F. Lee and Henry B. Rothblatt. *Complete Manual of Criminal Forms.* Federal and State. Rochester: Lawyers Cooperative, 1968. $35.00 ($7 annual upkeep)

2. Ballentine, James A. *Ballentine's Law Dictionary* (3d ed. by James A. Anderson) . Rochester: Lawyers Cooperative, 1969. $20.00

or

Black, Henry C. *Black's Law Dictionary* (Rev. 4th ed.) St. Paul: West, 1968. $14.50

3. Cohen, Morris L. *Legal Research in a Nutshell* (2d ed.) . St. Paul: West, 1971. $4.50

4. *Criminal Law Reporter.* Washington, D.C.: Bureau of National Affairs. Weekly. 2 vols. (looseleaf) $148.00 first year ($138 annually thereafter)

5. Fox, Sanford J. *Juvenile Courts in a Nutshell.* St. Paul: West, 1971. $4.50

6. Israel, Jerold H. and Wayne R. LaFave. *Criminal Procedure in a Nutshell.* St. Paul: West, 1971. $5.00

7. *Prison Law Reporter.* Seattle: Administration of Criminal Justice and Prison Reform Committee, Young Lawyers Section, American Bar Association, 1971–. Subscription: $14.00 a yr. ($1 a year for prisoners.)

8. Sokol, Ronald P. *Federal Habeas Corpus* (2d ed.) . Charlottesville, Va.: Michie, 1969. $25.00

II. Additional Materials for State Prisons

1. Reports of highest and intermediate appellate courts of state. 1960–.
2. State statutes compilation.
3. State digest of court decisions.
4. Shepard's Citations for state.
5. Treatise covering state criminal practice and procedure.
6. Volume containing rules of state courts, if available, otherwise, rules obtainable free from clerks of some state courts.

Note: All materials should be kept up to date by supplementation.

All prices are subject to change and do change from time to time.

Checklists of materials for each state are available on request from A.A.L.L. Special Committee on Law Library Services to Prisoners.

American Association of Law Libraries
Special Committee on
Law Library Services to Prisoners

CHECKLIST TWO:
EXPANDED COLLECTION FOR PRISON LAW LIBRARIES
Draft

I. Materials for both Federal and State Prisons
  A. Federal Materials
    1. *United States Code Annotated.* St. Paul: West. 164 vols. $902.00*

       or

       United States Code Service (Lawyer's Edition). Rochester: Lawyers Cooperative. 53 vols. $20.00 per month (until 6/30/75)
    2. *United States Reports.* Washington, D.C.: U.S. Government Printing Office. Vol. 340–, 1950–. 61 vols. $350.00 ($36.50 annual upkeep)

       or

       Supreme Court Reporter. St. Paul: West. Vol. 71–, 1950–. 31 vols. $354.00 ($45 annual upkeep)

       or

       United States Supreme Court Reports (Lawyers' Edition). Rochester: Lawyers Cooperative. Vol. 95–, 1950–. 34 vols. $564.50† ($70 annual upkeep)
    3. *Federal Reporter.* (2d Series). St. Paul: West. Vol. 179–, 1950–. 261 vols. $2,021.00 ($180 annual upkeep)
    4. *Federal Supplement.* St. Paul: West. Vol. 88–, 1950–. 237 vols. $1,857.00 ($180 annual upkeep)
    5. *Modern Federal Practice Digest.* St. Paul: West, 1960–61. 83 vols. $1,182.25 ($250 annual upkeep)
    6. *Shepard's United States Citations.* Colorado Springs: Shepard, 1968. 5 vols. $145.00 ($48 annual upkeep)
    7. *Shepard's Federal Citations.* Colorado Springs: Shepard, 1969. 4 vols. $145.00 ($48 annual upkeep)

---

*Includes 3 years pocket parts; 2 years of recompiled volumes; 2 years of *U.S. Code Congressional and Administrative News*; 2 years *Federal Tax Regulations.*
†Includes *United States Supreme Court Reports Digest.*

8. Wright, Charles A. *Federal Practice and Procedure*. St. Paul: West, 1969. Vols. 1–3 (Criminal) . $85.50 ($15 annual upkeep)

or

Orfield, Lester B. *Criminal Procedure Under The Federal Rules*. Rochester, N.Y.: Lawyers Cooperative, 1966–68. 7 vols. $192.50 ($17.50 annual upkeep)

9. Sokol, Ronald P. *Federal Habeas Corpus*. (2d ed.) Charlottesville, N.C.: Michie, 1969. $25.00

B. General Materials

1. Black, Henry C. *Black's Law Dictionary*. (Rev. 4th ed.) St. Paul: West, 1968. $14.50

or

Ballentine, James A. *Ballentine's Law Dictionary*. Rochester, N.Y.: Lawyers Cooperative, 1969. $20.00

2. *Criminal Law Reporter*. Washington, D.C.: Bureau of National Affairs. Weekly. 2 vols. (looseleaf) $148.00 first year ($138 annually thereafter)

3. One or more of the following:

   a. Anderson, Ronald A. *Wharton's Criminal Law and Procedure*. Rochester, N.Y.: Lawyers Cooperative, 1957. (13th ed.) 5 vols. (supplements) $115.00 ($18.50 annual upkeep)

   b. Israel, Jerold H. and Wayne R. LaFave. *Criminal Procedure in a Nutshell*. St. Paul: West, 1971. $5.00

   c. Perkins, Rollin M. *Criminal Law*. (3d ed.) Mineola, N.Y.: Foundation Press, 1966. $12.50

   d. LaFave, Wayne R. and Austin Scott, Jr. *Hornbook on Criminal Law*. St. Paul: West, 1972. $13.50

   e. Hall, Livingston, Yale Kamisar, Wayne LaFave and Jerold Israel. *Cases on Modern Criminal Procedure*, (3rd ed.) St. Paul: West, 1969. $17.50 Supplement, 1972. $3.50

4. Bailey, F. Lee and Henry Rothblatt. *Complete Manual of Criminal Forms, Federal and State*. Rochester, N.Y.: Lawyers Cooperative, 1968. $35.00 ($7 annual upkeep)

5. Cohen, Morris L. *Legal Research in a Nutshell*. (2d ed.) St. Paul: West, 1971. $4.50

6. Fox, Sanford J. *Juvenile Courts in a Nutshell*. St. Paul: West, 1971. $4.50

7. One or more of the following:

   a. *Prison Law Reporter*. Seattle: Administration of Criminal Justice and Prison Reform Committee, Young Lawyers Section, American Bar Association, 1971–. Monthly. $14.00 a year ($1 a year for prisoners)

   b. *Prisoners Rights Newsletter*. State University of New York, 1971–. Free?

      c. *Penal Digest International.* Iowa City, Iowa: Penal Digest International, 1971–. Monthly. $9.00 a year

    8. *Martindale–Hubbell Legal Directory.* Summit, N.J.: Martindale–Hubbell. Annual. 5 vols. $5.00 a year

    9. *Criminal Law Bulletin.* Boston: Warren, Gorham & Lamont. Monthly. $28.00 a year

II. Additional Materials for State Prisons

    1. Set of annotated statutes of State.

    2. State session laws subsequent to coverage in annotated statutes and supplements, if not covered by legislative service of annotated statutes publisher.

    3. Court reports of appellate courts of State, 1950–.

    4. Digest of court decisions of State.

    5. Shepard's citations for State.

    6. Rules of State courts not covered in annotated statutes. Single volume edition preferred, if available; otherwise, free copies may be obtained from clerks of some courts.

    7. State legal encyclopedia, if any.

    8. One or more state practice books (with forms) on evidence, criminal law and procedure.

Note: It is recommended that complete sets of the court reports listed be purchased, if funds are available, beginning with volume one of each set.

All materials should be kept up to date by subscriptions or supplementation.

All prices are subject to change and do change from time to time.

Checklists of materials for each State are available upon request from A.A.L.L. Special Committee on Law Library Services To Prisoners.

Table of Cases

The following cases are alphabetized and are cross-referenced to the chapters and footnotes where cited for a proposition of law. Some of the cross-references are also to pages or sections of different chapters.

Index

(References are to pages; n. refers to footnotes and App. refers to appendices.)